CHEMICAL PROCESS CONTROL

CONTROL

Second Edition

CHEMICAL PROCESS CONTROL

Second Edition

James B. Riggs

Department of Chemical Engineering

Texas Tech University

Ferret Publishing

Printed in the United States of America

ISBN 0-9669601-3-0

Ferret Publishing
2609 24th Street
Lubbock, Texas 79410 USA
1-806-747-3872

Table of Contents

PART I: INTRODUCTION

PART II: PROCESS DYNAMICS

PART III: PID CONTROL

PART IV: ADVANCED PID CONTROL

PART V: CONTROL OF MIMO PROCESSES

Preface to the First Edition

Over the past 15 years, process control engineering has emerged as a major technical specialty for chemical engineers. As a result, more and more chemical engineers are developing careers in the process control field. The objective of this text is to provide a framework for teaching undergraduate students the fundamentals of process dynamics and feedback systems while also teaching these students the critical skills necessary to function as process control engineers in industry.

An industrial process control engineer needs to be able to tune and troubleshoot control loops, make process control design decisions and understand the terminology of the profession. It is important to teach these skills in an undergraduate control class (if we are going to produce engineers who are productive when they begin work), but these skills by themselves can be limiting without a fundamental understanding of process dynamics and feedback systems. In addition, much of the terminology of the process control profession is strongly tied to the theoretical analysis of control systems. Professional terminology is crucial if control engineers are going to be able to convey their ideas and sell their approaches to their peers, their boss, and the process operators. (A summary of additional terminology is listed at the end of each chapter and the first time that a new term is used, it appears in bold letters in the text.) Clearly, there needs to be a proper balance between teaching industrially relevant process control skills and developing a fundamental understanding of process control theory.

This text is my attempt at this challenging balancing act. Moreover, I have attempted to clearly delineate within this text between material that directly relates to the industrial practice of process control and theoretical material that is presented for the fundamental understanding of process control systems and for the introduction to important terminology. For example, it is important for a student to understand that even though transfer functions (Chapter 4) are an important approach to analyzing and understanding the dynamic behavior of feedback systems, they are rarely directly used by industrial control engineers to analyze the behavior of their control loops. The material in this text that is primarily oriented toward control theory is contained in Chapter 4 (Laplace Transforms and Transfer Functions), Chapter 5 (Idealized Dynamic Behavior), Chapter 9 (Frequency Response Analysis) and a large part of Chapter 6 (PID Control). On the other hand, Chapter 2 (Control Loop Hardware) and Chapter 8 (Troubleshooting) are largely descriptive and are directly related to industrial control practice. But in general, most of the remaining chapters contain elements of both theory and practice. That is, the fundamental understanding of feedback systems and the analysis tools developed in theoretically oriented chapters are used to guide the study of control approaches relevant to industrial practice.

Certain industrial leaders in the field of process control have called for academia to put the "process" back into process control. That is, they would like for academia to teach process control with a process point of view. Industrial process control engineers use their knowledge of the entire process that they are working on along with their knowledge of control systems to solve control problems. Control engineers that do not understand the process are vulnerable to developing control solutions that appear fine to them, but in fact work against the overall objectives of the process. Moreover, this situation can result in serious safety problems.

In Chapter 3 (Dynamic Modeling), dynamic models of the actuator, the process, and the sensor are developed and combined to model the dynamic behavior of several process systems. Dynamic models for a thermal mixer, a composition mixer, a level in a tank, two continuous stirred tank reactors (CSTR's), and a heat exchanger are developed and used throughout the text. This approach to process modeling is quite simple and computationally efficient while exposing the student to process dynamics not unlike those demonstrated by industrial processes. The addition of sensor noise (Section 3.6) provides additional realism to these simple simulators. The exercises at the end of the chapters call for the student to use the simulators for a variety of functions including controller tuning and the application of advanced PID techniques. This approach provides the student with valuable hands-on dynamic and control experience and is quite different from the classical approach which is based on using transfer functions to study these problems. Also, the actuator/process/sensor view of process systems is used in Chapter 6 to evaluate the feedback behavior of a number of control loops commonly encountered in the chemical processing industries and provides an important process based view of control systems.

Chapter 7 presents an approach to process controller tuning which is based upon using an evaluation of the process nonlinearity and the magnitude of the disturbances affecting the process to determine the appropriate tuning criteria. This approach is developed by analyzing a nonlinear CSTR to demonstrate that process nonlinearity and disturbance magnitude can combine to produce unstable feedback behavior. Moreover, chemical engineering examples are used to introduce and demonstrate advanced PID techniques such as cascade, ratio, and feedforward (Chapter 10), inferential control and scheduling of controller settings (Chapter 11), and configuration selection for the control of multiple input/multiple output processes (Chapter 13).

Finally, the approach taken in this text is not to exhaustively cover the full range of process control topics, but rather to focus on material that develops a fundamental understanding of feedback systems and develop the skill set required for an industrial process control engineer. It is my hope that this text inspires more students to enter the important and interesting field of chemical process control.

James B. Riggs   August 1998
Lubbock, Texas

Preface to the Second Edition

Even though the first edition of the textbook was well received in many ways by the chemical engineering university community, professors and students who used the text pointed out that it suffered from a lack of examples in the text and did not have enough problems. The objective of the second edition is to retain the focus of the first edition while addressing these limitations. The opportunity was taken to add some new material and reorganize certain sections to improve their presentation.

Joe Pekny of Purdue University helped me understand that "most students learn by examples in textbooks". I came to understand that it is not enough to present examples to demonstrate the use of the technical material. Instead, a series of examples can be used to lead the student from the most basic application of the material to more complex applications. For example, in Chapter 2, I had originally considered adding an example for sizing a control valve after the equation for flow through a control valve was introduced. Then, I realized that this was too large a "conceptual jump" for most of the students. Instead, I added a series of examples from a simple application of the flow equation, to comparing installed valve characteristics, to sizing a control valve. In this manner, I have attempted to use examples as a means of communicating control approaches and principles to the uninitiated student and not just provide a verbal explanation.

A range of new material was added, including a capstone chapter on case studies for heat exchangers, CSTRs, and distillation columns, an appendix on piping and instrumentation diagrams, detailed examples that demonstrate the differences in installed valve characteristics between linear and equal percentage valves, a short section on controller tuning by pole placement, and a section for block diagram algebra. Upon reexamination of the first edition, I noticed that certain sections are quite long and lack organization. As a result, I subdivided these sections into a number of smaller sections to improve the presentation of the material. This approach is used for the material on transfer functions in Chapter 4, the presentation of types of PID controllers in Chapter 6, and the recommended approach to tuning in Chapter 7. The material on troubleshooting, which was previously included in Chapter 2, now appears as a separate chapter (Chapter 8) after controller tuning is addressed.

It is my hope that these modifications make this text a more effective teaching tool for providing undergraduates with the necessary skills to function in industry with a fundamental understanding of process dynamics and feedback control.

James B. Riggs
Lubbock,Texas

March, 2001

Note to Students

In this text, two general types of material are presented: theoretically- and industrially-oriented material. The theoretical material, which is largely based upon Laplace transforms, is presented to provide a fundamental understanding of the dynamic behavior of feedback control systems. In addition, much of the terminology used by control engineers is based upon the theoretical analysis of process control systems.

The industrially-oriented material involves an analysis of the hardware that actually makes up industrial control loops, presentations of a wide range of control approaches, and using a model-based approach to understand control loop behavior. The model-based approach analyzes the dynamic behavior of the components of a process control loop: controller, actuator, process and sensor. **It is important to keep track of what is theoretical material, which is intended for fundamental understanding, and what is directly related to the industrial practice of process control.**

The simulation software that goes with this textbook can be downloaded from

www.che.ttu.edu/pcoc/software

Each program contains the dynamic model of the process (i.e., actuator/process/sensor) and software for a variety of controllers. To complete certain homework exercises, the simulators are used by enabling or disabling certain sections of the program and applying the proper tuning parameters. These programs are available as FORTRAN and MATLAB files. In addition, a number of the simulators are available as "point-and-click" EXCEL files.

Note to Instructors

Teaching process control is a challenging task because it is generally the first time that the students are exposed to dynamic behavior, and it is difficult to keep the study of this field from becoming abstract to the student. One approach that I have found helpful in this regard is to use laboratory demonstrations of hardware to show the different types of hardware involved, process dynamics, and feedback behavior. It has been my observation that students tend to have an easier time learning technical material when they can physically see this equipment in operation. Our process control laboratory is a fluid-flow/heat-transfer process that uses industrial-type hardware with a distributed control system (DCS). Alternatively, a laboratory unit operation process without industrial hardware can be used to demonstrate process dynamics by having the instructor operate the process as the controller. In the latter case, control valves and a range of sensors donated by industry can be put on display for the student to examine.

The classical approach to homework problems for process control is based on developing analytical solutions for control problems using simplified transfer functions of a process, which generally do not consider the dynamics of the sensor or actuator system. The student gets a steady diet of tedious partial fraction expansions to arrive at the analytical solutions. The approach taken here is to use discussion questions and exercises with process simulators for homework problems. Simplified simulators that involve models of the actuator, process, and sensor along with software models for PID controllers, filters, autotune testing, and several advanced PID control functions are available as software that can be used with the text. In this manner, the student is able to have a hands-on experience with process dynamics, tuning, and advanced PID control.

Finally, I have found that it is important to expose the students to the components that make-up a feedback control loop (Chapter 2) before they study modeling and feedback behavior so that they understand how a feedback loop is actually implemented industrially. There are several terms and approaches that are discussed in Chapter 2 that may not be fully understood by the student. I have found it necessary to return to Chapter 2 near the end of the course to review the important aspects of control hardware after exposure to the full range of process control topics.

Acknowledgments

The revision of this book would not have been possible without the help of my graduate students: Hatim D. Al-Dekhiel, J. Govindhakannan, Kishor G. Gudekar, Rohit Kawathekar, Alpesh Shah, Dale D. Slaback, and Bryan M. Street. In the category of above and beyond the call, Govind provided detailed analysis of several technical topics, Dale (grammar man) significantly reduced the wordiness and increased the clarity of the text, and Bryan solved my computer software problems. Dale Green, one of my undergraduate students, developed visual basic versions of the simulators that execute as macros in Microsoft Excel.

A number of individuals from industry made major contributions to the chapter on control loop hardware. Dave Clough from the University of Colorado, who is a former industrial instrument engineer, provided extensive feedback on the material in Chapter 2. Ken Junk from Fisher-Rosemount supplied invaluable assistance by answering my questions and reviewing the material on final control elements. Bob Sogge of Fisher-Rosemount provided a number of photographs that are important for this chapter. Mohammad Khalfia from Yokogawa Corporation of America supplied information on flow indicators.

Karlene Hoo provided very valuable feedback on the chapters on transfer functions and frequency response analysis, and served as a valuable sounding board for issues related to control theory. Dominique Bonvin (I speeled it correctly this time!) contributed excellent reviews of several chapters and clarified a number of important issues as the result of the philosophical discussions on our trip through the desert on the way to Tucson. Jim Downs of Tennessee Eastman supplied information for sensor and controller tuning. Scott Boyden served as a technical sounding board for a number of technical topics. Charlie Cutler helped me better understand how DMC functions. Joe Pekny and Peter Rony shared ideas on ways to improve the first edition. My wife, Brenda, solved a number of problems with using the publication software.

Last but not least, H. R. Heichelheim provided copy editing and technical review of the manuscript. His 20-plus years of experience with teaching the uninitiated undergraduate student the principles of process control and his keen eye for detail contributed directly to the overall quality of this book.

Dedicated to my wife, Brenda, and our children, Michelle, James Michael, and Matthew.

PART I

INTRODUCTION

Chapter 1

Introduction

1.1 Chemical Process Control

Chemical Process Control (**CPC**) is concerned with operating a plant such that the product quality and production rate specifications are met in a safe and reliable manner. To attain these objectives, various flow rates, in most cases, are adjusted to maintain the operation (e.g., important levels, pressures, temperatures, and compositions) near the desired operating points. CPC is part of the larger field of automatic control, which ranges from controlling aircraft to controlling robots to controlling the critical systems in a computer.

Over the past 15 to 20 years, the **Chemical Processing Industries** (**CPI**, i.e., the companies that operate refineries and chemical plants) have been in a transition from a relatively young industry, largely driven by innovation in new products and new processing approaches, to a more mature industry in which the technology of the industry is changing much more slowly. In earlier times, new products such as nylon and Teflon® were developed, and new process designs such as fluidized catalytic cracking (FCC) and plastic processing technologies were implemented. These innovative products and processing approaches provided a major economic advantage to their developers. The resulting profit margins associated with these technological breakthroughs far outweighed the incremental benefits of optimal or near-optimal operation. For example, the addition of an FCC unit, which converts low-valued gas oils to high-valued gasoline, to a refinery provided much higher profit margins than the additional incremental benefit of optimal operation of the FCC unit. Optimal operation of an FCC unit is economically important but pales in comparison to the economic incentive of adding an FCC unit to a refinery in the first place. Today all refineries have FCC units; therefore, for a refinery to remain competitive, it must be concerned with the optimal operation of the FCC unit. CPC is an integral part of attaining the most efficient operation of an FCC unit and most other processes in the CPI.

During the 1970's and 1980's, significant advancements in instrumentation and process computers made the rapid development that has been observed in CPC possible. In the 1960's, the chemical engineering staff of a company consisted largely of process engineers and design engineers. During the 1970's and 1980's, CPC consulting companies and control experts within operating companies were able to

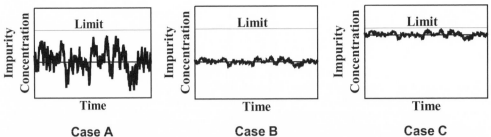

Figure 1.1 Comparison between impurity measurements and the upper limit on the impurity in a product for the original control system (case A), the improved control system with the original impurity target (case B), and the improved control system with a new impurity target (case C).

demonstrate that improved process control can provide significant economic return, usually with relatively low capital investment. As a result, today a typical chemical engineering staff of an operating company in the CPI consists of process engineers and process control engineers. Now, most operating companies in the CPI use consulting companies to provide design services.

CPC is intimately involved in the effort to meet the operational objectives of the process while striving for the most efficient operation of the plant. Minimizing the **variability** (i.e., magnitude of the deviations from the target) in the product is, many times, a key operational objective and is directly affected by the performance of the process control system. In fact, the performance of an overall process control system is many times expressed in terms of the variability in the products produced by the process. Figure 1.1 shows the measurement of the impurity in a product for the original control system (case A). Case B represents the performance of a new control system. The controller corresponding to case B produces a product with less variability in the impurity than for case A; therefore, case B is referred to as producing a lower variability product than case A. For many products, low variability is an important product specification. If a product does not meet its product variability specifications, the resulting product can be low-valued with low demand, while products that meet the variability specification can be high-valued with high demand. Because case B has a lower variability, the average impurity level can be moved closer to the impurity specification (case C), usually allowing greater production rates or lower energy usage, both of which result in more efficient operation of the process. Other types of operational limits are encountered resulting from environmental regulations, capacity limits on equipment, and safety limits. In a similar manner, operating close to these limits can also be economically important. Figure 1.2 shows the impurity distribution or frequency of impurity measurements for the three cases shown in Figure 1.1.

Summarizing, the benefits of improved control can be (a) producing a lower variability product, (b) increasing the process throughput, and/or (c) reducing the energy usage. It should be emphasized that these economic benefits can generally be attained with modest or no additional capital investment.

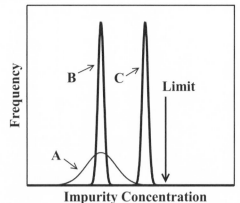

Figure 1.2 Frequency distribution for cases presented in Figure 1.1.

1.2 Everyday Examples of Process Control

Process control is commonplace in our everyday life. Several examples are considered here in an effort to introduce the concept of process control as well as some of the terminology of the field. The terminology introduced here is frequently used throughout the remainder of the text.

Controlling the Water Temperature of a Shower. Everyone is familiar with the problem of controlling the water temperature of a shower when you first get in the shower or after something has changed the water temperature (e.g., water heater starts running out of hot water). Assume that the valve (faucet) on the cold-water line is adjusted to control the temperature of the shower.

Consider the case in which the hot-water heater is starting to run out of hot water, which leads to a decrease in the temperature of the hot water. As a result, the person in the shower begins to close the valve on the cold-water line to maintain the desired temperature of the shower.

Let's analyze this process from a process control point of view. In this case, the shower is the **process**. The person's skin "senses" the shower temperature and is, therefore, referred to as the **sensor**. Controlling the shower temperature is the objective of the control operation; therefore, the shower temperature is the **controlled variable**. The desired shower temperature is called the **setpoint** of the control loop. The flow of cold water into the showerhead is used to control the temperature of the shower and is referred to as the **manipulated variable**. The valve on the cold-water line and the person's hand are used to change the flow rate of cold water and are referred to as the **actuator**, which is known industrially as the **final control element**. The person in the shower senses the temperature and combines this with past experience with the cold-water valve (i.e., process knowledge) to determine how much to turn the valve; therefore, the person in the shower is acting as the **controller**. Manipulating the flow rate of the cold water based on the sensed temperature of the shower is an example of **feedback control** or **closed-loop control**. The combination of the sensor, setpoint, controller, actuator, and process comprise the feedback control loop.

When a change in the valve on the cold-water line is made and the temperature of the shower is allowed to move to a new steady-state condition without any further changes in the cold-water flow, the resulting time behavior of the shower temperature is called the **open-loop response** of the process. Therefore, an open-loop response does not involve feedback from the measured controlled variable.

A changing hot-water temperature is called a **disturbance** to the process since it is not directly controlled, and it affects the shower temperature. Another disturbance can occur when someone flushes a nearby toilet if adequate supply pressure is not available for the cold water. After the toilet is flushed, the shower temperature increases sharply. When you hear someone flushing the toilet, if you adjust the cold water flow before the shower temperature increases in an effort to reduce the resulting temperature increase, that is an example of **feedforward control,** which involves compensating for known disturbances before they affect the process. If you step out of the shower to avoid being burned by the hot water when you hear someone flushing a toilet, that is an example of **override control**.

For a poorly designed shower, when the valve on the cold-water line is adjusted, it may take several seconds before the shower temperature changes. This can result when the velocity of water in the cold-water line is low and/or when the piping from the hot- and cold-water mixing point to the showerhead is excessively long. As a result, when a change in the cold-water valve is made, the person in the shower must wait until the effect on the shower temperature has occurred before making another adjustment to the valve. The time delay between a change in the cold-water valve and the resulting change in the shower temperature is the **deadtime** of the process, and deadtime makes feedback control more difficult.

Return to the case in which the hot-water heater is running out of hot water. As the temperature of the hot water decreases, the cold-water flow rate must also decrease to maintain the desired shower temperature. Eventually, the flow rate of cold water is shut off at which point the shower temperature equals the hot-water temperature. But as time goes on, the temperature of the hot water and, as a result, the shower temperature drops below the desired level. Since the cold-water flow rate cannot be negative, a zero flow rate for the cold water represents a **process constraint** or limit to the process.

An old valve on the cold-water line can exhibit significant "sticking". That is, if the valve is opened a small amount, no change in the flow results. If additional small changes are made, eventually a large change in the flow rate of the cold water results, causing a significant change in the shower temperature. Then, if the valve is closed in small steps, a number of steps is required before the flow rate of cold water decreases, and the resulting decrease in the shower temperature is relatively large. A sticking valve affects the metering precision of the flow rate that one can attain and is referred to as the **valve deadband.** The more a valve sticks, the larger the deadband it exhibits. Since the valve affects how accurately the manipulated variable is controlled, significant valve deadband can affect how precisely the controlled variable is controlled, i.e., variability in the shower temperature.

To this point, we have considered that the flow rate of the cold water is used to control the shower temperature, which is an example of a **Single-Input/Single-Output (SISO)** process since one manipulated variable (the flow rate of cold water) is used to control one controlled variable (the shower temperature). Assume now that it is desired to control the shower temperature using the flow rate of the cold water and to control the flow rate of the shower water using the hot-water flow rate. This is an example of a **Multiple-Input/Multiple-Output (MIMO)** process since there are two inputs (the flow rates of hot and cold water) and two outputs (the shower temperature and the flow rate of water for the shower). If the cold-water flow rate is adjusted to control the shower temperature, the shower flow rate also changes. Likewise, if the hot-water flow rate is adjusted to control the shower flow rate, the shower temperature also changes. This is an example of **coupling** or **interaction** between control loops in a MIMO process. Instead of using the cold-water flow rate to control the shower temperature and the hot-water flow rate to control the shower flow rate, the hot-water flow could be used to control the shower temperature and the cold-water flow rate could be used to control the shower flow rate. In addition, other manipulated variables can be used, e.g., the ratio of the cold-water flow rate to the hot-water flow rate. The **pairing of manipulated and controlled variables** has a very significant effect upon the control performance for MIMO processes (Chapter 13).

If a small change in the valve position results in a relatively large change in the shower temperature, the shower is a **high-gain process.** Conversely, if a large change in the valve results in a moderate or small change in the shower temperature, the process is a **low-gain process.** That is, the process gain is the ratio of the change in the controlled variable to the corresponding change in the manipulated variable. At the beginning of a shower when the hot water is at its highest temperature, and a relatively small amount of hot water is being used in the shower, small changes to the valve on the hot water can produce relatively large changes in the shower temperature, corresponding to a high-gain process. On the other hand, as the hot-water heater runs out of hot water, the temperature of the hot water is near the desired temperature for the shower, and the flow rate of the hot water is high, large changes in the valve on the hot water cause relatively small changes in the temperature of the shower, corresponding to a low-gain process.

Controlling the Water Temperature in a Bathtub. Consider filling a bath tub with water while attempting to maintain a specified temperature of the water in the tub. The process is the water in the bathtub. The setpoint is the desired bath-water temperature. The sensor is the person's hand immersed in the bath water to sense the water temperature. Also, the person's hand is used to sense the temperature of the water added to the tub. The manipulated variable used to control the temperature of the water in the bathtub is the temperature of the water entering the bathtub, and the actuator is the valve on the hot water line and the person's hand. The person is the controller for this process. This process is called a semi-batch process since water enters the tub but does not exit. The shower is an example of a **continuous process** since water continuously enters and leaves the shower. A batch process has neither feeds entering nor products leaving the system.

For the bathtub example, there are two separate control loops: the control loop for the tub-water temperature and the control loop for the temperature of the water entering the tub. If a person samples the tub water and finds that it is too hot, they must reduce the temperature of the water entering the tub by adjusting the valve on the hot-water line. This is an example of **cascade control** since the control loops are applied in tandem, i.e., the setpoint for the temperature controller on the water entering the tub is determined by the temperature controller for the tub water. As the setpoint for the temperature of the water entering the tub is changed, the valve on the hot-water line is adjusted.

When adjustments are required for the water temperature in the tub, it takes some time for a correction in the measured temperature to result. The "inertia" of the process is referred to as the **lag** of the process and depends on the volume of water in the tub and the volumetric flow rate of water into the tub. That is, as the size of the tub and the level of water in the tub is reduced for a set water feed rate, the temperature of the water in the tub changes faster than in a tub with more water in it, i.e., the smaller tub exhibits less thermal lag.

Driving a Car. Consider a person driving a car. The objective (i.e., setpoint) is to keep the car in its lane on the road. The sensor is the person's eyes and the controlled variable is the position of the car on the road. The manipulated variable is the steering wheel/power steering system/front wheel system while the actuator can be thought of as the person's hands and arms that turn the steering wheel. Loose steering (i.e., the steering wheel can be moved back and forth without changing the direction of the car) represents deadband in the actuator/manipulated variable. The controller is the person driving. Curves in the road are disturbances and driver anticipation of a curve is feedforward control. Wear on the tires, a worn suspension, or fouled spark plugs represent very slow disturbances to this process. When the driver sees that the car is drifting to the center or the shoulder of the road, the driver takes corrective action, which is feedback control.

Cruise Control on an Automobile. The sensor for the cruise control unit can be two magnets attached to the drive shaft in combination with an electrical coil that generates a current that is directly proportional to the revolutions per minute that the drive shaft is turning, which in turn is directly proportional to the speed of the automobile. When the automobile reaches the desired speed, the setpoint for the cruise control unit is specified by pushing the "set button". The setpoint for the controller is actually the electrical current that is generated by the sensor when the set button is pushed. The controlled variable is the generated electrical current from the sensor, which correlates directly with the speed of the automobile. The actuator is the throttle position on the engine while the manipulated variable is the flow of gasoline to the engine. Hills or a loss of power produced by the engine represent disturbances to the cruise control unit. Since changes to the throttle position made by the cruise control unit are directly proportional to the error from setpoint, the cruise control system acts as a **proportional-only controller**. When a steep hill is encountered, a small but persistent error from the specified automobile speed results. This constant error from setpoint is referred to as **offset**. If the driver pushes the resume button when the automobile is far below the setpoint speed, the throttle fully opens and the maximum flow rate of gasoline to the engine results. This is an example of a **saturated manipulated variable** since the manipulated variable of the process is at its highest level.

Balancing a Spoon on a Finger. Consider a person balancing a spoon on his/her finger. The objective is to keep the spoon pointing vertically, balanced on the finger. The sensor for this control system is the person's eyes, and the manipulated variable is the horizontal location of the finger. The actuator is the person's hand and arm. This is an example of an **open-loop unstable process** since if control is not applied, the spoon will not remain on the person's finger. For the shower example, if one were to stop adjusting the cold-water valve, the shower temperature stabilizes at some temperature even though it might not be the desired one. The shower process is an example of an **open-loop stable process**.

1.3 Chemical Engineering Process Control Examples

Flow Controller. The most common control loop in the CPI is a flow controller (Figure 1.3). This control system is used to track the flow rate changes called for by higher-level controllers. The sensor in this system is usually a combination of an orifice placed in the line and a device that measures the pressure drop across the orifice, which is directly related to the flow rate.   The actuator is the control valve in the line. The process is the fluid in the pipe and in the control valve. The flow controller (FC) compares the measured flow rate with the specified flow rate (i.e., the flow setpoint) and opens or closes the control valve accordingly. A more complete analysis of flow controller operation is presented in Section 6.10.

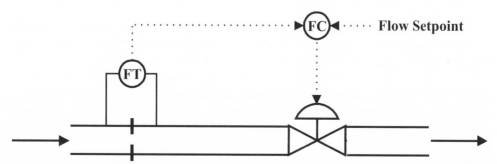

Figure 1.3 Schematic of a flow control loop. FT- flow sensor/transmitter and FC- flow controller.

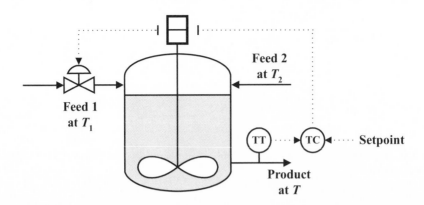

Figure 1.4 Schematic of a CST thermal mixer. TC - temperature controller and TT - temperature sensor/transmitter.

Continuous Stirred Tank (CST) Thermal Mixer. Figure 1.4 shows a schematic for a CST thermal mixer with two feed streams at different temperatures for which it is desired to maintain a specified temperature for the product. The setpoint is the desired product temperature and the controlled variable is the product temperature. The manipulated variable is the flow rate of Feed 1 to the mixer and the actuator is the control valve on that line. The sensor is a temperature sensor/transmitter (TT) located in the product line. The process is the fluid inside the CST thermal mixer. The temperature controller (TC) compares the measured temperature with its setpoint and makes changes to the control valve on the feed flow to the mixer. Disturbances to the process include changes in the temperature of the feed to the CST. The volume of the mixer divided by the total volumetric flow rate to the mixer is the **residence time** or the average time that an element of feed spends in the mixer, assuming that the liquid level in the CST is held constant. For this process, the **time constant** of the process is equal to the residence time. The time constant is a measure of how fast the temperature in the mixer can change. As a rule of thumb, **one can assume that it takes approximately four time constants to observe the full effect of a step change of an input to a process** under open-loop conditions provided no other input changes to the process occur.

Continuous Stirred Tank Composition (CST) Mixer. In a manner similar to the CST thermal mixer, the CST composition mixer combines two streams with different concentrations, and the control objective is to maintain a specified composition of the product. The setpoint is the desired concentration of the CST product, and the manipulated variable is the flow rate of one of the feed streams. The actuator is the control valve on the manipulated feed stream. The process is the fluid inside the CST composition mixer. The sensor is a composition analyzer that analyzes samples taken from the product line. Normally, gas chromatographs (GCs) are used as on-line analyzers, and provide new composition measurements typically every three to ten minutes. The time between new measurements is referred to as **analyzer deadtime** or **analyzer delay**. The controller compares the measured composition of the product with its setpoint and makes changes to the control valve on the feed flow to the mixer. The residence time and time constant of this process are equal to the volume of liquid

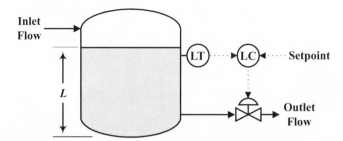

Figure 1.5 Schematic of a level in a tank. LT - level sensor/transmitter and LC - level controller.

in the mixer divided by the total volumetric feed rate to the mixer, assuming that the liquid level in the mixer is held constant.

Level Control in a Tank. Figure 1.5 shows a schematic for controlling the level in a tank. The setpoint is the desired level in the tank, and the controlled variable is the level in the tank. The manipulated variable is the exit flow from the tank and the actuator is the control valve on the outflow line. The sensor is the level indicator on the tank (LT) and changes in the inlet flow rate are disturbances to the process. The level controller (LC) compares the measured level with the setpoint for the level in the tank and makes a change to the control valve on the exit flow from the tank.

Endothermic Continuous Stirred Tank Reactor (CSTR).   An endothermic CSTR is shown schematically in Figure 1.6. The control objective for this system is to maintain the temperature of the product stream at a specified level. The controlled variable is the temperature of the product leaving the reactor, and the manipulated variable is the feed rate of steam to the heat exchanger. The process is the fluid in the CSTR, the heat exchanger, and associated lines.   The sensor is a temperature sensor/transmitter (TT) that measures the temperature of the product stream leaving the reactor. The temperature controller (TC) compares the measured value of the product temperature with its setpoint and makes changes to the control valve on the steam to the heat exchanger.

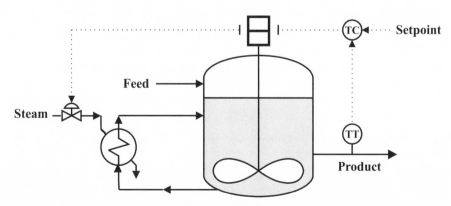

Figure 1.6 Schematic of an endothermic CSTR. TC - temperature controller and TT- temperature sensor/transmitter.

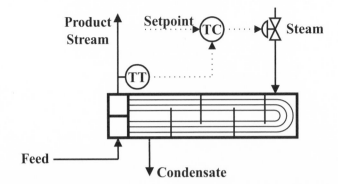

Figure 1.7 Schematic of a steam heated heat exchanger. TC - temperature controller and TT - temperature sensor/transmitter.

Stirred Tank Heater. If no reaction occurs in the tank, Figure 1.6 also represents a stirred tank heater. The control objective for this system is to maintain the temperature of the product stream at a specified level. In this system, the material in the tank is heated by passing it through the heat exchanger. The controlled variable is the temperature of the product leaving the tank and the manipulated variable is the flow rate of steam to the heat exchanger. The process is the fluid in the well-mixed vessel, the heat exchanger, and associated lines. The actuator is the valve on the steam line, and the sensor is the temperature sensor/transmitter, which is placed in the product line.   The temperature controller compares the measured value of the product temperature with its setpoint and makes changes in the control valve on the steam to the heat exchanger.

Heat Exchanger. Figure 1.7 shows a schematic of a steam-heated heat exchanger for which the flow of steam is used to maintain the product stream at a specified temperature. The feed enters the heat exchanger and flows through the tube side of the tube bundle as the steam heats it. The controlled variable is the temperature of the stream leaving the heat exchanger, and the manipulated variable is the flow rate of steam to the heat exchanger. The actuator is the valve on the steam line, and the sensor is the temperature sensor/transmitter (TT), which measures the temperature of the product stream leaving the heat exchanger. The process is the steam, process fluid, and heat exchanger tubes inside the heat exchanger. The temperature controller (TC) compares the temperature of the stream leaving the heat exchanger with its setpoint and makes changes in the control valve on the steam line.

1.4 Block Diagram of a General Feedback Control System

Figure 1.8 shows a block diagram representation of a generalized feedback control system. This diagram can represent each of the previous examples. That is, each of the examples has a controller, an actuator, a process, and a sensor, in that order,

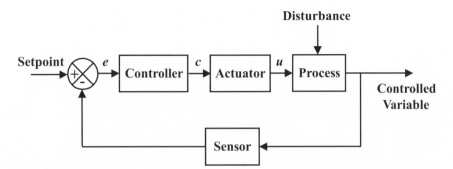

Figure 1.8 Block diagram of a generalized feedback system. *e* **is the error from setpoint,** *c* **is the controller output, and** *u* **is the manipulated variable.**

along with feedback of the measured value of the controlled variable to the controller. In addition, each of the examples is affected by disturbances. The sensor reading is compared with the setpoint to produce the **error from setpoint** (*e*) and the controller chooses control action (*c*) based upon this difference. The actuator system is responsible for making changes in the level of the manipulated variable (*u*). The "process" for a control loop is only the part of the system that determines the relationship between the controlled variable and the inputs (i.e., the manipulated variable and disturbances). The process considered here can be based upon a number of processing units or one small part of a unit operation.

The symbol $\otimes$ in Figure 1.8 represents a summation function. The negative sign on the measurement of the controlled variable results in forming the difference between the setpoint and the measured value of the controlled variable, which is the error from setpoint (*e*). A block diagram of an open-loop process (without feedback control) involves only the actuator, process, and sensor.

1.5 Types of Controllers

On-Off Control. An on-off controller applies two modes of control action: full control action and no control action. Initially, an on-off heater applies heat to the system as long as the controlled temperature is below a specified upper limit (Figure 1.9). When the upper temperature limit is reached, the addition of heat is stopped. Heat is not added to the process until the controlled temperature becomes less than a specified lower limit. In this manner, the heat is intermittently applied and the controlled temperature cycles between the specified upper and lower limits. Note that the control temperature exceeds the maximum temperature and becomes less than the minimum temperature due to the inertia of the process. In the case of overshoot and undershoot, the upper and lower temperature limits can be adjusted so that the effective maximum and minimum controlled temperatures correspond to the desired maximum and minimum temperatures. A typical room thermostat is an example of an on-off controller.

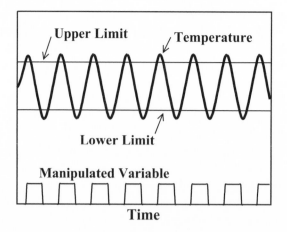

Figure 1.9 An example of the performance of an on-off temperature controller.

Manual Control. When process operators act as the controller, this is referred to as manual control. Operators typically make changes in manipulated variable levels and wait to see where the process settles before making the next manipulated variable change. In this manner, the operator adjusts the manipulated variable in a conservative fashion by using a series of steady-state or near steady-state steps. The time between manipulated variable changes is set by the **open-loop settling time** of the process, i.e., the time for the process to reach a new steady-state operating point after a single step change in the manipulated variable level has been applied to the process.

Consider manual control for a single change in a disturbance. Operators see the initial effect of the disturbance and make their estimate of the needed change in the manipulated variable. Then they observe the response of the process (i.e., wait for approximately one open-loop settling time). After the process has settled or nearly settled, they make another adjustment to the level of the manipulated variable and observe its effect. It typically takes several adjustments to return the process to the desired setpoint. Obviously, when the process is subjected to frequent disturbance upsets, operators are continually making changes to the process and observing the results in an effort to keep the controlled variable near its setpoint.

Proportional-Integral-Derivative (PID) Controllers. The most common controller in the CPI is the PID controller, which is the primary emphasis of this text. The PID controller provides adjustment to the actuator, which is proportional to the error from setpoint, proportional to the time integral of the error, and proportional to the time derivative of the error (Chapter 6). Properly implemented PID controllers provide substantial performance improvement over manual control. For a single disturbance, a properly tuned PID controller typically returns the process to or near setpoint in approximately one open-loop settling time. For a series of disturbances, the PID controller significantly outperforms manual control in terms of the resulting variability about setpoint.

Advanced PID Controllers. PID controller performance can be enhanced by a number of techniques including cascade control, ratio control, feedforward control, scheduling of controller tuning, decouplers, and anti-windup (Chapters 10 to 12). These techniques are designed to assist PID controllers with regard to more effectively handling disturbances, deadtime, coupling, etc.

Model-Based Controllers. Controllers that directly use process models to determine the control action can handle process nonlinearity, disturbances, coupling, and complex dynamics if the model used in the controller accurately represents these features. There is a variety of model-based controllers (Chapter 14) with the major classifications being linear and nonlinear. Also, there are a number of different types of controllers within each of these classifications. Model-based controllers can offer significant performance improvement over PID controllers in certain cases when properly implemented and maintained.

1.6 Responsibilities of a Chemical Process Control Engineer

Overview. From an overall point of view, process control engineers are responsible for using their process control skills and process knowledge **to make money** for the operating company. Specifically, process control engineers are responsible for seeing that a plant that was generally not designed with regard to process control performance operates safely, reliably, and efficiently while producing the desired product quality. Control engineers do this by transferring the variability that would otherwise go into important controlled variables (e.g., product compositions) to manipulated variables (e.g., steam flow rates) and less important controlled variables (e.g., byproduct compositions). To meet these objectives, it is essential that process control engineers use a complete knowledge of the process to attain the most desirable performance.

Controller Design. The control engineer is responsible for selecting the proper mode of the controller (P-only, PI or PID) depending upon the characteristics of the process. That is, the P-only controller uses only proportional feedback action, the PI controller uses proportional and integral action, and PID uses proportional, integral, and derivative action. Each of these controller options has advantages when applied in the proper situation. The control engineer is also responsible for applying advanced PID versions (cascade, ratio, feedforward, etc.) to the cases in which they offer significant advantages. Therefore, the control engineer must understand the advantages and disadvantages of standard and advanced PID techniques as well as understand the control-relevant aspects of the process in question, e.g., the proper pairing of manipulated and controlled variables.

Process Design. The process design can have a dominant effect on the ultimate control performance of the process. That is, the reduction in holdup of material in the process and the application of material recycle and energy recovery can each have a very significant economic advantage from a steady-state design point of view. On the other hand, these steady-state advantages can, in the extreme, render the process impossible to control. For this reason, many companies include a control engineer on their process design teams. Design modifications can sometimes convert an existing plant from a poorly performing process into a well performing system from a control standpoint. The control engineer may also be responsible for specifying the type of sensors and control valves.

Controller Tuning. Selecting the values of the controller settings (e.g., choosing the amount of proportional, integral, and derivative action to be used by a PID controller) is critically important for the proper functioning of a controller. Controller tuning involves considering how a control loop affects the overall process objectives and many times results in a compromise between controller performance and controller reliability (Chapter 7). For certain systems, the controllers can be tuned aggressively, resulting in very tight control while other systems require much more conservative controller settings. Controller tuning is needed for implementing new controllers, but is more frequently required for existing control loops due to changes in the behavior of the process or for changes in the magnitude or type of disturbances affecting the process.

Controller Troubleshooting. Even a properly designed and tuned controller may not function properly. For example, an erratic sensor or an improperly functioning actuator can seriously undermine the performance of a controller. Excessive disturbance levels can also be the source of unacceptable controller performance. It is the responsibility of the control engineer to identify the reasons for improperly functioning control loops and correct them as much as possible (Chapter 8).

Documentation of Process Control Changes. Any significant change to a process, including changes to the process controls, requires approval by a safety review committee for most companies in the CPI. Before approving changes in the controls for a process, the safety review committee typically requires that a data sheet for process changes, which describes the proposed process changes, be completed. The data sheet for process changes must be approved by the operational and management authorities for the affected area of the plant before the changes can be implemented. The process control engineer is responsible for completing the process change data sheet, obtaining the approval signatures, and presenting the process modifications to the safety review committee. The process control engineer usually serves on the safety review committee to assess the effects of process modifications to the process control systems.

Types of Process Control Engineers. There are, in general, several levels of responsibility to which control engineers are assigned. For example, for an entry-level assignment, process control engineers might have the responsibility for the process control tasks for an area of the plant. These engineers are responsible for the day-to-day operation of the control loops in their area (i.e., tuning and troubleshooting).   Control engineers with five or more years experience or with graduate training in process control may be responsible for larger, more challenging control projects throughout the plant.   These control engineers are involved in the design, tuning, and troubleshooting of the controllers.   Finally, corporate level control engineers typically are stationed at corporate engineering headquarters and are involved in long term control projects at a variety of plant sites.   These engineers typically have a Ph.D. degree in chemical process control or have worked their way up the ranks to be recognized as one of the company's top process control engineers.   For each of these job levels, effective process control engineers use their knowledge and experience on control systems combined with a thorough understanding of the chemical processes with which they are working to solve process control problems. The key point here is that for process control engineers to perform effectively, they must have a thorough knowledge of the process behavior and the operational objectives and constraints of the process, i.e., **process knowledge is a prerequisite for becoming a successful process control engineer**.

1.7 Operator Acceptance

A major issue in effectively functioning as a process control engineer is **operator acceptance**. Operator acceptance depends upon developing process control solutions that work effectively in an industrial setting as well as getting along with the operators. The quickest way to ensure that the operators not accept your control work is to deal with them in an arrogant and condescending manner. For example, if you come into the control room with an arrogant attitude, a significant number of operators will take it upon themselves to make sure that you are not successful in their plant. Regardless of how well your controller functions on the process, if you have offended the operators, they will see that your controller does not stay on-line. Remember that at 2 a.m., they are the "kings" of the process.

That said, the best way to interact with the operators is to give them the respect that they deserve and seek their advice and input whenever you start a control project. Remember that they are observing the process day in and day out. They may not correctly know why certain things happen in the process but you can count on them knowing what happens and under what conditions.   As a result, operators are a valuable resource of operating experience.

With regard to implementing controllers that function well in an industrial setting, the control engineer must ensure that the proper controller type (Chapters 6, 10, and 11) has been chosen for the process in question and that the controller is properly tuned (Chapter 7). Bumpless transfer (Chapter 12) and anti-windup (Chapter 12) should be used as well. Validity checks and filtering should also be applied to sensor readings. In this manner, controllers can provide good control performance in a highly reliable fashion. The best controllers are the ones that meet their control objectives, stay in service unless there is a sensor or actuator failure, and respond "gracefully" when the actuator or sensor failures occur.

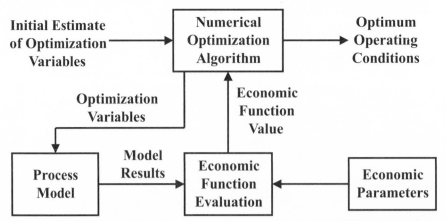

Figure 1.10 A logic flow diagram of a process optimization procedure.

1.8 Interfacing Process Control and Process Optimization

Process optimization is concerned with operating the plant so that the operation results in producing the highest rate of profit generation for the operating company consistent with the safety of personnel, equipment, and environment. For example, for many reactor systems, as the reactor temperature is increased the conversion of the reactants increases, but the ratio of products to byproducts (i.e., selectivity) decreases; therefore, there is an optimum reactor temperature that provides the best economic tradeoff between conversion and selectivity. The economic optimum temperature is related to a number of process variables (e.g., feed rate, feed composition, reactor volume) as well as economic parameters (e.g., product values, separation costs, feed costs). The optimal operation of a process may also involve producing as much product from the process as possible, which corresponds to maintaining operation against the most advantageous process constraints.

Figure 1.10 shows a logic flow diagram for a typical process optimization application. The optimization process starts with an initial estimate of the optimum operating conditions, which, in the case of the reactor example, is the initial estimate of the optimum reactor temperature. The numerical optimization algorithm passes the initial estimate of the optimum operating conditions to the model equations (Chapter 3) where all the operating conditions of the process are calculated. For the reactor example, the production rate of products and byproducts is calculated along with the utility usage for the process using material and energy balances around the reactor. The model results are then combined with economic parameters to calculate the rate of profit generation. An economic objective function is typically represented as follows:

$$\Phi = \sum P_i V_i - \sum F_i V_i - \sum U_i C_i \qquad \textbf{1.1}$$

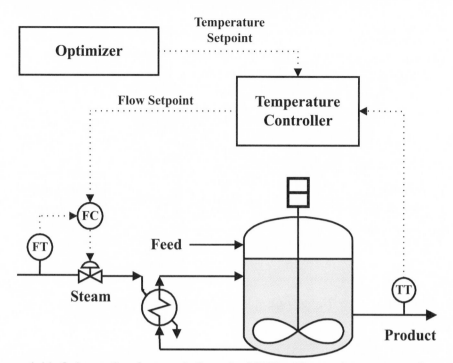

Figure 1.11 Schematic of an endothermic CSTR with regulatory control, supervisory control, and optimization. FC- flow controller; FT- flow sensor/ transmitter; TT-temperature sensor/transmitter.

where Φ is the rate of profit generation or the value of the economic objective function, P_i is a production rate of a product or byproduct, V_i is the value or cost per unit mass of a feed, product, or byproduct, F_i is a feed rate, U_i is a utility rate (e.g., steam flow rate), and C_i is the corresponding unit cost for utility usage. V_i and C_i correspond to the economic parameters shown in Figure 1.10. The economic objective function given by Equation 1.1 is applicable to existing processes and does not consider equipment costs.

In the optimization procedure shown in Figure 1.10, the numerical optimization algorithm calculates values of the optimization variables or the **optimization decision variables** until the optimal value of the economic objective function is identified. In the case of the reactor example, the reactor temperature is the optimization decision variable and, therefore, is adjusted until the optimum is identified. Each time a new reactor temperature is chosen by the optimization algorithm, the model equations are solved and the product and byproduct rates are used to determine the corresponding value of the economic objective function. Once the optimum value of Φ (e.g., the maximum value of Φ) is identified, the optimization calculation is finished. The corresponding values of the optimum operating conditions (i.e., the optimum values of the optimization decision variables) are typically applied to the process as setpoints for controllers on the process.

Figure 1.11 shows how optimization can be applied to an endothermic CSTR. Note that the result of the numerical optimizer, optimization model, and economic objective function is the optimum reactor temperature. This temperature becomes the setpoint for the reactor temperature controller, which is referred to as a **supervisory controller**. The output of the supervisory controller is the setpoint for the flow controller on the steam, which is referred to as a **regulatory controller**. Generally, composition and temperature control loops serve as supervisory control loops while pressure, level and flow control loops are used as regulatory control loops.   In summary, the process optimizer determines the setpoints for the supervisory control loops, which in turn select the setpoints for the regulatory control loops, which adjust control valves on the process.

Example 1.1 Optimization of a CSTR with a Series Reaction

Problem Statement. Determine the optimum reactor temperature based on the following economic parameters, operating conditions, and reaction parameters for a CSTR (Figure 1.11):

Reaction: $A \xrightarrow{r_1} B \xrightarrow{r_2} C$

$r_1 = k_1 \, C_A \exp(-E_1/RT)$ $r_2 = k_2 \, C_B \exp(-E_2/RT)$

$k_1 = 3.8604 \times 10^6 \text{ s}^{-1}$ $k_2 = 1.8628 \times 10^{13} \text{ s}^{-1}$

$E_1/R = 5033 \text{ K}$ $E_2/R = 10{,}065 \text{ K}$

$Q = 10 \text{ L/s}$ $V_r = 100 \text{ L}$

$C_{A0} = 1.0 \text{ gmole/L}$ $V_{AF} = \$0.15/\text{gmole}$

$V_A = \$0.10/\text{gmole}$ $V_B = \$0.50/\text{gmole}$

$V_C = \$0.20/\text{gmole}$

where Q is the volumetric feed rate, V_r is the volume of the reactor, T is the reaction temperature, V_{AF} is the cost of A in the feed, V_A is the value of A in the product, V_B is the value of the primary product B, V_C is the value of the secondary product C, and C_{A0} is the concentration of A in the feed to the reactor. Assume that the feed contains only A and neglect the utility costs in the optimization analysis of this system. Note that V_A is less than V_{AF}, indicating that the separation costs of recovering A from the product stream are significant. Applying optimization to this process ensures that the most economically preferred process operation is used.

Solution. When undertaking an optimization problem, it is best to develop a physical understanding of the process based on the competing factors that cause the nontrivial optimization problem. For this reactor, if the reaction temperature is too low, little reaction occurs and only a small amount of product is produced. On the other hand, if the temperature is too high, most of the primary product B reacts to form the lower-valued secondary product C; therefore, there is a temperature between these limits that maximizes the profitability of this reactor, i.e., the optimum reactor operating temperature, T^*. The optimization of this process is analyzed in terms of the logic flow diagram for optimization presented in Figure 1.10.

Model development. The model equations for this process are used to calculate all the values of the process operating conditions, which in turn are used to determine the value of the economic objective function Φ given the values of the economic parameters (i.e., V_{AF}, V_A, V_B, and V_C). In this case, given the reactor temperature, T, the concentrations of A, B, and C in the product (i.e., C_A, C_B, and C_C) can be calculated directly using steady-state material balances for A, B, and C, respectively. Applying a steady-state material balance for A (i.e., the flow rate of A entering the process minus the flow rate of A leaving the process minus the rate of consumption of A within the process is equal to zero) yields

$$Q C_{A0} - Q C_A - k_1 \exp[-E_1 / RT] C_A V_r = 0$$

Rearranging and solving for C_A results in

$$C_A = \frac{C_{A0}}{1 + \dfrac{k_1 \exp[-E_1 / RT] V_r}{Q}} \qquad \textbf{A}$$

Note that the reaction temperature and the process parameters are used in Equation A to calculate C_A. Similarly applying steady-state mole balances for B and C yield

$$C_B = \frac{k_1 \exp[-E_1 / RT] C_A V_r}{Q + k_2 \exp[-E_2 / RT] V_r} \qquad \textbf{B}$$

$$C_C = \frac{k_2 \exp[-E_2 / RT] C_B V_r}{Q} \qquad \textbf{C}$$

Equation B requires the value of C_A and Equation C requires the value of C_B; therefore, Equations A to C should be applied sequentially.

Formation of the objective function. Once the model equations are solved (i.e., Equations A-C), the value of Φ can be calculated by applying Equation 1.1 using the values of the economic parameters (i.e., V_A, V_B, V_C, and V_{AF}):

$$\Phi = Q C_A V_A + Q C_B V_B + Q C_C V_C - Q C_{A0} V_{AF} \qquad \textbf{D}$$

where Φ has units of \$/s. The solution procedure is as follows: (1) select a reactor temperature, (2) use Equation A to calculate C_A, (3) use Equation B to calculate C_B, (4) use Equation C to calculate C_C, (5) use Equation D to calculate Φ, and (6) repeat

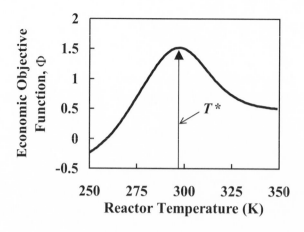

Figure 1.12 Graphical solution of Example 1.1

this process until the reactor temperature that produces the maximum profit is determined.

Results. Figure 1.12 shows the effect of the reactor temperature on the economic objective function as well as the optimum reactor temperature. At reactor temperatures below 260 K, Φ is negative indicating that the feed costs are greater than the product value because of a low reaction conversion. At high temperatures, Φ levels out at the profit level corresponding to converting all the feed to product C. The maximum profitability for the reactor occurs at a reactor temperature of 297 K (i.e., the optimum reactor temperature). In general, the numerical optimization algorithm as shown in Figure 1.10 numerically determines the optimum reactor temperature instead of using a graphical solution as shown in Figure 1.12. Since the reactor temperature is the only optimization variable, a plot of the value of Φ versus the reactor temperature is an easy and direct method to identify the optimum reactor temperature. Otherwise, a numerical optimization procedure is required if, for example, there are more than a couple of optimization variables, which eliminate the possible use of graphical techniques.

Periodic evaluation of the optimum reactor temperature may be required because variations in the reactor feed rate, feed composition, feed costs, or product values can result in significant variations in the optimum reactor temperature. In this manner, the optimum reactor temperature is calculated online to maintain operation at the optimum reactor temperature in the face of variations in process operating conditions and the values of the products. Finally, according to Figure 1.11, the optimum reactor temperature obtained in this procedure becomes the setpoint for the temperature controller on the reactor. This hierarchy of optimization/supervisory control/regulatory control is shown schematically in Figure 1.13 for this example. The connection from the process to the regulatory controls, supervisory controls, and the

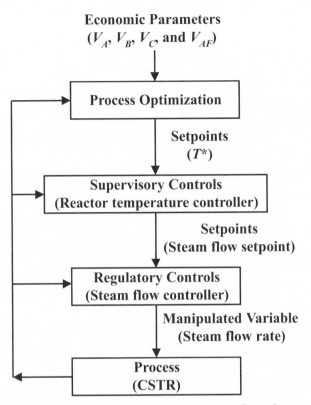

Economic Parameters
$(V_A, V_B, V_C,$ and $V_{AF})$

Process Optimization

Setpoints
(T^*)

Supervisory Controls
(Reactor temperature controller)

Setpoints
(Steam flow setpoint)

Regulatory Controls
(Steam flow controller)

Manipulated Variable
(Steam flow rate)

Process
(CSTR)

Figure 1.13 Block diagram showing the interconnections between process optimization, supervisory control, and regulatory control.

process optimizer represents the flow of process measurements to each of these functions. ♠

1.9 Illustrative Example of a Process Control System

Figure 1.14 shows a schematic of a control system for a distillation column. The purpose of this section is not to overwhelm the student with the complexity of material that has not yet been studied, but to introduce, from an overall point of view, the set of process control skills that are addressed in the remaining chapters of this text.

The overall objective of the control configuration shown in Figure 1.14 is to maintain the composition of the distillate product, D, and the bottoms product, B, at their respective setpoints in the face of process disturbances (e.g., feed flow rate, feed composition changes, cooling water temperature changes, and changes in reboiler steam pressure). In addition, when the column is fed more feed than it can separate, it is desired to maintain the purity of the distillate product at the expense of the bottoms product. Table 1.1 lists the symbols for the various control components (e.g., sensor/transmitters and controllers) that are used in this text. These symbols are used to depict the control loops presented in the remainder of the text.

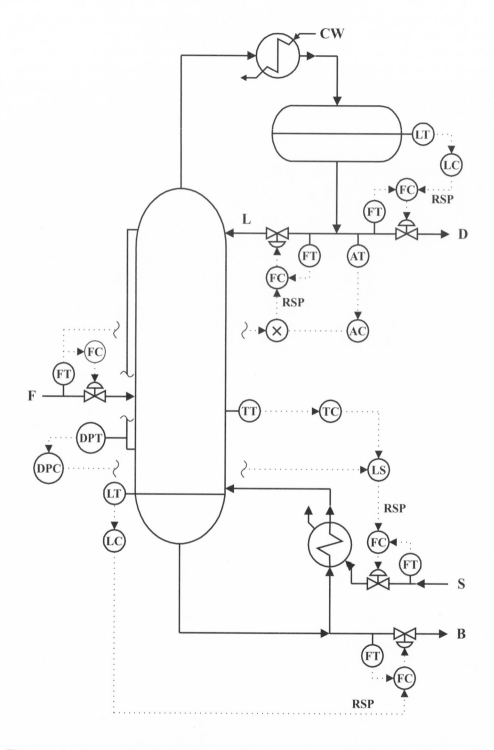

Figure 1.14 Schematic of a control system applied to a distillation column. F-column feed rate, D- distillate flow rate, L- reflux flow rate, B- bottoms flow rate, S- steam flow rate, CW- cooling water.

There are five controlled variables for this column: the composition of the distillate product, the temperature of a tray in the stripping section, the level in the accumulator, the level in the reboiler, and the feed flow rate to the column. The operator selects the setpoints for the level controllers on the accumulator and the reboiler, the temperature controller, and the distillate composition controller as well as the setpoint for the column feed rate controller. Also, there are four manipulated variables: the flow rates of the distillate product, the reflux, the bottoms product, and the steam to the reboiler. The flow rate of reflux is used to control the composition of the distillate product while the steam flow rate is adjusted to control the tray temperature in the stripping section, which leaves the distillate and bottoms flow rates to control the levels in the accumulator and reboiler, respectively. Chapter 13 addresses selecting the proper manipulated and controlled variable pairings.

The flow rates of the reflux, distillate, bottoms, and steam are each controlled by their respective flow controllers (FC). The setpoints for these flow controllers are provided by the corresponding supervisory controllers. For example, the level controller (LC) on the accumulator sets the **remote setpoint** (RSP) for the flow controller on the distillate. This is referred to as a remote setpoint since the setpoint for the flow rate controller on the distillate is determined "remotely" by the level controller. This is an example of cascade control, which is analyzed in Chapter 10. In this manner, the flow rates of the four manipulated variables are adjusted to meet the column control objectives.

The output of the overhead product composition controller is the ratio of reflux to feed so that, as the feed rate changes, the reflux flow rate changes proportionally. The measured feed rate to the column is multiplied ($\times$) by the output from the composition controller on the distillate product to set the flow rate for the reflux flow controller. As a result, when a feed rate change occurs, the remote setpoint (RSP) for the reflux rate flow controller is automatically changed to maintain the specified reflux-to-feed ratio, which is set by the distillate composition controller (AC). This is an example of ratio control, which is presented in Chapter 10.

The composition control loop on the bottoms product involves a tray temperature controller (TC). For this column, the temperature of the indicated tray correlates strongly with the composition of the bottoms product. Since this measurement of the tray temperature is available with much less deadtime than the laboratory analysis on the product stream, the tray temperature controller is used to select the remote setpoint (RSP) for the steam flow controller (FC). The setpoint for the tray temperature controller (TC) is set by the operator based upon the laboratory analysis of the bottom product composition; therefore, these TC and FC loops in tandem are another example of cascade control. In addition, using a tray temperature for composition control is an example of inferential control (i.e., the bottom product composition is "inferred" by the tray temperature), which is presented in Chapter 11.

Table 1.1
Definition of Symbols for Control Diagrams.

AC - analyzer controller (i.e., composition controller)

AT - analyzer transmitter (i.e., composition analyzer/transmitter)

DPC - differential pressure controller

DPT - differential pressure sensor/transmitter

FC - flow controller

FF - feedforward controller

FT - flow sensor/transmitter

HS - high select (this element selects the larger of two inputs)

LC - level controller

LS - low select (this element selects the smaller of two inputs)

LT - level sensor/transmitter

PC - pressure controller

pHC - pH controller

pHT - pH sensor/transmitter

PT - pressure sensor/transmitter

RSP - remote setpoint

S - select controller (i.e., chooses which manipulated variable to use)

TC - temperature controller

TT - temperature sensor/transmitter

$\otimes$ - summation block (i.e., for adding or subtracting inputs)

+ - an addition function (i.e., adds two inputs to determine the output)

$\times$ - multiplication function (i.e., forms the product of two inputs)

This control configuration is designed to prevent the column from flooding as the feed rate to the column is increased. The onset of flooding is marked by a sharp increase in the pressure drop across the column. A differential pressure controller (DPC) sets the steam flow rate necessary to prevent flooding. The low select (LS) chooses the lower steam flow rate setpoint between the differential pressure controller (DPC) and the tray temperature controller (TC) and sends the result to the steam flow controller (FC) as its remote setpoint (RSP). When operation is not near the flooding constraint, the DPC sets a steam flow rate that is considerably larger than the steam flow rate called for by the tray TC; therefore, the LS uses the output from the tray TC as the setpoint for the steam flow controller. When flooding is approached, the LS chooses the output from the DPC since it is lower than the tray TC. This is an example of override/select control, which is covered in Chapter 11.

The proper mode for the PID controller for each of the controllers in this system should be selected (Chapter 6) and each controller should be tuned to meet the operational objectives of the process (Chapter 7). Bumpless transfer and anti-windup strategies should be applied to provide smooth and reliable service for each control loop. Solving day-to-day operational problems on these control loops requires a thorough knowledge of the components that comprise each of the feedback loops (Chapter 2) as well as a knowledge of control loop troubleshooting techniques (Chapter 8).

It should be clear that there are a number of critical skills that are required to design, implement, and maintain process control systems. The remainder of this text is devoted to the study of these items from a fundamental and practical point of view.

This text uses control diagrams similar to Figure 1.14 to present various control approaches. Industry documents their controls using **piping and instrumentation diagrams (P&IDs)**. A P&ID for the stripping section of the distillation column and associated controls presented in Figure 1.14 is shown in Appendix A. Appendix A lists the general features of P&IDs. Note that the control diagrams used here and the P&IDs are similar, but they do have several differences.

1. In a P&ID, each instrument (e.g., temperature transmitters and field-mounted pressure gauge) is shown whether it is part of a control loop.
2. Each controller and sensor in a P&ID has a unique number.
3. P&IDs use the symbol 'FY' to represent a range of control functions, e.g., feedforward control and ratio control, while the diagrams in this text more explicitly differentiate between these functions.
4. P&IDs show all lines, valves, and instruments, and indicate whether the instruments provide a reading to the control computer.
5. Control diagrams show only the lines, valves, and instruments that are associated with the control loop of interest.
6. P&IDs, due to their detail, are complex and generally show only a small portion of the process, but are usually available for the entire plant. Therefore, the control engineer may have to use several P&IDs to understand the existing controls for a single process unit.

1.10 Summary

CPC is concerned with operating a plant so that the operational objectives are met in a safe and reliable manner. CPC directly affects the variability of the products and, therefore, affects product quality, production rates, and utility usage. In addition, CPC is a prerequisite for process optimization.

A single control loop combines a controller, an actuator, and a sensor with the process to maintain the controlled variable at its assigned setpoint. Disturbances enter the process and require the control system to take action to absorb their effect to keep the controlled variable near its setpoint.

PID controllers are the most commonly used controllers in the CPI. Nevertheless, in the extremes, manual control and model-based control are also widely used in industry.

Process control engineers are primarily responsible for controller design, controller tuning, and controller troubleshooting. For process control engineers to be successful, they must be able to work effectively with the operators, and they must rely upon their process understanding to guide their application of process control techniques.

1.11 Additional Terminology

Actuator - the system that changes the level of the manipulated variable. The actuator system usually involves a control valve and associated equipment.
Analyzer deadtime - the time from process stream sampling to the availability of the analyzer reading.
Analyzer delay - the time from process stream sampling to the availability of the analyzer reading.
CPC - chemical process control.
CPI - chemical processing industries (i.e., chemical plants and refineries).
Cascade control - manipulation of a regulatory controller setpoint by a supervisory controller.
Closed-loop control - use of the measured value of the controlled variable to select the manipulated variable level.
Constraint - a limit on process operation.
Continuous process - a process for which material continuously enters and leaves.
Controlled variable - the process variable that the control loop is attempting to maintain at its setpoint.
Controller - a unit which adjusts the manipulated variable level to keep the controlled variable at or near its setpoint.
Coupling - the interaction between control loops for a MIMO process.
Deadtime - the time difference between a manipulated variable change and significant process change.

Decision variables - the operating conditions of a process that are selected by an optimization algorithm for the optimum operation of the process.

Disturbance - a change to an input to the process that is not a manipulated variable.

Error from setpoint - the difference between the measured value of the controlled variable and its setpoint.

Feedback control - use of the sensor reading and the setpoint value to select the level for the manipulated variable for a process.

Feedforward control - a controller that makes adjustments to the manipulated variable level based upon measured disturbances in an effort to absorb the effect of the disturbance before it affects the process.

High-gain process - a process for which a relatively small input change causes a relatively large change in the output variable.

Interaction - the effect of control loops on each other in a MIMO system.

Final control element - the system that changes the level of the manipulated variable. The final control element usually involves a control valve and associated equipment.

Lag - the property of a process that keeps it from responding instantaneously to input changes.

Low-gain process - a process for which a relatively large input change causes a relatively small change in the output variable.

Manipulated variable - the process variable, usually a flow rate, which is adjusted to keep the controlled variable at its setpoint.

MIMO - multiple-input/multiple-output process, i.e., a process with two or more inputs and two or more outputs.

Offset - a persistent error between the measured value of the controlled variable and its setpoint.

Open-loop response - the measured value of the controlled variable as a function of time after a step change in the manipulated variable value without feedback control.

Open-loop settling time - the time for the controlled variable to attain 95% of its ultimate change after a step change in the manipulated variable.

Open-loop stable process - a process that reaches a new steady state after an input change.

Open-loop unstable process - a process that does not reach a new steady state after an input change.

Operator acceptance - having the operators routinely use a controller, i.e.,operator trust in reliable and effective controller operation.

Override control - the arrangement of control loops to prevent the violation of safety, environmental, or operational constraints.

Optimization decision variables - the operating conditions of a process that are selected by an optimization algorithm for the optimum operation of the process.

Pairing of manipulated and controlled variables - for MIMO processes, selecting which manipulated variable is to be used to control which controlled variable.

Process - the system whose outputs are affected by the inputs.

Process constraint - a limit on process operation.

Process optimization - selecting the setpoints for key controllers such that the process produces the highest rate of profit generation.

Proportional-only controller - a feedback controller that makes changes which are proportional to the error from setpoint to the manipulated variable value.

Regulatory controller - the lowest level of controls, usually flow controllers, pressure controllers and level controllers.

Remote setpoint - a setpoint for a regulatory control loop that is determined by a supervisory control loop.

Residence time - the average time that an element of feed spends in the process.

Saturated manipulated variable - a manipulated variable that is at its maximum or minimum level.

Sensor - the device that measures a process variable.

Setpoint - the desired or specified value for the controlled variable.

SISO - a single-input/single-output process.

Supervisory controller - the controllers that are responsible for meeting the setpoints applied by the optimizer or the operator, usually temperature or composition control loops.

Time constant - a measure of how fast a process changes for a change in an input.

Valve deadband - the maximum positive and negative change in the signal to the final control element that does not produce a measurable change in the flow rate in question.

Variability - the magnitude of the deviations from the setpoint for the controlled variable value.

1.12 Preliminary Questions

1.1 What is the overall purpose of process control?

1.2 What is improved process control performance? How is it measured?

1.3 How can improved control performance be used to improve the economic performance of a company in the CPI?

1.4 Why is process control financially attractive to companies in the CPI?

1.5 In general, what function does a controller perform?

1.6 In general, what function does a sensor perform?

1.7 In general, what function does an actuator perform?

1.8 How are a disturbance and a change in a manipulated variable alike? How are they different?

1.9 What is the difference between feedback control and feedforward control?

1.10 What is the sensor used in the shower example?

1.11 What is a typical sensor for a cruise control unit on an automobile?

1.12   Why must a control loop be arranged in the following order: controller-actuator-process-sensor?

1.13 What is the difference between c and u in Figure 1.8? How are they related?

1.14 Summarize the differences between manual, PID, advanced PID, and model-based control. How are they similar?

1.15 Why do process control engineers need to understand the processes to which they apply controls?

1.16 What behavior would cause an operator not to use a control loop? List as many reasons as possible.

1.17 What are the primary responsibilities of a process control engineer? Give an example of each one that you identify.

1.18 What is the difference between process design effects on process control and designing process control systems?

1.19 Why is a process model usually necessary to perform an optimization analysis? When is a model not necessary?

1.20 What is the economic objective function of a process?

1.21 What is the difference between PID and P&ID?

1.22 What is a summation block and how is it used in a feedback control loop?

1.23 What does a symbol on a control diagram that ends with a "C" (e.g., TC, FC, and DPC) represent?

1.24 What does a symbol on a control diagram that ends with a "T" (e.g., TT, FT, and PT) represent?

1.25 What does the symbol "FY" represent on a P&ID?

1.26 How are P&IDs different from the control schematics used in this text? How are they alike?

1.27 In P&IDs, how are pneumatic lines and electrical connections distinguished from each other?

1.13 Analytical Questions and Exercises

1.28 Identify a control process with which you interact daily. Choose an example that is different from the ones presented in the text. Identify the controller, actuator, process, and sensor and draw a block diagram for the control loop.

1.29 Give an everyday example for each of the following terms. Use examples different from those presented in the text.
   a. Disturbance
   b. Deadtime
   c. Process constraint
   d. Coupling
   e. Lag

1.30 Choose an industrial process control system to which you have been exposed. Identify the controller, actuator, process, and sensor and draw a block diagram for the control loop.

1.31 Identify a SISO process and a MIMO process used in industry.

1.32 Identify what constitutes the process for the control loop shown in Figure 1.7.

1.33 Consider the level control loop on the accumulator for the column shown in Figure 1.14. What constitutes the process for this control loop? What is a disturbance for this control loop?

1.34 Consider the control loop for the bottom product composition for the column shown in Figure 1.14. What constitutes the process for this control loop? What is a disturbance for this control loop?

1.35 Explain how process control is different from process optimization. Give an industrial example of each to substantiate your analysis.

1.36 Consider a distillation column that separates propane from butane shown in the figure for this problem. The overhead product (D) from the column, which is largely propane, is used as fuel while the bottoms product (B), which is largely butane, is a much more valuable product since it is a component blended directly into the gasoline pool. The greater the separation produced by the distillation column (i.e., the lower the mole fraction of butane in the overhead propane product and the lower the mole fraction of propane in the butane product), the larger the fraction of the butane recovered in the process, but at the expense of requiring a larger steam usage. Consider how optimization, supervisory control, and regulatory control are applied to this column.
   a. Write an equation for the economic objective function for this case. Remember that the butane that leaves with the propane in the overhead product is valued as fuel (V_F) and the propane in the butane in the bottoms product does not yield gasoline in the reformer reactors but is valued as fuel grade propane. The butane that is recovered in the bottoms product has a value V_B while the propane in the bottoms product is valued

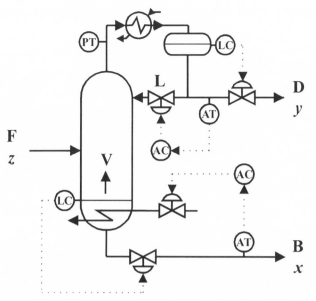

Schematic of distillation column for Problem 1.36.

as fuel, V_F. The cost per pound of steam is given as V_S.

b. Draw a control schematic of this column (i.e., similar to Figure 1.11) showing the connection between optimization, supervisory control, and regulatory control. Assume that the reflux flow rate is used to control the butane in the overhead product and the steam flow to the reboiler is used to control the propane in the bottoms product. In addition, assume that the flow rate of the reflux and the steam to the reboiler are controlled by flow control loops.

1.37 Identify an example of how you use optimization in your everyday life. List the degrees of freedom (the things that you are free to choose) and clearly define the process and how you determine the objective function.

1.38 Consider a separation train composed of a number of distillation columns that separates its feed into individual products based on boiling point differences. Assuming that each distillation column has specified impurity setpoints for its overhead and bottoms products, what is likely the optimum operation of this separation train.

1.39 Determine the optimum reactor temperature for the CSTR in Example 1.1 if the value of C (V_C) is decreased to -0.20/gmole. What can you conclude? What does a negative value of a byproduct signify?

1.40 Determine the optimum reactor temperature for the CSTR in Example 1.1 if the value of C (V_C) is decreased to 0.00/gmole. What can you conclude?

1.41 Determine the optimum reactor temperature for the CSTR in Example 1.1 if the value of B (V_B) is increased to \$1.00/gmole. What can you conclude?

1.42   Determine the optimum reactor temperature for the CSTR in Example 1.1 if the value of B (V_B) is decreased to \$0.35/gmole. What can you conclude?

1.43 Evaluate the effect of Q on the optimum reactor temperature in Example 1.1 by determining T^* for Q in L/s equal to [2, 5, 10, 20, 40].   What can you conclude?

1.44 Evaluate the effect of C_{A0} on the optimum reactor temperature in Example 1.1 by determining T^* for C_{A0} in gmoles/L equal to [0.2, 0.5, 1.0, 2.0, 4.0].   What can you conclude?

1.45 Explain in your own words how the overhead product composition is controlled for the distillation column shown in Figure 1.14.

1.46 Explain in your own words how the bottom composition is controlled for the distillation column shown in Figure 1.14.

1.47 For Figure 1.14, list each of the following items
    a. All sensors
    b. All controlled variables
    c. All manipulated variables
    d. All cascade control loops
    e. All process constraints

Chapter 2

Control Loop Hardware

2.1 Introduction

The hardware used to implement feedback control loops in the CPI has a direct effect on the performance of these control loops. Control loop hardware is comprised of mechanical and electrical devices that perform the functions of the actuator, sensor, and controller. For example, to implement the control loops shown in Section 1.3, control loop hardware is required. To maintain the efficient operation of control loops, the control engineer must understand the control-relevant aspects of these devices.

Choosing the proper hardware for a control application and ensuring that it operates effectively are major responsibilities of control engineers. In addition, when control loops are not functioning properly, control engineers must identify the source of the problem and correct it. Troubleshooting control loops is addressed in Chapter 8. To accomplish these tasks, control engineers must understand the control-relevant issues associated with each of the components that make up a control loop. This chapter describes the hardware components that comprise a typical feedback control loop used in the CPI by providing an overview of the design approaches and performance measures for these components. Since a complete description of these devices is beyond the scope of this text, the descriptions here focus on their control-relevant aspects.

Figure 2.1 is a schematic of a feedback control loop for a temperature controller on the CST thermal mixer (Figure 1.4). This feedback control loop consists of a controller, a final control element, a process, and a sensor. Figure 2.2 is a schematic of the hardware that comprises this feedback temperature control loop as well as the signals that are passed between the various hardware components. The sensor system in Figure 2.1 corresponds to the thermowell, thermocouple, and transmitter in Figure 2.2 while the actuator system in Figure 2.1 corresponds to the control valve, I/P (current-to-pressure) signal converter, and instrument air system in Figure 2.2. Likewise, the controller in Figure 2.1 consists of the A/D (analog-to-digital) and D/A (digital-to-analog) signal converters, the control computer, and the operator console in Figure 2.2. The abbreviations used in this paragraph are described in the next several sections.

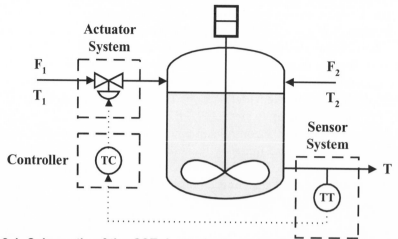

Figure 2.1 Schematic of the CST thermal mixer showing the actuator system, sensor system, controller, and the process.

A thermocouple is used to measure the temperature inside the mixing tank and is placed in thermal contact with the process fluid leaving the mixing tank by means of a thermowell in the product line. The temperature transmitter converts the millivolt signal generated by the thermocouple into a 4-20 mA (milliamperes) analog electrical signal that is proportional to the temperature inside the thermowell. When the thermocouple/transmitter system is calibrated properly and when the thermowell is correctly designed and located, the value of the analog signal corresponds closely to the temperature in the mixing tank. The thermocouple/thermowell/temperature transmitter comprises the sensor system for this process.

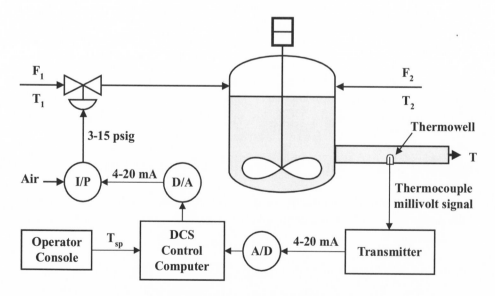

Figure 2.2 Schematic of the control system on the CST thermowell mixer showing each component along with the various signals.

The 4-20 mA analog signal from the temperature transmitter is converted into a digital reading by the **analog-to-digital (A/D) converter**. The output of the A/D converter is a digital measurement of the temperature that is used in the control calculations. The operator console shown in Figure 2.2 allows the operator or control engineer to observe the performance of the control loop and to change the setpoint, T_{sp}, and controller tuning parameters for this loop. The value of T_{sp} and the digital value of the measured mixer temperature are used by the control algorithm in the **distributed control system**, (**DCS**, i.e., the control computer). The output from the controller is a digital signal that is converted into a 4-20 mA analog signal by the **digital-to-analog (D/A) converter**. The DCS, D/A and A/D converters, and the operator consoles are typically located in a centralized control room while the remaining equipment resides in the field near the process equipment.

The 4-20 mA analog signal from the D/A converter goes to the **current-to-air pressure (I/P) converter**. The I/P converter uses a source of instrument air to change the air pressure (3-15 psig) applied to the control valve corresponding to the value of the analog signal. That is, if I is the value of the analog signal and P is the instrument air pressure delivered to the control valve,

$$\frac{I-4}{16} = \frac{P-3}{12}$$

2.1

since a 4 to 20 mA range in the analog signal corresponds to a 3 to 15 psig range in the instrument air pressure and the zero of the analog signal is 4 mA and the zero of the pneumatic signal is 3 psig. Changes of instrument air pressure to the control valve cause changes in the stem position of the control valve, which result in changes in the flow rate to the process. These changes in the flow rate to the process cause changes in the temperature of the mixer, which are measured by the sensor, completing the feedback control loop. The final control element consists of the I/P converter, the instrument air system, and the control valve.

The ability to effectively troubleshoot a control loop requires the knowledge of the components that actually implement the control loop as well as the signals that are passed between these elements. This chapter considers the design and control-relevant aspects of the DCS, the actuator system, and several commonly encountered sensors.

Example 2.1 Conversion of Signals within a Feedback Loop

Problem Statement. Determine the value of the 4-20 mA signal to the I/P converter and the pneumatic signal to the control valve in Figure 2.2 if the controller output is 75% of full range.

Solution. A controller output signal equal to 75% of full range results in a 4-20 mA signal of

$$I = 4 + 0.75 \left[20 - 4 \right] = 16 \ mA$$

since a zero controller output corresponds to a 4 mA signal and the range of the analog signal is the maximum reading (20 mA) minus the minimum reading (4 mA). To calculate the magnitude of the pneumatic signal, rearrange Equation 2.1, i.e.,

$$P = 3 + \frac{12}{16} \left[16 - 4 \right] = 12 \ psig$$

♠

2.2 Distributed Control Systems

Background. Pneumatic PID controllers were introduced in the 1920's and were in widespread use by the mid 1930's. Pneumatic controllers use bellows, baffles, and nozzles with a supply of air pressure to apply control action. That is, the pneumatic controller receives a pneumatic signal corresponding to the error between the measured value of the controlled variable and the setpoint and acts on this signal with a bellows, baffle, and nozzle in conjunction with the instrument air system to produce a pneumatic signal that is sent to the control valve. For the early versions of pneumatic controllers, the controllers were installed in the field near the sensors and control valves. In the late 1930's, transmitter-type pneumatic controllers began to replace the field-mounted pneumatic controllers because of the increase in size and complexity of the processes being controlled. For the transmitter-type pneumatic controllers, the sensor readings were converted into pneumatic signals (i.e., 3-15 psig) that were conveyed by metal tubing into the control room where the pneumatic controller determined the control action. In turn, the control action was pneumatically transmitted to the actuator on the process. Since the transmitter-type pneumatic controllers were typically located in a central control room, operators could conveniently address the overall control of the process using a number of controllers from a centralized location.

In the late 1950's, electronic controllers (i.e., electronic analog controllers) became commercially available.   These devices use capacitors, resistors and transistor-based amplifiers to implement control action. Since electronic transmitters were used (i.e., the output from the sensor was converted to a 4-20 mA signal and the 4-20 mA controller output signal was converted to a pneumatic signal by the I/P converter), the use of electronic analog controllers eliminated the need for long runs of metal tubing by using electrical wires, greatly reducing the installation costs and resulting in faster-responding controllers. By 1970, the sales of electronic controllers exceeded the sales of pneumatic controllers in the CPI[1].

The first supervisory computer control system was installed in a refinery in 1959. A simplified schematic of a supervisory computer control system is shown in Figure 2.3. Note that this system offered data storage and acquisition as well as control loop alarms that previous control systems did not offer. In addition, the centralized

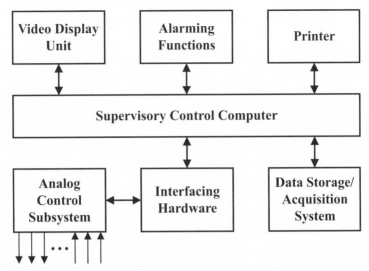

Figure 2.3 Block diagram of a supervisory control system.

computer could use the available operating data to determine the setpoints for certain key control loops in an effort to obtain the most efficient operation of the plant (i.e., process optimization).

The biggest disadvantage of the centralized control computer approach was that if the control computer failed, the entire control system was shut down. A redundant control computer was an expensive alternative and not always reliable. Due to the technological breakthroughs in computers and associated systems in the 1970's, a new computer control architecture was developed and introduced by vendors in the late 1970's. This architecture is based on using a number of **local control units (LCUs)**, which have their own microprocessors and are interconnected by **shared communication lines** (i.e., a **data highway**). The LCU network is connected to a data acquisition system, operator/engineer consoles, and a general purpose computer. This computer control architecture became known as a **distributed control system (DCS)** (Figure 2.4) since it involves a network with various control functions distributed for a variety of users.

The advantages of a DCS over a centralized control computer result from the use of microprocessors for the local control function. Even if a microprocessor were to fail, only the control loops serviced by that LCU would be affected. A redundant microprocessor that performs the same calculations as the primary microprocessor (i.e., a hot backup) greatly increases the system's reliability. As a result, the probability that all the control loops fail at the same time, or even a major portion of the control loops fail, is greatly reduced in comparison to a centralized control computer. In addition, the DCS is much easier to expand. To increase the number of control loops serviced by the DCS, only a primary and a redundant LCU need to be added. The modular nature of DCSs can be a major economic advantage for plants that undergo expansion. In comparing a DCS to electronic analog controllers, the application of

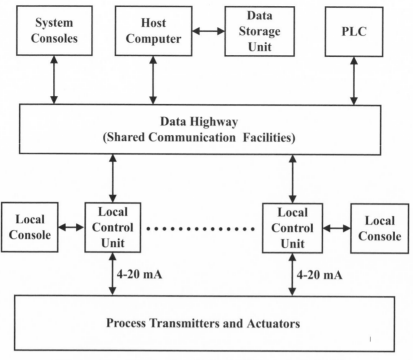

Figure 2.4 Generalized block diagram of a DCS.

conventional controls is generally equivalent, but implementing controllers is much easier and less expensive per loop using a DCS.

Structure of a DCS. A generalized schematic of a DCS is shown in Figure 2.4. A number of LCUs, which contain redundant microprocessors, perform the control functions for the process in a distributed fashion. Each LCU has several consoles attached to it. The consoles (**video display units**, **VDUs**), which utilize **cathode ray tubes** (**CRTs**), have video displays that show process schematics with current process measurements. Operators and control engineers use these displays to monitor the behavior of the process, set up control loops, and enter setpoints and tuning parameters. A photograph of a typical control room for a DCS is shown in Figure 2.5. Normally, these consoles have touch screen capability so that if operators want to make a change to a control loop, they touch the icon for the controller in which they are interested. Then a screen pops up that allows the operator to make the desired changes. On some DCSs, control loops can be conveniently set up by clicking and dragging the tags for the desired sensor readings and the final control elements and connecting them to the type of controller that is chosen. Since the LCU is attached to the shared communications facility, a local display console can view schematics and current operating data for other parts of the plant, but typically can make changes only to the control loops associated with its LCU. The local console can also be used to display historical trends of process measurements. To do this, the local console must access historical data in the data storage unit by using the data highway (i.e., the shared communication facilities).

Figure 2.5 Photograph of a control room for a DCS. Courtesy of Honeywell.

Data acquisition is accomplished by transferring the process measurements from the LCUs, through the data highway, and into the host computer where the process data are passed on to the data storage unit. The archived process data can be accessed from one of the system consoles or one of the local consoles. Previously, during the era of electronic analog controllers, data storage for important control loops was typically accomplished using a strip chart recorder, which printed measurements on a small roll of paper in different colors of ink.

The data highway holds the entire DCS together by allowing each modular element and each global element to share data and communicate with each other. The data highway is composed of one or more levels of communication hardware and the associated software. System consoles are directly attached to the data highway and can act as a local console for any of the local control units. In addition, system consoles can be used to change linking functions of the distributed elements. Operators have access to the local consoles, but they are usually restricted from modifying certain functions (e.g., altering control configurations). On the other hand, engineers have access to most of the DCS functions. The host computer is a mainframe computer that is used for data storage, process optimization calculations, and the application of advanced process control approaches. Attached to the host computer is the data storage unit (usually a magnetic tape-based system) where archived data are stored.

DCS Performance and Use. A goal of a DCS is to apply the control calculations for each control loop so fast that the control appears continuous. Since DCSs are based upon sequential processors, each control loop is applied at a discrete point in time and the control action is held constant at that level until the next time the controller is executed. The time between subsequent calls to a controller applied by the DCS is called the **controller cycle time** or the **control interval**. Unfortunately, **the fastest cycle times for controller calls within a DCS are typically in the range of 0.2 seconds while most loops are called only every 0.5 to 1.0 seconds. The regulatory control loops typically use control intervals in the range of 0.5 to 2.0 seconds while supervisory control is typically applied with control intervals of 20 seconds up to several minutes**. While this controller cycle time does not present a limitation for slower control loops such as level, temperature, and composition control loops, it does present a limitation for fast control loops such as flow controllers and some pressure controllers. A real-time control system for the DCS is used to enforce a priority ranking of control functions. That is, certain high-priority control loops are maintained at the expense of less important loops.

Since DCSs are based on digital controller calculations, a wide variety of special control options are available in self-contained modular form and can be easily selected by "click and drag" action on most DCSs. In this manner, complex control configurations can be conveniently assembled, interfaced, and implemented. In addition, a variety of signal conditioning techniques, including filtering and validity checks, can be applied to process measurements.

Programmable Logic Controllers (PLCs). **Programmable logic controllers** have been used primarily in the CPI for controlling batch processes and for sequencing of process startup and shutdown operations. PLCs have been traditionally based on **ladder logic**, which allows the user to specify a series of discrete operations, e.g., start the flow to the reactor until the level reaches a specified value, next start steam flow to the heat exchanger until the reactor temperature reaches a specified level, next start catalyst flow to the reactor, etc. A small PLC can be responsible for monitoring about 100 separate operations while a large PLC can handle over 1000 operations. Today the distinction between PLCs and DCSs has become less clear since PLCs are being designed to implement conventional and advanced control algorithms and DCSs that provide control for sequenced operations are being offered. PLCs are typically attached to the data highway in a DCS (Figure 2.4) and provide sequenced control functions during startup, shutdown, and override of the normal controllers in the event of an unsafe operating condition.

Fieldbus Technology. The fieldbus approach to distributed control is shown in Figure 2.6. The fieldbus approach distributes control to "smart" field-mounted devices (i.e., sensors, valves, and controllers with onboard microprocessors, which are used for complex operations and diagnostics) using a high-speed, digital two-way communication system that connects the field-mounted devices with **Local Area Networks (LANs)**, process automation systems, and the plant-wide network. This high-speed communication system is similar to the data highway used by DCSs. Optical fiber is used to provide communications between control rooms and is making inroads for other high-speed digital communications applications. While supervisory and advanced control functions are implemented in the LANs, the regulatory control functions are handled by the field mounted devices on

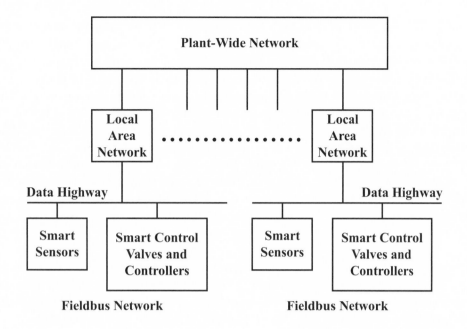

Figure 2.6 Schematic of the integration of the fieldbus with plant networks.

the fieldbus network. The advantage of the fieldbus design comes from the fact that instead of running electrical wires from each sensor/transmitter to the centralized control room and from the control room to each final control element, a large number of field mounted devices can be attached to a single two-wire communication line. This results in a significant reduction in the time and cost associated with system installation. Fieldbus technology is just beginning to be available commercially, but is expected to move regulatory controls from DCSs into the field in the future.

A conventional DCS is not equipped to handle the extra information associated with fieldbus devices.   DCSs are currently being designed with compatibility to fieldbus devices. As an example, Fisher-Rosemount's Delta-V DCS has an architecture that affords the complete utilization of fieldbus systems and other special purpose control hardware, and one DCS can service up to 30,000 control loops. The Delta-V DCS uses an Ethernet (i.e., a low-cost standard data highway) as its data highway and uses off-the-shelf PCs as its LCU microprocessors; therefore, this architecture is significantly less expensive than a traditional DCS.

2.3 Actuator Systems (Final Control Elements)

The actuator system for a process control system in the CPI is typically comprised of the control valve, which includes the valve body and the valve actuator, the I/P transmitter, and the instrument air system. The actuator system is known

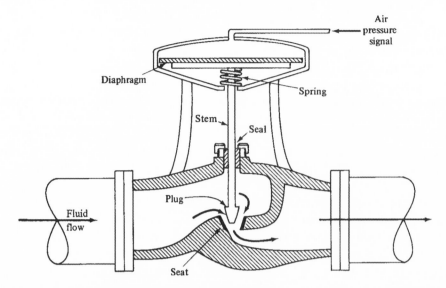

Figure 2.7   Schematic globe control valve.   Reprinted with permission from the McGraw-Hill Publishing Company.

industrially as the final control element. There is a variety of optional equipment, such as valve stem positioners and instrument air boosters, that is designed to enhance the performance of the actuator system. In a few cases, electrical heaters and variable speed devices are used as actuators.

       Control Valves. Control valves are broadly classified as sliding stem or rotary shaft devices. The most common type of control valve body in the CPI is the sliding stem valve shown schematically in Figure 2.7, which is known as a globe valve. They are called globe valves because of the globe shape of the flow chamber of the valve. Butterfly valves, which are discussed later in this section, are a rotary shaft valve. For globe valves, the closure member is a **valve plug** positioned at the end of the **valve stem**. As the valve stem is lowered, the plug approaches the **valve seat**, restricting the area for flow through the valve. When the plug makes contact with the valve seat, the valve is closed and flow through the valve is shut off. Globe valves are characterized by the fact that the plug travels in a direction perpendicular to the valve seat. The top of the valve stem is attached to a spring-and-diaphragm actuator, which is operated by the net force of instrument air and the actuator spring acting on the diaphragm. Consider Figure 2.7 for which, as the instrument air pressure is increased, the diaphragm moves against the spring, moving the stem downward, thus moving the valve plug closer to the valve seat, reducing the flow through the valve. Likewise, when the air pressure is decreased, the flow through the valve increases. Therefore, changes in the instrument air pressure coming from the I/P converter effect changes in the flow rate through the control valve. The flow direction through a control valve is usually opposite that shown in Figure 2.7 (i.e., flow is usually up through the plug/seat opening.

Figure 2.8 shows a detailed cross-section of a globe control valve with a plug in a **cage-guided valve** arrangement along with notation indicating some of the key components of a control valve and valve actuator. Note that the flow direction indicated in the inlet flow channel enters the plug/seat area from the bottom. The cage provides guidance for the plug as the plug moves toward or away from the valve seat. The cage also provides part of the flow restriction produced by the control valve. An example of a cage for a globe valve is shown in Figure 2.9. The valve packing reduces the leakage of the process stream into the environment but provides resistance to movement of the valve stem and contributes to sticking of the valve. The travel indicator provides a visual indication of the valve stem position.

Figure 2.10 shows the valve body assembly for a globe valve with an unbalanced plug. The unbalanced plug is subject to a static force directly related to the pressure drop across the valve and a flow force due to the fluid velocity past the plug. The greater these forces, the more force that is required to close the valve and the less force that is required to open the valve. Note that for Figure 2.7, it requires more force to open than to close due to the pressure drop and shear forces on the plug. Figure 2.11 shows the valve body assembly for a globe valve with balanced plugs. This valve is referred to as having balanced plugs because the top and bottom of the plug are subjected to the same downstream pressure when the valve is closed. Thus, the static force on the valve stem is low. In addition, the flow forces also cancel each other. Valves with balanced plugs are preferred because they are faster responding than valves with unbalanced plugs and require smaller valve actuators, but they should be used only with clean liquids and are not effective for tight shut-off of the flow. For example, an unbalanced plug is preferred for service with a liquid that tends to crystallize on the surface of the valve plug unless shear forces are present to prevent the buildup of crystals. A balanced plug is more susceptible to buildup due to the lower velocity by the plug because there are two separate flow paths.

Sizing of control valves is important because, if the valve is oversized or undersized, it can significantly affect the range over which the valve provides precise flow metering. When the valve is oversized, the valve is not sufficiently open to allow the valve to mechanically control the position of the valve plug. Typically for valve stem positions less than 10% open, the plug will regularly impact the valve seat, causing rapid wear to the valve. When the valve is undersized, the valve may be almost fully open so that accurate control is not possible or, in certain cases, the required flow cannot be met even when the valve is fully open. A simplified valve flow equation based on incompressible flow is given by

$$Q_f = K C_v(x) \sqrt{(P_1 - P_2)/\rho} \qquad \textbf{2.2}$$

where Q_f is the flow rate through the valve, K is a constant that depends on the units used in this equation, $C_v(x)$ is the valve coefficient, which is dependent upon the stem position (x) [i.e., $C_v(x) = C_v^{max}$ when the valve is fully open (i.e., x equal to 100%) and $C_v(x)=0$ when the valve is closed], ρ is the density of the fluid, P_1 is the pressure at the inlet to the control valve, and P_2 is the pressure at the exit of the control valve. **Note**

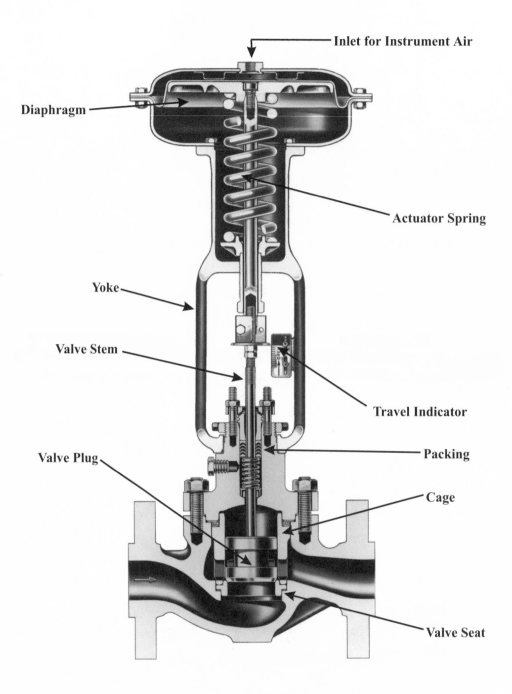

Figure 2.8 Cross-section of a globe valve with an unbalanced plug. Courtesy of Fisher-Rosemount.

Figure 2.9 Photograph of a cage for an equal percentage valve. Courtesy of Fisher-Rosemount.

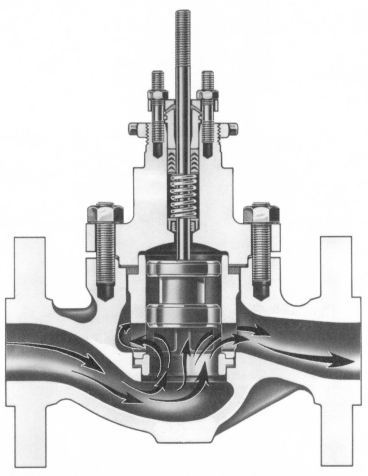

Figure 2.10 Cross-section of a globe valve body assembly with an unbalanced plug. Courtesy of Fisher-Rosemount.

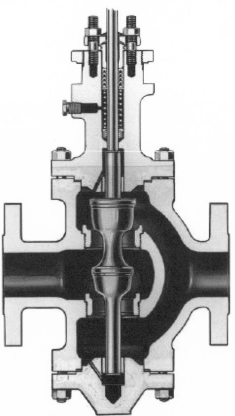

Figure 2.11 Cross-section of a globe valve body assembly with a balanced plug. Courtesy of Fisher-Rosemount.

that the values of C_v are chosen such that K is equal to unity when the density is expressed as the specific gravity, pressure drop (i.e., P_1-P_2) is given in psi, and the flow rate is expressed in GPM.   A more complex representation is required for compressible flow through a control valve, including the determination of the expansion factor and the sonic flow though the valve.

In general, control valves should be designed so that the valve provides accurate metering of the flow over a wide operating range conservatively below fully open and above the closed position. This reduces the likelihood that the valve will be expected to operate nearly fully open or fully closed where flow control performance is generally poor. The correct size of the valve should be selected as well as the proper type of valve to provide a wide operating range. Figure 2.12 shows how *f(x)* [Equation 2.3] varies with stem position for three types of valves: a quick-opening valve, an equal percentage valve, and a linear valve where

$$f(x) = \frac{C_v(x)}{C_v^{\max}}$$

2.3

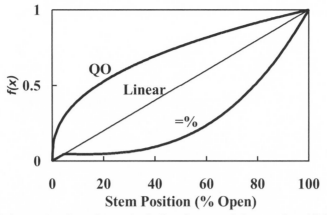

Figure 2.12 Inherent valve characteristics for a quick opening (QO), linear, and equal percentage valve (=%).

Table 2.1 Representative C_v's for an Equal Percentage Globe Valve.											
	Body Size (in)	Stem Position as a Percentage of Total Travel									
		10	20	30	40	50	60	70	80	90	100
C_v	1	0.79	1.25	1.80	2.53	3.63	5.28	7.59	10.7	12.7	13.2
	1.5	0.80	1.23	1.91	2.95	4.30	6.46	9.84	16.4	22.2	28.1
	2	1.65	2.61	4.30	6.62	11.1	20.7	32.8	44.7	50.0	53.8
	3	3.11	5.77	9.12	13.7	21.7	36.0	60.4	86.4	104	114
	4	4.90	8.19	13.5	20.1	31.2	52.6	96.7	140	170	190

Figure 2.12 shows the **inherent valve characteristics,** which indicate how the flow rate through the valve varies with stem position for a **fixed pressure drop across the valve**, for these types of control valves. The design of the plugs, valve seats, and cages (where applied) determine the particular flow versus stem position that a control valve provides and is also known as the **valve trim**. That is, the shape of the valve plug and the flow openings in the cage determine the shape of the flow restriction as the valve stem position is changed. For example for a quick-opening valve, as the valve is opened from fully closed, the cross-sectional area of the restriction of the valve increases much faster than the linear or equal percentage valves. Quick-opening valves are not usually used for feedback flow control applications but are used in cases where it is important to start a flow rate as quickly as possible (e.g., coolant flow through a by-pass around a control valve for an exothermic reactor). Linear and equal percentage valves are primarily used for flow control applications in the CPI. Table 2.1 list the C_v's for various sizes of a specific equal percentage valve as a function of

stem position expressed as a percentage of total travel. Other types of equal percentage valves have different values of C_v's than the ones listed in Table 2.1. Note that the values in Table 2.1 could be used to generate the inherent valve characteristics for the different valve sizes by applying Equation 2.3, recognizing that C_v^{max} is the value of C_v for the stem position a 100% open. The following equation represents C_v for a linear valve as a function of total valve travel, x.

$$C_v(x) = C_v^{max}\left[\frac{x}{100}\right] \qquad\qquad 2.4$$

Example 2.2 Flow Rate through a Control Valve

Problem Statement.   Calculate the flow rate of water through a 4-inch equal percentage control valve that is 80% open based on stem position with an available pressure drop across the valve of 30 psi. Obtain the C_v for this valve from Table 2.1

Solution.   Using Equation 2.2 with C_v equal to 140 from Table 2.1 and the specific gravity and K are equal to unity:

$$Q_f = 140\sqrt{30/1} = 767\ GPM \qquad\qquad ♠$$

Example 2.3 Pressure Drop Across a Control Valve

Problem Statement.   Calculate the required pressure drop across a 2-inch equal percentage control valve that is 40% open for a flow rate of water of 35 GPM. Obtain the C_v for this valve from Table 2.1

Solution.   Rearranging Equation 2.2 to solve for ΔP yields

$$\Delta P = \frac{\rho Q_f^2}{K^2 C_v^2}$$

Substituting C_v equal to 6.62 with the specific gravity and K equal to unity yields 28.0 psi.

♠

The inherent valve characteristics of a control valve are based on a fixed pressure drop across the valve. For most applications, however, the pressure drop across a control valve varies with the flow rate. The **installed valve characteristic** gives the flow rate through the valve as a function of stem position for a valve in service in a flow system. The pressure drop across the valve is a function of the flow rate; therefore, the installed valve characteristic depend on the particular flow system to which the valve is applied. From a process control standpoint, it is desirable to have a control valve that exhibits a linear relationship between flow rate and stem position over a wide range for the installed valve. As a rule of thumb, **the slope of the installed valve characteristic versus stem position should not vary greater than a factor of four over the range of operation for effective flow control.**

Table 2.2 Installed Pressure Drop For a Control Valve versus Flow Rate			
Q (GPM)	ΔP (psi)	Q (GPM)	ΔP (psi)
50	19.3	74	18.0
54	19.1	78	17.8
58	18.9	82	17.5
62	18.7	86	17.2
66	18.5	90	16.9
70	18.3	94	16.6

Example 2.4 Determine the Installed Flow Rate for a Known Valve Stem Position

Problem Statement.   Determine the flow rate though a 3-inch equal percentage control valve that is 40% open for the C_v data given in Table 2.1 and the installed pressure drop presented in Table 2.2.

Solution. From Table 2.2, ΔP is a function of flow rate; therefore, an iterative solution of Equation 2.2 is required. From Table 2.1, C_v is 13.7 for a 3-inch valve that is 40% open. From Table 2.2, it is clear that installed pressure drop is not a strong function of flow rate; therefore, a flow rate can be assumed to calculate the pressure drop for the installed valve, and this value used to update the flow rate. Assuming that the flow rate is 94 GPM, the installed pressure drop is equal to 16.6 psi using Table 2.2, and then Equation 2.2 yields a flow rate of 55.8 GPM. Using this flow rate in Table 2.2, the pressure drop for the installed valve is 19.0 psi by linear interpolation. Once again, Equation 2.2 is applied, yielding a calculated flow rate of 59.7 GPM. Updating ΔP (18.8 psi) yields a flow rate of 59.4 GPM, which is the converged solution for this problem.

♠

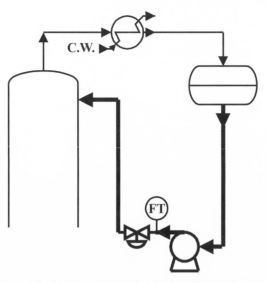

Figure 2.13 Schematic of a flow system for delivering reflux from the accumulator to the top tray of the column.

Example 2.5 Comparison between Linear and Equal Percentage Valves

Problem Statement. Consider the flow system shown schematically in Figure 2.13. This schematic represents the flow system that is used to deliver reflux from the accumulator to the top tray of the column. Compare the installed valve characteristics for a 4-inch linear and a 4-inch equal percentage valve for this system. Use the C_v's for the equal percentage valve from Table 2.1. Assume that the lines are 3-inch schedule 40 piping.

Solution. There are three sources of pressure changes in this flow system: (1) pressure drop through the straight run pipe, elbows and fittings, and the orifice for the flow sensor/transmitter, (2) the head increase provided by the pump, and (3) the pressure drop across the control valve. The first type of pressure drop varies directly with the square of the flow rate. The head increase provided by the pump (e.g., a centrifugal pump) decreases nonlinearly as the flow rate is increased. Because, for this example, the pressure above the liquid in the accumulator and the discharge pressure on the top tray of the column are approximately equal, the pressure drop across the control valve (ΔP_{valve}) is set by the difference between the head developed by the pump (ΔP_{pump}) and the pressure drop created by the line devices (ΔP_{line}), i.e.,

$$\Delta P_{valve} = \Delta P_{pump} - \Delta P_{line}$$

Figure 2.14 shows the pressure developed by the pump, the pressure drop due to line losses, and the available pressure drop for the control valve as a function of flow rate for the flow system shown in Figure 2.13. The relationships shown in this figure

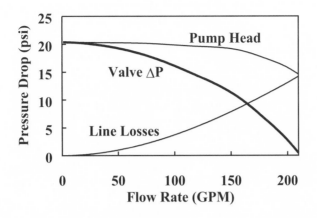

Figure 2.14 Pressure drops versus flow rate for the reflux flow system.

can be understood by recognizing that, at low flow rates, the pump head is at its largest value while the line losses are at their smallest. At this flow rate, the control valve must provide a relatively large pressure drop to maintain a low flow rate in the flow system. At large flow rates, the pump head is significantly reduced while the line losses are at their highest level. As a result, the control valve must provide a relatively small pressure drop to maintain the large flow rate in the flow system. For this case, the pressure drop across the control valve varies significantly with flow rate.

Using the pressure drop available for the control valve and the C_v's for a linear valve and an equal percentage valve (Table 2.1), the installed valve characteristics can be calculated using Equation 2.2. The C_v for a fully-open linear valve was assumed equal to the C_v for the fully open equal percentage valve. Then, the C_v for the linear valve is given using Equation 2.4. Since the available pressure drop is given as a function of flow rate in Figure 2.14, an iterative procedure as shown in Example 2.4 is

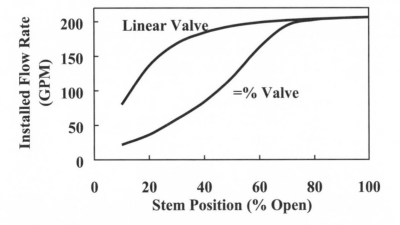

Figure 2.15 The installed valve characteristics of a linear and equal percentage valve for the reflux flow system.

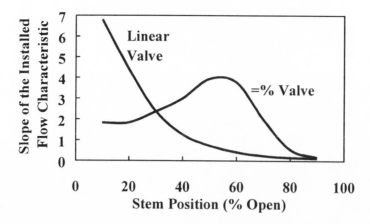

Figure 2.16 Slope of the installed valve characteristics for a linear and equal percentage valve.

required to calculate the installed valve characteristics. Figure 2.15 shows the installed valve characteristics for a linear and equal percentage valve for this example.

While it is clear from Figure 2.15 that there are differences between the installed valve characteristics for a linear and an equal percentage valve, at first glance the performance of these two valves may not appear to be significantly different. Since the performance criterion for a valve is based on the change in the slope of the installed valve characteristic, the slope of the installed valve characteristic (Figure 2.15) for the linear and equal percentage valves is shown in Figure 2.16. Based on the heuristic rule (i.e., the ratio of the maximum to the minimum slope of the installed valve characteristic should be less than 4), the linear valve could operate effectively between 10% and 50% or between 50% and 90%. On the other hand, the equal percentage valve can operate effectively between 10% and 85%. **This example demonstrates the advantage of equal percentage valves compared to linear valves for cases in which the pressure drop across the control valve varies significantly with flow rate.**

♠

Example 2.6 Comparison between Linear and Equal Percentage Valves

Problem Statement. Consider the flow system shown in Figure 2.17. The 5-inch line discharges liquid from the tank to an open reservoir. Compare the installed valve characteristics for a 4-inch linear and a 4-inch equal percentage valve for this system. Use the C_v's for the equal percentage valve from Table 2.1.

Solution. The hydrostatic head (30 ft) provides the driving force for flow through this system while the line losses and the control valve cause pressure drop. Similar to the previous example, since the pressure above the liquid in the tank and the discharge

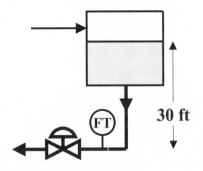

Figure 2.17 Schematic of a control valve in a line from an elevated tank to an open discharge.

pressure are assumed equal to atmospheric pressure, the pressure drop required by the control valve is given by

$$\Delta P_{valve} = \Delta P_{head} - \Delta P_{line}$$

Figure 2.18 shows the hydrostatic head, the pressure drop due to line losses, and the required pressure drop across the control valve as a function of flow rate. Since the level in the elevated tank is assumed to remain constant, the hydrostatic head is constant. Because **an oversized line was used for this example**, the line losses, which were modeled in a manner similar to the approach used for the last example, remain moderate even for the largest flow rate. As a result, the pressure drop for the control valve remains relatively constant for the full range of flow rates considered.

The installed valve characteristics for a linear valve and an equal percentage valve for this case are shown in Figure 2.19. These results were generated by choosing valve positions for the valves and applying the procedure demonstrated in Example 2.4 to determine the flow rate through the system. The available pressure drop for the

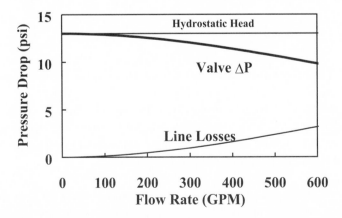

Figure 2.18 Pressure drop versus flow rate for the discharge line from the elevated tank.

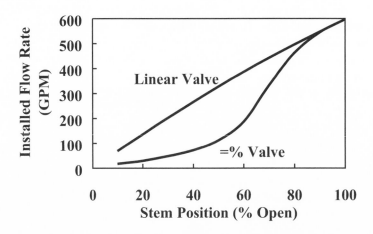

Figure 2.19 Installed valve characteristics for a linear and equal percentage valve applied to the discharge line for the elevated tank.

control valve versus flow rate shown in Figure 2.18 was used in this procedure. The C_v's for the equal percentage value were taken from Table 2.1. The C_v's for the linear valve were determined using Equation 2.4 assuming that the maximum value of C_v for the linear valve is equal to the maximum C_v for the equal percentage valve. From an examination of Figure 2.19, it is clear that the linear valve is the preferred choice in this case because its installed valve characteristic is much more linear than for the equal percentage valve. **This example demonstrates the advantage of linear valves compared to equal percentage valves for cases in which the pressure drop across the control valve does not vary significantly with flow rate.**

♠

In approximately 10% of the control valve applications in the CPI, the pressure drop across the control valve remains relatively constant, and a linear control valve is preferred. Figure 2.20 shows a case in which the flow rate of steam is

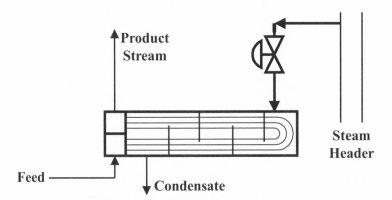

Figure 2.20 Schematic of a flow system from a steam header to a heat exchanger.

manipulated to heat a process stream. Since the pressure losses in the lines are usually relatively small compared to the pressure difference between the steam header and the steam pressure in the heat exchanger, the pressure drop across the control valve remains relatively constant for the wide range of steam flow rates to the heat exchanger. Since a linear control valve combined with a constant pressure drop across the valve results in a relatively linear installed characteristic, linear control valves are preferred when the pressure drop across a control valve remains relatively constant.

If the ratio of pressure drop across the control valve for lowest flow rate to highest flow rate is greater than 5, an equal percentage valve is recommended[2]. For Example 2.5 using Figure 2.15, the maximum flow rate is approximately 200 GPM. Then, using Figure 2.14, the maximum pressure drop is approximately 20 psi and the minimum is approximately 3 psi; therefore, the ratio is 6.6, indicating that an equal percentage valve should be used. For Example 2.6, using Figure 2.19, the maximum flow rate is approximately 600 GPM. Then, using Figure 2.18, the maximum pressure drop is approximately 13 psi and the minimum is approximately 10 psi; therefore, the ratio of the maximum to minimum pressure drop is 1.3, indicating that a linear valve should be used. It should be emphasized that the pressure drop remained relatively constant for Example 2.6 because an oversized line was used. Therefore, Examples 2.5 and 2.6 are consistent with this guideline. **A control valve can be converted to either a linear or equal percentage valve by changing the cage**, which is relatively easy to accomplish.

An important characteristic of a control valve is the **valve deadband**, which is a measure of how precisely a control valve can control the flow rate. The deadband for a steering system on an automobile is the maximum positive and negative turn in the steering wheel that does not result in a noticeable change in direction of the automobile. For a control valve, deadband is the maximum positive or negative change in the signal to a control valve that does not produce a measurable change in the flow rate. Valve deadband is caused by the friction between the valve stem and valve packing and other forces on the valve stem. Typically, industrial control valves without positioners have a deadband of 10 to 25%. That is, for a 25% deadband, a change in the signal to the control valve that is greater than 25% results in a measured change in the flow rate through the valve. On the other hand, a change that is less than 25% may not produce a change in the flow rate. Generally, the larger and older the control valve, the larger the deadband. A properly functioning valve with a valve positioner typically should have a deadband less than 0.5%. Note that deadband is reported in percent and represents the maximum relative change in the signal to the control valve that does not cause a measurable change in the flow rate through the valve.

Example 2.7 Control Valve Design Problem

Problem Statement. Size a control valve for service on a line carrying water with a maximum flow rate of 150 GPM and a minimum flow rate of 30 GPM. Assume an equal percentage valve with the pressure drop versus flow rate shown in Figure 2.14. The C_v's for equal percentage valves of different sizes are presented in Table 2.1.

Solution. A simplified design procedure is used to size the valve for this application. The average flow rate (90 GPM) is assumed to result when the valve is 67% open[3]. This allows us to size the valve, but after sizing, it is necessary to check to ensure that the valve can accurately control the flow at the maximum and minimum flow rates.

Equation 2.2 is used to determine the C_v of the valve at 67% open. Then, the valve size is selected based on matching C_v values listed in Table 2.1. To apply Equation 2.2, the pressure drop at the average flow rate is used. From Figure 2.14, ΔP is approximately 16 psi at a flow rate of 90 GPM. Using Equation 2.2, C_v is calculated equal to 25.0. Using the C_v values given in Table 2.1, a 1.5-inch control valve is approximately 90% open, a 2-inch valve is approximately 62% open, and a 3-inch valve is 51% open; therefore, based on the assumed design criterion, the 2-inch valve should be selected.

Now that the valve has been sized, check to ensure that accurate flow metering is available for the maximum and minimum flow rates. First, check the valve stem position for the maximum flow rate (150 GPM). From Figure 2.14, the available pressure drop is approximately 11 psi; therefore, using Equation 2.2, C_v is equal to 45.2, which corresponds to a valve position of 81% using linear interpolation applied to Table 2.1 for a 2-inch valve. For the minimum flow rate (30 GPM), the available pressure drop is approximately 19 psi; therefore, C_v is equal to 6.9, which corresponds to a valve position 40% open. While this sizing should work, the largest flow rate is near the upper limit for controllability for a 2-inch valve. For a 3-inch valve, it is 65% open at the maximum flow rate and 23% open at the minimum flow rate. From an examination of Figure 2.16, it is clear that the 3-inch valve is more nearly centered in the linear operation range of a control valve and, therefore, is preferred in this case. In fact, if the **turndown ratio** (i.e., the ratio of the maximum to minimum controllable flow rates) had been larger, approaching the upper limit for a control valve (i.e., a turndown ratio of 9) while keeping the maximum flow rate set at 150 GPM, a 2-inch valve would have been selected. Since the turndown ratio is only 5, a 3-inch valve provides a more flexible solution, affording larger flow rates if necessary in the future.

♠

As the turndown ratio for a control valve increases, the proper sizing of the valve and specification of the valve plug and valve cage geometry, to meet the controllability requirement for the maximum and minimum flows, becomes a much more challenging problem because the valve must be able to accurately control the flow rate at the minimum and maximum flow rates. Control valve vendors typically offer software to size control valves, but the control engineer should ensure that the available pressure drop across the control valve for the maximum and minimum flow rate used by the vendor to size the valve adequately represents the process.

When the turndown ratio is moderate (e.g., less than 3), a detailed valve sizing is not required. As a rule of thumb, when the turndown ratio is moderate, the valve size is usually set equal to the line size or one size smaller. For example, for a 4-inch line, a

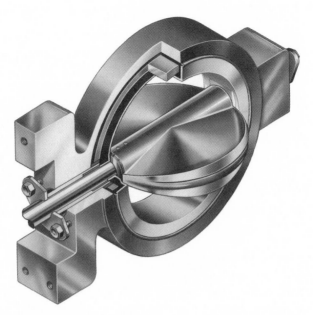

Figure 2.21 Partial cutaway view of a butterfly valve. Courtesy of Fisher-Rosemount.

3-inch or a 4-inch control valve is selected. The key issue here is to ensure that the control valve can handle the maximum flow rate. That is, the control valve should be no more than 80% open for the maximum anticipated flow rate.

Butterfly valves. Figure 2.21 shows a cutaway drawing of a butterfly valve. A disk is attached to a shaft so that, as the shaft is rotated, the restriction to flow is changed. Butterfly valves typically have a installed valve characteristic somewhere between a linear and quick-opening valve. Butterfly valves are flanged into a line and have a motor and positioner attached to move the disk to a specified orientation (i.e., a rotary actuator) and, therefore, regulate the flow rate through the valve. Butterfly valves are much less expensive than globe valves, but they usually have a range of accurate flow metering that is about half that of a globe valve. Butterfly valves become economically attractive as control valves for application with pipe diameters above 6 inches[2].

Cavitation. Cavitation results when the liquid vaporizes and then implodes inside the control valve. As a fluid flows through a control valve the pressure drops sharply near the restriction between the valve plug and the valve seat due to high velocity and friction losses in this region. As the fluid passes the valve restriction region and enters a region with a larger cross-section, the pressure increases sharply (i.e., pressure recovery) due to the drop in the fluid velocity. If the pressure in the valve restriction region is less than the vapor pressure of the liquid, a portion of the liquid vaporizes and, when the pressure recovers due to a drop in the velocity, the bubbles violently collapse at nucleation sites on the metal surface. Cavitation results in noise, vibration, reduced flow, and possibly rapid erosion of the body of the valve. In the field, cavitation sounds like marbles are flowing through the valve.

Valve Actuator. The valve actuator provides the force necessary to change the valve stem position and alter the flow rate through the valve. The valve actuator must provide the force necessary to overcome pressure forces, flow forces, friction from valve packing (the major contribution), and friction from the plug contacting the valve cage. For example, for a 15-inch diameter diaphragm with an instrument air pressure change of 12 psi (15 psig minus 3 psig) and for a valve stem travel of 0.75 inches, the spring constant for the spring in the valve actuator is nearly 3000 lb/in, which is usually sufficient to overcome the resistance to the movement of the stem.

Figure 2.22 shows a cross-section of a typical **air-to-close actuator**, which fails open when instrument air pressure is lost. The pressure of the instrument air acts on the diaphragm/spring system from the top causing the valve to close as the air pressure supplied to the valve actuator is increased. The diaphragm is constructed of an air impermeable, flexible material (typically fabric-reinforced neoprene) that allows the valve plug to move from fully open to closed as the instrument air pressure is increased from 3 to 15 psig. Note that the force generated by the instrument air pressure on the surface of the diaphragm is balanced by the force of the compressed actuator spring (Figures 2.7, 2.8, and 2.22). An actuator with a control valve with an air-to-close valve actuator is also known as a **reverse-acting final control element** because the valve position decreases as the air pressure to the valve is increased. For an **air-to-open actuator**, the instrument air enters below the diaphragm so that, as the air pressure is increased, the valve stem moves upward, opening the valve. An actuator with a control valve with an air-to-open valve actuator is also known as a **direct-acting final control element** because the valve position increases as the air pressure to the valve is increased. Valve actuators generally provide a fail-safe function. That is, in the event of a loss of instrument air pressure, the valve actuator causes the valve to open fully or to close. An actuator with an air-to-open unit fails closed and an air-to-close unit fails fully open. In this manner, a valve actuator can be chosen such that the proper failure mode is obtained. For example, consider the valve on the cooling water to an exothermic reactor. Obviously, an air-to-close actuator is selected so that the loss of instrument air pressure opens the value and, therefore, cool down the reactor instead of allowing a thermal runaway.

Example 2.8 Valve Actuator Selection

Problem Statement. Consider the control valves for the stripping section of a distillation column shown in Figure 2.23. Determine whether air-to-open or air-to-close valve actuators should be used for the two valves in this case.

Solution. First consider the valve on the product line from the reboiler. If this valve fails (e.g., a loss of instrument air pressure), is it better for the valve to fail open or fail closed? In this case, if the valve were to fail open, the reboiler level could be lost, and the reboiler tubes could be exposed, causing damage due to overheating by the steam; therefore, an air-to-open valve actuator should be selected for the valve actuator on the

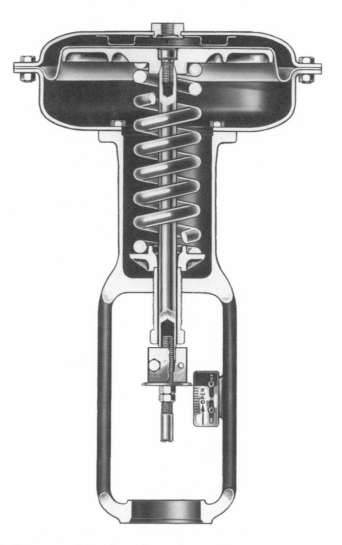

Figure 2.22 Cross-section of an air-to-close valve actuator. Courtesy of Fisher Rosemount.

valve on the bottoms product line. Likewise, an air-to-open valve should be selected to prevent excessive steam flow to the reboiler in the event that the actuator on the steam valve were to fail. Excessive steam flow to the reboiler could also expose the reboiler tubes even though the valve on the bottom product line is closed.   ♠

Example 2.9 Valve Actuator Selection

Problem Statement. Consider the control valve on the refrigerant for the overhead condenser for the rectifying section of a distillation column shown in Figure 2.24. Determine whether an air-to-open or an air-to-close valve actuator should be used for this valve.

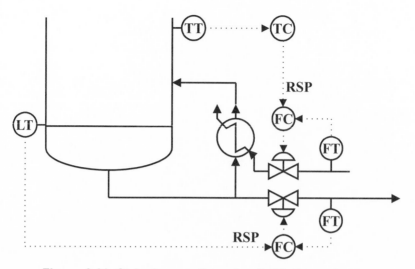

Figure 2.23 Stripping section of a distillation column.

Solution. If the valve on the refrigerant were to fail closed, the pressure in the column would increase sharply and require venting of a significant amount of overhead product; therefore, an air-to-close valve should be selected for this application. During a valve failure, the column uses more refrigerant than necessary and the column over-purifies the overhead product if an air-to-close actuator were used, but venting from the column is avoided.

♠

I/P Transmitter. The I/P transmitter is an electro-mechanical device, which converts the 4-20 mA signal from the controller to a 3-15 psig instrument air pressure signal to the valve actuator, which in turn affects the valve stem position.

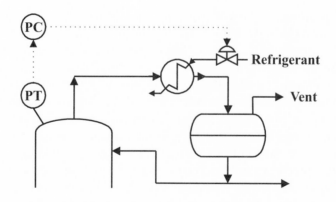

Figure 2.24 Schematic of an overhead condenser of a distillation column.

Figure 2.25 Photograph of a globe valve with a pneumatic valve positioner. Courtesy of Fisher-Rosemount.

Optional equipment. Several devices are available for improving the overall performance of final control elements.

Valve positioners. The **valve positioner** (Figure 2.25), which is usually contained in its own box and is mounted on the side of the valve actuator, is designed to control the valve stem position at a prescribed position in spite of packing friction and other forces on the stem. The valve positioner itself is a high-gain proportional controller that compares the measured stem position with the specified stem position and makes adjustments to the instrument air pressure to provide the desired stem position. In this case, the setpoint for the valve positioner can be a pneumatic signal coming from an I/P converter or the 4-20 mA analog signal coming directly from the controller. Due to the friction from the packing, it is not possible to move the valve stem position to a precise value. As a result, the valve positioner opens and closes the valve bracketing the desired stem position. This high-frequency, high-gain feedback provided by the valve positioner can result in precise metering of the **average** flow rate. A valve with a deadband of 25% can provide a repeatability of the flow rate of less than ±0.5% for the average flow rate using a valve positioner. Valves with low levels of valve friction can control the average flow rate to a precision approaching ±0.1% using a valve positioner, which corresponds to controlling valve position to within 0.001 inches. As a point of reference, a penny is 0.06 inches in thickness.

For flow control loops that are controlled by a DCS, a valve positioner is a necessity because the control interval for a DCS (i.e., 0.5 to 1.0 seconds) is not fast enough for most flow control loops. There are two general types of valve positioners: pneumatic positioners and digital positioners. Pneumatic positioners receive a pneumatic signal from the I/P converter and send a pneumatic signal to the valve actuator. A more modern type of valve positioner is a digital positioner, which receives the 4-20 mA analog signal directly and adjusts the instrument air pressure sent to the valve actuator. Digital positioners have the advantage that they can be calibrated, tuned, and tested remotely, and they can also be equipped with self-tuning capabilities. Valve positioners represent an additional cost and should be applied only in cases for which they are needed.

Booster relays. Booster relays are designed to provide extra flow capacity for the instrument air system, which decreases the **dynamic response time** of the control valve (i.e., the time for most of a change to occur). Booster relays are used on valve actuators for large valves that require a large volume of instrument air to move the valve stem. Booster relays use the pneumatic signal as input and adjust the pressure of a high flow rate capacity instrument air system that provides air pressure directly to the diaphragm of the valve actuator.

Adjustable speed pumps. Adjustable speed pumps can be used instead of the control valve systems just discussed. A centrifugal pump directly driven by a variable speed electric motor is the most commonly used form of adjustable speed pump. Another type of adjustable speed pump is based on using a variable speed electric motor combined with a positive displacement pump. Adjustable speed pumps have the following advantages compared with control valve-based actuators: 1) they use less energy; 2) they provide fast, accurate flow metering without additional device requirements; and 3) they do not require an instrument air system. Their major disadvantages are capital cost, particularly for large flow rate applications, and lower reliability than control valves. Another disadvantage of adjustable speed pumps is that they do not fail open or closed like a control valve with an air-to-close or air-to-open actuator, respectively. As a result, the CPI almost exclusively use control valve-based actuators except for low flow applications, such as catalyst addition systems or base injection pumps for wastewater neutralization, which typically use adjustable speed pumps.

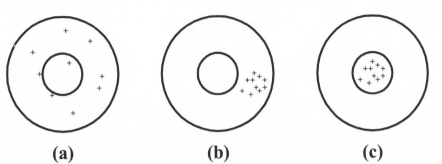

Figure 2.26 Targets which demonstrate the difference between accuracy and repeatability. (a) Neither accurate nor repeatable. (b) Repeatable but not accurate. (c) Accurate and repeatable.

2.4 Sensor Systems

Sensor systems are composed of the sensor, transmitter, and associated signal processing capabilities. The sensor measures certain quantities (e.g., voltage, current, or resistance) associated with devices in contact with the process such that the measured quantities correlate strongly with the actual controlled variable value. There are two general classifications for sensors: continuous measurements and discrete measurements. Continuous measurements are, as the term implies, generally continuously available while discrete measurements update at discrete times. Pressure, temperature, level, and flow sensors typically yield continuous measurements while certain composition analyzers (e.g., gas chromatographs) provide discrete-time measurements based on taking and analyzing samples periodically.

Several terms are used to characterize the performance of a sensor:

- **Zero** is the lowest reading available from the sensor/transmitter, i.e., the sensor reading corresponding to a transmitter output of 4 mA.
- **Span** is the difference between the largest measurement value made by the sensor/transmitter and the lowest.
- **Range** is the maximum and minimum sensor reading. For example, the range of a pressure sensor can be expressed as a maximum of 150 psig and a minimum of 50 psig, corresponding to a span of 100 psig.
- **Accuracy** is the difference between the value of the measured variable indicated by the sensor and its true value (Figure 2.26). The true value is never known; therefore, accuracy is estimated by the difference between the sensor value and an accepted standard.
- **Repeatability** is related to the difference between the sensor readings while the process conditions remain constant (Figure 2.26).
- **Process measurement dynamics** indicate how quickly the sensor responds to changes in the value of the measured variable.
- **Rangeability** is the ratio of the largest accurate sensor reading to the smallest accurate reading.

- **Calibration** involves the adjustment of the correlation between the sensor output and the predicted measurement so that the sensor reading agrees with a standard. Most plants calibrate their temperature and pressure sensors once every year or two. Many composition analyzers are calibrated every day.

Example 2.10 Sensor Signals

Problem Statement. Determine the temperature reading corresponding to a 10 mA analog signal from a temperature transmitter that has a span of 200°C and a zero equal to 20°C.

Solution. The position between the maximum and minimum analog signal is given by

$$\frac{10\,mA\ -\ 4\,mA}{20\,mA\ -\ 4\,mA} = 0.375$$

This corresponds to a 37.5% position on the temperature span of the transmitter or $0.375 \times 200°C$, i.e., 75°C. Then the temperature sensor reading is simply 75°C plus the temperature of the zero (20°C) for a sensor reading of 95°C.

♠

Example 2.11 Sensor Signals

Problem Statement. Determine the value of the electric analog reading in mA for an actual level of 45% for a level transmitter that has a span of 40% and a zero of 20%.

Solution. A 45% level measurement represents a position between the maximum level measurement (60%) and the minimum level measurement (20%) of

$$Position\ in\ span = \frac{45\% - 20\%}{60\% - 20\%} = 0.625$$

Then, the electric analog signal is given by

$$4\,mA + 0.625\left[20\,mA\ -\ 4\,mA\right] = 14\,mA$$

♠

Overview. A wide variety of sensors is available for measuring process variables[3]. Choosing the correct sensor for a particular application depends on the controlled variable, the properties of the process, accuracy and repeatability requirements, and costs, both initial and maintenance. Best practice[4] for instrument selection, for instrument installation, and to reduce maintenance costs has been identified for the CPI. Following is an analysis of the control-relevant issues associated with some of the most commonly used sensors for feedback control in the CPI.

Smart sensors. Smart sensors have built-in microprocessor-based diagnostics. For example, some smart pH sensors are able to identify the buildup of coatings on the pH electrode surface and trigger a wash cycle to reduce the effect of these coatings. In general, smart sensors are moderately more expensive than conventional sensors but, when they are properly selected and implemented, smart sensors can be an excellent investment due to greater sensor reliability and reduced maintenance.

Temperature Measurements. The two primary temperature sensing devices used in the CPI are **thermocouples (TCs)** and **resistance thermometer detectors (RTDs)**.

Thermocouples. Thermocouples are based on the fact that two metal junctions (i.e., the contacting of two different types of metal wire) at different temperatures generate a voltage and the magnitude of the voltage is proportional to the temperature difference. Thermocouples are constructed of two different types of wire that are connected to each other at both ends (i.e., junctions). The cold junction of a thermocouple is normally at ambient temperature, but is electrically compensated so that it behaves as if it were at a constant temperature. The hot junction is used to measure the process temperature of interest. In general, the voltage generated by the hot junction, inside a thermowell in contact with a process fluid, varies quite linearly with the process temperature. Thermocouples are constructed of metal pairs including iron-constantan, copper-constantan, chromel-alumel, and platinum-rhodium. The latter is the most popular material of construction and results in the most accurate thermocouples. (Alumel, chromel, and constantan are trade names for alloys that are used to make these thermocouples.)

RTDs. RTDs are based on the observation that the resistance of certain metals depends strongly upon their temperature. A Wheatstone bridge or other type of resistance measuring bridge can be used to measure the resistance of the RTD element and thus estimate the process temperature. Platinum and nickel are typically used for RTDs. Platinum has a much wider useful range (i.e., -200°C to 800°C) while nickel is more limited (-80°C to 320°C) but is less expensive than platinum. Each of these metals has a known temperature dependence for its resistance; therefore, calibration requires only applying the RTD to a known temperature condition. Unlike TCs, RTDs require a separate power supply.

Thermistors. Thermistors are also a popular temperature sensing device that is based on the temperature dependence of its resistance. Thermistors have a limited range measurement (e.g., ±10°F) and have a repeatability approximately equal to a TC, but they are much less expensive than an RTD. Because a thermistor has a much larger sensitivity (change in resistance for a change in temperature), the hardware necessary to make the resistance measurement is less expensive for a thermistor.

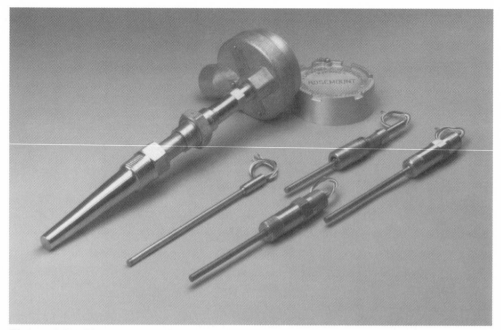

Figure 2.27 Photograph of hardware for measuring process temperature. Included are a thermowell and transmitter housing (left) and several TCs. Courtesy of Fisher-Rosemount.

Optical pyrometers.   Optical pyrometers are used to measure high temperatures (>1000°C) without requiring thermal contact with the temperature point. Optical pyrometers estimate the temperature from the wave length for the radiation of a hot body (e.g., furnace tubes).

Thermowells.   Thermowells are typically cylindrical metal tubes that are capped on one end and protrude into a process line or vessel to bring the TC or RTD in thermal contact with the process fluid.   Thermowells provide a rugged, corrosion resistant barrier between the process fluid and the sensor that allows for removal of the sensor while the process is still in operation.   Thermowells that are coated with polymer or other adhering material can significantly increase the lag associated with the temperature measurement, i.e., significantly increase the response time of the sensor.   Figure 2.27 shows a typical thermowell and housing as well as several thermocouples.

Overall comparison of TCs and RTDs.   TCs are less expensive and more rugged than RTDs but are an order of magnitude less repeatable than RTDs. Typically, RTDs should be used for important temperature control points, such as on reactors and distillation columns.

Repeatability, accuracy and dynamic response.   TCs typically have a repeatability of ±1°C while RTDs have a repeatability of ±0.1°C. Accuracy is a much more complex issue. Errors in the temperature reading can result from heat loss along the length of the thermowell, electronic error, sensor error, error from nonlinearity, calibration errors, and other sources[5].

Figure 2.28 Photograph of a differential pressure sensor/transmitter (DP cell). Courtesy of Fisher-Rosemount.

The dynamic response time of a TC or RTD sensor within a thermowell can vary over a wide range and is a function of the type of process fluid (i.e., gas or liquid), the fluid velocity past the thermowell, the separation between the sensor and inside wall of the thermowell, and material filling the thermowell (e.g., air or oil). Typical well-designed applications result in time constants of 6-20 seconds for measuring the temperature of most fluids.

Pressure Measurements. The most commonly used pressure sensing devices use mechanical elements to make process pressure measurements. A differential pressure cell (Figure 2.28) uses a balance bar that is deflected based on the pressure differential between two compartments that are in contact with opposite sides of the balance bar. A precision forcing motor is used to maintain the balance bar at a specific position. The measurement of the pressure is directly related to the force used by the forcing motor to balance the bar.

Strain gauges are used to measure high process pressures. Strain gauges are based upon the property that when a wire is stretched elastically, its length increases while its diameter decreases, both of which increase the resistance of the wire. Serpentine lengths of elastic resistance wires can be bonded to the surface of an elastic element (diaphragm). When deformation of the diaphragm occurs as the result of a pressure increase, the wires elongate and, therefore, the resistance of these wires increases, indicating an increased pressure reading. These pressure sensing devices actually measure the differential pressure across the diaphragm, but can be used to measure a process pressure in gauge pressure by exposing the low pressure side of the device to the atmosphere. Another approach is to use a strain gauge to measure the

Figure 2.29 Photograph of a paddle type orifice plate against a flanged pipe. Courtesy of Thermocouple Instruments, Limited.

effect of a pressure change on a coiled tube. The resistance of the strain gauge is usually measured using a Wheatstone bridge. Pressure sensors are very fast responding. Repeatability for pressure measurement is generally less than ±0.1%.

Flow Measurements. The most commonly used flow meter is an orifice meter. An orifice meter uses the measured pressure drop across a fixed-area flow restriction (an orifice) to predict the flow rate. An example of a paddle type orifice plate is shown in Figure 2.29. The pressure drop across an orifice is usually measured using a **DP cell** (Figure 2.28). The pressure drop across an orifice plate, ΔP, is related to the volumetric flow, Q, by the following equation:

$$Q = \frac{C_d A_2}{\sqrt{1-(A_2/A_1)^2}} \sqrt{\frac{2 g_c \Delta P}{\rho}} \qquad \qquad 2.5$$

where A_1 is the pipe cross-sectional area, A_2 is the cross-sectional area of the orifice, ρ is the density of the fluid, g_c is a unit conversion factor (32.2 lb$_m$-ft/lb$_f$-s^2), and C_d is the discharge coefficient. C_d is a function of the Reynolds number and the type of fluid, but typically is approximately 0.6. A straight run of pipe preceding the orifice meter is required to develop uniform flow at the orifice meter. If not, an error as large as 15% can result in the predicted flow rate. Since the orifice meter is based upon a measured pressure drop, it is a very fast-responding measurement. Orifice meters typically provide a repeatability in the range of ±0.3 to ±1%.

Example 2.12 Flow Rate through an Orifice Plate

Problem Statement. Calculate the flow rate of water through a 1.5-inch diameter orifice in a schedule 40 3-inch line if the pressure drop across the orifice is 5 psi.

Solution. The inside diameter of a schedule 40 3-inch line is 3.068 inches. Then A_2 is calculated to be 1.767 in^2 and A_1 is 7.393 in^2. The density of water is taken as 62.4 lb_m/ft^3. Equation 2.5 can be applied directly to solve this problem, but care should be taken with the associated unit conversions. For example, g_c (32.2 lb_m-ft/lb_f-s^2) and the conversion of in^2 to ft^2 is required to cancel the units. Applying Equation 2.5 yields

$$Q = \frac{(0.6)(1.767\,in^2)(ft^2\,/\,144\,in^2)}{\sqrt{1-(1.767\,/\,7.393)^2}}\sqrt{\frac{(2)(5\,lb_f\,/\,in^2)(32.2\,lb_m\cdot ft\,/\,lb_f\cdot s^2)}{(62.4\,lb_m\,/\,ft^3)(ft^2\,/\,144\,in^2)}}$$

$$= 0.2067\,ft^3\,/\,s = 92.8\,GPM$$

♠

Example 2.13 Pressure Drop across an Orifice Plate

Problem Statement. For the system described in Example 2.12, calculate the pressure drop across the orifice for a flow rate of 75 GPM.

Solution. Solving for ΔP by rearranging Equation 2.5 yields

$$\Delta P = \frac{Q^2\rho\left[1-(A_2\,/\,A_1)^2\right]}{2g_c\,C_d^2\,A_2^2}$$

Substituting the numerical values and performing the necessary unit conversions yields

$$\Delta P = \frac{(75\,gal\,/\,min)^2\,(min\,/\,60\,s)^2\,(ft^3\,/\,7.481\,gal)^2\,(62.4\,lb_m\,/\,ft^3)[1-(1.767\,/\,7.393)^2]}{(2)(32.2\,lb_m\cdot ft\,/\,lb_f\cdot s^2)(0.6)^2(1.767\,in^2)^2(ft^2\,/\,144\,in^2)}$$

$$\Delta P = 3.27\,psi$$

A simpler method to solve this problem is to apply Equation 2.5 twice, i.e., once for Example 2.12 and once for this example, and take the ratio, noting that all the parameters of the problem cancel except ΔP and Q. Then, the pressure drop for 75 GPM can be calculated directly by

$$\Delta P_{75\,GPM} = \Delta P_{92.8\,GPM} \left[\frac{75\,GPM}{92.8\,GPM} \right]^2 = 3.27\,psi$$

♠

Example 2.14 Sizing an Orifice Meter

Problem Statement. Size an orifice meter for service on a 2½-inch schedule 40 pipe carrying water with a maximum flow rate of 180 GPM and a minimum flow rate of 60 GPM. Assume that the line pressure is 150 psig.

Solution. The design of an orifice meter is directly related to the differential pressure sensor that is used. Typically, differential pressure sensors are available in various sizes indicated by the maximum pressure drop, e.g., 1 psi, 2 psi, 5 psi, and 10 psi sizes. Sizing an orifice meter involves choosing a pressure drop across the orifice plate and then calculating β, the ratio of the diameter of the opening in the orifice to the inside pipe diameter, while honoring the following three restrictions: (1) β should be greater than 0.2 and less than 0.7 for most orifice designs[3], (2) the pressure drop measured across the orifice should be less than 4% of the line pressure[3], and (3) the Reynolds number for flow in the pipe must be between 10^4 and 10^7 for normal operation[3]. Since the maximum turndown ratio for a differential pressure sensor is about 9 and because there is a square root relation between flow rate and pressure drop, the maximum turndown ratio for the flow rate through an orifice meter is about 3. On other hand, an orifice meter that uses a smart transmitter can provide a turndown ratio of 10:1.

Assume that a differential pressure sensor with a 2 psi maximum is used for this application. For the maximum flow, it is assumed that the resulting differential pressure is 1.33 psi (67% of full reading[3]). This result corresponds to 0.9% of the line pressure, which satisfies the second requirement. Recognizing that $D_2 = \beta D_1$ and rearranging Equation 2.5 to solve for β yields

$$\beta = \sqrt[4]{\frac{Q_f^2}{Q_f^2 + 2C_d^2 A_1^2 g_c \Delta P / \rho}}$$

This equation, with the diameter of 2½-inch schedule 40 ferrous pipe (2.469 in), a pressure drop of 1.33 psi, C_d equal to 0.61, and a flow rate of 180 GPM yields a β of 0.742. Because this β is greater than 0.7, this is not an acceptable design for an orifice meter. Since a larger pressure drop across the orifice is required, the next largest size differential pressure sensor should be used, i.e., a 5 psi differential sensor. For the maximum flow, it is now assumed that the resulting differential pressure is 3.33 psi (67% of full reading). This result corresponds to 2.2% of the line pressure, which satisfies the second restriction. Using the previous equation for β, a pressure drop of 3.33 psi at a flow rate of 180 GPM yields a β of 0.573. The Reynolds number for the pipe is 1.9×10^5, which is also within the specified range. The turndown ratio for the

Figure 2.30   Photograph of a vortex shedding flow meter. Courtesy of Yokogawa Corporation of America.

flow is 3; therefore, the low flow rate should also be accurately measured. As a result, β equal to 0.573 (i.e., an orifice bore equal to 1.41 inches) with a 5 psi differential pressure sensor is a viable orifice meter design for this application.

♠

Other types of flow meters, including vortex shedding flow meters and magnetic flow meters, are used for flow rate control in special situations. Vortex shedding flow meters (Figure 2.30) are based on inserting an unstreamlined obstruction (i.e., a blunt object) in the pipe and measuring the frequency of downstream pulses created by the flow past the obstruction. The flow rate is directly related to the frequency of the pulses. Vortex shedding meters are recommended for clean, low viscosity liquids and gases, and can typically provide a rangeability of about 15:1. Care should be taken to ensure that (1) cavitation does not occur in the measuring zone and (2) the velocity does not become less than its lower velocity limit.   Vapor bubbles resulting from cavitation increase the noise and decrease the accuracy of the measurement; therefore, care should be taken to ensure that the pressure in the line remains above a lower limit. Vortex shedding meters are usually accurate at Reynolds number greater than 10,000.

Figure 2.31 Photograph of a magnetic flow meter. Courtesy of Sparling, Inc.

Magnetic flow meters (Figure 2.31), which are low-pressure drop devices, can be used to measure the flow rate of electrically conducting fluids. The conductivity of typical tap water, which is not particularly conductive, is sufficient to use a magnetic flow meter. Magnetic flow meters are based on the principle that a voltage is generated by an electronically conducting fluid flowing through a magnetic field. The magnetic flow meter creates a magnetic field using an electromagnet and measures the resulting voltage, which is proportional to the flow rate in the pipe. Magnetic flow meters provide accurate flow measurements over a wide range of flow rates and are especially accurate at low flow rates. Deposition on the electrodes is a limitation of magnetic flow meters in certain cases. Typical applications of magnetic flow meters are for metering the flow rates of viscous fluids, slurries, and highly corrosive chemicals[6]. Magnetic flow meters are used extensively in water treatment facilities. The lower velocity limit for magnetic flow meters is about 1 ft/s for water and increases for more viscous fluids.

The purchase price of vortex shedding flow meters and magnetic flow meters is much higher than of orifice meters, but their maintenance costs are usually much lower since they do not use pressure taps, which are prone to plugging. **Flow meters**, whichever type is chosen, **are typically installed upstream of the control valve to provide the most accurate, lowest noise measurement** to avoid the effects of flashing and/or nonuniform flow. Installing the flow sensor downstream of a control

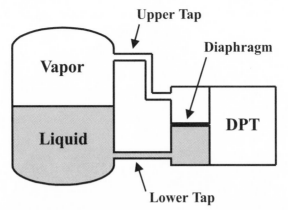

Figure 2.32 Schematic of a typical differential pressure level measurement system.

valve subjects the sensor to flow fluctuations and even two-phase flow, which reduce the sensor accuracy and increase the measurement noise.

Level measurements. The most common type of level measurement is based upon measuring the hydrostatic head in a vessel using a differential pressure measurement. This approach typically works well as long as there is a large difference between the density of the light and heavy phases. Because it is based on a pressure measurement, this approach usually has relatively fast measurement dynamics. If the pressure tap connections between the process and the DP cell become partially blocked, the dynamic response time of the sensor can be significantly increased, resulting in slower-responding level measurements. Level measurements typically have a repeatability of approximately ±1%.

Figure 2.32 shows how a differential pressure measurement can be used to determine the level in a vessel. This approach directly measures the hydrostatic head in the vessel. Because of plugging and corrosion problems, it may be necessary to keep the process fluid from entering the differential pressure transmitter. In addition, it is important to keep vapor from condensing in the upper tap and collecting in the low pressure side of the differential pressure transmitter. This can usually be accomplished by insulating the pressure tap and wrapping it with resistive heating tape. There are other level measuring approaches that are based upon a variety of physical phenomena and are used in special cases. Float activated devices, which are similar to the level measuring approach used in the water reservoir in toilets, are sometimes used in the CPI.

Chemical Composition Analyzers. The most commonly used on-line composition analyzer is the **gas chromatograph (GC)** while inroads have been recently made by infrared analyzers and ultraviolet and visible-radiation analyzers. On-line composition measurements are generally much more expensive than temperature, pressure, flow rate, and level measurements with much lower reliability. The annual cost of an on-line composition analyzer can easily be in excess of $100,000 due to high capital costs and large maintenance costs. Due to the large associated cost, the decision to use an on-line composition analyzer is normally based on process economics. For example, for refineries and high volume chemical intermediate plants, on-line analyzers (usually GCs) are used extensively because 1) due to the large flow rates used in these large plants, process improvement due to on-line composition analysis easily economically justifies the application and 2) the measurement techniques are generally well established for this industry. On the other hand, for the specialty chemicals industry, much less use of on-line analyzers is made due to 1) lower production rates and 2) unavailability of reliable analyzers.

Gas chromatographs. GCs process a vapor sample, along with a carrier gas, through a small diameter (approximately 3/8 inch) packed column. As a result of different affinities of the sample components for the column packing, the various sample components have different residence times in the packed column. As each component emerges from the column, it passes through a detector process. The most commonly used detectors are thermal conductivity detectors and hydrogen-flame ionization detectors. Hydrogen-flame ionization detectors are more complicated than thermal conductivity detectors but are much more sensitive for hydrocarbons and organic compounds. Repeatability for GCs can vary over a wide range and is dependent on the particular system being measured. New analyzer readings are typically updated every 3 to 10 minutes for GCs.

Infrared, ultraviolet and visible radiation. These analyzers are based on the property that each compound absorbs specific frequencies of radiation and the greater the concentration, the higher the degree of absorption. To identify a component from among several components, only the absorption frequencies of the component of interest are required.

Sampling system. The sampling system is responsible for collecting a representative sample of the process and delivering it to the analyzer for analysis. Obviously, the reliability of the sampling system directly affects the reliability of the overall composition analysis system. The transport delay associated with the sampling system contributes directly to the overall deadtime associated with an on-line composition measurement. For example, an improperly designed sampling system can result in a transport time of one hour for the sample to travel from the process to the analyzer while a properly designed system can result in a transport delay of 10 seconds or less. This difference in sampling deadtime can have a dramatic effect on the performance of a control loop. Table 2.3 summarizes the dynamic characteristics, repeatability, and rangeability or turndown ratio of control valve systems and several different types of sensors

Table 2.3

Summary of Control-Relevant Aspects of Actuators and Sensors

	Time Constant (sec)	Valve Deadband or Sensor Repeatability	Turndown Ratio, Rangeability or Range
Control valve *	3 - 15	10 - 25%	9:1
Control valve w/valve positioner*	0.5 - 2	0.1 - 0.5%	9:1
Flow control loop w/valve positioner*	0.5 - 2	0.1 - 0.5%	9:1
TC w/ thermowell	6 - 20	±1.0 °C	-200°C to 1300°C
RTD w/ thermowell	6 - 20	±0.1 °C	-200°C to 800°C
Magnetic flow meter	<1	±0.1%	20:1
Vortex shedding meter	<0.1	±0.2%	15:1
Orifice flow meter	<0.2	±0.3 - ±1%	3:1
Orifice meter w/smart transmitter	<0.2	±0.3 - ±1%	10:1
Differential Pressure Level Indicator	<1	±1%	9:1
Pressure sensor	<0.2	±0.1%	9:1

* Based on globe valves.

Transmitters. The transmitter converts the output from the sensor (i.e., a millivolt signal, a differential pressure, a displacement, etc.) into a 4-20 mA analog signal that represents the measured value of the controlled variable. Consider a transmitter that is applied to a temperature sensor. Assume that the maximum temperature that the transmitter is expected to handle is 200°C and that the minimum temperature is 50°C, then the span of the transmitter is 150 °C and the zero of the transmitter is 50°C. Transmitters are typically designed with two knobs that allow for independent adjustment of the span and the zero of the transmitter. Properly functioning and implemented transmitters are so fast that they do not normally contribute to the dynamic lag of the process measurement. Modern transmitters have features that, if not applied properly, can reduce the effectiveness of the control loop. For example, excessive filtering (Appendix C) of the measurement signal by the transmitter can add extra lag to the feedback loop, thus degrading control loop performance.

2.5 Summary

An industrial feedback control loop consists of a controller, an actuator system, a process, and a sensor system. The sensor generates an output that is related to the controlled variable and the transmitter converts this reading into a 4-20 mA analog signal. The A/D converter converts the analog signal into a digital value for the sensor reading. The DCS accepts the digital sensor reading, compares it to the setpoint, and calculates the digital value of the controller output. The D/A converter converts this digital reading into a 4-20 mA analog signal which, in turn, is converted to a 3-15 psig instrument air pressure by the I/P converter. The instrument air pressure acts on the control valve, which causes the manipulated flow to the process to change. This change to the process, as well as other input changes, causes the value of the controlled variable to change. The sensor reading changes and the control loop is complete.

The evolution of controllers from pneumatic controllers to analog controllers to DCSs has been driven by economics, functional performance, and reliability. From a process control performance perspective, the only influence from a controller is the effect of its control interval. Even though an analog controller has a smaller control interval than a DCS, the DCS has a much lower cost per control loop, greater functional capability, and superior reliability. The DCS is made up of a number of different elements and is held together by the data highway. The DCS is responsible for performing control calculations, providing displays of current and previous operating conditions, providing a means to modify control functions, archiving process data, providing process alarms, and performing process optimization.

The actuator system consists of the control valve, the valve actuator, the I/P converter, and the instrument air system. A typical industrial control valve has a deadband from 10% to 25%. If a valve positioner is installed, the deadband should drop to less than 0.5%. Depending on the design of the valve plug and valve seat, a control valve can have different inherent valve characteristics, i.e., different flow rate versus stem position for a constant pressure drop across the control valve. Equal percentage valves are used in about 90% of the control valve applications in the CPI while linear valves are used in the remaining cases for which the pressure drop across the valve remains relatively constant. The valve actuator determines whether the valve fails open or closed when instrument air pressure is lost.

The sensor system is composed of the sensor, the transmitter, and the associated signal processing. TCs and RTDs are used to measure process temperatures and are implemented on processes using thermowells. RTDs are more expensive and less rugged than TCs , but provide much more repeatable temperature measurements. Pressure measurements are typically made using strain gauges, which are based on measuring the resistance of a serpentine wire bonded to the surface of a flexible diaphragm. Flow measurements are typically made from the pressure drop across an orifice plate. Level measurements are commonly based upon the differential pressure between two taps on the process vessel. GCs are used to measure product compositions on-line by passing a sample through a packed column and detecting the separated components as they exit the GC column.

2.6 Additional Terminology

A/D Converter - analog-to-digital converter. Converts a 4-20 mA electrical analog signal into a digital reading that can be processed by the DCS.

Accuracy - the difference between the true value and the measurement.

Air-to-close actuator - a valve actuator that causes the valve to close as its instrument air pressure is increased (i.e., fails open).

Air-to-open actuator - a valve actuator that causes the valve to open as its instrument air pressure is increased (i.e., fails close).

Cage-guided valve - a valve with a cage around the valve plug that guides the plug toward the valve seat.

Calibration - an adjustment of the correlation between the sensor output and the predicted measurement so that the sensor reading agrees with the standard.

CRT - cathode ray tube. A computer console that allows the operators and engineers to access process operating conditions and adjust the process control activities of a DCS.

Control interval - the time period between adjacent calls to a controller from a DCS.

Controller cycle time - the time period between adjacent calls to a controller from a DCS.

D/A converter - digital-to-analog converter. Converts a digital value from the DCS into a 4-20 mA electrical analog signal.

Data highway - communication hardware and the associated software in a DCS that allows the distributed elements of a DCS to exchange data with each other.

Deadband - the maximum percentage change in the input that can be implemented without an observable change in the output.

DCS - distributed control system. A control computer that is made up of a number of distributed elements that are linked together by the data highway.

Direct-acting final control element - a final control element with an air-to-open valve actuator.

DP cell - a differential pressure sensor/transmitter.

Dynamic response time - the time for a system to make most of its change after an input change has occurred.

GC - gas chromatograph. A composition analyzer that is based on separating the components of a mixture in a small diameter packed column.

I/P converter - an electro-mechanical device that converts a 4-20 mA electrical signal to a 3-15 psig pneumatic signal, i.e., a current-to-pressure converter.

Inherent valve characteristics - the flow rate versus stem position for a fixed pressure drop across the valve.

Installed valve characteristics - the flow rate versus stem position for a valve installed in service.

LCU - local control unit. A microprocessor in a DCS that is responsible for performing control functions for a portion of a plant.

Ladder logic - a programming language used in PLCs to implement a sequence of actions.

LAN - local area network.

PLC - programmable logic controller. A process computer typically used to apply a sequence of control actions, e.g., startup, shutdown, and batch operations.

Process measurement dynamics - a measure of the speed with which a sensor responds to a change in the process.

RTD - resistance thermometer detector. A temperature sensor that is based on the known temperature dependence of a pure metal resistor.

Repeatability - the variation in a sensor reading not due to process changes. It provides an indication of consistency of the sensor reading.

Reverse-acting final control element - a final control element with an air-to-close valve actuator.

Shared communication facility - communication hardware and the associated software in a DCS that allows the distributed elements of a DCS to exchange data with each other.

Smart sensor - a sensor that is equipped with a microprocessor that provides onboard diagnostics and/or calibration.

Span - the difference between the maximum and the minimum value of a measurement that can be made by a sensor/transmitter.

TC - thermocouple. A temperature sensor that is based upon the fact that metal junctions at different temperatures generate an electrical voltage.

Turndown ratio - the ratio of the maximum to minimum controllable flow rates for a control valve.

VDU - video display unit. A computer console that allows the operators and engineers to access process operating conditions and adjust the process control activities of a DCS.

Valve deadband - the maximum percentage change in the input to the valve that can be implemented without an observable change in the flow rate through the valve.

Valve plug - the device in a valve that is responsible for restricting flow through the valve.

Valve positioner - a device that adjusts the instrument air pressure to a control valve to maintain a specified value for the stem position.

Valve seat - the portion of the valve against which the valve plug rests when the valve is fully closed.

Valve stem - a rod that connects the diaphragm in the valve actuator with the valve plug so that, as the air pressure acts on the diaphragm, the plug provides more or less restriction to flow through the valve.

Zero - the lowest sensor/transmitter reading possible, i.e., the sensor reading corresponding to a transmitter output of 4 mA.

Valve trim - the valve flow characteristics that are determined by the geometry of the valve plug, seat, and cage.

2.7 References

1. Lucas, M.P., *Distributed Control Systems*, Van Reinhold Company, New York, p. 4 (1986).

2. *Perry's Chemical Engineers Handbook*, 7th edition, R. H Perry and D. W. Green, editors, McGraw-Hill, p. 8-64 (1997).

3. Liptak, *Instrument Engineers Handbook*, Chilton, Philadelphia, (1995).

4. McMillan, G. K., G. E. Mertz, and V. L. Trevathan, "Troublefree Instrumentation", *Chemical Engineering*, p. 80-88 (Nov 1998).

5. McMillan, G.K. *Advanced Temperature Control*, Instrument Society of America, p. 133-155(1995).

6. *Perry's Chemical Engineers Handbook*, 7th edition, R. H Perry and D. W. Green, editors, McGraw-Hill , p. 8-48 (1997)

2.8 Preliminary Questions

2.1 For a typical feedback loop in the CPI, where are 4-20 mA signals used?

2.2 For a typical feedback loop in the CPI, where are 3-15 psig signals used?

2.3 For a typical feedback loop in the CPI, where are A/D and D/A converters used?

2.4 For Figure 2.2, what hardware is located in the field and what hardware is located in the control room?

2.5 For a pneumatic controller, what mechanical devices are used to implement PID control?

2.6 Why have electronic analog controllers replaced pneumatic controllers?

2.7 Why have DCSs replaced electronic analog controllers?

2.8 What type of device is used as a local control unit?

2.9 What system in a DCS allows a user on a local console to observe operation of the plant controlled by other LCUs?

2.10 Based on Figure 2.4, where are CRTs used in a DCS?

2.11 How frequently can a DCS execute most regulatory control loops?

2.12 Using Figure 2.4, explain how process data are stored and later displayed on a system console.

2.13 What is a PLC and how is it different from a DCS? How are they alike?

2.14 For what type of control function were PLCs originally designed?

2.15 What is the difference between a DCS and the fieldbus approach to distributed control?

2.16 For Figure 2.6, in what locations are control calculations performed?

2.17 What hardware comprises the final control element?

2.18 What is the difference between the actuator system and the final control element? What is the difference between the actuator system and the valve actuator?

2.19 How do you choose between selecting a globe valve with an unbalanced plug and one with a balanced plug?

2.20 Why are globe valves generally used for flow control applications?

2.21 What is the difference between inherent and installed valve characteristics?

2.22 Why are equal percentage valves generally selected over linear and quick-opening valves?

2.23 What determines whether a globe valve is linear, equal percentage, or quick-opening?

2.24 Using Figure 2.8, indicate how do you measure the stem position of a valve in operation.

2.25 Why is the pressure drop across a control valve in a flow system usually a strong function of flow rate?

2.26 When are butterfly valves preferred over globe valves for flow control applications? Why are they preferred?

2.27 Explain how cavitation in control valves occurs and what it causes.

2.28 What physical characteristic of the process determines whether a valve actuator is air-to-open or air-to-close?

2.29 Identify a case where an air-to-close valve actuator should be used and explain your reasoning.

2.30 Why has an increased usage of DCSs resulted in a greater use of valve positioners?

2.31 Under what conditions are adjustable speed pumps preferred over a flow control loop using a control valve?

2.32 From a process point of view, which is generally more important for a sensor, accuracy or repeatability? Explain your reasoning.

2.33 When is the dynamic response time of a sensor important to a process control system and when is it not important?

2.34 What are the two most important differences between TCs and RTDs ?

2.35 Why is a straight run of pipe preceding an orifice meter required?

2.36 Why are flow measurement devices usually located upstream of the control valve?

2.37 What determines whether an on-line analyzer should be installed?

2.9 Analytical Questions and Exercises

2.38 For the control loop shown in Figure 1.3, make a drawing similar to Figure 2.2 and list all signals on your diagram.

2.39 For the control loop shown in Figure 6.17, make a drawing similar to Figure 2.2 and list all signals on your diagram.

2.40 For the control loop shown in Figure 1.5, make a drawing similar to Figure 2.2 and list all signals on your diagram.

2.41 For the control loop shown in Figure 1.6, make a drawing similar to Figure 2.2 and list all signals on your diagram.

2.42 For the control loop shown in Figure 1.7, make a drawing similar to Figure 2.2 and list all signals on your diagram.

2.43 Choose an industrial process control loop and make a drawing similar to Figure 2.2 for your system and list all signals on your diagram.

2.44 Determine the 4-20 mA signal and the pneumatic signal if the controller output is 50% of its full-scale reading for a system corresponding to Figure 2.2.

2.45 Determine the 4-20 mA signal and the pneumatic signal if the controller output is 25% of its full-scale reading for a system corresponding to Figure 2.2.

2.46 Determine the 4-20 mA signal and the pneumatic signal if the controller output is 35% of its full-scale reading for a system corresponding to Figure 2.2.

2.47 Determine the 4-20 mA signal and the pneumatic signal if the controller output is 72% of its full-scale reading for a system corresponding to Figure 2.2.

2.48 Determine the 4-20 mA signal and the controller output in percent of full range, if the pneumatic signal is 9 psig for a system corresponding to Figure 2.2.

2.49 Determine the 4-20 mA signal and the controller output in percent of full range, if the pneumatic signal is 10 psig for a system corresponding to Figure 2.2.

2.50 Determine the 4-20 mA signal and the controller output in percent of full range, if the pneumatic signal is 14 psig for a system corresponding to Figure 2.2.

2.51 Determine the 4-20 mA signal and the controller output in percent of full range, if the pneumatic signal is 4 psig for a system corresponding to Figure 2.2.

2.52 Why have DCSs replaced analog controllers and supervisory control computers in the CPI? Why is fieldbus technology likely to begin replacing DCSs in the future? Can you identify a pattern?

2.53 Explain why a valve with a 10% deadband may not produce a change in the flow rate through the valve for a 9% change in the signal to the control valve. Explain why a 2% change in the signal to the control valve may, certain situations, produce a change in the flow rate through the same control valve.

2.54 Calculate the flow rate of water through a 3-inch control valve that is 50% open based on stem position with a pressure drop across the valve equal to 14 psi . Obtain the C_v for this valve from Table 2.1.

2.55 Calculate the flow rate of water through a 2-inch control valve that is 75% open based on stem position with a pressure drop across the valve equal to 35 psi. Obtain the C_v for this valve from Table 2.1.

2.56 Calculate the flow rate of a hydrocarbon stream with a density of 44 lb/ft^3 through a 3-inch control valve that is 80% open based on stem position with a pressure drop across the valve equal to 82 psi. Obtain the C_v for this valve from Table 2.1.

2.57 Calculate the flow rate of a hydrocarbon stream with a density of 44 lb/ft^3 through a 2-inch control valve that is 35% open based on stem position with a pressure drop across the valve equal to 14 psi. Obtain the C_v for this valve from Table 2.1.

2.58 Calculate the pressure drop across a 3-inch valve that is 50% open based on stem position for a flow of 65 GPM of water. Obtain the C_v for this valve from Table 2.1.

2.59 Calculate the pressure drop across a 4-inch valve that is 45% open based on stem position for a flow of 165 GPM of water. Obtain the C_v for this valve from Table 2.1.

2.60 Calculate the pressure drop across a 3-inch valve that is 40% open based on stem position for a flow of 100 GPM of a hydrocarbon stream with a density of 40 lb/ft^3. Obtain the C_v for this valve from Table 2.1.

2.61 Calculate the pressure drop across a 3-inch valve that is 63% open based on stem position for a flow of 95 GPM of a hydrocarbon stream with a density of 45 lb/ft^3. Obtain the C_v for this valve from Table 2.1.

2.62 Calculate the pressure drop across a 2-inch valve that is 80% open based on stem position for a flow of 35 GPM of a hydrocarbon stream with a density of 45 lb/ft^3. Obtain the C_v for this valve from Table 2.1.

2.63 Determine the flow rate of water though a 2-inch equal percentage valve that is 60% open based on stem position for the C_v given in Table 2.1 and the installed pressure drop presented in Table 2.2.

2.64 Determine the flow rate of water though a 1.5-inch equal percentage valve that is 80% open based on stem position for the C_v given in Table 2.1 and the installed pressure drop presented in Table 2.2.

2.65 Determine the flow rate of water though a 3-inch linear valve that is 15% open based on stem position for the maximum value of C_v equal to 100 and the installed pressure drop presented in Table 2.2.

2.66 Determine the flow rate of water though a 1.5-inch linear valve that is 70% open based on stem position for the maximum value of C_v equal to 30 and the installed pressure drop presented in Table 2.2.

2.67 Determine the flow rate of a hydrocarbon liquid (specific gravity equal to 0.65) though a 3-inch equal percentage valve that is 30% open based on stem position for the C_v given in Table 2.1 and the installed pressure drop presented in Table 2.2.

2.68 Determine the flow rate of a hydrocarbon liquid (specific gravity equal to 0.65) though a 2-inch equal percentage valve that is 50% open based on stem position for the C_v given in Table 2.1 and the installed pressure drop presented in Table 2.2.

2.69 Determine the valve stem position of a 4-inch equal percentage valve if 90 GPM of water flow through the system. Use Table 2.1 to determine the C_v and Table 2.2 for the available pressure drop across the control valve.

2.70 Determine the valve stem position of a 3-inch equal percentage valve if 82 GPM of water flow through the system. Use Table 2.1 to determine the C_v and Table 2.2 for the available pressure drop across the control valve.

2.71 Determine the valve stem position of a 2-inch equal percentage valve if 64 GPM of hydrocarbon liquid (specific gravity equal to 0.65) flow through the system. Use Table 2.1 to determine the C_v and Table 2.2 for the available pressure drop across the control valve.

2.72 Determine the valve stem position of a 2-inch equal percentage valve if 74 GPM of hydrocarbon liquid (specific gravity equal to 0.65) flow through the system. Use Table 2.1 to determine the C_v and Table 2.2 for the available pressure drop across the control valve.

2.73 Determine the valve position of a 4-inch equal percentage valve if 105 GPM of water flow through the system. Assume an equal percentage valve with the pressure drop versus stem position shown in the table for this problem. Use Table 2.1 to determine the C_v.

2.74 Size a control valve for service on a line carrying water with a maximum flow rate of 90 GPM and a minimum flow rate of 30 GPM. Assume an equal percentage valve with the pressure drop versus flow rate shown in the table for this problem. The C_v's for equal percentage valves of different sizes are presented in the Table 2.1.

2.75 Size a control valve for service on a line carrying a hydrocarbon liquid (specific gravity equal to 0.65) with a maximum flow rate of 80 GPM and a minimum flow rate of 20 GPM. Assume an equal percentage valve with the pressure drop versus flow rate shown in the table for this problem. The C_v's for equal percentage valves of different sizes are presented in the Table 2.1.

Pressure Drop of an Installed Valve versus Flow Rate for Problems 2.73-5			
Q (GPM)	ΔP (psi)	Q (GPM)	ΔP (psi)
0	28.5	55	21.4
5	28.4	60	20.1
10	28.2	65	18.8
15	27.9	70	17.4
20	27.4	75	15.8
25	27.0	80	14.0
30	26.3	85	11.7
35	25.6	90	9.3
40	24.7	95	6.7
45	23.7	100	3.9
50	22.6	105	0.6

2.76 Size a control valve for service on a line carrying water with a maximum flow rate of 400 GPM and a minimum flow rate of 100 GPM. Assume an equal percentage valve with the pressure drop versus stem position shown in the table for this problem. The C_v's for equal percentage valves of different sizes are presented in the Table 2.1.

2.77 Size a control valve for service on a line carrying a hydrocarbon liquid (specific gravity equal to 0.65) with a maximum flow rate of 500 GPM and a minimum flow rate of 50 GPM. Assume an equal percentage valve with the pressure drop versus stem position shown in the table for this problem. The C_v's for equal percentage valves of different sizes are presented in the Table 2.1.

2.78 Size a control valve for service on a line carrying a hydrocarbon liquid (specific gravity equal to 0.65) with a maximum flow rate of 500 GPM and a minimum flow rate of 100 GPM. Assume an equal percentage valve with the pressure drop versus stem position shown in the table for this problem. The C_v's for equal percentage valves of different sizes are presented in the Table 2.1.

Pressure Drop of an Installed Valve versus Flow Rate for Problems 2.76-8			
Q (GPM)	ΔP (psi)	Q (GPM)	ΔP (psi)
0	30.6	220	22.9
20	30.5	240	21.5
40	30.2	260	20.2
60	29.9	280	18.7
80	29.5	300	17.0
100	28.9	320	15.0
120	28.2	340	12.6
140	27.4	360	9.9
160	26.5	380	8.6
180	25.4	400	7.4
200	24.2	420	6.1

2.79 Determine the temperature reading corresponding to a 7 mA analog signal from a temperature transmitter that has a span of 150°C and a zero of 50°C.

2.80 Determine the pressure reading corresponding to a 5.5 mA analog signal from a pressure transmitter that has a span of 150 psi and a zero of 25 psig.

2.81 Determine the flow rate reading corresponding to a 12.2 mA analog signal from a flow transmitter that has a span of 10,000 lb/hr and a zero of 1,000 lb/hr.

2.82 Determine the temperature reading corresponding to a 3.7 mA analog signal from a temperature transmitter that has a span of 200°F and a zero of 100°F.

2.83 Determine the level reading corresponding to a 6.8 mA analog signal from a level transmitter that has a span of 75% and a zero of 10%.

2.84 Determine the value of the electric analog reading in mA from a temperature transmitter that has a span of 400°F and a zero of 100°F corresponding to a measured temperature of 300°F.

2.85   Determine the value of the electric analog reading in mA from a pressure transmitter that has a span of 250 psi and a zero of 14.7 psia corresponding to a measured pressure of 202 psia.

2.86   Determine the value of the electric analog reading in mA from a pressure transmitter that has a span of 250 psi and a zero of 14.7 psia corresponding to a measured pressure of 300 psia.

2.87   Determine the value of the electric analog reading in mA from a flow transmitter that has a span of 100,000 lb/hr and a zero of 15,000 lb/hr corresponding to a measured flow rate of 66,732 lb/hr.

2.88   Determine the value of the electric analog reading in mA from a level transmitter that has a span of 65% and a zero of 12% corresponding to a measured level of 47%.

2.89   Consider a pressure sensor/transmitter that reads 80 psig when the transmitter output is 8 mA and reads 100 psig when the transmitter output is 10 mA. What are the zero and span of this pressure sensor/transmitter?

2.90   Consider a temperature sensor/transmitter that reads 100°F when the transmitter output is 8 mA and reads 150 °F when the transmitter output is 10 mA. What are the zero and span of this temperature sensor/transmitter?

2.91   Consider a flow sensor/transmitter that reads 10,000 lb/h when the transmitter output is 7 mA and reads 15,000 lb/h when the transmitter output is 12 mA. What are the zero and span of this flow sensor/transmitter?

2.92   Consider a pressure sensor/transmitter that reads 180 psig when the transmitter output is 6 mA and reads 250 psig when the transmitter output is 10 mA. What are the zero and span of this pressure sensor/transmitter?

2.93   Calculate the flow rate of water through an orifice with β equal to 0.5 in a schedule 40 4-inch line if the pressure drop across the orifice is 2 psi.

2.94   Calculate the flow rate of water through an orifice with β equal to 0.6 in a schedule 40 3-inch line if the pressure drop across the orifice is 10 psi.

2.95   Calculate the flow rate of a hydrocarbon liquid (specific gravity equal to 0.65) through an orifice with β equal to 0.67 in a schedule 40 2-inch line if the pressure drop across the orifice is 1.5 psi.

2.96   Calculate the flow rate of a hydrocarbon liquid (specific gravity equal to 0.65) through an orifice with β equal to 0.45 in a schedule 40 2-inch line if the pressure drop across the orifice is 2.3 psi.

2.97 Calculate the flow rate of water through an orifice with β equal to 0.87 in a schedule 40 4-inch line if the pressure drop across the orifice is 2 psi.

2.98 Calculate the pressure drop across an orifice with β equal to 0.6 in a schedule 40 4-inch line for a flow rate of water of 150 GPM.

2.99 Calculate the pressure drop across an orifice with β equal to 0.4 in a schedule 40 4-inch line for a flow rate of water of 150 GPM.

2.100 Calculate the pressure drop across an orifice with β equal to 0.43 in a schedule 40 3-inch line for a flow rate of a hydrocarbon liquid (specific gravity equal to 0.65) of 60 GPM.

2.101 Calculate the pressure drop across an orifice with β equal to 0.23 in a schedule 40 3-inch line for a flow rate of a hydrocarbon liquid (specific gravity equal to 0.65) of 60 GPM.

2.102 Calculate the pressure drop across an orifice with β equal to 0.59 in a schedule 40 2-inch line for a flow rate of a hydrocarbon liquid (specific gravity equal to 0.65) of 40 GPM.

2.103 Size an orifice meter for service on a 3-inch schedule 40 pipe carrying water with a maximum flow rate of 150 GPM and a minimum flow rate of 60 GPM. Assume that the line pressure is 200 psig.

2.104 Size an orifice meter for service on a 4-inch schedule 40 pipe carrying water with a maximum flow rate of 350 GPM and a minimum flow rate of 150 GPM. Assume that the line pressure is 100 psig.

2.105 Size an orifice meter for service on a 4-inch schedule 40 pipe carrying water with a maximum flow rate of 350 GPM and a minimum flow rate of 150 GPM. Assume that the line pressure is 30 psig.

2.106 Size an orifice meter for service on a 2-inch schedule 40 pipe carrying a hydrocarbon liquid (specific gravity equal to 0.65) with a maximum flow rate of 75 GPM and a minimum flow rate of 25 GPM. Assume that the line pressure is 50 psig.

2.107 Size an orifice meter for service on a 3-inch schedule 40 pipe carrying a hydrocarbon liquid (specific gravity equal to 0.65) with a maximum flow rate of 175 GPM and a minimum flow rate of 75 GPM. Assume that the line pressure is 150 psig.

2.10 Projects

Specify the instruments and design the orifice meters and control valves for each of the following cases. Size the lines (i.e., to available cast iron schedule 40 pipe sizes) based on assuming that the linear velocity in the lines is approximately 7 ft/s. For each case, assume that water is the process fluid and the line pressure is 150 psig.

a. CST temperature mixer (Example 3.1) b. CST composition mixer (Example 3.2)

c. Level in a tank (Example 3.3)

PART II

PROCESS DYNAMICS

Chapter 3

Dynamic Modeling

3.1 Introduction

Most chemical engineering courses are concerned primarily with the steady-state aspects of chemical engineering systems. For example, thermodynamics is based solely on a steady-state analysis and heat transfer, fluid flow, mass transfer and kinetics are primarily studied from a steady-state point of view. The study of process design and the laboratory study of unit operations also typically focuses on the steady-state aspects of these subjects. It is no wonder that most undergraduate students enter their process control course with little experience or feel for the dynamic behavior of chemical processes.

One of the most common responses from recent chemical engineering graduates after industrial experience is "There is no such thing as steady state". Due to an almost continuous fluctuations in feed flow rate and composition to a process and other disturbances, such as steam pressure and cooling water temperature changes, most processes in the CPI are in a constant state of flux. The control systems of the units respond to these disturbances using changes in the manipulated variables to drive the controlled variables toward their setpoints. As a result, generally there are few periods, if any, that resemble steady-state operation. Therefore, dynamic behavior is an integral part of industrial operations, including process control operations. The first step in becoming knowledgeable in the field of process control is developing an understanding of process dynamics.

Understanding the dynamic behavior of chemical processes depends on understanding the steady-state behavior of these processes. For example, if a step change in an input to a process is made (e.g., a change in the manipulated variable), a steady-state analysis of the process using the new input level indicates where the process settles after a sufficient period of time. The dynamic characteristics of the process (e.g., the time constant and deadtime) determine how long it takes to approach the new steady-state and what path the process takes (see Figure 3.1). Understanding the dynamic behavior of a complex process made up of a number of separate unit operations (heat exchangers, reactors, holding tanks, etc.) requires combining the dynamic behavior of all the unit operations. Using the combined dynamic picture of the system, the control engineer can follow the transient behavior of the complex

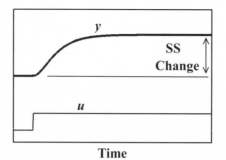

Figure 3.1 Dynamic response of a process to a step change in an input. SS-steady state. u **is the manipulated variable and** y **is the output variable.**

process by considering the effect of an input change as it propagates through the entire process.

Dynamic models predict the time-varying behavior of the outputs of the model based on the dynamic behavior of the inputs. Dynamic models can be as simple as a SISO system or as complex as a dynamic model of a major portion of a chemical plant. Simple dynamic models are used to illustrate the key features of process dynamics and feedback control. Complex dynamic models have a variety of important uses in the CPI.

3.2 Uses of Dynamic Models

Process Design. Dynamic models are used to design batch processing systems. For example, the volume of a batch reactor can be determined from a dynamic model of the reactor so that production rate and product quality specifications are met.

Analysis of Process Control Approaches. A range of potential process control configurations can be compared directly using dynamic models. Each control approach can be implemented on a dynamic model of the process, and the resulting control performance can be calculated for a standard upset disturbance test. In this manner, a controlled comparison between different control approaches can be quantitatively assessed, i.e., each controller can be applied to exactly the same process with exactly the same disturbance. As processes become more highly integrated (i.e., using material recycle and heat recovery) in an effort to become more cost effective, the use of dynamic models for process control evaluation is becoming increasingly important to ensure that these highly integrated processes produce on-specification products with safe and reliable operation.

Operator Training. A dynamic simulation of a process can be interfaced with the same type of DCS that controls the actual process, and the resulting system

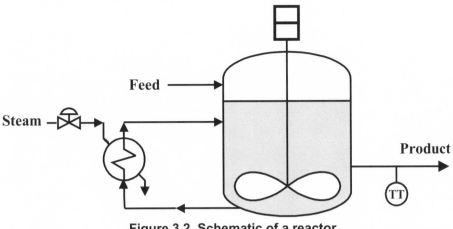

Figure 3.2 Schematic of a reactor.

can be used to train operators. In this manner, the operator can be exposed to a wide range of major upsets and potentially dangerous operational scenarios without upsetting or endangering the process.

Start-up/Shutdown Strategy Development. Viable process startup and shutdown strategies can be identified from dynamic process simulators. This class of dynamic simulators must be able to model process behavior over a much wider range of operation than the dynamic simulators used for process control evaluation.

3.3 Classifications of Phenomenological Models

There are two general classifications of phenomenological process models (i.e., models based on conservation of mass and energy): **lumped parameter models** and **distributed parameter models**. A lumped parameter model assumes that the dependent variables of the process are not a function of spatial location within the process. Consider the schematic of a reactor shown in Figure 3.2. A lumped parameter model of this reactor assumes that the composition of the chemical species present in the reactor and the temperature in the reactor are uniform throughout the reactor volume. If the mixer on the reactor is properly designed, this assumption can be quite good. **Macroscopic balances** are used to model lumped parameter systems and consider what enters or leaves the process and what is occurring inside the process as a whole. For Figure 3.2, feed enters the reactor, product is removed, heat is added by the heat exchanger, and the same reaction rate occurs throughout the reactor volume. A model developed from macroscopic balances is called a **macroscopic model**.

Models that consider the spatial variation in the dependent variables are referred to as **distributed parameter models**. If the mixer on the reactor in Figure 3.2

is not functioning properly, significant spatial variation in the concentrations of the reactor species and reactor temperature can result, requiring a distributed parameter model. The heat exchanger shown in Figure 1.7 is another example of a distributed parameter system since the tube-side temperature of the process fluid changes significantly as it flows through the heat exchanger. Microscopic balances, i.e., balances based on differential elements, are typically used to model distributed parameter processes. These microscopic balances are used to derive differential equations, which are applied over the full spatial region to develop a model that describes the entire process. A model developed by applying microscopic balances is called a **microscopic model**.

3.4 Dynamic Balance Equations

This section presents dynamic material and energy balances. Depending upon whether the balances are applied around an overall process or to a differential element within the process, these equations can be applied to develop either macroscopic or microscopic models, respectively.

Mass Balance Equation.   Mass balance equations relate the rate of accumulation of mass in the system of interest to the rate of mass entering and leaving the system:

$$
\begin{bmatrix} rate\ of\ accumulation \\ of\ mass\ in\ the \\ system \end{bmatrix} = \begin{bmatrix} rate\ of\ mass \\ entering\ the \\ system \end{bmatrix} - \begin{bmatrix} rate\ of\ mass \\ leaving\ the \\ system \end{bmatrix} \qquad \textbf{3.1}
$$

This equation applies to the total mass of a system whether chemical reactions are occurring or not, but applies to the mass of any one component only if no chemical reactions involving that component occur.

Mole Balance Equation.   The following equation represents the conservation of the number of moles in a reacting system.

$$
\begin{bmatrix} rate\ of\ accumulation \\ of\ moles\ in\ the \\ system \end{bmatrix} = \begin{bmatrix} rate\ of\ moles \\ entering\ the \\ system \end{bmatrix} - \begin{bmatrix} rate\ of\ moles \\ leaving\ the \\ system \end{bmatrix}
$$
$$
+ \begin{bmatrix} rate\ of\ generation \\ of\ moles\ by \\ reaction \end{bmatrix} - \begin{bmatrix} rate\ of \\ consumption\ of \\ moles\ by\ reaction \end{bmatrix} \qquad \textbf{3.2}
$$

This equation applies to the total number of moles or the moles of a particular component in the system.

Energy Balance Equation. For processes such as reactors, heat exchangers, and distillation columns, potential energy changes, kinetic energy changes, mechanical work, and the heat generated by frictional losses are typically small compared with convective heat transfer (i.e., the energy carried with streams entering or leaving the process), heat exchange across the boundaries of the system, and the energy generated or consumed by reaction. Therefore, the energy balance equation used in these cases is given by

$$
\begin{bmatrix} rate\ of \\ accumulation\ of \\ energy \end{bmatrix} = \begin{bmatrix} rate\ of\ convective \\ heat\ transfer \\ entering\ the\ system \end{bmatrix} - \begin{bmatrix} rate\ of\ convective \\ heat\ transfer \\ leaving\ the\ system \end{bmatrix}
$$

$$
+ \begin{bmatrix} net\ rate\ of\ energy \\ generation\ by \\ chemical\ reaction \end{bmatrix} + \begin{bmatrix} net\ rate\ of\ heat\ transfer \\ through\ the\ boundaries \\ of\ the\ system \end{bmatrix} \qquad 3.3
$$

It should be pointed out that for fluid flow through a piping system, kinetic energy, mechanical work, potential energy, and frictional losses are important and a mechanical energy balance, e.g., Bernoulli's equation[1], should be used to model these systems. Note that each of **the previous dynamic equations (i.e., Equations 3.1 to 3.3) can be converted into a steady-state equation by setting its accumulation term equal to zero.**

Constitutive Relationships. A number of physical relationships are required to implement the equations that result from the application of Equations 3.1 to 3.3. Examples of **constitutive relations** include:

- Gas laws
- Vapor/liquid equilibrium
- Heat-transfer correlations
- Expressions for rates of reaction
- Correlations for pressure drop as a function of flow rate
- Enthalpy correlations

Modeling the dynamic behavior of the temperature of a reactor requires rate expressions for the major reactions. A dynamic distillation column model uses vapor/liquid equilibrium relationships.

Degrees of Freedom Analysis. Developing a dynamic model of a complex process can involve a large number of differential equations and constitutive relationships, which are usually in the form of algebraic equations. A degrees of freedom analysis involves counting the total number of unknowns, N_v, i.e., variables that are unknown and must be calculated, and the total number of equations, N_e, both differential and algebraic. The degrees of freedom, N_f, of a model is given by

$$N_f = N_v - N_e$$

When N_f is equal to zero, the model is referred to as **exactly determined** or **exactly specified**.   For a solvable model, the number of degrees of freedom must be zero. When N_f is less than zero, the model is referred as **overdetermined** or **overspecified**. For this case, there are more equations than unknowns, which can result from redundant equations or an improperly formulated model. When N_f is greater than zero, the model is referred to as **underdetermined** or **underspecified**. For this case, there are more unknowns than equations. To solve such a model, additional equations must be identified or unknown variables eliminated. The variables that are specified by the user are the **independent variables** while the variables computed from the solution of the equations are the **dependent variables**. To make this distinction clearer, the independent and dependent variables are identified in the examples that follow. Constants used in the model equations, such as densities, heat capacities, heats of reaction and gas constants, are called **process parameters**.

3.5 Modeling Examples

In this section, dynamic models are developed and results from these models are presented.   The modeling examples considered here are simple and highly idealized.   The dynamic modeling of industrial processes is considerably more complex. Riggs[2] presents a systematic approach to process modeling, which includes a detailed model validation procedure. Bequette[3] analyzes dynamic process behavior and presents the development of a number of dynamic models.

The representation of a process for a control application involves the combination of models of the actuator, process, and sensor (i.e., sensor/transmitter) as shown in Figure 3.3. To affect a change in a process, the signal to the actuator must be changed, which results in a change in the flow rate of the input variable u to the process, which, in turn, causes the process to change. This causes the actual value of the output variable, y, to change, resulting in a change in the value of y measured by the sensor as y_s.

The actuator, process, and sensor each has its own dynamic behavior. Here, we first develop dynamic models for an actuator system and for several common types of sensors. Then, we use these results to develop actuator/process/sensor models for a thermal mixing tank, a composition mixing tank, the level in a tank, an endothermic and exothermic CSTR, a heat exchanger, and a fed-batch reactor. Finally, a model for sensor noise is presented. It should be pointed out that the dynamic models for the actuators, the sensors, and the sensor noise are empirical models that consider only the

Figure 3.3 Schematic of a system made up of an actuator, a process, and a sensor.

general behavior of these systems and are not based on phenomenological behavior. These empirical models assume a preset functional form and are not based on the conservation of mass or energy while the models for the various chemical processes considered here are phenomenological models.

Actuator System Models. The actuator system (final control element) consists of the I/P converter, the instrument air system, and the control valve. When a change in the analog signal to the I/P converter is made, the instrument air pressure to the valve changes. This causes the diaphragm in the control valve to expand or contract, which, in turn, causes the valve stem position to change, which affects the flow rate through the control valve. After the valve stem position changes, the flow rate through the valve changes very quickly. Because of the individual dynamics of the components of the final control element (i.e., the instrument air dynamics, the valve actuator dynamics, and the flow dynamics), the dynamic response of the valve actuator to changes in the instrument air pressure applied to the valve is usually considerably slower than either the response of the I/P instrument air system or the flow through the valve. Since the dynamic response of the actuator is based on the instrument air working against a spring in a first-order manner, the dynamic behavior of the control valve can be represented as a linear first-order process (Section 5.3). Therefore, the flow rate, F, through a control valve can be represented by the following equation

$$\frac{dF}{dt} = \frac{1}{\tau_v}(F_{spec} - F) \qquad\qquad \textbf{3.4}$$

where F_{spec} is the specified flow rate (input) and τ_v is the time constant of the valve. When the actuator is considered by itself, F is a dependent variable and t and F_{spec} are independent variables. τ_v depends upon the size of the valve and typically ranges between 3 and 15 seconds (Table 2.3) for cases in which a valve positioner is not used or the valve is not applied in a flow control loop. In fact, the flow rate changes for a control valve exhibit some deadtime and are not perfectly first-order responses, but the assumed first-order form shown is reasonably accurate and sufficient for the modeling examples considered here. When the actuator is part of a control loop, F_{spec} is the

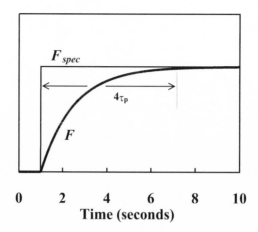

Figure 3.4 The dynamic response of the flow through a flow control loop in response to a step change in the specified flow rate, F_{spec}.

output of a supervisory controller. The dynamic behavior of a flow control loop or a control valve with a positioner can also be effectively modeled using Equation 3.4 where the time constant, τ_v, typically ranges between 0.5 and 2 seconds (Table 2.3). Usually the larger and older the control valve, the larger the value of τ_v. Figure 3.4 shows the resulting dynamic behavior for a step change in F_{spec} for a flow control loop with a τ_v of 1.5 sec.

For certain systems, it is convenient to represent the combined effect of flow rate and a heat-transfer process as a lumped system.   For example, when an input variable to a process is the rate of heat transfer, the actuator system for such a process usually involves the flow rate of a heat-transfer fluid (e.g., steam) and the transfer of heat through a contacting device (e.g., a heat exchanger). As a result, modeling the dynamic behavior of the actuator of such a process involves considering the dynamics of the flow control of the heat-transfer fluid and the dynamics of the heat-transfer process. For the flow control of the heat-transfer fluid, a flow controller is typically used and the previous analysis is valid. Therefore, the time constant for the flow controller is expected in the range of 0.5 to 2 seconds. The dynamics of the heat-transfer process are affected by the dynamics of heating or cooling the metal that passes the heat from the hot to the cold source and the transport delay for the process fluid to flow through the tubes of the heat exchanger. To increase the rate of heat transfer in a heat exchanger, the temperature of the metal tubes in the heat exchanger must be increased and the fluid must flow through the heat exchanger. The thermal lag associated with changing the temperature of the metal tubes provides the dynamic lag associated with heat transfer. The time constant for changing the temperature of the heat-exchanger tubes is typically in the range of 1 to 6 seconds, while the transport delay is in the range of 5 to 30 seconds. Modeling the combined dynamics of the actuator and the heat-transfer system can also be represented as a first-order process given by

$$\frac{dQ}{dt} = \frac{1}{\tau_H}(Q_{spec} - Q)$$ **3.5**

where Q_{spec} is the specified heat-transfer rate and τ_H is the effective time constant for heat transfer (6 - 40 seconds). Q is a dependent variable and t and Q_{spec} are independent variables. Clearly, if a more accurate dynamic model of a heat-transfer system is required, detailed models of each element (e.g., flow control loops, heat transfer from the hot fluid to the metal of the tubes, accumulation of thermal energy in the metal tubes, and heat transfer from the metal tubes to the cold fluid) should be used.

Sensor Models. Dynamic models for temperature sensors, level sensors, and composition analyzers are considered. The dynamic behavior of temperature sensors (e.g., a thermocouple or RTD) and level sensors (e.g., a differential pressure sensor) are well represented as linear first-order models similar to Equation 3.4. For example, for a temperature sensor, the following equation can be used to model the measured temperature, T_s,

$$\frac{dT_s}{dt} = \frac{1}{\tau_{Ts}}(T - T_s)$$ **3.6**

where T is the actual process temperature and τ_{Ts} is the time constant for the temperature sensor. τ_{Ts} typically ranges from 6 to 20 seconds depending on the mass of metal in the thermowell, the thermal resistance between the temperature sensor and the inner wall of the thermowell, and the velocity of process fluid past the thermowell. The separation between the temperature sensor and the surface of the thermowell, thickness of the thermowell walls, and the thickness of the heat-transfer boundary layer outside the thermowell affect the value of τ_{Ts}.

Similarly, the model for a level sensor is given by

$$\frac{dL_s}{dt} = \frac{1}{\tau_{Ls}}(L - L_s)$$ **3.7**

where L_s is the measured level, L is the actual process level, and τ_{Ls} is the time constant for the level sensor. Since a differential pressure measurement is typically used to determine the level and the dynamics of differential pressure measurements are relatively fast, τ_{Ls} is typically less than one second. As a result, it is usually reasonable to neglect the dynamics of the level sensor and assume that the level sensor makes an instantaneous measurement. Differential pressure sensors are used to measure flow rates, levels, and system gauge pressure, which can also usually be assumed to have fast sensor dynamics. For level sensors, improperly designed or partially plugged liquid lines from the pressure taps to the differential pressure cell can significantly

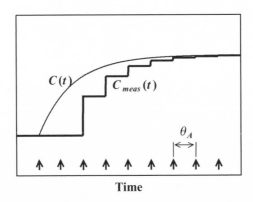

Time

Figure 3.5 The dynamic response of the actual composition and the measured composition.

increase the value of τ_{Ls}. Flow indicators, such as orifice, vortex shedding, and magnetic flow meters, have time constants that are small enough that their dynamic response can be assumed instantaneous in most cases.

The most common composition analyzer in the CPI is the gas chromatograph (GC). Since a GC is a packed column, the analysis requires time for the sample to migrate, by plug flow, the length of the separation column. Therefore, the dynamic model of a GC is a pure time delay, i.e.,

$$C_s(t) = C(t - \theta_A) \qquad\qquad\qquad \textbf{3.8}$$

where $C_s(t)$ is the measured composition and $C(t - \theta_A)$ is the actual composition in the process θ_A time units earlier. θ_A is the cycle time for the analyzer or the time for the sample to flow through the packed column before it is introduced to the detector. Figure 3.5 shows a plot of $C_s(t)$ and $C(t)$. The arrows above the x-axis indicate when samples were injected into the GC. Note that the value $C_s(t)$ remains constant for θ_A time units, indicating the cycle time.

Example 3.1 CST Thermal Mixing Tank

Problem Statement. Develop the dynamic model equations for the **continuous stirred tank (CST)** thermal mixer shown in Figure 3.6. The process parameters and variables are defined as:

- M - mass of liquid in the mixer (100 kg)
- T - temperature of the mixed liquid (50°C)
- F_1 - mass flow rate of stream 1 (5 kg/s)
- T_1 - temperature of stream 1 (25°C)
- F_2 - mass flow rate of stream 2 (5 kg/s)
- T_2 - temperature of stream 2 (75°C)

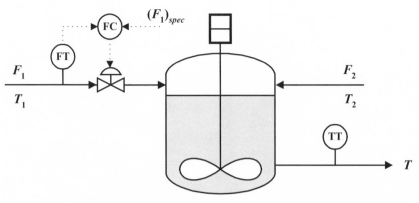

Figure 3.6 Schematic of the CST thermal mixing process.

These conditions represent the initial steady-state conditions. At time equal to 10 seconds, a step change in the specified flow rate for stream 1 is made from 5 kg/s to 4 kg/s. The flow control loop on stream 1 is assumed to have a τ_v equal to 2 seconds while the temperature sensor has a time constant, τ_{Ts}, of 6 seconds.

Solution. Assuming that the mixer volume is perfectly mixed, this process can be treated as a lumped parameter process, suitably represented by a macroscopic model. Applying Equation 3.3, noting that there are no chemical reactions and no heat transfer, yields:

$$M \frac{dT}{dt} = F_1 T_1 + F_2 T_2 - (F_1 + F_2) T \qquad \textbf{3.9}$$

assuming perfect level control (i.e., $F_T = F_1 + F_2$), the heat capacity of each stream is the same, and the heat capacities at constant volume are equal to the heat capacities at constant pressure. The actuator is modeled using Equation 3.4 and the sensor is modeled using Equation 3.6. Therefore, the model equations used to represent the CST thermal mixer are

Actuator $\qquad\qquad \dfrac{dF_1}{dt} = \dfrac{1}{\tau_v}(F_{1,spec} - F_1)$

Process $\qquad\qquad M \dfrac{dT}{dt} = F_1 T_1 + F_2 T_2 - (F_1 + F_2) T$

Sensor $\qquad\qquad \dfrac{dT_s}{dt} = \dfrac{1}{\tau_{Ts}}(T - T_s)$

Figure 3.7 shows the resulting dynamic behavior of the measured temperature of the mixed liquid for this process. After a change in the input, the process reaches a

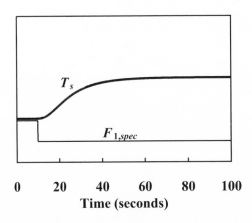

Figure 3.7 Dynamic response of the CST thermal mixer to a step change in $(F_1)_{spec}$.

new steady-state condition; therefore, this process is referred to as a **self-regulating process**. These results were obtained by simultaneously integrating Equations 3.4, 3.6, and 3.9, which represent the combined effects of the flow controller, the thermal mixing process, and the temperature sensor.

The process model is affected by changing $F_{1,spec}$, which changes F_1, resulting in a change in T, which is measured by the sensor as T_s. F_1, T, and T_s are dependent variables and t, $F_{1,spec}$, F_2, T_1, and T_2 are independent variables. τ_v, M, and τ_{Ts} are process parameters. Figure 3.8 shows a comparison between the actuator/process/sensor model and a model of the mixer process by itself. For the mixer model without the actuator and sensor included, the temperature of the product changes as soon as the specified value of F_1 changes, while there is a noticeable time period before a significant change in the product temperature results for the

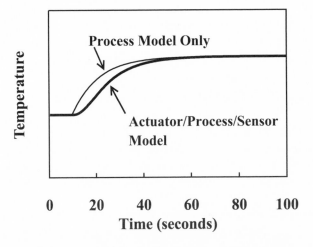

Figure 3.8 Comparison between the dynamic response of the model of the process by itself and a model of the actuator/process/sensor.

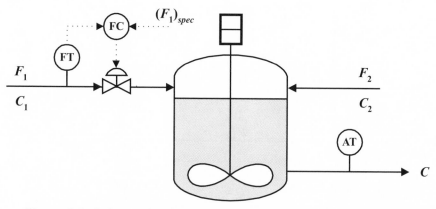

Figure 3.9 Schematic of the CST composition mixing process.

actuator/process/sensor model. If the dynamics of the actuator and sensor are not included, the model has a very different dynamic response, particularly when the initial responses of the two models are compared. Therefore, when dynamic models of a process are developed for process control purposes, the dynamics of the actuator and sensor should usually be considered. The simulation software that accompanies this text contains a simulator of this process based on the model developed here.

♠

Example 3.2 CST Composition Mixing Tank

Problem Statement. Develop a dynamic model for the CST composition mixing process shown in Figure 3.9. The process parameters and variables are given by

- V - the volume of the mixer (1000 L)
- C - the concentration of the component in the mixed stream (0.75 gmoles/L)
- C_1 - the concentration of the component in stream 1 (0.5 gmoles/L)
- F_1 - the mass flow rate of stream 1 (500 kg/min)
- C_2 - the concentration of the component in stream 2 (1.0 gmoles/L)
- F_2 - the mass flow rate of stream 2 (500 kg/min)
- ρ - the density of the feed and product streams (1 kg/L)

These conditions represent the initial steady-state conditions. At time equal to 5 minutes, a step change in the specified feed rate for stream 1 is made from 500 kg/min to 400 kg/min. The flow control loop on stream 1 is assumed to have a τ_v equal to 2 seconds while the composition analyzer has an analyzer delay, θ_A, of 5 minutes.

Solution. Assuming that the mixer volume is perfectly mixed, this process can be treated as a lumped parameter process and a macroscopic model can be applied. With

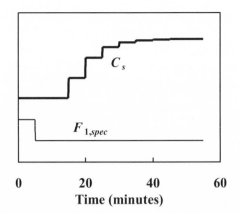

Figure 3.10 Dynamic response of the CST composition mixer for a step change in the specified value of F_1.

no chemical reactions, uniform densities, and constant level (i.e., $F_T = F_1 + F_2$), Equation 3.2 becomes:

$$\rho V \frac{dC}{dt} = F_1 C_1 + F_2 C_2 - (F_1 + F_2) C \qquad \textbf{3.10}$$

The model for the actuator is given by Equation 3.4 and the model for the composition analyzer is given by Equation 3.8. The equations that represent the CST composition mixer are as follows:

Actuator $$\frac{dF_1}{dt} = \frac{1}{\tau_v}(F_{1,spec} - F_1)$$

Process $$\rho V \frac{dC}{dt} = F_1 C_1 + F_2 C_2 - (F_1 + F_2) C$$

Sensor $$C_s(t) = C(t - \theta_A)$$

Figure 3.10 shows the simulated measured mixer composition as a function of time. This process is self-regulating because the open-loop response moves to a new steady-state condition after an input change. These results were obtained by simultaneously integrating Equations 3.4 and 3.10 while applying Equation 3.8. These equations represent the combined effects of the flow controller, mixer, and the composition analyzer. F_1, C, and C_s are dependent variables and t, $F_{1,spec}$, F_2, C_1, and C_2 are independent variables. τ_v, ρ, V, and θ_A are process parameters. The simulation software that accompanies this text contains a simulator of this process based on the model developed here.

♠

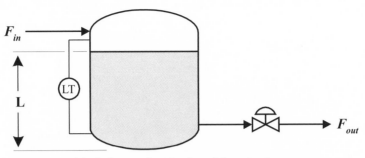

Figure 3.11 Schematic of a level in a tank process.

Example 3.3 Level in a Tank

Problem Statement. Develop a dynamic model of a level in the tank shown in Figure 3.11. The process parameters and variables are given by

- A_c - cross-sectional area (0.3 m^2)
- L - the level of liquid in the tank (2 meters)
- ρ - the fluid density (1 kg/L)
- F_{in} - the mass flow rate of liquid into the tank (1.0 kg/s)
- F_{out} - the mass flow rate of liquid leaving the tank (1.0 kg/s).

These conditions represent the initial conditions. At time equal to 10 seconds, the specified value of F_{out} is changed from 1.0 to 0.9 kg/s by changing the signal to the control valve. The control valve on the outlet stream from the tank has a τ_v of 5 seconds while the dynamics of the level sensor are assumed instantaneous.

Solution. Applying a macroscopic mass balance to this process, using the indicated systems variables yields

$$\rho A_c \frac{dL}{dt} = F_{in} - F_{out} \qquad \textbf{3.11}$$

Using Equation 3.4 to model the dynamic behavior of the actuator, neglecting the dynamics of the level sensor, and using the process model for this system (Equation 3.11) yields the following system of ODEs that represent the dynamic model of this system.

Actuator $\qquad \dfrac{dF_{out}}{dt} = \dfrac{1}{\tau_v}\left(F_{out,spec} - F_{out} \right)$

Process $\qquad \rho A_c \dfrac{dL}{dt} = F_{in} - F_{out}$

Sensor $\qquad L_s = L$

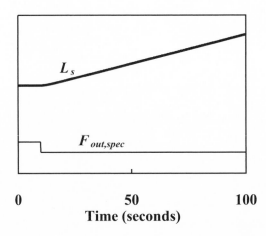

Figure 3.12 Dynamic response of a level in a tank to a step change in the flow rate leaving the tank.

Figure 3.12 shows the level in the tank as a function of time. This process does not move to a new steady-state condition; therefore, this system is referred to as a **non-self-regulating process**. These results were obtained by simultaneously integrating Equations 3.4 and 3.11, which represent the combined effects of the flow controller and the level process. F_{out}, L, and L_s are dependent variables and t, $F_{out,spec}$ and F_{in} are independent variables. A_c and ρ are process parameters. This is an example of an integrating process. The simulation software that accompanies this text contains a simulator of this process based on the model developed here.

♠

Example 3.4 Endothermic CSTR

Problem Statement. Develop a dynamic model for the endothermic CSTR shown in Figure 3.13. The process parameters and variables are given by

- V_r - reactor volume (100 L)
- F - mass feed rate (10 kg/s)
- C_{A0} - feed composition (1.0 gmoles/L)
- ρ - density of the reactor feed and product (1 kg/L)
- C_p - heat capacity of the reactor feed and product (1 cal/g - K)
- C_v - assumed equal to C_p
- ΔH- heat of reaction (160,000 cal/gmole)
- T_o - feed temperature (400 K)
- E/R- normalized activation energy (20,000 K)
- C_A - reactant concentration (0.25 gmoles/L)

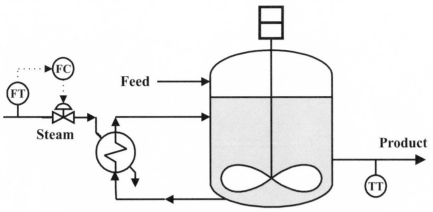

Figure 3.13 Schematic of an endothermic CSTR.

- k_o - rate constant (1.97×10^{24} s^{-1})
- T - reactor temperature (350 K)
- Q - heat addition rate (700,000 cal/s)

These conditions represent the initial steady-state conditions. At time equal to 10 seconds, a step change in the specified heat addition rate (Q_{spec}) is made from 700,000 cal/s to 900,000 cal/s. Since heat addition by the heat exchanger involves a change in the flow rate of the steam as well as heat transfer in the heat exchanger, the dynamics of heat addition is modeled as a first-order process with a time constant, τ_H, of 5 seconds. In addition, the temperature sensor is assumed to have a time constant, τ_{Ts}, of 6 seconds.

Solution. Assuming that the CSTR is perfectly mixed, the process can be modeled as a lumped parameter process. Applying Equation 3.2 for a first-order irreversible reaction and Arrhenius temperature dependence for the reaction rate constant results in

$$V_r \frac{dC_A}{dt} = \frac{F}{\rho}(C_{A0} - C_A) - V_r\, k_o\, C_A\, e^{-E/RT} \qquad \textbf{3.12}$$

which models the composition of the reactant assuming that the reactor volume is constant. In addition, Equation 3.3 is applied to model the reactor temperature

$$V_r\, \rho\, C_v \frac{dT}{dt} = F C_p (T_o - T) - V_r\, \Delta H C_A\, k_o\, e^{-E/RT} + Q \qquad \textbf{3.13}$$

Using Equation 3.5 to represent the actuator, Equation 3.6 to model the temperature sensor, and Equations 3.12 and 3.13, the actuator/process/sensor model for this process is given as:

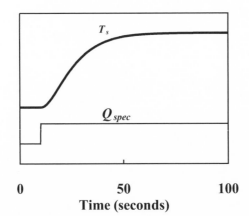

0   50   100
Time (seconds)

Figure 3.14 Dynamic response of the endothermic CSTR to a step increase in the heat addition rate to the reactor.

Lumped Actuator
$$\frac{dQ}{dt} = \frac{1}{\tau_H}(Q_{spec} - Q)$$

Process
$$V_r \frac{dC_A}{dt} = \frac{F(C_{A0} - C_A)}{\rho} - V_r k_0 C_A e^{-E/RT}$$

$$V_r \rho C_p \frac{dT}{dt} = F C_p (T_0 - T) - V_r \Delta H C_A k_0 e^{-E/RT} + Q$$

Sensor
$$\frac{dT_s}{dt} = \frac{1}{\tau_{Ts}}(T - T_s)$$

Figure 3.14 shows the measured reactor temperature as a function of time for a step change in heat addition rate. These results were obtained by simultaneously integrating Equation 3.5, Equation 3.12, Equation 3.13, and Equation 3.6. The reactant concentration must be modeled because C_A appears in Equation 3.13. Q, C_A, T, and T_s are dependent variables and t, Q_{spec}, T_0, C_{A0}, F, and V_r are independent variables. τ_H, ρ, C_p, ΔH, k_0, E, R, and τ_{Ts} are process parameters. The simulation software that accompanies this text contains a simulator of this process based on the model developed here.

♠

Example 3.5 Exothermic CSTR

Problem Statement. Develop a dynamic model for an exothermic CSTR. The exothermic CSTR considered here is identical to the endothermic CSTR shown in Figure 3.13 except that an exothermic reaction occurs in the reactor and heat is removed in the heat exchanger by cooling water. The process parameters are also the

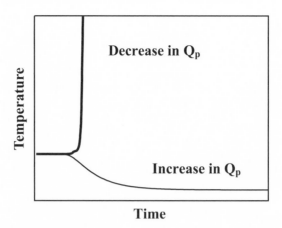

Figure 3.15 Open-loop response of the exothermic CSTR to a 1% increase and decrease in the heat removal rate.

same except that $Q_{spec} = -1,173,540$ cal/s; $C_A = 0.6415$ gmoles/L; $T = 340$ K; and $\Delta H = -160,000$ cal/gmole.

Solution. The equations used to model this process are all exactly the same as the equations used to model the endothermic CSTR with several of the model parameters and independent variables set to different values. Figure 3.15 shows the open-loop response of the exothermic CSTR to a 1% increase and a 1% decrease in the specified heat removal rate for the heat exchanger. This process is an example of an **open-loop unstable process** since a decrease in the heat removed by the heat exchanger causes a temperature runaway and an increase causes the reaction to extinguish. Not all exothermic reactors are open-loop unstable processes. For the case in which the reaction is extinguished (i.e., an increase in Q_{spec}), the outlet temperature is determined almost exclusively by the inlet feed temperature and the heat removal rate because the reaction rate is essentially zero. This process is another example of a non-self-regulating process.

♠

Example 3.6 Steam-Heated Heat Exchanger.

Problem Statement. Develop a dynamic model of the steam-heated heat exchanger shown in Figure 3.16. The feed enters the heat exchanger and flows through a number of parallel tubes that absorb heat from the condensing steam. The outlet temperature of the feed stream is measured by a temperature sensor/transmitter.

Solution. Figure 3.17 shows a cross-section of one of the heat exchanger tubes. An energy balance for this cross-section indicates that the rate of accumulation of heat in the metal is equal to the rate of heat transfer from the condensing steam minus the rate of heat transfer from the metal tube to the tube-side liquid, i.e., after rearranging,

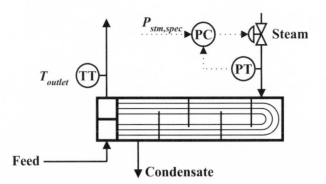

Figure 3.16 Schematic of a steam heated heat exchanger.

$$\frac{C_{vm}\,\rho_m}{4}(D_o^2 - D_i^2)\frac{dT_m}{dt} = D_o\,h_o\,(T_{stm} - T_m) - D_i\,h_i\,(T_m - T) \qquad \textbf{3.14}$$

where

- T_m - the temperature of the metal tube (°F)
- T_{stm} - the temperature of the condensing steam (°F)
- T - the temperature of the tube-side liquid (°F)
- C_{vm} is the heat capacity of the metal tube (0.092 Btu/lb-°F)
- ρ_m - the density of the metal tube (556 lb/ft^3)
- D_o - the outside diameter of the metal tube (1.05 in)
- D_i - the inside diameter of the metal tube (0.824 in)
- h_o - the heat-transfer coefficient between the steam and the tube metal (3000 Btu/ft^2-°F)
- h_i - the heat-transfer coefficient between the tube-side liquid and the tube metal (1000 Btu/ft^2-°F).

Equation 3.14 is valid for any point along the length of a heat exchanger tube and is based upon neglecting heat conduction along the length of the metal tube.

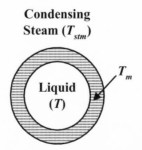

Figure 3.17 Cross-section of a tube in the steam heated heat exchanger.

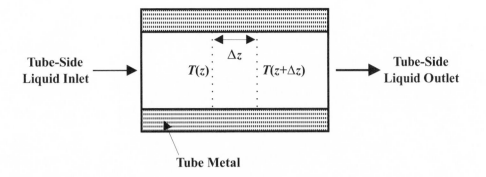

Figure 3.18 Cross-section of a tube from a steam-heated heat exchanger. Note that a differential volume is indicated inside the tube.

Consider the cross-section of a tube containing a differential volume shown in Figure 3.18. Applying Equation 3.3 to the differential volume,[4] noting that there are no reactions occurring, results in

$$\rho\, C_v A\, \Delta z\, \frac{dT}{dt} = \rho\, C_p v A\, T(z) - \rho\, C_p v A\, T(z + \Delta z) + Q\,\pi\, D_i\,\Delta z$$

where A is the cross-sectional area of the tube and Q is the heat flux from the metal tube to the tube-side liquid. Rearranging this equation, assuming that C_v is equal to C_p and using the expression for the cross-sectional area of the tube ($A = \pi\, D_i^2 / 4$), yields

$$\frac{dT}{dt} = v\,\frac{T(z) - T(z + \Delta z)}{\Delta z} + \frac{4Q}{\rho\, C_p D_i}$$

Substituting the equation for the heat flux [$Q = h_i\,(T_m - T)$] and taking the limit as Δz goes to zero results in the following partial differential equation:

$$\frac{\partial T}{\partial t} + v\,\frac{\partial T}{\partial z} = \frac{4h_i}{\rho_l\, C_{pl} D_i}(T_m - T) \qquad\qquad \textbf{3.15}$$

where

- T is the temperature of the tube-side fluid (°F)
- T_m is the metal temperature (°F)
- t is time (s)
- v is the average velocity of the tube-side fluid (7 ft/s)
- z is the axial position (ft)
- ρ_l is the density of the tube-side fluid (62.4 lb/ft^3)

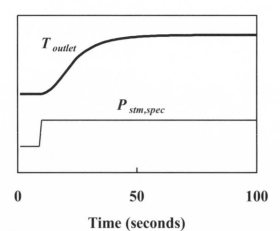

Figure 3.19 Open-loop response of the measured value of the outlet temperature of the steam-heated heat exchanger to a step increase in the specified value of the steam pressure applied to the heat exchanger.

- C_{pl} is the heat capacity of the tube-side liquid (1 Btu/lb-°F)

The dependent variables are T and T_m at each node point along the length of the tube, T_{stm} and T_{outlet} and the independent variable is $P_{stm,spec}$. This model is a distributed parameter model because the temperatures of the tube-side fluid and the metal tube vary over the length of the heat exchanger tube and are also functions of time. The inlet temperature of the feed is 80°F, the length of each tube is 80 ft, and initially the steam temperature is 250 °F. The temperature sensor dynamics were modeled using Equation 3.6 with a time constant of 10 seconds while the dynamics of the pressure controller were neglected. At time equal to 10 seconds, the setpoint for the steam pressure controller was increased, resulting in a 10°F increase in the steam temperature. Equation 3.15 is a partial differential equation that constitutes an initial value problem.

To solve Equation 3.15, the method of lines[5] can be applied, resulting in an ordinary differential equation for each node point along the length of the heat exchanger tube. Equation 3.14 is also applied at each node point. In addition, the model for the temperature sensor on the outlet from the heat exchanger is applied. The resulting set of ordinary differential equations is stiff, requiring an implicit integrator such as LSODE[6]. The dynamic response of this process is shown in Figure 3.19. The simulation software that accompanies this text contains a simulator of this process based on the model developed here.

♠

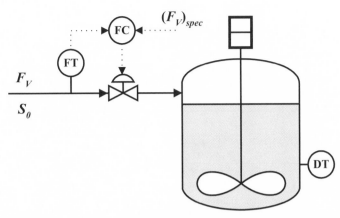

Figure 3.20 Schematic of a fed-batch reactor. DT - density sensor/transmitter.

Example 3.7 Fed-Batch Reactor for Ethanol Production

Problem Statement. Develop a dynamic model for the fed-batch fermentation process used to produce ethanol (EtOH) shown in Figure 3.20. Grains, such as corn, are converted to glucose by enzyme reactions and provide the feed for the fed-batch reactor modeled here. EtOH is recovered from the product produced by the fed-batch reactor by distillation. EtOH is added to gasoline to levels of approximately 10 percent by volume to produce gasohol, which is a common type of motor gasoline.

The variables for this process are

- k_s - Monod constant (0.22 g/L)
- k_s' - Monod constant (0.44 g/L)
- μ_0 - maximum specific growth rate (0.408 h^{-1})
- μ - specific growth rate (h^{-1})
- ε_0 - maximum specific productivity (1.0 h^{-1})
- ε - specific productivity (h^{-1})
- Y - yield coefficient (0.1 g-cell produced per g of glucose consumed)
- k_p - inhibition constant (16.0 g/L)
- k_p' - inhibition constant (71.5 g/L)
- x - yeast cell concentration (g/L)
- x_i - initial yeast cell concentration in the fermentor (1.0 g/L)
- V - volume of reaction mixture in the fermentor (L)
- V_i - initial volume of reaction mixture in the fermentor (10 L)
- F_V - volumetric feed rate to the fermentor (L/h).
- S - concentration of glucose in the fermentor (g/L).
- S_i - initial concentration of glucose in the fermentor (150 g/L).

- S_0 - concentration of glucose in the feed to the fermentor (150 g/L).
- P - concentration of EtOH in the fermentor (g/L)
- P_i - initial concentration of EtOH in the fermentor (0.0 g/L)
- m_S - total mass of glucose in the fermentor (g).
- m_x - total mass of yeast cells in the fermentor (g).
- m_P - total mass of EtOH in the fermentor (g).

The duration of a batch is 50 h. For the initial 13 h, feed is not added to the fed-batch fermentor to allow the yeast to grow to a sufficient level. After 13 h, the feed is added at a constant rate of 3,000 L/h until the end of the batch. The flow controller on the feed to the fermentor has an effective time constant of 2 s. An online density measurement is taken to infer the EtOH concentration in the fermentor; the sensor has an effective time constant of 20 s.

Solution. Assuming that the fermentor is perfectly mixed, the process can be modeled as a lumped parameter process. Equation 3.2 is applied to describe the dynamic behavior of the glucose, yeast cell, and EtOH concentrations, except that it is based on mass (g) and not moles. The fermentation reactions are modeled using the specific growth of the yeast cells (μ)

$$\mu = \left[\frac{\mu_0}{1 + P / k_P}\right]\left[\frac{S}{k_S + S}\right]$$

and the specific production rate of EtOH (ε)

$$\varepsilon = \left[\frac{\varepsilon_0}{1 + P / k_P'}\right]\left[\frac{S}{k_S' + S}\right]$$

using Monod kinetics[7]. Then, the growth rate of yeast cells is given as $\mu \cdot x \cdot V$, the consumption rate of glucose is $\mu \cdot x \cdot V / Y$, and the production rate of EtOH is $\varepsilon \cdot x \cdot V$.

Since the products are not removed from the fermentor during the batch, V is a function of time described by

$$\frac{dV}{dt} = F_V$$

The material balance for glucose is given by the following equation, which includes the effect of reaction and changes in the volume of material in the fermentor.

$$\frac{dm_S}{dt} = \frac{d}{dt}(VS) = V\frac{dS}{dt} + S\frac{dV}{dt} = F_V S_0 - \frac{\mu x V}{Y}$$

The first term on the right hand side of the equation represents the flow rate of glucose into the fermentor and the last term is the rate of consumption of glucose by the yeast cells. Using the dynamic description of the volume of the fermentor and rearranging results in

$$\frac{dS}{dt} = \frac{F_V(S_0 - S)}{V} - \frac{\mu x}{Y}$$

Likewise, the material balance for EtOH is given by the following equation, which includes the effect of reaction and changes in the volume of material in the fermentor.

$$\frac{dm_P}{dt} = \frac{d}{dt}(VP) = V\frac{dP}{dt} + P\frac{dV}{dt} = \varepsilon x V$$

Using the dynamic description of the volume of the fermentor, rearranging results in

$$\frac{dP}{dt} = \varepsilon x - \frac{F_V P}{V}$$

The material balance for yeast cells is given by the following equation, which includes the effect of generation of yeast cells and changes in the volume of material in the fermentor due to feed addition.

$$\frac{dm_x}{dt} = \frac{d}{dt}(Vx) = V\frac{dx}{dt} + x\frac{dV}{dt} = \mu x V$$

Using the dynamic description of the volume of the fermentor, rearranging results in

$$\frac{dx}{dt} = \mu x - \frac{F_V x}{V}$$

Because the process is slow responding, the actuator and sensor dynamics are neglected in this case (time constants of the order of seconds can be neglected when the time scale of the simulation is 50 h). Therefore, the model equations that are used to represent the fed-batch fermentor are given by

Actuator $F_V = F_{V,spec}$

Process $\dfrac{dV}{dt} = F_V$

$$\frac{dS}{dt} = \frac{F_V(S_0 - S)}{V} - \frac{\mu x}{Y}$$

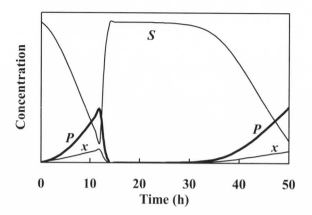

Figure 3.21 Dynamic behavior of the fed-batch reactor where S is the glucose concentrations, P is the EtOH concentration, and x is the concentration of yeast cells.

$$\frac{dP}{dt} = \varepsilon x - \frac{F_V P}{V}$$

$$\frac{dx}{dt} = \mu x - \frac{F_V x}{V}$$

where

$$\mu = \left[\frac{\mu_0}{1 + P / k_P}\right]\left[\frac{S}{k_S + S}\right]$$

and

$$\varepsilon = \left[\frac{\varepsilon_0}{1 + P / k'_P}\right]\left[\frac{S}{k'_S + S}\right]$$

Sensor $$P_S = P$$

Figure 3.21 shows the resulting dynamic behavior of the glucose concentration, the yeast cell concentration, and the measured EtOH concentration in the fermentor during the 50 h batch. These results were obtained by simultaneously integrating the model equations that describe this fed-batch reactor.   The concentrations of yeast cells and EtOH drop sharply when the feed to the fermentor is started (13 h), but both recover afterwards.

♠

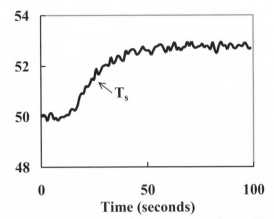

Figure 3.22 Dynamic response of the CST thermal mixer with noise modeled on the sensor reading.

3.6 Sensor Noise

Modeling of sensor noise is important for the realistic modeling of industrial processes. To reduce the effect of noise on feedback control, the process measurement is routinely filtered for industrial applications. Filtering of the process measurement can add extra lag to the overall dynamic response of a feedback loop; therefore, neglecting sensor noise can result in a dynamic model that responds faster than a corresponding industrial process that uses filtering of sensor readings.

Sensor noise can usually be modeled by assuming that it is **Gaussian-distributed white noise**. To model Gaussian-distributed white noise, one has to choose only the standard deviation of the noise, σ. Then the following equation[8] can be used to approximate a "bell-shaped" Gaussian distribution.

$$y_n = \frac{1.961\,\sigma\,(x_n - 0.5)}{[(x_n + 0.002432)(1.002432 - x_n)]^{0.203}} \qquad \textbf{3.16}$$

where y_n is the noise contribution to the measured value of the controlled variable and x_n is a random number between 0 and 1. Since $0 < x_n < 1$ with a mean of 0.5, y_n has approximately the same number of positive and negative values. Appendix B presents a simple algorithm for generating numbers that are very nearly random.

The procedure for modeling a sensor reading with noise is as follows.

1. Select the standard deviation of the noise. Remember that 4σ (i.e., $\pm 2\sigma$) should contain 95% of the readings.

2. Identify the noise-free sensor reading, y_{nf}. For example, Figure 3.14 shows the noise-free sensor readings for a step change for the endothermic CSTR.

3. Generate a random number with values between 0 and 1, x_n (Appendix B).

4. Apply Equation 3.16 to calculate y_n.
5. Then calculate the sensor reading, y_s, as

$$y_s = y_{nf} + y_n$$

Each time a new sensor reading is required, apply steps 2 to 5. The repeatability of the sensor reading of interest (Table 2.3) can be used to estimate the value of σ to use to model the sensor noise. For example, consider a level indicator. From Table 2.3, the repeatability is about ±1% corresponding to 4σ; therefore, σ is equal to 0.5%.

Figure 3.22 shows the results of adding sensor noise to the CST thermal mixer for a step change in the flow rate of stream 1. The noise on the temperature sensor reading is modeled using a σ of 0.05°C. The noise free temperature results are shown in Figure 3.7.

Example 3.8 Noise Model for an Orifice Flow Meter

Problem Statement. Develop a noise model for an orifice flow meter assuming that it has a repeatability of ±0.8% where the nominal flow measurement is 10,000 lbs/h.

Solution. Since the repeatability (i.e., ±0.8%) is assumed equal to 4σ (i.e., ±2σ), σ is equal to 0.4% or 40 lb/h at the nominal flow rate. The procedure for modeling noise on a flow measurement from an orifice flow meter is as follows.

1. Determine the noise-free value of the flow, F_{nf}. Note that F_{nf} contains the effects of the sensor lag.

2. Determine a random number $(0,1)$ x_n.

3. Calculate σ as $\sigma = 0.004\, F_{nf}$.

4. Apply Equation 3.16 to calculate F_n.

5. Calculate the sensor reading as

$$F_s = F_{nf} + F_n$$

♠

3.7 Numerical Integration of ODEs

The differential equation that represents a dynamic system has the general form

$$\frac{dy}{dt} = f(t, y, u, d) \qquad\qquad \textbf{3.17}$$

with initial conditions $t = t_0, \ y = y_0$

which is referred to as an initial-valued ordinary differential equation (IV-ODE) where y is the dependent variable, t is time, u is the manipulated variable (independent variable), and d is a disturbance (independent variable). When $f(t,y,u,d)$ is a linear function, an analytical solution is available (e.g., Laplace transforms, Chapter 4). When $f(t,y,u,d)$ is nonlinear, a numerical solution procedure is generally required. The dynamic model equations for the modeling examples in this chapter are consistent with the form of Equation 3.17.

With regard to the numerical solution of IV-ODEs, there are two key issues: solution accuracy and stability of the numerical procedure. Accuracy is related to the error between the exact solution and the numerical approximation. As the step size, Δt, used by the integration method is reduced, the error between the exact solution and the numerical approximation, E_T, is also reduced. In general, E_T can be represented by

$$E_T = K \Delta t^n \qquad\qquad \textbf{3.18}$$

where n is the order of the numerical integration technique and K is a constant. This relationship indicates that the magnitude of Δt should be kept small to produce an accurate solution. The parameter n indicates the accuracy of an integration technique. For example, if n is equal to 1, E_T decreases linearly as Δt is reduced. For n equal to 2, E_T decreases with the square of Δt, which means that E_T decreases much faster than for n equal 1 as Δt is decreased. Likewise, for a fourth-order method (i.e., $n = 4$), the accuracy of the numerical solution is much greater than for a first-order or second-order method with the same Δt. Therefore, **higher-order integration methods provide greater accuracy than lower-order integration methods.**

The numerical stability of an ODE integrator is determined by whether the round-off error damps out or grows with each step in time, Δt. If it damps out, the numerical integration is stable. If it does not, the round-off error grows without bound and soon dominates the numerical solution. There are two general types of ODE integrators: explicit and implicit integrators, and they each have a very different sensitivity to numerical stability. Explicit integrators integrate ODEs by solving a series of explicit equations while implicit integrators use implicit equation solutions. An example of an explicit equation is

$$y = a\,e^x + b\,x^2 + c$$

since the right hand side of the equation can be determined directly using the value of x and the constants a, b, and c. An example of an implicit equation is given by

$$y = a\,e^y + b\,x^2 + c$$

since the right hand side of the equation is a function of y; therefore, to solve for the value of y from this equation, an iterative numerical procedure is generally required.

The simplest ODE integrator is the explicit Euler method

$$y(t+\Delta t) = y(t) + \Delta t\, f\big(t,y,u,d\big)\big|_t \qquad\qquad \textbf{3.19}$$

where $f(t,y,u,d)$ is evaluated at time equal to t. The Euler method is a first-order method (i.e., $n=1$). It is referred to as explicit since the right hand side of Equation 3.19 is not a function of $y(t+\Delta t)$. The stability limit for integration by the explicit Euler method can be derived analytically[9] and is given by

$$\Delta t < \frac{2}{\big|\lambda(t)\big|} \qquad\qquad \textbf{3.20}$$

where $\lambda(t)$ can be roughly approximated by

$$\lambda(t) = \frac{f(t,y,u)}{y(t)} \qquad\qquad \textbf{3.21}$$

$\lambda(t)$ can be viewed as the relative rate of change of y. Equation 3.20 indicates that the stability of an explicit integrator can be improved by reducing the time step size, Δt. ODEs that have values of λ in the neighborhood of 1000 are referred to as **stiff ODEs**. From an analysis of Equation 3.20, it is clear that an explicit Euler integrator must use very small values of Δt to maintain numerical stability for the integration of stiff ODEs.

Another popular explicit integration method is the fourth-order Runge-Kutta method. It uses evaluations of $f(t,y,u,d)$ at t, $t+\frac{1}{2}\Delta t$, and $t+\Delta t$ to more accurately approximate the effective slope for the time step, Δt. Since it is a fourth-order method, it is much more accurate than the Euler method but has approximately the same stability dependence on Δt.

A well-known implicit integration method is the trapezoidal method.

$$y(t+\Delta t) = y(t) + \frac{\Delta t}{2}\big[f(t,y,u,d)\big|_t + f(t,y,u,d)\big|_{t+\Delta t}\big] \qquad\qquad \textbf{3.22}$$

This is referred to as an implicit method because $y(t + \Delta t)$ appears on the right hand side of Equation 3.22 and, in general, solving for $y(t + \Delta t)$ using Equation 3.22 requires the iterative solution of a nonlinear equation. **Implicit methods overcome stability limits on Δt but are usually much more difficult and computationally expensive to apply.** When λ is large, Δt must accordingly be reduced to retain stability for explicit methods; therefore, for these cases, implicit methods can offer significant advantages over explicit methods.

Well-behaved dynamic equations (i.e., ODEs that are nonstiff) are usually solved using high-order explicit methods because numerical stability is not a controlling factor for nonstiff equations and high-order methods provide computationally efficient solutions. Dynamic model equations that are stiff ($\lambda > 500$) present a challenge for explicit methods due to numerical stability, but can be effectively solved using implicit integrators. Because of their inherent numerical stability, implicit integrators (e.g., trapezoidal method) are much more computationally efficient for stiff problems even though they require more computations per time step. Implicit methods must still keep Δt below a certain level to meet the accuracy requirements.

For moderately stiff systems of ODEs (i.e., $100 < \lambda < 500$), the explicit Euler method offers computational advantages and is much simpler to apply than other methods. Since most control-loop dynamic models are nonstiff to moderately stiff, the explicit Euler is a convenient and reliable integration technique for this class of problems. Even so, most dynamic models used for process control analysis do not usually have λ's that are large enough to warrant the use of implicit integration techniques. More details concerning the issues of accuracy and stability for ODE integration can be found in Riggs[9].

Example 3.9 Stiffness Evaluation

Problem Statement. Analyze the stiffness of the model equations of the CST thermal mixer example (Example 3.1).

Solution. The application of Equation 3.21 to the models of the actuator, process, and sensor determines that the fastest-acting component of the actuator/process/sensor system for the CST thermal mixer is the actuator. The largest value of λ is 0.33 sec^{-1} (i.e., $1/\tau_v$). As a result, this problem does not require an implicit integrator since the application of Equation 3.20 indicates that a maximum stable step size of 6 seconds can be used. In fact, the results shown in Figure 3.7 were obtained using an Euler integrator with $\Delta t = 0.1$ seconds.

3.8 Summary

Dynamic process models are useful for analyzing process control behavior. Quantitative comparisons of control alternatives can be developed using dynamic process models. Dynamic process models can be developed using conservation of mass, moles, or energy, which consider accumulation, as well as the appropriate constitutive relations. When developing dynamic models for process control analysis, dynamic models of the actuator and sensors should be explicitly considered and, if appropriate, added to the dynamic model of the process to form an actuator/process/sensor model. In addition, the modeling of most sensors should include measurement noise, with the standard deviation of the noise estimated from the repeatability of the sensor (Table 2.3). The resulting dynamic equations for the actuator, process, and sensor can usually be integrated conveniently using an Euler integrator.

3.9 Additional Terminology

Constitutive relations - algebraic equations such as kinetic expressions or gas laws that are necessary to solve model equations.

CST - continuous stirred tank, i.e., a vessel in which the temperature and composition throughout the tank are uniform.

CSTR - continuous stirred tank reactor, i.e., a reactor in which the composition and temperature are uniform throughout the reactor volume since the fluid in the reactor is well mixed.

Dependent variable - a process variable that is determined by the solution of the model equations.

Distributed parameter model - a process model that can be applied to a system for which the dependent variables vary with spatial location within the process.

Exactly determined - a system of equations with the same number of unknowns as equations.

Exactly specified - a system of equations with the same number of unknowns as equations.

Gaussian-distributed white noise - noise that follows an equal probability-based Gaussian distribution.

Independent variable - a process variable that is specified independently of the process model results.

Lumped parameter model - a process model that assumes that the dependent variables are uniform throughout the spatial region of the process.

Macroscopic balances - balances based on what enters or leaves the process boundaries and treats the process in a lumped manner.

Macroscopic model - a model that is based upon macroscopic balances.

Microscopic balances - balances that consider that the dependent variables vary with spatial location within the process; .

Microscopic model - a model that is based upon microscopic balances.

Non-self-regulating process - a process that does not move to a new steady-state condition after a change in a process input is made.

Overdetermined - a system of equations with more equations than unknowns.

Overspecified - a system of equations with more equations than unknowns.

Process parameter - a constant appearing in a model equation, e.g., physical parameters, rate constants, gas constants, etc.

Self-regulating process - a process that moves to a new steady-state after a change in a process input is made.

Stiff ODE - an ODE with a λ (Equation 3.21) that is equal to or greater than 500.

Underdetermined - a system of equations with more unknowns than equations.

Underspecified - a system of equations with more unknowns than equations.

3.10 References

1. Bird, R.B., Stewart, W.E., and Lightfoot, E.N., *Transport Phenomena*, John Wiley and Sons, New York, p. 216 (1960).

2. Riggs, J.B., *An Introduction to Numerical Methods for Chemical Engineers,* Second Edition, Texas Tech University Press, Lubbock, Texas, pp. 387-420 (1994).

3. Bequette, B.W., *Modeling and Analysis of Dynamic Systems*, Prentice Hall, Englewood, New Jersey, (1998).

4. Stephanopoulos, G., *Chemical Process Control*, Prentice-Hall, Englewood, New Jersey, pp. 69-70 (1984).

5. Riggs, J.B., *An Introduction to Numerical Methods for Chemical Engineers,* Second Edition, Texas Tech University Press, Lubbock, Texas, pp. 220-228 (1994).

6. Ibid, pp. 200-207.

7. Aiba, S., M. Shoda, and M. Nagatani, *Biotechnol. Bioeng.*, 10, 845 (1968).

8. Unpublished work from R. Russel Rhinehart.

9. Riggs, J.B., *An Introduction to Numerical Methods for Chemical Engineers,* Second Edition, Texas Tech University Press, Lubbock, Texas, pp. 172-179 (1994).

3.11 Preliminary Questions

3.1 Why are undergraduate chemical engineering students generally unfamiliar with process dynamics before studying process control?

3.2 How can dynamic process simulators be used to choose the best control configuration for a new process?

3.3 Why are dynamic models for control and startup/shutdown analysis not generally the same?

3.4 What advantages does training operators on process simulators have compared to training them on the process?

3.5 What are the differences between lumped parameter and distributed parameter models? Give an example of each.

3.6 Why are macroscopic models generally used for lumped parameter processes and microscopic models used for distributed parameter processes?

3.7 When does the application of a mass balance and a mole balance yield the same equation?

3.8 What form do constitutive equations take and how are they used in models?

3.9 Does an overspecified system of equations have more equations than unknowns or more unknowns than equations?

3.10 Why are actuator systems represented as linear first-order systems?

3.11 What individual physical processes are modeled in a lumped fashion by Equation 3.5?

3.12 What distinguishes independent variables from dependent variables?

3.13 If sensor measurements with noise average out to the sensor reading without noise, why should one model sensor noise when dynamically modeling a feedback control loop?

3.14 What are the sources of sensor noise?

3.15 Why is a random number used to model sensor noise?

3.16 Indicate how each of the model equations for the endothermic CSTR (Example 3.4) is consistent with the general equation for an ODE given by Equation 3.17.

3.17 What are the two most important factors when numerically integrating ODEs?

3.18 Does meeting accuracy requirements affect explicit methods differently than implicit methods?

3.19 Does meeting numerical stability requirements affect explicit methods differently than implicit methods?

3.20 How are the explicit Euler method and the trapezoidal method alike? How are they different?

3.21 Why are most dynamic models of process control systems integrated using the explicit Euler method?

3.12 Analytical Questions and Exercises

3.22 When can the dynamics of a sensor or actuator be assumed instantaneous?

3.23 Estimate a reasonable range for the standard deviation of the noise for a level sensor.

3.24 Estimate a reasonable range for the standard deviation of the noise for a pressure sensor.

3.25 Estimate a reasonable range for the standard deviation of the noise for a differential pressure/orifice flow sensor.

3.26 Consider the level process shown in Figure 3.11 except that the inlet flow is the input and the outlet flow is given by

$$F_{out} = K \sqrt{L}$$

where K is a constant and L is the level in the tank. Develop an actuator/process/sensor model for this process. Assume that the flow controller on the feed stream has a time constant of 2 seconds. Identify all process variables and process parameters along with their dimensional units. Identify the dependent variables, the independent variables, and the parameters for this model.

3.27 Consider a vertical cylindrical tank that is 3 feet in diameter and has a water level of 6 feet. Assume that electrical heaters are placed inside the tank and can provide an instantaneous change in the heat addition rate to the tank. A thermocouple and thermowell with a dynamic time constant of 10 seconds are used to measure the temperature, and the contents of the tank are well mixed. Develop the dynamic model

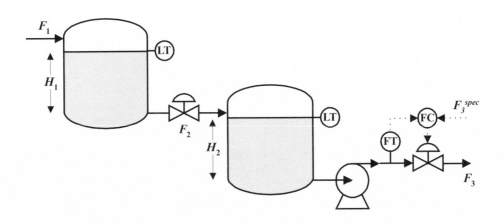

Figure for Problem 3.29. Schematic for a series of noninteracting tank levels.

equations for this batch process that describe the measured temperature of the water in the tank assuming that the water is initially at 25°C and that a fixed heating rate, Q, is applied to the tank by the electrical heaters. Assume that the specific gravity is unity and the heat capacity per unit mass is 1 cal/°C·g. Identify the dependent variables, the independent variables, and the parameters for this model.

3.28 Consider a vertical cylindrical tank that is 3 feet in diameter and has a water level of 6 feet. Assume that there is flow into the tank(F_{in}) and that the flow out of the tank (F_{out})is given by

$$F_{out} = k\sqrt{H}$$

where H is the height of the liquid in the tank. Develop the dynamic equations for this system assuming that initially the system is at steady state and then F_{in} is increased by 20%. Assume that a flow controller with a time constant of τ_v is used to implement the change in F_{in}. Assume that the specific gravity of water is unity. Identify the dependent variables, the independent variables, and the parameters for this model.

3.29 Consider the two noninteracting tank levels shown in the figure for this problem in which the F's represent volumetric flow rates. Develop the dynamic models for H_1 and H_2 assuming that F_2 is given by

$$F_2 = k\sqrt{H_1}$$

which represents the effect of the valve in the line between the first and second tank. A_1 and A_2 are the cross-sectional areas of the first and second tanks, respectively. Since this valve has a fixed stem position, which determines the value of k, the flow dynamics associated with this valve can be assumed instantaneous. Also assume that the dynamics of the level sensors are instantaneous. The changes in F_3 have a time

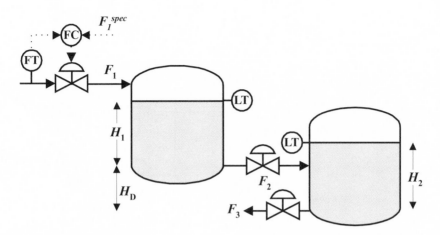

Figure for Problem 3.30. Schematic for a series of interacting tank levels.

constant τ_v and F_1 is assumed constant. Identify the dependent variables, the independent variables, and the parameters for this model.

3.30 Consider the two interacting tank levels shown in the figure for this problem in which the F's represent volumetric flow rates. Develop the dynamic models for H_1 and H_2 assuming that F_2 and F_3 are given by

$$F_2 = k_1 \sqrt{H_1 + H_D - H_2}$$

$$F_3 = k_2 \sqrt{H_2}$$

which represent the effect of the valves in the exit lines and the hydrostatic head for the two tanks. A_1 and A_2 are the cross-sectional areas of the first and second tanks, respectively. Since the valves have a fixed stem position, which determines the value of k, the flow dynamics associated with these valves can be assumed instantaneous. Also assume that the dynamics of the level sensors are instantaneous. The changes in F_1 have a time constant τ_v. Identify the dependent variables, the independent variables, and the parameters for this model.

3.31 Develop the dynamic modeling equations for the concentration of A in the product stream as a function of the specified flow rates for the feed and the recycle stream for the two mixing tanks shown in the figure for this problem. Note that all the F's are expressed as volumetric flow rates, and both flow controllers have the same dynamic response, which is described by τ_v. Assume perfect level control for both tanks and assume that both tanks are perfectly mixed and have the same holdup of liquid of volume V. The analyzer on the product stream has an analyzer delay of 3 minutes. Identify the dependent variables, the independent variables, and the parameters for this model.

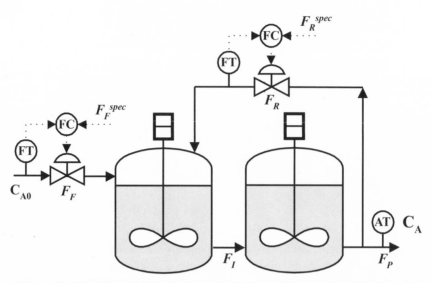

Figure for Problem 3.31. Schematic for a mixing tank with recycle.

3.32 Develop the model equations that can be used to represent the dynamic behavior of a stirred tank heater considering the combined models of the actuator, process, and sensor. Assume that the stirred tank heater is identical to the endothermic CSTR given in Section 3.5 except that no reactions take place. Identify the dependent variables, the independent variables, and the parameters for this model.

3.33 Develop the set of dynamic equations that describe an isothermal CSTR in which series reactions occur using an actuator/process/sensor modeling approach. Assume that one feed stream enters the reactor and one product stream leaves the reactor. The reaction scheme is given by

$$A \xrightarrow{r_1} B \xrightarrow{r_2} C$$

where $r_1 = k_1 C_A$ and $r_2 = k_2 C_B$. Assume that the feed rate is the input variable and that the time constant for the flow controller for the feed rate has a value of 2 seconds and that the feed stream contains only component A at a concentration C_{A0}. The output variable is the concentration of B in the reactor product. Assume an analyzer delay of 3 minutes for the B analyzer on the product stream. Also assume perfect level control in the reactor (i.e., the flow rate out of the reactor equals the flow rate into the reactor). Identify all process variables and process parameters along with their dimensional units. Identify the dependent variables, the independent variables, and the parameters for this model.

3.34 Develop the set of dynamic equations that describes a nonisothermal endothermic CSTR with the same series reactions given in Problem 3.33. Assume that the first-order Arrhenius rate expressions and heats of reaction are known. Assume

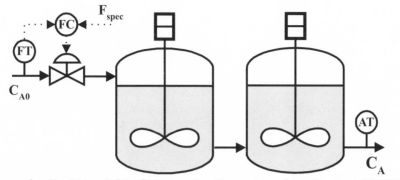

Figure for Problem 3.35. Schematic of a series of isothermal CSTR's.

that the inputs are the feed rate and the heat addition rate with time constants of 2 and 6 seconds, respectively. The output variables are the concentration of B and the temperature of the reaction mixture. Assume a 5 minute analyzer delay for the composition measurement and a time constant for the temperature measurement of 20 seconds. Also assume perfect level control in the reactor (i.e., the flow rate out of the reactor equals the flow rate into the reactor). Identify the dependent variables, the independent variables, and the parameters for this model.

3.35 Develop the set of dynamic equations that describe two isothermal CSTR's in series shown in the figure for this problem using an actuator/process/sensor modeling approach. Assume that a single irreversible reaction occurs in this system given by

$$A \xrightarrow{\ r\ } B$$

where $r = k\, C_A^2$. Assume that the feed rate to the first reactor is the input variable and that the flow controller on the feed has a time constant of 2 seconds. The inlet feed contains only component A at a concentration of C_{A0}. The output variable of this process is the concentration of B in the outlet product stream and the analyzer on this stream has an analyzer delay of 5 minutes. Also assume perfect level control in each reactor (i.e., the flow rate out of the reactor equals the flow rate into the reactor). Identify the dependent variables, the independent variables, and the parameters for this model.

3.36 Develop a macroscopic model of a steam-heated heat exchanger using an actuator/process/sensor modeling approach. The output variable is the outlet temperature of the process fluid and the input variable is the specified steam pressure. For a macroscopic model of a heat exchanger, the metal of the heat exchanger is at one temperature and the temperature of the process stream used for heat-transfer calculations is the average between the inlet temperature and the exit temperature for the heat exchanger, i.e., the heat-transfer rate from the metal to the process fluid and the heat transfer rate from the steam to the metal are given by

$$Q = U\, A(\overline{T}_m - \overline{T}) \qquad\qquad Q_{stm} = U_{stm} A(T_{stm} - \overline{T}_m)$$

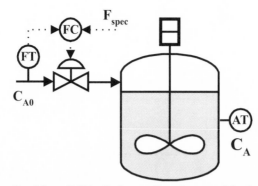

Figure for Problem 3.37. Schematic of a semi-batch reactor.

respectively, where U is the overall heat-transfer coefficient, A is the surface area for heat transfer, $\overline{T}$ is the average temperature for the process fluid inside the heat exchanger, $\overline{T_m}$ is the average temperature for the metal tubes in the heat exchanger, T_{stm} is the steam temperature, and U_{stm} is the heat-transfer coefficient between the steam and the metal tubes. The result for the heat-transfer rate can be used to calculate the outlet temperature of the process fluid. Assume that the pressure controller on the steam has a time constant of 2 seconds and the outlet temperature sensor for the process fluid has a time constant of 20 seconds. Identify the dependent variables, the independent variables, and the parameters for this model.

3.37 Develop the set of dynamic equations that describe an isothermal semi-batch reactor as shown in the figure for this problem using an actuator/process/sensor modeling approach. For a semi-batch reactor feed is added to the reactor, but product is not removed. Assume the same reaction scheme and rate expression as used in Problem 3.35. Assume that a flow controller with a time constant of 2 seconds controls the feed to the reactor and that the product composition is measured by an analyzer with a analyzer delay of 5 minutes. Identify all process variables and process parameters along with their dimensional units. (Hint: Remember to model the volume of the reactor as a function of time.) Identify the dependent variables, the independent variables, and the parameters for this model.

3.38 Consider the moonshine still shown in the figure for this problem. This batch process consists of putting sour mash (i.e., largely water and ethyl alcohol) into the still and adding heat. The ethyl alcohol is lighter than water; therefore, the distillate from the still is rich in alcohol. Write a set of model equations for this process using the actuator/process/sensor approach, assuming that the charge is already heated to the boiling point of the mixture. The heat input rate, Q, is the input variable and has a dynamic time constant of 20 seconds while the output variable is the concentration of ethyl alcohol in the product stream. Since the composition analysis is done by drawing a sample and measuring the density of the product, the analyzer delay is 30 seconds. Assume that the mixture has a constant heat of vaporization and that the mass fraction of the alcohol in the vapor leaving the still, y, is related to the mass fraction of alcohol remaining in the still, x, by the following equation

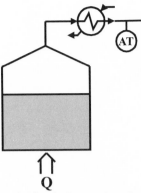

Figure for Problem 3.38. Schematic of a moonshine still.

$$y = \frac{\alpha x}{1+(\alpha-1)x}$$

Identify the dependent variables, the independent variables, and the parameters for this model.

3.39 Consider a pressure vessel for which there is a fixed gas flow into the vessel and an exit line that has a control valve on it. Assume that the input to this process is the signal to the control valve on the exit line and the output variable is the pressure of the gas in the vessel. Assume that τ_v is equal to 10 seconds. Develop a dynamic model for this process using the combined models of the actuator, process, and sensor. Identify the dependent variables, the independent variables, and the parameters for this model. (Hint: Use the ideal gas law to relate pressure to the number of moles of gas in the vessel.)

3.40 Develop the model equations for a hot-water heater. Consider that the hot-water heater is well mixed and has a water holdup of 30 gallons. Assume that initially the water temperature is 120°F. At time equal to zero, hot water is withdrawn at rate of 5 gallons per minute and 5 gallons per minute of cold water at 60°F are simultaneously added. Assume that the heat addition rate to the hot-water heater is constant at 6×10^4 BTU/h and is applied at the instant the hot water is removed from the tank. For this case neglect actuator and sensor dynamics. Also, determine how long it takes for the hot-water temperature to drop to less than 90°F.

3.41 Develop a dynamic model for the level in a cone-shaped bin. The equation for volume of fluid in a cone is given by

$$V = \frac{\pi r^2 h}{3}$$

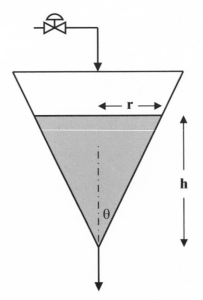

Figure for Problem 3.41. Schematic of a cone-shaped tank

where h is the height of the fluid in the cone and r is the radius of the cone at the fluid level in the cone. Note that r is a function of h. Consider the flow into and out of the cone, the actuator dynamics, and the level sensor dynamics. Assume that the flow rate leaving the tank is given by

$$F_{out} = k\sqrt{h}$$

3.42 What type of numerical integrator would you use to integrate the equations in Example 3.4? Use the stiffness of the equations to justify your answer.

Chapter 4

Laplace Transforms and Transfer Functions

4.1 Introduction

Laplace transforms represent a simple means to develop analytical solutions of **linear differential equations**. In addition, Laplace transforms can be used to develop transfer functions, which conveniently and meaningfully represent the input/output behavior of a linear process. Laplace transforms and transfer functions provide insight into the fundamental behavior of dynamic systems while introducing important terminology relevant to the process control field, but they are not typically used for process control applications in industry. Using the techniques presented in this chapter, transfer functions will be used in Chapters 6 and 7 to analyze the behavior of feedback systems.

4.2 Laplace Transforms

The Laplace transform of a function, $f(t)$, is defined by

$$\mathscr{L}\{f(t)\} = \int_0^\infty f(t)\, e^{-st}\, dt = F(s) \qquad \textbf{4.1}$$

where $f(t)$ is a relatively general function of time, t, for $t \geq 0$, $\mathscr{L}$ is the Laplace operator, s is a complex variable, and $F(s)$ is the symbol for the Laplace transform of $f(t)$. Equation 4.1 can be rearranged to yield the expression for the inverse Laplace transform.

$$\mathscr{L}^{-1}\{F(s)\} = f(t) \qquad \textbf{4.2}$$

Laplace transforms are useful for solving linear dynamic equations. The time domain equations are transformed into the Laplace domain (Equation 4.1) where they are solved algebraically, yielding an equation for the output variable in the Laplace domain. The output variable in the Laplace domain is then be transformed back to the time domain using inverse Laplace transforms (Equation 4.2).

The Laplace transformation is a linear operation. That is, the Laplace transform of a sum of two input functions is the sum of Laplace transform of the individual functions, i.e.,

$$\mathscr{L}\{a f_1(t) + b f_2(t)\} = a \mathscr{L}\{f_1(t)\} + b \mathscr{L}\{f_2(t)\} \qquad\qquad \mathbf{4.3}$$

where a and b are constants. On the other hand,

$$\mathscr{L}\{f_1(t)f_2(t)\} \neq \mathscr{L}\{f_1(t)\}\mathscr{L}\{f_2(t)\}$$

One can observe this relationship by comparing the Laplace transform of $e^{-at}\sin\omega t$ with the Laplace transforms of e^{-at} and $\sin\omega t$ in Table 4.1.

Table 4.1 lists the Laplace transforms of several commonly encountered functions. Table 4.1 can also be used to apply inverse Laplace transforms by going from the Laplace transform to the corresponding time function, $f(t)$.

Example 4.1 The Laplace Transform of a Series of Functions

Problem Statement. Determine the Laplace transform of $f(t)$ if

$$f(t) = t^2 + t^2 e^{-3t}$$

Solution. By defining

$$f_1(t) = t^2$$
$$f_2(t) = t^2 e^{-3t}$$

and using the property of a linear operation (Equation 4.3),

$$\mathscr{L}\{f(t)\} = F(s) = \mathscr{L}\{t^2\} + \mathscr{L}\{t^2 e^{-3t}\}$$

Then, using Table 4.1,

$$F(s) = \frac{2}{s^3} + \frac{2}{(s+3)^3}$$

Table 4.1	
Laplace Transforms of Commonly Encountered Functions	
f(t)	**Laplace transform of *f(t)***
f(t)	*F(s)*
K f(t)	*K F(s)*
Unit impulse at $t = 0$	1
Unit step at $t = 0$	$1/s$
Unit ramp, t	$1/s^2$
t^2	$\dfrac{2}{s^3}$
t^n	$\dfrac{n!}{s^{n+1}}$
e^{-at}	$\dfrac{1}{s+a}$
$t^n e^{-at}$	$\dfrac{n!}{(s+a)^{n+1}}$
$\sin \omega t$	$\dfrac{\omega}{s^2 + \omega^2}$
$\cos \omega t$	$\dfrac{s}{s^2 + \omega^2}$
$e^{-at} \sin \omega t$	$\dfrac{\omega}{(s+a)^2 + \omega^2}$
$e^{-at} \cos \omega t$	$\dfrac{s+a}{(s+a)^2 + \omega^2}$
$\dfrac{d f(t)}{dt}$	$s F(s) - f(0)$
$\dfrac{d^2 f(t)}{d t^2}$	$s^2 F(s) - s f(0) - \left[\dfrac{df}{dt}\right]_{t=0}$
$\displaystyle\int_0^t f(\tau)\, d\tau$	$\dfrac{1}{s} F(s)$
$f(t - \theta)$	$F(s) e^{-\theta s}$

4.3 Laplace Transform Solutions of Linear Differential Equations

Laplace transforms can be used to solve linear dynamic equations. Figure 4.1 schematically shows this process. A linear differential equation in the time domain is transformed into the Laplace domain by taking the Laplace transform of each term on both sides of the equation, which is illustrated in Figure 4.1 by the vertical arrow between the upper and lower left-hand blocks. That is, from the linear operation property of Laplace transforms (Equation 4.3), the equality of the equation can be maintained by applying Laplace transforms to the entire equation. For example, consider the following equation

$$\frac{d\,y(t)}{dt} = -\,y(t) \qquad at \quad t=0 \quad y(t)=y(0)$$

If Laplace transforms are applied to each term in the equation, the following equation in the Laplace transform domain results.

$$s\,Y(s) - y(0) = -\,Y(s)$$

Next, the transformed equation is rearranged algebraically to solve explicitly for the dependent variable in the Laplace domain, $Y(s)$, which is represented by the horizontal arrow between the upper left- and right-hand blocks in Figure 4.1. Even though the previous equation represents the differential equation in the Laplace domain, it contains $y(0)$, which is the initial condition (i.e., a constant) from the time domain. For the example under consideration,

$$Y(s) = \frac{y(0)}{s+1} = H(s)$$

Finally, the time dependent behavior of the dependent variable, $y(t)$, is obtained by applying the inverse Laplace transform to $Y(s)$, as shown by the vertical arrow between the upper and lower right-hand blocks in Figure 4.1 . That is, $F(s)$ must be converted to a form consistent with one of the entries in the right column of Table 4.1. Then the time domain form corresponding to this entry sets the functional form of the time domain solution, and the values for its parameters come directly from the parameter values in the Laplace domain. For the example under consideration, $Y(s)$ corresponds to $1/(s+a)$ in Table 4.1, which in turn corresponds to e^{-at} in the time domain. Since $y(0)$ is a constant and a is equal to 1 in this case, the time domain solution is given by

$$y(t) = y(0)\,e^{-t}$$

The key advantage of using Laplace transforms to solve linear differential equations is that, when the differential equation is transformed to the Laplace domain, algebraic equations, which are generally easier to manipulate, result.

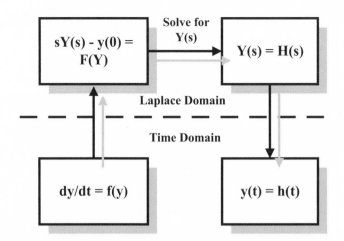

Figure 4.1 Schematic that shows how Laplace transforms can be used to solve linear differential equations.

Example 4.2   Solution of a General First-Order Equation

Problem Statement. Consider the following first-order differential equation

$$\frac{dy}{dt} = \frac{1}{\tau}(u - y)$$

where $y(0) = 0$ and τ is a constant. u undergoes a step change from zero to u at time equal to zero. Determine $y(t)$ using Laplace transforms.

Solution. The first step is to apply Laplace transforms to each term in the differential equation. Applying the Laplace transforms listed in Table 4.1 to each term of the differential equation yields

$$sY(s) - y(0) = \frac{u}{\tau s} - \frac{Y(s)}{\tau}$$

Rearranging and solving for $Y(s)$ yields

$$Y(s) = \frac{u/\tau}{s(s+1/\tau)} \qquad\qquad \text{A}$$

To apply the inverse Laplace transform, this equation must be converted into the following form

$$Y(s) = \frac{C_1}{s} + \frac{C_2}{s+1/\tau} \qquad\qquad \text{B}$$

where C_1 and C_2 are constants. Combining the two terms on the right-hand side of Equation B yields

$$Y(s) = \frac{C_1 s + C_1 / \tau + C_2 s}{s(s + 1/\tau)} \qquad \textbf{C}$$

For Equations A and C to be equivalent, the coefficients of s in the numerators of both equations must be equal, i.e., equating the coefficients of s yields:

$$C_1 + C_2 = 0 \qquad \textbf{D}$$

Likewise, the constant terms in both numerators must be equal, i.e.,

$$C_1 = u$$

Using Equation D, $C_2 = -u$

Thus,

$$Y(s) = \frac{u}{s} - \frac{u}{s + 1/\tau}$$

Now Table 4.1 can be used to convert each term in this equation to the time domain (i.e., applying inverse Laplace transforms to each term) resulting in

$$y(t) = u(1 - e^{-t/\tau})$$

                                                             ♠

      In the previous example, it was necessary to convert Equation A into the form of Equation B so that inverse Laplace transforms could be easily applied. A general procedure for implementing the following equation

$$\frac{K}{(s + a_1)(s + a_2)\cdots(s + a_n)} = \frac{C_1}{s + a_1} + \frac{C_2}{s + a_2} + \cdots + \frac{C_n}{s + a_n}$$

is **partial fraction expansion**. Note that the coefficients of s in the factors are all unity in this equation. The terms on the right-hand side of this equation are recombined into the form of the term on the left-hand side, and by equating terms of equal powers of s, a systems of equations is generated that yields the values of C_i. If repeated roots occur, they are handled differently, e.g.,

$$\frac{K}{(s + a)^2 (s + b)} = \frac{C_1}{(s + a)} + \frac{C_2}{(s + a)^2} + \frac{C_3}{(s + b)}$$

In a fashion similar to the previous case, the C's are determined by recombining the right-hand side of the equation and equating the coefficients of like powers of s.

Example 4.3 Application of Partial Fraction Expansion

Problem Statement. Consider the following function in the Laplace domain:

$$F(s) = \frac{1}{(s+1)(s+2)}$$

Apply partial fraction expansion to $F(s)$.

Solution. To apply partial fraction expansion, $F(s)$ is expressed as

$$F(s) = \frac{C_1}{s+1} + \frac{C_2}{s+2}$$

Recombining the previous equation using a common denominator results in the following equation:

$$F(s) = \frac{C_1(s+2) + C_2(s+1)}{(s+1)(s+2)}$$

Equating the original equation for $F(s)$ to this equation yields

$$F(s) = \frac{1}{(s+1)(s+2)} = \frac{C_1(s+2) + C_2(s+1)}{(s+1)(s+2)}$$

Since both sides of the equation have the same denominator, the following equation results

$$1 = C_2(s+1) + C_1(s+2)$$

Because the left-hand side of this equation does not have terms containing s,

$$C_1 + C_2 = 0$$

In addition, the equation resulting from equating the constant terms is

$$2C_1 + C_2 = 1$$

Solving the last two equation simultaneously results in

$$C_1 = 1$$
$$C_2 = -1$$

Finally, $F(s)$ is given by

$$F(s) = \frac{1}{s+1} - \frac{1}{s+2}$$

♠

Example 4.4 Application of Partial Fraction Expansion

Problem Statement. Consider the following function in the Laplace domain:

$$F(s) = \frac{1}{(2s+1)^2 (s+1)}$$

Apply partial fraction expansion to $F(s)$.

Solution. First, the numerator and denominator of $F(s)$ are divided by 4 to convert it into a form for which the coefficients of s in the factors are unity, i.e.,

$$F(s) = \frac{\frac{1}{4}}{(s+\frac{1}{2})^2 (s+1)}$$

Now $F(s)$ is expressed as a series of individual factors.

$$F(s) = \frac{\frac{1}{4}}{(s+\frac{1}{2})^2 (s+1)} = \frac{C_1}{(s+\frac{1}{2})} + \frac{C_2}{(s+\frac{1}{2})^2} + \frac{C_3}{(s+1)}$$

Recombining the previous equation using a common denominator results in the following equation:

$$F(s) = \frac{C_1(s^2+1.5s+\frac{1}{2}) + C_2(s+1) + C_3(s^2+s+\frac{1}{4})}{(s+\frac{1}{2})^2 (s+1)}$$

Collecting equal powers of s and equating the original equation for $F(s)$ to this equation yields

$$F(s) = \frac{\frac{1}{4}}{(s+\frac{1}{2})^2 (s+1)} = \frac{(C_1+C_3)s^2 + (1.5C_1+C_2+C_3)s + (\frac{1}{2}C_1+C_2+\frac{1}{4}C_3)}{(s+\frac{1}{2})^2 (s+1)}$$

Since both sides of the equation have the same denominator, the following equations result

$$C_1 + C_3 = 0$$
$$1.5C_1 + C_2 + C_3 = 0$$
$$\tfrac{1}{2}C_1 + C_2 + \tfrac{1}{4}C_3 = \tfrac{1}{4}$$

Solving these equation simultaneously, yields

$$C_1 = -1$$
$$C_2 = \tfrac{1}{2}$$
$$C_3 = 1$$

Finally, $F(s)$ is given by

$$F(s) = \frac{-1}{s + \tfrac{1}{2}} + \frac{\tfrac{1}{2}}{(s + \tfrac{1}{2})^2} + \frac{1}{s + 1}$$

♠

Example 4.5   Solution of the CST Thermal Mixer Equation

Problem Statement. The dynamic equation for a CST thermal mixing tank is given by Equation 3.9, i.e.,

$$M\frac{dT}{dt} = F_1 T_1 + F_2 T_2 - (F_1 + F_2)T$$

where T is the dependent variable of the process and F_1, F_2, T_1, and T_2 are inputs to the process. Determine the time behavior of T, assuming that at time equal to zero, T is equal to T_0 and a step change in T_1 of magnitude ΔT_1 is implemented at time equal to zero while all other inputs remain constant.

Solution. The first step is to take the Laplace transform of each term in the previous equation (Table 4.1).

$$M[sT(s) - T_0] = \frac{F_1[T_1 + \Delta T_1] + F_2 T_2}{s} - (F_1 + F_2)T(s)$$

Algebraically solving for $T(s)$ yields

$$T(s) = \frac{M T_0 + \dfrac{F_1 \Delta T_1 + F_1 T_1 + F_2 T_2}{s}}{M s + (F_1 + F_2)}$$

Rearranging yields

$$T(s) = \frac{T_0 s + F_1 \Delta T_1 / M + F_1 T_1 / M + F_2 T_2 / M}{s[s + (F_1 + F_2)/M]} \qquad \textbf{A}$$

To apply the inverse Laplace transforms, we need to use partial fraction expansion, i.e.,

$$T(s) = \frac{C_1}{s} + \frac{C_2}{s + (F_1 + F_2)/M}$$

By recombining the terms on the right-hand side of this equation, the following results

$$T(s) = \frac{C_1 s + C_1 (F_1 + F_2)/M + C_2 s}{s[s + (F_1 + F_2)/M]} \qquad \textbf{B}$$

To solve for the values of C_1 and C_2, we equate the coefficients of like powers of s in the numerators for Equation A and Equation B.

(s) $$C_1 + C_2 = T_0$$

(Constant) $$C_1 (F_1 + F_2) = F_1 \Delta T_1 + F_1 T_1 + F_2 T_2$$

Thus $$C_1 = \frac{F_1 \Delta T_1 + F_1 T_1 + F_2 T_2}{F_1 + F_2}$$

$$C_2 = T_0 - \frac{F_1 \Delta T_1 + F_1 T_1 + F_2 T_2}{F_1 + F_2}$$

Then

$$T(s) = \frac{F_1 \Delta T_1 + F_1 T_1 + F_2 T_2}{s(F_1 + F_2)} + \left[T_0 - \frac{F_1 \Delta T_1 + F_1 T_1 + F_2 T_2}{F_1 + F_2} \right] \frac{1}{s + (F_1 + F_2)/M}$$

Applying the inverse Laplace transform yields:

$$T(t) = \frac{F_1 \Delta T_1 + F_1 T_1 + F_2 T_2}{F_1 + F_2} + \left[T_0 - \frac{F_1 \Delta T_1 + F_1 T_1 + F_2 T_2}{F_1 + F_2} \right] e^{-t(F_1 + F_2)/M}$$

Note that at $t = 0$, $T = T_0$ and as $t \rightarrow \infty$

$$T \rightarrow \frac{F_1 \, \Delta T_1 + F_1 \, T_1 + F_2 \, T_2}{F_1 + F_2} = T_\infty$$

The solution can also be written as

$$T = T_\infty - (T_\infty - T_0) e^{-t(F_1 + F_2)/M}$$

♠

There are two additional important properties of Laplace transform: the **final-value theorem** and the **initial-value theorem**. The final-value theorem states that

$$\lim_{t \rightarrow \infty} \{f(t)\} = \lim_{s \rightarrow 0} \{s F(s)\} \qquad \textbf{4.4}$$

if the limit of $f(t)$ as $t \rightarrow \infty$ exists. The final-value theorem can be used to determine the steady-state conditions of a process if a model of the process is available in the Laplace domain. The initial-value theorem is given by

$$\lim_{t \rightarrow 0} \{f(t)\} = \lim_{s \rightarrow \infty} \{s F(s)\} \qquad \textbf{4.5}$$

The initial-value theorem can be used to determine the initial conditions of a function if the Laplace transform of the function is known. Note that when time becomes large, s approaches zero and *vice-versa*.

Example 4.6 Application of the Initial-Value and Final-Value Theorems

Problem Statement. Apply the initial-value and final-value theorems to the Laplace transform of

$$f(t) = e^{-at} \sin \omega t$$

Solution. From Table 4.1, the Laplace equation for this function is

$$F(s) = \frac{\omega}{(s+a)^2 + \omega^2}$$

Applying Equation 4.5 yields

$$\lim_{t \rightarrow 0} \{f(t)\} = \lim_{s \rightarrow \infty} \left[\frac{s\omega}{(s+a)^2 + \omega^2} \right] = 0$$

Note that when t equal to zero is substituted into the time domain version of the function, the same result is obtained.

Applying Equation 4.4 yields

$$\lim_{t \to \infty} \{f(t)\} = \lim_{s \to 0} \left[\frac{s\omega}{(s+a)^2 + \omega^2} \right] = 0$$

which is also consistent with the time domain function.

♠

Example 4.7 Solution of Second-Order Differential Equations

Problem Statement. Consider a general second-order differential equation

$$\frac{d^2 y}{dt^2} + a\frac{dy}{dt} + by = f(t)$$

where
$$\left(\frac{dy}{dt}\right)_{t=0} = 0$$
$$y(0) = 0$$

and $f(t)$ is a step change from 0 to 1 at $t = 0$. Evaluate the solutions for this differential equation. Note that because this is a second-order differential equation, two initial conditions are required to solve it.

Solution. Using Table 4.1 to apply Laplace transforms to each term in the differential equation results in

$$\left[s^2 Y(s) - s\, y(0) - \left(\frac{dy}{dt}\right)_{t=o} \right] + a[s Y(s) - y(0)] + b Y(s) = 1/s$$

Simplifying and solving for $Y(s)$,

$$Y(s) = \frac{1}{s(s^2 + as + b)}$$

Before this equation can be converted back to the time domain by applying inverse Laplace transforms, the roots of the denominator must be calculated so that partial fraction expansion can be used. Applying the quadratic formula to factor the denominator into its roots yields

$$Y(s) = \frac{1}{s\left(s + \dfrac{a + \sqrt{a^2 - 4b}}{2}\right)\left(s + \dfrac{a - \sqrt{a^2 - 4b}}{2}\right)}$$

Three cases can result for this system:

Case 1 $a^2 - 4b > 0$

Case 2 $a^2 - 4b = 0$

Case 3 $a^2 - 4b < 0$

Case 1 Consider the case in which $a = 5$ and $b = 6$ (i.e., $a^2 - 4b = 1$)

$$Y(s) = \frac{1}{s(s^2 + 5s + 6)} = \frac{1}{s(s+2)(s+3)}$$

Applying standard partial fraction expansion

$$Y(s) = \frac{1}{s(s+2)(s+3)} = \frac{C_1}{s} + \frac{C_2}{s+2} + \frac{C_3}{s+3}$$

$$Y(s) = \frac{1}{6s} - \frac{1}{2(s+2)} + \frac{1}{3(s+3)}$$

Applying the inverse Laplace transformation to each term yields

$$y(t) = \mathcal{L}^{-1}[Y(s)] = \mathcal{L}^{-1}\left(\frac{1/6}{s}\right) - \mathcal{L}^{-1}\left(\frac{1/2}{s+2}\right) + \mathcal{L}^{-1}\left(\frac{1/3}{s+3}\right)$$

$$y(t) = \frac{1}{6} - \frac{1}{2}e^{-2t} + \frac{1}{3}e^{-3t}$$

Case 2 Consider the case in which $a = 6$ and $b = 9$ (i.e., $a^2 - 4b = 0$)

$$Y(s) = \frac{1}{s(s^2 + 6s + 9)} = \frac{1}{s(s+3)(s+3)}$$

Applying partial fraction expansion,

$$Y(s) = \frac{1}{s(s+3)(s+3)} = \frac{C_1}{s} + \frac{C_2}{s+3} + \frac{C_3}{(s+3)^2}$$

Note that because of the repeated root (i.e., $s = -3$), a term with $(s+3)^2$ must be used. Solving for C_1, C_2, and C_3 using partial fraction expansion results in

$$Y(s) = \frac{1}{9s} - \frac{1}{9(s+3)} - \frac{1}{3(s+3)^2}$$

Applying the inverse Laplace transformation to each term,

$$y(t) = \frac{1}{9} - \frac{1}{9}e^{-3t} - \frac{1}{3}te^{-3t}$$

$$y(t) = \frac{1}{9}[1 - e^{-3t}(1+3t)]$$

This result corresponds to a critically damped response, which will be discussed in Section 5.4.

Case 3 Consider the case in which $a = 4$, and $b = 8$ (i.e., $a^2 - 4b = -4$).

$$Y(s) = \frac{1}{s(s^2 + 4s + 8)} = \frac{1}{s(s+2-2i)(s+2+2i)}$$

where $i = \sqrt{-1}$ and $i^2 = -1$.

Applying partial fraction expansion,

$$Y(s) = \frac{1}{s(s+2-2i)(s+2+2i)} = \frac{C_1}{s} + \frac{C_2}{s+2-2i} + \frac{C_3}{s+2+2i}$$

Solving for C_1, C_2, and C_3 yields

$$Y(s) = \frac{1}{8s} - \frac{(1-i)}{16(s+2-2i)} - \frac{i+1}{16(s+2+2i)}$$

Applying the inverse Laplace transformation to each term yields the following after considerable algebraic manipulations and the use of several identities from trigonometry[1].

$$y(t) = \frac{1}{8}[1 - \sqrt{2}\,e^{-2t}\sin(2t+\phi)]$$

where $\phi = 45°$. This result corresponds to damped sinusoidal behavior, which will be described in more detail later in this chapter. It is damped because the term (e^{-2t}) becomes small as time increases.

♠

4.4 General Characteristics of Transfer Functions

In the previous section, Laplace transforms were used to solve linear differential equations based on specified inputs. In this section, Laplace transforms will be used to develop transfer functions to relate the output (dependent variable) to the input (independent variable). Transfer functions have the advantages that they can be combined with a wide variety of inputs to determine the output of the process, and combinations of transfer function can be analyzed to study the behavior of more complex systems (e.g., feedback control loops). Moreover, the general form of the transfer function indicates the fundamental dynamic characteristics of the corresponding process.

A transfer function is defined as

$$G(s) = \frac{Y(s)}{U(s)} \qquad\qquad \textbf{4.6}$$

where $Y(s)$ is the Laplace transform of the output variable and $U(s)$ is the Laplace transform of the input variable, both written in **deviation variable** form. Deviation variables [i.e., $\Delta y(t)$ and $\Delta u(t)$] represent changes in a variable from initial steady-state conditions. The procedure for converting an equation into deviation variable form is as follows: (1) select the steady-state or equilibrium values for the independent variables, i.e., $\Delta u(t) = u(t) - \bar{u}$ for which $\bar{u}$ is the steady-state or equilibrium value of u, an independent variable , and (2) compute the corresponding equilibrium values for the dependent variables, i.e., $\Delta y(t) = y(t) - \bar{y}$ for which $\bar{y}$ is the steady-state or equilibrium value of y, a dependent variable. Equilibrium conditions correspond to steady-state conditions; therefore, **the initial conditions for $\Delta y(t)$ and $\Delta u(t)$ are zero for transfer functions**.

Example 4.8 Conversion of a Differential Equation to Deviation Variable Form

Problem Statement. Convert Equation 3.11 into deviation variable form.

Solution. Equation 3.11 is given as

$$\rho A_c \frac{dL}{dt} = F_{in} - F_{out}$$

L, F_{in}, and F_{out} require conversion to deviation variable form; therefore, equilibrium values (e.g., steady-state conditions) should be selected for level ($\bar{L}$) and flow rate ($\bar{F}$). Then, the deviation variable can be defined as

$$\Delta L = L - \bar{L}$$

$$\Delta F_{in} = F_{in} - \bar{F}$$

$$\Delta F_{out} = F_{out} - \bar{F}$$

Solving for the original variables (L, F_{in}, and F_{out}) and substituting into Equation 3.11 yields

$$\rho A_c \frac{d(\Delta L + \bar{L})}{dt} = (\Delta F_{in} + \bar{F}) - (\Delta F_{out} + \bar{F})$$

Simplifying results in the deviation variable form of this differential equation,

$$\rho A_c \frac{d\Delta L}{dt} = \Delta F_{in} - \Delta F_{out}$$

♠

Example 4.9 Conversion of a Differential Equation to Deviation Variable Form

Problem Statement. Convert Equation 3.10 into deviation variable form where C and C_1 are considered as the only variables in the equation and the system is initially at steady state at

$$C = \bar{C} \quad C_1 = \bar{C}_1 \quad C_2 = \bar{C}_2$$

Solution. Equation 3.10 is given as

$$\rho V \frac{dC}{dt} = F_1 C_1 + F_2 C_2 - (F_1 + F_2) C$$

The deviation variables are written as

$$\Delta C = C - \bar{C} \qquad \Delta C_1 = C_1 - \bar{C}_1$$

Rearranging the equations for the deviation variables and substituting into Equation 3.10, noting that C_2 remains constant, yields

$$\rho V \frac{d(\Delta C + \bar{C})}{dt} = F_1 (\Delta C_1 + \bar{C}_1) + F_2 \bar{C}_2 - (F_1 + F_2)(\Delta C + \bar{C})$$

Simplifying and rearranging results in

$$\rho V \frac{d\Delta C}{dt} = F_1 \Delta C_1 - (F_1 + F_2)\Delta C + F_1\overline{C}_1 + F_2\overline{C}_2 - (F_1 + F_2)\overline{C} \qquad \text{A}$$

Because the process is initially at steady state, i.e.,

$$\rho V \frac{d\overline{C}}{dt} = F_1 \overline{C}_1 + F_2 \overline{C}_2 - (F_1 + F_2)\overline{C} = 0$$

the sum of the last three term in Equation A is zero. Therefore,

$$\rho V \frac{d\Delta C}{dt} = F_1 \Delta C_1 - (F_1 + F_2)\Delta C$$

♠

Example 4.10   Derivation of a Transfer Function

Problem Statement. Convert the differential equation in Example 4.2 into deviation variable form and determine the transfer function for the process.

Solution. The first-order equation is given by

$$\frac{dy}{dt} = \frac{1}{\tau}(y_{ss} - y)$$

where y and y_{ss} are equal to $\overline{y}$ at time equal to zero. First, write each variable (y - output variable and y_{ss} - input variable) in deviation variable form

$$\Delta y = y - \overline{y}$$
$$\Delta y_{ss} = y_{ss} - \overline{y}$$

Rearranging yields

$$y = \Delta y + \overline{y}$$
$$y_{ss} = \Delta y_{ss} + \overline{y}$$

Substituting these equations into the differential equation results in

$$\frac{d\Delta y}{dt} = \frac{1}{\tau}(\Delta y_{ss} - \Delta y)$$

Taking the Laplace transform of this equation using the initial conditions $\Delta y = \Delta y_{ss} = 0$ at $t = 0$ yields

$$sY(s) = \frac{1}{\tau} [Y_{ss}(s) - Y(s)]$$

Solving for $Y(s)$ yields

$$Y(s) = \frac{Y_{ss}(s)}{\tau s + 1}$$

Then the transfer function of this system is given by

$$G(s) = \frac{Y(s)}{Y_{ss}(s)} = \frac{1}{\tau s + 1}$$

♠

Example 4.11 Derivation of the Transfer Function for a PID Controller

Problem Statement. Develop the transfer function for a PID controller in which the input is $e(t)$ [the error from setpoint] and the output is $c(t)$ [the controller output], i.e.,

$$c(t) = c_0 + K_c \left[e(t) + \frac{1}{\tau_I} \int_0^t e(t)\,dt + \tau_D \frac{d\,e(t)}{dt} \right]$$

where K_c, τ_I and τ_D are tuning constants and c_0 is the initial value of $c(t)$.

Solution. $e(t)$ is already in deviation variable form and the deviation variable for $c(t)$ is given as

$$\Delta c(t) = c(t) - c_0$$

Applying Laplace transforms and rearranging results in

$$G_c(s) = \frac{C(s)}{E(s)} = K_c \left[1 + \frac{1}{\tau_I s} + \tau_D s \right]$$

♠

Example 4.12 Predicting the Dynamic Behavior Using a Transfer Function.

Problem Statement. Determine the time domain behavior of the first-order system considered in Example 4.10 for (a) a step input change of magnitude A, (b) a unit impulse input change, and (c) a ramp input of slope B.

Solution. (a) For a step input change of magnitude A, from Table 4.1, the Laplace transform for the input variable $Y_{ss}(s)$ is given as

$$Y_{ss}(s) = \frac{A}{s}$$

Noting that multiplying $G(s)$ by $Y_{ss}(s)$ yields $Y(s)$, rearranging , i.e.,

$$Y(s) = \frac{A/\tau}{s(s+1/\tau)}$$

To develop a time domain solution for this equation, partial fraction expansion is required, i.e.,

$$Y(s) = \frac{A}{s} - \frac{A}{s+1/\tau}$$

Using Table 4.1 to apply inverse Laplace transforms results in

$$\Delta y(t) = A(1 - e^{-t/\tau})$$

(b) If an impulse input were used, $Y_{ss}(s)$ becomes

$$Y_{ss}(s) = 1$$

Then
$$Y(s) = \frac{1/\tau}{s+1/\tau}$$

and applying an inverse Laplace transform yields the time domain solution,

$$\Delta y(t) = \frac{1}{\tau} e^{-t/\tau}$$

(c) If a ramp input is used, $\quad Y_{ss}(s) = B/s^2$

and
$$Y(s) = \frac{B/\tau}{s^2(s+1/\tau)}$$

The time domain solution can be obtained by partial fraction expansion followed by the application of inverse Laplace transforms applied to each term, resulting in

$$\Delta y(t) = Bt + B\tau(1 - e^{-t/\tau})$$

Thus, **transfer functions can be used with a wide variety of inputs to determine the output behavior**. Moreover, a transfer function indicates the general dynamic behavior of the process it represents. For this example, each of the time domain solutions had exponential time dependence (i.e., $e^{-t/\tau}$), which is indicated by the denominator of the transfer function.

♠

4.5 Poles of a Transfer Function

Consider the general form of a transfer function

$$G(s) = \frac{K}{P(s)} \qquad \qquad \textbf{4.8}$$

The roots of $P(s)=0$ [i.e., the values of s that render $P(s) = 0$] are called the **poles of the transfer function.** Assume that $P(s)$ can be factored into a series of real poles, p_i.

$$G(s) = \frac{K}{(s - p_1)(s - p_2)....(s - p_n)} = \frac{Y(s)}{U(s)} \qquad \qquad \textbf{4.9}$$

Assume that a unit step input $(U(s) = 1/s)$ is applied to the process in question.

$$Y(s) = \frac{K}{s(s - p_1)(s - p_2).......(s - p_n)} \qquad \qquad \textbf{4.10}$$

By partial fraction expansion, this transfer function can be written as

$$Y(s) = \frac{C_0}{s} + \frac{C_1}{s - p_1} + \frac{C_2}{s - p_2} + ... + \frac{C_n}{s - p_n} \qquad \qquad \textbf{4.11}$$

Taking the inverse Laplace transform yields

$$\Delta y(t) = C_0 + C_1 e^{p_1 t} + C_2 e^{p_2 t} + ... + C_n e^{p_n t} \qquad \qquad \textbf{4.12}$$

Although the values of the constant terms are not known, the dynamic behavior of the process can be determined directly from the poles of the transfer function. Figure 4.2 shows the time behavior of $e^{p_i t}$ for positive and negative values of p_i. Note that

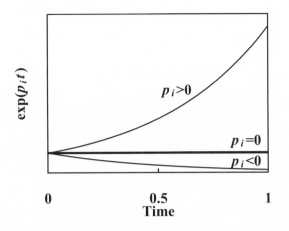

Figure 4.2 Different types of exponential behavior, i.e., exponential growth (p_i>0); constant value (p_i=0); and exponential decay (p_i<0).

positive values of p_i result in exponential growth with time, and negative values of p_i result in exponential decay approaching zero.

Now assume that one of the factors of $P(s)$ is $(s^2 + p^2)$. After partial fraction expansion, a term with the following form results

$$\frac{C}{s^2 + p^2}$$

The roots of this term are $s = i\,p$ and $s = -i\,p$. The inverse Laplace transform yields

$$\frac{C}{p} \sin p\,t$$

which corresponds to sinusoidal behavior with an amplitude of C/p.

Now assume that one of the factors of $P(s)$ is $(s^2 + as + b)$. After partial fraction expansion, a term with the following form results

$$\frac{C}{s^2 + as + b}$$

Now factoring yields

$$\frac{C}{\left(s + \dfrac{a - \sqrt{a^2 - 4b}}{2}\right)\left(s + \dfrac{a + \sqrt{a^2 - 4b}}{2}\right)}$$

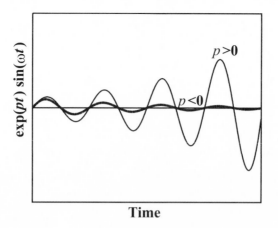

Figure 4.3 Exponentially growing ($p > 0$) and exponentially damped ($p < 0$) sinusoidal behavior.

If $a^2 - 4b > 0$, then real roots exist and the previous results for real roots apply.

If $a^2 - 4b = 0$, there are two real roots that are equal and critically damped behavior (see Section 5.4) results.

If $a^2 - 4b < 0$, the following, where $i\omega = \sqrt{a^2 - 4b}$, results

$$\frac{C}{\left(s + \dfrac{a - i\omega}{2}\right)\left(s + \dfrac{a + i\omega}{2}\right)}$$

This set of complex roots is called a **complex conjugate pair**. The inverse Laplace transform yields a term of the following form

$$C\, e^{pt} \sin(\omega t + \phi)$$

Figure 4.3 shows the time behavior of this term for $p > 0$ and $p < 0$, which show exponentially growing sinusoidal behavior and damped sinusoidal behavior, respectively. When $p < 0$, the larger the magnitude of p, the faster the sinusoidal response will damp out with time, i.e., approach zero. Likewise, when $p > 0$, the larger the magnitude of p the faster the sinusoidal response will grow.

Figure 4.4 shows a plot of poles in the complex plane, which plots the real and imaginary parts of each pole. The pole represented by a circle ($\bullet$) correspond to a real negative pole; therefore, this pole results in exponential decay (Figure 4.5a -b).

The complex conjugate poles represented by the triangles ($\blacktriangle$) have a negative real component with equal magnitude positive and negative imaginary parts; therefore, these poles result in damped oscillatory behavior (Figure 4.5c-f). Since the poles in

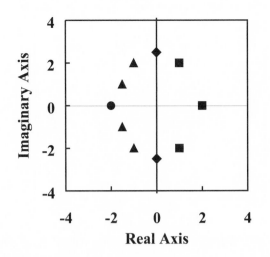

Figure 4.4 A complex plane with different types of poles: (●) exponential decay; (▲) damped sinusoidal; (♦) sustained oscillations; (■) unbounded sinusoidal growth and unbounded exponential growth.

Figure 4.5e have a real part with a smaller magnitude, the oscillations of the response in Figure 4.5f do not damp out as fast as the ones in Figure 4.5d. The poles represented by diamonds (♦) correspond to sustained oscillations (Figures 4.5g-h).

The complex conjugate poles represented by squares (■) have a positive real part; therefore, these poles result in oscillatory behavior that grows exponentially in amplitude (Figures 4.5i-j). The real pole represented by a square (■) indicates unbounded exponential growth. Note that poles in the right-half plane (i.e., the real part of the pole is positive) of this figure have exponential behavior that grows without bound as time increases, referred to as **unstable behavior**. That is, a process is unstable when bounded (i.e., fixed) input changes result in unbounded growth in the dependent variable.

These results show that **the poles of a transfer function [i.e., the roots of $P(s)$] indicate very specifically the type of dynamic behavior for the systems that the transfer function represents**. In other words, by simply determining the poles of a transfer function, one will automatically know the general dynamic behavior of the process represented by the transfer function. Table 4.2 shows different types of transfer functions and their corresponding dynamic behavior. This table shows that the dynamic behavior of a process can be determined directly by examining the denominator of the transfer function of the process.

A more general representation of a transfer function is given by

$$G(s) = \frac{Q(s)}{P(s)}$$

The roots of $P(s)$ are the poles of the transfer function and have a similar effect on the response to input changes as just shown.   For the general case, $Q(s)$ also has an effect on the response of the system.   The roots of $Q(s)$ are called the **zeros of the transfer function**.   A zero for a transfer function that is positive (i.e., a right-half-plane zero) indicates a special type of response (i.e., inverse action, Section 5.9).

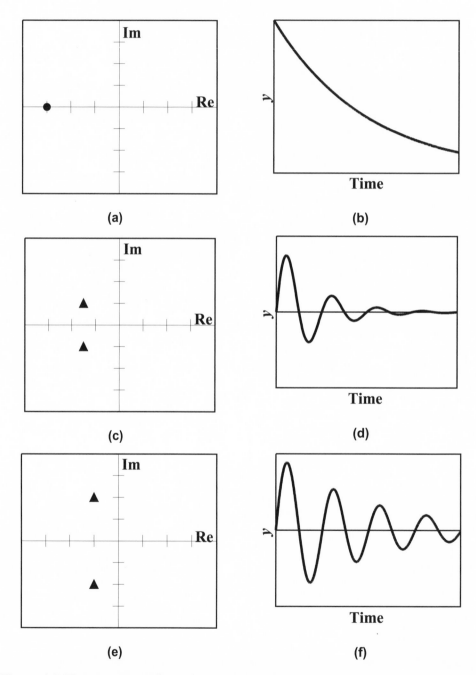

(a)   (b)

(c)   (d)

(e)   (f)

Figure 4.5 **The correspondence between poles on a complex plane and dynamic behavior.   (a) and (b) exponential decay;   (c) and (d) damped sinusoidal behavior;   (e) and (f) damped sinusoidal behavior.**

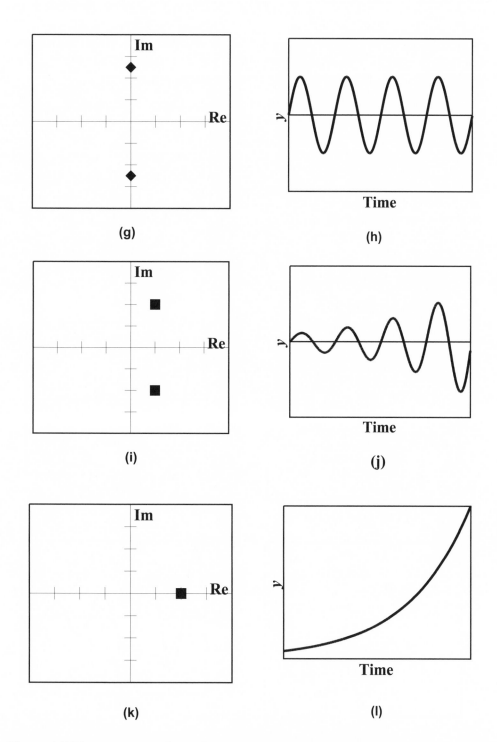

Figure 4.5 The correspondence between poles on a complex plane and dynamic behavior. (g) and (h) sustained oscillations; (i) and (j) exponential growing sinusoidal behavior; (k) and (l) unbounded exponential growth.

Table 4.2

Different Types of Transfer Functions and their Corresponding Dynamic Behavior

$G(s) = \dfrac{3}{s+1}$	Exponential decay of the form e^{-t}
$G(s) = \dfrac{3}{s-1}$	Unbounded exponential growth of the form e^{t} (i.e., unstable behavior)
$G(s) = \dfrac{3s+1}{(s+1)\,(s+3)}$	Exponential decay involving terms of the form e^{-t} and e^{-3t}
$G(s) = \dfrac{4}{s^2 + 9}$	Sinusoidal behavior of the form $sin\ 3t$
$G(s) = \dfrac{2}{(s+1)^2 + 4}$	Damped sinusoidal behavior of the form $e^{-t} sin\ 2t$
$G(s) = \dfrac{2}{(s-1)^2 + 4}$	Exponentially growing sinusoidal behavior of the form $e^{t} sin\ 2t$ (i.e., unstable behavior)

4.6 Block Diagrams using Transfer Functions

Block diagrams using transfer functions can be useful in understanding complicated control systems. To accomplish this, the properties of a sequence of transfer functions and some simple block diagram representations must be understood.

A Sequence of Transfer Functions. Consider the generalized sequence of transfer functions shown in Figure 4.6. From the definition of a transfer function, the following equation represents the input/output relationship for any of the transfer functions in this sequence

$$G_i(s) = \frac{Y_{i+1}(s)}{Y_i(s)}$$

To determine the relationship between $Y_3(s)$ and $Y_1(s)$, the previous equation will be applied for $G_1(s)$ and $G_2(s)$, i.e.,

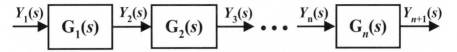

Figure 4.6 Schematic of a general sequence of transfer functions.

$$G_1(s) = \frac{Y_2(s)}{Y_1(s)}$$

$$G_2(s) = \frac{Y_3(s)}{Y_2(s)}$$

Note that by simply multiplying $G_1(s)$ and $G_2(s)$, the relationship between $Y_3(s)$ and $Y_1(s)$ is obtained.

$$\frac{Y_3(s)}{Y_1(s)} = G_1(s)G_2(s)$$

When considering a longer sequence of transfer functions, the product of the sequence of transfer functions eliminates the intermediate values so that **the transfer function for a sequence of transfer functions is simply the product of transfer functions in the sequence.** Therefore, the overall transfer function for the general sequence of individual transfer functions shown in Figure 4.6 is

$$G_{overall}(s) = \frac{Y_{n+1}(s)}{Y_1(s)} = G_1(s)G_2(s)\cdots G_n(s) \qquad \textbf{4.13}$$

where the overall transfer function is defined as the ratio of the output of the sequence divided by the input to the sequence. This property of transfer functions in series is particularly useful when analyzing the block diagrams of feedback control loops and other control related systems.

Example 4.13 Transfer Function of an Actuator, Process, and Sensor System

Problem Statement. Determine the overall transfer function of an actuator, process and sensor (Figure 4.7). Assume that the actuator, process and sensor each exhibit first-order dynamics, i.e.,

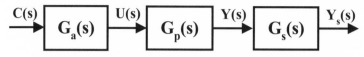

Figure 4.7   Schematic of a transfer function representation of an actuator/process/sensor system.

$$G_a(s) = \frac{K_a}{\tau_a s + 1}$$

$$G_p(s) = \frac{K_p}{\tau_p s + 1}$$

$$G_s(s) = \frac{K_s}{\tau_s s + 1}$$

Solution. Applying Equation 4.13 yields

$$G_{oa}(s) = \frac{Y_s(s)}{C(s)} = \left(\frac{K_a}{\tau_a s + 1}\right)\left(\frac{K_p}{\tau_p s + 1}\right)\left(\frac{K_s}{\tau_s s + 1}\right) = \frac{K_a K_p K_s}{(\tau_a s + 1)(\tau_p s + 1)(\tau_s s + 1)}$$

Note that this result shows that the combined system of the actuator/process/sensor behaves as a third-order process if the actuator, process, and the sensor each behaves as a first-order process (see Chapter 5).

♠

Block Diagram Algebra.   The properties of block diagrams and transfer functions can be used to develop general input/output relationships for process control systems.   The input/output relationship for a series of transfer functions developed in the last section can be combined with the properties of a summation function (Figure 4.8a and Figure 4.8b) and a divider (Figure 4.9).   For the summation function in Figure 4.8a, the following relationship results

$$Y_1(s) + Y_2(s) = Y_3(s)$$

For the summation function in Figure 4.8b, the following relationship results

$$Y_1(s) - Y_2(s) = Y_3(s)$$

The following relationship holds for the divider shown in Figure 4.9.

$$Y_1(s) = Y_2(s) = Y_3(s)$$

Using these rules with the properties of a series of transfer functions, input/output relationships can be derived for a wide range of systems.

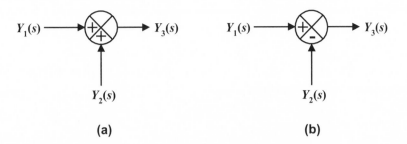

Figure 4.8 Examples of summation functions for block diagrams. (a) Addition (b) Subtraction.

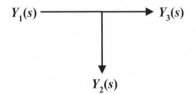

Figure 4.9 Schematic of a signal divider.

Example 4.14   Derivation of an Overall Transfer Function for a Block Diagram

Problem Statement. Develop a transfer function for the effect of $U(s)$ on $Y(s)$ for the system shown schematically in Figure 4.10.

Solution. Using the properties of a divider,

$$U(s) = C(s) = F(s) \qquad\qquad\qquad \textbf{A}$$

Using the properties of a sequence of transfer functions (Equation 4.13) results in the following equations

$$E(s) = G_1(s)G_2(s)C(s) \qquad\qquad\qquad \textbf{B}$$

$$H(s) = G_3(s)F(s) \qquad\qquad\qquad \textbf{C}$$

Finally, applying the properties of a summation function yields

$$E(s) + H(s) = Y(s) \qquad\qquad\qquad \textbf{D}$$

Substituting Equations B and C into Equation D results in

$$Y(s) = G_1(s)G_2(s)C(s) + G_3(s)F(s)$$

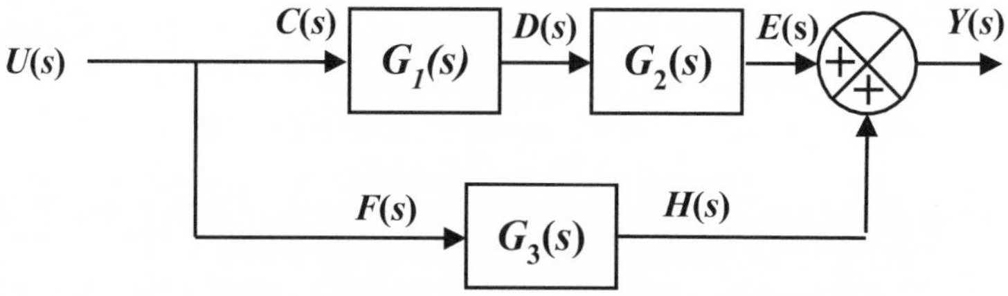

$Y = G_1 G_2 U + G_3 U$

$G_P = 1/0$

Figure 4.10 Block diagram for Example 4.14.

Using the divider relation (Equation A) to replace $C(s)$ and $F(s)$ with $U(s)$ and dividing both sides of the equation by $U(s)$ results in the overall transfer function for this system.

$$G_p(s) = \frac{Y(s)}{U(s)} = G_1(s)G_2(s) + G_3(s)$$

♠

4.7 Linearization of Nonlinear Differential Equations

The use of Laplace transforms to solve differential equations and to develop transfer functions is restricted to linear differential equations. But all real processes have some degree of nonlinearity. Changes in process gains and time constants represent examples of process nonlinearity. A number of processes are inherently nonlinear: (a) temperature control of a reactor with reaction rates that are exponential functions of temperature, (b) composition control in a distillation column with upper and lower limits on product purity, and (c) neutralization of an acid with a base due to an s-shaped titration curve.

When the model equations of a process are nonlinear, the equations can be **linearized** about an operating point, thus converting the nonlinear equations into a linear form that allows the application of Laplace transforms. Consider a nonlinear dynamic equation,

$$\frac{dy}{dt} = f(y,u)$$

at $t = 0$, $y = y_0$, $u = u_0$, and $f(y_0,u_0)=0$

where y is the output and u is the input variable. Because $f(y_0,u_0)=0$, u_0 and y_0 represent an equilibrium point and a basis for deviation variables. The linear approximation of $f(y,u)$ about (u_0,y_0) can be obtained by applying a Taylor series expansion[2] to this function and truncating the terms that are second-order and higher, i.e.,

$$\frac{dy}{dt} = f(y,u) \cong f(y,u)\Big|_{y_0,u_0} + (y - y_0)\frac{\partial f(y,u)}{\partial y}\Big|_{y_0,u_0} + (u - u_0)\frac{\partial f(y,u)}{\partial u}\Big|_{y_0,u_0} \quad \textbf{4.14}$$

Converting to deviation variables results in

$$\frac{d\Delta y}{dt} = \Delta y\,\frac{\partial f(y,u)}{\partial y}\Big|_{y_0,u_0} + \Delta u\,\frac{\partial f(y,u)}{\partial u}\Big|_{y_0,u_0} \quad \textbf{4.15}$$

This approximation is accurate in the vicinity of (u_0, y_0). Taking the Laplace transform of each term in Equation 4.15 and rearranging yields the transfer function of the process at the operating point (u_0, y_0).

$$\frac{Y(s)}{U(s)} = \frac{\dfrac{\partial f}{\partial u}\Big|_{y_0,u_0}}{s - \dfrac{\partial f}{\partial y}\Big|_{y_0,u_0}} \quad \textbf{4.16}$$

Example 4.15 Linearization of a Quadratic Function

Problem Statement. Linearize the following function

$$f(x) = a x^2 + b x + c$$

about x_0.

Solution. Applying Equation 4.14 yields

$$f(x) \approx f(x_0) + (x - x_0)\frac{d f(x)}{dx}\Big|_{x_0}$$

Evaluating the derivative of $f(x)$ and simplifying results in

$$f(x) \approx a x_0^2 + 2 a x_0(x - x_0) + b x + c$$

♠

Example 4.16 Linearization of a Bilinear Function

Problem Statement. Linearize the following function

$$f(y,u) = A u y$$

about y_0 and u_0. Note that the right-hand side of the equation is referred to as a bilinear term since it is formed by the product of two variables.

Solution. Applying Equation 4.14

$$f(y,u) \approx A u_0 y_0 + (y - y_0) A u_0 + (u - u_0) A y_0$$

Simplifying yields

$$f(y,u) \approx A[u_0 y_0 + u_0(y - y_0) + y_0(u - u_0)]$$

♠

Example 4.17 Transfer Function for the CST Thermal Mixer

Problem Statement. Use Equation 3.9 to develop a transfer function for the effect of changes of F_1 on T.

Solution. Equation 3.9 is given by

$$M \frac{dT}{dt} = F_1 T_1 + F_2 T_2 - (F_1 + F_2) T$$

Since there is a bilinear term involving F_1 and T, this equation is nonlinear. As a result, this equation must be linearized using Equation 4.14 before the transfer function can be developed. The linear approximation for Equation 3.9 about $\bar{F}_1$ and $\bar{T}$ is given by

$$M \frac{dT}{dt} = \bar{F}_1 T_1 + F_2 T_2 - (\bar{F}_1 + F_2)\bar{T} + (T_1 - \bar{T})(F_1 - \bar{F}) - (\bar{F}_1 + F_2)(T - \bar{T})$$

Define the deviation variables as follows.

$$\Delta F_1 = F_1 - \bar{F}_1$$
$$\Delta T = T - \bar{T}$$

Note that in this case we are assuming that T and F_1 are changing; therefore, deviation variables for only these terms are required. Substituting into the linearized model equation yields

$$M \frac{d(\Delta T + \bar{T})}{dt} = \bar{F}_1 T_1 + F_2 T_2 - (\bar{F}_1 + F_2)\bar{T} + (T_1 - \bar{T})\Delta F_1 - (\bar{F}_1 + F_2)\Delta T$$

This equation becomes

$$M \frac{d\Delta T}{dt} = (T_1 - \bar{T})\Delta F_1 - (\bar{F}_1 + F_2)\Delta T$$

because the following equation holds

$$M \frac{d\bar{T}}{dt} = \bar{F}_1 T_1 + F_2 T_2 - (\bar{F}_1 + F_2)\bar{T} = 0$$

initially at steady-state conditions.

The application of Laplace transforms to Equation 3.9 in deviation variable form yields

$$M s T(s) = (T_1 - \bar{T})F_1(s) - (\bar{F}_1 + F_2)T(s)$$

Rearranging this equation results in the desired form for the transfer function,

$$G_p(s) = \frac{T(s)}{F_1(s)} = \frac{\dfrac{T_1 - \bar{T}}{M}}{s + \dfrac{\bar{F}_1 + F_2}{M}}$$

♠

Example 4.18 Transfer Function for the CSTR Model Equation with Exponential Temperature Dependence

Problem Statement. Develop a transfer function for the effect of Q on T for Equation 3.13 evaluated at $T=T_0$. Assume that C_A is constant.

Solution. To apply Equation 4.16, $\dfrac{\partial f}{\partial T}$ and $\dfrac{\partial f}{\partial Q}$ must be calculated and evaluated at $T=T_0$.

$$\frac{\partial f}{\partial T}\bigg|_{T=T_0} = \left[\frac{-F C_p + \dfrac{V_r \Delta H C_A k_0 E}{R T_0^2}\exp\left(\dfrac{-E}{R T_0}\right)}{V_r \rho C_v}\right]$$

$$\frac{\partial f}{\partial Q} = \frac{1}{V_r \rho C_v}$$

Applying Equation 4.16 yields

$$G(s) = \frac{T(s)}{Q(s)} = \frac{\dfrac{1}{V_r \rho C_v}}{\left\{ s - \left[\dfrac{-FC_p + \dfrac{V_r \Delta H C_A k_0 E}{R T_0^2} \exp\left(\dfrac{-E}{R T_0}\right)}{V_r \rho C_v} \right] \right\}}$$

This approximation shows that the pole of this transfer function is a strong function of T_0, which is the temperature about which the nonlinear equation is linearized.

♠

Example 4.19　Analysis of the Linearization of a Level in a Tank[3]

Problem Statement. Consider the level in the tank shown in Figure 4.11. The tank is 10 ft in height and 6 ft in diameter. The discharge flow from the tank is given by

$$F_{out} = C_v \sqrt{h}$$

where C_v is 447 lb/h-ft$^{1/2}$. Initially the feed rate of water to the tank (F_{in}) is 1000 lb/h, which corresponds to a steady-state liquid level of 5 ft. Develop a nonlinear dynamic model for this process and linearize the nonlinear model about the initial conditions. Compare the steady-state change for the linearized model with the nonlinear model for a step increase in F_{in} to 1450 lb/h.

Solution. Applying an unsteady-state macroscopic mass balance to this process results in the following nonlinear equation

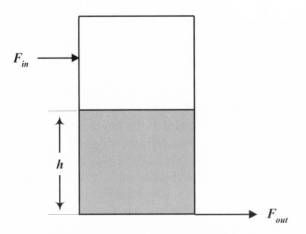

Figure 4.11 Schematic of a level in a tank for Example 4.19.

$$A\rho \frac{dh}{dt} = F_{in} - C_v \sqrt{h}$$

$$t = 0 \qquad h = h_0$$

A

where A is the cross-sectional area of the tank, ρ is the density of the water in the tank, and h is the height of water in the tank. The analytical solution of Equation A can be developed by using a variable transformation and separation of variables followed by integration, but is not presented here due to its complexity.

Equation A can be linearized by linearizing the square root of h, which is the only nonlinear term in the equation. That is,

$$\sqrt{h} \approx \sqrt{h_0} + \frac{1}{2\sqrt{h_0}}\left(h - h_0\right)$$

where h_0 is the operating condition about which the equation was linearized (i.e., a liquid level of 5 ft). Then, the linearized equation for this process is given by

$$A\rho \frac{dh}{dt} = F_{in} - C_v \left[\sqrt{h_0} + \frac{1}{2\sqrt{h_0}}(h - h_0)\right]$$

B

The analytical solution of the linear differential equation can be obtained by applying separation of variables and integrating, and the solution is given by

$$h = h_0 + \frac{2F'_{in}\sqrt{h_0}}{C_v}\left[1 - \exp\left\{-\frac{C_v t}{2A\rho\sqrt{h_0}}\right\}\right]$$

where F'_{in} is the inlet flow in deviation variable form.

The steady-state liquid level in the tank after the change in the inlet flow can be determined for the linear and nonlinear models of this system by either of two means: (1) by setting dh/dt equal to zero for the differential equation (i.e., Equation A or B) and solving for the liquid level, h or (2) using the time domain solutions and determining the tank level in the limit of time approaching infinity. The linear representation of the process with F_{in} equal to 1450 lb/h, and h_0 equal to 5 ft yields a steady-state liquid level in the tank of 9.51 ft. On the other hand, if these values are applied to the nonlinear equation, the steady-state liquid level in the tank corresponding to a feed rate 1450 lb/h is 10.52 ft. Therefore, the linearized model predicts that the liquid level was still within the 10 ft height of the tank while the nonlinear model indicates that the tank would overflow for this feed rate. In this case a 45% increase in inlet feed rate resulted in a one foot error in the steady-state level for the linear model, which, in this case, would cause the actual process to overflow while the linear model would predict only a high level. Clearly, the larger the change from the point about which the nonlinear model is linearized, the larger the error between the

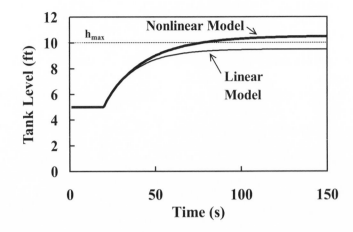

Figure 4.12 Comparison between the dynamic response of a nonlinear and a linear model of the level in a tank (Example 4.19).

nonlinear model and the linear approximation. Figure 4.12 shows the dynamic behavior of the linearized model and the nonlinear model for a step change in the inlet flow rate from 1000 to 1450 lb/h at time equal to 20 s. In addition, this figure also indicates the maximum tank level (10 ft).

♠

4.8 Summary

Laplace transforms are a convenient means for solving linear differential equations. The dynamic equation is transformed to the Laplace domain where the dependent variable can be solved for algebraically. Finally, the dependent variable in the Laplace domain is transformed back into the time domain, yielding the time domain solution to the original differential equation.

Transfer functions are the ratio of the Laplace transform of the dependent variable (output) to the Laplace transform of the independent variable (input) and can be derived from linear dynamic time domain equations by applying Laplace transforms once the dynamic equations have been expressed in deviation variable form. An advantage of transfer functions is that they can be combined with a wide variety of inputs to predict the dynamic behavior of the process. In addition, the roots of the denominator of a transfer function, i.e., the poles of the transfer function, directly indicate the dynamic behavior of the process.

4.9 Additional Terminology

Complex conjugate pairs - poles of a transfer function that indicate oscillatory time behavior.

Deviation variable - a variable that results from subtracting a nominal or constant value from the dependent variable.

Final-value theorem - An application of Laplace transforms that yields the long-term behavior of a dependent variable.

Initial-value theorem - An application of Laplace transforms that yields the initial conditions of a dependent variable.

Linearization - developing a linear approximation of a nonlinear model.

Partial fractional expansion - expansion of a transfer function into a sum of terms, each of which contains one of the factors of the denominator of the transfer function.

Poles of a transfer function - the roots of the equation $P(s) = 0$ where $P(s)$ is the denominator of the transfer function.

Unstable behavior - unbounded growth of a dependent variable for a bounded input.

Zeros of a transfer function - the roots of the numerator of a transfer function.

4.10 References

1. Stephanopoulos, G., *Chemical Process Control*, McGraw-Hill, pp. 145-157 (1984)

2. Riggs, J.B., An Introduction to Numerical Methods for Chemical Engineers, Texas Tech University Press, p. 78 (1994).

3. Example suggested by Karlene Hoo.

4.11 Preliminary Questions

4.1 What is the definition of the Laplace transform of a function, $g(t)$?

4.2 Give an example of a nonlinear equation not given in the text.

4.3 Explain how Laplace transforms are used to analytically solve differential equations.

4.4 If Laplace transforms and transfer functions are not typically used industrially, why is it important to study these topics?

4.5 What is the major limitation of using Laplace transforms to solve ODE problems?

4.6 How can the final-value theorem be used?

4.7 How can the initial-value theorem be used?

4.8 What advantages do Laplace transforms offer for solving linear ODEs?

4.9 What three types of dynamic behavior result from second-order differential equations?

4.10 In general terms, what does a transfer function represent?

4.11 How can the form of a transfer function be used to determine the dynamic behavior of the process it represents?

4.12 What are the poles of a transfer function and what are their significance?

4.13 What factor in the denominator of a transfer function indicates damped exponential behavior?

4.14 What factor in the denominator of a transfer function indicates damped oscillatory behavior?

4.15 What factor in the denominator of a transfer function indicates unbounded oscillatory growth?

4.16 What factor in the denominator of a transfer function indicates unbounded exponential growth?

4.17 What is a complex plane and how is it used to demonstrate the dynamic behavior of a process?

4.18 What are the three elements of block diagram algebra?

4.19 How can one obtain a transfer function of a nonlinear process model?

4.20 When a Taylor series expansion is used to linearize a single nonlinear function, what general type of dynamic behavior results?

4.12 Analytical Questions and Exercises

4.21 Determine the Laplace transform of $f(t)$ for the following functions using Table 4.1

a. $f(t) = e^{-at} + e^{-at} \sin \omega t$ b. $f(t) = \dfrac{d\,g(t)}{dt} - e^{-2t} \cos 5t$

c. $f(t) = \displaystyle\int_0^t g(t)\,dt - t^3 e^{-5t}$ d. $f(t) = 7g(t-10) + \sin 10t$

4.22 Apply the initial- and final-value theorems to $f(t)$ for the following functions.

a. $f(t) = e^{-at} \sin \omega t$ b. $f(t) = t^2 e^{-5t} + \sin 5t$

c. $f(t) = e^{-2t} \sin 2t - e^{-2t}$ d. $f(t) = \sin \omega t + \cos \omega t$

4.23 Apply partial fraction expansion to the following functions.

a. $F(s) = \dfrac{2}{(s+2)(s+3)}$ b. $F(s) = \dfrac{2}{s^2 + 11s + 30}$

c. $F(s) = \dfrac{7}{(s+1)(s+2)(s+6)}$ d. $F(s) = \dfrac{3s}{(s+1)(s+7)}$

4.24 Determine $y(t)$ by applying partial fraction expansion and inverse Laplace transforms for the following cases

a. $Y(s) = \dfrac{s+1}{(s+2)(s+3)}$ b. $Y(s) = \dfrac{1}{(s+1)(s+2)}$

c. $Y(s) = \dfrac{s+3}{(s+1)^2}$ d. $Y(s) = \dfrac{s+2}{(s+1)(s+6)(s+7)}$

4.25 For Problem 4.24, apply the initial-value theorem and the final-value theorem.

4.26 Solve the following differential equation using Laplace transforms.

$$\frac{dy}{dt} = t^2 \qquad y(0) = 0$$

4.27 Determine $y(t)$ for each of the following differential equations, assuming that

$$y(0) = \left(\frac{dy}{dt}\right)_{t=0} = 0$$

a. $\dfrac{d^2y}{dt^2} + 5\dfrac{dy}{dt} + 6y = 2$ b. $\dfrac{d^2y}{dt^2} + 3\dfrac{dy}{dt} = 5$

c. $\dfrac{d^2y}{dt^2} + 4\dfrac{dy}{dt} - 5y = 4$ d. $\dfrac{d^2y}{dt^2} + 4\dfrac{dy}{dt} + 4y = 1$

e. $2\dfrac{d^2y}{dt^2} + 11\dfrac{dy}{dt} + 12y = 5$ f. $3\dfrac{d^2y}{dt^2} + 7\dfrac{dy}{dt} + 2y = 6t$

Also, indicate whether each of the solutions exhibits stable or unstable behavior.

4.28* For the following set of ODEs

$$\frac{dy_1}{dt} + 2y_1 + y_2 = 2 \qquad y_1(0) = 0$$

$$\frac{dy_2}{dt} + y_2 + y_1 = 0 \qquad y_2(0) = 0$$

a. Solve for Y_1(s) by eliminating Y_2(s). Then determine Y_2(s).

b. Solve for $y_1(t)$ and $y_2(t)$.

* indicates a challenging problem

4.29 Convert the following differential equations into deviation variable form. In each case assume that steady state exists at the initial conditions. Assume that A, B, and C are constants.

a. $A\dfrac{dy}{dt} = BF_1 - CF_2$ where the initial conditions are $y=\bar{y}$ and $F_1=F_2=\bar{F}$.

b. $A\dfrac{dy}{dt} = By + Cu$ where the initial conditions are $u=\bar{u}$ and $y=\bar{y}$.

c. $A\dfrac{dy}{dt} = By + Cu + D$ where the initial conditions are $u=\bar{u}$ and $y=\bar{y}$.

4.30 Develop the transfer function for the effect of u on y for the following differential equations, assuming $y(0)=0$.

a. $\dfrac{d^2y}{dt^2} + 5\dfrac{dy}{dt} + 6y = u$

b. $\dfrac{d^2y}{dt^2} + 3\dfrac{dy}{dt} = u$

c. $\dfrac{d^2y}{dt^2} + 4\dfrac{dy}{dt} - 5y = u$

d. $\dfrac{d^2y}{dt^2} + 4\dfrac{dy}{dt} + 4y = u$

e. $2\dfrac{d^2y}{dt^2} + 11\dfrac{dy}{dt} + 12y = 5u$

f. $3\dfrac{d^2y}{dt^2} + 7\dfrac{dy}{dt} + 2y = u$

4.31 Describe the dynamic behavior indicated by each of the following transfer functions.

a. $G(s) = \dfrac{2}{2s+1}$

b. $G(s) = \dfrac{3}{(s+1)(s+4)}$

c. $G(s) = \dfrac{1}{s^2+s+1}$

d. $G(s) = \dfrac{1}{s^2-s+1}$

e. $G(s) = \dfrac{1}{s^2+9}$

f. $G(s) = \dfrac{1}{s^2+2s+4}$

4.32 Determine $y(t)$ for an unit impulse input and a step input of unit magnitude for

    a. Problem 4.30 a

    b. Problem 4.30 b

4.33 From Equation 3.6, develop the transfer function for a temperature sensor.

4.34 From Equation 3.8, develop the transfer function for a composition analyzer.

4.35 For Example 3.3, develop the transfer function for the effect of inlet flow rate changes on the actual level in the tank (Equation 3.11).

4.36 For Example 3.1, develop the transfer function for the effect of changes in T_1 on the **measured** temperature of the product.

4.37 For Example 3.1, develop the transfer function for the effect of the specified flow rate for F_1 on the **measured** value of T. Note that this problem requires that Equation 3.9 be linearized.

4.38 For Example 3.2, develop the transfer function for the effect of the specified flow rate for F_1 on the **measured** value of product composition. Note that this problem requires that Equation 3.10 be linearized.

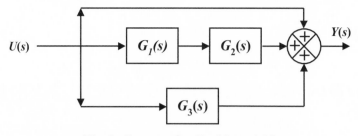

Block diagram for Problem 4.39.

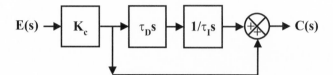

Block diagram for Problem 4.40.

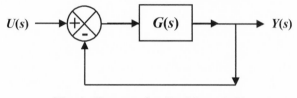

Block diagram for Problem 4.41.

4.39 For the block diagram for this problem, develop the transfer function between $Y(s)$ and $U(s)$.

4.40 For the block diagram for this problem, develop the transfer function between $C(s)$ and $E(s)$.

4.41 For the block diagram for this problem, develop the transfer function between $Y(s)$ and $U(s)$.

4.42 For the block diagram for this problem, develop the transfer function between $Y(s)$ and $U(s)$.

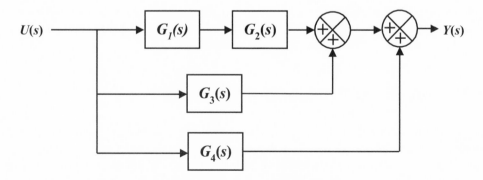

Block diagram for Problem 4.42.

Chapter 5

Dynamic Behavior of Ideal Systems

5.1   Introduction

In the previous chapter, Laplace transform solutions and transfer functions were developed for several simple cases. In this chapter, the dynamic behavior of a variety of idealized systems is presented along with their corresponding transfer functions, e.g., a first-order process, a second-order process, an integrating process, etc. From this chapter, it should become clear that a full range of process behavior can be represented using these idealized representations. Moreover, even one type of idealized dynamic behavior can represent widely varying processes. For example, a CST composition mixer, a CSTR with a first-order reaction, flow through a control valve, temperature measurement from a thermocouple, and charge storage in a capacitor are all well represented with a simple first-order dynamic model. Then for this example, the parameters of the first-order dynamic model clearly indicate the dynamic behavior of the process, i.e., the speed of the response and the sensitivity of the process to changes in the input. It may be necessary to combine two or more of these idealized elements to represent complex process dynamics, e.g., first-order plus deadtime model or inverse acting behavior.

The material in this chapter is not usually used in the industrial practice of process control. Even though an idealized model may accurately represent an industrial process, more direct means are available for applying control loop analysis without developing process models. Idealized models are, however, critically important to the understanding of process dynamics and the terminology of the process control profession. Understanding second-order dynamic behavior is important when tuning controllers. Underdamped or overdamped behavior, decay ratio, and settling time are important aspects of second-order dynamic behavior as well as terms that are commonly used by process control engineers to describe controller performance.

5.2   Idealized Process Inputs

Process inputs include manipulated variables, measured disturbances, and unmeasured disturbances. Each of the input types considered here can be applied using a manipulated variable, while only ramp and sinusoidal inputs are usually used to describe the effect of disturbances. By understanding how a process responds to one or more of these idealized inputs, one should be able to understand the general dynamic behavior of the process in question.

Unit impulse input.   A unit impulse input has infinite height for an infinitesimal duration so that the area under the impulse is unity.   An **impulse input** is shown graphically in Figure 5.1a.   The Laplace transform of a unit impulse input applied at t=0 is (Table 4.1)

$$U(s) = 1 \qquad\qquad \textbf{5.1}$$

While physical implementation of an impulse is not possible, a rectangular pulse can be a realistic approximation of an impulse.

Step input.   One of the easiest input changes to implement is the **step change**, which is a sudden and sustained change.   A step change of magnitude A at $t=t_0$ can be represented as

$$
\begin{aligned}
u(t) &= 0 \qquad & t < t_0 \\
u(t) &= A \qquad & t \geq t_0
\end{aligned}
\qquad\qquad \textbf{5.2}
$$

The Laplace transform for a step change of A applied at t_0=0 is given by (Table 4.1)

$$U(s) = \frac{A}{s} \qquad\qquad \textbf{5.3}$$

An idealized step change is shown graphically in Figure 5.1b.   In chemical process control, manipulated variables are normally flow rates; therefore, due to valve dynamics and other factors, the actual flow rate does not change instantaneously.   If the specified flow rate or the signal to the final control element is considered as the input to the process, virtually instantaneous step changes in inputs can be implemented on industrial processes.

Rectangular pulse.   A **rectangular pulse** is similar to a step change except that the input is returned to its original value after a specified amount of time.   Thus, a rectangular pulse can be considered as a series of two step changes.   A rectangular pulse is given by

$$
\begin{aligned}
u(t) &= 0 \qquad & t < t_0 \\
u(t) &= A \qquad & t_0 \leq t < t_0 + \Delta t \\
u(t) &= 0 \qquad & t \geq t_0 + \Delta t
\end{aligned}
\qquad\qquad \textbf{5.4}
$$

The rectangular pulse is said to have a strength of $A\Delta t$.   Figure 5.1c graphically shows a rectangular pulse.   The Laplace transform of a rectangular pulse is given by (Table 4.1)

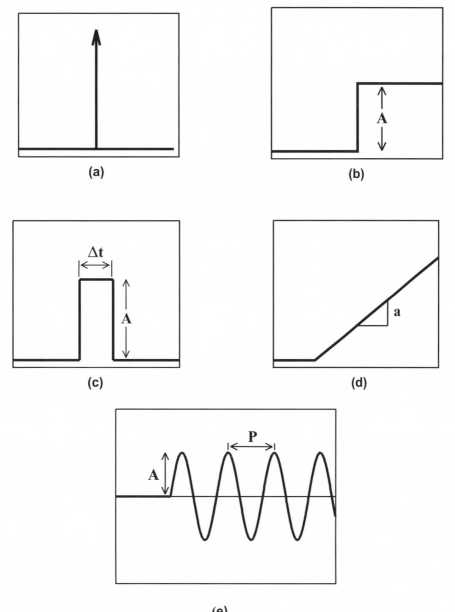

Figure 5.1   Idealized inputs (a) impulse (b) step (c) pulse (d) ramp (e) sinusoidal.

$$U(s) = \frac{A}{s}[1 - e^{-\Delta t s}]$$ **5.5**

when t_0 is equal to zero.

   Ramp input. Certain types of disturbances can be reasonably represented as ramps. For example, air temperature or cooling-water temperature can change steadily with a relatively constant slope during certain portions of the day. A **ramp input** is given by

$$u(t) = 0 \qquad t < t_0$$
$$u(t) = a\,t \qquad t \geq t_0$$

     5.6

and is illustrated in Figure 5.1d. The Laplace transform of a ramp input is given by (Table 4.1)

$$U(s) = \frac{a}{s^2}$$

     5.7

for t_0 equal to zero.

Sinusoidal inputs. The time scale over which inputs change can have an important effect on feedback control performance (see Chapter 9). For example, air temperature disturbances have a 24 hour period due to day-to-night variations. On the other hand, feed flow rate changes to a process can have a period of minutes or seconds. Since the frequency is directly related to the time scale of the input, one way to evaluate the effect of different time scales for inputs is to use sinusoidal inputs with different frequencies.

A **sinusoidal input** is given by

$$u(t) = 0 \qquad t < 0$$
$$u(t) = A \sin \omega t \qquad t \geq 0$$

     5.8

where ω is the radian frequency and A is the amplitude of the sinusoidal input. An example of a sinusoidal input is given in Figure 5.1e. The period, P, is equal to $2\pi/\omega$. The Laplace transform for a sinusoidal input is (Table 4.1)

$$U(s) = \frac{A\omega}{s^2 + \omega^2}$$

     5.9

5.3   First-Order Processes

A CST composition mixer, a CST thermal mixer, and an isothermal CSTR with a first-order reaction are examples of **first-order processes**. The differential equation for a first-order process written in the standard form is given by

$$\tau_p \frac{dy(t)}{dt} + y(t) = K_p\,u(t)$$

     5.10

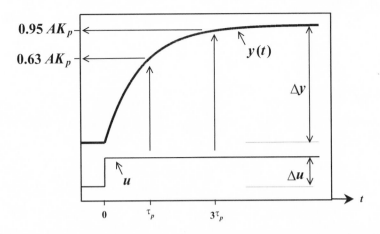

Figure 5.2 Dynamic response of a first-order process to a step input change.

where y is the output variable, u is the input variable, K_p is the steady-state process gain, and τ_p is the process time constant. The process gain is the steady-state change in y divided by the corresponding change in u (Figure 5.2), i.e.,

$$K_p = \frac{\Delta y}{\Delta u}$$

The time constant for the CST thermal mixer and the CST composition mixer is the volume of liquid in the CST mixer divided by the total volumetric feed rate, i.e., the residence time of the CST mixer.

The transfer function for a first-order process is given by

$$G_p(s) = \frac{K_p}{\tau_p s + 1} \qquad \text{5.11}$$

Note that the denominator of the transfer function contains s to the first power for a first-order process. Since the differential equation for a thermal mixer [Equation 3.9] can be rearranged into the same form as Equation 5.10, considering T_1 as the only input, the thermal mixer is a first-order process. Likewise, the transfer function of any first-order process can be rearranged into the same form as Equation 5.11. In each case, the process gain and process time constant can be identified directly. The standard form for a first-order differential equation (Equation 5.10) requires that the coefficient of y be unity while the standard form for the transfer function of a first-order process (Equation 5.11) requires that the constant term in the denominator be unity.

Figure 5.2 shows the response of a first-order process (y) to a step change in u. The analytical solution of Equation 5.10 for a step change, A, in u is given by

$$y(t) = A K_p (1 - e^{-t/\tau_p}) \qquad\qquad \textbf{5.12}$$

The process gain, K_p, and the size of the step change, A, determine the new steady-state value of y. The time constant, τ_p, determines the dynamic path the process takes as it approaches the new steady-state, i.e., how long it takes to approach the new steady-state. Note that 63.2% of the final change occurs in one time constant after the input change; 95% of the change occurs in three time constants; and 98% of the change occurs in four time constants (Figure 5.2).

Example 5.1   Characteristics of a First-Order Process

Problem Statement.   For the following first-order transfer function, calculate the process gain and the time constant. Also, determine the time required after a step input change for 98% of the change in the output variable to occur.

$$G_p(s) = \frac{16}{s+2}$$

Solution.   Rearrange the transfer function into the standard form for a first-order process by dividing the numerator and denominator by 2 resulting in

$$G_p(s) = \frac{8}{0.5 s + 1}$$

Therefore, the process gain, K_p, is 8 and the process time constant, τ_p, is 0.5 time units. Finally, 98% of the total change occurs in four time constants, which corresponds to 2 time units.

♠

Example 5.2   Estimation of a First-Order Model from Plant Observations

Problem Statement.   After observing a process, the operator indicates to the control engineer that an increase of 1,000 lb/h of steam (the input) to a reactor produces a 5°F increase in the reactor temperature (the output). When a change in the steam flow rate is made, it takes approximately 40 minutes for the full effect on the reactor temperature to be observed. Using this process information, develop a first-order model for this process.

Solution.   The gain of the process, K_p, can be estimated based on the steady-state changes observed for the process, i.e.,

$$K_p = \frac{\Delta y}{\Delta u} = \frac{5° F}{1000 \ lb / h} = 0.005 \ °F \cdot h / lb$$

The open-loop settling time is 40 minutes, which is approximately equal to $4\tau_p$. Therefore, the time constant is 10 minutes. The first-order transfer function for this process is

$$G(s) = \frac{0.005}{10s + 1}$$

where time is given in minutes and the gain has units of (°F·h/lb).

♠

5.4   Second-Order Processes

A series of two first-order processes or a first-order process with a PI feedback controller behaves as a **second-order process**. The differential equation for a second-order process written in the standard form is given by

$$\tau_p^2 \frac{d^2 y(t)}{dt^2} + 2\zeta\tau_p \frac{dy(t)}{dt} + y(t) = K_p u(t) \qquad \textbf{5.13}$$

where K_p is the steady-state process gain, τ_p is the time constant, and ζ is the **damping factor**, which determines the general shape of the dynamic response. The transfer function for a second-order process is given by

$$G_p(s) = \frac{K_p}{\tau_p^2 s^2 + 2\zeta\tau_p s + 1} \qquad \textbf{5.14}$$

Note that the denominator of the transfer function of a second-order process contains s^2 as the highest power of s. Similar to a first-order process, either the second-order differential equation or the transfer function can be put into these standard forms to directly determine K_p, τ_p, and ζ. To put the differential equation into the standard form corresponding to Equation 5.13, the coefficient of y is unity. Likewise, the standard form for the transfer function of a second-order process requires that the constant term in the denominator be unity.

Figure 5.3 shows the response of a second-order process to a step change, A, in the input for several cases for which $\zeta < 1$ (**underdamped behavior**) and $\zeta = 1$ (**critically damped**). Figure 5.4 shows the step response for $\zeta = 1$ (critically damped) and $\zeta > 1$ (**overdamped behavior**). Note that the value of ζ determines the general shape of the dynamic behavior of a second-order process, τ_p indicates the time scale of the response, and K_p indicates the steady-state sensitivity to input changes. In Chapter 4, it was shown that the poles of the transfer function determine the dynamic behavior of the process. In the case of a second-order process, real distinct roots correspond to an overdamped system, repeated real roots correspond to a critically damped system,

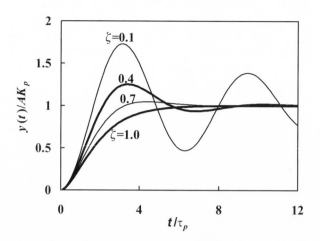

Figure 5.3 Dynamic response of an underdamped second-order process (0.1<ζ<1.0).

and complex roots correspond to underdamped behavior. Figure 5.5 shows a typical second-order underdamped response, along with its key characteristics, to a step input:

   1. Rise time, t_{rise}, is the time required for $y(t)$ to first cross its new steady-state value and is given by the following analytical expression

$$t_{rise} = \tau_p \frac{\pi - \phi}{\sqrt{1 - \zeta^2}}$$

where

$$\phi = \tan^{-1}\left[\frac{\sqrt{1 - \zeta^2}}{\zeta}\right]$$

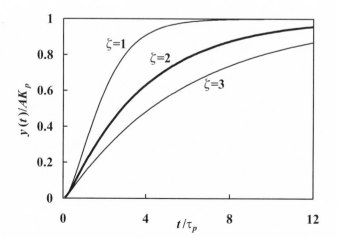

Figure 5.4 Dynamic response of an overdamped second-order process (ζ>1).

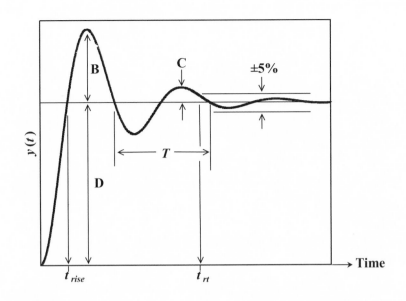

Figure 5.5 The key characteristics of an underdamped second-order response.

2. Percentage overshoot, $B/D \times 100\%$., is the maximum amount by which the response exceeds the resting value of y. The analytical expression for percentage overshoot is

$$\% \, Overshoot = 100 \exp\left\{\frac{-\pi\zeta}{\sqrt{1-\zeta^2}}\right\}$$

                                                                                                                    5.15

Therefore, one can estimate ζ by measuring the percentage overshoot and algebraically solving Equation 5.15 for ζ.

3. Decay ratio, C/B, is the ratio of successive peaks in the response. The analytical expression for decay ratio is

$$Decay \; Ratio = \exp\left\{\frac{-2\pi\zeta}{\sqrt{1-\zeta^2}}\right\}$$

                                                                                                                    5.16

Again, one can estimate ζ by measuring the decay ratio and algebraically solving Equation 5.16 for ζ.

4. Period of oscillations, T, is the time for a complete cycle. The analytical expression for period of oscillation is

$$T = \frac{2\pi\tau_p}{\sqrt{1 - \zeta^2}}$$ **5.17**

5. Response time or **settling time**, t_{rt}, is the time required for the response to remain within a $\pm 5\%$ band, based upon the steady-state change in y. That is, the $\pm 5\%$ band corresponds to $D \pm 0.05D$ for Figure 5.5. The above expressions are strictly valid only for second-order processes.

Decay ratio, percentage overshoot, settling time, and damping factor (ζ) can each be used as a basis for tuning. For example, a decay ratio of $\frac{1}{4}$ (i.e., quarter-amplitude damping) is a common tuning criterion. Selecting a damping factor specifies the decay ratio and percentage overshoot for a second-order process (Equations 5.15 and 5.16). Tuning based on minimum response time can also be used.

Example 5.3   Characteristics of a Second-Order Process

Problem Statement. For the following second-order transfer function, calculate the process gain, the time constant, and the damping factor. In addition, determine the percentage overshoot and the decay ratio.

$$G_p(s) = \frac{1}{2s^2 + 1.5s + 0.5}$$

Solution. Rearranging the second-order transfer function into the standard form yields

$$G_p(s) = \frac{2}{4s^2 + 3s + 1}$$

Since the coefficient of s^2 is equal to τ_p^2, the time constant is equal to 2 time units. Also, since the coefficient of s is equal to $2\tau_p\zeta$, the damping factor, ζ, is equal to 0.75. Finally, the process gain is 2. Using Equation 5.15 with ζ equal to 0.75, the percentage overshoot is equal to 2.8%; using Equation 5.16, the decay ratio is equal to 0.000805 or 1/1242.

♠

Example 5.4 Determine the Decay Ratio from the Percentage Overshoot

Problem Statement. Consider an underdamped second-order process that results in a 20% overshoot for a step input change. Determine the decay ratio for this second-order system.

Solution. Applying Equation 5.15 in the text results in

$$20 = 100 \exp\left\{\frac{-\pi\zeta}{\sqrt{1-\zeta^2}}\right\}$$

Dividing through by 100 and taking the natural logarithm of both sides yields the following after rearranging

$$\sqrt{1-\zeta^2} = \frac{\pi\zeta}{1.6094}$$

Squaring both sides of the equation and solving for ζ yields $\zeta = 0.4559$. Applying Equation 5.16, a decay ratio of 1/25 is calculated.

♠

Example 5.5 Develop a Second-Order Transfer Function from Process Information.

Problem Statement. Consider a temperature control loop that exhibits underdamped behavior. The temperature control loop is tuned for a 1/6 decay ratio, and the time period for oscillations is 20 minutes. The control loop is tuned properly so that, after the process reaches steady-state operation, there is no noticeable offset between the setpoint and the measured value of the temperature. Develop a second-order transfer function for this closed-loop system assuming that the input is the temperature setpoint and the output is the measured value of the process temperature.

Solution. Since there is no offset for this temperature controller, the process gain is one. The damping factor can be determined from Equation 5.16 using the specified decay ratio, and the time constant can be determined from Equation 5.17. Since Equation 5.17 depends on ζ, Equation 5.16 should be solved first to determine the value for ζ. Rearranging Equation 5.16 and using the specified decay ratio yields ζ equal to 0.274. Rearranging Equation 5.17 and using the value of T and ζ yields τ_p equal to 3.06 minutes; therefore, the transfer function for this closed-loop process is

$$G(s) = \frac{1}{9.38s^2 + 1.69s + 1}$$

where time is in minutes and the gain is in deg/deg.   ♠

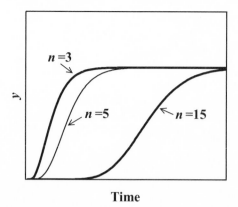

Figure 5.6 Dynamic response of three high-order systems (n=3, 5, and 15).

5.5   High-Order Processes

Staged separation devices, such as distillation and absorption columns, can be represented as a series of first-order processes. For example, for a distillation column, each tray can be considered a first-order process. Since the overall transfer function for a process composed of a number of transfer functions in series is the product of each individual transfer function (Equation 4.13), the transfer function for a series of first-order process with equal time constants is given by

$$G_p(s) = \frac{K_p}{\left(\tau_p\, s + 1\right)^n} \qquad\qquad 5.18$$

Since the largest power of s in the denominator is n, Equation 5.18 represents an nth-order process. Figure 5.6 shows the response to a step input for an nth-order process for various values of n (i.e., $n = 3, 5, 15$). As n becomes larger, the response becomes more **sluggish**, i.e., the slope of the initial response becomes smaller. For larger values of n, there is a period of time before a noticeable change in the output variable can be observed, and this period of time (deadtime) increases as n increases. A first-order plus deadtime (FOPDT) model can provide a good approximation of a high-order system, as shown later in this chapter. The response for $n=3$ is similar to the open-loop response of the CST thermal mixer, which is also a third-order linear process since the actuator, process, and sensor were each modeled as first-order processes.

5.6 Integrating Processes

The most common type of **integrating process** is the level in a tank for which the outflow and inflow are set independently of the level. The differential equation describing the dynamic behavior of a level in a tank is given by

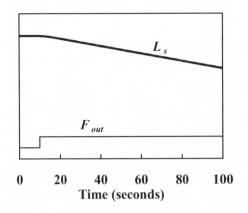

Figure 5.7 Dynamic response of an integrating process to a step input change.

$$\rho A_c \frac{dL}{dt} = F_{in} - F_{out} \qquad\qquad \textbf{5.19}$$

where A_c is the cross-sectional area of the tank, L is the height of liquid in the tank, ρ is the density of the feed and product, F_{in} is the mass flow rate into the tank, and F_{out} is the mass flow rate out of the tank. Assuming the inflow, F_{in}, is constant, the transfer function for this process is

$$G_p(s) = \frac{L(s)}{F_{out}(s)} = \frac{-1}{\rho A_c\, s} \qquad\qquad \textbf{5.20}$$

The s factor in the denominator of the transfer function indicates that this process is integrating in behavior. Using the final-value theorem (Equation 4.4), one can easily determine that this process is non-self regulating. Figure 5.7 shows the response of an integrating process to a step increase in F_{out}.

Example 5.6 Developing a Transfer Function for an Integrating Process

Problem Statement. An open-loop test is applied to a tank level process. Initially, the level is constant at a value of 40%. The outflow from the tank is increased by 1000 lb/h. After 5 minutes the level reading is 30%. Develop a transfer function for this process for which the input is the change in the outflow rate and the output is the change in the level in the tank.

Solution. For a tank level initially at steady state, a change in outflow rate produces a constant slope change similar to Figure 5.7. In this case, the slope is calculated as the change in the level per time or 2% min^{-1}, which corresponds to a flow rate change of 1000 lb/h; therefore, the transfer function for this system in units of %-h/lb is

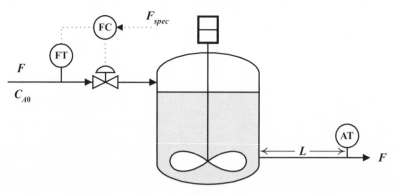

Figure 5.8 Schematic of a CSTR with transport delay.

$$G(s) = \frac{L(s)}{F_{out}(s)} = -\frac{0.002}{s}$$

♠

5.7 Deadtime

Deadtime or **transport delay** can result from plug flow transport through a pipe or from transport of solids by a conveyor belt. Figure 5.8 shows a CSTR with a product line attached. It is assumed that reaction occurs only in the reactor and the product flows by plug flow a length, L, at which point an on-line analyzer measures the product composition. Turbulent flow through a pipe is well represented as plug flow. The time, θ, that it takes the reaction mixture to flow by plug flow from the CSTR to the analyzer is

$$\theta = \frac{\rho L A_c}{F} \qquad\qquad 5.21$$

where A_c is the cross-sectional area of the product line, ρ is the density of the fluid, and F is the mass flow rate of the product through the product line. If the composition measurement is fast compared to θ, the measured composition, $C_s(t)$, is the reactor composition, $C(t)$, θ time units before, i.e.,

$$C_s(t) = C(t - \theta) \qquad\qquad 5.22$$

where θ is the deadtime or transport delay for this process. From Table 4.1, the transfer function for deadtime is

$$G_p(s) = e^{-\theta s} \qquad\qquad 5.23$$

Gas chromatographs (GC's) exhibit **analyzer deadtime** or **delay**. That is, the sample enters the GC and must flow through a separation column before the analysis is

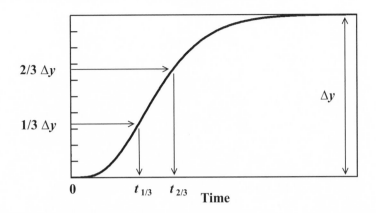

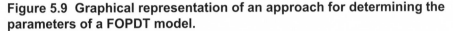

Figure 5.9 Graphical representation of an approach for determining the parameters of a FOPDT model.

complete. The analyzer delay for a dedicated GC typically ranges between 3 and 10 minutes.

Process deadtime and/or analyzer deadtime can have a significant effect on feedback controller tuning and control performance when the deadtime is significant compared to the time constant of the process. A five minute analyzer delay does not significantly affect feedback control performance for a large distillation column with a time constant of three hours for composition dynamics. On the other hand, a five minute analyzer delay dramatically affects a column with a time constant of five minutes for its composition dynamics.

Deadtime is usually combined with other models to take into account the effect of process and analyzer deadtime as well as the initial response of a highly overdamped process (e.g., a first-order plus deadtime model or an integrator plus deadtime model).

5.8 First-Order Plus Deadtime (FOPDT) Model

A **FOPDT** model is the combination of a first-order model with deadtime:

$$G_p(s) = \frac{K_p\, e^{-\theta_p s}}{\tau_p\, s + 1}$$

5.24

A step test can be conveniently used to develop a FOPDT model. Figure 5.9 shows one such approach. First, identify the resulting change in y (i.e., Δy) and the step change in the input, Δu. Then, from the step response, identify the time required for one-third of the total change in y to occur, $t_{1/3}$. Next, identify the time required for

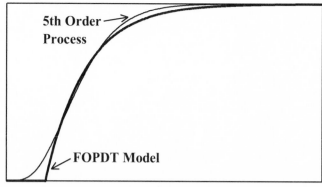

Figure 5.10 Comparison between a FOPDT model and an overdamped 5th order process.

two-thirds of the total change in y to occur, $t_{\frac{2}{3}}$. Then the following estimates can be used.

$$\tau_p = \frac{t_{\frac{2}{3}} - t_{\frac{1}{3}}}{0.7}$$

$$\theta_p = t_{\frac{1}{3}} - 0.4\tau_p \qquad\qquad \textbf{5.25}$$

$$K_p = \frac{\Delta y}{\Delta u}$$

Note that $t_{\frac{1}{3}}$ and $t_{\frac{2}{3}}$ are based upon assuming that time is equal to zero when the step change in u is implemented. This modeling approach is particularly well suited for modeling high-order processes. Figure 5.10 shows a fifth order process and a FOPDT model that was selected to match this high-order process. There is slight mismatch initially between the FOPDT model and the high-order process model, but overall the FOPDT model provides a good approximation for overdamped process behavior; therefore, the FOPDT model is one of the best idealized models to represent industrial processes.

Example 5.7 Estimation of FOPDT Parameters

Problem Statement. Estimate the FOPDT parameters from the following step test results.

Time	Input (u)	Output (y)
0	1	5.5
1	1	5.5
2	1	5.5
3	2	5.5
4	2	5.5
5	2	5.4
6	2	5.0
7	2	4.5
8	2	4.3
9	2	4.2
10	2	4.1
11	2	4.0
12	2	4.0

Solution. The process gain is calculated from the steady-state change in y divided by the change in u, i.e.,

$$K_p = \frac{4.0 - 5.5}{2 - 1} = -1.5$$

Since $t_{1/3}$ and $t_{2/3}$ are based on when the input change is applied, time equal to zero for their calculation is $t=3$. Because the total change in y is -1.5, $y_{1/3}$ is 5.0 and $y_{2/3}$ is 4.5; therefore, from the open-loop response, $t_{1/3}$ is equal to 3 (i.e., 6-3) and $t_{2/3}$ is equal to 4. Applying the formula for τ_p

$$\tau_p = \frac{4 - 3}{0.7} = 1.43$$

Then $$\theta_p = 3.0 - (0.4)(1.43) = 2.43$$

The FOPDT transfer function is given by

$$G_p(s) = \frac{-1.5 \, e^{-2.43 s}}{1.43 s + 1}$$

♠

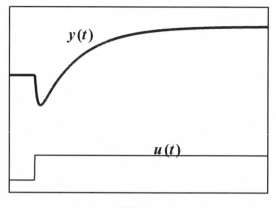

Figure 5.11   Dynamic response of an inverse-acting process to a step input change.

5.9 Inverse Acting Processes

An **inverse-acting process** can occur when opposing factors are acting within the process: one that is faster responding but with less steady-state gain than the other, e.g.,

$$G_p(s) = \frac{K_p}{\tau_p s + 1} - \frac{K'_p}{\tau'_p s + 1} \qquad\qquad \textbf{5.26}$$

where $|K'_p| < |K_p|$ and $\tau'_p << \tau_p$. The response of an inverse-acting process to a step change input is shown in Figure 5.11. For a short time the second term is controlling but, as time proceeds, the first term, due to its larger steady-state gain, dominates the response. Combining the terms in Equation 5.26 results in

$$G_p(s) = \frac{(K_p \tau'_p - K'_p \tau_p)s + (K_p - K'_p)}{(\tau_p s + 1)(\tau'_p s + 1)}$$

The zero of this transfer function is

$$s = \frac{K_p - K'_p}{K'_p \tau_p - K_p \tau'_p}$$

When this equation is positive (i.e., a right-half-plane zero), inverse action results. In general, **if a transfer function has at least one right-half-plane zero, it exhibits inverse action**.

Consider a mercury-in-glass thermometer, initially at ambient temperature, that is submersed in hot water. The glass can be viewed as a container for the mercury.

The height of the mercury column is used to measure temperature. After the thermometer is put into the hot water, the temperature of the glass around the mercury column increases before the temperature of the mercury. Since glass expands when heated, the inside **diameter** of the glass container increases slightly, causing the height of the mercury column to decrease slightly. Soon after this decrease in the height of the mercury column, the temperature of the mercury begins to rise, causing the overall height of the mercury column to increase rapidly. The effect of the expansion of the glass on the measured temperature is the low-gain, small time constant effect while the expansion of the mercury column due to a temperature increase is the high-gain, slower-responding process. Together, the two processes result in inverse action.

Certain types of reboilers can exhibit inverse-acting behavior for a step change in the steam flow rate to the reboiler[1]. An increase in steam flow to the reboiler causes the number and volume of bubbles produced on the shell side of the reboiler to immediately increase. This "swell" effect can cause the measured level to show an initial increase after a steam rate increase. Of course, since the reboiler duty is increased, the vapor boilup rate increases, which eventually results in a decrease in the level in the reboiler. The swell is the low-gain, quick-responding behavior that yields inverse action while the increase in vapor rate from the reboiler is the high-gain, slow-responding behavior. When the heat addition rate to the reboiler is used to control the level in a reboiler that exhibits significant inverse action, a much more challenging control problem is encountered than is usually observed for conventional level control systems.

Example 5.8 Identifying Inverse Action from $G_p(s)$

Problem Statement. Determine whether the following transfer function exhibits inverse action.

$$G_p(s) = \frac{2s^2 - s - 1}{4s^3 + 3s^2 + 5s + 1}$$

Solution. This system representation exhibits inverse action if there are any RHP zeros. Therefore, setting the numerator of the transfer function equal to zero,

$$2s^2 - s - 1 = 0$$

Because the roots of this equation are -0.5 and 1.0 and a positive RHP zero is determined, inverse action is indicated.

♠

5.10 Lead-Lag Element

Lead-lag elements are used to provide dynamic compensation for feedforward control (Chapter 10) and decouplers (Chapter 13). The transfer function for a lead-lag element is given as

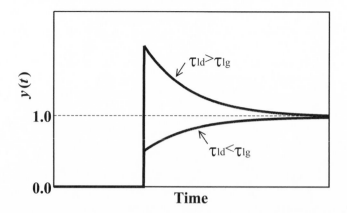

Figure 5.12 The effect of the ratio of τ_{ld} to τ_{lg} on the dynamic response of a lead-lag element.

$$G_{lead-lag}(s) = \frac{\tau_{ld}s+1}{\tau_{lg}s+1}$$

The time-domain behavior of a lead-lag element for a unit step input change is given by

$$y(t) = e^{-t/\tau_{lg}}\left[\frac{\tau_{ld}}{\tau_{lg}}-1\right]+1 \qquad\qquad 5.27$$

This result is obtained by combining the transfer function for a lead-lag element with a unit step in the input (i.e., $U(s)=1/s$) and applying partial fraction expansion before it is converted to the time domain. Figure 5.12 shows the output of a lead-lag element for a unit step input change when τ_{ld} is larger than τ_{lg} and when τ_{ld} is less than τ_{lg}. The dynamic behavior of a lead-lag element can be understood by examining the terms inside the bracket in Equation 5.27. When τ_{ld} is greater than τ_{lg}, the terms in the bracket have a positive result and initially $y(t)$ is larger than one. If t_{ld} is less than τ_{lg}, the terms inside the bracket have a negative result, and the initial response is less than one.

5.11 Recycle Processes

Recycle processes are used industrially to improve the economic performance of a process from a steady-state point of view. Material recycle is used to recover unreacted reactants and recycle them to the reactor as feed to increase overall conversion, and energy recycle or heat recovery is used to recycle heat within a process and thus reduce overall energy usage. Even though processes with recycle can have significant economic advantages compared to the corresponding processes without recycle, the process control problems associated with recycle processes can be much

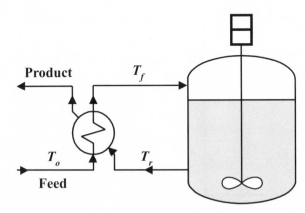

Figure 5.13 Schematic of an exothermic CSTR with heat integration.

more challenging. Recycling (also termed **process integration**) can have a dominant effect on the overall process dynamics and resulting control performance.

Example 5.9 Analysis of an Energy Recycle Case

Problem Statement. Analyze the dynamics of the CSTR with heat integration shown in Figure 5.13.

Energy Recycle. This process is an exothermic CSTR for which the product stream is used to preheat the feed to the reactor[2]. The temperature of the feed entering the reactor is T_f, which is given by

$$T_f(s) = T_o(s) + \Delta T_f(s) \qquad \textbf{5.28}$$

where $\Delta T_f(s)$ represents the change in the temperature of the reactor feed caused by the heat exchanger. Note that since transfer functions are used, each term in Equation 5.28 is written in deviation variable form. Heat transfer to the feed depends on the temperature of the reactor, T_r. Using a transfer function model of the heat exchanger yields

$$\Delta T_f(s) = T_r(s)\, G_H(s) \qquad \textbf{5.29}$$

Likewise, the temperature of the reactor, T_r, is a function of the reactor feed temperature, T_f. This relationship can be expressed using a transfer function, $G_R(s)$, as

$$T_r(s) = T_f(s)\, G_R(s) \qquad \textbf{5.30}$$

Substituting Equation 5.28 into Equation 5.30 and rearranging results in

$$T_r(s) = G_R(s)\, [T_o(s) + \Delta T_f(s)] \qquad \textbf{5.31}$$

Then Equation 5.29 is used to eliminate $\Delta T_f(s)$ from Equation 5.31.

$$T_r(s) = G_R(s)[T_o(s) + G_H(s)T_r(s)] \qquad\qquad \textbf{5.32}$$

The overall transfer function, $G_{overall}(s)$, for this process becomes

$$G_{overall}(s) = \frac{T_r(s)}{T_o(s)} = \frac{G_R(s)}{1 - G_R(s)G_H(s)} \qquad\qquad \textbf{5.33}$$

Assuming the following forms for $G_R(s)$ and $G_H(s)$

$$G_R(s) = \frac{K_R}{\tau_R s + 1}$$

$$G_H(s) = K_H$$

results in the following, after rearranging into the standard form for a first-order process

$$G_{overall}(s) = \frac{\dfrac{K_R}{1 - K_H K_R}}{\dfrac{\tau_R}{1 - K_H K_R} s + 1} \qquad\qquad \textbf{5.34}$$

Assuming the following numerical values

$$K_H \;=\; 0.5$$
$$K_R \;=\; 1.9$$
$$\tau_R \;=\; 1.0$$

yields

$$G_R(s) = \frac{1.9}{s + 1} \qquad \text{(without heat integration)} \qquad \textbf{5.35}$$

$$G_{overall}(s) = \frac{38}{20 s + 1} \qquad \text{(with heat integration)} \qquad \textbf{5.36}$$

The gain and the time constant have both increased by a factor of 20 for the system with recycle. This is an extreme example, but one can easily see that material recycle and/or heat integration increases the process gain while slowing the overall process response.

♠

Material Recycle. Due to economic driving forces that require operating companies to produce as much product as possible from every pound of feed, material recycle is quite common in the CPI. Figure 5.14 shows a simple reactor/stripper

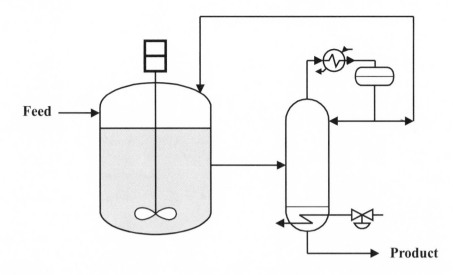

Figure 5.14 Schematic of a reactor/stripper process with material recycle.

recycle system. For such systems it can be very important to operate at low conversion levels in the reactor to minimize the production of waste products. Therefore, it is essential to recover the unreacted feed and recycle it back to the reactor. In this case, the reactor may operate at a relatively low conversion per pass while, for the overall process with recycle, the conversion can approach 100%. Material recycle can also increase the process gain and the time constant of the overall response and, therefore, complicate the application of process control.

5.12 Summary

The dynamic behavior of real processes can be described using idealized dynamic models. In this chapter, the dynamic behavior of first-order processes, second-order processes, high-order processes, integrating processes, processes with deadtime, FOPDT processes, inverse-acting processes, and recycle processes were considered.

5.13 Additional Terminology

Critically damped - $\zeta=1$, which corresponds to the transition point between overdamped and underdamped behavior.

Damping factor (ζ) - the characteristic of a second-order process that determines the general shape of the dynamic response.

Deadtime - the time delay associated with a composition analyzer or the delay a process experiences after input changes.

Decay ratio - the ratio of the successive peaks for a second-order underdamped response.

First-order process - a process with a transfer function that has unity as the highest power of s in the denominator.

FOPDT model - A First-Order Plus DeadTime model. A model combining a first-order process with deadtime.

Impulse input - an input with an infinite height and an infinitesimal duration.

Integrating process - a process that accumulates or depletes mass or energy.

Inverse-acting process - a process that has two competing factors: one that is faster responding but with less steady-state gain than the other.

K_p - the steady-state process gain ($\Delta y/\Delta u$).

Overdamped process - a second- or higher-order process which does not exhibit oscillatory behavior.

Percentage overshoot - the magnitude of the overshoot divided by the steady-state change times 100.

Period of oscillation - the time required for a complete cycle.

Process integration - a term for using mass and energy recycle to make a process more economically efficient.

Ramp input - an input that increases or decreases at a constant rate.

Rectangular pulse - a step increase followed after a time by a step decrease that returns the input to its original value.

Recycle process - a process that recovers mass or energy from a process stream before it leaves the process.

Response time - the time after a step change for the process to settle to within ±5% of the steady-state change.

Rise time - the time after a step input change for an underdamped response to cross the ultimate steady-state condition for the first time.

Second-order process - a process with a transfer function that has two as the highest power of s in the denominator.

Settling time - the time after a step change for the process to settle to within ±5% of the steady-state change.

Sinusoidal input - a process input that has a sine wave shape.

Sluggish - behavior of a process for which the output variable is slow to respond to input changes.

Step change - a sudden and sustained change.

Transport delay - the time for material to move from one point in the process to another.

Underdamped process - a second- or higher-order process, which exhibits oscillatory behavior.

τ_p - process time constant, i.e., determines the speed of dynamic response.

θ_p - process deadtime.

5.14 References

1. Munsif, HP and Riggs, J.B. "An Analysis of Inverse Acting Column Levels", *Ind & Eng Chem Res,* Vol. 35, p. 2640 (1996).

2. Marlin, T.E., Process Control, McGraw-Hill, pp. 173-176 (1995).

5.15 Preliminary Questions

5.1 Why are rectangular pulse inputs more feasible to apply to industrial processes than impulse inputs?

5.2 Why are ideal models of processes not normally used for tuning control loops in the CPI?

5.3 What is the parameter for a ramp input?

5.4 What are the two parameters for a sinusoidal input?

5.5 What are the characteristics of a first-order process subjected to a step input change?

5.6 What does K_p represent?

5.7 What does the time constant for a process represent?

5.8 For a first-order process, how many time constants are required after an input change to observe 98% of the total change?

5.9 What is the difference between an underdamped response with $\zeta=0.1$ and $\zeta=0.5$?

5.10 What is the difference between an overdamped response with $\zeta=2$ and $\zeta=6$?

5.11 Qualitatively describe what the rise time is. Does a first-order process have a rise time? Why or why not?

5.12 Qualitatively describe what the decay ratio is.

5.13 What characteristic behavior does a high-order process exhibit?

5.14 Why are high-order processes well represented by FOPDT models?

5.15 What is the difference between analyzer delay and transport delay? How are they similar?

5.16 In general terms, describe why analyzer deadtime can affect the performance of a controller.

5.17 Is the process gain, K_p, for a FOPDT model different from the K_p for a first-order process model or the K_p for a second-order process model?

5.18 What causes inverse action?

5.19 How can a thermometer exhibit inverse action?

5.20 What is energy recycle?

5.21 What is material recycle?

5.16 Analytical Questions and Exercises

5.22 Consider the following first-order transfer functions. What characteristics of the process can you identify from these transfer functions?

a. $G_p(s) = \dfrac{16}{456s + 100}$
    b. $G_p(s) = \dfrac{1}{s + 0.1}$

c. $G_p(s) = \dfrac{300}{600s + 10}$
    d. $G_p(s) = \dfrac{0.1}{3s + 0.01}$

5.23 A one-dimensional model of a thermocouple yields the following differential equation

$$M C_p \frac{dT_s}{dt} = A h (T_p - T_s)$$

where M is the mass of the thermocouple per unit length (1g/cm), C_p is the heat capacity of the thermocouple (0.1 cal/g·°C), T_s is the temperature of the thermocouple, A is the surface area per unit length (4 cm²/cm), h is the heat transfer coefficient between the thermocouple and the process fluid (25 cal/cm²·h·°C), and T_p is the temperature of the process fluid. Calculate the time constant, in seconds, for this thermocouple system based on this one-dimensional model.

5.24 Using the approach given in Problem 3.36, estimate the time constant for changing the temperature of the metal of a heat exchanger. Assume that the tubes are ½ inch schedule 40 copper tubes. Also, use "ballpark" values for the heat-transfer coefficients for a liquid water/liquid water heat exchanger.

5.25 Section 1.3 states "As a rule of thumb, one can assume that it takes approximately four time constants to observe the full effect of a step change of an input to a process under open-loop conditions". Evaluate this statement using a FOPDT model.

5.26 By observing a process, an operator indicates that an increase of 200 lb/h of steam (input) to a heat exchanger produces a 20 psi increase in the measured pressure of steam on the shell side of the heat exchanger (output). In addition, when a change in the steam flow rate is made, it takes approximately 40 s for the full effect on the steam pressure to be observed. Using this process information, develop a first-order model for this process.

5.27 By observing a process, an operator indicates that an increase of 5,000 lb/h of steam (input) to the reboiler on a distillation column produces a 3% decrease in the impurity level in the bottoms product (output). When a change in the steam flow rate is made, it takes approximately 120 minutes for the full effect on the product composition to be observed. Using this process information, develop a first-order model for this process.

5.28 By observing a process, an operator indicates that an increase of 1,000 lb/h of feed (input) to a tank produces a 8% increase in a self-regulating tank level (output). In addition, when a change in the feed rate is made, it takes approximately 20 minutes for the full effect on the tank to be observed. Using this process information, develop a first-order model for this process.

5.29 By observing a process, an operator indicates that an increase of 2,000 lb/h in cooling water flow rate (input) to a heat exchanger produces a 10°F decrease in the temperature of the process stream leaving the heat exchanger (output). In addition, when a change in the cooling water flow rate is made, it takes 18 minutes for the full effect on the outlet temperature of the process fluid to be observed. Using this process information, develop a first-order model for this process.

5.30 Tuning controllers such that the resulting dynamic response has a decay ratio of 1/4 is an industrial practice. Assuming a second-order response for the feedback system, what value of ζ corresponds to a decay ratio of 1/4?

5.31 Determine the percentage overshoot for a second-order system if the decay ratio is 1/6.

5.32 For the following second-order transfer functions, determine K_p, τ_p, and ζ.

a. $G_p(s) = \dfrac{6}{4s^2 + s + 4}$ b. $G_p(s) = \dfrac{3}{5s^2 + 10s + 10}$

c. $G_p(s) = \dfrac{10}{s^2 + 2s + 0.5}$ d. $G_p(s) = \dfrac{0.5}{0.1s^2 + 6s + 0.1}$

5.33 Determine the percentage overshoot of a second-order process if the decay ratio is 1/4.

5.34 Determine the decay ratio of a second-order process if the percentage overshoot is 60%.

5.35 Determine the percentage overshoot of a second-order process if the decay ratio is 1/10.

5.36 Determine the decay ratio of a second-order process if the percentage overshoot is 20%.

5.37 Consider a pressure control loop that exhibits underdamped behavior. The pressure control loop is tuned for 10% overshoot, and the time period for oscillations is 1 minute. The control loop is tuned properly so that after the process reaches steady-state operation, there is no noticeable offset between the setpoint and the measured value of the pressure. Develop a second-order transfer function for this closed-loop system assuming that the input is the pressure setpoint and the output is the measured value of the process pressure.

5.38 Consider a composition control loop that exhibits underdamped behavior. The composition control loop is tuned for a 1/4 decay ratio, and the time period for oscillations is 60 minutes. The control loop is tuned properly so that after the process reaches steady-state operation, there is no noticeable offset between the setpoint and the measured value of the composition. Develop a second-order transfer function for this closed-loop system assuming that the input is the composition setpoint and the output is the measured value of the process composition.

5.39 Consider a temperature control loop that exhibits underdamped behavior. The temperature control loop is tuned for a 1/8 decay ratio, and the time period for oscillations is 14 minutes. The control loop is tuned properly so that after the process reaches steady-state operation, there is no noticeable offset between the setpoint and the measured value of the temperature. Develop a second-order transfer function for this closed-loop system assuming that the input is the temperature setpoint and the output is the measured value of the process temperature.

5.40 Consider a flow control loop that exhibits underdamped behavior. The temperature control loop is tuned for 25% overshoot, and the time period for oscillations is 8 s. The control loop is tuned properly so that after the process reaches steady-state operation, there is no noticeable offset between the setpoint and the measured value of the flow rate. Develop a second-order transfer function for this closed-loop system assuming that the input is the flow rate setpoint and the output is the measured value of the flow rate.

5.41 Consider the following differential equation

$$\frac{d^2 y}{dt^2} + K \frac{dy}{dt} + y = u$$

Discuss the dynamic behavior of this system for $-5 \leq K \leq 5$.

5.42 An open-loop test is applied to a tank level process. Initially, the level is constant at a value of 35%. The inflow to the tank is increased by 500 lb/h. After 3 minutes the level reading is 45%. Develop a transfer function for this process for which the input is the change in the inflow rate and the output is the level in the tank.

5.43 An open-loop test is applied to a tank level process. Initially, the level is constant at a value of 30%. The outflow from the tank is decreased by 2000 lb/h. After 15 minutes the level reading is 47%. Develop a transfer function for this process for which the input is the change in the outflow rate and the output is the level in the tank.

5.44 An open-loop test is applied to a tank level process. Initially, the level is constant at a value of 25%. The inflow to the tank is increased by 800 lb/h. After 13 minutes the level reading is 38%. Develop a transfer function for this process for which the input is the change in the outflow rate and the output is the level in the tank.

5.45 An open-loop test is applied to a tank level process. Initially, the level is constant at a value of 35%. The outflow from the tank is increased by 1500 lb/h. After 16 minutes the level reading is 26%. Develop a transfer function for this process for which the input is the change in the outflow rate and the output is the level in the tank.

5.46 Consider the following transfer function. Indicate as many characteristics of the process corresponding to this transfer function as possible.

$$G_p(s) = \frac{323\, e^{-3s}}{4s^2 + 16s + 4}$$

5.47 Consider the CST thermal mixing process presented in Section 3.5. Assume that the effluent from the mixer goes to a mixing tank with the same volume as the first. Determine the dynamic behavior of the overall process.

5.48 Consider four CSTR's in series. If there is a single irreversible first-order reaction occurring in each reactor, what is the dynamic response of the process?

Time	Input	Output	Time	Input	Output
0	0	1.0	7	1	1.6
1	0	1.0	8	1	1.8
2	1	1.0	9	1	1.9
3	1	1.05	10	1	1.95
4	1	1.1	11	1	2.0
5	1	1.2	12	1	2.0
6	1	1.4			

5.49 Consider the previous set of input/output data. Develop a FOPDT model for this input/output system and plot your approximation against the data.

5.50 Consider the following set of input/output data.

Time	Input	Output	Time	Input	Output
0	0	1.0	7	1	1.2
1	0	1.0	8	1	1.3
2	1	1.0	9	1	1.4
3	1	1.0	10	1	1.5
4	1	1.0	11	1	1.6
5	1	1.0	12	1	1.7
6	1	1.1	13	1	1.7

Develop a transfer function model based on this data.

5.51 Consider the following set of input/output data

Time	Input	Output	Time	Input	Output
0	3.3	17.3	7	2.5	20.3
1	3.3	17.3	8	2.5	23.2
2	3.3	17.3	9	2.5	24.0
3	2.5	17.3	10	2.5	24.5
4	2.5	17.4	11	2.5	24.7
5	2.5	17.6	12	2.5	24.8
6	2.5	18.4	13	2.5	24.8

Develop a FOPDT model for this input/output system and plot your approximation against the data.

5.52 Consider the following set of input/output data

Time	Input	Output	Time	Input	Output
0	223	77.2	7	202	76.3
1	223	77.2	8	202	76.0
2	202	77.2	9	202	75.8
3	202	77.2	10	202	75.6
4	202	77.1	11	202	75.5
5	202	77.0	12	202	75.4
6	202	76.8	13	202	75.4

Develop a FOPDT model for this input/output system and plot your approximation against the data.

5.53 Determine whether the following transfer functions exhibit inverse action.

a. $G_p(s) = \dfrac{2s^2 + 5s - 3}{s^3 + 2s^2 + 5s + 1}$

b. $G_p(s) = \dfrac{2s^2 + 7s + 3}{5s^3 + s^2 + 2s + 1}$

c. $G_p(s) = \dfrac{s^2 + 9.99s - 0.01}{3s^3 + 2s^2 + 7s + 1}$

d. $G_p(s) = \dfrac{s^2 - 4s + 3}{s^3 + 7s^2 + 2s + 1}$

e. $G_p(s) = \dfrac{s^3 - 3s - 2}{s^4 + 5s^3 + 3s^2 + 2s + 1}$

f. $G_p(s) = \dfrac{s^3 + 3s^2 - s - 3}{s^4 + 4s^3 + 3s^2 + 5s + 1}$

5.17 Projects

Develop FOPDT models using the simulations that accompany the text. Step tests should be applied for ±3% and ±10% changes in the manipulated variable while starting at the nominal, lined out conditions. Average each of the FOPDT parameters obtained from four open-loop step tests. Using the results of the individual step tests, compare the variation in the FOPDT model parameters.

a. CST thermal mixer^S

b. CST composition mixer^S

c. Level in a tank^S

d. CSTR^S

e. Heat exchanger^S

A superscript "S" indicates that the simulators are required to perform these problems.

PART III

PID CONTROL

Chapter 6

PID Control

6.1 Introduction

Feedback control compares the measured value of the controlled variable to its setpoint and adjusts the manipulated variable in an effort to drive the controlled variable to its setpoint. For the everyday examples of feedback control cited in Chapter 1 (i.e., the shower, bathtub, driving a car, and balancing a spoon) a human serves as the feedback controller. In the CPI, the **Proportional-Integral-Derivative (PID) controller** is the most common controller used and is used almost exclusively for flow control loops, pressure control loops, and level control loops, as well as many composition and temperature control loops. Operators also serve as controllers for certain loops, e.g., a composition loop based upon laboratory composition analysis once each eight-hour shift. This chapter is concerned with the forms, characteristics, and types of PID controllers.

PID controllers came into use in the CPI in the 1930's in the form of pneumatic controllers. Today PID controllers are implemented in DCSs while some older installations still use analog electrical controllers. The digital controllers in a DCS are less expensive per control loop than analog controllers for large installations with many control loops, and DCSs are much more reliable due to their redundancy and distributed nature. In addition, many of the clever controller designs associated with analog devices became trivial in the digital world of a DCS.

As you will see later in this chapter, PID controllers are simple to implement and are extremely flexible as evidenced by the fact that PID controllers have been applied to almost any conceivable process ranging from refineries to spacecraft to electronic devices to power plants. The PID algorithm is computationally quite efficient and much of the flexibility of a PID controller comes from the unique characteristics of proportional, integral, and derivative action.

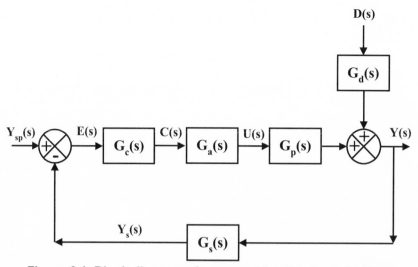

Figure 6.1 Block diagram of a general feedback control loop.

6.2 Closed-Loop Transfer Functions

The transfer function for a feedback control loop is derived in this section and used later to determine the fundamental characteristics of proportional action, integral action, and derivative action as well as to examine the stability properties of a feedback loop. Consider the schematic for a feedback loop shown in Figure 6.1 where $G_c(s)$, $G_a(s)$, $G_p(s)$, $G_d(s)$, and $G_s(s)$ are the transfer functions for the controller, actuator, process as affected by the manipulated variable, process as affected by the disturbance, and sensor, respectively. Applying the properties of transfer functions and summation blocks (Section 4.6), the following relationships can be formulated:

(Process) $Y(s) = G_p(s)\,U(s) + G_d(s)\,D(s)$ **6.1**

(Actuator) $U(s) = G_a(s)\,C(s)$ **6.2**

(Controller) $C(s) = G_c(s)\,E(s)$ **6.3**

(Summation) $E(s) = Y_{sp}(s) - Y_s(s)$ **6.4**

(Sensor) $Y_s(s) = G_s(s)\,Y(s)$ **6.5**

First, substitute Equation 6.2 into Equation 6.1 to eliminate $U(s)$ resulting in

$$Y(s) = G_d(s)D(s) + G_p(s)G_a(s)C(s)$$

Next, substitute Equation 6.3 into this equation to eliminate $C(s)$ yielding

$$Y(s) = G_d(s)D(s) + G_p(s)\, G_a(s)G_c(s)E(s)$$

Then, substitute Equation 6.4 into this equation to eliminate $E(s)$ giving

$$Y(s) = G_d(s)D(s) + G_p(s)\, G_a(s)G_c(s)[Y_{sp}(s)-Y_s(s)]$$

Finally, substitute Equation 6.5 into this equation to eliminate $Y_s(s)$ producing

$$Y(s) = G_d(s)D(s) + G_p(s)\, G_a(s)G_c(s)[Y_{sp}(s)-G_s(s)Y(s)]$$

Collecting terms and solving for $Y(s)$ results in

$$Y(s) = \frac{G_d(s)D(s) + G_p(s)\, G_a(s)\, G_c(s)\, Y_{sp}(s)}{G_c(s)\, G_a(s)\, G_p(s)\, G_s(s) + 1}$$

If $D(s)$ is zero (i.e., no change in the disturbance level is occurring), the closed-loop transfer function for **setpoint tracking**, controlling for setpoint changes, is given by

$$\frac{Y(s)}{Y_{sp}(s)} = \frac{G_p(s)\, G_a(s)\, G_c(s)}{G_c(s)\, G_a(s)\, G_p(s)\, G_s(s) + 1} \qquad \textbf{6.6}$$

Setpoint tracking is also referred to as **servo control**.

If $Y_{sp}(s)$ is zero (i.e., a fixed setpoint is being applied), the closed-loop transfer function for **disturbance rejection**, controlling to a fixed setpoint in the face of disturbance upsets, is given by

$$\frac{Y(s)}{D(s)} = \frac{G_d(s)}{G_c(s)\, G_a(s)\, G_p(s)\, G_s(s) + 1} \qquad \textbf{6.7}$$

Controlling for disturbance rejection is also called **regulatory control**.

Note that the denominator of the closed-loop transfer function for setpoint tracking and disturbance rejection is the same. If the denominator of the closed-loop transfer function is set equal to zero, the following equation,

$$G_c(s)\, G_a(s)\, G_p(s)\, G_s(s) + 1 = 0 \qquad \textbf{6.8}$$

which is called the **characteristic equation** of the feedback loop, results. The roots of the characteristic equation are the poles of the feedback process and, therefore, determine the dynamic behavior of the closed-loop process. For example, if all the roots of the characteristic equation are real negative values, the closed-loop dynamic behavior is overdamped. Further, if there are complex roots, oscillatory closed-loop behavior results. Finally, if any of the roots have positive real parts, the closed-loop system is unstable.

Example 6.1 Dynamic Behavior of P-only Controller Applied to a Second-Order Process

Problem Statement. Determine the dynamic behavior of a P-only controller (i.e., $G_c(s) = K_c$) with K_c equal to 2 applied to a second-order process ($K_p=1$; $\tau_p=5$; $\zeta=1.5$). Assume that the second-order process model represents the combined effect of the actuator, process, and sensor.

Solution. Since the roots of the characteristic equation are the poles of the closed-loop system and determine its dynamic behavior, the characteristic equation is used here to determine the dynamic behavior of the closed-loop system. Using the specified properties of the second-order process model, $G_p(s)$ is given as

$$G_p(s) = \frac{1}{25s^2 + 15s + 1}$$

Substituting the specifications of the problem into the characteristic equation (Equation 6.8) and setting the result equal to zero yields

$$2\left[\frac{1}{25s^2 + 15s + 1}\right] + 1 = 0$$

Rearranging yields
$$25s^2 + 15s + 3 = 0$$

Putting this equation into the standard form for a second-order transfer function results in

$$8.33s^2 + 5s + 1 = 0$$

which indicates that the closed-loop second-order time constant, τ'_p, is 2.89 and the closed-loop damping factor, ζ', is 0.866, which corresponds to underdamped behavior. That is, the poles of the closed-loop transfer function are a complex conjugate pair with a negative real part, indicating damped oscillatory behavior.

♠

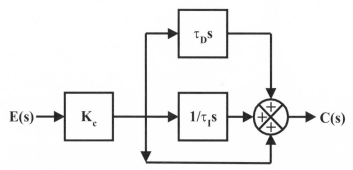

Figure 6.2 Block diagram of a conventional PID algorithm.

6.3 Position Forms of the PID Algorithm

The ISA (Instrument Society of America) standard for the PID algorithm in the **position form** is given as

$$c(t) = c_0 + K_c \left[e(t) + \frac{1}{\tau_I} \int_0^t e(t)\,dt + \tau_D \frac{d\,e(t)}{dt} \right] \qquad 6.9$$

where K_c, τ_I, and τ_D are the user-selected tuning parameters, $c(t)$ is the output from the controller and $e(t)$ is $[y_{sp} - y_s(t)]$. **Note that c_0 is the value of the controller output when the controller is turned on**. Proportional action is provided by the first term inside the bracket [i.e., $e(t)$]; the second term provides integral action; the third term provides derivative action. K_c is the controller gain and should not be confused with the process gain K_p. K_p has units of $\Delta y_s/\Delta c$ while K_c has units corresponding to $\Delta c/\Delta y_s$. The controller gain, K_c, can have a variety of units depending on the units used for c and y. For example, if the controller output is expressed as a 0 to 100% signal, and the controlled variable is temperature in °F, the controller gain has units of %/°F. On the other hand, if the controller output is expressed as a flow rate (i.e., lb/h), and the controlled variable is a pressure in psi, the controller gain has units of lb/h·psi.

The transfer function for a PID controller (Example 4.11) is given by

$$G_c(s) = \frac{C(s)}{E(s)} = K_c \left[1 + \frac{1}{\tau_I\, s} + \tau_D\, s \right] \qquad 6.10$$

A block diagram for the PID algorithm is shown in Figure 6.2, which assumes that the derivative action is based on the error from setpoint. As shown proportional, integral, and derivative action act in parallel with each other.

Example 6.2   Dynamic Behavior of a PI Controller Applied to a Second-Order Process

Problem Statement. Determine the dynamic behavior of a PI controller with K_c equal to 1 and τ_I equal to 1 applied to a second-order process ($K_p=1$, $\tau_p=5$, and $\zeta=2$). Assume that the second-order process model represents the combined effect of the actuator, process, and sensor.

Solution. Substituting this information into the characteristic equation (Equation 6.8) and setting the result equal to zero yields

$$\frac{1}{25s^2 + 20s + 1}\left[1 + \frac{1}{s}\right] + 1 = 0$$

Rearranging yields

$$25s^3 + 20s^2 + 2s + 1 = 0$$

By numerical root finding, a real root of this cubic equation is determined (i.e., s=-0.764). Factoring out this root by long division yields

$$25s^2 + 0.905s + 1.309 = 0$$

Rearranging into the standard form for a second-order function,

$$19.1s^2 + 0.692s + 1 = 0$$

which indicates that τ_p is 4.37 and ζ is 0.08, which corresponds to stable but highly oscillatory underdamped behavior. The poles of this system are (-0.764; -0.0181 ± 0.228 i).

♠

Another way to represent the controller gain is the **proportional band (PB)**, which is an approach that was in more frequent use 10 to 15 years ago. *PB* can be expressed in terms of K_c when K_c is expressed in dimensionless form, as K_c^D. For example, the controller output and the error from setpoint can be scaled 0-100% yielding a dimensionless K_c.

$$PB = \frac{100\%}{K_c^D} \qquad\qquad\qquad \textbf{6.11}$$

The proportional band is small when the controller gain is large and *PB* is large when K_c is small. Also note that *PB* is expressed as a percentage. The position form of the PID algorithm using proportional band is given as

$$c(t) = c_0 + \frac{100\%}{PB}\left[e(t) + \frac{1}{\tau_I}\int_0^t e(t)\,dt + \tau_D\frac{d\,e(t)}{dt}\right]$$

When proportional band is used with a controller, output is expressed as a percentage. Since the controller output becomes a 4-20 mA signal, PB is a convenient form for the controller gain.

Example 6.3 Conversion from Proportional Band to K_c

Problem Statement. Determine the dimensional version of the controller gain corresponding to a proportional band of 200%. The range of the error from setpoint is 200 psi and the controller output is 0% to 100%.

Solution. Applying Equation 6.11 yields K_c^D equal to 0.5. Then, using the range of the error from setpoint and the controller output results in

$$K_c = 0.5\left(\frac{100\%}{200\ psi}\right) = 0.25\ \%\,/\,psi$$

♠

Example 6.4 Conversion from K_c to Proportional Band

Problem Statement. Determine the proportional band corresponding to a controller gain of 15 %/°F. The range of the error from setpoint is 25°F and the controller output is 0% to 100%.

Solution. First, the process gain must be converted into a dimensionless form. Using the range of the error and the range of the controller output,

$$K_c^D = \left(\frac{15\%}{°F}\right)\left(\frac{25°F}{100\%}\right) = 3.75$$

Then, application of Equation 6.11 yields

$$PB = \frac{100\%}{3.75} = 26.7\%$$

♠

When a setpoint change is made to a process using the PID algorithm given by Equation 6.9, a spike in the calculated value of $de(t)/dt$ occurs, causing a spike in $c(t)$. The spike in the derivative of the error from setpoint results because the difference between the setpoint and the controlled variable value changes instantaneously when a setpoint change is implemented. This behavior is called **derivative kick** and can be eliminated by replacing $de(t)/dt$ with $-dy_s(t)/dt$ yielding

$$c(t) = c_0 + K_c \left[e(t) + \frac{1}{\tau_I} \int_0^t e(t)\,dt - \tau_D \frac{d\,y_s(t)}{dt} \right] \qquad \textbf{6.12}$$

In fact, there is no need to have derivative action on the error from setpoint, and Equation 6.12 and Equation 6.9 are equivalent as long as there are not changes in the value of the setpoint. The **derivative-on-measurement** form of the PID algorithm is recommended because it provides derivative action, but it is not susceptible to derivative kick.

Other commonly used forms of the PID algorithm are the proportional-integral (PI) and proportional-only (P-only) controllers. The PI controller results from setting τ_D equal to zero.

$$\text{PI-controller:}\quad c(t) = c_0 + K_c \left[e(t) + \frac{1}{\tau_I} \int_0^t e(t)\,dt \right] \qquad \textbf{6.13}$$

The P-only controller has neither derivative nor integral action.

$$\text{P-only:}\qquad\qquad c(t) = c_0 + K_c\, e(t) \qquad\qquad \textbf{6.14}$$

Equation 6.12 can be implemented in a digital form by using the following approximations

$$\int_0^t e(t)\,dt \approx \sum_{i=1}^n e(i\,\Delta t)\,\Delta t$$

where n is equal to $t\,/\,\Delta t$ and

$$\frac{d\,y_s(t)}{dt} \approx \frac{y_s(t) - y_s(t-\Delta t)}{\Delta t}$$

where Δt is the time interval between applications of the PID algorithm, i.e., the **control interval**. These approximations result in the digital version of the position form of the PID controller.

$$c(t) = c_0 + K_c \left[e(t) + \frac{\Delta t}{\tau_I} \sum_{i=1}^n e(i\cdot\Delta t) - \tau_D \left[\frac{y_s(t) - y_s(t-\Delta t)}{\Delta t} \right] \right] \qquad \textbf{6.15}$$

6.4 Velocity Forms of the PID Algorithm

The PID algorithm can be also applied in the **velocity form**, i.e., a form that determines changes to the current controller output. Applying Equation 6.15 at $t - \Delta t$ results in the following equation

$$c(t-\Delta t)=c_0 +K_c \left[e(t-\Delta t)+\frac{\Delta t}{\tau_I} \sum_{i=1}^{n-1} e(i \cdot \Delta t) - \tau_D \left[\frac{y_s(t-\Delta t)-y_s(t-2\Delta t)}{\Delta t} \right] \right]$$

6.16

Subtracting Equation 6.16 from Equation 6.15 results in the velocity form of the PID algorithm.

$$\Delta c(t) = K_c \left[e(t)-e(t-\Delta t) + \frac{\Delta t}{\tau_I} e(t) - \tau_D \left[\frac{y_s(t)-2y_s(t-\Delta t)+y_s(t-2\Delta t)}{\Delta t} \right] \right]$$

6.17

where
$$c(t) = c(t-\Delta t) + \Delta c(t)$$
6.18

The velocity form for the derivative on the error from setpoint is given by

$$\Delta c(t) = K_c \left(e(t)-e(t-\Delta t) + \frac{\Delta t}{\tau_I} e(t) + \tau_D \left[\frac{e(t)-2e(t-\Delta t)+e(t-2\Delta t)}{\Delta t} \right] \right)$$ **6.19**

Another popular version of the velocity form of the PID algorithm can be developed by eliminating proportional action for setpoint changes. For many control systems, implementing large setpoint changes unduly upsets the process. That is, a setpoint change abruptly affects the process. Because the error from setpoint changes as soon as the setpoint change is implemented, the response of a standard proportional controller to a setpoint change is virtually instantaneous. The sharp response of a process to a setpoint change is called **proportional kick.** Noticing that the proportional part of Equation 6.17 is simply the difference between $y(t)$ and $y(t-\Delta t)$ when the setpoint remains unchanged leads one to replace the difference between errors from setpoint with the difference between measured values of the controlled variable in the velocity form of the PID controller, i.e.,

$$\Delta c(t)=K_c \left[y_s(t-\Delta t)-y_s(t)+\frac{\Delta t}{\tau_I} e(t)-\tau_D \left(\frac{y_s(t)-2y_s(t-\Delta t)+y_s(t-2\Delta t)}{\Delta t} \right) \right]$$

6.20

The advantage of this form of the PID controller is that it does not act as abruptly to setpoint changes as Equation 6.17, i.e., this form eliminates proportional kick. In fact, from Equation 6.20 only the integral action moves the process toward a new setpoint. This reduction in aggressive setpoint tracking has an effect that is similar to bumpless transfer, which is introduced in Chapter 12.

Note that the position form of the PID algorithm calculates the absolute value of the output of the controller while the velocity form calculates the change in the controller output, which should be added to the current level of the controller output. The position and velocity modes are different forms of the same equation; therefore, they are generally equivalent while the velocity form is usually used industrially. In general, **DCSs offer the velocity form of the PID controller in three forms: the velocity form in which P, I, and D are based upon the error from setpoint (Equation 6.19), the velocity form in which P and I only are based upon the error from setpoint (Equation 6.17), and the velocity form in which only integral action is based upon the error from setpoint (Equation 6.20).**

6.5 Direct- and Reverse-Acting Controllers

Depending on the process and the actuator used in the final control element, the change in the controller output, $\Delta c(t)$ can be either added to or subtracted from the control action previously implemented, $\Delta c(t-\Delta t)$.   A PID controller that adds $\Delta c(t)$ to the previous control action is called a **reverse-acting** controller, and a controller that subtracts $\Delta c(t)$ is referred to as a **direct-acting** controller, i.e., for a PID controller in the velocity form,

$$\text{Direct-acting controller} \qquad c(t) = c(t - \Delta t) - \Delta c(t) \qquad\qquad \textbf{6.21}$$

$$\text{Reverse-acting controller} \qquad c(t) = c(t - \Delta t) + \Delta c(t) \qquad\qquad \textbf{6.22}$$

Equation 6.21 is called a direct-acting controller because it is direct-acting with regard to the process measurement. Because $\Delta c(t)$ is proportional to the error from setpoint $[e(t)=y_{sp}-y_s(t)]$, subtracting $\Delta c(t)$ from $\Delta c(t-\Delta t)$ increases the value of $y_s(t)$ for a process with a positive process gain. A reverse-acting controller increases the value of $y_s(t)$ for a process with a negative process gain.

The decision between using a direct-acting controller (Equation 6.21) or a reverse-acting controller (Equation 6.22) depends on the sign of the process gain and whether a direct- or reverse-acting final control element is used. To illustrate this, consider a heat exchanger in which the steam flow rate to the heat exchanger is manipulated to control the temperature of the process stream leaving the heat exchanger. Since an increase in steam flow to the heat exchanger results in an increase in the outlet temperature of the process stream, the process gain of this system is positive. Also, consider a direct-acting final control element on the steam, which causes an increase in steam flow rate when the signal to the final control element is increased. Further, consider the case in which the measured outlet temperature is below its setpoint [i.e., $e(t)$ and $\Delta c(t)$ are positive]. Since it is desired to move the controlled variable toward its setpoint, the steam flow rate to the heat exchanger should be increased; therefore, from an examination of Equations 6.17, 6.21 and 6.22, it is clear that a reverse-acting controller (Equation 6.22) should be used. On the other hand, if the direct-acting final control element is replaced with a reverse-acting final control element, a decrease in the signal to the final control element is required; therefore, a direct-acting controller (Equation 6.21) is required. **Remember that the choice between a reverse- and direct-acting final control element usually depends upon whether the final control element should fail open or closed when instrument air pressure is lost.** Also, recall that a direct-acting final control element uses an air-to-open valve actuator, and a reverse-acting final control element uses an air-to-close valve actuator.

Now consider a heat exchanger in which the flow rate of cooling water to the heat exchanger is manipulated to control the temperature of the process stream leaving the heat exchanger. Since an increase in the flow rate of cooling water to the heat exchanger results in a decrease in the controlled variable for this process, the process gain is negative. Also, consider a direct-acting final control element. Similar to the previous example, consider the case in which the controlled variable is below its setpoint. Under these conditions, a decrease in the flow rate of cooling water is required; therefore, a direct-acting controller should be used. Finally, if a reverse-acting final control element is substituted for the direct-acting final control element, a reverse-acting controller should be used. Table 6.1 summarizes these results. Obviously, these different combinations of positive and negative process gains and reverse- and direct-acting final control elements can each occur in the implementation of process control in industry. As a result, the process control engineer needs a way to conveniently choose a direct-acting or a reverse-acting controller. On a DCS, when a control loop is set up, there is typically a box to check to select a direct- or reverse-acting controller. For analog controllers, there is a switch on the back of the controller that allows the user to select the proper form for the controller, direct- or reverse-acting.

Table 6.1		
Guidelines for Selecting Direct- and Reverse-Acting Controllers		
Process Gain	**Direct-Acting Actuator**	**Reverse-Acting Actuator**
Positive	Reverse-Acting PID	Direct-Acting PID
Negative	Direct-Acting PID	Reverse-Acting PID

If the position form of the PID controller is used, whether a direct-acting or reverse-acting controller is used determines whether the proportional, integral, and derivative terms are added or subtracted, respectively, from c_0. That is, Equation 6.9 represents a reverse-acting PID controller in the position form and the following equation represents a direct-acting position form PID controller.

$$c(t) = c_0 - K_c \left[e(t) + \frac{1}{\tau_I} \int_0^t e(t)\,dt + \tau_D \frac{d\,e(t)}{dt} \right]$$

Example 6.5 Selecting the Proper Form of the PID Algorithm

Problem Statement. Write the position form of the PID algorithm similar to Equation 6.9 for Example 3.1, and assume that the control valve on the feed has an air-to-open actuator. Use the form that is not susceptible to derivative kick.

Solution. From Example 3.1, since T_1 is less than T_2, as F_1 is increased, the outlet temperature from the CST thermal mixer decreases; therefore, the process gain is negative. Because an air-to-open valve actuator, which is a direct-acting actuator, is used, Table 6.1 indicates that a direct-acting controller should be used. To eliminate derivative kick, the derivative action should be based on the process measurement. The resulting PID algorithm is given by

$$c(t) = c_0 - K_c \left[e(t) + \frac{1}{\tau_I} \int_0^t e(t)\,dt - \tau_D \frac{d\,y_s(t)}{dt} \right]$$

♠

Example 6.6 Selecting the Proper Form of the PID Algorithm

Problem Statement. Write the digital version of the position form of the PID algorithm similar to Equation 6.15 for Example 3.4, and assume that the control valve on the steam line to the heat exchanger for the CSTR has an air-to-close actuator. Use the form that is not susceptible to derivative kick.

Solution. From Example 3.4, as the steam flow to the heat exchanger on the reactor is increased, the outlet temperature from the CSTR increases; therefore, the process gain is positive. Because an air-to-close valve actuator, which is a reverse-acting actuator, is used, Table 6.1 indicates that a direct-acting controller should be used. To eliminate derivative kick, the derivative action should be based on the process measurement. The resulting digital form of the PID algorithm is given by

$$c(t) = c_0 - K_c \left[e(t) + \frac{\Delta t}{\tau_I} \sum_{i=1}^{n} e(i \cdot \Delta t) - \tau_D \left[\frac{y_s(t) - y_s(t - \Delta t)}{\Delta t} \right] \right]$$

♠

Example 6.7 Selecting the Proper Form of the PID Algorithm

Problem Statement. Write the velocity form of the PID algorithm similar to Equation 6.17 for Example 3.6, and assume that the control valve on steam line to the heat exchanger has an air-to-close actuator. Use the form that is not susceptible to derivative kick or proportional kick.

Solution. From Example 3.6, as the steam flow to the heat exchanger is increased, the outlet temperature of the process fluid increases; therefore, the process gain is positive. Because an air-to-close valve actuator, which is a reverse-acting actuator, is used, Table 6.1 indicates that a direct-acting controller should be used. To eliminate derivative kick, the derivative should be based on the measured value of the controlled variable, and to eliminate proportional kick, the proportional action should also be based on the measured value of the controlled variable. The resulting PID algorithm is given by

$$\Delta c(t) = K_c \left[y_s(t-\Delta t) - y_s(t) + \frac{\Delta t}{\tau_I} e(t) - \tau_D \left[\frac{y_s(t) - 2y_s(t-\Delta t) + y_s(t-2\Delta t)}{\Delta t} \right] \right]$$

$$c(t) = c(t-\Delta t) - \Delta c(t)$$

♠

6.6 Filtering of Sensor Measurements

Sensor measurements are well known to contain some degree of noise (Section 3.6). Sensor noise is the variation in the sensor reading that does not correspond to changes in the process and can be caused by background electrical interference and mechanical vibrations. In feedback control loops, sensor measurements containing significant levels of noise result in noisy errors from setpoint, noisy controller output, and noisy actuator behavior. Consider the proportional term in a PID controller, i.e., $K_c(y_{sp} - y_s)$. Clearly, if the magnitude of the noise is large, a major portion of the proportional control action results directly from the noise because K_c and y_{sp} are constant.

Figure 6.3 shows the effect of excessive sensor noise on the feedback control performance of the CST thermal mixer (Example 3.1) for a setpoint increase of 5°C. The effect of the noise ($\sigma = 1.5$°C) on the temperature sensor reading can be seen in the strong variations in the sensor readings. The feedback controller reacts to these variations as evidenced by the variation in the manipulated variable. The thick line in Figure 6.3 represents the temperature sensor reading without noise (i.e., the noise-free reading). The variability in the noise-free value of the temperature is caused by the response of the feedback controller to the larger variations in the sensor reading caused by the sensor noise. The variations in the temperature measurement due to noise do not reflect real process changes. On the other hand, because of the action of the feedback controller on the noisy sensor measurement, the noise does affect the process as shown by the variations in the noise-free sensor reading.

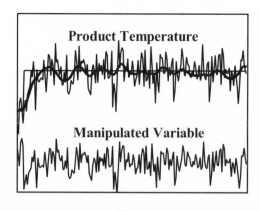

Time

Figure 6.3 Feedback control results for the CST thermal mixer for a noisy sensor. For the product temperature, the thin line is the noisy temperature senor reading and the thick line is the actual noise-free temperature reading.

Filters are used to reduce the effect of noise on control loops. Filters, in effect, average a number of sensor readings to reduce the amount of noise to which a feedback controller is exposed. A first-order **digital filter** is given by

$$y_f(t) = f\, y_s(t) + (1-f)\, y_f(t-\Delta t) \qquad\qquad 6.23$$

where $y_f(t)$ is the sensor reading after a digital filter has been applied, $y_s(t)$ is the current sensor reading, and f is the filter constant, which is normally between 0.01 and 0.5. A value of 0.1 for the filter factor is roughly equivalent to a running average of the last 10 sensor measurements while a filter factor of 0.01 is equivalent to an average of the last 100 sensor measurements. A more complete discussion of signal filtering is presented in Appendix C. The digital filter provides a running average and absorbs the short term variations caused by the noise. The transfer function for a first-order filter is given by

$$G_f(s) = \frac{1}{\tau_f s + 1}$$

$$\tau_f = \Delta t\left[\frac{1}{f} - 1\right] \qquad\qquad 6.24$$

where Δt is the time between applications of the filter.

Figure 6.4 shows the results of the application of sensor filtering to the CST thermal mixer with the sensor noise shown in Figure 6.3. A digital filter (Equation 6.23) was applied to the noisy sensor reading to produce a filtered temperature reading (thin line in Figure 6.4), which is used as the measurement of the controlled variable by the feedback temperature controller. A filter factor of 0.05 was used in this case. Note that the noise-free value of the product temperature (thick line in Figure 6.4) shows

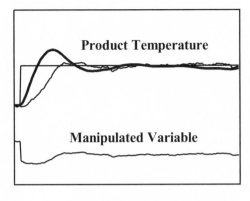

Time

Figure 6.4 Feedback control results for the CST thermal mixer with sensor filtering. For the product temperature, the thin line is the filtered sensor reading and the thick line is the noise-free product temperature reading.

significantly lower variability about the setpoint than for the case without sensor filtering (Figure 6.3). Also, the filter was able to significantly reduce the variation in the manipulated variable.   To produce the desired dynamic response, the aggressiveness of the controller was reduced when filtering was applied. Filtering of the controlled variable adds additional lag to the overall process, requiring less aggressive tuning. The use of less aggressive tuning for the controller and the delay caused by the filtering process causes the filtered case to respond more slowly than in the case without filtering, i.e., compare Figures 6.3 and 6.4.

Derivative action is much more sensitive than proportional action to noise. In the case of noisy sensor readings, erratic derivative action can result because the difference between successive sensor readings can be dominated by the noise, instead of by real process changes. Figure 6.5 shows a sensor reading with noise and the corresponding value of the derivative. Figure 6.5 also shows the value of the

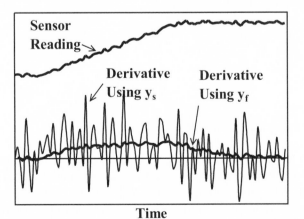

Time

Figure 6.5 The instantaneous and filtered value for the derivative of a noisy sensor reading.

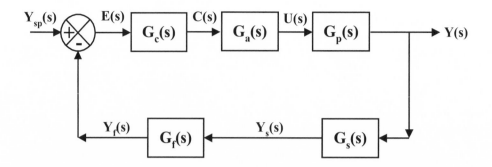

Figure 6.6 Schematic of a feedback control loop with sensor filtering.

derivative calculated using filtered values of $y_s(t)$ with a filter factor of 0.08. In this manner, filtered values of the controlled variable can be used in calculating the derivative used in the PID control equation, i.e.,

$$c(t) = c_0 + K_c \left(e(t) + \frac{1}{\tau_I} \sum_{i=1}^{n} e(i\Delta t)\Delta t - \tau_D \frac{y_f(t) - y_f(t - \Delta t)}{\Delta t} \right) \qquad \textbf{6.25}$$

In general, derivative action should not be used for a control loop with a noisy sensor. In cases in which there is a large relative amount of noise, the degree of filtering necessary to effectively apply derivative action usually adds so much extra lag to the loop that it negates the benefit of derivative action. It should be clear from this example that filtering is necessary in certain cases, but **a minimum level of filtering should be used to minimize the detrimental effect of filtering on control performance**.

Example 6.8 Analysis of the Dynamic Behavior of a Feedback System with a Filter on the Sensor Reading

Problem Statement. Analyze the effect of a filter for the sensor reading on the dynamic behavior of a first-order process with a P-only controller, i.e., $G_c(s) = K_c$ (Figure 6.6). Assume that the first-order process represents the combined effect of the actuator, process, and sensor.

Solution. Figure 6.6 shows a block diagram of a feedback controller for which filtering is used on the measurement of the controlled variable. The input to the filter is the sensor reading and the output is the filtered value of the sensor reading, which is compared with the setpoint value.

In a manner similar to the derivation presented in Section 6.2, the characteristic equation for the system given in Figure 6.6 is

$$G_p(s)G_a(s)G_c(s)G_s(s)G_f(s) + 1 = 0$$

From Equation 6.24, the transfer function of a first-order filter is given by

$$G_f(s) = \frac{1}{\tau_f s + 1}$$

Note that as τ_f is increased, more filtering is applied (i.e., f is decreased). The characteristic equation for this case is given by

$$K_c \left[\frac{K_p}{\tau_p s + 1} \right] \left[\frac{1}{\tau_f s + 1} \right] + 1 = 0$$

Rearranging this equation and putting it into the standard form for a second-order system (Equation 5.13) yields

$$\frac{\tau_p \tau_f}{K_c K_p + 1} s^2 + \frac{\tau_p + \tau_f}{K_c K_p + 1} s + 1 = 0$$

which indicates that

$$\tau'_p = \sqrt{\frac{\tau_p \tau_f}{K_c K_p + 1}}$$

$$\zeta' = \frac{\tau_p + \tau_f}{2\sqrt{\tau_p \tau_f (K_c K_p + 1)}}$$

Therefore, as τ_f is increased (i.e., an increased amount of filtering), the closed-loop response becomes slower and the damping factor increases, i.e., it becomes more overdamped. ζ' increases because as τ_f is increased, the linear term in the numerator increases at a faster rate than the square root term in the denominator. The comparison of Figures 6.4 and 6.5 showed that filtering the sensor reading slowed the closed-loop response of the CST thermal mixer, which is consistent with the results of this example.

♠

6.7 Interactive Form of the PID Controller

An older version of the PID algorithm, originally applied using analog devices, is called an **interactive PID controller**. Figure 6.7 shows a block diagram of this controller, which is also referred to as **"rate before reset"** since the derivative action is in series with and precedes the integral action. A PI or a P-only interactive

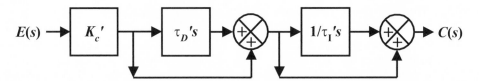

Figure 6.7 Block diagram for an interactive PID controller.

controller is no different from the earlier form presented (i.e., non-interactive PID, Equation 6.9). This can be seen by comparing Figures 6.2 and 6.7 with τ_D equal to zero. The only difference between an interactive and a non-interactive controller occurs for the PID controller. While there are differences in the tuning constants, both controllers apply the PID algorithm. That is, for the same amount of proportional, integral and derivative action, the interactive and non-interactive controllers have different values of the tuning constants (i.e., K_c, τ_I, and τ_D). Following are formulas for converting from interactive tuning parameters (i.e., the tuning parameters with primes) to tuning parameters for the conventional non-interactive PID form

$$K_c = K'_c\,(1+\tau'_D\,/\,\tau'_I)$$

$$\tau_I = \tau'_I\,(1+\tau'_D\,/\,\tau'_I)$$

$$\tau_D = \tau'_D\left[\frac{1}{1+\tau'_D\,/\,\tau'_I}\right]$$

Even though **interactive controllers** are an option on most DCSs, it is not recommended to use this form because it can cause confusion concerning the tuning parameters and **offers no advantage over the non-interactive form of the PID controller**. As a result, only the formulas for converting the settings from the interactive form to the non-interactive form are presented here.

6.8 Analysis of P, I, and D Action

In this section, we assume that the combination of the actuator, process and sensor is represented as a first-order process, i.e.,

$$G_a(s)G_p(s)G_s(s) = \frac{K_p}{\tau_p s+1}$$

Then the closed-loop transfer function for a setpoint change (Equation 6.6) is used to analyze the fundamental characteristics of proportional, integral, and derivative action.

The major objectives of feedback control are to:

- Minimize the response time of the closed-loop process.
- Maintain reliable operation.
- Control to setpoints, i.e., reduce deviations from setpoint and eliminate offset.
- Reject disturbances

Proportional, integral, and derivative action each affects feedback control performance with regard to these objectives. Moreover, controller tuning (selecting the individual levels of each of these feedback components) represents a compromise among these objectives. Chapter 7 addresses controller tuning.

Proportional action. Feedback control based on **proportional action**,

$$c(t) = c_0 + K_c \, e(t)$$

takes action based on the latest error from setpoint where K_c is the **controller gain**. The larger the error, the larger the control action. The transfer function for a proportional controller is

$$G_c(s) = K_c$$

The closed-loop transfer function for a setpoint change (Equation 6.6) for the case of a first-order actuator/process/sensor becomes

$$\frac{Y(s)}{Y_{sp}(s)} = \frac{\dfrac{K_c \, K_p}{\tau_p \, s + 1}}{\dfrac{K_c \, K_p}{\tau_p \, s + 1} + 1} = \frac{K_c \, K_p}{\tau_p \, s + 1 + K_c \, K_p}$$

Putting this result into the standard form for a first-order process results in

$$\frac{Y(s)}{Y_{sp}(s)} = \frac{\dfrac{K_c \, K_p}{K_c \, K_p + 1}}{\dfrac{\tau_p}{K_c \, K_p + 1} \, s + 1}$$

This result can be used to identify several fundamental characteristics of proportional action:

1. The closed-loop response of a first-order process remains first-order. In general, proportional action does not change the order of the process.
2. The closed-loop time constant $[\tau_p / (K_c K_p + 1)]$ is smaller than the open-loop time constant, τ_p. That is, proportional action makes the closed-loop process

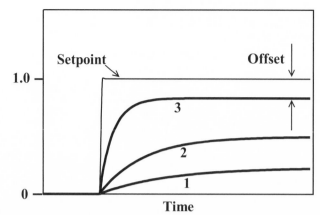

Figure 6.8 The effect of K_c on the response of a P-only controller for a first-order process to a setpoint change. K_c is increased from "1" to "3".

respond faster than the open-loop process. **Increasing the speed of the response of the process is the primary benefit of proportional control.**

3. The steady-state gain is not equal to unity. Figure 6.8 shows setpoint changes for three different values of K_c. Note that the steady-state closed-loop response differs from the setpoint value, which indicates **offset**. Offset is the error between the new setpoint and the new steady-state controlled variable value. As K_c increases, the offset is reduced. In fact, for this case the offset is given by

$$\text{Offset} = \frac{1}{1 + K_p K_c}$$

for a setpoint change of 1. Note that the same three conclusions can be reached if a disturbance were considered instead of a setpoint change.

Figure 6.9 shows the portion of a controller signal resulting from proportional action for a PI controller, applying a setpoint change. The proportional control action is positive when y is below y_{sp} and negative when y is above y_{sp} and its magnitude is directly proportional to the error from setpoint. Initially, the setpoint change causes a spike in proportional action but, as y moves toward the setpoint, the proportional action is reduced and eventually diminishes as y settles at the setpoint.

Integral action. Feedback control based on **integral action**, i.e.,

$$c(t) = c_0 + \frac{K_c}{\tau_I} \int_0^t e(t)\, dt$$

acts on the long term error from setpoint. Integral action is a much slower-responding form of feedback control than proportional action. τ_I is the **reset time (integral time)**, which is the tuning parameter for integral action and has units of time. The term reset comes from the fact that integral action is responsible for driving a process to a new value. Consider Equation 6.9 after a setpoint change or a disturbance has affected the

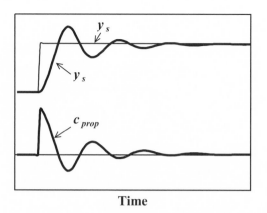

Time

Figure 6.9 The portion of the controller output resulting from proportional control (c_{prop}) for a setpoint change applied by a PI controller.

process. Further, assume that the process has reached steady-state conditions at the specified setpoint after the effects of the disturbances or the setpoint changes have been absorbed by the controller. Under these conditions, $e(t)$ and $dy(t)/dt$ are both zero, which indicates that the proportional action and derivative action are also zero. Because a setpoint change or a disturbance change has occurred, $c(t)$ must be significantly different from c_0; therefore, the integral term is responsible for providing the incremental change at steady-state from c_0 necessary to maintain operation at the new operating condition. As a result, integral action is a critically important feature of PID feedback control. The transfer function for an integral-only controller is

$$G_c = \frac{K_c}{\tau_I s}$$

The closed-loop transfer function for a setpoint change (Equation 6.6) for a first-order process becomes

$$\frac{Y(s)}{Y_{sp}(s)} = \frac{\dfrac{K_c K_p}{\tau_I s(\tau_p s + 1)}}{\dfrac{K_c K_p}{\tau_I s(\tau_p s + 1)} + 1} = \frac{K_c K_p}{\tau_I \tau_p s^2 + \tau_I s + K_c K_p}$$

Putting this result into the standard form for a second-order process (i.e., Equation 5.14) results in

$$\frac{Y(s)}{Y_{sp}(s)} = \frac{1}{\dfrac{\tau_I \tau_p}{K_p K_c} s^2 + \dfrac{\tau_I}{K_p K_c} s + 1}$$

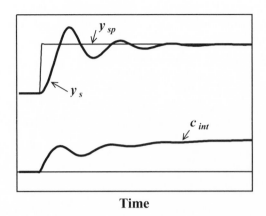

Time

Figure 6.10 The portion of the manipulated variable level resulting from integral action (c_{int}) for a setpoint change applied by a PI controller.

By comparing this equation with the standard second-order form, the closed-loop time constant τ'_p is given as

$$\tau'_p = \sqrt{\frac{\tau_I \, \tau_p}{K_p \, K_c}}$$

and solving for the closed-loop damping factor, ζ', yields

$$\zeta' = \frac{1}{2}\sqrt{\frac{\tau_I}{\tau_p \, K_c \, K_p}}$$

and the closed-loop gain is 1. These results, along with the previous analysis, provide several fundamental characteristics of integral action.

1. All the steady-state corrections for disturbances or setpoint changes must come from integral action.

2. Since the gain of the closed-loop transfer function is 1, there is no offset at steady state. **Eliminating offset is the primary advantage provided by integral action.**

3. Integral action increases the order of the process dynamics by 1.

4. Based upon the equations for τ'_p and ζ', as τ_I is decreased, the process becomes faster but at the expense of larger overshoots and more sustained oscillations. For example, assume that $K_p K_c = 1$. If $\tau_I = \tau_p$, then $\zeta' = 0.5$ and $\tau'_p = \tau_p$. If $\tau_I = \frac{1}{4}\tau_p$, then $\zeta' = 0.25$ and $\tau'_p = 0.5\tau_p$. Therefore, increasing the amount of integral action (decreasing τ_I) results in a faster-responding feedback process, but increases the degree of oscillatory behavior.

Figure 6.10 shows the portion of the controller output resulting from integral action for a PI controller for the same process shown in Figure 6.9. Note that the peaks and valleys in c_{int} occur when y_s crosses y_{sp}. Also note that, as the process lines out at the setpoint, c_{int} lines out at a non-zero value.

Derivative Action. Feedback control based on **derivative action** is given by

$$c(t) = c_0 - K_c \tau_D \frac{d\,y_s(t)}{dt}$$

which indicates that derivative action acts to oppose the slope of the controlled variable in an effort to stabilize the feedback process. As the slope of the controlled variable increases, derivative control action also increases in an effort to reduce the slope to allow for more gradual changes in the controlled variable regardless of whether the controlled variable is moving away from or toward the setpoint. τ_D is the **derivative time**, which is the tuning parameter for derivative action and has the units of time.

The transfer function for derivative action is

$$G_c(s) = K_c \tau_D s$$

The closed-loop transfer function for a setpoint change (Equation 6.6) for a first-order process becomes

$$\frac{Y(s)}{Y_{sp}(s)} = \frac{\dfrac{K_c K_p \tau_D s}{\tau_p s + 1}}{\dfrac{K_c K_p \tau_D s}{\tau_p s + 1} + 1} = \frac{K_c K_p \tau_D s}{(K_c K_p \tau_D + \tau_p)s + 1}$$

which indicates that derivative action does not change the order of the process or eliminate offset, but does increase the time constant for a first-order process.

It is also instructive to consider the effect of derivative action applied to a second-order process. The closed-loop transfer function for a setpoint change applied to this case yields

$$\frac{Y(s)}{Y_{sp}(s)} = \frac{\dfrac{K_p}{\tau_p^2 s^2 + 2\zeta \tau_p s + 1} K_c \tau_D s}{\dfrac{K_p}{\tau_p^2 s^2 + 2\zeta \tau_p s + 1} K_c \tau_D s + 1}$$

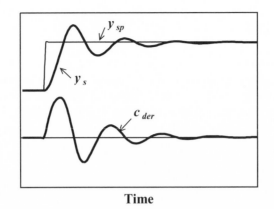

Figure 6.11 The portion of the manipulated variable level resulting from derivative action (c_{der}) for a setpoint change applied using a PID controller.

Rearranging

$$\frac{Y(s)}{Y_{sp}(s)} = \frac{K_p K_c \tau_D s}{\tau_p^2 s^2 + (2\zeta\tau_p + K_p K_c \tau_D)s + 1}$$

For a second-order process, τ_p remains unchanged while the closed-loop damping factor is larger than the open-loop damping factor. These results indicate several fundamental characteristics of derivative action:

1. Derivative action does not change the order of the process.
2. Derivative action slows down the response of a first-order process.
3. Derivative action does not eliminate offset.
4. Derivative action reduces the oscillatory nature of feedback control. **Reducing the oscillatory nature of a feedback response is the primary advantage of derivative action.**

Figure 6.11 shows the portion of the manipulated variable level resulting from derivative action (c_{der}) for a setpoint change using a PID controller. Note that c_{der} is zero at the peaks and valleys of y since it is directly related to the slope of y_s.

6.9 Controller Design Issues

When choosing between P-only, PI, or PID controllers, one should consider the dynamics of the combined actuator/process/sensor system and the objectives of the control loop. For the conventional control loops in the CPI, it has been estimated[1] that approximately 93% use PI controllers, 2% use P-only controllers, and 5% use PID controllers. The following guidelines, based on process dynamics and control objectives, can be used to choose the proper controller mode.

P-only control. P-only control is used for processes that are not sluggish and for which some degree of offset is acceptable. A sluggish process is characterized by the fact that the process does not respond quickly to changes in the manipulated variable (i.e., not a first-order-like response). Typical applications are level control and pressure control. There are many control loops that should use P-only controllers, but instead use typical PI or PI with a relatively small amount of integral action since most operators do not want offset from setpoint.

PI control. PI controllers are used for processes that are not sluggish and for which it is necessary to have offset-free operation. Typical applications are flow control, level control, pressure control, temperature control, and composition control.

PID control. PID controllers are useful for certain sluggish processes. Typical applications are temperature control and composition control. Because of the inertia of a sluggish process, the process exhibits a tendency to cycle under PI control. Derivative action reduces cycling and allows more proportional action to be used, both of which contribute to improved control performance. A key issue here is to determine whether a process is sluggish enough to warrant a PID controller. Assume that a FOPDT model has been fit to an open-loop step test. If the resulting deadtime, θ_p, and time constant, τ_p, are such that

$$\frac{\theta_p}{\tau_p} < \frac{1}{2}$$

the process is not sufficiently sluggish to warrant a PID controller. **If**

$$\frac{\theta_p}{\tau_p} > 1$$

the process is sufficiently sluggish that a PID controller should offer significant benefits over a PI controller. For

$$\frac{1}{2} < \frac{\theta_p}{\tau_p} < 1$$

either PI or PID can be preferred. In the event that FOPDT models are not available, excessive oscillations of a PI controller or a sluggishly responding PI controller are indications that a PID controller may provide improved control performance. Measurements of the controlled variable with significant noise levels can make the use of derivative action ineffective because of the sensitivity of the derivative to noise on the measurement. That is, since the measurements of the controlled variable have so

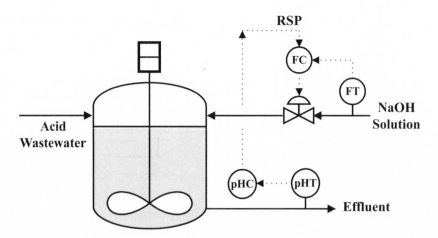

Figure 6.12   Schematic of a control system on a wastewater neutralization process.

much noise, the lag added by a filter can negate any benefit produced by the derivative action.

Example 6.9 Selection of the Proper Mode of a PID Controller

Problem Statement. Consider the wastewater neutralization process shown in Figure 6.12. The objective of this process is to maintain the pH of the effluent stream at a pH value of 7 (neutrality). Determine the proper mode of a PID controller for this process if the residence time for the reactor is 3 minutes and the time constant for the pH sensor/transmitter is 3 s.

Solution. Since the objective is to maintain neutrality, integral action should be used. Since they are primarily strong acid/strong base reactions occurring in the reactor, the reactions can be assumed instantaneous. Therefore, the reactor should behave as a first-order process. Because the sensor dynamics and the dynamics of the final control element are much faster than the process in this case, the overall dynamic behavior should be similar to a first-order process; therefore, the effective deadtime-to-time constant ratio of this system should be relatively small. As a result, a PI controller should be selected for this application.

♠

6.10 Commonly Encountered Control Loops

In this section, five control loops commonly encountered in the CPI are analyzed: a flow control loop, level control loop, pressure control loop, temperature control loop, and composition control loop. The relevant control characteristics of

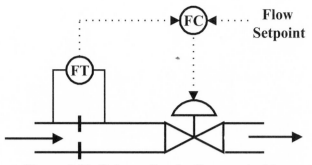

Figure 6.13 Schematic of a flow control loop.

each loop are discussed from an actuator/process/sensor point of view and the problem of selecting a P-only, PI, or PID controller is addressed for each case.

Flow Control Loop. A flow control loop is the most common control loop used in the CPI. Most of the control loops in the CPI, other than a flow control loop itself, use a setpoint to a flow controller as their manipulated variable in a cascade control arrangement. A schematic of a flow control loop is shown in Figure 6.13. An orifice meter/differential pressure sensor is used to measure the flow rate and the actuator is a final control element (I/P converter, instrument air, and assembled control valve). The objective of this control loop is to maintain the flow rate at the setpoint for changes in the upstream and downstream pressures and for changes in the setpoint to the flow controller.

The dynamics of the process (i.e., flow rate changes for changes in the valve stem position) and the sensor (i.e., changes in the measured pressure drop for changes in the flow rate) are quite fast compared with the dynamics of the control valve (i.e., changes in valve stem position for changes in signal to the final control element). Since the overall process is relatively fast and accurate control to setpoint is required, a PI controller is the proper choice for most flow control applications.

The most interesting aspect of flow control loops is that, in spite of the fact that industrial control valves have a deadband of 10% to 25%, flow control loops are able to precisely meter the average flow rate typically to within a deadband of ±0.5% and down to ±0.1%. Figure 6.14 shows a plot of the actual valve position and the instrument air pressure delivered to the valve in an open-loop case as a function of time. This behavior is caused by deadband in the valve primarily from friction between the valve stem and the valve packing. As a result of the drag of the packing on the valve stem, a minimum force is necessary to cause the valve to move and when it does move, it breaks loose and significant valve travel results, thus causing a significant deadband.

To understand how a flow control loop can very accurately control the flow rate using such an imprecise actuator, consider the measured flow rate and specified flow rate shown in Figure 6.15. The significant variation in the flow rate (i.e., sustained oscillations) is due to the deadband of the valve, but the average flow is

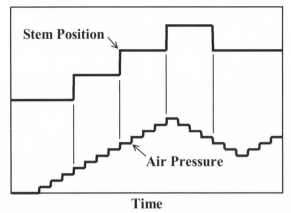

Figure 6.14 Valve stem position versus air pressure to the valve actuator for a valve with significant deadband.

precisely controlled due to the high frequency feedback control provided by the flow controller. Since the period of the flow variations is in the range of seconds and most chemical processes have time constants several minutes or larger, the process is sensitive only to the average flow and not to flow fluctuations; therefore, flow control loops can provide very precise metering of the **average flow rate** in spite of the fact that a very imprecise actuator is used. Because the primary objective of a flow control loop is to control the average flow rate and short-term deviations from setpoint are unimportant, PI flow controllers are usually tuned with much more integral action than proportional action. If a valve positioner is used, the valve positioner provides the high-frequency feedback necessary to counteract the detrimental effects of the deadband of the control valve on the metering precision of the average flow rate. That is, the high-gain P-only controller applied by the valve positioner opens and closes the valve in a manner similar to the results shown in Figure 6.15. A flow control loop applied to a control valve with a positioner eliminates the offset for which the positioner does not account and absorbs unmeasured disturbances such as changes in upstream and downstream pressures.

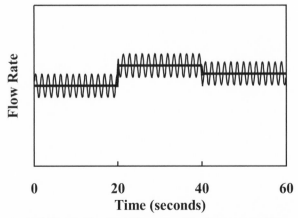

Figure 6.15 Measured flow rate and the specified average flow rate for a valve with a positioner. Thin line - measured flow rate. Thick line - flow rate setpoint.

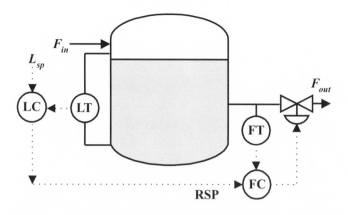

Figure 6.16 Schematic of a level controller applied to a tank.

Level Control Loop. Level control loops are used to control the liquid levels in the accumulator and reboiler of distillation columns, steam boilers, reactors, and intermediate storage tanks. A schematic for a level control loop used to control the level in a tank is shown in Figure 6.16. A differential pressure sensor is used to measure the liquid level and the actuator is a flow control loop that controls the flow rate from the tank. The manipulated variable determined by the level controller is the setpoint for the flow controller on the line leaving the tank. This is an example of cascade control, which is discussed in detail in Chapter 10. Some level controllers send their outputs directly to the valve on the line, but most level controllers in the CPI are implemented as shown in Figure 6.16, using flow control loops. The objective of this loop is to maintain the level within a certain range, for example, from 30 to 40% of full for changes in the feed rate to the tank and changes in operating conditions. On the other hand, many operators want levels controlled to specified setpoints and are not satisfied if, for example, the level is 32% or 38% when the setpoint is 35%.

The dynamics of the sensor are quite fast and the dynamics of the actuator are usually fast compared with the dynamics of the process (i.e., percentage level changes for changes in flow leaving the tank). Since level systems are integrating processes, the rate of change of the level depends upon the change in flow rate and the cross-sectional area of the vessel. For a typical system under open-loop conditions, a 5% level change can occur in about one minute for about a 10% change in feed rate to the tank. Thus, the response of the actuator/process/sensor system is typically controlled by the process dynamics. Since the overall process is not generally sluggish, a P-only controller is the proper choice when offset elimination is not required. When offset elimination is required (e.g., level control for a reactor), a PI controller should be used.

Pressure Control Loop. Pressure control loops are used to maintain system pressure for distillation columns, reactors, and other process units. A pressure control loop for maintaining overhead pressure in a column is shown in Figure 6.17. The actuator is a control valve on the vent line and the sensor is a pressure sensor mounted on the top of the column. Note that the output from the pressure controller goes directly to the control valve on the vent line. The objective of this loop is to

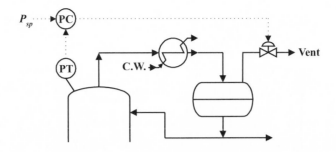

Figure 6.17 Schematic of a pressure controller for the overhead of a distillation column.

maintain the column overhead pressure at or near setpoint for changes in condenser duty and changes in vapor flow rate up the column.

The pressure sensor is quite fast while the process (changes in pressure for changes in vent valve stem position) and the actuator are generally the slowest elements in the feedback system, making this a relatively fast-responding process. A P-only controller can be used if offset elimination is not important and a PI controller can be used when offset elimination is important.

Temperature Control Loop. Temperature control loops can be applied to control the temperature of a stream exiting a heat exchanger, the temperature of a tray in a distillation column, and the temperature of a CSTR. Figure 6.18 shows a schematic of a temperature controller applied to the temperature of a process stream leaving a gas-fired heater. The sensor is a RTD element placed in a thermowell located in the line leaving the heater and the actuator is a flow control loop on the gas line to the heater. The objective of the temperature control loop is to maintain the temperature of the exiting process stream at setpoint in the face of changes in the temperature of the process stream entering the heater and changes in the heating value of the gas.

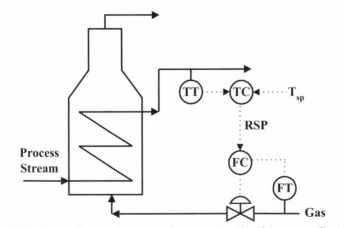

Figure 6.18 Schematic of a temperature controller for a gas-fired heater.

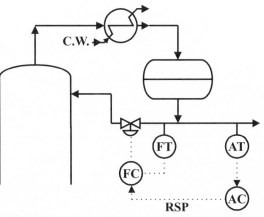

Figure 6.19 Schematic of a composition controller for the overhead of a distillation column.

The dynamics of the actuator are generally much faster than the dynamics of the process (i.e., change in outlet process temperature for a change in gas flow rate to the heater) and the sensor, which typically has a dynamic time constant between 6 and 20 seconds for a properly installed RTD. The process fluid entering the gas-fired heater flows by plug flow through the furnace tubes that are exposed to high-temperature combustion gas. There is a thermal lag associated with changing the temperature of the metal of the furnace tubes as well as transport delay caused by plug flow through the heater tubes. The transport delay and resulting overall process deadtime increases as the feed rate of the process fluid is reduced. As a result, the process can be sluggish particularly for low feed rate operations. Since the heater is likely to behave as a sluggish process, a PID controller should be selected in this example. Excessive sensor noise can make the use of derivative action ineffective, which is why an RTD is preferred in this application over a TC. If this process were less sluggish, a PI controller is preferable. The guidelines presented in the previous section should be used to determine if the process is sufficiently sluggish to warrant the use of PID control.

Composition Control Loop. Composition control loops are used to keep products produced by distillation columns on specification, to maintain constant conversion in a reactor, and to maintain oxygen levels in the flue gas of a boiler to eliminate carbon monoxide emissions. Figure 6.19 shows a schematic of a composition loop that controls the impurity level in the overhead product of a distillation column. The sensor is a gas chromatograph that samples the distillation product and the output of the controller for this loop is the setpoint for the reflux flow controller. The objective of the composition control loop is to keep the impurity level in the overhead product at setpoint during changes in the feed flow rate and feed composition to the column.

The actuator dynamics are relatively fast while the sensor typically can have three to ten minutes of analyzer delay. The process (i.e., the change in impurity level in the overhead product for a change in the setpoint for the reflux flow controller) can be sluggish and the sensor delay is usually significant; therefore, the dynamics of the process and sensor typically determine the dynamic response of this type of process. If the process and analyzer delay result in a sluggish actuator/process/sensor system, a PID controller may be preferred. Once again, the guidelines presented in the previous section should be used to determine if the process is sluggish enough to warrant the use of PID control.

Table 6.2 Summary of PID Controller Modes for Commonly Encountered Control Loops

	\multicolumn{3}{c}{Are dynamics important to the control loop performance?}	Preferred Mode of a PID Controller
	Actuator	**Process**	**Sensor**	
Flow controllers	√			PI
Pressure controllers	√	√		P-only or PI
Level controllers		√		P-only or PI
Temperature controllers		√	√	PI or PID
Composition Controllers		√	√	PI or PID

6.11 Summary

The roots of the characteristic equation of the closed-loop transfer function define the dynamic behavior of a feedback loop. PID controllers are extremely flexible and are the most commonly used controllers in the CPI. A PID controller has individual terms that separately apply proportional, integral, and derivative action. PID control is implemented using digital approximations of the integral of the error from setpoint and the derivative of the controlled variable value. Sensor filtering is implemented to reduce the effect of noise on feedback control performance. Because filtering adds lag to the dynamic response of the feedback system, the minimum level of filtering should be used.

It is shown that (1) proportional action makes the process respond faster but does not eliminate offset, (2) integral action eliminates offset but increases the oscillatory nature of the feedback response, and (3) derivative action reduces the oscillatory nature of the closed-loop response but does not eliminate offset.

When deciding among P-only, PI, and PID control, one should consider the combined dynamic behavior of the actuator, process, and sensor. Processes with non-sluggish dynamic behavior should use P-only control when offset is not important and should use PI control when offset elimination is important. PID control should be used for sluggish processes, i.e., when the effective deadtime-to-time constant ratio is significant. Otherwise, a PI controller should be used.

6.12 Additional Terminology

c_0 - the value of the controller signal to the actuator when a PID controller is turned on.

Characteristic equation - the equation formed by setting the denominator of the closed-loop transfer function equal to zero. The roots of the characteristic equation determine the dynamic behavior of the closed-loop system.

Control interval - the cycle time for applying control action, i.e., equal to the time interval between executions of the controller.

Controller gain (K_c) - tuning parameter in a PID controller that determines the aggressiveness of the controller.

Derivative action - control action that is proportional to the derivative of the controlled variable.

Derivative kick - a spike in control action resulting from a setpoint change when the derivative is based on the error from setpoint.

Derivative-on-measurement - derivative action in a PID controller that is calculated based upon the slope of the measurement and, therefore, does not suffer from derivative kick.

Derivative time (τ_D) - the tuning parameter for derivative action in a PID controller.

Digital filter - a numerical running average that is used to reduce the effect of noisy sensor readings.

Direct-acting controller - a controller that subtracts the proportional, integral, and derivative correction to the previous control action (velocity form) or to c_0 (position form).

Disturbance rejection - controlling to setpoint in the face of disturbance upsets.

Integral action - control action that is proportional to the time integral of the error from setpoint.

Integral time (τ_I) - the tuning parameter for integral action in a PID controller.

Interactive PID controllers - an older form of PID control based upon the sequential application of derivative and integral action. Also known as "rate-before-reset".

K_c - PID controller gain, tuning parameter for proportional action.

Offset - a sustained error from setpoint.

PB - the proportional band tuning constant.

PID controller - a linear controller that applies proportional, integral, and derivative action.

Position form - PID algorithm that calculates the total value of the controller output.

Proportional action - control action that is proportional to the latest error from setpoint.

Proportional band - a term that indicates the amount of proportional action used by a PID controller (inversely related to K_c).

Proportional kick - the sharp response of a PI controller to a setpoint change when the proportional term is based on the error from setpoint.

Rate-before-reset - an older form of PID control based on the sequential application of derivative and integral action.

Regulatory control - controlling to setpoint in the face of disturbance upsets.

Reset time (τ_I) - the tuning parameter for integral action in a PID controller.

Reverse-acting controller - a controller that adds the proportional, integral, and derivative correction from the previous control action (velocity form) or from c_0 (position form).

Servo control - controlling to setpoint in the face of setpoint changes.

Setpoint tracking - controlling to setpoint in the face of setpoint changes.

Velocity form of PID - PID algorithm that calculates the change in the controller output.

τ_D - PID derivative time, the tuning parameter for derivative action.

τ_I - PID reset time, the tuning parameter for integral action.

6.13 References

1. Private communication, Jim Downs, Tennessee Eastman Company (Nov 1998).

6.14 Preliminary Questions

6.1 What is the characteristic equation of a feedback loop and what is its significance?

6.2 What does the characteristic equation indicate about the dynamics of feedback systems for setpoint changes and disturbance rejection?

6.3 What is the difference between servo control and regulatory control?

6.4 What is "c_0" in the position form of the PID algorithm?

6.5 How are the units of the controller gain related to the units of the process gain?

6.6 How can derivative kick be eliminated?

6.7 How can proportional kick be eliminated?

6.8 How is Equation 6.9 converted into the digital version of the position form of the PID algorithm?

6.9 How does the control interval affect the digital version of the position form of the PID algorithm?

6.10 The term "$e(t)$-$e(t$-$\Delta t)$" in the velocity form of the PID algorithm represents what type of control action?

6.11 The term "$e(t)$" in the velocity form of the PID algorithm represents what type of control action?

6.12 How can proportional kick be eliminated using the position form of the PID algorithm?

6.13 How can one determine whether a process gain is positive or negative?

6.14 What is a direct-acting final control element? Why is it called direct acting? Under what conditions is it chosen?

6.15 What is a reverse-acting final control element? Why is it called reverse acting? Under what conditions is it chosen?

6.16 Explain how an increase in the noise level for a sensor can cause an increase in the variability produced by the control loop using the sensor.

6.17 How does filtering a sensor measurement reduce the variation in the manipulated variable value for a control loop?

6.18 What price, in terms of controller performance, does one pay for using a filter on sensor readings?

6.19 Is sensor noise more detrimental to proportional or derivative action?

6.20 What is the purpose of a digital filter? How do you decide how much filtering is appropriate?

6.21 Explain why one cannot simply add enough filtering to remove all the noise from a noisy measurement of the controlled variable before applying derivative action.

6.22 What is the noninteractive form of the PID algorithm?

6.23 Why are the interactive and noninteractive forms of a PI controller equivalent?

6.24 What are the three key characteristics of proportional control?

6.25 What are the four key characteristics of integral control?

6.26 What are the four key characteristics of derivative control?

6.27 Compare and contrast the fundamental characteristics of proportional, integral, and derivative action.

6.28 What is the most commonly used mode of a PID controller?

6.29 In general, what kind of processes use P-only controllers?

6.30 In general, what kind of processes use PI controllers?

6.31 In general, what kind of processes use PID controllers?

6.32 What are the relative dynamics (i.e., fastest to slowest) of the actuator, process, and sensor for a typical flow control loop?

6.33 What are the relative dynamics (i.e., fastest to slowest) of the actuator, process, and sensor for a typical pressure control loop?

6.34 What are the relative dynamics (i.e., fastest to slowest) of the actuator, process, and sensor for a typical level control loop?

6.35 What are the relative dynamics (i.e., fastest to slowest) of the actuator, process, and sensor for a typical temperature control loop?

6.36 What are the relative dynamics (i.e., fastest to slowest) of the actuator, process, and sensor for a typical composition control loop?

6.37 How do you decide between a PID and a PI controller?

6.38 How can a control valve with a deadband of 10% be used to control the flow rate to a deadband of less than 0.5%?

6.15 Analytical Questions and Exercises

6.39 Determine the dynamic behavior of a PI controller with K_c equal to 3 and τ_I equal to 20 applied to a first-order process in which the process gain is equal to 0.5 and the time constant is equal to 9. Assume that $G_s(s)$ and $G_a(s)$ are equal to one.

6.40 Determine the dynamic behavior of a P-only controller with K_c equal to 2 applied to a first-order process in which the process gain is equal to 0.5 and the time constant is equal to 15. Assume a first-order model with a time constant of 6 for $G_s(s)$ and $G_a(s)$ is equal to one.

6.41 Determine the dynamic behavior of a P-only controller with K_c equal to 1 applied to a first-order process in which the process gain is equal to 2 and the time constant is equal to 22. Assume that $G_s(s)$ is equal to one and $G_a(s)$ behaves as a first-order process with a time constant of 5.

6.42 Determine the dynamic behavior of a PI controller with K_c equal to 0.1 and τ_I equal to 10 applied to a first-order process in which the process gain is equal to 12 and the time constant is equal to 9. Assume that $G_s(s)$ and $G_a(s)$ are equal to unity.

6.43 Determine the dynamic behavior of a PI controller with K_c equal to 2 and τ_I equal to 10 applied to a first-order process in which the process gain is equal to 6 and the time constant is equal to 3. Assume that $G_s(s)$ and $G_a(s)$ are equal to unity.

6.44 Determine the dynamic behavior of a PI controller with K_c equal to 1 and τ_I equal to 5 applied to a second-order process (K_p=0.7, τ_p=4, and ζ=3). Assume that $G_s(s)$ and $G_a(s)$ are equal to unity.

6.45 Determine the dynamic behavior of a PI controller with K_c equal to 2 and τ_I equal to 4 applied to a second-order process (K_p=2, τ_p=5, and ζ=1.5). Assume that $G_s(s)$ and $G_a(s)$ are equal to unity.

6.46 Determine the dynamic behavior of a P-only controller with K_c equal to 3 applied to a second-order process (K_p=0.3, τ_p=5, and ζ=2). Assume that $G_s(s)$ and $G_a(s)$ are equal to unity.

6.47 Determine the dynamic behavior of a PI controller with K_c equal to 1 and τ_I equal to 1 applied to a second-order process (K_p=0.2, τ_p=5, and ζ=2). Assume that $G_s(s)$ and $G_a(s)$ are equal to unity.

6.48 Determine the dimensional version of the controller gain corresponding to a proportional band of 900%. The range of the error from setpoint is 5 mole % and the controller output is 0 to 100%.

6.49 Determine the dimensional version of the controller gain corresponding to a proportional band of 35%. The range of the error from setpoint is 20 °C and the controller output is 0 to 100%.

6.50 Determine the dimensional version of the controller gain corresponding to a proportional band of 400%. The range of the error from setpoint is 1000 lb/h and the controller output is 0 to 100%.

6.51 Determine the dimensional version of the controller gain corresponding to a proportional band of 50%. The range of the error (level reading) from setpoint is 100% and the controller output is 0 to 100%.

6.52   Determine the proportional band corresponding to a controller gain of 15 %/mole%. The range of the error from setpoint is 10 mole % and the controller output 0 to 100%.

6.53   Determine the proportional band corresponding to a controller gain of 35 %/°F. The range of the error from setpoint is 100°F and the controller output is 0 to 100%.

6.54   Determine the proportional band corresponding to a controller gain of 7 %/psi. The range of the error from setpoint is 150 psi and the controller output is 0 to 100%.

6.55   Determine the proportional band corresponding to a controller gain of 0.01 %-h/lb. The range of the error from setpoint is 3000 lb/h and the controller output is 0 to 100%.

6.56   Write the position form of the PID algorithm similar to Equation 6.9 for Example 3.3, and assume that the control valve on the exit stream has an air-to-open actuator. Use the form that is not susceptible to derivative kick.

6.57   Write the position form of the PID algorithm similar to Equation 6.9 for Example 3.6, and assume that the control valve on the steam line has an air-to-close actuator. Use the form that is susceptible to derivative kick.

6.58   Write the position form of the PID algorithm similar to Equation 6.9 for Example 3.4, and assume that the control valve on the steam line has an air-to-open actuator. Use the form that is not susceptible to derivative kick and use proportional band instead of K_c.

6.59   Write the digital version of the position form of the PID algorithm similar to Equation 6.15 for Example 3.6, and assume that the control valve on the steam line to the heat exchanger has an air-to-open actuator. Use the form that is not susceptible to derivative kick.

6.60   Write the digital version of the position form of the PID algorithm similar to Equation 6.15 for Example 3.2, and assume that the control valve on the feed line to the mixer has an air-to-close actuator. Use the form that is susceptible to derivative kick.

6.61   Write the digital version of the position form of the PID algorithm similar to Equation 6.15 for Example 3.1, and assume that the control valve on the feed line to the mixer has an air-to-open actuator. Use the form that is not susceptible to derivative kick and use proportional band instead of K_c.

6.62   Write the velocity form of the PID algorithm similar to Equation 6.17 for Example 3.3, and assume that the control valve on the exit line has an air-to-open actuator. Use the form that is not susceptible to derivative kick, but is susceptible to proportional kick.

6.63   Write the velocity form of the PID algorithm similar to Equation 6.17 for Example 3.6, and assume that the control valve on the steam line to the heat exchanger has an air-to-close actuator. Use the form that is susceptible to derivative kick and proportional kick.

6.64 Write the velocity form of the PID algorithm similar to Equation 6.17 for Example 3.2, and assume that the control valve on the feed line to the mixer has an air-to-close actuator. Use the form that is not susceptible to derivative kick or proportional kick.

6.65 Write the velocity form of the PID algorithm similar to Equation 6.17 for Example 3.1, and assume that the control valve on the feed line to the mixer has an air-to-open actuator. Use the form that is not susceptible to derivative kick or proportional kick. Use proportional band instead of K_c.

6.66 Derive the velocity form of the PID algorithm starting with Equation 6.9.

6.67 Determine the dynamic behavior of a P-only controller with K_c equal to 2 applied to a first-order process with a process gain of 0.5 and a time constant of 15. Assume that a first-order filter is applied to the sensor reading and uses a time constant of 3. Assume that $G_s(s)$ and $G_a(s)$ are equal to unity.

6.68 Determine the dynamic behavior of a P-only controller with K_c equal to 2 applied to a first-order process with a process gain of 0.5 and a time constant of 5. Assume that a first-order filter is applied to the sensor reading and uses a filter factor (f) of 0.1 with a control interval of 1. Assume that $G_s(s)$ and $G_a(s)$ are equal to unity.

6.69 Determine the dynamic behavior of a P-only controller with K_c equal to 5 applied to a first-order process with a process gain of 0.05 and a time constant of 17. Assume that a first-order filter is applied to the sensor reading and uses a filter factor (f) of 0.3 with a control interval of 1. Assume that $G_s(s)$ and $G_a(s)$ are equal to unity.

6.70 Determine the dynamic behavior of a P-only controller with K_c equal to 0.1 applied to a first-order process with a process gain of 3 and a time constant of 200. Assume that a first-order filter is applied to the sensor reading and uses a filter factor (f) of 0.05 with a control interval of 1. Assume that $G_s(s)$ and $G_a(s)$ are equal to unity.

6.71[S] Apply a P-only controller to the following process simulators provided with this text and tune for reasonable performance.

    a. CST thermal mixer.   b. CST composition mixer.

    c. Level process.   d. Endothermic CSTR.

    e. Heat exchanger.

6.72[S] Apply an integral-only controller to the following process simulators provided with this text and tune for reasonable performance.

    a. CST thermal mixer.   b. CST composition mixer.

    c . Level process.   d. Endothermic CSTR.

    e. Heat exchanger.

6.73 When are the dynamics of the actuator system important to the overall dynamic behavior of the feedback loop? Give an example.

6.74 When are the dynamics of the sensor system important to the overall dynamic behavior of the feedback loop? Give an example.

6.75 Give an example in which the dynamics of the process are insignificant compared to the actuator.

6.76 Under what conditions are the dynamics of an actuator of a level control process significant compared with the dynamics of the process? Be specific.

6.77 For Figure 6.4, explain why the noise-free value of the controlled variable exhibits overshoot.

A superscript "S" after a problem number indicates the use of the simulators is required.

Chapter 7

PID Controller Tuning

7.1 Introduction

Tuning PID loops is one of the major responsibilities of a process control engineer, and the resulting controller settings have a dominant effect on the performance of a PID control loop. Tuning a PID controller requires selecting values for K_c, τ_I, and τ_D that meet the operational objectives of the control loop, which usually requires making a proper compromise between performance (minimizing deviations from setpoint) and reliability (the controller's ability to remain in service while handling major disturbances). At other times, controller tuning is determined by the overall objectives of the process. This chapter presents tuning criteria and performance assessment approaches, analyzes the effect of controller tuning parameters on feedback control performance, presents an overview of pole placement, describes several well-known tuning approaches, and finally presents a controller tuning procedure that is recommended for tuning industrial PID controllers.

7.2 Tuning Criteria and Performance Assessment

Tuning Criteria. Following are some controller tuning objectives.

- Minimize deviations from setpoint
- Attain good setpoint tracking performance
- Avoid excessive variation of the manipulated variables
- Maintain process stability for major disturbance upsets
- Eliminate offset

It is not possible to simultaneously satisfy each of these objectives; therefore, tuning is a compromise among these objectives. For example, tuning for minimum deviation from setpoint for normal disturbances is contrary to tuning the controller to remain stable for major disturbances. If the controller is tuned for normal disturbances, the closed-loop system may go unstable when a major disturbance enters the process. On the other hand, if the controller is tuned for the largest possible disturbance, control performance is likely to be excessively sluggish for normal disturbances.

Performance Assessment. There are a number of performance statistics that can be used to evaluate **control performance**:

Integral Absolute Error (*IAE*)

$$IAE = \int_0^\infty \left| y_{sp}(t) - y_s(t) \right| dt$$

Integral Time Absolute Error (*ITAE*)

$$ITAE = \int_0^\infty t \left| y_{sp}(t) - y_s(t) \right| dt$$

Integral Square Error (*ISE*)

$$ISE = \int_0^\infty \left[y_{sp}(t) - y_s(t) \right]^2 dt$$

Integral Time Square Error (*ITSE*)

$$ITSE = \int_0^\infty t \left[y_{sp}(t) - y_s(t) \right]^2 dt$$

Each of these statistical measures values the error from setpoint differently. *ITAE* and *ITSE* penalize later deviations more severely than *IAE* and *ISE*. *ISE* and *ITSE* penalize larger deviations more severely than *IAE* and *ITAE*.

Figure 7.1 shows the setpoint response of a process tuned for sluggish performance (Figure 7.1a), for a decay ratio of 1/10 (Figure 7.1b), for a decay ratio of 1/4 (**quarter-amplitude damping, QAD**, Figure 7.1c), and for a decay ratio of 1/1.5 (Figure 7.1d). The decay ratio is a convenient measurement of the closed-loop dynamic response because it can be easily estimated from setpoint changes and some disturbance upsets. The 1/1.5 decay ratio results in excessive cycling, which is called **ringing**. QAD results in the best control performance for this case. The aggressiveness of the controller is increased from Figure 7.1a to Figure 7.1d. Table 7.1 lists the IAE, ITAE, ISE, and ITSE for a range of decay ratios for this process. Note that QAD tuning results in the best overall performance without regard to **reliability** (i.e., the ability to maintain stable operation in the face of significant disturbances). Also, each of these statistics goes through a minimum as the decay ratio is increased. It should be emphasized that these statistics are used in academic research to compare the control performance for different controllers using dynamic process simulations, but are not usually used in industry.

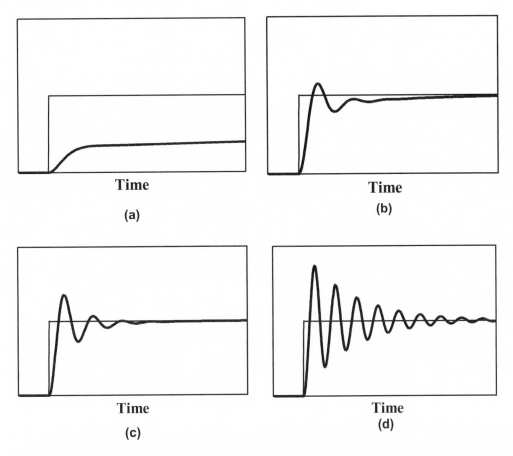

Figure 7.1   Control response for a setpoint change. (a) Controller tuned for sluggish response. (b) Controller tuned for 1/10 decay ratio. (c) Controller tuned for QAD. (d) Controller tuned for ringing response.

Table 7.1				
Several Performance Statistics as a Function of Decay Ratio				
Decay Ratio	IAE	ITAE	ISE	ITSE
1/1.5	39.6	1244	31.1	470
1/2.0	28.3	628	22.8	231
1/3.0	20.9	347	17.8	117
1/4.0	19.8	387	16.8	92.8
1/5.0	20.7	503	16.8	91.2
1/6.0	22.0	635	17.1	97.4
1/8.0	24.9	903	17.9	119
1/10.0	27.4	1141	18.8	145

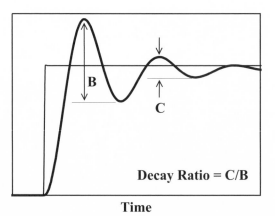

Time

Figure 7.2 A method for estimating the decay ratio using peak-to-valley measurements.

The classical definition of the decay ratio (Figure 5.5) is difficult to apply to the cases shown in Figures 7.1b and 7.1c because the oscillations are not symmetric about the setpoint. The decay ratio can be estimated using the difference between a peak and a valley (Figure 7.2). That is, the decay ratio can be calculated by the ratio of the peak-to-valley difference for two adjacent cycles. As a result, symmetric oscillations about the setpoint are not required to estimate the decay ratio from the closed-loop response to a setpoint change.

Industrial control performance is often assessed by the variability in the final products. The deviation from setpoint (σ) can be used as a measure of product variability and thus as a measure of control performance. Deviation from setpoint is defined as

$$\sigma = \sqrt{\frac{\sum_{i=1}^{N}[y_s(t_i) - y_{sp}]^2}{N}}$$

where $y_s(t_i)$ is the sampled controlled variable value at time equal to t_i and N is the number of samples. The smaller the deviation from setpoint, the better the control performance. Remember that this statistic is based on the error from setpoint while the standard deviation is based on the error from the average value of a set of data.

Most companies keep statistical process control (SPC) charts that track the laboratory analysis of final products, which are typically sampled one to three times daily. Figure 7.3 is an example of an industrial SPC chart. Note the upper and lower limits on the product composition. This chart shows control results for two different controllers for two different seven day periods. It is easy to see which controller performed better.

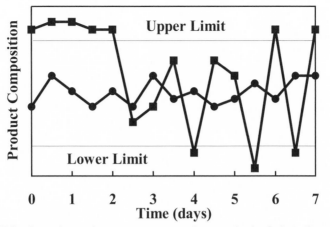

Figure 7.3 SPC chart based upon a seven day period of data for two different controllers on the same process.

7.3 Effect of Tuning Parameters on P-only Control

P-only controllers are used industrially for some pressure and level control loops. It was shown in Section 6.8 that a P-only controller increases the speed of the dynamic response of a process but does not change the order of the process. Because P-only control uses only one tuning parameter, K_c, it is the simplest form of PID control.

Example 7.1 Effect of K_c on Closed-Loop Dynamics for a FOPDT Process

Problem Statement. Determine the effect of controller gain, K_c, for a P-only controller applied to a FOPDT process. The transfer function for a FOPDT process is

$$G_p(s) = \frac{K_p e^{-\theta_p s}}{\tau_p s + 1} \qquad \text{A}$$

Solution. Using the first-order Padé approximation[1] for the deadtime term, $e^{-\theta_p s}$,

$$e^{-\theta_p s} \approx \frac{1 - \frac{1}{2}\theta_p s}{1 + \frac{1}{2}\theta_p s}$$

Substituting this into Equation A results in

$$G_p(s) = \frac{K_p(1 - \frac{1}{2}\theta_p s)}{(\tau_p s + 1)(1 + \frac{1}{2}\theta_p s)}$$

Then, using the closed-loop transfer function for a setpoint change (Equation 6.6) for P-only control and assuming $G_a(s) = G_s(s) = 1$ yields

$$\frac{Y(s)}{Y_{sp}(s)} = \frac{\dfrac{K_c K_p (1-\frac{1}{2}\theta_p s)}{(\tau_p s+1)(1+\frac{1}{2}\theta_p s)}}{\dfrac{K_c K_p (1-\frac{1}{2}\theta_p s)}{(\tau_p s+1)(1+\frac{1}{2}\theta_p s)} + 1}$$

Rearranging results in

$$\frac{Y(s)}{Y_{sp}(s)} = \frac{K_c K_p (1-\frac{1}{2}\theta_p s)}{\frac{1}{2}\tau_p\theta_p\, s^2 + [\tau_p +\frac{1}{2}\theta_p(1-K_c K_p)]s +1+ K_c K_p}$$

The poles of the transfer function determine the dynamic behavior of the closed-loop system. The poles of the previous closed-loop transfer function are the roots of the denominator and can be evaluated analytically using the quadratic formula, i.e.,.

$$p_1 = \frac{-(\tau_p +\frac{1}{2}\theta_p[1 -K_c K_p]) + \sqrt{(\tau_p +\frac{1}{2}\theta_p[1-K_c K_p])^2 - 2\tau_p \theta_p (1+K_c K_p)}}{\tau_p \theta_p}$$

B

$$p_2 = \frac{-(\tau_p +\frac{1}{2}\theta_p[1-K_c K_p]) - \sqrt{(\tau_p +\frac{1}{2}\theta_p[1-K_c K_p])^2 - 2\tau_p \theta_p (1+K_c K_p)}}{\tau_p \theta_p}$$

C

Figure 7.4 shows plots of the two poles, p_1 and p_2, on a complex plane (Section 4.5) as a function of K_c assuming that $K_p = 1$, $\tau_p = 1$, and $\theta_p = 0.5$, where the real portion of the pole is plotted on the x-axis and the imaginary portion on the y-axis. This plot is called a **root locus diagram** and graphically shows the effect of K_c on the dynamic characteristics of the feedback system. The arrows on the lines in Figure 7.4 indicate the direction of increasing values of K_c.

A root locus diagram is an analysis tool based on a specific theoretical framework with significant analytical capabilities. The theoretical development of the root locus diagram is beyond the scope of this text. On the other hand, root locus diagrams are used here as a convenient visual representation of the range of dynamic behavior resulting from feedback control. The root locus diagram is a plot in the complex plane of the poles of the characteristic equation of the closed-loop transfer function in which a parameter, usually a controller tuning parameter (e.g., K_c or τ_I), is varied over a range. By knowing the dynamic character indicated by the poles of a transfer function (Section 4.5), one can identify the transition from one type of dynamic behavior to another as the parameter of interest is varied. For example, point c in Figure 7.4 (K_c=0.35) indicates the boundary between overdamped and

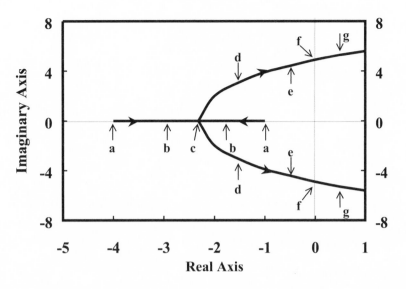

Figure 7.4   Root locus diagram for the results of Example 7.1.   A P-only controller applied to a FOPDT process (K_p=1; τ_p=1; θ_p=0.5) with a controller gain, K_c, that increases from points a to points g: (a) K_c=0, (b) K_c=0.30, (c) K_c=0.35, (d) K_c=1.0, (e) K_c =3.0, (f) K_c =5.0, (g) K_c=6.0.

underdamped behavior, and point f (K_c=5.0) represents the boundary between stable and unstable behavior.   The root locus diagram presented here is representative of a major portion of industrial process. While root locus diagrams are a convenient means to represent the dynamics of feedback control and assist in the fundamental understanding of feedback dynamics, they are not generally used industrially because their use requires process models, which are not generally available.

Between points a and c in Figure 7.4 (0 $< K_c <$ 0.35), the poles are real and negative, indicating overdamped dynamic behavior. Remember from Section 4.5 that real negative poles yield time domain solutions that involve exponential decay with time (e^{-at}). At point c (K_c = 0.35), the closed-loop system is critically damped since both poles are -2.32 and any increase in K_c results in oscillatory behavior. For the poles between points c and f (0.35 $< K_c <$ 5.0), the system is underdamped. The poles in this region are complex conjugate pairs (p_1 = a +$i\omega$ and p_2 = a - $i\omega$), which in the time domain result in terms of the form $e^{-at} \sin \omega t$. Since the real part of these complex conjugate poles is negative, damped oscillatory behavior is indicated. Moreover, the magnitude of the real portion of the complex conjugate (a) decreases as K_c is increased from 0.35 to 5, which indicates that the rate of damping of the oscillations is also decreasing. For the poles between points c and f, the magnitude of the imaginary part of the pole increases, indicating an increase in the oscillatory nature of the response. At point f (K_c = 5), sustained oscillations result. This marks the boundary between stable operation ($K_c <$ 5) and unstable operation ($K_c >$ 5) and is indicated as a vertical line in Figure 7.4. Poles to the right of this vertical line are said to lie in the right-half plane

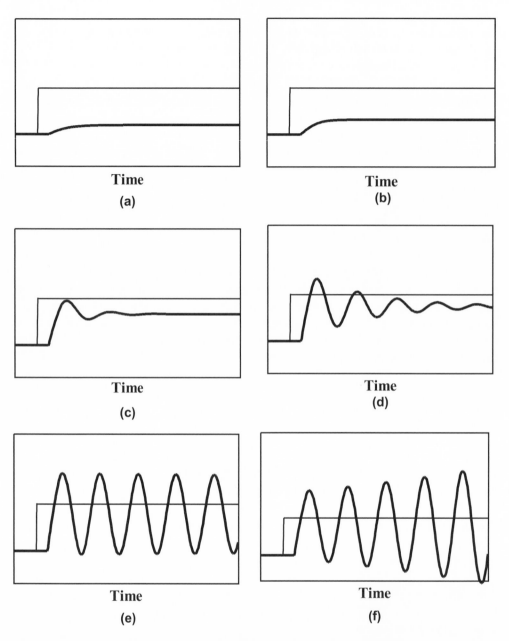

Figure 7.5 The response of a FOPDT process with a P-only controller to a setpoint change. (a) K_c**=0.25; (b)** K_c**=0.35; (c)** K_c**=1.0; (d)** K_c**=3.0; (e)** K_c**=5.0; (f)** K_c**=5.2.**

and represent unstable behavior. As K_c is increased above 5, the rate of exponential growth increases because the magnitude of the real part of the pole increases.

Figure 7.5 shows the time domain response of the FOPDT model (K_p=1; τ_p=1; θ_p=0.5) for several values of K_c (0.25, 0.35, 1.0, 3.0, 5.0, 5.2) for a setpoint change in y. The dynamic response of the closed-loop system corresponds to (a) sluggish behavior,

(b) critically damped, (c) oscillatory performance, (d) ringing, (e) sustained oscillations, and (f) unstable behavior. Note that as K_c increases, the system response becomes faster. Although this is a simple case, industrial control loops show the same general behavior; that is, **as the controller gain is increased, an open-loop overdamped process moves from overdamped behavior to critically damped to underdamped to ringing to sustained oscillations to unstable oscillations.** Therefore, for a P-only controller, determining whether a controller is tuned too aggressively (i.e., K_c is too large) or too sluggishly (i.e., K_c is too small) is relatively simple by comparing the dynamic response of the process to the sequence of dynamic behavior shown in Figure 7.5. If the dynamic response of the process is similar to Figure 7.5a, the value of K_c used in the P-only controller is probably too small. On the other hand, if the dynamic response is similar to one of the responses shown in Figures 7.5d-f, the value of K_c is too large and should be reduced.

Since the application of a P-only controller to the FOPDT model considered here results in a second-order closed-loop response, the closed-loop damping factor and time constant can be used to characterize the dynamic behavior of this system. Figure 7.6 shows the closed-loop damping factor and time constant for this system as functions of the controller gain, K_c. Note that the same modes of dynamic behavior that were observed in Figures 7.5a-f are shown in Figure 7.6a. In Figure 7.6b, the closed-loop second-order time constant is shown to decrease monotonically as the controller gain is increased.

♠

Example 7.2 Evaluation of the Effect of K_c on the Closed-Loop Dynamics of a P-Only Controller Applied to a Second-Order Process.

Problem Statement. Determine the effect of controller gain, K_c, for a P-only controller applied to a second-order process, assuming that the second-order process represents the combined effect of the actuator, process, and sensor.

Solution. Applying the characteristic equation (Equation 6.8) using a transfer function for a second-order process (Equation 5.14) and a P-only controller [$G_c(s)=K_c$] results in the following equation.

$$\frac{K_c K_p}{\tau_p^2 s^2 + 2\tau_p \zeta s + 1} + 1 = 0$$

Rearranging and transforming this equation into the standard form for a second-order process yields

$$\frac{\tau_p^2}{K_c K_p + 1} s^2 + \frac{2\tau_p \zeta}{K_c K_p + 1} s + 1 = 0$$

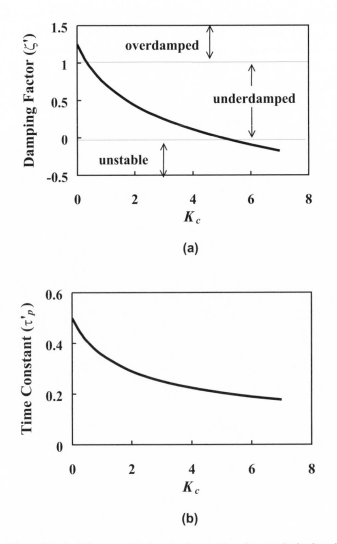

(a)

(b)

Figure 7.6 The effect of the controller gain on the dynamic behavior of a FOPDT process (K_p=1; τ_p=1; θ_p=0.5). (a) shows how the closed-loop damping factor changes with K_c and (b) shows how the closed-loop time constant varies with K_c.

Then, the closed-loop time constant (τ'_p) and the closed-loop damping factor (ζ') are given as

$$\tau'_p = \tau_p \sqrt{\frac{1}{K_c K_p + 1}}$$

$$\zeta' = \zeta \sqrt{\frac{1}{K_c K_p + 1}}$$

As K_cK_p is increased, both the closed-loop time constant and the closed-loop damping factor decrease. As K_cK_p is increased, the response of the closed-loop process becomes faster and, eventually, more oscillatory. But no matter how large the controller gain becomes, the response of the system remains stable (i.e., $\zeta' > 0$). Real processes become unstable if the process gain is sufficiently increased. Therefore, a second-order model without deadtime does not represent a real process for large values of K_cK_p.

♠

Example 7.3 Dynamics of a P-only Controller applied to a First-Order Process

Problem Statement. Analyze the dynamic behavior of a first-order process with a P-only controller.

Solution. Applying the characteristic equation (Equation 6.8) using the transfer function for a first-order process and $G_c(s)=K_c$ results in the following equation after rearranging.

$$\frac{\tau_p}{K_c K_p + 1} s + 1 = 0$$

This indicates that the closed-loop response remains first-order regardless of the value of K_c, and becomes faster (i.e., the time constant becomes smaller) as K_c is increased. This result indicates that the best approach is to operate at very large controller gains since the response becomes virtually instantaneous and the offset becomes negligibly small. If this situation existed for real processes, process control would be extremely simple. Unfortunately, this analysis does not apply to real processes because it is based on assuming that the process is described as a first-order system without deadtime. Even if a process, by itself, behaves as a first-order process, as K_c is increased and the response of the closed-loop system becomes faster, the dynamics of the actuator and sensor at some point become significant, and the process is no longer first order. More importantly, the first-order models for the actuator and sensors neglect deadtime because it is usually small compared to the time constant of the response for these systems. As K_c is increased, even a small amount of deadtime affects the dynamics of the system and leads to oscillatory behavior as in Example 7.1. **The analysis of a P-only controller applied to a first-order process is physically unrealistic in the extreme because no real process behaves as a first-order system without deadtime at large controller gains.** The analysis of a FOPDT model is much more realistic than even a high-order linear model without deadtime because of the sensitivity of feedback control to deadtime.

♠

7.4 Effect of Tuning Parameters for PI Control

PI controllers are the most commonly used form of PID controllers, accounting for over 90% of industrial PID applications. Tuning a PI controller involves setting the controller gain, K_c, and the reset time, τ_I. Proportional action increases the speed of the closed-loop response, and integral action ensures offset-free operation. As a result, combining proportional and integral action achieves the advantages of both approaches, but tuning a PI controller is more complicated because two tuning parameters must be specified. To better understand the effect of the PI tuning parameters, the following examples are presented to illustrate the individual effects of K_c and τ_I on a PI controller applied to a process represented by a FOPDT model.

Example 7.4 Evaluation of the Effect of K_c on the Closed-Loop Dynamics for a PI Controller applied to a FOPDT Model of a Process

Problem Statement. Analyze the effect of the controller gain on the dynamic behavior of a PI controller applied to a FOPDT model of a process. Assume that the reset time ($\tau_I = 1$) and the FOPDT parameters ($K_p = 1$; $\tau_p = 1$; $\theta_p = 0.5$) are constant. Assume that the FOPDT model represents the actuator, process, and sensor.

Solution. Substituting the transfer function of a general FOPDT model as the process and the transfer function of the controller,

$$G_c(s) = K_c\left(1 + \frac{1}{\tau_I s}\right)$$

into the characteristic equation for this system assuming $G_a(s) = G_s(s) = 1$ results in

$$\frac{K_c\left[1 + \dfrac{1}{\tau_I s}\right]K_p(1 - \frac{1}{2}\theta_p s)}{(\tau_p s + 1)(1 + \frac{1}{2}\theta_p s)} + 1 = 0 \qquad\qquad \mathbf{A}$$

using the Padé approximation for deadtime.

Figure 7.7 shows the root locus diagram of the characteristic equation for a range of K_c's for $\tau_I = 1.0$, $K_p = 1.0$, $\tau_p = 1.0$, and $\theta_p = 0.5$. Since the rearrangement of Equation A results in a cubic equation in s in the denominator, there are three poles for this closed-loop system. Using the parameter values, the characteristic equation for this system reduces to

$$\frac{1}{4}s^3 + (1.25 - \frac{1}{4}K_c)s^2 + (1 + \frac{3}{4}K_c)s + K_c = 0$$

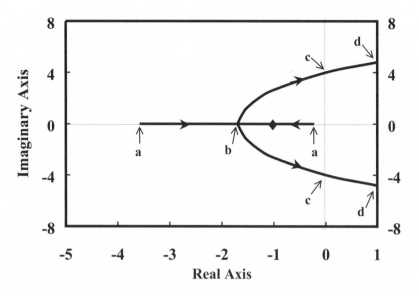

Figure 7.7 Root locus diagram for the results of Example 7.4. A PI controller applied to a FOPDT process (K_p=1; τ_p=1; θ_p=0.5; τ_I=1) with a controller gain, K_c, that increases from points a to points d: (a) K_c=0.2, (b) K_c=0.75, (c) K_c=4.0, (d) K_c=6.0.

As K_c is increased, the dynamic behavior goes from overdamped to critically damped to underdamped to sustained oscillations to unstable behavior, which is consistent with the results obtained in Example 7.1. One pole ($p_3 = -1.0$) remains invariant for the full range of controller gains and is denoted in Figure 7.7 by a diamond. Figure 7.8 plots the damping factor of the complex conjugate pair for this system as a function of K_c, which shows the transition from overdamped to unstable. The complex conjugate

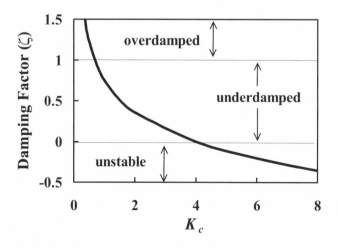

Figure 7.8 The effect of the controller gain on the damping factor for a PI controller applied to a FOPDT process (K_p=1; τ_p=1; θ_p=0.5, τ_I=1).

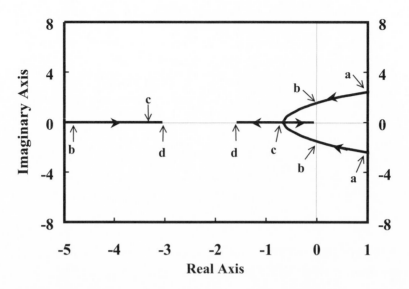

Figure 7.9 Root locus diagram for the results of Example 7.5. A PI controller applied to a FOPDT process (K_p=1; τ_p=1; θ_p=0.5, K_c=0.3) with a controller reset time, τ_I, that increases from points a to points d: (a) τ_I =0.04, (b) τ_I= 0.17, (c) τ_I= 0.9, (d) τ_I =4.0.

determines the oscillatory component of the dynamic response. By comparing Figures 7.8 and 7.6a, one can see that integral action causes the damping factor to be more sensitive to changes in K_c. The addition of integral action provides offset-free operation but produces a more sensitive closed-loop system. The closed-loop time constant for this system decreases with K_c in a similar fashion to the results shown in Figure 7.6b.

♠

Example 7.5 Evaluation of the Effect of τ_I on the Closed-Loop Dynamics for a PI Controller applied to a FOPDT Model of a Process

Problem Statement. Analyze the effect of the reset time on the dynamic behavior of a PI controller applied to a FOPDT model of a process. Assume that the controller gain (K_c = 0.3) and the FOPDT parameters (K_p = 1; τ_p = 1; θ_p = 0.5) are constant, and the combined effect of the actuator, process, and sensor is represented by the FOPDT model.

Solution. The closed-loop transfer function developed in Example 7.4 can be applied to this case. As in the previous example, solving for the roots of the characteristic equation requires the solution of a cubic equation. Figure 7.9 shows the poles for the closed-loop transfer function for a range of values of reset times from 0.04 to 4.0. In this case, as τ_I is increased, the dynamic behavior goes from unstable oscillations to

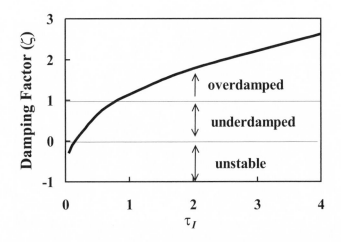

Figure 7.10 The effect of the controller reset time on the damping factor for a PI controller applied to a FOPDT process (K_p=1; τ_p=1; θ_p=0.5, K_c=0.3).

sustained oscillations to critically damped to overdamped. As the amount of integral action is increased (i.e., as τ_I is decreased), the dynamic behavior goes through the same sequence of phases as an increase in proportional action produced. Figure 7.10 shows the effect of τ_I on the damping factor of the complex conjugate pair for this system.

♠

Figure 7.11 shows the dynamic behavior of the same FOPDT process with a PI controller considered in Examples 7.4 and 7.5 with different amounts of proportional action. Figure 7.11b shows the results for a PI controller for which both K_c and τ_I were adjusted to provide a QAD response. In addition, the QAD tuning was modified by increasing K_c (Figure 7.11c) while keeping τ_I constant and by decreasing K_c (Figure 7.11a) while keeping τ_I constant. The increase in K_c results in ringing while the decrease in K_c results in sluggish behavior. Note that too much or too little proportional action results in longer settling times than the QAD tuned controller.

Figure 7.12 shows similar results for the effect of variations in τ_I. Figure 7.12b shows the results for QAD tuning and is the same result as shown in Figure 7.11b. A decrease in τ_I from QAD settings results in ringing (Figure 7.12c) and an increase results in a slow removal of offset (Figure 7.12a). By comparing Figures 7.11a and 7.12a, it can be seen that when K_c is too low, long rise times and sluggish behavior result, and when integral action is too low (i.e., τ_I is too large), offset elimination is slow. Therefore, determining that a PI controller has too little proportional or too little integral action is relatively straightforward. On the other hand, ringing from too much proportional action (Figure 7.11c) and ringing from too much integral action (Figure 7.12c) are quite similar; therefore, when controller

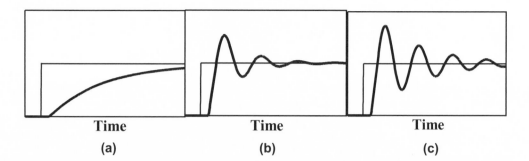

Figure 7.11 PI controller response for a FOPDT process with varying amounts of proportional action. (A) K_c **is too low. (B)** K_c **tuned for QAD. (C)** K_c **is too large.**

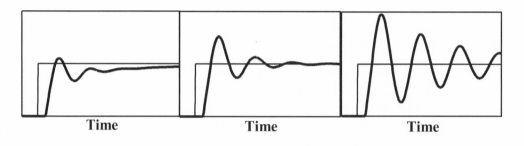

Figure 7.12 PI controller response for a FOPDT process with varying levels of integral action. (a) τ_I **is too large. (b)** τ_I **tuned for QAD. (c)** τ_I **is too small.**

ringing results, it is difficult to tell whether it is caused by excessive proportional action, excessive integral action, or both.

Figure 7.13 shows the controller output and controlled variables for a QAD tuned controller. Note that the controller output "lags" behind the controlled variable

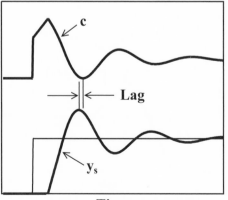

Figure 7.13 The lag between the controller output and controlled variable for a QAD tuned PI controller. c **is the controller output and** y_s **is the controlled variable value.**

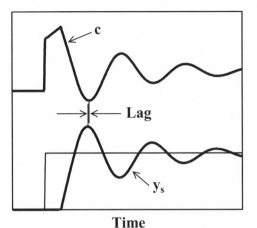
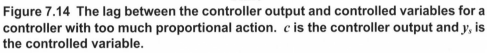

Figure 7.14 The lag between the controller output and controlled variables for a controller with too much proportional action. c **is the controller output and** y_s **is the controlled variable.**

for this case. The lag between the controlled variable and the controller output is discussed in more detail in Chapter 9. Figure 7.14 shows the same system with K_c increased by 25% and τ_I increased by a factor of 2 (i.e., the ringing is caused by too much proportional action). Note that the lag between the controlled variable and the controller output is significantly reduced. Excessive gain reduces the lag between the controlled variable and the controller output. Figure 7.15 shows the case in which K_c and τ_I are both reduced by a factor of 2 compared with the QAD settings. In this case, the lag increases significantly. Excessive integral action results in an increase in the lag of the system. **Therefore, the lag between the controller output and the controlled variable can be used to determine if a controlled process is ringing from too much proportional action or too much integral action.** If a controller is ringing and there is a small amount of lag between the controller output and the controlled variable, the ringing is probably caused by an excess amount of proportional action. On the other hand, if a controller is ringing and there is an appreciable amount

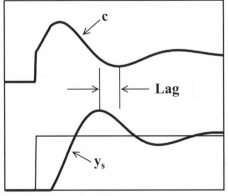

Figure 7.15 The lag between the controller output and controlled variable for a controller with too much integral action. c **is the controller output and** y_s **is the controlled variable value.**

of lag between the controller output and the controlled variable, the ringing is probably caused by an excessive amount of integral action. In the case in which there is an excessive amount of proportional and integral action, there should be some degree of lag between the controller output and the controlled variable, but when the integral is reduced, the response usually still exhibits some degree of ringing.

With proportional-only control action, the maximum c (controller output) occurs at the maximum deviation from setpoint, which corresponds to zero lag (i.e., **in-phase**). For integral-only control action, the maximum c occurs when the error from setpoint changes sign, which corresponds to a large lag.

7.5 Effect of Tuning Parameters on PID Control

PID controllers are used for certain temperature and composition control loops. Derivative action is the least understood and the least used mode in a PID controller, but can provide significant benefits in specific cases. Section 6.9 indicates that derivative action improves control performance for processes that have deadtime-to-time constant ratios greater than one. Since derivative action opposes the slope of the controlled variable, it reduces the oscillatory nature of the feedback response. The effect of proportional and integral action on the feedback behavior of a PID controller is similar to that observed for the PI controller studied in Examples 7.4 and 7.5.

Figure 7.16a shows the results of PID and PI control applied to a FOPDT process: ($K_p = 1$, $\tau_p = 1$, $\theta_p = 0.1$). Figure 7.16b shows the results of PID control and PI control applied to another FOPDT process with more deadtime: ($K_p = 1$, $\tau_p = 1$, $\theta_p = 2$). These results support the conclusion that derivative action is useful for processes that have large deadtime-to-time constant ratios. Figure 7.17 shows a case that has too much derivative action in the PID controller. Note that a

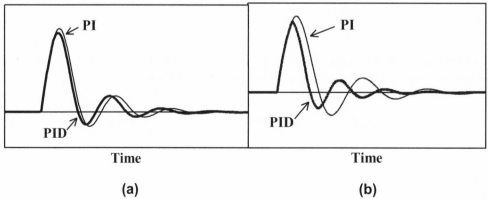

| (a) | (b) |

Figure 7.16 Comparison between a PI and PID controller for a process with (a) low deadtime and (b) large deadtime.

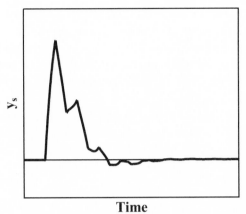

Figure 7.17 The control performance of a PID controller with too much derivative action.

"stair-step" feedback response indicates that too much derivative action is being used. The stair-step behavior is caused because, as the process moves toward the setpoint, excessive derivative action causes the process to stall or level out. After the process stalls, the proportional and integral action act on the process to move the controlled variable toward the setpoint. When this occurs, the derivative of the controlled variable builds up and the derivative action acts against it, causing the response to stall again, resulting the stair-step effect.

Example 7.6 Evaluation of the Effect of τ_D on the Closed-Loop Dynamics for a PID controller applied to a FOPDT Process

Problem Statement. Evaluate the effect of τ_D on the closed-loop dynamics of a PID controller ($K_c=1$; $\tau_I=2$) applied to a FOPDT process ($K_p = 1$; $\tau_p = 1$; $\theta_p = 2$).

Solution. Substituting the transfer function for a PID controller, i.e.,

$$G_c(s) = K_c\left[1+\frac{1}{\tau_I s}+\tau_D s\right]$$

and the transfer function for a FOPDT process model with the Padé approximation for deadtime into the characteristic equation (Equation 6.8) result in

$$K_c\left[1+\frac{1}{\tau_I s}+\tau_D s\right]\frac{K_p(1-\frac{1}{2}\theta_p s)}{(\tau_p s+1)(1+\frac{1}{2}\theta_p s)}+1=0$$

Substituting the controller and process parameters results in the following cubic equation in s after rearranging.

$$2(1-\tau_D)s^3+2(\tau_D+1)s^2+3s+1=0$$

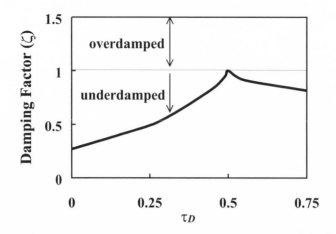

Figure 7.18 The effect of the controller derivative time on the damping factor for a PID controller applied to a FOPDT process (K_p=1; τ_p=1; θ_p=2, K_c=1; τ_I=2).

As τ_D is increased from 0 to 0.75, one of the poles of the characteristic equation, which is a real pole, changes from -0.4 to -6. The other two poles form a complex conjugate pair that determine the oscillatory nature of the closed-loop response. Figure 7.18 plots the damping factor for the complex conjugate pair as a function of the derivative time. As τ_D is increased from 0 to 0.5, the damping factor increases, indicating that the oscillatory nature of the system is reduced by the derivative action. On the other hand, as the derivative time is increased above 0.5, the oscillatory nature of the response increases. Derivative action reduces the oscillatory nature of the response up to a point, but, above that point, a further increase in τ_D increases oscillatory behavior, which corresponds to the results shown in Figure 7.17.

♠

7.6 Controller Tuning by Pole Placement

One way to tune a PID controller using transfer function process models is to use a pole-placement approach (also known as direct synthesis). For pole placement applied to PID tuning, the poles of the closed-loop response (i.e., the desired dynamic response of the closed-loop system) are specified, and the PID tuning parameters are then calculated. Tuning the control loop using pole placement specifies the closed-loop dynamics (e.g., by specifying the closed-loop time constant, τ'_p, and the damping factor, ζ'). Consider the characteristic equation for a first-order process with a PI controller, i.e.,

$$K_c \left[1 + \frac{1}{\tau_1 s} \right] \frac{K_p}{\tau_p s + 1} + 1 = 0$$

Rearranging into the standard form for a second-order equation results in

$$\frac{\tau_I \tau_p}{K_c K_p} s^2 + \tau_I \left[1 + \frac{1}{K_c K_p}\right] s + 1 = 0$$

Then, the closed-loop time constant and damping factor are given by

$$\tau'_p = \sqrt{\frac{\tau_I \tau_p}{K_c K_p}} \qquad\qquad 7.1$$

$$\zeta' = \frac{1}{2}\sqrt{\frac{\tau_I}{\tau_p}}\left[\sqrt{K_c K_p} + \frac{1}{\sqrt{K_c K_p}}\right] \qquad\qquad 7.2$$

Assume that we have specified the values of τ'_p and ζ' (i.e., the dynamic response of the closed-loop system). Specifying τ'_p and ζ' is, in effect, specifying the poles of the closed-loop response, which can be calculated directly by applying the quadratic formula to the following equation.

$$(\tau'_p)^2 s^2 + 2\tau'_p \zeta' s + 1 = 0$$

Solving Equations 7.1 and 7.2 simultaneously for K_c and τ_I yields

$$K_c = \frac{1}{K_p} F \qquad\qquad 7.3$$

$$\tau_I = \frac{(\tau'_p)^2}{\tau_p} F \qquad\qquad 7.4$$

where

$$F = \left[2\zeta'\frac{\tau_p}{\tau'_p} - 1\right] \qquad\qquad 7.5$$

F must be greater than zero to maintain proper values of K_c and τ_I. For a conservatively tuned controller ($\tau'_p = \tau_p$ and $\zeta'=1$), F is equal to 1. For an aggressively tuned controller ($\tau'_p = \tau_p/4$ and $\zeta'=0.5$), F is equal to 3. Therefore, F is an indication of the aggressiveness of the controller.

Example 7.7 Application of Pole Placement for Tuning a PI Controller

Problem Statement. Determine the PI controller settings for a first-order process $(K_p = 3; \tau_p = 10)$ if it is desired to obtain a closed-loop damping factor of 0.4 and a closed-loop time constant of 3.

Solution. From Equation 7.5, F is equal to 1.67 for this case. Then, using the value of K_p, K_c is calculated equal to 0.556. Likewise, τ_I is calculated directly as 1.50. The two closed-loop poles that correspond to a damping factor of 0.4 and a time constant of 3 are $(-.133 \pm 0.306\, i)$; therefore, specifying the closed-loop time constant and damping factor is equivalent to selecting the poles of the closed-loop response.

♠

Example 7.8 Application of Pole Placement for Tuning a PI Controller

Problem Statement. Determine the PI controller settings for a first-order process $(K_p = 3; \tau_p = 10)$ if it is desired to obtain a closed-loop damping factor of 0.4 and a closed-loop time constant of 10.

Solution. From Equation 7.5, F is equal to -0.2 for this case. The negative sign for F indicates that the specifications for τ'_p and ζ' were not consistent. For this case, to obtain a closed-loop damping factor of 0.4, the closed-loop time constant would be significantly smaller than τ_p. Therefore, when using this approach, consistent performance specification must be used because the values of τ'_p and ζ' are not completely independent.

♠

The concept of pole placement leads to the derivation of a general transfer function representation of a controller based on a specified closed-loop response and a transfer function for the process. Let us now assume that we want a specific second-order response for a first-order process. Then the closed-loop transfer function for setpoint changes (Equation 6.6) is set equal to a specified second-order transfer function, i.e.,

$$\frac{G_c(s)\dfrac{K_p}{\tau_p s+1}}{G_c(s)\dfrac{K_p}{\tau_p s+1}+1} = \frac{1}{(\tau'_p)^2 s^2 + 2\tau'_p \zeta' s+1}$$

Here τ'_p and ζ' are specified by the user to set the desired second-order response. Because an offset-free response is desired, the gain of the specified second-order response is one. Rearranging and solving for $G_c(s)$ yields

$$G_c(s) = \dfrac{\dfrac{1}{(\tau'_p)^2 s^2 + 2\tau'_p \zeta' s + 1}}{\dfrac{K_p}{\tau_p s + 1}\left[1 - \dfrac{1}{(\tau'_p)^2 s^2 + 2\tau'_p \zeta' s + 1}\right]}$$

Combining the two terms in the denominator and simplifying yields

$$G_c(s) = \dfrac{\tau_p s + 1}{K_p \tau'_p s\left(\tau'_p s + 2\zeta'\right)}$$

Since the formulation of the problem was based on a general unknown controller, the functional form of this controller does not correspond to a PID controller. Earlier in this section, it was demonstrated that a PI controller could, under certain circumstances, be tuned for a specified second-order closed-loop response. This general controller reduces to a PI controller under certain conditions. There are limits on the closed-loop performance specifications that one can choose when using a PID controller, and these limits correspond to the conditions necessary to transform this general controller into a PI controller.

Consider the problem of deriving a general controller, $G_c(s)$, for a general closed-loop performance specification, $S_{cl}(s)$. Once again, we can equate the closed-loop transfer function for a setpoint change (Equation 6.6) to the use-selected performance specification:

$$\dfrac{G_c(s)G_p(s)}{G_c(s)G_p(s) + 1} = S_{cl}(s)$$

Rearranging and solving for $G_c(s)$ yields

$$G_c(s) = \dfrac{S_{cl}(s)}{G_p(s)[1 - S_{cl}(s)]} \qquad \text{7.6}$$

Example 7.9 Derivation of a General Controller

Problem statement. Derive the transfer function for the controller for a first-order process that provides a specified first-order response.

Solution. In this case,

$$S_{cl}(s) = \frac{1}{\tau'_p s + 1}$$

Applying Equation 7.6 results in

$$G_c(s) = \frac{\dfrac{1}{\tau'_p s + 1}}{\dfrac{K_p}{\tau_p s + 1}\left[1 - \dfrac{1}{\tau'_p s + 1}\right]}$$

Simplifying,

$$G_c(s) = \frac{\tau_p s + 1}{K_p \tau'_p s} = \frac{\tau_p}{K_p \tau'_p}\left[1 + \frac{1}{\tau_p s}\right]$$

which is equivalent to a PI controller with the following settings.

$$K_c = \frac{\tau_p}{K_p \tau'_p} \qquad \tau_I = \tau_p$$

As the specifications for the closed-loop response become more aggressive (i.e., the ratio of τ_p to τ'_p becomes larger), K_c increases proportionally. If the reset time is less than the process time constant, an oscillatory response results. In addition, the general controller can also be reduced to a P-only controller by placing restrictions on the values of τ'_p. ♠

Overview. Pole placement provides an important perspective for PID controller tuning and provides an important insight: closed-loop performance specifications must be consistent. Moreover, the concept of pole placement can be extended to a methodology for developing a general controller (i.e., not limited to a PID controller) that is designed to meet the preset performance specifications.

While pole placement provides useful insights and fundamental understanding, it is not usually used to tune PID controllers in the CPI or to develop general controllers that are applied in the CPI. This results primarily because process models are not generally available, and the time required to develop a process model far exceeds the time required to tune a loop using other methods. In addition, PID controllers are a standard function on control computers whereas implementation of a general controller requires the development and implementation of custom software. Sections 7.8-7.15 present the recommended procedure for tuning PID controllers in the CPI.

7.7 Classical Tuning Methods

A wide range of PID tuning methods has been proposed. This section considers two of the earliest methods: Cohen and Coon method[2] and the Ziegler-Nichols method[3]. In addition, a more recent technique (the Cianione and Marlin method[4]) is also considered.

Each of these methods is based upon a preset tuning criterion. As a result, even when they are used industrially, they are usually used as initial controller settings. Then control engineers use their knowledge of the nonlinearity and the severity of disturbances for the particular control loop in question to adjust the controller tuning to meet the proper compromise between reliability and performance for that particular loop. The methods presented here can be used for initial controller settings (Example 7.11) using process knowledge. These methods also provide insight into the relative tuning of P-only, PI, and PID controllers. The next section presents the recommended tuning procedure for industrial control loops.

Table 7.2

Cohen and Coon PID Settings Based on a FOPDT Model

Controller	K_c	τ_I	τ_D
P-only	$\dfrac{1}{K_p}\dfrac{\tau_p}{\theta_p}\left(1+\dfrac{\theta_p}{3\tau_p}\right)$		
PI	$\dfrac{1}{K_p}\dfrac{\tau_p}{\theta_p}\left[0.9+\dfrac{\theta_p}{12\tau_p}\right]$	$\dfrac{\theta_p\left[30+\dfrac{3\theta_p}{\tau_p}\right]}{9+20\left[\dfrac{\theta_p}{\tau_p}\right]}$	
PID	$\dfrac{1}{K_p}\dfrac{\tau_p}{\theta_p}\left(\dfrac{16+3\dfrac{\theta_p}{\tau_p}}{12}\right)$	$\dfrac{\theta_p\left[32+\dfrac{6\theta_p}{\tau_p}\right]}{13+8\left[\dfrac{\theta_p}{\tau_p}\right]}$	$\dfrac{4\theta_p}{11+2\left[\dfrac{\theta_p}{\tau_p}\right]}$

Cohen and Coon Method. The Cohen and Coon approach[2] assumes that a FOPDT model of the process (i.e., the combined effect of the actuator, process, and sensor) is available. The Cohen and Coon parameters for P-only, PI, and PID controllers are listed in Table 7.2. These results are based on a combination of QAD, minimum ISE, and minimum offset tuning for a FOPDT process model.

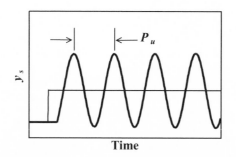

Figure 7.19 The controlled variable for a ZN ultimate test, i.e., operation at sustained oscillations with a P-only controller.

Ziegler-Nichols Tuning. Ziegler-Nichols (**ZN**) tuning[4] uses experimental measurements of the **ultimate gain**, K_u, and the **ultimate period**, P_u to calculate the controller settings. The ultimate parameters are obtained by operating a P-only controller under sustained oscillations and measuring the period of the oscillations and noting the gain of the P-only controller. The procedure is as follows

1. Turn off integral and derivative action to give a P-only controller.
2. Increase K_c until oscillations are sustained for a relatively small setpoint change (Figure 7.19).
3. K_u is the P-only controller gain that results in the sustained oscillations.
4. P_u is the period of the sustained oscillations (Figure 7.19).
5. Calculate the controller settings using Table 7.3.

Table 7.3 Ziegler-Nichols PID Settings			
Controller	K_c	τ_I	τ_D
P	$0.5 K_u$	—	—
PI	$0.45 K_u$	$P_u/1.2$	—
PID	$0.6 K_u$	$P_u/2$	$P_u/8$

The Ziegler-Nichols settings are based on a QAD tuned response. A QAD response for a second-order process corresponds to a damping factor (ζ) of 0.22 with a 50% overshoot. According to these settings, PID uses a 33% larger K_c than a corresponding PI controller and a P-only controller uses a K_c that is 10% larger than a corresponding PI controller.

Cianione and Marlin Tuning. The Cianione and Marlin controller tuning approach[4] uses FOPDT parameters along with dimensionless tuning parameter plots to determine the controller settings. This approach was derived using the closed-loop transfer function to develop dimensionless relationships that can be used to select tuning parameters. Consider a FOPDT model of the process

$$G_a(s)G_p(s)G_s(s) = G'_p(s) \cong \frac{K_p e^{-\theta_p s}}{\tau_p s + 1} \qquad 7.7$$

Then, the closed-loop transfer function for disturbance rejection is given by

$$\frac{Y(s)}{D(s)} = \frac{G_d(s)}{G_c(s)G'_p(s) + 1} = \frac{G_d(s)}{K_c\left(1 + \dfrac{1}{\tau_I s} + \tau_D s\right)\left(\dfrac{K_p e^{-\theta_p s}}{\tau_p s + 1}\right) + 1} \qquad 7.8$$

The following relationship can be used to convert this equation into dimensionless form

$$\bar{s} = s(\theta_p + \tau_p) \qquad 7.9$$

Eliminating s from the closed-loop transfer function for disturbance rejection yields

$$\frac{Y(\bar{s})}{D(\bar{s})} = \frac{G_d(\bar{s})}{1 + K_c K_p\left(1 + \dfrac{1}{\tau_I \bar{s}/(\theta_p + \tau_p)} + \dfrac{\tau_D \bar{s}}{\theta_p + \tau_p}\right)\left(\dfrac{e^{-\theta_p \bar{s}/(\theta_p + \tau_p)}}{1 + \dfrac{\tau_p \bar{s}}{\theta_p + \tau_p}}\right)} \qquad 7.10$$

Note that

$$\frac{\tau_p}{(\theta_p + \tau_p)} = 1 - \frac{\theta_p}{\theta_p + \tau_p} \qquad 7.11$$

and $[\theta_p/(\theta_p + \tau_p)]$ is referred to as the **fractional deadtime**[5]. Therefore, the process model is converted from six parameters $(K_c, \tau_I, \tau_D, K_p, \tau_p, \theta_p)$ into four parameters $[K_p K_c, \theta_p/(\theta_p + \tau_p), \tau_I/(\theta_p + \tau_p), \tau_D/(\theta_p + \tau_p)]$. Using this approach, dimensionless forms of the tuning parameters are obtained, i.e.,

$$\text{Dimensionless Gain} = K_c K_p$$

$$\text{Dimensionless Reset Time} = \frac{\tau_I}{\theta_p + \tau_p}$$

$$\text{Dimensionless Derivative Time} = \frac{\tau_D}{\theta_p + \tau_p}$$

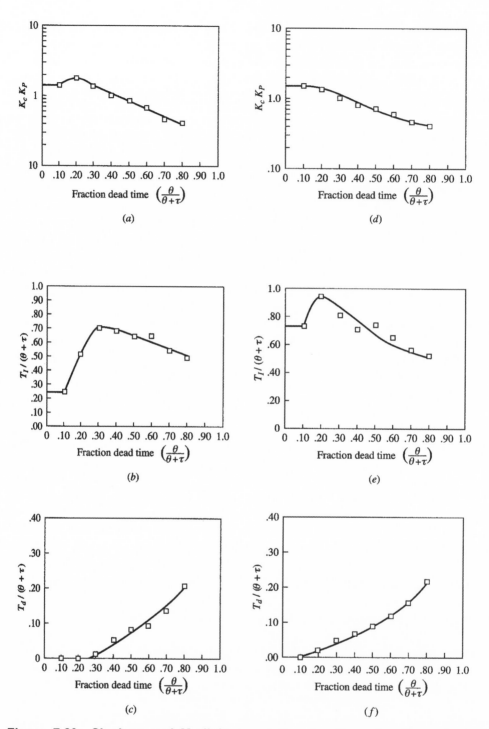

Figure 7.20   Cianione and Marlin's correlation functions for dimensionless tuning constants. For disturbance rejection (a) K_c (b) τ_I (c) τ_D . For setpoint changes   (d) K_c (e) τ_I (f) τ_D . Note that T_d and T_I in this figure correspond to τ_D and τ_I. This figure is reprinted with permission from McGraw-Hill Publishing Co.

Cianione and Marlin[5] correlations for the dimensionless gain, reset time and derivative time as a function of the fractional deadtime are shown in Figure 7.20. These correlations are based on tuning for minimum IAE performance considering ±25% error in the model parameters (i.e., variations in K_p, τ_p, and θ_p). These results show some of the differences between tuning for setpoint changes and disturbance rejection. The correlations for disturbances and setpoint changes are similar, but the dimensionless reset time for disturbances is quite different at low values of fractional deadtime $[\theta_p / (\theta_p + \tau_p) < 0.3]$. Note that more integral action is used for disturbances than for setpoint changes. There is some difference between the dimensionless derivative time at low fractional deadtime for setpoint tracking and disturbance rejection.

While the FOPDT model is flexible enough to reasonably model a wide range of real processes, developing accurate FOPDT models for industrial processes can be a difficult and time-consuming process. The assumption of ±25% parameter uncertainty is arbitrary. Relatively linear processes with low disturbance levels can be expected to result in FOPDT parameters that are much more uniform than ±25%. On the other hand, highly nonlinear processes are expected to result in FOPDT parameter variations well in excess of ±25% for major disturbance upsets. While this approach is certainly interesting and provides insight into the PID tuning process, it should be viewed as providing only initial estimates of tuning parameters.

Overview. The Cohen and Coon method and the Cianione and Marlin method require a FOPDT process model, which is difficult and time consuming to develop. The settings for these tuning methods are based on a tuning criterion that may not be consistent with the requirements of the control loop under consideration.

The Ziegler-Nichols method requires an ultimate test that can unnecessarily upset the process. It does have the advantage that it is a direct measurement on the process. But once again, the controller settings are based on QAD, and nonlinear processes using these settings can lead to ringing or unstable behavior. A very large number of tuning methods have been proposed. Each of these methods suffers from one or more of the same limitations as the three tuning methods presented here.

Example 7.10 Comparison of Classical Tuning Methods

Problem Statement. Determine the PID controller setting for the Cohen and Coon and the Cianione and Marlin methods using the FOPDT model determined in Example 5.7. Use the Cianione and Marlin settings for disturbance rejection.

Solution. Using the FOPDT model parameters from Example 5.7 ($K_p = -1.5$; $\tau_p = 1.43$; $\theta_p = 2.43$) in the equations from Table 7.2 results in the following PID settings.

$$K_c = 0.690$$
$$\tau_I = 3.86$$
$$\tau_D = 0.675$$

For the Cianione and Marlin method, the fractional deadtime is the independent variable for the dimensionless correlations and has a value of 0.63 for this case. The values of the dimensionless tuning parameters can be read directly from Figure 7.20 (i.e., the dimensionless gain is 0.55, the dimensionless reset time is 0.60, and the dimensionless derivative time is 0.12). Using the definitions of the dimensionless tuning parameters to solve for the PID tuning parameters results in

$$K_c = 0.367$$
$$\tau_I = 2.32$$
$$\tau_D = 0.463$$

Note that the Cohen and Coon settings have almost twice the controller gain as the Cianione and Marlin settings. Also, note that even though the process gain is negative, the controller gain is specified as a positive number because the effect of the negative gain is addressed by whether a direct-acting or a reverse-acting controller is used.

♠

Example 7.11 Initial Controller Tuning Estimates

Problem Statement.   Using the Cianione and Marlin method, develop initial controller settings for a PI controller applied to a temperature control loop on a steam-heated heat exchanger, which operates under regulatory control. By observing the process operation, it has been estimated that the process gain is approximately 0.01 °F·hr/lb. The response time of the process has been estimated equal to approximately 10 minutes. Further, by observing the process, it has been determined that the amount of deadtime in the system is relatively small, i.e., the process responds quickly to changes in the flow rate of steam to the heat exchanger.

Solution. Figure 7.20d, assuming a fractional deadtime equal to approximately zero, yields a value of $K_c K_p$ of 1.3. This results in a controller gain of 130 lb/hr·°F. From Figure 7.20e, the dimensionless reset time is 0.73. From the response time, the process time constant is estimated as 2.5 minutes. Neglecting the deadtime, the reset time is calculated as 1.83 minutes.

♠

7.8 Recommended Approach to Controller Tuning

The following procedure is recommended for tuning PID control loops.

1. Select the tuning criterion for the control loop. The tuning criterion depends on how the control loops affect the overall process objectives and can involve applying a compromise between performance and reliability (Sections 7.9 and 7.10).

2. Apply filtering to the sensor reading. Sensor filtering (Section 7.11) reduces the effect of sensor noise on the variability in the controlled variable but introduces lag to the feedback system, which is detrimental to control performance. Therefore, filtering should be applied carefully.

3. Determine if the control loop is a fast- or slow-responding control loop. The distinction between fast- and slow-responding control loops is concerned with the closed-loop response time of the system. If a set of controller settings can be tested using setpoint changes in a reasonable period of time (e.g., less than 10 minutes), the process is a fast-responding control loop. If not, it is a slow-responding control loop.

4. For fast-responding control loops, apply field tuning (Section 7.12).

5. For slow-responding control loops, apply the ATV-based tuning procedure (Section 7.13).

Table 7.4			
Typical Tuning Parameters for Common Loops in the CPI			
Loop Type	**PB**	$\tau_I(s)$	$\tau_D(s)$
Flow Controller	100 - 500%	0.2 - 2.0	0
Gas Pressure Controller	1 - 15%	5-100	0
Liquid Pressure controller	100 - 500%	0.2 - 2.0	0
Level Controller	5 - 50%	5 - 60	0
Temperature Controller	10 - 50%	40 - 4000	30 - 2000*
Composition Controller	100 - 1000%	100 - 5000	30 - 4000*
*τ_D should always be smaller than τ_I.			

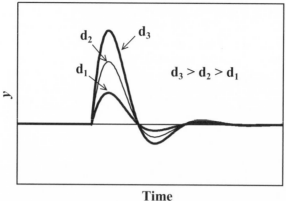

Figure 7.21 The effect of disturbance magnitude on the dynamic response of a linear process.

Table 7.4 lists ranges of PID tuning parameters for flow controllers, gas pressure controllers, liquid pressure controllers, level controllers, temperature controllers, and composition controllers.   Note that the gain is expressed in proportional band (Section 6.3) and the larger the *PB*, the lower the value of K_c. Flow control loops are actually a special case for tuning.   Because of the sustained oscillations that result about the setpoint (Figure 6.15), flow control loops are usually tuned with more integral action than proportional action compared with most other control loops, which is consistent with Table 7.4.

7.9 Controller Reliability

Controller reliability is concerned with whether a controller remains stable during severe upsets.   Consider the closed-loop transfer function for disturbance rejection (Equation 6.7):

$$\frac{Y(s)}{D(s)} = \frac{G_d(s)}{G_c(s)\,G_a(s)\,G_p(s)\,G_s(s) + 1}$$

For a particular set of controller tuning parameters and fixed process models (i.e., $G_a(s)$, $G_p(s)$, and $G_s(s)$ remain unchanged), this equation indicates that the dynamic behavior of the process, i.e., the roots of the characteristic equation, are fixed and remain unchanged regardless of the size or the character of the disturbance. Figure 7.21 shows the dynamic behavior of a linear process subjected to several different levels of a disturbance. Note that the larger disturbances produce larger deviations, but the dynamic behavior (decay ratio and time constant) remains unchanged.

It is well known from industrial experience that certain controlled processes, which are stable under normal conditions, can become unstable when subjected to

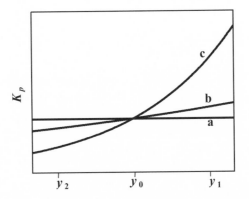

Figure 7.22 Process gain as a function of the controlled variable for (a) a linear process, (b) a moderately nonlinear process, and (c) a severely nonlinear process.

severe upsets, thus indicating that the dynamic characteristics of feedback processes are **not** always constant. Let's examine this apparent discrepancy.

Up until this point we have assumed that the dynamic characteristics of the process, sensor, and actuator all remain constant as the operating conditions change. In fact, these models can change with operating conditions. For example, all real processes exhibit some degree of nonlinearity. Figure 7.22 shows the process gain, K_p, as a function of the controlled variable, y, for (a) a linear process, (b) a moderately nonlinear process, and (c) a severely nonlinear process. For a very narrow region near y_0, even the severely nonlinear process behaves relatively linearly (i.e., exhibits a relatively constant process gain). The farther removed from y_0, the larger the resulting gain change.

Feed flow rate changes can cause process time constant and deadtime changes, which represent another type of process nonlinearity. For the CST thermal mixer (Section 3.5), the process time constant, τ_p, is given by

$$\tau_p = \frac{\rho V_r}{F_1 + F_2}$$

This equation shows that the process time constant varies inversely with the total feed rate to the process. Also, Section 5.7 shows transport deadtime varies inversely with flow rate.

To demonstrate the effect of process nonlinearity combined with disturbances, consider the application of a PI controller to the endothermic CSTR presented in Example 3.4. This process exhibits changes in both process gain and time constant as the operating conditions change. A PI controller was tuned for a setpoint change using the QAD tuning criterion. Table 7.5 shows the results of this system for different magnitude upsets in the inlet feed composition, ΔC_{A_o}.

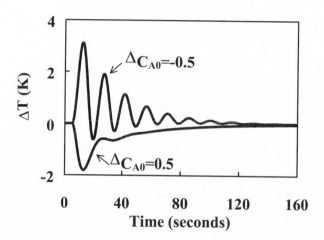

Figure 7.23 The effect of the disturbance direction on the dynamic behavior of the endothermic CSTR.

The decay ratio decreases sharply with an increase in the disturbance magnitude, which leads to ringing for a large reduction in the feed composition. For the largest feed composition upset, unstable closed-loop dynamics result. Therefore, for this nonlinear process, as the disturbance magnitude increases, the dynamic behavior of the process goes through the same sequence of phases that was observed for the controller tuning in previous sections. Remember from Figure 7.21, decay ratio remains constant irrespective of the disturbance size for a linear system

Figure 7.23 shows the closed-loop results for the endothermic CSTR for a positive and negative 0.5 gmole/L feed composition upset. The negative feed composition change results in ringing while the positive change results in sluggish behavior. The effect of process nonlinearity and disturbance magnitude on dynamic behavior can be understood by recognizing that a disturbance moves the controlled variable from its normal operating range, resulting in process gain and time constant changes. These changes to the process parameters cause changes in the dynamic behavior of the closed-loop process. Consider the severely nonlinear process gain depicted in Figure 7.22. A disturbance enters this process and results in an increase in y from y_0 to y_1, where the process gain is over twice the gain at y_0. Likewise, if a different disturbance moves the process to y_2, the process gain would be less than half the original process gain at y_0. Increasing the process gain by a factor of two can cause a properly tuned controller to exhibit ringing while a reduction in the process gain by a factor of two can cause a properly tuned controller to become sluggish. As a result, a nonlinear process can exhibit severe ringing or instability and, at other times, behave in a very sluggish manner depending upon the type, magnitude, and direction of the disturbance. **A process is highly nonlinear when a control system with constant controller settings applied to the process exhibits ringing and, at other times, exhibits sluggish behavior.**

Table 7.5	
Effect of Disturbance Magnitude on Closed-Loop Dynamic Behavior	
$\Delta C_{A_0} \, (gmole \, / \, L)$	**Decay Ratio**
-0.1	1/2.50
-0.2	1/2.35
-0.3	1/2.18
-0.4	1/1.94
-0.5	1/1.64
-0.6	1/1.34
-0.7	1/0.91 (unstable)

Table 7.6 shows the effect of disturbance magnitude on the dynamic behavior of the endothermic CSTR with a reaction rate expression with a lower activation energy ($E/R = 2000$ K). The lower activation energy results in a more linear process than the original endothermic CSTR. For the case with a reduced activation energy, the decay ratio also depends on the magnitude of the disturbance, but is a much weaker function of the disturbance magnitude. In fact, the PI controller remains stable for the full range of changes in the magnitude of the disturbance.

Table 7.6	
Effect of Disturbance Magnitude on closed-loop Dynamic Behavior ($E/R = 2000$ K)	
$\Delta C_{A_0} \, (gmole \, / \, l)$	**Decay Ratio**
-0.1	1/3.05
-0.2	1/2.88
-0.3	1/2.65
-0.4	1/2.48
-0.5	1/2.28
-0.6	1/2.12
-0.7	1/2.01

This analysis shows that **the combined effect of the nonlinearity of a process and the type and severity of disturbances affects the reliability of a controller**. If a controller proves unreliable, reducing the aggressiveness of the controller usually improves its reliability but at the expense of control performance.

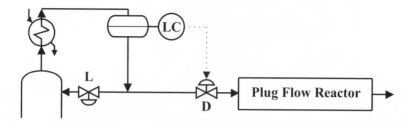

Figure 7.24 Schematic of an accumulator of a distillation column feeding a plug flow reactor.

Many times, selecting the proper tuning parameters for a controller is a compromise between reliability and performance.

7.10 Selection of Tuning Criterion

The first step in tuning a controller is selecting the tuning criterion (Section 7.2). It was shown in Section 7.6 that one cannot arbitrarily select the desired dynamic response for a PID controller. For example, choosing the closed-loop damping factor limits the closed-loop time constant that is attainable. In fact, Figure 7.5 shows that as the controller gain of the P-only controller is increased, the closed-loop time constant and the damping factor decrease in a consistent manner. The same general behavior occurs for PI and PID controllers. Therefore, selecting the damping factor, in effect, determines the closed-loop time constant for a particular control loop. As a result, the aggressiveness of a controller can be specified in terms of the damping factor of the closed-loop system. Because the decay ratio, which is directly related to the damping factor (see Equation 5.16), is relatively easy to estimate from a response (see Figure 7.2), it is the preferred form for the tuning criterion.

Selecting the tuning criterion for a control loop is equivalent to determining the aggressiveness of the feedback controller. If one were to choose a critically damped response as the tuning criterion, a controller with a low aggressiveness would result.   On the other hand, QAD tuning criterion corresponds to a very aggressively-tuned controller.

The first factor that should be considered when choosing the proper tuning criterion is how the control loop affects the overall objectives of the process. Consider the accumulator of a distillation column that feeds a plug flow reactor (Figure 7.24). Tight level control for the accumulator results in sharp changes in the feed to the reactor. Sharp, frequent changes to the feed rate to the plug flow reactor significantly upset the operation of the reactor because the residence time of the reactor is directly related to the feed rate, and changes in the residence time affect the

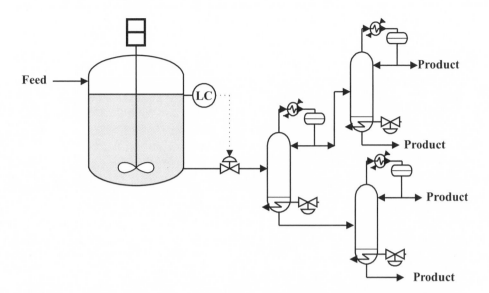

Figure 7.25 Schematic of a level in a CSTR that feeds a separation train.

degree of conversion. On the other hand, if the level controller for the accumulator is tuned for sluggish performance, the changes in the feed rate to the reactor are much more gradual and smooth, allowing for better operation of the reactor. From an overall process point of view, maintaining smooth operation of the reactor is much more economically important than maintaining tight level control in the accumulator; therefore, a critically damped or overdamped tuning criterion is the proper choice for the level controller on the accumulator in this example.

As another example of how the overall process objective can affect the selection of the tuning criterion, consider the CSTR and separation train shown in Figure 7.25.   If the level controller for the CSTR is tuned loosely, the CSTR level can change significantly. Because the production rates of the various products is related to the residence time in the reactor, large variations in the CSTR level directly affect the product distribution produced by the reactor. The resulting composition changes in the stream leaving the CSTR represent major upsets for the composition controllers for the distillation columns that comprise the separation train. Even though tight level control for the CSTR causes short term variations in the feed to the first column, these upsets are much easier to handle than composition changes; therefore, considering the overall process objectives, a tuning criterion corresponding to tight level control should be chosen for the level controller on the CSTR. From these two examples, it should be clear that it is important to consider how a control loop affects the overall process when selecting its tuning criterion.

If consideration of the overall process objectives do not place a limit on the aggressiveness of the tuning criterion or if the overall process objectives dictate that minimum variability in the controlled variable of the loop in question is desirable, the selection of the tuning criterion should be based on a compromise

between performance and reliability. From the previous section, it was shown that process nonlinearity and disturbances determine the reliability of a controller. If a process is highly nonlinear and subject to large disturbances, controller reliability will likely be a problem, and a more conservative tuning criterion should be selected (e.g., a critically damped response). On the other hand, if the process is relatively linear and the disturbances are relatively mild, a more aggressive tuning criterion should be selected (e.g., a 1/6 decay ratio). Therefore, **when control engineers are faced with choosing a tuning criterion that is a compromise between performance and reliability, they must use their knowledge of the process to evaluate the relative nonlinearity of the process and the relative degree of severity of the disturbances.**

Even though Table 7.1 shows that QAD provides the best overall performance in terms of errors from setpoint, many companies are reluctant to have their control engineers tune even well-behaved control loops for QAD because of the 50% overshoot associated with QAD and because QAD is too close to the onset of instability. In addition, since QAD causes significant variation in the manipulated variable levels, QAD can result in unduly upsetting other parts of the process. For these reasons, it is probably better to tune well-behaved loops for decay ratios of 1/6 to 1/8. For a process that is more nonlinear with more severe disturbances 1/10 amplitude damping or a critically damped response is more appropriate. In extreme cases, an overdamped tuning criterion may be the proper choice. From Figure 7.5b, the controller gain for critically damped performance is 0.35, and it is approximately 1.0 for a controller tuned for a 1/6 decay ratio; therefore, the range in the tuning parameters from a 1/6 decay ratio to critically damped is relatively large. **No single tuning criterion works effectively for all control loops because the process nonlinearity, disturbance type and magnitude, and operational objectives must all be considered when choosing the proper tuning criterion, and these factors change from control loop to control loop.**

7.11 Tuning the Filter on Sensor Readings

Sensor readings should usually be filtered to reduce the influence of sensor noise on feedback control performance, as demonstrated in Section 6.6. Filtering, however, adds lag to the closed-loop response (Example 6.8). In certain cases, tuning a filter on a sensor can involve balancing the benefits of reducing the noise against the detrimental effects of adding lag to the overall process. In other cases, if possible, the time constant of the filter should be significantly smaller than the other dominant time constants in the actuator/process/sensor system so that filtering does not slow down the response of the system.

It is usually more convenient to use the filter time (i.e., the time constant of the first-order filter), τ_f, to specify the amount of filtering applied to a sensor reading. In this manner, the time constant of the filter can be directly compared to the time constants of the actuator, process, and sensor to determine whether it affects the closed-loop dynamics. The filter factor, f, and the cycle time for applying the filter, Δt_f, can be used to calculate the filter time constant by the following equation.

$$\tau_f = \Delta t_f \left[\frac{1}{f} - 1 \right]$$

For most DCSs, sensor readings are updated 5 or 6 times per second (i.e., Δt_f is 0.16 to 0.2 s). For a filter time constant of 3 s, the filter factor is equal to 0.06; therefore, relatively extensive sensor filtering can result for most sensors using high-frequency updating by a DCS.

The amount of sensor filtering required is dependent on the amount of noise on the reading. For example, a reading from a thermocouple is expected to require more filtering than a reading from an RTD, which has an order of magnitude smaller repeatability (Table 2.3), for the same application. From an examination of Table 2.3, one can see that a properly functioning sensor usually has a relatively small amount of noise. As a result, most flow, level, pressure and temperature sensors can be filtered effectively using a filter time constant of 3 to 5 s, which does not normally affect the closed-loop dynamics. Composition analyzer readings from GCs are updated so infrequently that filtering is usually not used for them. On the other hand, if composition measurements are available at a sufficiently high frequency, filtering can be used effectively.

In certain cases, the filtering of a noisy sensor is required. Noisy sensors present a challenge. A nuclear-based level sensor, a pressure sensor located too close to a 90° elbow in a line, or an orifice flow meter located immediately downstream of a control valve are examples of noisy sensors. For these cases, tuning the filter is a compromise between removing the noise from the sensor reading and adding lag to the closed-loop response when one is forced to use a noisy sensor reading.

7.12 Tuning Fast-Responding Control Loops

Fast-Responding Loops. For fast-responding loops, such as flow control and pressure control loops, the simplest and quickest tuning method available is field tuning, which is based upon a trial-and-error selection of tuning parameters. Some level and temperature loops also behave as fast-responding control loops. A fast-responding control loop is defined here as a control loop that has a closed-loop response time of 10 minutes or less. Since these processes respond quickly, trial-and-error tuning is effective. It is usually easier to field tune a fast-responding loop rather than identify FOPDT parameters, use initial tuning parameters from a chosen tuning method, and adjust the tuning to meet the selected tuning criterion. The recommended procedure for field tuning, assuming that the tuning criterion has been selected and the sensor reading filtered, follows.

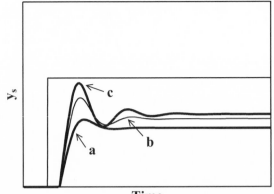

Time

Figure 7.26 Selection of K$_c$ during field tuning (a) Results for initial value of K$_c$ (b) Results for an increase in K$_c$ (c) Results for final value of K$_c$ (1/6 decay ratio).

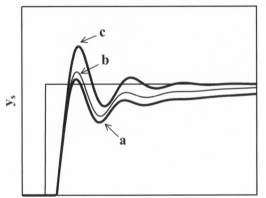

Time

Figure 7.27 Selection of τ$_I$ during field tuning (a) Results for initial value of τ$_I$ (b) Results for a decrease in τ$_I$ (c) Results for the final value of τ$_I$ (1/6 decay ratio).

1. Turn off the derivative action ($\tau_D = 0$) and the integral action ($\tau_I \rightarrow \infty$).

2. Use an initial estimate of K_c , e.g., $K_c = \dfrac{1}{2K_p}$. Estimate K_p from process knowledge.

3. Using setpoint changes, increase K_c in small increments until the response meets the tuning criterion. (See Figure 7.26, which is based upon a 1/6 decay ratio). For tuning a P-only controller, the tuning procedure is completed.

4. Decrease K_c by 10%.

5. Use an initial value of τ_I , i.e., $\tau_I \cong 5\tau_p$. Estimate τ_p from process knowledge.

6. Decrease τ_I until offset is eliminated and the tuning criterion is met for setpoint changes. (See Figure 7.27, which is also based upon a 1/6 decay ratio).

7. Check to ensure that adequate levels of proportional and integral action are being used.

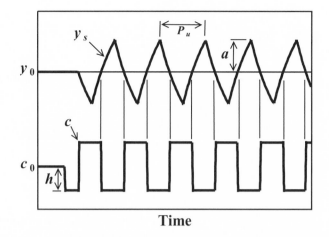

Figure 7.28 Graphical representation of an ATV test.

PID controllers, which are not usually required for fast-responding processes, are discussed in Section 7.14

7.13 Tuning Slow-Responding Control Loops

Slow-Responding Processes. For slow-responding loops (e.g., certain temperature and composition control loops), field tuning can be a time-consuming procedure that leads to less than satisfactory results. Step test results can be used to generate FOPDT models and tuning parameters can be calculated from a variety of techniques. This approach suffers from the fact that it takes approximately the open-loop response time of the process to implement a step test and during that time, measured and unmeasured disturbances can affect the process, thus corrupting the results from the step test. In addition, it is unlikely that the tuning approach selected is based on the proper tuning criterion.   Because of model mismatch and the likely selection of an inappropriate tuning criterion, significant adjustments to the tuning are usually required.

The **ATV**[6] (autotune variation) method determines the ultimate gain and period in a manner similar to that of the ultimate method, but ATV tests can be implemented without unduly upsetting the process. Controller settings are calculated, and the controller is then tuned online to meet the selected tuning criterion.

Figure 7.28 graphically demonstrates the ATV method. The user selects h, the relay height used or the change in the manipulated variable applied. The chosen value of h should be small enough that the process is not unnecessarily upset, yet large enough that the resulting amplitude, a, can be accurately measured.

To initiate an ATV test, the process should be at or near steady-state conditions, c_0 and y_0. Next, the controller output is set to $c_0 + h$ (or $c_0 - h$) until y deviates noticeably from y_0. At that point, the controller output is set to $c_0 - h$ (or $c_0 + h$), which turns the process back toward y_0. Then, each time y crosses y_0, the controller output is switched from $c_0 + h$ to $c_0 - h$ or vice versa. This process is also referred to as a relay feedback experiment. A standing wave is established after 3 to 4 cycles; therefore, the values of a and the ultimate period, P_u, can be measured directly and the ATV test is concluded. The **ultimate controller gain**, K_u, is calculated by

$$K_u = \frac{4h}{\pi a} \qquad\qquad 7.12$$

The **ultimate period** is obtained directly from the ATV test (see Figure 7.28). K_u and P_u can be used in one of several tuning schemes. One tuning approach is the Ziegler-Nichols (ZN) ultimate settings (Table 7.3). Consider the ZN settings for a PI controller:

$$K_c^{ZN} = 0.45\,K_u$$
$$\tau_I^{ZN} = P_u / 1.2$$

ZN settings are fairly aggressive and can lead to ringing behavior for nonlinear processes due to the relatively small value of τ_I (i.e., large integral action).

Another tuning approach that was developed for processes that behave like an integrator plus deadtime system is the Tyreus and Luyben (TL) settings[7]:

$$K_c^{TL} = 0.31\,K_u$$
$$\tau_I^{TL} = P_u / 0.45$$

The TL settings are less aggressive with considerably less integral action than the ZN settings. The TL settings are recommended for more sluggish processes that are well represented as integrator plus deadtime for a good portion of its step test (e.g., a sluggish distillation column). After the ZN or TL settings are calculated, they may require on-line tuning, particularly for the ZN settings to meet the desired tuning criterion (e.g., 1/6 decay ratio or critical damping). For example, the ZN settings are tuned on-line as follows:

$$K_c = K_u^{ZN} / F_T \qquad\qquad 7.13$$
$$\tau_I = \tau_I^{ZN} \times F_T$$

by adjusting F_T on-line. As F_T is increased, K_c decreases while τ_I increases by the same proportion (detuning). The tuning factor, F_T, can be adjusted to meet the performance requirements for each individual application. Therefore, on-line tuning has been reduced to a one-dimensional search for the proper level of controller

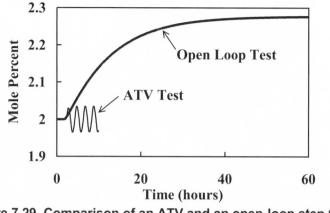

Figure 7.29 Comparison of an ATV and an open-loop step test.

aggressiveness for a PI controller. If the controller is too aggressive, F_T is increased; if the controller is too sluggish, F_T is decreased.

The procedure based on ATV identification with on-line tuning is applicable to PI controllers. For certain cases, after this procedure has been applied, it will be evident that the proper balance between proportional and integral action has not been found, e.g., if offset elimination is slow. In these cases, adjustments in the relative amount of proportional or integral action may be required. For example, if the TL settings were used and not enough integral action resulted, the 0.45 factor in the TL settings for integral action (i.e., P_u /0.45) could be increased to speed up offset elimination. Figures 7.11 and 7.12 can be helpful in determining if not enough proportional action or not enough integral action is being used.

Consider the application of an ATV test to a dynamic simulator of a C_3 (propylene/propane) splitter. Figure 7.29 shows an ATV test and an open-loop step test on the same time scale for the bottom product composition control loop. Note that the four cycles of the ATV test require 6-8 hours while the open-loop test requires in excess of 60 hours. The ATV results were used with TL settings and the results for three different tuning factors are shown in Figure 7.30.

In certain cases, plant operations do not allow ATV tests applied to their processes. In such cases for slow-responding loops, an approach similar to the one used in Example 7.11 is recommended for obtaining the initial controller settings. That is, using process knowledge, one can make crude estimates of FOPDT model parameters and use either the Cohen and Coon or Cianione and Marlin method as the initial controller settings. Then, Equation 7.13 can be applied to fine tune the settings to meet the tuning criterion specification. The control results obtained using this approach are usually inferior to those from ATV-based tuning.

Summarizing, identifying the ultimate controller gain and ultimate period of a slow-responding loop using the ATV method is relatively fast, providing a "snap shot" of the process without unduly upsetting the system. In addition, the on-line tuning

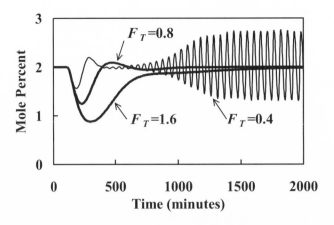

Figure 7.30 Effect of F_T on dynamic response.

procedure provides a systematic method of selecting the proper degree of controller aggressiveness. Therefore, the ATV test with on-line tuning represents an industrially relevant means of attaining high quality controller tuning for loops with large response times.

Example 7.12   Example of ATV Identification and On-line Tuning

Problem Statement. Apply ATV identification with on-line tuning to a PI controller applied to the CST composition mixer process given in Example 3.2. Tune for a 1/6 decay ratio.

Solution. Figure 7.31 shows an ATV test using a value of h equal to 0.5 kg/s applied to the specified value of F_1. From Figure 7.31, the values of a and P_u are

$$a = 0.107 \text{ gmoles/L}$$

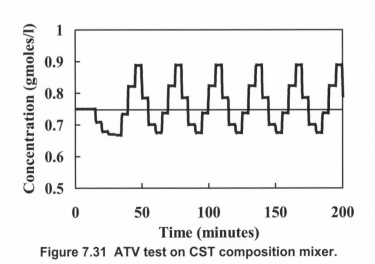

Figure 7.31 ATV test on CST composition mixer.

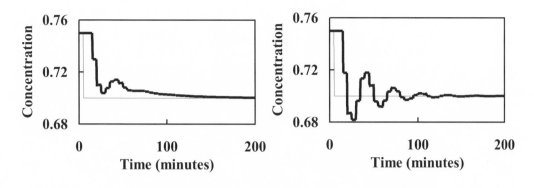

(a)   **(b)**

Figure 7.32 Dynamic response for the CST composition mixer for different tuning factors. (a) F_T=0.75 (b) F_T=0.5.

$$P_u = 30 \text{ min}$$

Since y_s is not symmetric about y_0, an average value of a is computed. Then, using Equation 7.12 results in

$$K_u = 5.96 \text{ (kg/s) /(gmole/L)}$$

Then, the ZN settings are

$$K_c^{ZN} = 2.68 \text{ (kg/s) / (gmole/L)}$$

$$\tau_I^{ZN} = 25 \text{ min}$$

Figures 7.32 shows the closed-loop results for a setpoint change in the product composition for F_T equal to 0.75 and 0.5, respectively. For F_T equal to 0.75 (Figure 7.32a), the decay ratio is 1/12 and for F_T equal to 0.5 (Figure 7.32b) the decay ratio is 1/2.6; therefore, the tuning factor for a decay ratio of 1/6 is between 0.5 and 0.75. In fact, for a decay ratio of 1/6, F_T is equal to 0.61. In this case, because the oscillations are not always symmetric about the setpoint, the decay ratio can be determined based upon adjacent peak to valley heights. Figure 7.33 shows the control performance for the tuned controller for a step change in feed composition for stream 1 from 0.5 to 0.55 gmole/L. The results shown in Figure 7.33 indicate that, since the oscillations are not symmetric about the setpoint and the offset is removed slowly, not enough integral action was applied. The results shown in Figure 7.34 correspond to a 30% reduction in the reset time. Note that the oscillations are much more symmetric about the setpoint.

♠

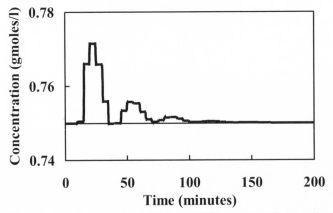

Figure 7.33 Control performance for the CST composition mixer for a feed composition upset.

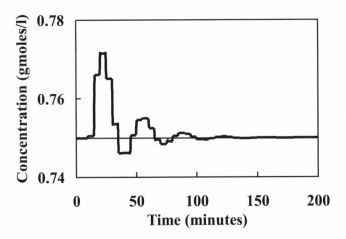

Figure 7.34 Control performance for the CST composition mixer for a feed composition upset with 30% additional integral action.

7.14 PID Tuning

The tuning of PID controllers applied to slow-responding processes is less systematic than tuning PI controllers since the on-line tuning procedure (Section 7.13) is not generally effective for PID controllers. That is, applying a tuning factor, F_T, to the derivative time and tuning a PID controller by adjusting only F_T does not, in general, lead to a well-tuned PID controller. The recommended procedure for tuning PID controllers is as follows

1. Tune a PI controller using ATV identification with on-line tuning. Make sure that the proper balance between proportional and integral action is used. It may be necessary to reduce τ_I to produce symmetric oscillations about the new setpoint.

2. Add derivative action and tune τ_D for minimum response time for a setpoint change. Initially set τ_D equal to $P_u/8$ where P_u comes from the ATV test.

3. Since the application of step 2 moves the dynamic response toward critically damped behavior, increase K_c and τ_D by the same factor until the desired dynamic response is obtained.

4. Check the response to ensure that the correct level of integral action is being used.

Example 7.13 PID Tuning Example

Problem Statement. Apply the proposed PID tuning procedure to tune a PID controller applied to a FOPDT process ($K_p = 1$, $\tau_p = 1$, $\theta_p = 2$) for a 1/4 decay ratio.

Solution. An ATV test was applied to a simulation of this FOPDT process and the amplitude of the resulting standing wave was 0.0859 with an ultimate period of 5.2 for a relay height (h) of 0.1. The TL settings were applied because of the deadtime-to-time constant ratio of the process, and the online tuning factor was adjusted until a 1/4 decay ratio was obtained for a setpoint change from 0.0 to 1.0, resulting in F_T equal to 0.58. It was observed that oscillations in y_s were not symmetric about the setpoint, indicating that inadequate integral action was being applied. The value of τ_I was reduced by 60%, which resulted in proper integral action. Next, derivative action was added and τ_D was set equal to $P_u/8$. The resulting controller provided a decay ratio of 1/6. Then K_c and τ_D were both increased by 10% yielding QAD performance. When the PID controller performance was compared with the PI controller, the PID controller provided 50% less overshoot and a 40% shorter settling time than the corresponding PI controller tuned for QAD.

♠

7.15 Tuning Level Controllers

Level Controller Tuning. If a level control process is fast responding, then field tuning is effective. If the level control process is relatively slow responding, it can be helpful to use the following approach to select the initial settings for the level controller. Marlin[8] developed closed-form solutions for the dynamic behavior of PI and P-only control of level in a constant cross-section tank. He used these expressions to derive analytical expressions for the tuning parameters that result in a **critically damped response** for the closed-loop level control process:

$$K_c = \left. \frac{-F'_{MAX}}{L'_{max}} \right\} \; P-only \; control \qquad\qquad \textbf{7.14}$$

$$K_c = \left. \begin{array}{l} \dfrac{-0.736\, F'_{MAX}}{L'_{MAX}} \\[2em] \tau_I = \dfrac{4A_c\, \rho}{-K_c} \end{array} \right\} PI\ control \qquad\qquad \textbf{7.15}$$

where A_c is the cross-sectional area of the tank, ρ is the density of the liquid, F'_{MAX} is the maximum expected step change in the feed rate to the tank, and L'_{MAX} is the maximum level change that F'_{MAX} should cause under feedback conditions.

These tuning relations can be used for both tight level control and loose level control depending upon the selection of L'_{MAX}. If L'_{MAX} is selected to correspond to about a 2% level change, it represents tight level control and K_c has a correspondingly high value. On the other hand, if L'_{MAX} is selected to correspond to a 20% level change, it represents quite loose level control and K_c is correspondingly lower.

This analysis is based on an idealized model of the level of a tank and does not consider sensor or actuator dynamics and does not consider that horizontal cylindrical tanks do not have a constant cross-section. For these reasons, it is recommended that Equation 7.14 and 7.15 be used as initial estimates of the tuning parameters and that an on-line tuning factor, F_T, be used to tune for the desired level control performance:

$$K'_c = K_c / F_T$$
$$\tau'_I = \tau_I \times F_T$$

Example 7.14   Calculation of Initial Tuning Parameters for a Level Controller

Problem Statement. Consider level control in a horizontal cylindrical tank 6 feet in diameter and 20 feet long. Normally, the feed rate to the tank is 10,000 pounds per hour of a dilute aqueous solution. Feed rate step changes are normally within the range of ± 10% of the normal feed rate. The setpoint for the level is usually 20%. The pressure taps for the level indicator are located at the top and bottom of the tank. Determine the tuning parameters for a PI controller that maintain the level within ±5% of setpoint based upon Equation 7.15 for ±10% feed rate changes.

Solution. By geometric analysis, the width of the liquid level in the tank at 20% full is 4.8 feet; therefore, the cross-sectional area is 96 ft^2. Using the density of water,

$$F'_{MAX} = (0.1)(10{,}000\ lb/h)\left(\frac{h}{60\,min}\right) = 16.67\ lb/min$$

$$K_c = \frac{-0.736(1000\,lb/h)}{5\%} = -147.4\ \frac{lb/h}{\%}$$

$$\tau_I = \frac{(4)\,(96\,ft^2)(62.4\ lb\ /\ ft^3)(6\,ft\ /\ 100\%)}{(147.4\dfrac{lb\ /\ h}{\%})(\dfrac{h}{60\,min})} = 585\,min$$

♠

7.16 Control Interval

The PID control results presented so far have been based on a continuous application of the controller. The digital application of feedback control is applied at discrete points in time, i.e., the controller is periodically called and the resulting control action implemented. DCSs use sequential microprocessors that perform control calculations for a large number of control loops. Typical control loops are executed every 0.5 to 1.0 seconds for regulatory loops and 30 to 120 seconds for supervisory loops. The time between control applications is the control interval, Δt. PID control is applied industrially on DCSs using digital formulas, which are applied at discrete control intervals (Equations 6.17 to 6.20).

Consider a QAD tuned continuous PI controller applied to a FOPDT process ($K_p = 1$, $\tau_p = 1$, $\theta_p = 0.5$) resulting in the response labeled continuous in Figure 7.35. Applying the same PI controller settings using a DCS with a control interval of 0.5 results in unstable behavior. Reduction of the controller gain by 60% is required to restore stability ($\Delta t = 0.5$ in Figure 7.35) at the cost of longer settling times.

As a general rule[9], **the control interval should be selected such that**

$$\Delta t \ \leq \ \mathbf{0.05}\,(\theta_p + \tau_p) \qquad\qquad \textbf{7.16}$$

to obtain control performance approaching that of continuous control for which θ_p and τ_p are the FOPDT model parameters of the process. For Δt above this limit, the control performance deteriorates as Δt is increased. For Δt below this limit, no significant improvement in control performance results as Δt is decreased. Equation 7.16 only indicates if control performance is improved by reducing Δt.

For feedback control using an on-line GC, the control interval is set by the cycle time for the analyzer updates (typically 3-10 minutes). No advantage is gained by applying control action more frequently than the GC updates since new information on the process response is available only when the GC updates. Based on Equation 7.16, for a 5 minute analyzer delay for an analyzer applied to a column with an open-loop time constant of 5 hours, the control performance is not improved by reducing the analyzer delay. On the other hand, for a 5 minute analyzer delay for an analyzer applied to a column with an open-loop time constant of 30 minutes, the control performance is expected to improve if the analyzer delay were reduced.   For sensors that provide continuous readings (e.g., temperature sensor), the maximum

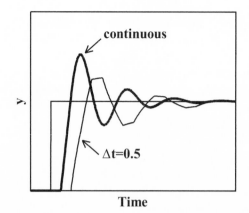

Figure 7.35 Comparison between a continuous PI controller and a PI controller applied each 0.5 time units.

recommended control interval is typically equal to one sensor time constant. For level, pressure, and flow loops, sensor dynamics do not usually present a significant constraint for the choice of the control interval.

Example 7.15 Estimation of the Control Interval

Problem Statement. Estimate the maximum control interval that can be used on the process studied in Example 5.7 without affecting the control performance.

Solution. From the results of Example 5.7, θ_p=2.43 and τ_p=1.43. Applying Equation 7.16 yields Δt <0.193; therefore, if the control interval is less than 0.193, the control performance should be equivalent to the continuous application of feedback control. ♠

7.17 Summary

One of the major responsibilities of a process control engineer is PID controller tuning, which is generally a compromise between controller performance and controller reliability with consideration given to the operational objectives of the process. Control performance is measured by the error from setpoint while reliability is determined by the severity of the disturbances that a controller is able to absorb effectively without becoming unstable. The control engineer should consider the combined effect of process nonlinearity, the severity of disturbances, and the operational objectives of the process when selecting the tuning criterion (e.g. 1/6 decay ratio or critically damped in the extremes) for a particular control loop.

As the amount of proportional action or integral action is increased, the dynamic behavior of a feedback system can change from overdamped to critically damped to oscillatory to ringing to sustained oscillations to unstable. As the amount of derivative action is increased, the damping rate increases and the rate of oscillations decreases.

Classical tuning methods based on one preset tuning criterion, e.g., QAD or minimum IAE can result in control loops that are excessively aggressive or excessively sluggish, depending on the combined effect of process nonlinearity and disturbance severity for a particular process.

The recommended tuning procedure is to first determine the tuning criterion based upon an analysis of the process nonlinearity, disturbance severity, and process objectives. Next, adjust the degree of filtering applied to the measured value of the controlled variable. Then, if the process is fast acting (e.g., flow or pressure control loops), a field tuning procedure is used to match the closed-loop performance to the selected tuning criterion. If the process is slow responding, ATV identification of the ultimate controller gain and period followed by online tuning to attain closed-loop performance consistent with the selected tuning criterion is recommended.

7.18 Additional Terminology

ATV - autotune variation; a relay feedback experiment designed to measure the ultimate controller gain and ultimate period of a control loop.
Cohen and Coon tuning - control settings for P-only, PI, and PID controllers based on a minimum IAE tuning criterion using FOPDT process models.
Controller performance - a measure of the error from setpoint.
Controller reliability - a measure of how well a controller stays in service. It can be quantified by the maximum severity of a disturbance that a control loop can handle and remain in service.
F_T - the on-line tuning factor for PI controller tuning.
Fractional deadtime - $\theta_p / (\theta_p + \tau_p)$

IAE - integral absolute error.
ISE - integral squared error.
ITAE - integral time absolute error.
ITSE - integral time squared error.
In-phase - y_s is in-phase with c when the peaks or valleys for y_s and c both occur at the same point in time.
K_u - the ultimate controller gain of a loop, i.e., the controller gain for a P-only controller that causes sustained oscillations.
P_u - the period of sustained oscillations using a P-only control.
Quarter amplitude damping (QAD) - a decay ratio of 1/4.
Reliability - the ability of a controlled process to remain stable when subjected to severe disturbances.
Ringing - oscillatory behavior with low amplitude damping (e.g., a decay ratio of 1/1.5).

Root locus diagram - a plot of the real and imaginary components of the poles of a closed-loop transfer function as a function of the controller tuning parameters.
Ultimate controller gain - the gain of a P-only controller that corresponds to sustained oscillations.
Ultimate period - the period of sustained oscillations for a P-only controller.
Ziegler-Nichols (ZN) tuning - controller settings for P-only, PI, or PID controllers using K_u and P_u which is based upon a QAD tuning criterion.

7.19 References

1. Stephanopoulos, G., *Chemical Process Control*, Prentice-Hall, Inc., p. 215 (1984).

2. Cohen, G.H. and G.A. Coon, "Theoretical Considerations of Retarded Control", *Trans ASME*, Vol. 75, p. 827 (1953).

3. Ziegler, J.G. and N.B. Nichols, "Optimum Settings for Automatic Controllers", *Trans ASME*, Vol. 64, p. 759 (1942).

4. Marlin, T.E., *Process Control*, McGraw-Hill, p. 300 (1995).

5. Cianione, R. and T.E. Marlin, "Tune Controllers to Meet Plant Objectives", *Control*, Vol. 5, p. 50 (1992).

6. Astrom, K.J. and T. Hagglund, *Automatic Tuning of PID Controllers,* Instrument Society of America, p. 233 (1998).

7. Tyreus, B.D. and W.L. Luyben, "Tuning PI Controllers for Integrator/Deadtime Processes", *Ind. Eng. Chem. Res.*, Vol. 31, p. 2625 (1992).

8. Marlin, T.E., *Process Control*, McGraw-Hill, p. 588-590 (1995).

9. Marlin, T.E., Process Control, McGraw-Hill, p. 393 (1995).

7.20 Preliminary Questions

7.1 List several commonly used tuning objectives and explain why they cannot be simultaneously met.

7.2 How is using a minimum IAE tuning criterion different from using a minimum ITAE tuning criterion?

7.3 How is using a minimum IAE tuning criterion different from using a minimum ISE tuning criterion?

7.4 Why is using a decay ratio a convenient tuning criterion for tuning PID control loops?

7.5 Explain what a statistical process control chart is and how it can be used to assess control performance.

7.6 How do many companies track the variability of the products that they produce?

7.7 From a process control point of view, why is it better to use the standard deviation from the setpoint instead of the standard deviation as a measure of variability for a controller?

7.8 For a process that is open-loop overdamped, how do the poles of the closed-loop response change as the controller gain is increased for a P-only controller?

7.9 Define a root locus diagram and explain what it shows.

7.10 Where is a critically damped response located on a root locus diagram?

7.11 Where is a response with sustained oscillations located on a root locus diagram?

7.12 For a plot of the closed-loop damping factor versus the controller gain, what point corresponds to critically damped behavior?

7.13 For a plot of the closed-loop damping factor versus the controller gain, what point corresponds to sustained oscillations?

7.14 Why does a first-order process model without deadtime not adequately represent the closed-loop behavior of a process with an aggressively tuned controller?

7.15 For a PI controller, how does the reset time affect the aggressiveness of the controller?

7.16 How are the dynamic responses of a PI and a P-only controller alike? How are they different?

7.17 Consider a PI controller. How can you tell if there is too little proportional action? How can you tell if there is too little integral action?

7.18 Consider a PI controller that results in ringing. How can you tell if there is too much proportional action or too much integral action?

7.19 How does the derivative time of a PID controller affect the closed-loop damping factor?

7.20 How does one determine if too much derivative action is used in a PID controller?

7.21 How is control performance affected by the size of the control interval?

7.22 How is pole placement used to tune a PID controller?

7.23 How can one specify a general feedback controller, which is not necessarily a PID type controller, to attain a prescribed feedback behavior.

7.24 What knowledge about the process is necessary to apply the Cohen and Coon tuning method?

7.25 What knowledge about the process is necessary to apply the Ziegler-Nichols tuning method?

7.26 How are the dynamics of the sensor and actuator related to the process models used in the Cohen and Coon method?

7.27 What information about the process is required to use the Cianione and Marlin tuning method?

7.28 Why are the classical tuning methods presented in Section 7.7 not recommended for tuning industrial control loops?

7.29 Why does a linear process model not explain the controller reliability limitations of industrial processes?

7.30 How does process nonlinearity affect the dynamic character of the closed-loop response?

7.31 How do disturbances affect the dynamic character of the closed-loop response?

7.32 If a control loop exhibits ringing and, at other times, sluggish behavior with the same controller settings, what process characteristic does this represent?

7.33 What factors determine the tuning criterion for a control loop?

7.34 In general, how can the overall process objectives affect the choice of the tuning criterion of a control loop in the process?

7.35 Explain in your own words how controllers are tuned when one must make a tradeoff between performance and reliability.

7.36 From Table 7.1, it is clear that QAD tuning provides the best performance. Why are industrial control loops not normally tuned for QAD behavior?

7.37 Why is filtering of the sensor reading applied before tuning of a PID controller is started?

7.38 How is the filter on a sensor reading tuned?

7.39 What determines whether one should use field tuning or ATV-based tuning?

7.40 What determines whether a process is fast responding or slow responding?

7.41 What tuning procedure should be applied to fast-responding processes?

7.42 What is an ATV test and how is it used to tune a controller?

7.43 Why should one use an ATV test for tuning a slow-responding process?

7.44 How does the PI-control tuning factor, F_T, affect the closed-loop dynamics?

7.45 To apply Equation 7.15 for tuning of a level controller, what two terms must be selected before this equation can be applied?

7.21 Analytical Questions and Exercises

7.46 Develop a root locus plot for a P-only controller applied to a second-order process (K_p=2, τ_p=3, ζ=2). Why does this root locus diagram not represent a real process?

7.47 Develop a root locus plot for a P-only controller applied to a second-order process (K_p=1, τ_p=1, ζ=1.5). Why does this root locus diagram not represent a real process?

7.48 Develop a root locus plot for a P-only controller applied to a second-order process (K_p=0.5, τ_p=10, ζ=5). Why does this root locus diagram not represent a real process?

7.49 Develop a root locus plot for a P-only controller applied to a second-order process (K_p=10, τ_p=6, ζ=10). Why does this root locus diagram not represent a real process?

7.50 Develop a root locus plot for a PI controller (τ_I=3) applied to a first-order process (K_p=2, τ_p=3) for which the controller gain is varied. Why does this root locus diagram not represent a real process?

7.51 Develop a root locus plot for a PI controller (τ_I=2) applied to a first-order process (K_p=1, τ_p=3) for which the controller gain is varied. Why does this root locus diagram not represent a real process?

7.52 Develop a root locus plot for a PI controller (τ_I=1) applied to a first-order process (K_p=10, τ_p=3) for which the controller gain is varied. Why does this root locus diagram not represent a real process?

7.53 Develop a root locus plot for a PI controller (τ_I=0.5) applied to a first-order process (K_p=0.5, τ_p=3) for which the controller gain is varied. Why does this root locus diagram not represent a real process?

7.54 Develop a root locus plot for a PI controller (K_c=3) applied to a first-order process (K_p=0.2, τ_p=1) for which the reset time is varied. Why does this root locus diagram not represent a real process?

7.55 Develop a root locus plot for a PI controller (K_c=2) applied to a first-order process (K_p=0.5, τ_p=2) for which the reset time is varied. Why does this root locus diagram not represent a real process?

7.56 Develop a root locus plot for a PI controller (K_c=1) applied to a first-order process (K_p=2, τ_p=3) for which the reset time is varied. Why does this root locus diagram not represent a real process?

7.57 Develop a root locus plot for a PI controller (K_c=6) applied to a first-order process (K_p=2, τ_p=4) for which the reset time is varied. Why does this root locus diagram not represent a real process?

7.58 Develop a root locus plot for a PID controller (K_c=0.5, τ_I=2) applied to a first-order process (K_p=2, τ_p=4) for which the derivative time is varied.

7.59 Develop a root locus plot for a PID controller (K_c=1, τ_I=3) applied to a first-order process (K_p=2, τ_p=4) for which the derivative time is varied.

7.60 Develop a root locus plot for a PID controller (K_c=2, τ_I=2) applied to a first-order process (K_p=0.4, τ_p=4) for which the derivative time is varied.

7.61 Develop a root locus plot for a PID controller (K_c=0.5, τ_I=2) applied to a first-order process (K_p=1, τ_p=4) for which the derivative time is varied.

7.62 Determine the PI controller settings for a first-order process ($K_p = 1$; $\tau_p = 4$) if it is desired to obtain a closed-loop damping factor of 0.4 and a closed-loop time constant of 2.

7.63 Determine the PI controller settings for a first-order process ($K_p = 6$; $\tau_p = 5$) if it is desired to obtain a closed-loop damping factor of 0.3 and a closed-loop time constant of 3.

7.64 Determine the PI controller settings for a first-order process ($K_p = 13$; $\tau_p = 15$) if it is desired to obtain a closed-loop damping factor of 0.7 and a closed-loop time constant of 3.

7.65 Determine the PI controller settings for a first-order process ($K_p = 3$; $\tau_p = 10$) if it is desired to obtain a closed-loop damping factor of 0.6 and a closed-loop time constant of 3.

7.66 Consider a FOPDT process (i.e., $K_p=1$, $\tau_p=2$, $\theta_p=0.5$). What is the maximum size of the control interval that should be used for this case without the control performance deteriorating? What happens if a larger or a smaller control interval is used?

7.67 Consider a FOPDT process (i.e., $K_p=4$, $\tau_p=10$, $\theta_p=4.5$). What is the maximum size of the control interval that should be used for this case without the control performance deteriorating? What happens if a larger or a smaller control interval is used?

7.68 Consider a FOPDT process (i.e., $K_p=12$, $\tau_p=15$, $\theta_p=3$). What is the maximum size of the control interval that should be used for this case without the control performance deteriorating? What happens if a larger or a smaller control interval is used?

7.69 Consider a FOPDT process (i.e., $K_p=2$, $\tau_p=1$, $\theta_p=3$). What is the maximum size of the control interval that should be used for this case without the control performance deteriorating? What happens if a larger or a smaller control interval is used?

7.70 Determine the PID controller setting for the Cohen and Coon and Cianione and Marlin methods using the following FOPDT model (i.e., $K_p=2$, $\tau_p=6$, $\theta_p=3$). Use the Cianione and Marlin settings for disturbance rejection.

7.71 Determine the PID controller setting for the Cohen and Coon and Cianione and Marlin methods using the following FOPDT model (i.e., $K_p=0.5$, $\tau_p=5$, $\theta_p=2$). Use the Cianione and Marlin settings for setpoint tracking.

7.72 Determine the PID controller setting for the Cohen and Coon and Cianione and Marlin methods using the following FOPDT model (i.e., $K_p=10$, $\tau_p=3$, $\theta_p=1$). Use the Cianione and Marlin settings for disturbance rejection.

7.73 Determine the PID controller setting for the Cohen and Coon and Cianione and Marlin methods using the following FOPDT model (i.e., $K_p=4$, $\tau_p=1$, $\theta_p=3$). Use the Cianione and Marlin settings for setpoint tracking.

7.74 Using the Cianione and Marlin method, develop initial controller settings for a PI controller applied to a temperature control loop on a water-cooled heat exchanger that operates under regulatory control. By observing the process operation, it has been estimated that the process gain is approximately -0.005 °F·hr/lb. The response time of the process has been estimated to be approximately 12 minutes. Further, by observing the process, it has been determined that the amount of deadtime in the system is approximately 1.5 minutes.

7.75 Using the Cohen and Coon method, develop initial controller settings for a PI controller applied to a temperature control loop on a water-cooled CSTR that operates under regulatory control. By observing the process operation, it has been estimated that the process gain is approximately -0.03 °F·hr/lb. The response time of the process has been estimated to be approximately 6 minutes. Further, by observing the process, it has been determined that the amount of deadtime in the system is approximately 1 minute.

7.76 Using the Cianione and Marlin method, develop initial controller settings for a PI controller applied to a pressure control loop on a distillation column that operates under regulatory control. By observing the process operation, it has been estimated that the process gain is approximately -0.05 psi·hr/lb. The response time of the process has been estimated to be approximately 6 minutes. Further, by observing the process, it has been determined that the amount of deadtime in the system is approximately 0.5 minutes.

7.77 Using the Cianione and Marlin method, develop initial controller settings for a PI controller applied to a temperature control loop on a water-cooled heat exchanger that operates under regulatory control. By observing the process operation, it has been estimated that the process gain is approximately -0.05 °F·hr/lb. The response time of the process has been estimated to be approximately 12 minutes. Further, by observing the process, it has been determined that the amount of deadtime in the system is approximately 4 minutes.

7.78[S] For each of the following process simulators provided with the text, apply filtering to the measured value of the controlled variable. Compare the filtered sensor data with the unfiltered data for lined out periods and periods when the controlled variable is changing. Next, double the standard deviation of the noise and repeat the filter tuning procedure. Then, take the original noise level and divide it by a factor of two and repeat the filter tuning procedure. Compare the results of this exercise.

    a. CST thermal mixer   b. CST composition mixer

    c. Level control process   d. Endothermic CSTR

    e. Heat exchanger

7.79[S] For each of the following process simulators provided with the text, tune the filter on the measured value of the controlled variable. Applying field tuning techniques, tune a PI controller for the process for a 1/6 decay ratio*. Next, apply a filter factor of 0.5 and retune the controller. Finally, apply a filter factor of 0.01 and retune the controller. What can you conclude from this exercise?

a. CST thermal mixer

b. CST composition mixer

c. Level control process

d. Endothermic CSTR

e. Heat exchanger

7.80[S] For each of the following process simulators provided with the text, apply an ATV test to determine the ultimate controller gain and ultimate period. Apply ZN settings and tune a PI controller for a 1/8 decay ratio* using the on-line tuning factor. Apply TL settings and tune a PI controller for a 1/8 decay ratio* using the on-line tuning factor. Remember that fine tuning adjustments may be required to ensure that the correct amount of proportional and integral action are being used.

a. CST thermal mixer

b. CST composition mixer

c. Level control process

d. Endothermic CSTR

e. Heat exchanger

7.81[S] For each of the following process simulators provided with the text, apply an ATV test to determine the ultimate controller gain and ultimate period. Using ZN settings and the on-line tuning factor, tune the process for a dynamic response corresponding to critically damped behavior, a 1/10 decay ratio*, and a 1/6 decay ratio* for a setpoint change. Test each controller with a step change in the disturbance level and plot all the disturbance result tests on the same figure.

a. CST thermal mixer

b. CST composition mixer

c. Level control process

d. Endothermic CSTR

e. Heat exchanger

7.82[S] For each of the following process simulators provided with the text, apply the field tuning procedure. Tune the process for a dynamic response corresponding to critically damped behavior, a 1/10 decay ratio*, and a 1/6 decay ratio* for a setpoint change. Test each controller with a step change in the disturbance level and plot all the disturbance test results on the same figure.

a. CST thermal mixer

b. CST composition mixer

c. Level control process   d. Endothermic CSTR

e. Heat exchanger

7.83[S] For the heat exchanger process simulator provided with the text, tune a PI and a PID controller for a 1/8 decay ratio* using small amplitude setpoint changes. Then test both controllers for a step disturbance upset and compare the results.

7.84[S] Apply a PI and a PID controller to each of the following FOPDT processes for which K_p and τ_p are equal to unity. Tune both controllers for setpoint changes and test them for step disturbances.

a. $\theta_p = 0.3$ b. $\theta_p = 0.6$

c. $\theta_p = 1.2$ d. $\theta_p = 2.4$

7.85 Calculate the initial PI controller settings for a level controller with a critically damped response for a 10 ft diameter tank (i.e., a cylinder placed on its end) with a measured height of 10 ft that normally handles a feed rate of 1000 lb/h. Assume that it is desired to have a maximum level change of 5% for a 20% feed rate change and that the liquid has a density corresponding to that of water.

7.86 Calculate the initial PI controller settings for a level controller with a critically damped response for a 6 ft diameter tank (i.e., a cylinder placed on its end) with a measured height of 6 ft that normally handles a feed rate of 1000 lb/h. Assume that it is desired to have a maximum level change of 4% for a 10% feed rate change and that the liquid has a density corresponding to that of water.

7.87 Calculate the initial P-only controller settings for a level controller with a critically damped response for a 16 ft diameter tank (i.e., a cylinder placed on its end) with a measured height of 16 ft that normally handles a feed rate of 10,000 lb/h. Assume that it is desired to have a maximum level change of 10% for a 10% feed rate change and that the liquid has a density corresponding to that of water.

7.88 Calculate the initial PI controller settings for a level controller with a critically damped response for a 9 ft diameter tank (i.e., a cylinder placed on its end) with a measured height of 6 ft that normally handles a feed rate of 5000 lb/h. Assume that it is desired to have a maximum level change of 8% for a 15% feed rate change and that the liquid has a density corresponding to that of water.

7.89 Calculate the initial PI controller settings for a level controller with a critically damped response for a 12 ft diameter tank (i.e., a cylinder placed on its end) with a measured height of 6 ft that normally handles a feed rate of 3000 lb/h. Assume that it is desired to have a maximum level change of 14% for a 10% feed rate change and that the liquid has a density corresponding to that of water.

A problem number with a **superscript S** denotes that the problem requires the use of the simulators.

* When measuring the decay ratio of a response, it is generally easier and more accurate to take the ratio of the difference from the peak-to-valley height for the first two oscillations.

Chapter 8

Troubleshooting Control Loops

8.1 Introduction

Chemical process control engineers spend a major portion of their time troubleshooting control loops. An operator may point out that a particular loop has been behaving erratically and ask the control engineer to improve the performance of the control loop. The control engineer may discover that an important control loop is under manual operation (open-loop operation). A final product may have excessive variability in its impurity levels and the control engineer's job is to reduce the variability to an acceptable level. In this latter example, a number of control loops may require scrutiny. When one or more loops are not performing properly, troubleshooting is required to return them to the expected performance levels, or at least identify the source of the problem. To effectively troubleshoot control loops, the control engineer must understand the proper design and expected performance of the hardware that comprise a control loop, which are addressed in Chapter 2.

Troubleshooting control loops involves identifying the source of the problem with a control loop from an overwhelming number of possible causes. The size of this problem requires a systematic approach when troubleshooting. Control loop troubleshooting is too often treated as an afterthought and performed haphazardly. This chapter presents a general troubleshooting procedure as well as a detailed analysis of fault detection for the final control element, the sensor system, the control computer or DCS, and the process.

8.2 Overall Approach to Troubleshooting

The key to effective troubleshooting is expressed in the old adage, "divide and conquer". It is important to locate the portion of the control-loop hardware that is causing the poor performance: the final control element, the sensor system, the controller, or the process. The place to start is to test each system separately to determine whether that portion of the control loop is operating properly. The final control element can be evaluated by applying a series of input step tests. That is, the input to the final control element, which is normally set by the controller, can be manually adjusted. The test allows the determination of the dynamic response and deadband of the actuator system. If the performance in these two areas is satisfactory, there is no need to evaluate the actuator system further. Section 8.3 addresses troubleshooting actuator systems and contains a listing of common failure modes.

The sensor system is more difficult to check than the actuator system. Using the DCS to track the measured value of the controlled variable can be helpful to point out certain abnormalities. The repeatability of the sensor can be estimated during a steady-state period. Determining the time constant for the sensor dynamics is usually much more difficult. A time history of the actual control variable must be compared to the time history of the sensor reading to estimate the sensor time constant. The sensor may also require calibration. Section 8.4 addresses troubleshooting sensor systems and contains a listing of common failure modes for a number of sensor types.

Controllers are implemented by the DCS or control computer and affect the control performance through the controller tuning, the control interval, and sensor filtering. The controller tuning is very often the source of erratic control performance and can be corrected by simply retuning the control loop. Controller tuning is the easiest thing to change, but retuning the controller may mask the real problem with the control loop. When a component of the feedback system is not functioning properly and the controller is retuned, erratic behavior may not be present, but a sacrifice in control performance results. Controller design and implementation issues can be the source of poor control loop performance, e.g., using the wrong mode of the PID controller, using a reverse-acting controller for a system that requires a direct-acting controller, and having the controller output go to the wrong manipulated variable. Section 8.5 addresses troubleshooting the controller and contains a listing of common problems.

The process should be evaluated with regard to its effect on controller performance. Excessive disturbances entering the process can be reduced by modifying upstream operations. Fouling or mechanical failure can create a situation in which it is not possible for the controller to maintain the controlled variable at its setpoint. The control of the process may not be satisfactory because an unidentified constraint prevents normal control of the process. Section 8.6 addresses troubleshooting the process to identify process problems or limitations affecting control loop performance.

Finally, the entire loop should be tested under closed-loop conditions. First, the **closed-loop deadband** should be determined, i.e., the largest positive and negative setpoint changes that can be implemented without causing measurable changes in the controlled variable. The dynamic response of the closed-loop process can also be assessed from the results of the closed-loop deadband test. Section 8.7 addresses evaluating the closed-loop performance of a control loop.

Sudden changes in control loop performance from satisfactory to unacceptable may be caused by recent changes in the process. Considering what changes have been made to the process can expedite the troubleshooting process. For example, the controller could have been retuned. A new analyzer could have been

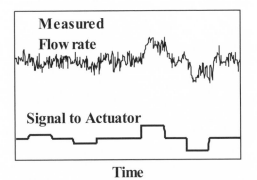

Figure 8.1 Graphical representation of a block sine wave test applied to an actuator system.

installed. A new instrument technician could be responsible for calibrating and maintaining an analyzer. The feed to the unit could have significantly changed. These examples and many more can be directly related to the source of poor control-loop performance. When something significant has changed, it can provide a valuable clue that allows quicker determination of the source of the problem with a poorly performing control loop.

When troubleshooting a more complex control system, it is advisable to start by comparing the existing control loops with those from the P&ID. The current problem may be due to inappropriate modifications of the original control configuration.

8.3 Final Control Element

The final control element consists of the instrument air system, the I/P converter, and the control valve (the valve and the valve actuator). The fastest way to identify gross problems with the final control element is to plot both the manipulated variable and the controller output. If the manipulated variable does not follow the controller output, there is probably a problem with the final control element.

Even if the manipulated variable seems to follow the controller output, there could be a problem with the actuator. Estimates of the actuator deadband and dynamic response are required to determine if the actuator system is performing properly (both of which can be determined by a **block sine wave** test). A block sine wave test is shown in Figure 8.1. A block sine wave (Figure 8.2) is a series of equal sized step changes that approximate a sine wave. For the test shown in Figure 8.1, initially the amplitude of the step change used in the block sine wave is small enough that consistent positive and negative changes in the measured value of the flow rate of the manipulated variable are not observed. The next block sine wave uses a larger amplitude step change, and for this case, the measured manipulated variable can be

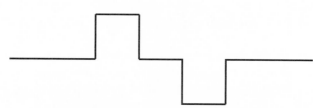

Figure 8.2 A block sine wave.

seen to make both positive and negative changes corresponding to the positive and negative changes in the controller output. Therefore, the deadband of the actuator in this case is larger than the step size used in the first block sine wave and smaller than the one used in the second. The same block sine wave test can be used to estimate the time constant of the final control element. If the time between step changes used in the block sine wave is large enough, the settling time of the actuator can be estimated. Then, the time constant of the actuator is estimated as one-quarter of the settling time.

Table 8.1
Common Problems with the Final Control Element

- Excessive lag in the instrument air system.
- Wrong type of instrument air connected to control valve. Some plants have high and low pressure instrument air.
- Low instrument air pressure.
- Wet or dirty instrument air.
- Excessive deadband.*
- Improperly sized control valve*.
- Excessive resistance to movement of valve stem*.
- Leak in diaphragm of control valve.
- Debris stuck in opening to control valve.
- Plugged or obstructed instrument air line.
- Plug/seat erosion in the control valve.
- By-pass line open or leaking.
- Flashing and cavitation.
- Improperly tuned valve positioner*.
  * More frequently observed problems

Once the deadband and time constant of the actuator have been determined, the performance of the actuator can be assessed. The deadband for valves with positioners typically ranges from 0.1 to 0.5 % of the flow rate for properly implemented systems and depends on the size of the valves, the pressure drop across the valve, the fluid properties, etc. Deadband for an industrial valve without a positioner typically ranges from 10 to 25%, and even higher for older valves that have not been maintained. The time constant of a properly functioning final control element is less than 2 s for a valve with a positioner or a control valve in a flow control loop. Otherwise, the actuator time constant is usually between 3 and 15 s.

If it has been determined that the actuator system is not functioning properly, one should first determine if the instrument air pressure system is operating properly. This can be done by observing the instrument air pressure at the control valve after a step change in the signal to the final control element has been implemented in the DCS or in the control computer. If the instrument air pressure at the control valve increases sharply after the step test has been implemented, then the control valve is the source of the slow or erratic response. Another common problem is valve packing that is over tightened, which primarily increases the valve deadband. A valve that is operating below 10% or above 90% opening typically performs below standards. Another problem is an improperly tuned valve positioner. If the valve positioner is tuned too aggressively, oscillatory control performance results for the control valve, resulting in an increase in the actuator deadband. If the valve positioner is not tuned aggressively enough, the dynamic response of the actuator is slower than it should be. Table 8.1 lists a number of common problems with the components of the actuator system.

8.4 Sensor Systems

The sensor system is composed of the sensor, the transmitter, and the sampling system that allows the sensor to make its measurement. The performance of a sensor can be assessed by determining its repeatability and time constant, and sometimes its accuracy. Accuracy is important for a composition analyzer on a final product to ensure that the product meets specifications. The accuracy of a flow transmitter is usually not important because the flow rate is adjusted incrementally by a supervisory controller so that its actual flow rate is unimportant. The dynamics of the sensor can affect the feedback control performance if it is too slow, and a large repeatability can increase the variability in the controlled variable.

The accuracy of the sensor can be checked by comparing the sensor reading to a standard or known condition. For example, a composition standard can be processed to verify the accuracy of the GC or a thermocouple can be placed in boiling water to check its accuracy. The repeatability of a sensor can be estimated by observing sensor readings during a period of relatively steady-state operation. The repeatability is the variation in the sensor reading caused by noise. One would assume that during steady operation, the process was not, in fact, changing.

Determining the time constant of the sensor is usually more difficult than estimating the repeatability. To determine the time constant of the sensor system, one needs to know the actual process measurement. Consider a temperature measurement. A measurement of the actual process temperature is required to estimate the time constant of a sensor. Instead, the thermal resistance, which causes the excessive thermal lag of the temperature sensor, can be evaluated. The location of the thermowell should be checked to ensure that it extends far enough into the line so that the fluid velocity past the thermowell is sufficient; the possibility of buildup of insulating material on the outside of the thermowell should be assessed; and the thermal contact between the end of the temperature probe and the walls of the thermowell should be evaluated. In this manner, an indirect estimate of the responsiveness of the temperature sensor can be developed. The velocity of a sample in the line, which delivers a sample from a process line to a gas chromatograph, can indicate the transport delay associated with the sample system. A low velocity in the sample line from the process stream to a GC can result in excessive transport delay, which can greatly reduce controller effectiveness.

One should be careful to determine if the sensor used is really measuring the controlled variable of interest. Differential pressure sensors are used for pressure, flow, and level measurements. They are particularly susceptible to plugging of the sensing lines that connect the differential pressure sensor to the process itself. Plugging of the sensing lines can result from the buildup of coatings or solids or from freezing of the fluid in the pressure taps (Figure 2.32). The calibration of a differential pressure sensor is quite sensitive to the conditions of the fluid in the sensing lines. Condensate buildup in lines that should be dry can lead to large calibration errors. Table 8.2 lists some commonly encountered sources of problems for sensor systems. For a complete analysis of the sensor system, an instrument engineer or other expert familiar with that particular sensor may be required. Table 2.3 lists the expected ranges for the repeatability and the time constant for several commonly used sensors in the CPI. Deviation of the apparent repeatability or time constant from these expected values identifies a poorly performing sensor

Table 8.2
Commonly Encountered Problems with Components of a Sensor System

Sensor	• Common Problems
Transmitter	• Not calibrated correctly*. • Low resolution • Excessive signal filtering* • Slow sampling
Thermocouple/ RTD	• Off-calibration*. • Short in the electrical circuit. • Improperly located thermowell*. • Thermowell with excessive thermal resistance (e.g. stainless steel thermowells). • Partially burned out thermocouple. • Interference from heat tracing. • Buildup of material on the outside surface of the thermowell.

Table 8.2 (Continued) **Commonly Encountered Problems with Components of a Sensor System**	
Sensor	**• Common Problems**
Pressure Indicators	• Plugged line to pressure indicator*. • Confusion about absolute pressure readings, gauge pressure readings and vacuum pressure readings. • Condensation in lines to pressure indicator*
Sampling System For GC	• Excessive transport delay for an analyzer. • Sample drawn from wrong process point. • Plugged sample system*. • Sample system closed off.
GC	• Out of calibration. • Plugging in the GC column. • Failure of electrical components in GC. • Excessive noise on measurement.
Flow Indicator	• Square root compensation applied for non-DP-type flow indicator not applied properly. • Orifice plate installed backwards. • Damaged orifice plate. • Plugged line to DP sensor*. • Flashing of liquids as they flow through an orifice meter.
Level Indicator	• Plugged line from process to DP cell*. • Leak in line to DP cell or in DP cell itself. • Boiling of liquid in line to or from DP cell due to a steam leak in the steam tracing line. • Solidification of liquid in line to or from process to DP cell due to failure in steam tracing. • Formation of emulsions, which can confound interface level measurements. • Leak in float type level indicators. • Formation of foams which can interfere with level measurements.
* Indicates a more frequently observed problem	

8.5 Control Computer/DCS System

The control computer/DCS system consists of controllers, A/D and D/A converters, and the signal conditioning hardware and software, i.e., filtering and validation. Each of these components requires separate evaluation. Table 8.3 lists possible problems with the controller/DCS system. One way to initially check controller tuning is to place the control loop in manual (open the control loop) and observe whether the controlled variable lines out to a steady-state or near steady-state value. Comparing the open-loop and closed-loop performance indicates if the controller is upsetting the process. If the controller is not upsetting the process, disturbances to the control loop in question are the primary source of the upsets.

Table 8.3

Possible Problems with the Controller/DCS System

- Improperly tuned controller*.
- Wrong scaling for A/D and D/A converter.
- Improper or lack of pressure/temperature compensation for flow measurement.
- Improper selection of reverse-acting or direct-acting controller (Chapter 6).
- Too much or not enough filtering of the measured controlled variable*.
- Signal aliasing due to excessive control interval (see Appendix B).
- Poor resolution on A/D or D/A converters.
- Derivative action based on error from the setpoint instead of the measurement.

* More frequently observed problems

8.6 Process Effects

The effect of the process on the closed-loop behavior can be examined directly by opening the control loop in question and observing the process behavior. Open-loop oscillatory behavior indicates a problem internal to the process. The noise level on the analyzer reading can also be assessed under open-loop conditions.

Fluctuating disturbances and process gain changes due to nonlinearity are a natural part of process control. Extraordinary disturbances combined with nonlinearity can cause an otherwise properly tuned controller to oscillate or go unstable during upset periods. Severe process nonlinearity can be identified if a closed-loop process exhibits ringing and sluggish behavior during different periods with the same controller tuning. Scheduling the controller tuning (Chapter 11) is one way to compensate for process nonlinearity. It may be possible to reduce the magnitude of the disturbances to acceptable levels by modifying the upstream operations (e.g., tuning upstream controllers). Excessive disturbances, when not measurable, can be inferred by observing the range of the average manipulated variable levels. If large magnitude disturbances are affecting the process, large changes in the average manipulated variable level are required to maintain the process near its desired operating point. Excessive fouling of heat exchangers or deactivation of catalyst can result in process gain changes that result in sluggish or unstable behavior.

Process changes that require manipulated variable levels in excess of what is physically available can also occur. After feed rate increases to a distillation column, the reboiler might be unable to provide enough heat transfer to maintain the purity of the bottom product. When this occurs, it is a physical limitation of the process and not the fault of the controller. Loss of steam pressure can also cause a constraint that can affect control loop performance. Downstream pressure changes can cause a constraint on the maximum flow rate due to an inadequate pressure driving force. Constraint control techniques (Chapter 11) should be used when manipulated variables saturate. It should be clear that a thorough understanding of the process is a prerequisite for control loop troubleshooting.

8.7 Testing the Entire Control Loop

After each of the components has been evaluated and corrected, wherever possible, the closed-loop system should be checked. From an overall point of view, there are three general factors that affect the closed-loop performance of a control loop: (1) the type and magnitude of disturbances, (2) the lag associated with the components that comprise the control loop, and (3) the precision to which each component of the control loop performs. Actuator deadband affects the variability in the controlled variable. The addition of lag to a control loop (e.g., sensor filtering) results in slower disturbance rejection, which can increase the variability in the controlled variable. Disturbance magnitude directly affects variability.

The performance of a closed-loop system can be assessed by the settling time, closed-loop deadband, and the variability of the controlled variable evaluated over an extended period of time. The settling time and the closed-loop deadband can be determined using a closed-loop block sine wave test (Figure 8.3). For a closed-loop block sine wave test, the setpoint for the control loop is applied in the form of a block sine wave, and the amplitude of the block sine wave is varied until the deadband is determined. During these tests, the settling time of the controller can also be estimated. An accurate determination of the variability of a controlled variable generally requires an extended period of operation. An evaluation of the variability based on a short period of time may not be representative of the true performance of the system.

Consider a control system with an excessive lag (e.g., buildup of scale on the exterior of a thermowell) added to a control loop. The controller can be tuned for any

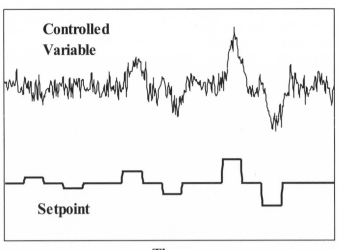

Figure 8.3 An example of a closed-loop block sine wave test.

tuning criterion (e.g., a decay ratio of 1/6 to critically damped); therefore, tuning a control loop to the desired tuning criterion is not, in itself, an indication of the performance of the control system. The settling time and the variability provide a measure of the performance of the control system. A process with the additional lag exhibits a longer settling time than a process without the additional lag. The average variability in the controlled variable over an extended period also shows that the system without the additional lag exhibits superior control performance. The variability is usually a direct measure of controller performance that generally can be related to the overall objectives of the process, but requires a significant operating period (e.g., a week) to accurately determine. On the other hand, the settling time can be determined much more quickly and easily, but provides only a relative measure of control performance. One can determine the relative change in controller performance by comparing the settling time before control loop troubleshooting was undertaken to it afterwards.

The closed-loop deadband is an indication of the variability in the controlled variable that results from the combined effects of actuator deadband, sensor noise, and resolution of the A/D and D/A converters. The closed-loop settling time is an indication of the combined lags of the control loop components. The closed-loop performance assessment is a means of determining if all the major problems within a control loop have been rectified.

Example 8.1 Troubleshooting Example

Problem Statement. Present a step-by-step troubleshooting process, along with intermediate results, for a temperature controller that results in sluggish closed-loop performance.

Solution. Step 1: Determine the deadband of the final control element using a series of block sine wave tests. **Result:** The deadband of the final control element is less than 0.4% and the dynamic response time of the final control element is 2 seconds; therefore, the final control element is functioning properly.

Step 2: Retune the temperature controller. **Result:** The controller settings do not change significantly; therefore, the controller tuning does not appear to be the problem.

Step 3: Evaluate the sensor. Check the repeatability of the sensor by observing the temperature measurements during a steady-state or near steady-state period. **Result:** The repeatability is less than 0.1 °C, which is good for an RTD. An independent measurement of the temperature is made and compared with the sensor reading. **Result:** The sensor reading is observed to have excessive lag, i.e., a dynamic response time for the sensor is estimated equal to about 5 minutes. Based on Table 2.3, the maximum response time for a properly functioning temperature sensor is less than 80 s. It is determined upon further examination that there was an excessive air space between the RTD element and the surface of the thermowell. The proper installation of the RTD in the thermowell is made and the dynamic lag of the sensor is found in the proper range. The controller is retuned and control performance is significantly improved.

♠

Example 8.2 Troubleshooting Example

Problem Statement. Present a step-by-step troubleshooting process, along with intermediate results, for a reactor temperature controller that exhibits excessive reactor temperature excursions from setpoint. Reactor temperature control is achieved by manipulating the heat added to the reactor feed. The reactor temperature controller is supervisory and selects the setpoint for the flow controller on the steam to the feed preheater, which is the regulatory controller.

Solution. Step 1: First, the performance of the flow controller on the steam line is evaluated. Perform a series of closed-loop block sine wave tests on the steam flow controller. **Result:** The repeatability of the flow measurement is observed to be larger than it should be. It is determined that the differential pressure sensor has a partially plugged pressure tap. This problem is corrected and the flow controller is tested over the expected flow rate range. **Result:** It is observed that in the low flow rate range the flow control performance is poor. Upon examination of the control valve it is determined that an equal percentage valve is used while a linear valve should have been used since the pressure drop across the valve remains relatively constant. The valve plug and cage are replaced with ones that result in linear inherent valve characteristics and good controllability of the steam flow over the entire flow rate range is observed after the flow controller is retuned.

Step 2: Evaluate the temperature sensor on the product stream from the reactor. **Result:** It is determined that the repeatability and dynamic response of the temperature sensor are good.

Step 3: Retune the temperature controller on the reactor exit temperature. **Result:** After the temperature control loop is retuned, the variability in the reactor temperature from setpoint is observed to be a factor of three lower than was previously observed, thus meeting the operational objectives of this control loop.

♠

Example 8.3 Troubleshooting Example

Problem Statement. Present a step-by-step troubleshooting procedure for a composition control loop on the overhead of a distillation column for which the variability of the impurity level in the overhead product is in excess of the product specifications. The output of the composition controller goes to a flow control loop on the reflux flow.

Solution. Step 1: Evaluate the deadband of the reflux flow controller. **Result:** The deadband of the flow control loop is found equal to ±0.3% with a time constant of approximately 1.5 seconds; therefore, the flow control loop is functioning properly.

Step 2: Check the tuning for the composition controller. **Result:** The controller is properly tuned.

Step 3: Evaluate the on-line GC. **Result:** The repeatability of the analyzer is found equal to ±2% by observing GC readings during a steady-state period. This repeatability is well within the product variability limits and is consistent with the analysis of this type of mixture. Upon further examination it is determined that there is excessive sample transport delay; therefore, the sample pump is replaced and the sample transport delay is reduced to an acceptable level because the velocity through the sample line is increased to a proper level. After this change and the retuning of the composition controller, the variability of the overhead product is reduced, but it is found to periodically exceed the product variability specifications.

Step 4: Evaluate the closed-loop deadband for the composition control loop. **Result**: It is found that the deadband is acceptable, but the dynamic response is slower than expected. Upon further evaluation it is determined that excessive filtering of the analyzer reading is being used. The proper level of filtering is applied and the composition controller is retuned. The resulting product variability is found to be well within the product specifications.

♠

8.8 Summary

The key to troubleshooting control loops is to independently check the actuator system, the sensor system, the process, and the control computer to isolate the source of the problem. The actuator system is the easiest to check since the flow measurement is generally available. The sensor system may require an instrument technician to determine whether it is functioning properly. Checking the control computer generally involves evaluating the controller tuning but can also involve A/D and D/A converters, sensor signal conditioning, or simple oversights, such as specifying a direct-acting controller for a case that requires a reverse-acting controller. Changes to the process (e.g., changes in the type or magnitude of disturbance) can also be the source of a poorly performing control loop. Finally, the closed-loop performance of the control loop should be tested.

8.9 Additional Terminology

Block sine wave - a series of step changes that approximate a sine wave.

Closed-loop deadband - the maximum positive and negative setpoint change to a control loop that can be implemented without a noticeable change in the measured value of the controlled variable.

8.10 Preliminary Questions

8.1 What is troubleshooting control loops?

8.2 Since there are a very large number of possible faults that can undermine the performance of a control loop, how does the control engineer check each of these potential faults?

8.3 Summarize the recommended approach to troubleshooting a process control loop.

8.4 What are the most frequently observed problems with the actuator systems?

8.5 How can a control engineer determine if the final control element is functioning properly?

8.6 What is a block sine wave?

8.7 How is a block sine wave used to evaluate the performance of an actuator system?

8.8 How is the deadband of a final control element determined from a block sine wave test?

8.9 How is a block sine wave test used to determine the time constant of the actuator system?

8.10 What is the usual cause of excessive valve deadband?

8.11 What is the most common problem with sensors based on a differential pressure measurement?

8.12 Explain how you determine whether a sensor system is functioning properly.

8.13 How can one estimate the repeatability of a sensor?

8.14 Is the accuracy of a sensor always important to the performance of a control loop?

8.15 Is the repeatability of a sensor always important to the performance of a control loop?

8.16 Is the time constant of a sensor always important to the performance of a control loop?

8.17 Why do some engineers prefer a vortex shedding meter or a magnetic flow meter to an orifice flow meter?

8.18 How can condensate in a pressure tap affect a level reading?

8.19 What is the most common problem with the DCS/controller system?

8.20 Explain how controller tuning can mask problems with the hardware in a control loop. Give an example.

8.21 How can the wrong level of sensor filtering affect control performance.

8.22 What is the resolution of an A/D converter?

8.23 How does a control engineer determine if a process has excessive nonlinearity?

8.24 How can one determine if large disturbances are entering a process?

8.25 How do control engineers test the closed-loop performance of a control loop? What metrics do they use?

8.26 How is a closed-loop block sine wave test different from a block sine wave test applied to an actuator system?

8.27 What information is contained in the deadband obtained from a closed-loop block sine wave test?

8.28 How is the variability of a control loop measured?

8.29 What information does the closed-loop settling time of a control loop contain?

8.11 Analytical Questions and Exercises

8.30 In a manner similar to Examples 8.1, 8.2, and 8.3, present a troubleshooting study and results for

a. A level controller malfunctioning because of a plugged line to the DP sensor in the level indicator.

b. A pressure controller malfunctioning because of an improperly tuned valve positioner on the control valve.

c. A flow control loop malfunctioning because of low resolution of the A/D and D/A converters.

8.31 What would happen if the output of a controller were sent to the valve on the manipulated variable and to a valve that affects a disturbance of the process? How difficult would it be to identify this fault during a troubleshooting effort?

Chapter 9

Frequency Response Analysis

9.1 Introduction

To this point, dynamic process behavior, both open-loop and closed-loop, has been studied primarily for step changes in manipulated variables, setpoints, and disturbances. In this chapter, the effect of sinusoidal inputs over a range of frequencies, ω's, is studied where

$$u(t) = a \sin \omega t$$

This procedure is called **frequency response analysis**.

The frequency of an input can have a very significant effect upon the resulting behavior of the process. Consider a mixing tank with a time constant of 10 minutes for its composition dynamics. If sinusoidal variations in one of the inlet concentrations are applied at a frequency of 10 cycles per second, no measurable sinusoidal variation in the outlet concentration results. Since the time constant of the process is 10 minutes, the peaks and the valleys of the sinusoidal variation of the input average out because the input changes are occurring faster than the process can respond. If the frequency of the input were 0.01 cycles/second, significant variation in the output would result. If the frequency were extremely slow, e.g., one cycle per day, the process would appear to be at steady-state even though it would, in fact, be changing very slowly. By analyzing the frequencies of disturbances that pass through a number of controllers, one can evaluate the propagation of variability through a multiple unit process.

The frequency response behavior of a control loop can be an important perspective to use in understanding the performance of process control systems. While it is not recommended to apply frequency response analysis techniques directly to industrial processes (e.g., tuning control loops), frequency response analysis is still important to the understanding of the feedback control behavior of industrial processes. Important process control terminology is also based on frequency response analysis.

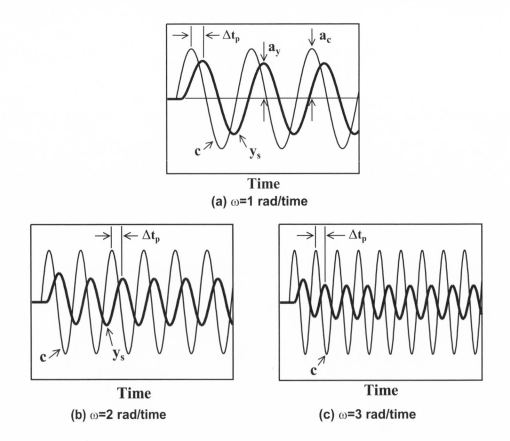

Time

(a) ω=1 rad/time

Time

(b) ω=2 rad/time

Time

(c) ω=3 rad/time

Figure 9.1 The effect of frequency on the amplitude and phase lag of a FOPDT process.

9.2 Bode Plot

Figure 9.1 shows the dynamic behavior of a FOPDT process model ($K_p =1$, $\tau_p =1$, $\theta_p =0.5$) that represents the combined effect of the actuator, process, and sensor subjected to sinusoidal inputs with different frequencies. Sinusoidal changes in c are the input to the process and the output is y_s. The amplitude of the variations in y_s and the difference in the timing of the peaks in y_s and c at each frequency characterize the frequency response behavior of this process. To normalize the results, the **amplitude ratio** is used, i.e.,

$$A_r = \frac{a_y}{a_c}$$

where a_y is the amplitude of the sinusoidal variation in the controlled variable, y_s, and a_c is the amplitude of the sinusoidal variations in the controller output, c. The time difference between peaks, Δt_p can be converted into an angle and is referred to as the **phase angle** of the response, ϕ,

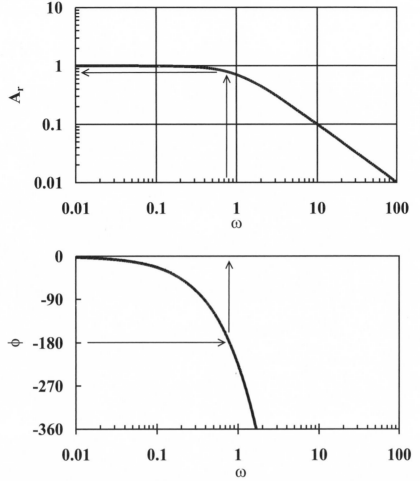

Figure 9.2 Bode plot for a FOPDT process (a) The upper plot is the amplitude ratio (b) The lower plot is the phase angle.

$$\phi = \frac{\omega \, \Delta t_p}{2\pi} \times 360°$$

where ω is the frequency of the input variations in radians per second. $\Delta \tau_p$ in this equation is positive when c lags y_s. For Figure 9.1, $\Delta \tau_p$ is negative because y_s lags c. A **Bode plot** of a process is a plot of ϕ and the logarithm of A_r versus the logarithm of ω. Note that these are common logarithms with base 10. Figure 9.2 shows the Bode plot for the previous FOPDT process model. From Figure 9.1, as the frequency increases, the amplitude ratio decreases, which is consistent with Figure 9.2. Since y_s lags c in Figure 9.1, the phase angle is negative as is shown in Figure 9.2. Therefore, the direct way to generate a Bode plot is to excite the process with sinusoidal inputs of varying frequencies, wait until standing waves have been established, and measure the amplitude ratio and phase angle.

The Bode plot of a process can also be generated by using the transfer function of the process. Consider a first-order process without deadtime

$$G_p(s) = \frac{K_p}{\tau_p s + 1}$$

with a sinusoidal input $$C(s) = \frac{a_c \omega}{s^2 + \omega^2}$$

Then, combining the transfer function with the input yields

$$Y(s) = \frac{K_p a_c \omega}{(\tau_p s + 1)(s^2 + \omega^2)} = \frac{K_p a_c}{\tau_p^2 \omega^2 + 1}\left[\frac{\omega \tau_p^2}{\tau_p s + 1} - \frac{s \omega \tau_p}{s^2 + \omega^2} + \frac{\omega}{s^2 + \omega^2}\right]$$

Taking the inverse Laplace transform yields

$$y(t) = \frac{K_p a_c}{\tau_p^2 \omega^2 + 1}\left[\omega \tau_p e^{-t/\tau_p} - \omega \tau_p \cos \omega t + \sin \omega t\right]$$

and applying trigonometric relations results in

$$y(t) = \frac{K_p a_c \omega \tau_p}{\omega^2 \tau_p^2 + 1} e^{-t/\tau_p} + \frac{K_p a_c}{\sqrt{\omega^2 \tau_p^2 + 1}} \sin(\omega t + \phi)$$

where $\phi = \tan^{-1}(-\omega \tau_p)$. The first term on the right-hand-side of the equation is the transient response, and it decays to zero at long time. The second term is the forced response, and it describes the standing wave in y_s that results from the sinusoidal input. Therefore, the amplitude ratio is determined by the forced response and is given by

$$A_r = \frac{K_p}{\sqrt{\omega^2 \tau_p^2 + 1}}$$

and the phase angle is simply ϕ. A Bode plot can also be derived using the transfer function with a sinusoidal input.

Another way to use a transfer function to generate a Bode plot is to substitute $s = i\omega$ into $G_p(s)$ and factor the result into the real and imaginary components in polar coordinates, i.e.,

$$G_p(i\omega) = R(\omega) + iI(\omega) \qquad\qquad \textbf{9.1}$$

then

$$A_r = \left| G_p(i\omega) \right| = \sqrt{R^2(\omega) + I^2(\omega)}$$

and

$$\phi = \tan^{-1}\left[I(\omega)/R(\omega) \right]$$

For example, consider a first-order process without deadtime. Substituting $s=i\omega$,

$$G_p(i\omega) = \frac{K_p}{i\omega\tau_p + 1}$$

To remove i from the denominator, multiply both the numerator and denominator by the complex conjugate of the denominator , i.e., $(1 - i\,\omega\tau_p)$

$$G_p(i\omega) = \frac{-iK_p\,\omega\tau_p + K_p}{\omega^2\tau_p^2 + 1} = \frac{K_p}{\omega^2\tau_p^2 + 1} - i\frac{K_p\,\omega\tau_p}{\omega^2\tau_p^2 + 1}$$

Then, using Equation 9.1,

$$A_r = \left| G_p(i\omega) \right| = \frac{\sqrt{K_p^2 + K_p^2\,\omega^2\tau_p^2}}{\omega^2\tau_p^2 + 1} = \frac{K_p}{\sqrt{\omega^2\tau_p^2 + 1}} \qquad \textbf{9.2}$$

and

$$\phi = \angle G_p(i\omega) = \tan^{-1}(-\omega\tau_p)$$

This method agrees with the results of the earlier approach and is generally simpler to apply.

Consider a transfer function given by

$$G_p(s) = \frac{G_a(s)\,G_b(s)}{G_c(s)\,G_d(s)}$$

The overall amplitude ratio is given by

$$(A_r)_{overall} = \left| G_p(i\omega) \right| = \frac{\left| G_a(i\omega) \right|\left| G_b(i\omega) \right|}{\left| G_c(i\omega) \right|\left| G_d(i\omega) \right|}$$

Since $\left| G_j(i\omega) \right|$ is equal to the amplitude ratio of the jth transfer function,

$$(A_r)_{overall} = \frac{(A_r)_a\,(A_r)_b}{(A_r)_c\,(A_r)_d} \qquad \textbf{9.3}$$

and $\quad \phi = \angle G_p(i\omega) = \angle G_a(i\omega) + \angle G_b(i\omega) - \angle G_c(i\omega) - \angle G_d(i\omega) \qquad \textbf{9.4}$

Bode plots of individual transfer functions can be graphically combined to yield the Bode plot of the product of the transfer functions. Taking the logarithm of Equation 9.3 results in

$$\log(A_r)_{overall} = \log(A_r)_a + \log(A_r)_b - \log(A_r)_c - \log(A_r)_d$$

Since a Bode plot contains the logarithm of A_r, the above equation shows that the logarithm of A_r of a process that is composed of the product of several transfer function is the sum of the logarithms of the A_r's of the individual transfer functions. Likewise, Equation 9.4 indicates that the phase angle of a process that is composed of the product of several transfer functions is simply the sum of the phase angles of the individual transfer functions. In this way, the Bode plots of complex transfer functions can easily be constructed using the known Bode plots of the individual components.

Table 9.1 lists A_r and ϕ as a function of ω for several commonly encountered transfer functions. The transfer functions considered are for a constant, a first-order process, a second-order process, a deadtime element, an integrator, and a PI controller, respectively.

Example 9.1 Developing a Bode Plot for a FOPDT Process

Problem Statement. Using the functions listed in Table 9.1, develop the equations that describe the dependence of the amplitude ratio and phase angle of a FOPDT process ($K_p = 2$, $\tau_p = 3$, $\theta_p = 1.5$) on the frequency of the input.

Solution. Using Table 9.1, the amplitude ratio and phase angle for a first-order transfer function and deadtime with the given parameter values are

$$(A_r)_{first-order} = \frac{2}{\sqrt{9\omega^2 + 1}} \qquad \phi_{first-order} = \tan^{-1}(-3\omega)$$

$$(A_r)_{deadtime} = 1 \qquad \phi_{deadtime} = -85.9\omega$$

Using Equation 9.3,

$$(A_r)_{FOPDT} = (A_r)_{first-order}(A_r)_{deadtime} = \frac{2}{\sqrt{9\omega^2 + 1}} \qquad \qquad \textbf{A}$$

$$\phi_{FOPDT} = \phi_{first-order} + \phi_{deadtime} = \tan^{-1}(-3\omega) - 85.9\omega \qquad \qquad \textbf{B}$$

Equations A and B allow one to directly generate a Bode plot for the FOPDT system by specifying a range of frequencies and calculating the corresponding values of the amplitude ratio and the phase angle at each frequency.

♠

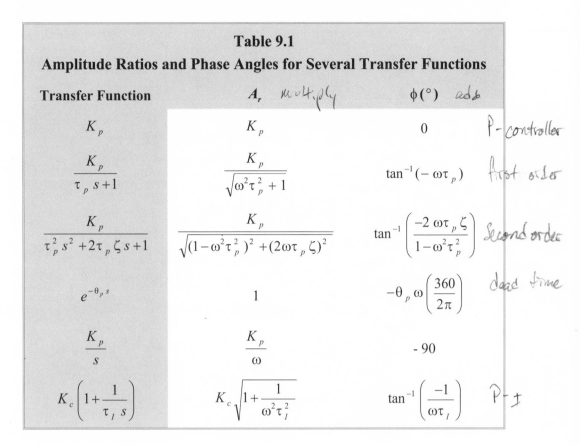

Table 9.1
Amplitude Ratios and Phase Angles for Several Transfer Functions

Transfer Function	A_r	$\phi(°)$	
K_p	K_p	0	P-controller
$\dfrac{K_p}{\tau_p s + 1}$	$\dfrac{K_p}{\sqrt{\omega^2 \tau_p^2 + 1}}$	$\tan^{-1}(-\omega\tau_p)$	first order
$\dfrac{K_p}{\tau_p^2 s^2 + 2\tau_p \zeta s + 1}$	$\dfrac{K_p}{\sqrt{(1 - \omega^2\tau_p^2)^2 + (2\omega\tau_p\zeta)^2}}$	$\tan^{-1}\left(\dfrac{-2\,\omega\tau_p\,\zeta}{1 - \omega^2\tau_p^2}\right)$	Second order
$e^{-\theta_p s}$	1	$-\theta_p\,\omega\left(\dfrac{360}{2\pi}\right)$	dead time
$\dfrac{K_p}{s}$	$\dfrac{K_p}{\omega}$	-90	
$K_c\left(1 + \dfrac{1}{\tau_I s}\right)$	$K_c\sqrt{1 + \dfrac{1}{\omega^2\tau_I^2}}$	$\tan^{-1}\left(\dfrac{-1}{\omega\tau_I}\right)$	P + I

(handwritten annotations: "multiply" above A_r; "adds" above $\phi(°)$)

Example 9.2 Developing a Bode Plot for a PI Controller Applied to a First-Order Process

Problem Statement. Develop the equations that can be used to construct a Bode plot for a PI controller ($K_c = 2$; $\tau_I = 3$) applied to a first-order process ($K_p = 0.7$, $\tau_p = 5$).

Solution. Using Table 9.1 for the amplitude ratio and phase angle for each component in this system,

$$(A_r)_{PI} = 2\sqrt{1 + \frac{1}{9\omega^2}} \qquad \phi_{PI} = \tan^{-1}\left(\frac{-1}{3\omega}\right)$$

$$(A_r)_{first-order} = \frac{0.7}{\sqrt{25\omega^2 + 1}} \qquad \phi_{first-order} = \tan^{-1}(-5\omega)$$

Then $\qquad (A_r)_{overall} = \dfrac{0.467}{\omega}\sqrt{\dfrac{9\omega^2 + 1}{25\omega^2 + 1}} \qquad \phi_{overall} = \tan^{-1}\left(\dfrac{-1}{3\omega}\right) + \tan^{-1}(-5\omega)$

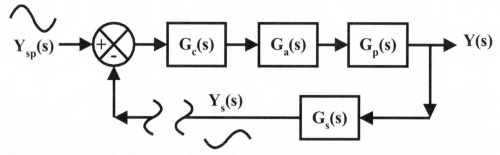

Figure 9.3a Block diagram of a feedback loop with the feedback broken and a sinusoidal variation in the setpoint.

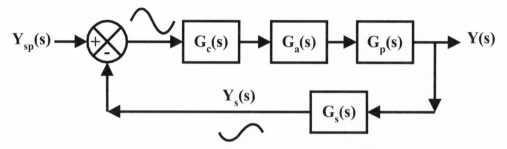

Figure 9.3b Block diagram of a feedback loop with simultaneous termination of the setpoint variation and closing of the loop.

9.3 Gain Margin and Phase Margin

Consider the frequency in Figure 9.2 that corresponds to a phase angle of -180°, i.e., from Figure 9.2, $\omega = 0.79$ radians per time. Figure 9.3a is a schematic of a loop with a sinusoidally varying setpoint with a frequency of 0.79 radians per second. A P-only controller with a gain of 1.0 is used, but the feedback of the measurement is broken before it is compared with the setpoint value (an open-loop process). Since the amplitude ratio at $\omega = 0.79$ radians per second is 0.78, the amplitude of the variation of the measured value of y is 0.78. Note that, since the phase angle is -180°, the sinusoidal variation in the measured value of y is the negative of the setpoint variation, i.e.,

$$y_{sp} = 1.0\sin(\omega t)$$
$$y_s = -0.78\sin(\omega t)$$

since $\sin(\omega t - 180°) = -\sin(\omega t)$

Figure 9.3b represents simultaneously closing the feedback loop and replacing the sinusoidal variation in the setpoint with a constant setpoint. Note that since the measured value of the controlled variable is subtracted from the setpoint, the variations in y_s are in phase with the original variations in y_{sp}. Once the loop is closed, the sinusoidal variations are fed back around the loop, but since the amplitude ratio is 0.78, the variation in y_s damps out with each subsequent cycle of the loop. The second time around the loop y_s has a sinusoidal amplitude of 0.61 (i.e., 0.78×0.78), the third time

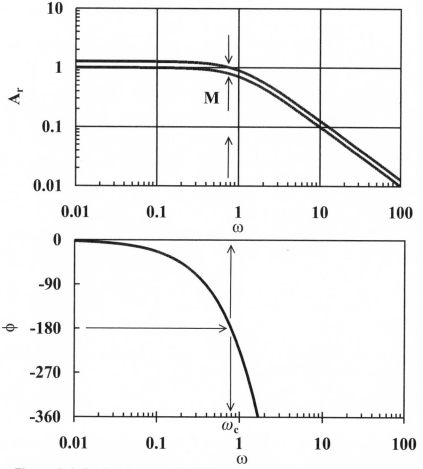

Figure 9.4 Bode plot of a FOPDT process that shows the gain margin.

has an amplitude of 0.48, and so on. If the amplitude ratio were exactly 1.0, the oscillations would be sustained. If the amplitude ratio were greater than 1.0, y_s would grow without bound (i.e., unstable operation). Therefore, the amplitude ratio at a phase angle of -180° indicates the stability of a system and is called the **Bode stability criterion**. The frequency at which the phase angle is equal to -180° is referred to as the **critical frequency**, ω_c.

Figure 9.4 shows the Bode plot of the FOPDT process for a P-only controller in an open-loop configuration. It shows the results for $K_c = 1.0$ and $K_c = 1.28$, which corresponds to underdamped stable operation and sustained oscillations at the critical frequency, respectively. The difference between the amplitude ratio for $K_c = 1.0$ and $K_c = 1.28$, denoted by M in Figure 9.4, is a measure of how close the controller with $K_c = 1.0$ is to the onset of instability. The **gain margin (GM)** is defined by

$$GM = \frac{1}{A_r^*} \qquad\qquad 9.5$$

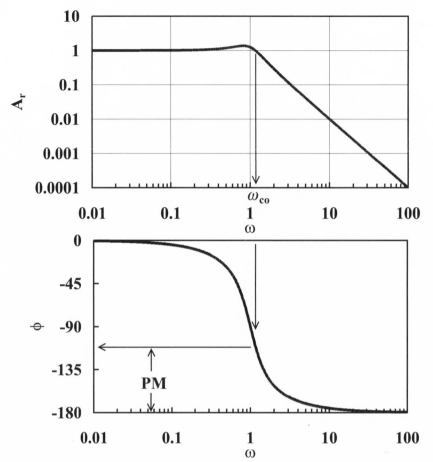

Figure 9.5 Bode plot of a second-order process that shows the phase margin.

where A_r^* is the amplitude ratio at the critical frequency, or 0.78 for Figure 9.2. In this latter case, the GM is equal to 1/0.78 or 1.28. When the $GM > 1$, the system is stable.

Figure 9.5 shows a Bode plot for a second-order process with a P-only controller with $K_c = 1.0$. The **phase margin** (**PM**), is the difference between a phase angle corresponding to an amplitude ratio of 1.0 and a phase angle of -180°, i.e.,

$$PM = \phi^* - (-180°)$$ **9.6**

where ϕ^* is the phase angle that corresponds to $A_r = 1$. For Figure 9.5, the PM is 67.5°. When $PM > 0$, the system is stable. The **crossover frequency**, ω_{co}, is the frequency that corresponds to $A_r = 1$. Gain margin and phase margin can be used to tune controllers. The larger the GM or PM values used for tuning, the more conservative the controller. Typical GM values used for tuning range from 1.4 to 1.8 while PM values typically range from 30° to 45°. GM and PM can be used like the decay ratio was used in

Chapter 7 to select the controller tuning criterion, i.e., the more nonlinear a process and the larger the magnitude of disturbances, the larger the values of PM or GM.

Example 9.3 Tuning a Controller for a Specified Gain Margin

Problem Statement. Determine the controller gain, K_c, for a P-only controller applied to a FOPDT process ($K_p = 2$, $\tau_p = 3$, $\theta_p = 1.5$) for a gain margin equal to 1.7.

Solution. From Table 9.1, the amplitude ratio and the phase angle are

$$(A_r)_{overall} = \frac{2K_c}{\sqrt{9\omega^2 + 1}} \qquad\qquad \textbf{A}$$

$$\phi_{overall} = \tan^{-1}(-3\omega) - 85.9\omega$$

First, the critical frequency, ω_c, is determined by setting the overall phase angle equal to (-180°) and solving for the corresponding frequency, i.e.,

$$-180° = \tan^{-1}(-3\omega_c) - 85.9\omega_c$$

By trial-and-error, the critical frequency is calculated equal to 1.218 radians per time.

The gain margin allows for the calculation of the amplitude ratio at the critical frequency (A_r^*), i.e.,

$$A_r^* = \frac{1}{1.7} = 0.588$$

Finally, the controller gain can be determined by applying Equation A at the critical frequency, i.e.,

$$A_r^* = \frac{2K_c}{\sqrt{9\omega_c^2 + 1}}$$

Rearranging and solving results in the controller gain equal to 1.12.

♠

Example 9.4 Tuning a Controller for a Specified Phase Margin

Problem Statement. Determine the controller gain, K_c, for a P-only controller applied to a second-order process ($K_p = 2$, $\tau_p = 3$, $\zeta = 1.5$) for a phase margin equal to 40°.

Solution. From Table 9.1 in a manner similar to Examples 9.1 and 9.2, the amplitude ratio and the phase angle can be expressed by

$$(A_r)_{overall} = \frac{2K_c}{\sqrt{(1-9\omega^2)^2 + (9\omega)^2}}$$

$$\phi_{overall} = \tan^{-1}\left(\frac{-9\omega}{1-9\omega^2}\right)$$

The $40°$ phase margin determines the crossover frequency by applying the equation for the phase angle.

$$40° - 180° = \tan^{-1}\left(\frac{-9\omega_{co}}{1-9\omega_{co}^2}\right)$$

Rearranging yields $7.55\omega_{co}^2 - 9\omega_{co} - 0.839 = 0$

Solving for the positive root of this equation determines that the crossover frequency is equal to 1.28 radians per unit time. At the crossover frequency, the amplitude ratio is equal to unity; therefore, applying the amplitude ratio equation results in

$$1 = \frac{2K_c}{\sqrt{(1-9\omega_{co}^2)^2 + (9\omega_{co})^2}}$$

Using the value of the crossover frequency in this equation and solving for the controller gain yields the controller gain equal to 8.95.

♠

9.4 Pulse Test

Earlier in this chapter, testing the process directly and using the transfer function of the process were presented for developing a Bode plot of a process. A **pulse test** is an experimental approach that can be used to generate a Bode plot of an industrial process without directly using transfer functions. The process considered here is the combined system of the actuator, process, and sensor, i.e.,

$$G_p'(s) = G_a(s)G_p(s)G_s(s)$$

The input to this process is the output of the controller. For a pulse test, a rectangular pulse (Chapter 5) is used and the resulting measured values of the controlled variable

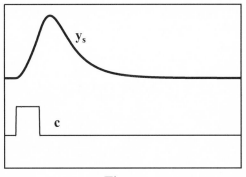

Figure 9.6 Example of a pulse test.

are recorded (Figure 9.6). This is an open-loop test and y_s should return to or near its starting point in the response time of the process if no significant disturbance occurs during the test. The transfer function for this process is given by

$$G'_p(s) = \frac{Y_s(s)}{C(s)} = \frac{\int_0^\infty \Delta y_s(t) e^{-st} dt}{\int_0^\infty \Delta c(t) e^{-st} dt} \qquad \textbf{9.7}$$

which is based upon the definition of the Laplace transform and where $\Delta y_s(t)$ and $\Delta c(t)$ are deviation variables. The transfer function can be converted into a Bode plot by substituting $s = i\omega$. Thus

$$G'_p(i\omega) = \frac{\int_0^\infty \Delta y_s(t) e^{-i\omega t} dt}{\int_0^\infty \Delta c(t) e^{-i\omega t} dt} \qquad \textbf{9.8}$$

Using the Euler identity

$$e^{-i\omega t} = \cos \omega t - i \sin \omega t$$

results in

$$G'_p(i\omega) = \frac{A(\omega) - i B(\omega)}{C(\omega) - i D(\omega)} \qquad \textbf{9.9}$$

where

$$A(\omega) = \int_0^\infty \Delta y_s(t) \cos \omega t \, dt$$

$$B(\omega) = \int_0^\infty \Delta y_s(t) \sin \omega t \, dt$$

$$C(\omega) = \int_0^\infty \Delta c(t) \cos \omega t \, dt$$ **9.10**

$$D(\omega) = \int_0^\infty \Delta c(t) \sin \omega t \, dt$$

After multiplying by the complex conjugate of the denominator, the real and imaginary components of $G'_p(i\omega)$ are given by

$$R(\omega) = \frac{A(\omega)C(\omega) + B(\omega)D(\omega)}{C^2(\omega) + D^2(\omega)}$$ **9.11**

$$I(\omega) = \frac{A(\omega)D(\omega) - B(\omega)C(\omega)}{C^2(\omega) + D^2(\omega)}$$ **9.12**

where $R(\omega)$ and $I(\omega)$ are the real and imaginary components of $G'_p(i\omega)$, respectively. Then, finally, the amplitude ratio, A_r, and the phase angle, ϕ, can be calculated directly

$$A_r(\omega) = \left| G'_p(i\omega) \right| = \sqrt{R^2(\omega) + I^2(\omega)}$$ **9.13**

$$\phi(\omega) = \angle G'_p(i\omega) = \tan^{-1}\left(\frac{I(\omega)}{R(\omega)} \right)$$ **9.14**

After the experimental pulse test is generated, Equations 9.9 to 9.13 are applied at each value of ω to generate the Bode plot. A value ω_1 is selected and the values of $A(\omega_1)$, $B(\omega_1)$, $C(\omega_1)$, and $D(\omega_1)$ [Equation 9.10] are calculated using the pulse test results and a numerical integration method (e.g., the trapezoidal method[1]). Then, $R(\omega_1)$ and $I(\omega_1)$ are calculated using Equations 9.11 and 9.12. Finally, $A_r(\omega_1)$ and $\phi(\omega_1)$ are determined from Equations 9.13 and 9.14. Another frequency is selected and the procedure is repeated until the Bode plot is complete.

Once the Bode plot is generated, the Bode plot of a P-only, PI, or PID controller can be combined with it and used to tune a controller to meet gain margin or phase margin specifications. The Bode plot of the controller can be plotted on the Bode diagram developed from the experimental pulse test. For a set of tuning parameters, the A_r's and ϕ's for the controller and the process can be added together to yield the overall Bode plot. A_r's are added because they are plotted as logarithms and adding logarithms is equivalent to multiplying the A_r's. In this manner, controller tuning parameters can be adjusted until the desired *GM* or *PM* is obtained.

This approach[2] was first used in the 1960's because it allowed for a systematic procedure to tune PID controllers applied to complex industrial processes. This approach to tuning suffers from the following limitations.

1. It requires an open-loop response time to complete the pulse test.
2. Disturbances during the test can corrupt the results.
3. Bode plots developed by this approach can be noisy, particularly around the crossover frequency, affecting the accuracy of the resulting *PM* or *GM* used for tuning.

The ATV method of identification with on-line tuning (Section 7.13) can be applied with much less time and effort and yields more accurate results. As a result, ATV-based tuning is recommended over pulse-based tuning for slow-responding loops.

9.5 Nyquist Diagram

The **Nyquist diagram** is an alternate method for presenting frequency response behavior. Bode plots present separate curves for the amplitude ratio and phase angle as a function of frequency. The Nyquist diagram presents the frequency response behavior in a more compact form, i.e., with a single curve. At a specific frequency, the amplitude ratio is the length of a vector from the origin and the phase angle is the angle of the vector with respect to the *x*-axis, which together define a point on the Nyquist diagram. The Nyquist diagram is generated by varying the frequency over a given range. The methods previously discussed for generating Bode plots can be used to generated a Nyquist diagram by simply plotting the amplitude ratio and phase angle on the complex plane. Nyquist diagrams, like Bode plots, can be used to tune controllers and analyze closed-loop stability, but the presentation of these approaches is beyond the scope of this text.

Figure 9.7 shows a Nyquist diagram for a FOPDT process model ($K_p = 1$, $\tau_p = 1$, $\theta_p = 0.5$). The amplitude ratio and phase angle of G_p ($i\omega$) are plotted in a complex plane for a range of values of frequency, ω. Each point on the Nyquist plot corresponds to a different frequency.

9.6 Closed-Loop Frequency Response

A Bode plot provides frequency response information about a process or a process and a controller in an open-loop form. It is also informative to consider the frequency dependence of a closed-loop system for disturbance upsets.

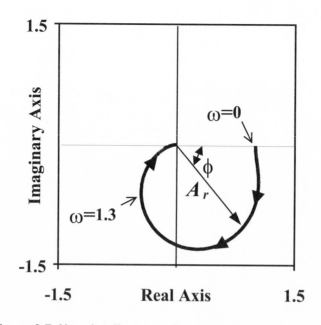

Figure 9.7 Nyquist diagram of a FOPDT process.

Figure 9.8 is a schematic of a closed-loop feedback system subjected to a sinusoidally-varying disturbance.   Figure 9.9 shows the **closed-loop frequency response** for a FOPDT process model ($K_p = 1$, $\tau_p = 1$, $\theta_p = 0.5$) and a FOPDT disturbance model ($K_d = 1$, $\tau_d = 1$, $\theta_d = 0.5$) for sinusoidal disturbance changes with a P-only controller ($K_c = 1$). Note that A_r is plotted on a linear scale in Figure 9.9. **The closed-loop amplitude ratio, A_r, is defined here as the ratio of the amplitude of the variations in the controlled variable divided by the amplitude of the variations in the disturbance.** The phase angle is the phase lag between the disturbance and the controlled variable.

At high frequencies, A_r drops off sharply because the process is not fast enough to respond to high-frequency variations in the disturbance level, and the variations become filtered out (i.e., averaged out by the process). At low frequencies, A_r drops off as well because, for very slow-varying disturbances, the feedback controller has time to absorb the disturbance and maintain operation at the setpoint. At frequencies between these extremes, ω is large enough that the feedback controller is unable to remove all the variations and ω is small enough that the process does not filter out the variations in the disturbance. The peak in the closed-loop frequency response is called the **closed-loop peak amplitude**. The **peak frequency** is the input frequency that corresponds to the closed-loop peak amplitude and represents the frequency at which the maximum sensitivity to the disturbance occurs.

Industrial feedback controllers exhibit the same general behavior as shown in Figure 9.9. There is a range of disturbance frequencies to which a controller is most sensitive. Analyzing the peak frequencies of the individual loops of a number of

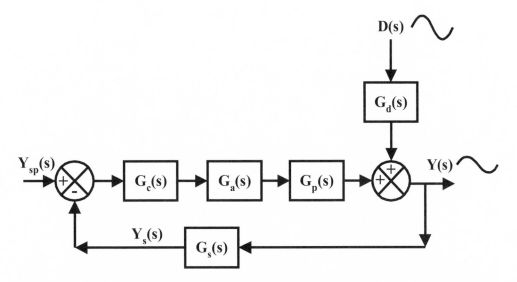

Figure 9.8 Block diagram of a feedback loop that is excited by a sinusoidal disturbance.

processing units in a series can provide insight into the disturbance rejection performance of the overall system.

Consider two distillation columns in series (Figure 9.10) for which the bottoms of the first column is the feed to the second column. First, consider the case in which the peak frequency for the bottom loop of the first column is equal to the peak frequency for both the top and bottom composition loops of the second column. In this case, the disturbance frequencies for which the two loops on the second column are

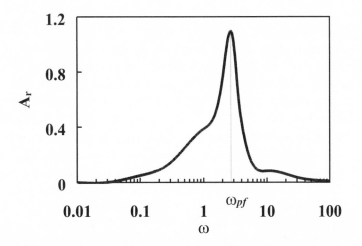

Figure 9.9 The closed-loop amplitude ratios for a FOPDT process. Note that A_r is plotted on a linear scale instead of the log scale used for a Bode plot. ω_{pf} is the peak frequency.

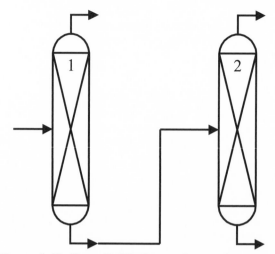

Figure 9.10 Two distillation columns in series.

most sensitive are the same as the frequencies for which the bottom loop on the first column is most sensitive. Therefore, the largest variations in the bottom product are expected to significantly affect both loops on the second column.

Next, consider the case in which the peak frequency of the bottom loop on the first column is significantly lower than the peak frequency for the two loops on the second column (Figure 9.11). For this case, the control loops on the second column should be able to handle the largest variations coming from the first column. From Figure 9.11, one can see that the disturbances that pass through the bottoms controller on the first column do not significantly affect the control loops for the second column. The controllers on the second column have sufficient time to handle these frequencies.

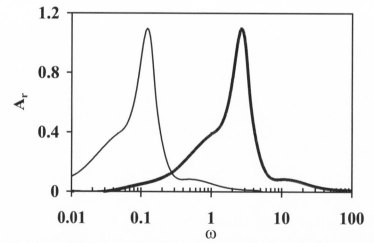

Figure 9.11 Closed-loop amplitude ratios for two control loops with very different frequencies corresponding to the closed-loop peak amplitude. Thin line-bottom control loop on column 1. Thick line-control loops on column 2.

Finally, assume that the bottom loop of the first column is much faster than the control loops on the second column. For this case, the largest variations coming from the first column are filtered out by the slower responding second column. Qualitatively using closed-loop frequency analysis can be helpful in analyzing the propagation of disturbances through a sequence of processing units.

9.7 Summary

The frequency or time scale of inputs to a process can have a significant effect on the resulting closed-loop behavior. For example, if high-frequency disturbances (i.e., short-time variations) enter a process, the process filters out the variations and the resulting controlled variable is relatively unaffected. If low-frequency disturbances (i.e., long-time variations) enter a process, the feedback controller has ample time to respond to them and deviation from setpoint is small. Therefore, control systems are typically most sensitive to intermediate frequencies. Frequency response analysis provides a methodology to analyze the frequency-dependent characteristics of a process.

Bode plots, which are plots of $\log(A_r)$ versus $\log(\omega)$ and ϕ versus $\log(\omega)$, are a convenient means to present the frequency-dependent characteristics of a process. Bode plots can be generated by (1) directly exciting the process with sinusoidal inputs, (2) applying a sinusoidal input to the transfer function of the process, (3) substituting $s = i\omega$ into the transfer function, and (4) applying a pulse test.

The Bode plot of the combined process and controller can be used to determine the closed-loop stability of the system using the Bode stability criterion. The gain margin and the phase margin can be used as tuning specifications for PID controllers.

Nyquist diagrams are another way to represent the frequency dependent behavior of a process. The Nyquist diagram is a plot of the magnitude and phase angle of $G_p(i\omega)$ on a complex plane for a range of frequencies.

The closed-loop frequency response of a process indicates the disturbance frequencies for which the controller is most sensitive. This information can be used to analyze how disturbances damp out or propagate from one control loop to another through a sequence of processes.

9.8 Additional Terminology

Amplitude ratio - (A_r) the ratio of the amplitude of the variations in y_s divided by the amplitude of the sinusoidal variations in an input to the process.

Bode plot - a plot of $\log(A_r)$ versus $\log(\omega)$ and a plot of ϕ versus $\log(\omega)$.

Bode stability criterion - states that a process is stable if $A_r < 1$ at the critical frequency.

Closed-loop frequency response - a Bode plot for a closed-loop process subjected to sinusoidally varying disturbance inputs.

Closed-loop peak amplitude - the maximum A_r for a closed-loop frequency response.

Critical frequency - the frequency that corresponds to $\phi = -180°$.

Crossover frequency - the frequency that corresponds to $A_r=1$.

Frequency response analysis - the study of the effect of varying input frequencies on process behavior.

Gain margin (GM) - defined by Equation 9.5 and indicates how aggressively a controller is tuned.

Nyquist diagram - a polar-coordinate plot of $G_p(i\omega)$ for a range of frequencies.

Peak frequency - the frequency that corresponds to the closed-loop peak amplitude.

Phase angle - (ϕ) an indication of how much the controller output lags behind the controlled variable.

Phase margin (PM) - defined by Equation 9.6 and indicates how aggressively a controller is tuned.

Pulse test - the response of a process to a rectangular pulse input that can be used to develop a Bode plot for an experimental system.

9.9 References

1. Riggs, J.B., *An Introduction to Numerical Methods for Chemical Engineers*, Texas Tech University Press, pp. 136-143 (1994).

2. Hougen, J.O., *Methods for Solving Process Plant Problems*, Instrument Society of America (1996).

9.10 Preliminary Questions

9.1 Even though frequency response analysis is not generally used by industrial process control engineers, why is frequency response analysis important to the understanding of feedback systems?

9.2 Explain what a Bode plot is. Indicate how you would directly generate a Bode plot for the CST thermal mixer.

9.3 Explain, using equations, how you would generate a Bode plot from the transfer function of a process.

9.4 What is the amplitude ratio used in a Bode plot?

9.5 What is the phase angle used in a Bode plot?

9.6 What information does a Bode plot contain?

9.7 How does one calculate the amplitude ratio of a sequence of transfer functions?

9.8 How does one calculate the phase angle of a sequence of transfer functions?

9.9 Explain the Bode stability criterion in your own words.

9.10 How are the gain margin and the phase margin alike and how are they different?

9.11 Using the results from Table 9.1, describe how the *PM* could be used to tune a PI controller applied to a second-order process.

9.12 Explain how a pulse test can be used to identify the Bode plot of an experimental process.

9.13 Describe how a pulse test can be used to tune a controller on an industrial process. Why would you not use this approach on an industrial process?

9.14 Define what a Nyquist diagram is and how it can be generated.

9.15 Define what a closed-loop Bode plot is and how it can be used to determine the propagation of variability from one processing unit to another.

9.16 What does the peak frequency of a controller indicate?

9.17 What input is varied to generate a closed-loop Bode plot?

9.18 What information does a closed-loop Bode plot provide?

9.19 What four methods shown in this chapter can be used to generate a Bode plot?

9.11 Analytical Questions and Exercises

9.20 Using Table 9.1, develop equations, in terms of the frequency of the input, for the amplitude ratio and phase angle:

     a.   For a PI controller (K_c=4; τ_I=5) applied to a FOPDT process ($K_p = 0.4$; $\tau_p = 6$; $\theta_p = 1$).

b. For a P-only controller (K_c=2) applied to a second-order plus deadtime process ($K_p = 1$; $\tau_p = 3$; $\zeta = 2$; $\theta_p = 1.5$).

c. For a PI controller (K_c=1; τ_I=5) applied to an integrating process (K_p=-3).

d. For a PI controller (K_c=3; τ_I=5) applied to an integrator plus dead time process ($K_p = 0.4$; $\theta_p = 1$).

e. For a PI controller (K_c=13; τ_I=10) applied to a second-order plus deadtime process ($K_p = 0.1$; $\tau_p = 30$; $\zeta = 4$; $\theta_p = 15$).

f. For a PI controller (K_c=3; τ_I=1) applied to a FOPDT process ($K_p = 2$; $\tau_p = 4$; $\theta_p = 2$).

g. For a PI controller (K_c=23; τ_I=15) applied to an integrator plus dead time process ($K_p = 3$; $\theta_p = 3$).

h. For a P-only controller (K_c=20) applied to a second-order plus deadtime process ($K_p = 0.25$; $\tau_p = 30$; $\zeta = 2$; $\theta_p = 10$).

9.21 Determine the controller gain for the following process models and gain margin specifications.

a. For a PI controller (τ_I=5) applied to a FOPDT process ($K_p = 0.4$; $\tau_p = 6$; $\theta_p = 1$) with a gain margin equal to 1.6.

b. For a PI controller (τ_I=3) applied to a FOPDT process ($K_p = 1.4$; $\tau_p = 5$; $\theta_p = 2$) with a gain margin equal to 1.4.

c. For a P-only controller applied to a second-order plus deadtime process ($K_p = 0.25$; $\tau_p = 30$; $\zeta = 2$; $\theta_p = 10$) with a gain margin equal to 1.8.

d. For a P-only controller applied to a second-order plus deadtime process ($K_p = 25$; $\tau_p = 3$; $\zeta = 1.5$; $\theta_p = 2$) with a gain margin equal to 1.5.

9.22 Determine the controller gain for the following process models and phase margin specifications.

a. For a PI controller (τ_I=5) applied to a FOPDT process ($K_p = 0.4$; $\tau_p = 6$; $\theta_p = 1$) with a phase margin equal to 30°.

b. For a PI controller (τ_I=3) applied to a FOPDT process ($K_p = 1.4$; $\tau_p = 5$; $\theta_p = 2$) with a phase margin equal to 45°.

c. For a P-only controller applied to a second-order plus deadtime process ($K_p = 0.25$; $\tau_p = 30$; $\zeta = 2$; $\theta_p = 10$) with a phase margin equal to 35°.

    d. For a P-only controller applied to a second-order plus deadtime process $(K_p = 25; \tau_p = 3; \zeta = 1.5; \theta_p = 2)$ with a phase margin equal to 40°.

9.23 Determine the change in the controller gain corresponding to a change in the gain margin from 1.6 to 1.4 for Problem 9.21a.

9.24 Determine the change in the controller gain corresponding to a change in the gain margin from 1.4 to 1.6 for Problem 9.21b.

9.25 Determine the change in the controller gain corresponding to a change in the phase margin from 30° to 45° for Problem 9.22a.

9.26 Determine the change in the controller gain corresponding to a change in the phase margin from 45° to 30° for Problem 9.22b

9.27 Explain how the reset time for a PI controller can be calculated to meet a specific gain margin if the controller gain is known.

9.28 Explain how the reset time for a PI controller can be calculated to meet a specific phase margin if the controller gain is known.

9.29 Consider a second-order model of a process without deadtime. Is there a gain margin for a controller applied to this model? If not, explain.

9.30 Consider a first-order model of a process without deadtime. Is there a phase margin for a controller applied to this model? If not, explain.

PART IV

ADVANCED
PID CONTROL

Chapter 10

Cascade, Ratio, and Feedforward Control

10.1 Introduction

This chapter considers cascade, ratio, and feedforward control. The advantage of each of these advanced PID controllers is related to its ability to reject disturbances more effectively than conventional PID controllers. Cascade control rejects specific types of disturbance upsets, which can either be measured or unmeasured. Ratio control effectively handles feed flow rate disturbances for a wide range of processes. Feedforward control is a general methodology for directly compensating for measured disturbances.

When a disturbance upsets a conventional PID control loop, all the correction comes from feedback action. No corrective action is taken until the disturbance has affected the process. Return to the everyday control example of driving a car, which was presented in Chapter 1. When driving a car, if one looks only at the car's position on the road when negotiating a turn (e.g., looking right in front of the car), the safe car speed through a turn is greatly reduced compared with the feedforward approach wherein the driver anticipates the curve. Cascade, ratio and feedforward control provide performance enhancement for chemical process control because, in each case, corrective action is taken before the disturbance has significantly affected the process. As a result, the amount of corrective action required from the PID controller, the resulting maximum deviation from setpoint, and response time of the feedback system can each be significantly reduced.

10.2 Cascade Control

Cascade control offers a means of reducing the effect of certain disturbances on the primary control objective of a control loop. Cascade control uses two control loops in tandem (Figure 10.1). The inner loop (A) receives its setpoint from the outer loop (B). The inner loop is used to react to certain disturbances on a high-frequency basis before these disturbances can significantly upset the process by maintaining y_A at

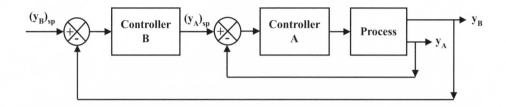

Figure 10.1 Block diagram of a cascade control loop. Controller A is the secondary controller and controller B is the primary controller.

its setpoint. The outer loop is applied to maintain the primary control objective (y_B) on setpoint. The inner loop is called the **secondary loop**, and the outer loop is called the **primary loop**. The secondary loop is also referred to as the **slave loop**, and the primary loop is referred to as the **master loop**. For an effective cascade arrangement, y_A in Figure 10.1 must have a strong and immediate effect on y_B, and the closed-loop dynamics of the secondary loop must be much faster than those of the primary loop. Maintaining y_A at its setpoint should reject specific disturbances.

Example 10.1 A Steam-Heated Heat Exchanger

Problem Statement. Consider the steam-heated heat exchanger without cascade control shown in Figure 10.2a. Apply cascade control and qualitatively analyze the control performance differences for this process with and without cascade control.

Solution. Considering the control configuration without cascade (Figure 10.2a), assume that the steam supply pressure increases. The steam pressure in the heat exchanger increases, causing an increase in the temperature of the process stream leaving the heat exchanger. As the outlet temperature begins to rise, the PID controller on the temperature of the outlet stream takes corrective action by reducing the stem position of the valve on the steam line. By the time the PID controller starts to take corrective action, an excessive amount of heat has already been transferred from the steam to the process fluid in the heat exchanger.

Figure 10.2b shows the steam-heated heat exchanger with a cascade control configuration. The pressure control loop is the secondary or inner loop. The temperature control loop is the primary or outer loop. The output of the temperature controller for the cascade control case is the setpoint for the pressure controller, while the output from the temperature controller for the case without cascade control goes directly to the control valve on the steam line. For the cascade control case, the setpoint of the pressure controller is manipulated to maintain the outlet temperature of the process stream. In relation to Figure 10.1, steam pressure corresponds to y_A and the outlet temperature of the feed corresponds to y_B. For the cascade control case, when the steam supply pressure increases, the pressure of steam inside the heat exchanger

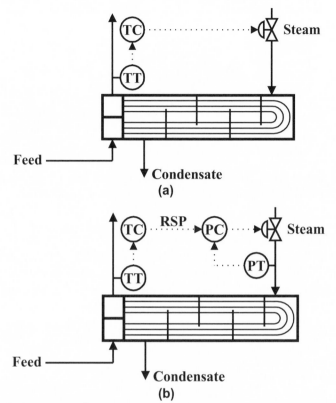

Figure 10.2 Schematic of a steam-heated heat exchanger with a temperature controller for controlling the temperature of the exiting process fluid. (a) without cascade and (b) with cascade control.

increases, but the pressure controller reacts quickly by closing the valve until the desired pressure of steam in the heat exchanger is reinstated. The steam pressure disturbance is almost completely absorbed by the secondary loop before the disturbance can affect the primary loop. Because the pressure control loop (secondary loop) is much faster-responding than the temperature control loop (primary loop), the pressure control loop can quickly compensate for changes in the steam pressure before they affect the temperature loop.

♠

Example 10.2 An Exothermic CSTR with a Water-Jacket Heat Exchanger

Problem Statement. Consider the exothermic CSTR with a water-jacket heat exchanger without cascade control shown in Figure 10.3a. Apply cascade control and qualitatively analyze the control performance with and without cascade control.

Solution. Considering the control configuration without cascade (Figure 10.3a), assume that significant changes in the temperature of the cooling water occur. A

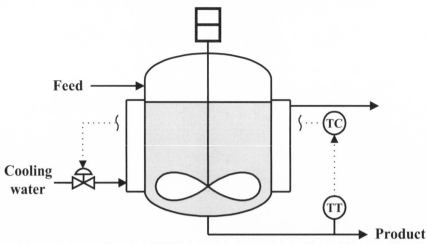

Figure 10.3a Schematic of a CSTR temperature controller without cascade control.

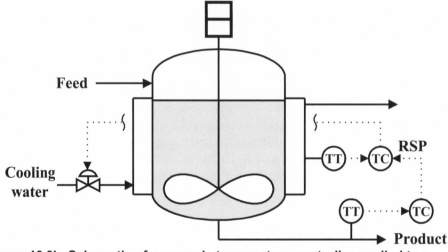

Figure 10.3b Schematic of a cascade temperature controller applied to a CSTR.

change in the inlet cooling water temperature results in a reactor temperature change. A significant change in the reactor temperature occurs before changes in the flow rate of the inlet cooling water are made because the reactor temperature responds relatively slowly. Figure 10.3b shows the CSTR with a cascade configuration. The temperature control loop on the cooling water is the secondary control loop while the temperature control loop on the product is the primary loop.   When an inlet cooling water temperature change occurs, a change in the jacket water temperature occurs long before the reactor temperature starts to change. The secondary loop (the water-jacket temperature loop) can react quickly to inlet cooling water temperature changes, thus significantly reducing the effect of cooling water temperature changes on the reactor temperature control loop.   ♠

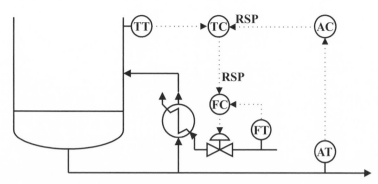

Figure 10.4 Schematic of a multiple cascade configuration applied for bottoms composition control of a distillation column.

Example 10.3 Stripping Section of a Distillation Column

Problem Statement. Consider the stripping section of a distillation column with multiple cascade control loops applied as shown in Figure 10.4. Analyze the control performance differences for this process with and without cascade control.

Solution. Figure 10.4 shows a multiple cascade configuration that is designed to maintain the impurity level in the bottoms product of a distillation column at its setpoint. The innermost loop is flow control on the steam to the reboiler. Cascade controllers, which use flow controllers as the secondary loop, are the most commonly used form of cascade control in the CPI. The flow controller provides fast response to steam pressure changes. The setpoint for the flow control loop is the manipulated variable of the intermediate loop.

Tray temperature correlates strongly with product composition for a large class of industrial columns. Utilizing such correlations is the basis of inferential control (Section 11.2). The advantage of controlling tray temperatures on distillation columns is that composition changes are measured much more quickly using tray temperatures than using on-line analyzers. For fast-acting columns (when the reflux ratio is relatively low), feedback control using the GC can result in poor control performance because the deadtime-to-time constant ratio of the process is too large. The fast response of temperature sensors gives tray temperature control loops a much smaller deadtime-to-time constant ratio and, therefore, tray temperature control loops exhibit better control performance with shorter closed-loop response times than control directly from the GC.

As the feed composition changes, the proper tray temperature setpoint changes; therefore, adjustments to the setpoint for the tray temperature controller are made by the composition control loop, which is the overall primary loop for this cascade arrangement. This multiple cascade arrangement works effectively because

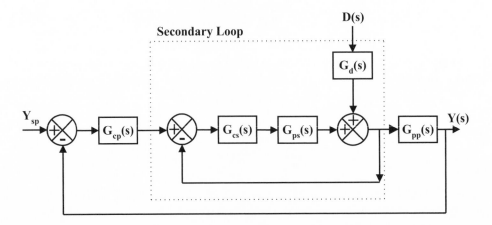

Figure 10.5 Block diagram of a generalized cascade control loop. Note that the actuators and sensors are omitted from this diagram.

the flow control loop is much faster than the temperature control loop, which is much faster than the composition control loop.

♠

From an analysis of these examples of cascade control, the following conclusions can be drawn:

1. The inner loop (secondary loop) must be considerably faster than the outer loop (primary loop) for effective cascade control.

2. High-frequency feedback action of the secondary loop eliminates specific disturbances before they can significantly affect the primary loop. Since the process responds much faster to the secondary loop than to the primary loop, the secondary loop can absorb these specific disturbances much more quickly.

3. The controlled variable of the secondary loop acts as the manipulated variable of the primary loop.

Theoretical Analysis. Figure 10.5 shows a block diagram of a generalized cascade loop. For the heat exchanger example, the inner loop is the pressure control loop wherein the output of the pressure controller goes directly to the control valve. $G_{ps}(s)$ represents the effect of valve stem position on steam pressure in the heat exchanger. $G_{pp}(s)$ represents the effect of steam pressure on the outlet temperature of the process fluid leaving the heat exchanger. The output of the temperature controller is the setpoint for the pressure controller. Note that the disturbance, $D(s)$, enters the secondary loop and, therefore, can be effectively absorbed by the action of the secondary loop. The transfer function for the effect of the disturbance $D(s)$ on the primary control loop $Y(s)$ can be derived using the properties of a block diagram

$$\frac{Y(s)}{D(s)} = \frac{G_d(s)G_{pp}(s)}{1+G_{cs}(s)G_{ps}(s)+G_{cp}(s)G_{pp}(s)G_{cs}(s)G_{ps}(s)} \qquad \textbf{10.1}$$

Assuming first-order processes for $G_{pp}(s)$ and $G_{ps}(s)$ and P-only controllers for the primary and secondary loops, a second-order response results. The closed-loop second-order process time constant, τ', is given by

$$\tau'_p = \sqrt{\frac{\tau_{pp}\tau_{ps}}{1+K_{cs}K_{ps}(1+K_{cp}K_{pp})}} \qquad \textbf{10.2}$$

where τ_{pp} is the time constant and K_{pp} is the gain of the primary process $[G_{pp}(s)]$, τ_{ps} is the time constant and K_{ps} is the gain of the secondary process $[G_{ps}(s)]$, K_{cp} is the gain of the controller on the primary loop, and K_{cs} is the gain for the secondary loop. From Equation 10.2, τ'_p can be significantly smaller than τ_{pp}.

Example 10.4 The Effect of the Relative Dynamics of the Primary and Secondary Loops

Problem Statement. Evaluate the control performance of a cascade control loop using a FOPDT process model for the primary and secondary loops:

$$G_{pp}(s) = \frac{1.0\,e^{-0.5\,s}}{s+1} \qquad \textbf{A}$$

$$G_{ps}(s) = \frac{1.0\,e^{-(0.5/r)\,s}}{s/r+1} \qquad \textbf{B}$$

$$r = \frac{\tau_{pp}}{\tau_{ps}}$$

where r is the relative speed of the secondary loop compared to the primary loop.

Solution. Figure 10.6 shows that the relative control performance (ratio of IAE for a faster secondary loop divided by IAE for a secondary loop with the same dynamics as the primary loop) improves as r increases. Note that these results are based on the disturbance, D(s), affecting the primary loop only through the secondary loop (see Figure 10.5). As a general rule, **the secondary loop should be at least three times as fast as the primary loop** to justify the use of cascade control. This point corresponds to the "knee" of the curve shown in Figure 10.6. To obtain this advantage for cascade control, **the secondary loop must be tuned tightly**, i.e., allowing only short term deviations from the setpoint of the secondary loop. ♠

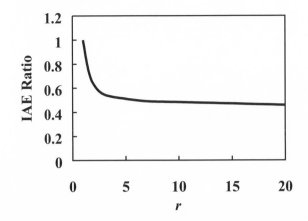

Figure 10.6 The effect of the relative speed of the secondary loop compared to the primary loop on the relative control performance of cascade control.

Example 10.5 Schematic Development for a Cascade Control System

Problem Statement. Consider the steam-heated heat exchanger shown in Figure 10.7. This process has a temperature measurement of the outlet temperature of the process fluid, a pressure measurement on the steam on the shell side of the exchanger, and a control valve on the condensate leaving the exchanger. The valve on the condensate affects the level of condensate in the exchanger which, in turn, affects the area available for condensation of the steam (heat transfer). The heat-transfer rate is directly related to the steam pressure. The heat-transfer rate determines the outlet temperature of the process stream. Draw the schematic of a control system for which a temperature controller on the outlet of the process stream is cascaded to a pressure controller on the steam, the output of which is sent to the control valve on the condensate.

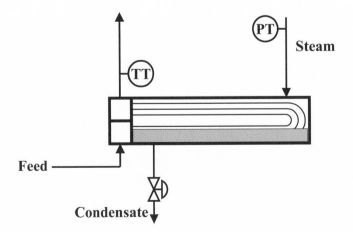

Figure 10.7 Schematic of a steam-heated heat exchanger without controls.

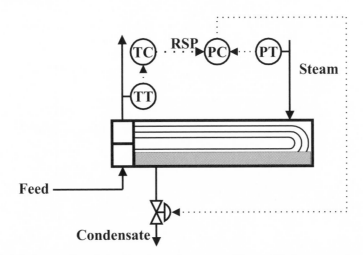

Figure 10.8 Schematic of the heat exchanger with multiple cascade controls.

Solution. The cascade system for the steam-heated heat exchanger is shown in Figure 10.8. The output of the temperature controller on the outlet of the process fluid becomes the setpoint for the pressure controller on the steam. The output of the pressure controller goes directly to the valve on the condensate. This configuration has the advantage that it can absorb changes in the steam pressure, and it uses a relatively small control valve (less expensive) because the condensate line is a small diameter line.

♠

10.3 Ratio Control

The flow rates associated with many processes scale directly with the feed rate to the process, e.g., distillation and wastewater neutralization. For distillation, all the liquid and vapor flow rates within the column are directly proportional to the feed rate if the product purities are maintained and the tray efficiency is constant. For wastewater neutralization, the amount of reagent necessary to maintain a neutral pH for the effluent varies directly with the flow rate of the wastewater feed, as long as the titration curve of the wastewater remains constant.

When the manipulated variable of a process is directly proportional to the feed rate, ratio control can significantly reduce the effect of feed rate disturbances on the process. Figure 10.9 shows how a ratio controller can be applied for a general case. When a feed flow rate change is measured, the manipulated variable is proportionally adjusted immediately, i.e., the measured flow rate of the feed is multiplied by the manipulated variable-to-feed rate ratio (output of the composition controller).

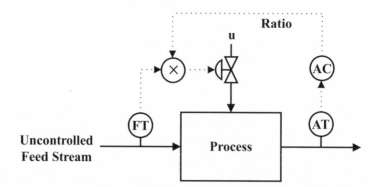

Figure 10.9 Schematic of a general ratio controller applied for composition control.

Feedback corrections (i.e., changes in the output from the controller) are made to the ratio based on analyzer readings. That is, **the controller output is a ratio**.

Figure 10.10 shows a comparison between a conventional feedback controller and a ratio controller for a distillation column. The controlled variable is the overhead composition and the disturbance is a change in the feed rate. Note that the maximum deviation from setpoint and the settling time for this disturbance are significantly reduced by ratio control. The manipulated variable for a ratio controller is a ratio; therefore, during an ATV test to tune a ratio controller, the ratio is adjusted to create the standing wave in the controlled variable.

Example 10.6 Ratio Control applied to a pH Neutralization Process

Problem Statement. Consider the pH neutralization process based on a mixing tank shown in Figure 10.11. Analyze the control performance of this process with and without ratio control.

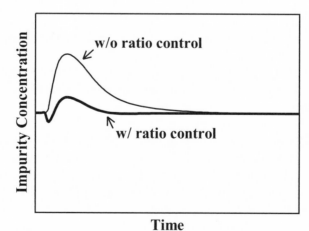

Figure 10.10 Distillation overhead composition with and without ratio control.

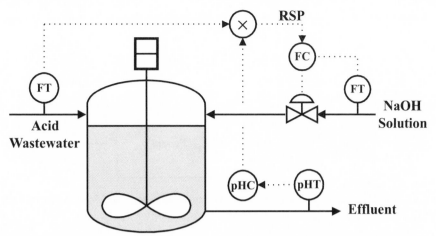

Figure 10.11 Schematic of ratio control applied for pH control of an acid wastewater neutralization process.

Solution. Without ratio control, acid wastewater flow rate changes cause significant pH excursions for the effluent. The wastewater is typically discharged to a biological treatment pond. If the pH of the pond is more than 9 or less than 6, the biological agents go into shock and are unable to remove the organic matter from the wastewater. Smaller changes in pH can also reduce the effectiveness of the treatment pond.

When the chemical makeup of the wastewater remains relatively constant, the ratio controller shown in Figure 10.11 can effectively handle wastewater feed flow rate changes and prevent feed flow rate changes from upsetting the treatment pond. Small changes in the chemical makeup of the wastewater can usually be handled by the feedback controller, which adjusts the reagent-to-wastewater ratio to maintain the specified effluent pH.

♠

Example 10.7 The Application of Ratio Control for a Distillation Column

Problem Statement. Consider the stripping section of a distillation column shown in Figure 10.12. Analyze the control performance differences for this process with and without ratio control.

Solution.   Consider the system shown in Figure 10.12 without ratio control. In this case, as feed flow rate changes to the column occur, the feedback controller from the bottoms product analyzer to the flow controller on the steam must absorb the entire upset, which can be significant. On the other hand, the application of ratio control can significantly reduce the size of the upset that the feedback controller must handle. This results because, at steady-state conditions, the steam rate necessary to maintain the product purities scales directly with the feed rate to the column.

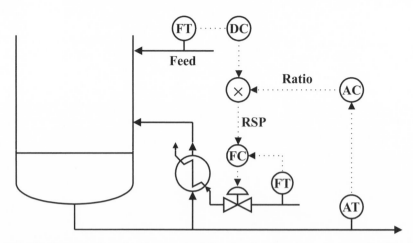

Figure 10.12 Schematic of ratio control for feed rate changes applied to the stripping section of a distillation column.

This application of ratio control is similar to the previous example except that dynamic compensation is added to the measured column feed rate. If the steam flow to the reboiler is increased immediately after an increase in column feed rate, the corrective action is initially an over-correction. This results because, when a feed rate change occurs, it takes some time for the bottom product composition to be affected. The purpose of the dynamic compensation (DC) element is to allow for the correct timing for the compensation for feed rate changes. The dynamic element for this case could be simply a lag element, e.g., a digital filter described by Equation 6.23. The wastewater neutralization case (Figure 10.11) does not require dynamic compensation because the process pH responses to feed rate and NaOH flow rate changes have similar dynamic behavior. In this case, the bottom composition responds differently to feed rate changes than to reboiler steam changes; therefore, dynamic compensation is required for ratio control.

♠

Example 10.8 Schematic of a Ratio Control System

Problem Statement. Consider the gas-fired furnace shown in Figure 10.13a. The furnace has a temperature measurement of the outlet temperature of the process fluid, a flow rate measurement on the process fluid, a flow measurement for the fuel to the furnace, and a control valve on the fuel line to the furnace. Draw the schematic of a control system that adjusts the ratio of fuel flow to the flow rate of the process fluid to control the outlet temperature of the process fluid. A flow control loop is used to maintain the measured fuel flow rate at the level specified by the ratio controller.

Solution. The ratio controller for the gas-fired furnace is shown in Figure 10.13b. The output of the temperature controller on the process fluid is the specified ratio of fuel

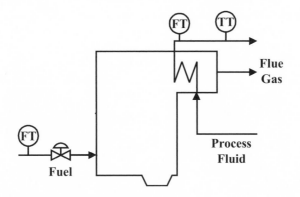

Figure 10.13a Schematic of a gas-fired furnace without controls.

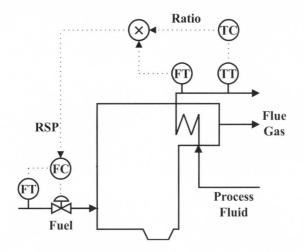

Figure 10.13b Schematic of a gas-fired furnace with ratio control.

flow rate to process fluid flow rate. This ratio is multiplied by the measured value of the process fluid flow rate and the result is the setpoint for the flow controller on the fuel. The application of ratio control to this case should reduce the magnitude of upsets caused by changes in flow rate of the process stream. Dynamic compensation may not be required in this case because feed rate and fuel flow changes are expected to have approximately the same dynamic behavior.

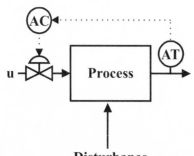

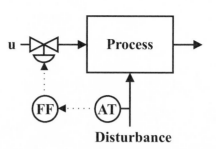

Figure 10.14a Schematic of a feedback controller.

Figure 10.14b Schematic of a feedforward controller.

10.4 Feedforward Control

Feedforward control can be applied to process control loops that are significantly affected by disturbances that are measurable (or estimatable) on-line. A feedback controller (Figure 10.14a) reacts to deviations from setpoint caused by the disturbance until the process is returned to setpoint. As was pointed out in Chapter 7, since the proportional and derivative terms are zero during steady-state operation at the setpoint, the integral term in the PID controller is responsible for the long term compensation for disturbances. A feedforward controller (Figure 10.14b) anticipates the effects of a measured change in a disturbance (i.e., a **load change**) and takes corrective action before the disturbance affects the process. In effect, the feedforward controller applies corrective manipulated variable changes corresponding to the integral action that a feedback controller generates; therefore, when a feedback controller and feedforward controller are used together, the feedback controller has much less "work" to do to compensate for a measured disturbance.

Example 10.9 Feedforward and Feedback Control of a Boiler Drum Level

Problem Statement. Evaluate feedforward, feedback, and combined feedforward and feedback control applied for level control of a boiler drum.

Solution. Figure 10.15a shows a feedback controller applied for the level control of a boiler drum. The feedback controller compares the measured value of the level with the setpoint and adjusts the flow rate of the feedwater to the drum. Therefore, when changes in the demand for steam occur, changes in the drum level result. If large changes in steam demand occur, a large gain is required for the feedback controller to maintain the level near its setpoint. But, for large controller gains, the process is more susceptible to oscillatory or unstable behavior. Also, high-gain controllers are sensitive to noisy measurements of the controlled variable and, in this case, level indicators can have significant noise levels.

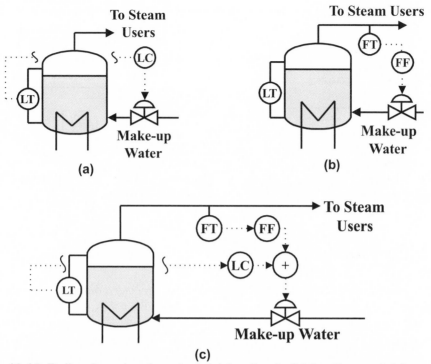

Figure 10.15 Boiler drum level control (a) feedback (b) feedforward (c) feedback and feedforward combined.

Figure 10.15b is a schematic of a feedforward controller applied for steam drum level control. The idea is quite simple: if the flow rate of the makeup feedwater is equal to the steam usage, the drum level remains constant. One is tempted to conclude that the feedforward controller is all that is needed for this application. Unfortunately, the measurements of the steam usage and the feedwater flow rate are not perfectly accurate. Even small errors in measured flow rates add up over time, leading to one of two undesirable extremes. The drum can fill with water and put water into the steam system or the liquid level can drop, exposing the boiler tubes, which can damage the boiler tubes. As a result, neither feedback nor feedforward are effective by themselves for this case. In general, feedforward-only controllers are susceptible to measurement errors and unmeasured disturbances and, as a result, some type of feedback correction is typically required.

Figure 10.15c shows a combined feedforward and feedback controller for the control of the level in the steam drum. The feedforward controller provides most of the control action required by responding to the measured steam usage. The feedback controller can be a relatively low-gain controller since it is required to compensate only for measurement errors and unmeasured disturbances.

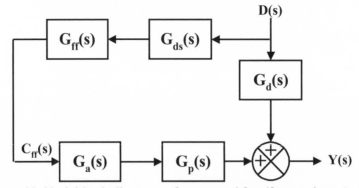

Figure 10.16 A block diagram of a general feedforward controller.

General feedforward controller. The previous example demonstrates how a feedforward controller can be developed from an analysis of the process. A more generalized feedforward controller design procedure can also be used. Consider a block diagram for a generalized feedforward controller shown in Figure 10.16. The disturbance is measured by a sensor with a dynamic response given by $G_{ds}(s)$. The feedforward controller $[G_{ff}(s)]$ uses the measured value of the disturbance to calculate its feedforward correction $[C_{ff}(s)]$. The feedforward correction affects the actuator, which, in turn, changes the manipulated variable level, which changes the controlled variable. Notice that the controlled variable changes are due to changes in the feedforward controller output, $C_{ff}(s)$, and in the disturbance, $D(s)$.

$$Y(s) = C_{ff}(s)G_a(s)G_p(s) + D(s)G_d(s) \qquad\qquad \textbf{10.3}$$

The feedforward controller determines the control action $C_{ff}(s)$, i.e.,

$$C_{ff}(s) = G_{ff}(s)G_{ds}(s)D(s) \qquad\qquad \textbf{10.4}$$

where $G_{ds}(s)$ represents the sensor response to the measured disturbance, then

$$Y(s) = D(s)G_{ds}(s)G_{ff}(s)G_a(s)G_p(s) + D(s)G_d(s)$$

Since we want to design a feedforward controller that keeps the process at setpoint in spite of disturbances, we set $Y(s)$ equal to zero and solve for $G_{ff}(s)$ yielding

$$G_{ff}(s) = \frac{-G_d(s)}{G_{ds}(s)G_a(s)G_p(s)} \qquad\qquad \textbf{10.5}$$

This equation gives us a means of directly determining the feedforward controller using a model of the effect of the disturbance on the process and a model of the effect of the manipulated variable on the process. Let's assume that we have FOPDT models for $G_d(s)$ and the product $G_{ds}(s)\,G_a(s)\,G_p(s)$, i.e.,

$$G_{ds}(s)G_a(s)G_p(s) = \frac{K_p\, e^{-\theta_p s}}{\tau_p\, s+1}$$

$$G_d(s) = \frac{K_d\, e^{-\theta_d s}}{\tau_d\, s+1}$$

Then the application of Equation 10.5 using the FOPDT models yields

$$G_{ff}(s) = -\frac{K_d(\tau_p s+1)\, e^{-\theta_d s}}{K_p(\tau_d s+1)\, e^{-\theta_p s}} = \frac{K_{ff}(\tau_{ld}\, s+1)\, e^{-\theta_{ff} s}}{(\tau_{lg}\, s+1)} \qquad \textbf{10.6}$$

The feedforward controller gain is given by

$$K_{ff} = \frac{-K_d}{K_p} \qquad \textbf{10.7}$$

The lead of the feedforward controller, τ_{ld}, is

$$\tau_{ld} = \tau_p \qquad \textbf{10.8}$$

The lag of the feedforward controller, τ_{lg}, is

$$\tau_{lg} = \tau_d \qquad \textbf{10.9}$$

The deadtime of the feedforward controller is

$$\theta_{ff} = \theta_d - \theta_p \qquad \textbf{10.10}$$

Equation 10.6 represents a lead-lag element (Section 5.10) with deadtime, which is a standard feature on a DCS. A feedforward controller can be implemented on a DCS by applying a lead-lag element with deadtime with the proper values of $K_{ff}, \tau_{ld}, \tau_{lg}$, and θ_{ff} to measured changes in the disturbance. Figure 10.17 shows the effect of the ratio of τ_{ld}/τ_{lg} on the dynamic response of a lead-lag element. When τ_{ld}/τ_{lg} is greater than one, an initial overcompensation is used. That is, when the process responds faster to the disturbance than to the controller output, larger than steady-state changes in the controller output are required to initially compensate for dynamic mismatch. On the other hand, when τ_{ld}/τ_{lg} is less than one, the application of the controller output is more gradual, eventually approaching its steady-state level. That is, when the process responds faster to the controller output than to the disturbance, a more gradual increase in the controller output level is used to compensate for a disturbance. Figure 10.18 shows the effect of τ_{lg} on the dynamic response of a lead-lag element for which the ratio of lead to lag is maintained constant

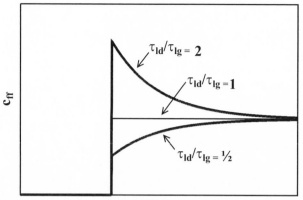

Figure 10.17 **The effect of the ratio of τ_{ld} to τ_{lg} on the dynamic response of a lead-lag element.** c_{ff} **is the output from the feedforward controller for a step input.**

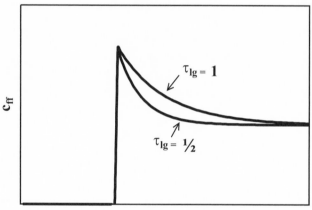

Figure 10.18 **The effect of τ_{lg} on the dynamic response of a lead-lag element.** c_{ff} **is the output of the feedforward controller for a step input.**

at a value of 2. As one would expect, the case with the larger value of the lag requires a longer time to settle to the steady-state value.

Example 10.10 Static Feedforward Controller

Problem Statement. Develop a feedforward controller for inlet feed temperature changes for a stirred-tank heater. The stirred-tank heater is equivalent to an endothermic CSTR (Example 3.4) without reactions occurring.

Solution. The dynamic energy balance for a stirred-tank heater is given by

$$V\rho C_v \frac{dT}{dt} = FC_p(T_0 - T) + Q$$

where V is the volume of fluid in the stirred-tank heater, ρ is the density of the fluid, C_v and C_p are heat capacities of the fluid, T is the temperature of the product leaving the stirred-tank heater, T_0 is the temperature of the feed entering the stirred-tank heater, and Q is the rate of heat addition. Converting this equation to deviation variables, applying Laplace transform, and rearranging results in the process transfer function,

$$G_p(s) = \frac{1}{FC_p} \left[\frac{1}{\dfrac{V\rho}{F}s + 1} \right]$$

and the transfer function for the effect of changes in the feed temperature, i.e.,

$$G_d(s) = \frac{1}{\dfrac{V\rho}{F}s + 1}$$

assuming that the heat capacity at constant volume is equal to the heat capacity at constant pressure. Applying Equation 10.5, assuming that $G_{ds}(s)$ and $G_a(s)$ are one (i.e., the dynamics of $G_{ds}(s)$ and $G_a(s)$ are relatively fast), the feedforward controller is given as

$$G_{ff}(s) = \frac{-G_d(s)}{G_p(s)} = -FC_p$$

Because the feedforward controller does not provide dynamic compensation, it is called a **static feedforward controller**. The effect of the manipulated variable and the effect of the disturbance on the process have the same dynamic behavior; therefore, the dynamic terms cancel in Equation 10.5, and a static feedforward controller results. The response of a static feedforward controller to a step input is shown in Figure 10.17 for τ_{ld} / τ_{lg} equal to one. In general, **a static feedforward controller can be used when the process has the same dynamic response to changes in the manipulated variable and the disturbance.** The feedforward controller for the boiler level in Example 10.9 is another example of a static feedforward controller.

♠

Example 10.11 Feedforward Controller When τ_p is Small

Problem Statement. Evaluate feedforward control for changes in the feed flow rate for the liquid/liquid heat exchanger shown in Figure 10.19.

Solution. A qualitative examination of the liquid/liquid heat exchanger shown in Figure 10.19 yields the following conclusions: (1) the product temperature is expected

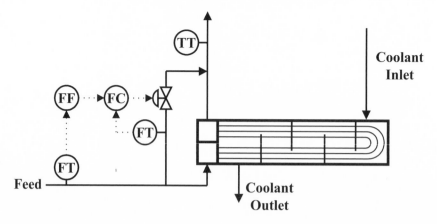

Figure 10.19 Schematic of a feedforward-only controller for a liquid/liquid heat exchanger.

to respond relatively quickly to changes in the manipulated variable (i.e., the bypass flow rate) and (2) the product temperature should respond much more slowly to changes in the feed rate of the process stream because its response depends on the dynamic response of the heat exchanger to a feed rate change. Therefore, application of Equation 10.6 for this problem results in a feedforward controller with the following form:

$$G_{ff}(s) = \frac{K_{ff} \, e^{-\theta_{ff} s}}{(\tau_{lg} \, s + 1)}$$

because τ_{ld} can be assumed to equal to zero in this case (i.e., τ_p is small). As a result, the feedforward controller provides a first-order plus deadtime compensation for changes in the feed rate to the system. From Figure 10.17, one can observe that in the limit of τ_{ld} approaching zero, the feedforward response becomes first order.

♠

Example 10.12   Feedforward Controller When the Process Responds Sightly More Quickly to the Manipulated Variable

Problem Statement. Evaluate feedforward control for changes in the feed composition for the stripping section of a distillation column (Figure 10.20).

Solution. For this case, the process should respond more quickly to changes in the manipulated variable than to changes in the disturbance. That is, once a change in the setpoint to the flow controller on the steam is implemented, the bottoms product composition changes more quickly than for a change in the feed composition. This results because the feed composition change must work its way down the column

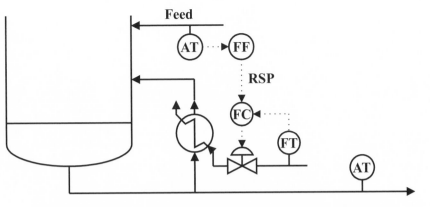

Figure 10.20 Schematic of a steam-heated heat exchanger.

tray-by-tray before it affects the bottom product composition. As a result, if compensation for feed composition changes is implemented immediately using a static feedforward controller, overcompensation results. Unlike Example 10.11, the dynamics of $G_p(s)$ are not fast enough to be neglected. As a result, the complete version of Equation 10.6 is required in this case, i.e.,

$$G_{ff}(s) = \frac{K_{ff}(\tau_{ld}\, s + 1)\, e^{-\theta_{ff}\, s}}{(\tau_{lg}\, s + 1)}$$

and the response of the feedforward controller for this case should be similar to the response shown in Figure 10.17 in which τ_{ld} is less than τ_{lg}. Because manipulated variables that have the most immediate effect on the process are usually selected, this case (i.e., the process responds more quickly to the manipulated variable than to the disturbance) represents the most common form for feedforward controllers.

♠

Example 10.13   Feedforward Controller When the Process Responds More Quickly to the Disturbance

Problem Statement. Evaluate a feedforward controller for inlet temperature changes for a pipe wrapped in resistive tape (Figure 10.21). The controlled variable is the outlet

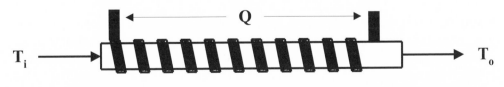

Figure 10.21 Drawing of a pipe wrapped with resistive heating tape.

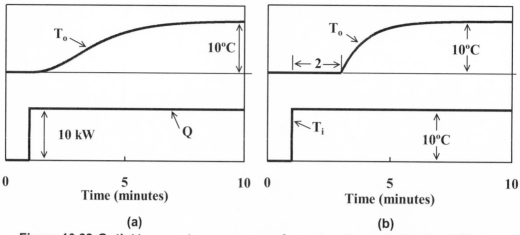

Figure 10.22 Outlet temperature responses for a step change in (a) Q and (b) T$_i$.

temperature, T_o, the manipulated variable is the power, Q, applied to the resistive tape and the measured disturbance is the inlet temperature, T_i.

Solution. Figure 10.22a shows the effect of a 10 kW increase in Q on the outlet temperature, T_o. T_o responds sluggishly to a change in Q with a response time of seven minutes. Figure 10.22b shows the response of T_o to a 10°C increase in the inlet temperature, T_i. The process responds more slowly to changes in the resistive heat input than to inlet temperature changes because of the thermal resistance between the electrical heating elements and the fluid inside the pipe. The response of T_o for a change in T_i can be represented as a FOPDT process with two minutes of deadtime.

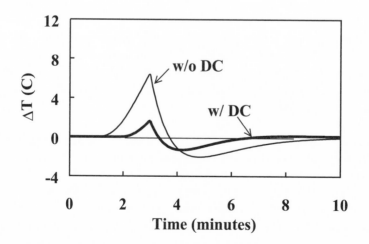

Figure 10.23 Comparison between feedforward control with and without dynamic compensation (DC).

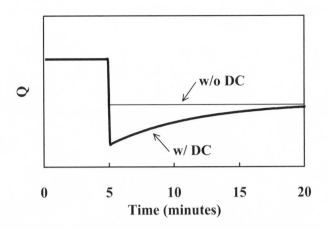

Figure 10.24 Comparison between the feedforward controller output for a static feedforward controller and one with dynamic compensation. DC- dynamic compensation.

Consider a step decrease of 20°C in T_i. Q should be increased by 20 kW to compensate for the 20°C drop in the inlet temperature. The results of a dynamically compensated feedforward controller (Equation 10.6) are shown in Figure 10.23 along with the results without dynamic compensation, i.e., a static feedforward controller. The corresponding manipulated variable level are shown in Figure 10.24. Note that, because the process responds more quickly to the disturbance than to the manipulated variable, a positive error from setpoint results for a positive increase in the inlet temperature. A comparison between the static feedforward controller and the feedforward controller with dynamic compensation (Equation 10.6) for this case indicates that dynamic compensation results in a shorter settling time and smaller deviation from setpoint.

♠

Tuning. Tuning a feedforward controller involves selecting the values of K_{ff}, τ_{ld}, τ_{lg}, and θ_{ff}. Equations 10.7 to 10.10 can be used to estimate these tuning parameters if FOPDT models are available. Since identifying $G_d(s)$ can be difficult, it is usually advisable to field tune feedforward controllers. The following field tuning procedure is recommended.

1. Make initial estimates of K_{ff}, τ_{ld}, τ_{lg}, and θ_{ff} based on process knowledge.
2. Under open-loop conditions, adjust K_{ff} while maintaining the rest of the tuning parameters at their initial levels to minimize the steady-state deviation from setpoint. Figure 10.25a shows the dynamic response of a feedforward controller for a step change in the disturbance after K_{ff} has been adjusted to eliminate offset.
3. By analyzing the dynamic mismatch, adjust θ_{ff}. The direction of the deviation should indicate whether the feedforward correction is applied too soon or too late,

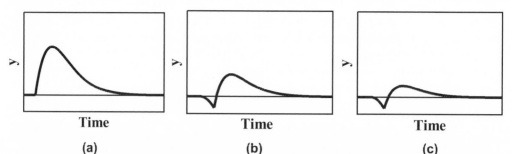

Figure 10.25 Tuning results for a feedforward controller for a step change in the disturbance. (a) Results for initial settings with correct feedforward gain. (b) Results after deadtime tuned. (c) Final tuning results.

causing dynamic mismatch.　Figure 10.25b shows the feedforward control performance after θ_{ff} is tuned.

4. Finally, adjust either τ_{ld} or τ_{lg} until approximately equal areas above and below the setpoint result.　Figure 10.25c shows the results after τ_{ld} and τ_{lg} are adjusted.

Overview.　Table 10.1 summarizes the advantages and disadvantages of feedforward and feedback control.　Feedforward and feedback control are complementary, i.e., they each can overcome the disadvantages of the other so that together they are superior to either method alone.　Feedforward control does not offer a significant advantage for fast-responding processes because a feedback-only controller can usually absorb disturbances efficiently for these cases.　But for slow-responding processes or processes with significant deadtime, by the time a feedback-only controller starts to respond to the effects of a disturbance, the process can already be severely upset.　For these cases, the effect of the disturbance can cause the controlled variable to change significantly from its setpoint, resulting in relatively large process parameter changes (K_p, τ_p, and θ_p).　In some cases this can lead to closed-loop instability.　When feedforward control is added to a slow process or a process with significant deadtime, the deviation of the controlled variable from setpoint can be significantly reduced, resulting in smaller process parameter changes. Therefore, feedforward control can provide significantly more reliable feedback control performance when the feedforward control performance compensates for a major disturbance to the process.　In general, feedforward control is useful when (1) feedback control by itself is not satisfactory, i.e., for slow-responding processes or processes with significant deadtime, and (2) the major disturbance to a process is measured online.

Feedforward control provides a linear correction and, therefore, can provide only partial compensation to a nonlinear process.　Nevertheless, feedforward control can be effective when properly implemented since it can reduce the amount of feedback correction required.　When tuning a feedforward controller for a nonlinear process, care should be taken to ensure that the feedforward controller is tuned considering both increases and decreases in the disturbance level.　For example, if the feedforward controller is tuned for a certain size increase in the disturbance, it may work quite well for that case but actually contribute to poorer performance when a different size disturbance decrease is encountered. Figure 10.26 shows how a feedforward controller and a feedback controller are combined. The changes in the manipulated variable calculated by the feedforward and feedback controllers are simply added.

Table 10.1 Comparison of Feedback and Feedforward Control	
Feedback	
Advantages	**Disadvantages**
1. Does not require a measurement of the disturbance.	1. Waits until the disturbance has affected the process before taking action.
2. Can effectively reject disturbances for fast-responding process.	2. Susceptible to disturbances when the process is slow or when significant deadtime is present.
3. Simple to implement.	3. Can lead to instability of the closed loop system due to nonlinearity.

Feedforward	
1. Compensates for disturbances before they affect the process.	1. Requires measurement or estimation of the disturbance.
2. Can improve the reliability of the feedback controller by reducing the deviation from setpoint.	2. Does not compensate for unmeasured disturbances.
3. Offers noticeable advantages for slow processes or processes with significant deadtime.	3. Since it is a linear based correction, its performance deteriorates with nonlinearity.

Example 10.14 Feedforward Control Applied to the Endothermic CSTR

Problem Statement. Apply a feedforward controller for feed temperature changes to the endothermic CSTR.

Solution. Using open-loop step tests, the following FOPDT models were developed for $G_d(s)$ and $G_p(s)$

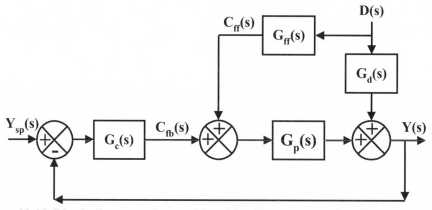

Figure 10.26 Block diagram of a combined feedforward and feedback controller. Note that the actuator and sensor are omitted.

$$G_d(s) = \frac{0.381\ e^{-5.62s}}{6.57\ s+1}\ (^\circ C/^\circ C)$$

$$G_p(s) = \frac{1.50\times10^{-4}\ e^{-4.31s}}{10.7\ s+1}\left(\frac{^\circ C}{cal\,/\,s}\right)$$

where time constants and deadtimes are reported in seconds. The process responds more quickly to the manipulated variable than to the disturbance, but not so fast that the dynamics of $G_p(s)$ can be neglected. The feedforward controller was tuned for a 100°C increase in feed temperature (T_0). Using a static feedforward controller (i.e., no dynamic compensation), K_{ff} was set at -1.09 × 10^4 cal/sec/°C. Next, θ_{ff} was evaluated and it was found that θ_{ff} should be set to zero. Due to positive deviations of the reactor temperature from setpoint, τ_{ld} was increased from 10.7 s (i.e., τ_p) to 12.9 s, which reduced the maximum deviation from setpoint without resulting in excessive negative deviations. τ_{lg} was maintained equal to τ_d or 6.57 seconds. Figure 10.27 shows the results for a step increase in T_0 from 400 K to 500K for the feedforward controller, a feedback controller, and the combined feedforward and feedback controller. The open-loop effect of this disturbance resulted in a 38K increase in reactor temperature while the combined feedforward and feedback controller had a maximum deviation of only 1.7 K. The results in Figure 10.27 show that combined feedforward and feedback outperform either feedforward or feedback alone. The feedforward-only controller significantly reduces the initial deviation from setpoint compared to the feedback-only controller, but is sluggish in returning to the setpoint. The combined feedforward and feedback controller uses the feedforward action to reduce the initial deviation from setpoint and uses the feedback action to quickly settle at the setpoint. Figure 10.28 shows a schematic representing a combined feedforward and feedback controller applied to the endothermic CSTR.

♠

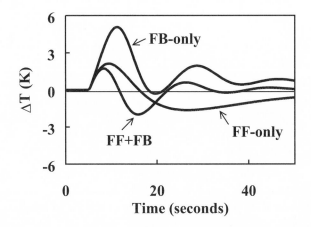

Figure 10.27 Comparison among feedforward (FF-only), feedback (FB-only), and combined feedforward and feedback (FF+FB) for a disturbance upset.

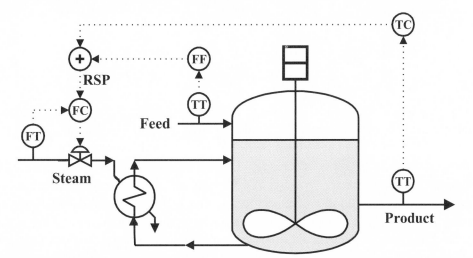

Figure 10.28 Schematic of an endothermic CSTR with combined feedforward and feedback control.

Example 10.15   Schematic of a Combined Feedforward and Feedback Control System

Problem Statement. Consider the steam-heated heat exchanger shown in Figure 10.29 for which there is a temperature measurement on the inlet and outlet of the feed to the exchanger, a pressure measurement on the steam to the exchanger, and a control valve on the steam to the exchanger. Draw a schematic of a combined feedforward and feedback control system for which the inlet temperature is the feedforward variable and the outlet temperature is the feedback variable. The combined feedforward and feedback control action is the setpoint for a pressure controller on the steam.

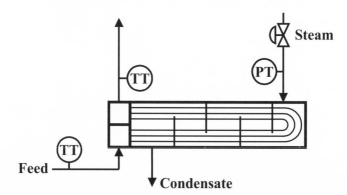

Figure 10.29 Schematic of a steam-heated heat exchanger without controls.

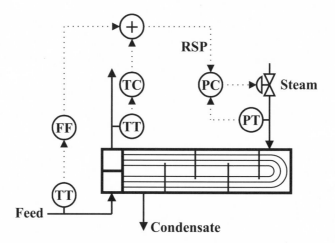

Figure 10.30 Schematic of a steam-heated heat exchanger with combined feedback and feedforward controls.

Solution. The combined feedforward and feedback controller is shown in Figure 10.30. The inlet temperature of the feed is the input to the feedforward controller while the outlet temperature of the feed is the input to the feedback controller. The outputs from the feedback and feedforward controllers are added together, and the resultant is the setpoint for the pressure controller on the steam.

♠

10.5 Summary

Cascade, ratio, and feedforward control are each designed to reduce the effect of disturbances on feedback control performance. Since disturbances tend to undermine controller reliability, cascade, ratio, and feedforward control can contribute to controller performance and reliability when they are properly implemented.

Cascade control involves applying two controllers in tandem instead of using a single control loop. The control loops are arranged such that the primary loop provides the setpoint for the secondary loop. In this manner, the secondary loop acts as the manipulated variable for the primary loop. Since the secondary loop responds more quickly than the primary loop, the secondary loop is able to more effectively reject certain disturbances than if the primary loop were applied by itself.

Ratio controllers can effectively handle process feed rate changes for processes that generally scale with feed rate. For ratio controllers, the controller selects the manipulated stream flow rate-to-feed flow rate ratio. Then, this ratio is multiplied by the measured feed rate to give the setpoint for the flow controller on the manipulated stream. In certain cases, dynamic compensation provides improvement for ratio control applications.

Feedforward control offers significant benefits to a feedback controller when (1) the process is slow responding or when significant deadtime is present and (2) the major disturbances to a process are measurable. A feedforward controller is typically implemented using a lead-lag element with deadtime.

10.6 Additional Terminology

Lead-lag element - the ratio of two FOPDT transfer function models; defined by Equation 10.6.

Load change - a change in the disturbance level to a process.

Master loop - the outer loop for a cascade controller. Also, the slowest loop in a cascade arrangement.

Primary loop - the outer loop for a cascade controller. Also, the slowest loop in a cascade arrangement.

Secondary loop - the inner loop for a cascade controller. Also, the fastest loop in a cascade arrangement.

Slave loop - the inner loop for a cascade controller. Also, the fastest loop in a cascade arrangement.

Static feedforward controller - a feedforward controller which contains only a gain, i.e., it contains no dynamic compensation.

10.7 Preliminary Questions

10.1 What do cascade, ratio, and feedforward control have in common?

10.2 What relationships between the primary and secondary loops are required for effective cascade control?

10.3 What disturbances does a flow control cascade reject?

10.4 What factors are necessary for an effective cascade arrangement?

10.5 Is a typical flow control loop on a DCS an example of cascade control? Explain your reasoning.

10.6 What kinds of disturbances does the cascade arrangement shown in Figure 10.4 reject effectively.

10.7 What kinds of disturbances does the cascade arrangement shown in Figure 10.8 reject effectively.

10.8 For Figure 10.2b, what does the primary loop adjust to control the outlet temperature of the process stream?

10.9 For Figure 10.3b, what does the primary loop adjust to control the product temperature?

10.10 For Figure 10.4, what does the outermost primary loop adjust to control the product composition?

10.11 What disturbances does the cascade controller shown in Figure 10.2b reject that the controller without cascade control can not effectively reject?

10.12 What disturbances does the cascade controller shown in Figure 10.3b reject that the controller without cascade control can not effectively reject?

10.13 What disturbances does the cascade controller shown in Figure 10.4 reject that the controller without cascade control can not effectively reject?

10.14 What kinds of processes benefit from ratio control?

10.15 When is dynamic compensation required and when is it not required for ratio control?

10.16 Explain how the ratio controller shown in Figure 10.11 reduces the effect of feed flow rate disturbances on the effluent pH.

10.17 Explain how the ratio controller shown in Figure 10.12 reduces the effect of feed flow rate disturbances on the bottoms product composition.

10.18 How are ratio control and feedforward control alike and how are they different?

10.19 For the combined feedforward-feedback controller shown in Figure 10.15c, indicate how the control structure is able to overcome the limitations of the feedback-only and feedforward-only controller while retaining their advantages.

10.20 For a feedforward controller using a lead-lag element, what kinds of systems result in a lead that is larger than its lag?

10.21 When is it advisable to use a static feedforward controller?

10.22 When the process exhibits the same dynamic response for changes in the manipulated variable and the disturbance, what form of feedforward controller should be used?

10.23 When a process responds more quickly to the manipulated variable than to the disturbance, what form of the dynamic response does a feedforward controller provide for a step change in the measured disturbance.

10.24 When a process responds more slowly to the manipulated variable than to the disturbance, what form of the dynamic response does a feedforward controller provide for a step change in the measured disturbance.

10.25 When tuning a lead-lag element with deadtime for a feedforward controller, in what order are the parameters tuned?

10.26 How can a feedforward controller improve the reliability of a feedback controller?

10.27 To what types of processes does feedforward control provide the most significant benefits?

10.28 How are a feedforward and a feedback controller combined?

10.8 Analytical Question and Exercises

10.29 Derive Equation 10.1 using Figure 10.5 and the properties of block diagrams.

10.30 Draw a schematic showing a process controlled with and without cascade control for a case not presented in this text.

10.31 Consider the CST thermal mixer presented in Example 3.1. Draw a schematic for this process demonstrating the application of cascade control.

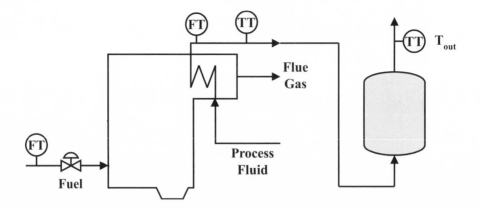

Figure for Problem 10.34

10.32 Consider the CST composition mixer presented in Example 3.2. Draw a schematic for this process demonstrating the application of cascade control.

10.33 Consider the tank level process presented in Example 3.3. Draw a schematic for this process demonstrating the application of cascade control.

10.34 Consider the fixed-bed reactor in which the feed is preheated by a gas-fired heater shown in the figure for this problem. The current control configuration has a temperature controller on the outlet from the fixed-bed reactor setting the setpoint for the flow controller on the gas to the furnace. Draw a schematic showing a further application of cascade control (i.e., beyond flow control on the gas flow rate) that provides improved control for this process for changes in the heating value of the gas fired to the heater.

10.35 Consider a heat exchanger that cools a process stream using a liquid refrigerant. The process stream is on the tube-side of the exchanger and the liquid refrigerant is maintained as a level on the shell-side. The vast majority of the heat transfer from the refrigerant to the process stream occurs from the liquid refrigerant due to the larger heat-transfer coefficient for the liquid than for the vapor refrigerant. As heat is transferred from the process stream to the liquid refrigerant, the refrigerant boils and leaves the heat exchanger as a vapor. The cascade control configuration has a temperature controller on the exit of the process stream setting the setpoint for the level controller on the liquid level of refrigerant in the exchanger. The level controller sets the valve position for a valve on the inlet flow of liquid refrigerant to the heat exchanger. What advantage does this cascade control arrangement have compared to having the output of the temperature controller go directly to the valve on the liquid refrigerant?

10.36 Draw a schematic of a rectifying section of a distillation column (see Figure for this problem) that has a composition controller for the overhead product cascaded to a

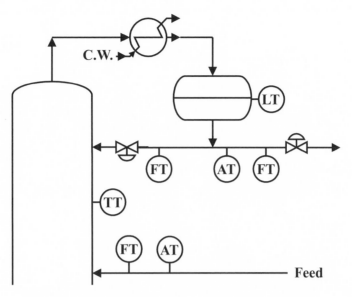

Figure for Problems 10.36 - 10.41, 10-47-10.48.

tray temperature controller, which is cascaded to a flow controller for the reflux. In addition, the level controller for the accumulator is cascaded to a flow controller on the distillate product.

10.37 Draw a schematic of a rectifying section of a distillation column (see Figure for this problem) that has a composition controller for the overhead product cascaded to a tray temperature controller, which is cascaded to a flow controller for the distillate product. In addition, the level controller for the accumulator is cascaded to a flow controller on the reflux.

10.38 Draw a schematic for the rectifying section of a distillation column (see figure for this problem) in which the ratio of the distillate product rate to column feed rate is set by a composition controller on the overhead product. Remember to set up a level control scheme for the accumulator.

10.39 Draw a schematic for the rectifying section of a distillation column (see figure for this problem) in which the ratio of reflux flow rate to distillate flow rate is set by a composition controller on the overhead product. (Hint: Use a level controller to set either the reflux flow rate or the distillate flow rate and determine the other flow rate using the ratio).

10.40 Draw a schematic for the rectifying section of a distillation column (see figure for this problem) in which the ratio of reflux flow rate to distillate flow rate is set by a composition controller on the overhead product, which is cascaded to a tray temperature controller. The tray temperature controller is cascaded to a flow controller

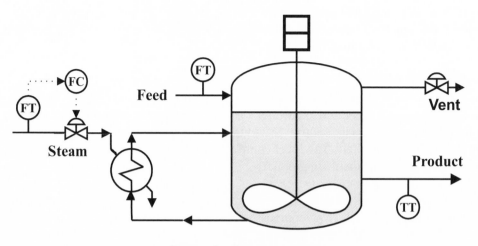

Figure for Problem 10.42.

on the reflux. In addition, the level controller for the accumulator is cascaded to a flow controller on the distillate product.

10.41 Draw a schematic for the rectifying section of a distillation column (see figure for this problem) in which a composition controller on the overhead product is cascaded to a tray temperature controller. The tray temperature controller is a ratio controller (i.e., the controller output is the reflux-to-feed ratio) and its output is combined with the measured feed rate to form the setpoint for the flow controller on the reflux. In addition, the level controller for the accumulator is cascaded to a flow controller on the distillate product.

10.42 Draw a schematic by modifying Figure 3.13 so that the CSTR is equipped with a vent stream so that light impurities do not accumulate in the vapor space above the reaction mixture in the reactor. Add a ratio controller that adjusts the ratio of the flow rate of the vent stream to the reactor feed flow rate to maintain the composition of the light component in the reactor vapor space at a prescribed setpoint.

10.43 Draw a schematic of a ratio controller applied to the CST thermal mixer (Figure 3.6) in which the ratio controller for the temperature sets the ratio of F_1 to F_2.

10.44 Draw a schematic of a control system that provides the same function as the ratio control system shown in Figure 10.12 using a combined feedforward and feedback controller.

10.45 Consider the steam-heated heat exchanger (Figure 3.16). Draw a schematic for this process for combined feedforward and feedback control where the feedforward disturbance is the temperature of the process stream entering the heat exchanger.

10.46 Consider the level process shown in Figure 3.11. Draw a schematic for this process for combined feedforward and feedback control where the feedforward disturbance is the inlet flow to the tank.

10.47 Draw a schematic for the rectifying section of a distillation column (see figure for this problem) in which a composition controller on the overhead product is cascaded to a tray temperature controller. The tray temperature controller is cascaded to the flow controller on the reflux. In addition, the feed composition is fed forward to the reflux flow controller. The level controller for the accumulator is cascaded to a flow controller on the distillate product.

10.48 Draw a schematic for the rectifying section of a distillation column (see figure for this problem) in which a composition controller on the overhead product is cascaded to a tray temperature controller. The tray temperature controller is a ratio controller (i.e., the controller output is the reflux-to-feed ratio) and its output is combined with the measured feed rate to form the setpoint for the flow controller on the reflux. In addition, the feed composition is fed forward to the reflux flow controller. The level controller for the accumulator is cascaded to a flow controller on the distillate product.

10.49[S] Apply and tune a feedforward controller to each of the following process simulators that are provided with this text. Develop FOPDT models of $G_p(s)$ and $G_d(s)$ using step test applied to the simulators. From these models, make initial guesses of the tuning parameters for the feedforward controller. Fine tune the feedforward controller and show results for a series of step changes in the measured disturbance.

    a. CST thermal mixer   b. CST composition mixer

    c. Endothermic CSTR   d. Heat exchanger

10.50[S] Apply and tune a combined feedforward-feedback controller to each of the following process simulators that are provided with this text.

    a. CST thermal mixer   b. CST composition mixer

    c. Endothermic CSTR   d. Heat exchanger

A superscript "**S**" indicates that the problem requires the use of one of process simulators.

Chapter 11

PID Enhancements

11.1 Introduction

This chapter is concerned with enhancements that are designed to overcome the effects of measurement deadtime, process nonlinearity, and process constraints on PID controllers. Inferential control can greatly reduce the effect of measurement deadtime, scheduling of controller tuning can compensate for process nonlinearity, and override/select control provides a direct means to use PID controls on systems that encounter process constraints. Computed manipulated variable control can be used to reduce the effect of certain types of disturbances.

11.2 Inferential Control

To this point, it has been assumed that the sensor in a control loop provides a direct measurement of the controlled variable. In fact, the output of the sensor only correlates with the value of the measured variable. For example, from Chapter 2, a thermocouple exposed to a process stream at a specific temperature generates a millivolt signal that correlates strongly with the temperature of the process stream. Likewise, the level in a tank can be inferred from the pressure difference between the top and the bottom of the tank, and a flow rate can be estimated from the pressure drop across an orifice plate. In this section, it is shown that **easily measured quantities, such as pressures, temperatures, and flow rates, can be effectively used to infer quantities which are more difficult to measure, such as composition, molecular weight, and extent of reaction**. The inferred value of the controlled variable can be used as the value of the controlled variable in a feedback control loop, greatly reducing the associated measurement delay.

There are three main reasons for using inferential measurement of a controlled variable:

1. Excessive analyzer deadtime undermines the performance of a feedback loop. In Chapter 7, it was shown that a deadtime-to-time constant ratio in excess of 0.5 requires reduction to the aggressiveness of the controller and, therefore, the

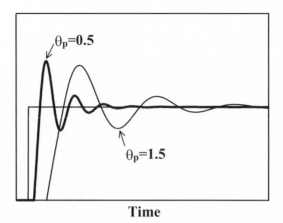

Figure 11.1 Setpoint tracking performance showing the effect of deadtime on closed-loop performance.

performance of the control loop suffers. Figure 11.1 shows the setpoint tracking performance for two FOPDT processes (K_p=1, τ_p=1, θ_p=0.5; K_p=1, τ_p=1, θ_p=1.5). Both systems are tuned for QAD, but the process with the larger deadtime results in a much longer response time than the smaller deadtime process. Certain techniques, such as **Smith Predictors**, have been developed to directly compensate for the deadtime of a process using process models. Smith Predictors have been studied extensively in academia, but have rarely been applied industrially because the incremental improvement provided by the Smith Predictor is generally much less than the improvement associated with an inferential measurement. Smith Predictors are typically difficult to implement and their effectiveness is sensitive to modeling errors. Therefore, inferential measurements are the industrial method of choice for counteracting large measurement delays for controlled variables.   Inferential measurements can greatly reduce the measurement deadtime because they are based on measurements (e.g., temperatures, pressures, and flows) that have relatively low levels of measurement deadtime.

2. The total cost (the purchase price and maintenance cost) of an online analyzer can be excessive. Since inferential measurements are typically based on temperature, pressure, and flow measurements, they are much less expensive to install and maintain.

3. An online analyzer may not be available, making inferential measurement the only option for feedback control.

For inferential control to be effective, the inferential measurement must correlate strongly with the controlled variable of interest, and this correlation should be relatively insensitive to unmeasured disturbances. Following are several examples that illustrate how inferential measurements can be effectively applied in the CPI.

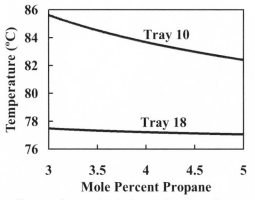

Figure 11.2 The effect of product impurity level on two different tray temperatures.

Example 11.1 Inferential Temperature Control for Distillation

Problem Statement. Evaluate the use of tray temperature measurements to infer product compositions for distillation columns.

Solution. Tray temperatures correlate very well with product compositions for many distillation columns; therefore, inferential control of distillation product composition is a widely used form of inferential control. Figure 11.2 shows the correlation between propane content in the bottoms product and the tray temperature for two trays in the stripping section of a propane/butane binary column. Since this is a binary separation, the temperature and pressure of a tray define the composition on that tray. The largest temperature change for a fixed change in the bottom product composition occurs for tray number 10; therefore, the temperature of tray 10 can be used to infer the bottom product purity of this column. Figure 11.3 shows the arrangement for inferential

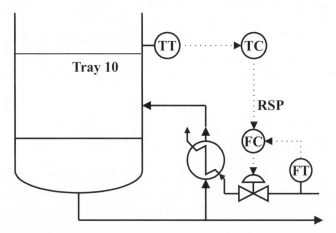

Figure 11.3 Schematic for inferential control of the bottoms product composition of a distillation column.

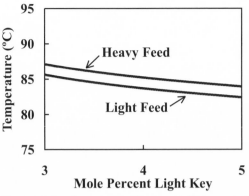

Figure 11.4 The effect of feed composition on the correlation between tray temperature and impurity level in the bottoms product.

temperature control of the bottom product composition for this column. The tray temperature controller is cascaded to a flow controller.

For a multicomponent distillation column, the tray temperature does not define the product composition. The liquid on a tray can have the same concentration of light and heavy keys with different relative amounts of heavy non-key and light non-key, and the resulting equilibrium temperature changes significantly. As the amount of heavy non-key is increased and the amount of light non-key is decreased, the tray temperature increases even though the proportions of light and heavy keys remain unchanged. Figure 11.4 shows a tray temperature in the stripping section of a multicomponent distillation column as a function of the light key in the bottoms product for different ratios of heavy non-key to light non-key (i.e., a light and a heavy feed). Note that the two curves are parallel with a difference of about 2°C. As a result, controlling a tray temperature to a fixed temperature results in offset as the feed composition changes. To remove this offset, a composition controller that uses an online composition analyzer can be cascaded to the tray temperature control loop

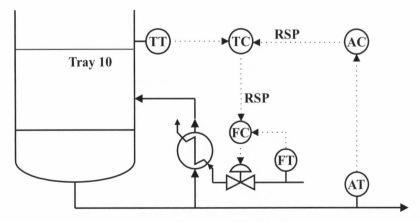

Figure 11.5 Schematic of an analyzer controller cascaded to a temperature controller for bottoms composition control of a distillation column.

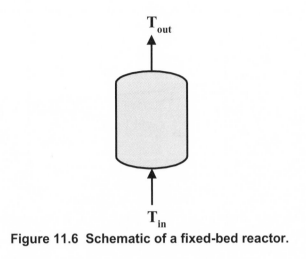

Figure 11.6 Schematic of a fixed-bed reactor.

(Figure 11.5). In certain cases, laboratory analysis results taken once per shift or once per day are used by the operator to select the setpoint for the temperature controller in an effort to remove the offset.

♠

Example 11.2 Inferential Reaction Conversion Control

Problem Statement. Consider an adiabatic fixed-bed reactor (Figure 11.6). Using material and energy balances for this system, develop an inferential estimate of the conversion in this reactor. Assume an irreversible first-order reaction.

Solution. For a single irreversible reaction, $A \to B$, the macroscopic steady-state energy balance, assuming no phase change, is given by

$$X_A C_{A_{in}} (-\Delta H_{rxn}) = \rho C_P (T_{out} - T_{in})$$ **11.1**

where X_A is the fractional conversion of reactant A, $C_{A_{in}}$ is the inlet concentration of A to the reactor, ΔH_{rxn} is the heat of reaction, ρ is the average density of the process stream, C_P is the average heat capacity of the process stream, T_{out} is the temperature of the outlet stream from the reactor, and T_{in} is the temperature of the inlet stream to the reactor. Rearranging Equation 11.1

$$X_A = \frac{\rho C_P}{C_{A_{in}} (-\Delta H_{rxn})} (T_{out} - T_{in})$$ **11.2**

Note that this relationship is not affected by changes in the feed rate although feed rate affects T_{out} and, thus, X_A. In an industrial reactor, there are heat losses, side reactions,

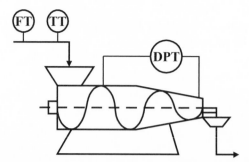

Figure 11.7 Schematic of a polymer extruder.

and variations in the physical parameters; therefore, the assumed inferential relationship is

$$X_A = a(T_{out} - T_{in}) + b \qquad\qquad 11.3$$

A plot of the experimental data for a reactor (X_A, T_{out}, and T_{in}) can be used to determine a and b as well as check the validity of this functional form. Note that the temperature difference across the reactor needs to be large enough that noise on the temperature measurement does not significantly affect the measured temperature drop across the reactor. Once a and b are identified, the inlet temperature (T_{in}) can be adjusted to maintain a fixed reaction conversion, X_A. Periodically, composition measurements for the product leaving the reactor can be made and the results used to update the value of b in the previous equation. The value of b, instead of the value of a, should be updated with plant data because a is less likely to change significantly with changes in the operating conditions compared with b.

♠

Example 11.3   Inferential Measurement of the Molecular Weight of a Polymer

Problem Statement. Figure 11.7 shows a schematic of a polymer extruder. An extruder is a screw device that forces a polymer melt through a set of dies creating a number of polymer strands. Develop a method for inferring the molecular weight of the polymer in the extruder from the process measurements shown in Figure 11.7.

Solution. From fluid dynamics, it is known that the pressure drop across the extruder is directly related to the viscosity of the polymer. As the molecular weight of the polymer increases, its viscosity increases. The temperature of the polymer melt inside the extruder also affects the viscosity.

The procedure for estimating the molecular weight of a polymer is as follows. First, the flow rate, F, and pressure drop across the extruder, ΔP, are measured. A fluid dynamic relationship is used to calculate the corresponding viscosity of the polymer melt at the prevailing temperature, T,

$$\mu(T) = f_1(\Delta P, F)$$

The viscosity is corrected for temperature so that the viscosity of the melt is calculated at a standard temperature, T_o.

$$\mu(T_o) = f_2[T, \mu(T)]$$

A correlation between $\mu(T_o)$ and the molecular weight of the polymer melt is developed using laboratory measurements of the molecular weight (M_{wt}) for a range of $\mu(T_o)$ values, i.e.,

$$M_{wt} = f_3[\mu(T_o)]$$

From measurements of the flow rate of the polymer melt, the pressure drop across the extruder, and the temperature of the polymer in the extruder, the molecular weight of the polymer can be estimated online. This value can be used by a feedback controller to make adjustments to the polymer reactor to control the molecular weight of the polymer product. Without this inferential estimator, samples of the extruded polymer have to be tested in the laboratory, requiring about 10 hours for each test. Because the residence time of the reactor/extruder process is typically significantly less than 1 hour, a 10 hour analysis deadtime makes feedback molecular weight control extremely difficult if not impossible. The samples, which are taken 1-3 times per day, could be used to make corrections to the molecular weight/viscosity correlation.

♠

Soft Sensors Based on Neural Networks. In electric power generating stations, restricting the NO_x (nitrogen oxide compounds) emissions in the flue gas to acceptable levels is important because NO_x compounds contribute to air pollution. Typically, online analyzers are used to measure the NO_x in the flue gas from the boilers. Occasionally, the NO_x analyzers on a boiler fail. If the NO_x level is not measured, the power companies must pay a fine for emissions. Instead of installing additional online NO_x analyzers, which are quite expensive, a number of power companies have applied a type of inferential estimator to predict the NO_x level in their flue gas.

Instead of using one or two process measurements, all the measured process conditions (e.g., fuel feed rate, oxygen in the flue gas, heating value of the fuel, ambient air temperature, etc.) can be empirically correlated to predict the NO_x concentration in the flue gas. The empirical correlation is based on training an **artificial neural network** (ANN) to predict the flue gas NO_x concentration from all the available data. A network with three input nodes, four nodes in the hidden layer,

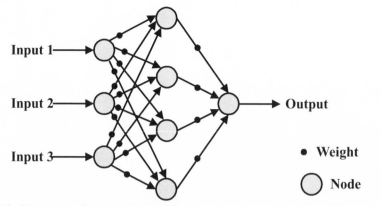

Figure 11.8 Diagram of a network with three input nodes, four nodes in the hidden layer, and one output node.

and one output node is shown schematically in Figure 11.8. Inputs to each node are summed and the resultant is transformed by a nonlinear function to calculate the node output. Weights are multiplied by the values that pass through them and are selected to emphasize or de-emphasize individual inputs to a node. For Figure 11.8, there are a total of 16 adjustable weights for the neural network that can be selected such that the neural network matches the available process data. As a result, neural networks can be used as empirical nonlinear input/output models. A neural network for a NO_x analyzer could have over 500 weights (adjustable parameters). This inferential NO_x analyzer is also referred to as a **soft sensor** since the neural network software, along with the process measurements, is used to provide the online measurement.

11.3 Scheduling Controller Tuning

In Chapter 7, it was demonstrated that a controller on a nonlinear process becomes unstable in certain situations, and can become extremely sluggish (e.g., Figure 11.9) at other times. If the process gain increases by over 100%, the controller is likely to become unstable, and if the process gain decreases by 50% or more, the process can be expected to behave sluggishly. Tuning PID controllers for the case with the largest process gain can eliminate unstable operation, but at the expense of largely sluggish performance. The combination of the magnitude of the disturbances and the inherent process nonlinearity determine the degree of variation in the FOPDT model parameters of the process. For a number of processes, certain measurements (e.g., the controlled variable or a measured disturbance) directly indicate whether the process parameters have increased or decreased and by how much; therefore, **scheduling of the controller tuning based on process measurements can be an effective means of compensating for process nonlinearity**. The controlled variable and the feed rate are examples of such key process measurements that can typically be used to schedule the controller tuning.

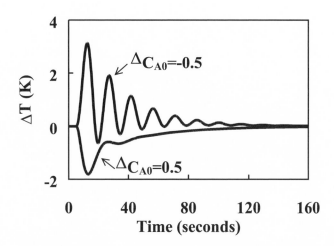

Figure 11.9 The effect of feed composition upsets on the PI feedback behavior for the endothermic CSTR. Thin line is for a feed composition decrease and thick line is for a feed composition increase.

Example 11.4 The Application of Scheduling of the Tuning Parameters for a CSTR

Problem Statement. Develop a scheduling procedure for a PI controller for the CSTR process presented in Example 3.4.

Solution. For the CSTR in Example 3.4, the reaction rate constant is represented by an Arrhenius rate expression, i.e.,

$$k = k_o \, e^{-E/RT}$$

which indicates strong nonlinearity for this process with regard to changes in the reactor temperature.   Figure 11.9 shows the response of temperature to feed composition disturbances under PI control. The controller is tuned for a region near the setpoint.   The feed composition decrease causes the reactor temperature to increase, and a feed composition increase causes the reactor temperature to decrease. Note that when the reaction temperature increases, the closed-loop response begins to ring, and when the temperature decreases, the closed-loop response becomes sluggish.

Now consider an approach for which the controller aggressiveness is adjusted based on the reactor temperature. The PI tuning factor, F_T, is scheduled as a function of the reactor temperature (Table 11.1).   Figure 11.10 shows a comparison between a conventional PI controller and a PI controller with scheduling for a severe feed composition upset for the endothermic CSTR. For the scheduled controller, F_T (Equation 7.13) is adjusted based on the error from setpoint according to Table 11.1. For this case, scheduling of the controller tuning was able to maintain stability while a conventional PI controller was not.   The slow movement towards setpoint indicates

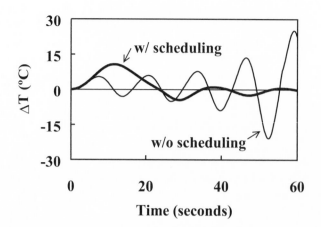

Figure 11.10 Comparison between a conventional PI controller and a PI controller with scheduling of the controller tuning for a severe feed composition upset for the endothermic CSTR.

that not enough integral action is used when the reactor temperature is below setpoint. Scheduling the entire set of controller parameters can provide the correct integral action for each temperature region. This can be accomplished by tuning the controller at several different reactor temperatures and using the results to schedule the tuning parameters.   ♠

Table 11.1 Scheduling of Controller Tuning for the CSTR Case	
$(T - T_{sp})$	F_T
- 4	1.4
- 2	1.6
0	1.8
2	2.8
4	3.8
6	4.8
8	5.8
10	6.8

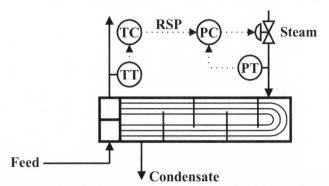

Figure 11.11 Schematic of a heat exchanger for which the outlet temperature is controlled by the steam pressure.

Example 11.5 The Application of Scheduling of the Tuning Parameters for a Heat Exchanger

Problem Statement. Develop a scheduling procedure for a PI controller for the heat exchanger process presented in Example 3.6.

Solution. Consider the heat exchanger shown in Figure 11.11. As the feed to the heat exchanger flows through the tube bundle, it is heated by steam condensing on the shell side. As the feed rate changes, the residence time of the feed in the tubes changes. Figure 11.12 shows the open-loop responses for three different feed rates for a step change in the setpoint of the steam pressure controller. The feed rate is represented by the average fluid velocity (v) in the tubes. Both the gain and the dynamic response change as the feed rate is changed. Table 11.2 lists the FOPDT parameters for each flow rate. Note that the gain and the deadtime of each change by a factor of about 2.5. The PI Cohen and Coon settings (Table 7.2) at each flow rate are also listed in Table 11.2. The controller gain changes by a factor of 5 while the reset time changes are more gradual. It is clear from these results that it is not reasonable to expect one set of

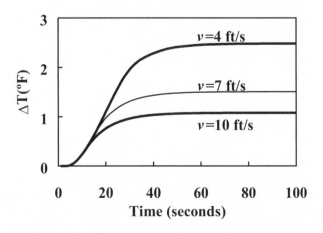

Figure 11.12 Open-loop response for a heat exchanger for different feed rates.

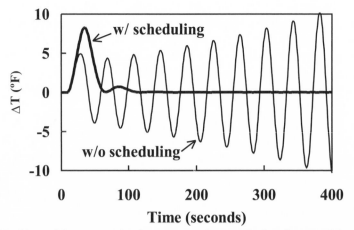

Figure 11.13 Closed-loop results for a step change in feed rate with and without scheduling of the controller tuning for the heat exchanger case.

PI controller settings to work effectively for significant changes in the feed rate to this heat exchanger. The temperature controller for the outlet of the heat exchanger tuned for $v=7$ ft/s becomes unstable when the feed rate is reduced to $v=4$ ft/s. Conversely, if the controller is tuned for the low flow rate condition, it performs sluggishly for the high flow rate conditions. Figure 11.13 shows results with and without scheduling of the controller tuning based on feed rate for a change in the velocity through the tubes from 7 to 4 ft/s. The controller without scheduling was tuned for a feed rate corresponding to $v=7$ ft/s.

		Table 11.2	
	FOPDT and PI Tuning Parameters for the Heat Exchanger Case as a Function of Feed Rate		
	$v=4$ ft/s	$v=7$ ft/s	$v=10$ ft/s
K_p	0.25	0.15	0.11
τ_p	10.7	9.9	10.0
θ_p	10.2	5.8	4.0
K_c	4.2	10.8	21.3
τ_I	12.0	8.8	7.3

♠

Non-stationary Behavior. Consider a wastewater neutralization process (Figure 10.11). If the titration curve of the wastewater and the other process parameters remain fixed, the process is referred to as **stationary** or **time-invariant**. If the titration curve changes with respect to time, the process is **non-stationary** or

time-varying. In the case of this pH control example, changes in the titration curve can have an overwhelming effect on the process gains. There are many more examples of non-stationary behavior that result in much more gradual process gain changes. The following are several examples of non-stationary behavior in the CPI:

1. Catalyst deactivation
2. Heat exchanger fouling
3. Fouling of trays in a distillation column
4. Feed composition changes that affect the process parameters (K_p, τ_p, and θ_p)

These effects can be large enough that controller retuning is required. If an overall tuning factor, F_T (Equation 7.13) has been used, one can adjust F_T in a straightforward manner to compensate for the non-stationary behavior. Control methods that adjust controller tuning to adapt to non-stationary behavior are referred to as **adaptive control** techniques. Adaptive control techniques can be effectively applied for processes that vary slowly. An adaptive controller is expected to handle gradual catalyst deactivation that occurs over several days, but is not expected to handle sharp changes in catalyst activity that occur within one hour. A number of commercially available adaptive controllers are referred to as **self-tuning controllers** and can usually be installed on a DCS. While there is a range of approaches used for self-tuning controllers, they are generally limited to processes that vary in a gradual, consistent manner.

11.4 Override/Select Control

Constraints are a natural part of industrial process control. As processes are pushed to produce as much product as possible, process limits are inevitably encountered. When an upper or lower limit on a manipulated variable is encountered, or when an upper or lower value of a controlled or output variable from the process is reached, it is necessary to alter the control configuration. **Effective industrial controller implementation requires that safeguards be installed to prevent the process from violating safety, environmental, or economic constraints.** These constraints can be met using override/select controls.

Example 11.6 Override/Select Control of a Gas-Fired Heater

Problem Statement. Analyze the operation of the override/select controls for the gas-fired heater shown in Figure 11.14.

Solution. Under normal operating conditions, the fuel flow rate is adjusted to control the exit temperature of the process fluid. As the feed rate of the process fluid increases, the furnace tube temperature increases. At some point, the upper limit on furnace tube temperature (an operational constraint) is encountered. The fuel flow rate to the furnace must be adjusted to keep the furnace tube temperature from exceeding its

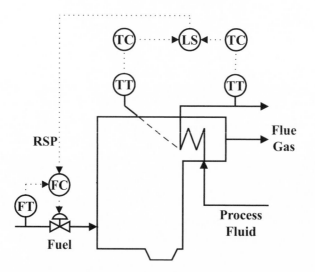

Figure 11.14 A schematic of a furnace fired heater with low select firing controls.

upper limit. If the tube temperature constraint is exceeded, damage to the furnace tubes results, significantly reducing their useful life. Figure 11.14 shows that the output of both control loops (the temperature controller on the process fluid and the temperature controller on the furnace tubes) are combined and the lower fuel feed rate is actually applied. The "LS" symbol in Figure 11.14 is called a **low select (LS)** and indicates that the lower fuel feed rate is chosen. When the feed rate is sufficiently low that the temperature of the process fluid can be controlled to setpoint, the output of the process fluid temperature controller is selected since it is lower than the output of the tube temperature controller. Likewise, when the tube temperature approaches its upper limit, the output of the tube temperature controller is selected. When the tube temperature controller is controlling the furnace, the outlet temperature is not controlled to setpoint. There are two separate loops that use fuel flow rate as a manipulated variable and the LS controller switches between them as the flow rate of the process fluid changes.

♠

Example 11.7 Override/Select Control of a Distillation Column

Problem Statement. Analyze the operation of the override/select controls for the stripping section of the distillation column shown in Figure 11.15.

Solution. Flooding in a distillation column can result as the feed to a column is increased. The onset of flooding is usually identified when the pressure drop across the column or a portion of the column increases sharply. When the pressure drop across

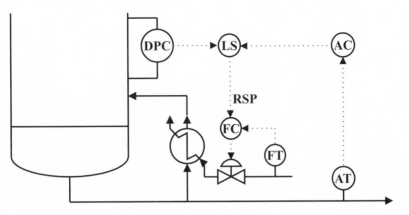

Figure 11.15 Schematic of the stripping section of a distillation column with low select controls applied to prevent flooding of the column.

the column reaches an upper operational limit (usually identified by experience), the reboiler duty is switched from controlling the bottom product composition to maintaining operation at the maximum pressure drop across the column (Figure 11.15). A LS controller is used for this application. When the column feed rate is reduced while operating at the maximum differential pressure across the column, the composition of the impurity in the bottoms product becomes less than its setpoint, and the reboiler duty called for by the composition control loop is less than that called for by the differential pressure controller. At this point, the LS controller uses the output from the composition controller. The control loop is switched when the column differential pressure reaches its upper limit and switches back when the bottom product is over purified. Two separate control loops use reboiler duty as a manipulated variable and the LS controller switches between them as the feed rate to the process changes.

♠

Example 11.8 High Select Control of a Fixed-Bed Reactor

Problem Statement. Analyze the operation of the high select controls for the fixed-bed reactor shown in Figure 11.16.

Solution. A **high select (HS)** controller (Figure 11.16) can be used to control the maximum temperature in a fixed-bed reactor even when the maximum reactor temperature occurs at different locations in the reactor. For certain reactors, if the catalyst in the reactor exceeds an upper temperature limit, damage to the catalyst occurs. The HS controller chooses the largest temperature measurement from a number of temperature measurements, and the largest reading is sent to the temperature controller. In this manner, the highest reactor temperature can be maintained below a preset upper limit. Low select (LS) controllers can also be used

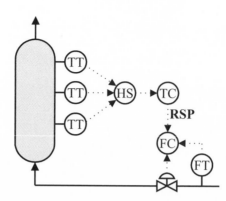

Figure 11.16 Schematic of a fixed-bed reactor with a high select controller applied to control the maximum reactor temperature.

where the lowest reading is selected from several readings.   ♠

Example 11.9 Override/Select Control of a Reboiler

Problem Statement. Analyze the operation of the override/select controls for the stripping section of the distillation column shown in Figure 11.17, which has an upper limit on its reboiler duty.

Solution. When the remote setpoint for the steam flow rate to the reboiler is consistently greater than the measured steam flow, a select controller switches to using the column feed rate as a manipulated variable to keep the bottom product purity on specification. When the column feed rate is adjusted back to its normal level and the control valve on the steam to the reboiler is no longer saturated (i.e., fully open), the

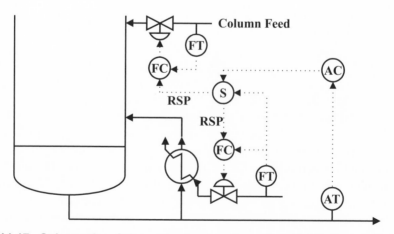

Figure 11.17 Schematic of the stripping section of a distillation column with select control to maintain bottom product purity when a maximum reboiler constraint is encountered.

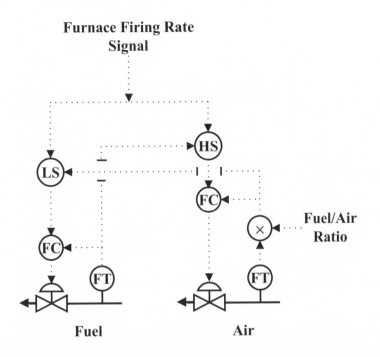

Figure 11.18 Schematic of cross-limiting firing controls, which are designed to prevent CO formation during changes in the furnace firing rate.

control configuration is changed so that the reboiler duty is manipulated to control the bottom product purity. This is an example of the selection of a secondary manipulated variable when the primary manipulated variable reaches a limit (becomes saturated). ♠

Example 11.10 Cross-Limiting Firing Controls for a Boiler

Problem Statement. Analyze the operation of the cross-limiting firing controls for a boiler shown in Figure 11.18.

Solution. For furnaces, it is important to ensure that excess air is always supplied with the fuel to prevent the formation of carbon monoxide (CO), a serious safety hazard. Furnaces are normally equipped with CO sensors that shut down the furnace if CO levels exceed specified limits. **Cross-limiting firing controls** (Figure 11.18) are designed to reduce the likelihood that CO is formed during changes in the firing rate to the furnace. To understand the schematic of cross-limiting firing controls, one must understand the flow control loop for the air addition to the furnace. The setpoint to this flow controller is the fuel equivalent to the desired air flow rate. The measured air flow rate is multiplied by the fuel-to-air ratio, and the resultant is compared with the setpoint by the flow controller. Therefore, both FCs, the LS, and the HS are based on the fuel firing rate.

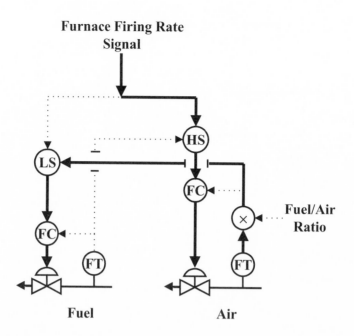

Figure 11.19 Schematic of cross-limiting firing controls showing the signal route for an increase in the firing rate.

In the case in which the firing rate increases, the air feed rate increases immediately and the fuel feed rate follows the air flow rate to ensure that combustion occurs with excess air. The fuel to air ratio is applied so that the fuel firing rate can be used in the air flow control loop. An increase in the firing rate signal (Figure 11.19) does not directly affect the fuel control loop because of the LS, but the air flow control loop accepts the firing rate increase because of the HS; therefore, the setpoint for the air flow controller increases immediately. As the air flow rate increases, the fuel flow rate corresponding to the increased air flow rate is transferred to the LS, which sends it on to the fuel flow controller as its setpoint; therefore, the fuel flow rate begins to increase, but only after the air flow rate, ensuring that excess air is present during this transient period. Similarly, when the firing signal is decreased (Figure 11.20), it does not directly affect the air flow because of the HS, but the setpoint for the fuel flow rate controller decreases immediately because of the LS. As the measured value of the fuel flow rate decreases, the HS chooses the measured fuel flow; therefore, excess air is maintained during a firing rate decrease.

♠

11.5 Computed Manipulated Variable Control

In certain cases, it is not possible to directly adjust the desired manipulated variable for a particular process. In these cases, by indirectly adjusting the desired manipulated variable, specific disturbances are effectively rejected. For example,

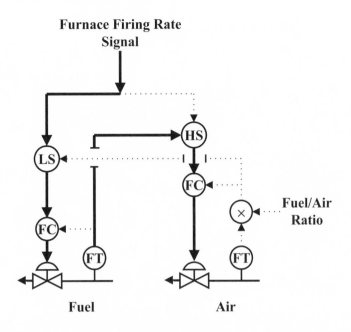

Figure 11.20 Schematic of cross-limiting firing controls showing the signal route for a decrease in the firing rate.

consider the reboiler on a distillation column that uses waste heat in the form of quench water (water used to cool hot gases) to provide reboiler duty (Figure 11.21). The inlet temperature of the quench water can vary over a wide range, which is a significant disturbance for the distillation column. When the inlet temperature increases, extra boilup results for the column and the bottoms product becomes over purified. The composition controller on the bottoms product can eventually compensate for this disturbance, but this affects the variability in the products produced by the distillation column. The desired operation of the reboiler has the composition controller setting

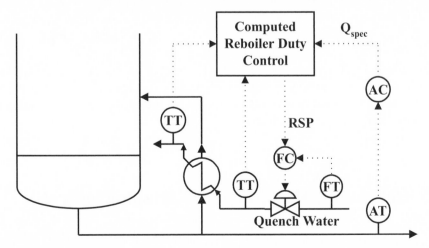

Figure 11.21 Schematic for applying computed reboiler duty control for a distillation column.

the reboiler duty directly. For steam-heated reboilers with constant enthalpy steam, the reboiler duty is directly related to the steam flow rate, but, for the case under consideration, the reboiler duty changes with inlet temperature as well as the flow rate of the quench water. The solution is to use a steady-state energy balance on the quench water to calculate the flow rate of the quench water that provides the desired reboiler duty. That is,

$$F_{sp} = \frac{Q_{spec}}{C_p (T_{in} - T_{out})}$$ **11.4**

where F_{sp} is the setpoint for the flow controller on the quench water to the reboiler, Q_{spec} is the reboiler heat duty specified by the bottom product composition controller, C_p is the heat capacity of the quench water, T_{in} and T_{out} are the measured inlet and outlet temperatures of the quench water, respectively. In this manner, as the inlet and outlet temperatures for the quench water change, its flow rate can be adjusted accordingly before affecting the product compositions of the distillation column. Figure 11.21 shows how computed manipulated variable control can be applied to this case. The inlet and outlet temperatures, along with the specified reboiler duty, are input to the computation block where Equation 11.4 calculates the required flow rate which, in turn, is passed on as the setpoint for the flow controller on the quench water.

Example 11.11 Computed Manipulated Variable Control for a Furnace

Problem Statement. Analyze the operation of the computed manipulated variable control for a furnace that is fired using two different types of gas with different heats of combustion.

Solution. Computed manipulated variable control can also be used to control a furnace that uses two different grades of fuel. Consider a process that produces a low-heating-value gas as a byproduct. It is desirable to burn all the low-heating-value gas in a furnace that is used to heat a process stream. Unfortunately, the production rate of the low-heating-value gas is not sufficient to provide all the heat duty for the furnace; therefore, natural gas is also fed to the furnace and the flow rate of natural gas is adjusted to control the temperature of the process stream leaving the furnace. Since the flow rate of the low-heating-value gas varies over a wide range, it represents a major disturbance for the temperature controller on the process stream leaving the furnace. A computed manipulated variable controller (Figure 11.22) can be used to calculate the flow rate of natural gas necessary to meet the heat duty requirements specified by the temperature controller using an energy balance for the heat duty of the furnace along with the heats of combustion for the low-heating-value gas and the natural gas, i.e.,

$$F_{sp,NG} = \frac{Q_{spec} + F_{LHV} \Delta H_{c,LHV}}{-\Delta H_{c,NG}}$$

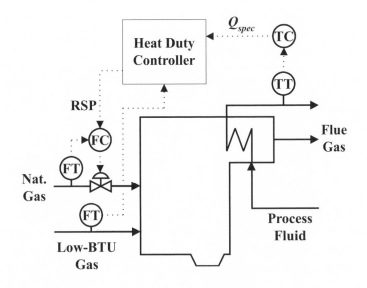

Figure 11.22 Schematic of computed manipulated variable control of a furnace with two grades of fuel.

where $F_{sp,NG}$ is the computed setpoint for the natural gas firing rate, Q_{spec} is the heat duty specified by the temperature controller, F_{LHV} is the measured flow rate of the low-heating value gas, $\Delta H_{c,LHV}$ is the heat of combustion of the low-heating-value gas, and $\Delta H_{c,NG}$ is the heat of combustion of the natural gas. Note that $\Delta H_{c,LHV}$ and $\Delta H_{c,NG}$ have negative values because combustion is an exothermic process. In this manner, flow rate changes in the low-heating-value gas can be readily compensated for by the computed manipulated variable controller. Computed manipulated variable control is an effective means of providing heat duty control in certain cases.

♠

Example 11.12 Internal Reflux Control

Problem Statement. Analyze the operation of internal reflux control applied to the column shown in Figure 11.23.

Solution. Distillation columns are particularly sensitive to sudden changes in ambient conditions, which usually accompany weather fronts and thundershowers. The reflux returned to the top of the column is cooled through increased heat loss to the cooler ambient air. This subcooled reflux causes added condensation from the vapor in the top of the column, increasing the internal reflux ratio, and improving the separation in the top portion of the column. It is much more desirable to control the internal reflux flow rate than the external reflux flow rate because ambient changes can effect the internal reflux of a column.

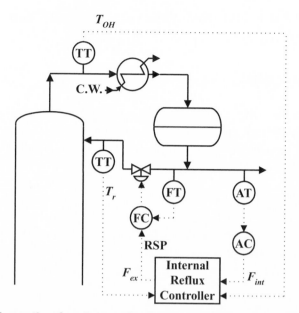

Figure 11.23 Schematic of an internal reflux controller applied for composition control of the overhead of a column.

Equating the heat lost by the condensing vapor to the heat required to heat the subcooled reflux to the temperature of the top tray results in the following equation

$$C_p F_{ex} (T_{oh} - T_r) = \Delta F_{int} \Delta H_{vap}$$

where C_p is the heat capacity of the reflux, T_{oh} is the overhead temperature, T_r is the subcooled reflux temperature, F_{ex} is the external reflux (the setpoint for the flow controller on the reflux), ΔF_{int} is the change in the reflux caused by the condensing vapor, and ΔH_{vap} is the heat of vaporization of the vapor. ΔF_{int} combines with the external reflux to form the internal reflux. The equation for the internal reflux flow (F_{int}) is given by

$$F_{int} = F_{ex} (1 + C_p [T_{oh} - T_r] / \Delta H_{vap})$$

This equation can be rearranged to calculate the external reflux that maintains a specified internal reflux (F_{int}^{spec}), i.e.,

$$F_{ex} = \frac{F_{int}^{spec}}{1 + C_p (T_{oh} - T_r) / \Delta H_{vap}} \qquad\qquad \textbf{11.5}$$

This approach is called internal reflux control and is shown schematically in Figure 11.23. The composition controller sets the specified value of the internal reflux flow rate and the internal reflux controller calculates the corresponding external reflux flow rate, which is used as the setpoint for the flow controller on the reflux.   ♠

11.6   Summary

Inferential control uses fast-responding process measurements, such as pressures, temperatures and flow rates, to estimate the value of the controlled variable. Less deadtime associated with the measurement of the controlled variable results and better feedback control performance is obtained.

When the characteristics of a process (K_p, τ_p, and θ_p) change significantly with the value of a measured process variable, scheduling of the controller tuning parameters results in improved control performance and reliability. For these cases, scheduling of the tuning parameters allows for the variation in the controller tuning as the process conditions change to maintain stable controller performance without sluggish behavior.

Override/select control switches between control loops when process constraints are encountered. High and low select controllers are applied to cases where the same manipulated variable is used by two different control loops to maintain process constraints. Override/select controls switch between manipulated variables and possible control loops to meet the operational objectives of the process as process conditions change.

Computed manipulated variable control is used when direct manipulation of the desired manipulated variable is not possible.   For these cases, process measurements are used to calculate the flow rate that is adjusted to maintain the desired manipulated variable at its prescribed level.

11.7   Additional Terminology

Adaptive controller - a controller that adjusts its tuning parameters online in response to changes in the process.
Artificial neural networks   - (ANN) a special class of nonlinear empirical models.
Cross-limiting firing controls - firing controls based on low and high selects that maintain excess air during changes in the firing rate to a furnace.
HS - high select controller.
Inferential control - the use of readily measured quantities, such as pressures, flows, and temperatures, to estimate values of the controlled variables for control purposes.
LS - low select controller.

Non-stationary process - a process whose characteristics (K_p, τ_p, θ_p) change in response to disturbances entering the process.

Self-tuning control - a controller that adjusts its tuning parameters online in response to changes in the process.

Smith Predictor - an approach that uses a process model to reduce the effects of deadtime.

Soft sensor - an algorithm that estimates the value of difficult-to-measure process variables using correlation functions based on available process measurements.

Stationary process - a process whose process characteristics (K_p, τ_p, θ_p) remain constant with time.

Time-invariant process - a process whose process characteristics (K_p, τ_p, θ_p) remain constant with time.

Time-varying process - a process whose characteristics (K_p, τ_p, θ_p) change in response to disturbances entering the process.

11.8 Preliminary Questions

11.1 Why are inferential measurements used industrially?

11.2 How do you determine which tray temperature should be used to infer the product composition of a distillation column?

11.3 Explain why inferential temperature control is extensively used industrially.

11.4 How do changes in the feed composition affect the use of inferential temperature control? How does one compensate for feed composition changes?

11.5 What assumptions were used in the derivations of Equation 11.2?

11.6 Indicate how an energy balance on a CSTR can be used to estimate the amount of conversion occurring in the reactor. What assumptions and limitations does this inferential estimator have?

11.7 How would one evaluate parameters a and b in Equation 11.3 using plant data?

11.8 For the inferential molecular weight estimator shown in Example 11.3, why is the viscosity of the polymer converted to a reference temperature?

11.9 Explain how a neural network can be trained and then used as a soft sensor.

11.10 How does scheduling controller tuning prevent a nonlinear process from going unstable or behaving sluggishly?

11.11   How do you determine whether scheduling of the tuning parameters of a controller will be effective?

11.12   Identify a process for which scheduling of the controller tuning parameters is likely to be beneficial. Outline how the scheduling of the controller tuning parameters could be accomplished. Choose a system not described in the text.

11.13   Explain how the control configuration shown in Figure 11.14 can prevent the furnace tubes from overheating.

11.14   Explain how the control configuration shown in Figure 11.15 can prevent the distillation column from flooding.

11.15   Explain how the control configuration shown in Figure 11.17 can maintain the bottom product composition at setpoint for a full range of operation.

11.16   Explain how the control configuration shown in Figure 11.20 can prevent CO formation for a decrease in the firing rate.

11.17   Explain how the control configuration shown in Figure 11.21 can reduce the effect of changes in the quench water temperature on the bottoms product composition.

11.18   Explain how the control configuration shown in Figure 11.22 can reduce the effect of changes in the production rate of the low-BTU gas on the temperature of the stream heated by the furnace.

11.19   Explain how the control configuration shown in Figure 11.23 can reduce the effect of changes in the subcooling of the reflux on the overhead product composition.

11.9 Analytical Questions and Exercises

11.20 The operating pressure of a distillation column has a significant effect on the temperatures of the trays of the column. Indicate how a tray temperature used to infer the product composition can be compensated for pressure changes. Assume that the tray temperature varies linearly with column pressure. Indicate how you would determine all unknown parameters.

11.21 Construct an inferential estimate of the fouling of the heat exchanger shown in Figure 11.11. Indicate how this estimator could be used to schedule cleaning of the tube bundle.

11.22 Consider the accumulator for a distillation column for which the distillate product flow rate is used to control the accumulator level and the reflux flow rate is used to control the composition of the overhead product similar to Figure 1.14. Draw a schematic showing select controls that will prevent the level from exceeding 95% or becoming less than 5% by overriding the composition controller on the overhead when the level is too high or too low.

11.23 Consider the stripping section of the distillation column shown in Figure 10.12. Modify this schematic by adding override controls that prevent the column pressure from exceeding its upper limit by overriding the composition controller when the pressure reaches its upper limit.

11.24 Consider the stripping section of the distillation column shown in Figure 10.12. Under certain conditions, the column floods if the steam addition rate is not restricted and, under other conditions, excess steam flow to the reboiler causes the maximum temperature limit on the reboiler to be exceeded, resulting in severe fouling of the reboiler. Draw a schematic showing the override/select controls that simultaneously prevents the column from flooding and from exceeding the upper limit on the reboiler temperature.

11.25 From your fluids course, you know that the mass flow rate of a gas through an orifice meter is dependent on the pressure drop across the orifice plate and the temperature and pressure of the gas. Therefore, if the temperature and pressure of a gas change significantly, using the pressure drop across an orifice meter as a measurement of flow rate can result in significant error. Devise a computed manipulated variable controller for the mass flow rate of a gas for which the temperature and pressure of the gas change significantly. List all the necessary equations and draw a schematic showing the computed mass flow rate controller.

11.26 Consider the schematic for an exothermic CSTR shown in the figure for this problem in which the heat produced by the reactor is used to generate steam [after W.L. Luyben, *Process Modeling, Simulation and Control for Chemical Engineers*, Second Edition, McGraw-Hill, p. 292 (1990)]. Draw a schematic for this process including each of the following control features:

    a. The level in the steam drum is controlled by the make-up water.

    b. The pressure of the steam drum is controlled by the valve on the steam line to the steam header.

    c. The temperature controller for the reactor is cascaded to the steam pressure control loop.

    d. The level in the reactor is controlled by the product flow rate.

    e. A low level in the steam drum overrides the setpoint for the flow controller on the feed to the reactor and cuts back on the feed to the reactor.

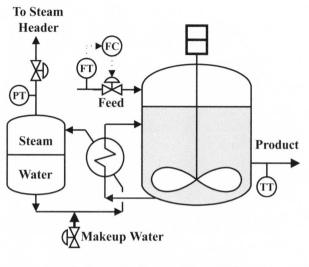

**To Steam
Header**

FC

FT

PT

Feed

Steam

Water

Product

TT

Makeup Water

Schematic for Problem 11.26

f. A high reactor temperature overrides the setpoint for the flow controller on the feed to the reactor and cuts back on the feed to the reactor.

11.27 Develop a computed manipulated variable controller for the reboiler shown in Figure 11.21, assuming that steam is used for reboiler duty instead of quench water. The computed manipulated variable controller should be able to make adjustments in the steam flow rate to account for changes in the steam enthalpy; therefore, the steam temperature and pressure upstream of the control valve should be measured and used by the computed manipulated variable. Assume that there is no condensed water in the steam.

Chapter 12

PID Implementation Issues

12.1 Introduction

This chapter is concerned with several techniques that have been developed to solve PID implementation problems. Anti-reset windup procedures protect against integral windup when a manipulated variable reaches an upper or lower limit or when either of two control loops is used with the same manipulated variable (e.g., override/select control). Bumpless transfer is a strategy for bringing a controller on-line in a manner that does not unduly upset the process. Split-range control uses two separate control loops to provide better performance than a single loop for a wide range of operation.

12.2 Anti-Windup Strategies

Figure 12.1a shows the manipulated and controlled variables for a standard PI controller for which the manipulated variable reaches a limit, i.e., the control valve is fully open or fully closed (saturated). Valve saturation can occur when a large disturbance enters the process or when the process is operated over a wide region (e.g., large setpoint changes). Since the manipulated variable cannot be increased further, the PI controller is unable to return the controlled variable to its setpoint. As long as there is an error between the controlled variable and its setpoint, the integral term in the PI controller (Equation 6.9) continues to accumulate, which is referred to as **reset windup** or **integral windup**. After some time, the disturbance level returns to its original value or the operation returns to its original setpoints. At this point, integral windup in the PI controller keeps the manipulated variable at its maximum level even though the value of the controlled variable is now above its setpoint. In effect, before the process can return to steady-state, an equal area "B" above the setpoint must be generated to compensate for area "A" shown in Figure 12.1a.

This behavior results because the integral action is allowed to continue accumulating after control of the process has been lost (**manipulated variable saturation**). Figure 12.1b shows the same case as Figure 12.1a except that, when the manipulated variable saturates, the integral action is not allowed to accumulate (**windup**). Note that when control returns to the process (i.e., when the manipulated

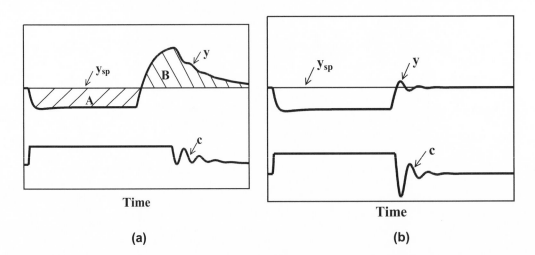

Figure 12.1 Response of a feedback system to a saturated manipulated variable. (a) Conventional PI controller. (b) PI controller with anti-reset windup.

variable is no longer saturated), the controlled variable moves directly back to its setpoint and does not exhibit prolonged deviations from setpoint as before. Because the integral action was turned off when the manipulated variable became saturated, the PI controller does not have to generate an area equivalent to area "A" above the setpoint (area "B").

Anti-reset windup can be implemented by simply not allowing the integral to accumulate when the manipulated variable is saturated. The manipulated variable is saturated when the control valve on the line supplying the manipulated variable is either closed or fully open. A saturated control valve can be identified when there is sustained offset between the manipulated variable level requested by the flow controller and the actual flow rate of the manipulated variable.

Clamping the Controller Output. Since DCSs use the velocity form of the PID controller, the output from the controller can be restricted or "clamped" so that it does not become less than 0% or more than 100%. In most cases, clamping the controller output prevents severe reaction to reset windup, but clamping the controller output still allows some degree of windup to occur.

Internal Reset Feedback. Figure 12.2a shows a block diagram for a conventional PI controller. Figure 12.2b shows a block diagram for **internal reset feedback**. Applying a balance around the summation block in Figure 12.2b for the internal reset feedback case yields

$$K_c\, E(s) + F(s) \;=\; C(s)$$

where

$$F(s) \;=\; \frac{C(s)}{\tau_I\, s + 1}$$

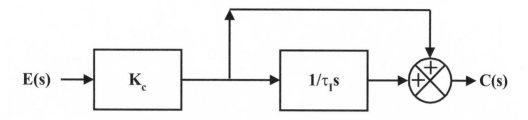

Figure 12.2a Block diagram of a conventional PI controller.

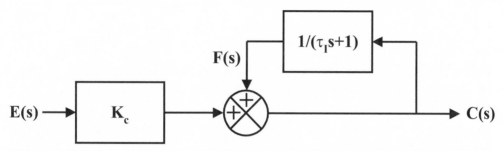

Figure 12.2b Block diagram of a PI controller with internal reset feedback.

Substituting and collecting terms results in

$$C(s)\left[1 - \frac{1}{\tau_I s + 1}\right] = K_c\, E(s)$$

Solving for $C(s)$ yields

$$C(s) = K_c\left[1 + \frac{1}{\tau_I s}\right]E(s)$$

which is the transfer function for a PI controller; therefore, internal reset feedback (Figure 12.2b) is equivalent to PI control (Figure 12.2a). Since it is equivalent to a conventional PI controller, internal reset feedback will also windup, but since $C(s)$ can be clamped, it does not windup above 100% or below 0%. Therefore, internal reset feedback does not offer any advantage over using the velocity form of the PI controller and clamping the controller output. It is, however, a natural step from internal reset feedback to external reset feedback, which is superior to controller output clamping.

External Reset Feedback. Figure 12.3 shows a block diagram for **external reset feedback**. For this case the measured value of the manipulated variable, instead of the output from the controller is fed back through the filter to the summation block. The advantage of external reset feedback is that shortly after the manipulated variable saturates, i.e., $F(s)$ becomes constant, reset windup is turned off and $C(s)$ becomes

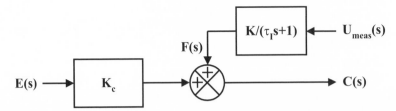

Figure 12.3 Block diagram of a PI controller with external reset feedback.

constant. For internal reset feedback, reset windup continues until the controller output reaches 0% or 100%. External reset feedback turns off the integral action much sooner than internal reset feedback. The disadvantage of external reset feedback is that a measurement of the manipulated variable, which is not available in all cases, is required. It should be pointed out that the measured value of the manipulated variable must be scaled so that it has the same units as the controller output (i.e., %).

It is a standard control practice to apply some type of anti-windup strategy (e.g., external reset feedback or turning off the integral action when the manipulated variable saturates) to all control loops that use integral action to prevent reset windup. This is essential for override/select loops because, when one loop is controlling the process, the other is not in service; therefore, the inactive loop can experience severe windup if anti-reset windup measures are not taken. Figure 12.4 demonstrates how external reset feedback is applied to a tray temperature controller on the stripping section of a distillation column. As shown in Figures 12.3 and 12.4, external reset feedback requires that the measurement of the steam flow be input to the controller.

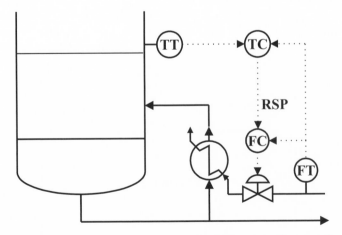

Figure 12.4 A schematic of the implementation of external reset feedback for a tray temperature controller on the stripping section of a distillation column.

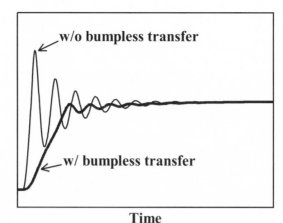

Time

Figure 12.5 The startup response of a feedback system (a) without bumpless transfer and (b) with bumpless transfer.

12.3 Bumpless Transfer

Figure 12.5 shows the process behavior with and without **bumpless transfer**. Without bumpless transfer, if the controller is turned on when the controlled variable is far removed from setpoint, the controller takes immediate action and drives the process to setpoint in an underdamped fashion. In certain cases, the controlled variable can be far enough away from setpoint and the process can be sufficiently nonlinear that the control loop becomes unstable. Even if the control loop does not become unstable, the abrupt action of the feedback controller can significantly upset other control loops on the process. As a result, operators find that the behavior of a controller without bumpless transfer is generally unacceptable, particularly for key loops such as composition and temperature control loops.

For bumpless transfer, there are two types of setpoints: the true setpoint, which corresponds to the desired operating point and the internal setpoint that is used

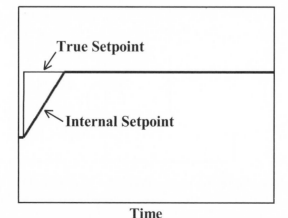

Time

Figure 12.6 Comparison between the true setpoint and the internal setpoint for the bumpless transfer example.

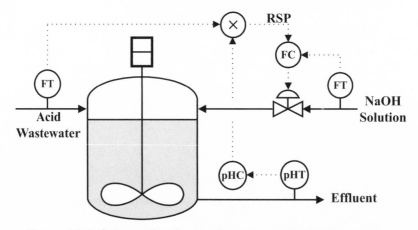

Figure 12.7 Schematic of a wastewater neutralization process.

for bumpless transfer (Figure 12.6). When a control loop is turned on, the setpoint used by the controller is actually different than the true setpoint when applying bumpless transfer. When the controller is turned on, the internal setpoint is set equal to the current controlled variable value; therefore, there is no change in the manipulated variable level. After this, the internal setpoint is ramped toward the true setpoint and the process begins moving toward the true setpoint in a gradual fashion. After the internal setpoint reaches the true setpoint value, it remains constant. By selecting a proper setpoint ramping rate, smooth and consistent startups for control loops result. Prevention of overly aggressive startup of a control loop or response to setpoint changes can also be attained by using the form of the PID algorithm that is not susceptible to proportional kick (Equation 6.20).

12.4 Split-Range Control

The basic idea behind split-range control is to use two or more actuators or manipulated variables so that the flexibility of a number of actuators or manipulated

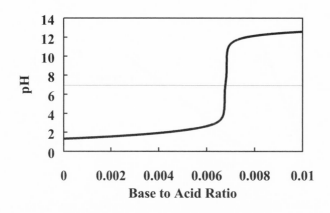

Figure 12.8 Titration curve for a strong acid/strong base system.

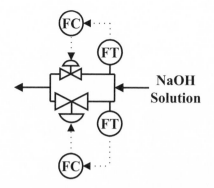

Figure 12.9 Schematic of a split range flow controller.

variables can be used by the controller. Split-range flow control and split-range temperature control are considered here.

Split-Range Flow Control. Consider the wastewater neutralization process shown in Figure 12.7. The titration curve for the wastewater is shown in Figure 12.8. To control the pH to ± 1.0 pH unit at a setpoint of pH 7, the base flow rate must be metered accurately to within ±0.5%. A single flow-control loop with a control valve with a positioner can meet this metering precision. If the total flow rate of base were to range from 0.1 to 10 gallons per minute, one flow control loop could not simultaneously meter the base flow rate to within ±0.5% at both extremes.

Two flow control loops that work together, as shown in Figure 12.9, can meet this requirement. At low flow rates, the large control valve is closed and the flow control loop with the smaller control valve can accurately meter the low-flow operation (Figure 12.10). As the total flow increases, the smaller control valve begins to approach saturation. Before this happens, the flow control loop with the larger control valve comes into service. At large flow rates, the small control valve is

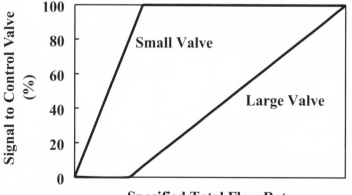

Figure 12.10 Controller output to the large and small valves in the split-range flow control arrangement shown in Figure 12.9.

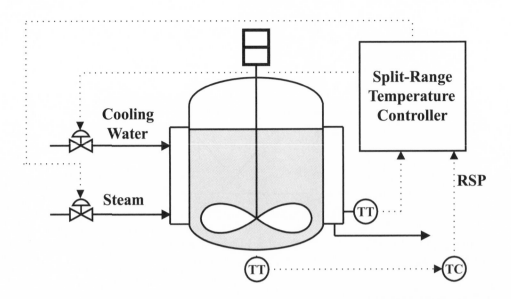

Figure 12.11 Schematic of a split-range temperature controller applied to water jacket of a batch reactor.

completely open and the flow control loop with the larger valve is accurately metering the base flow rate. This is an example of **split-range flow control**, which is used when accurate flow control is required over a wider operating range than one control valve can provide.

     Split-Range Reactor Temperature Control.   Figure 12.11 shows a schematic of an exothermic batch reactor for which steam is used to bring the reaction mixture up to the normal operating temperature and cooling water is used to maintain the reactor at the operating temperature.   Initially, the reactor is near ambient temperature and the reactions are essentially extinguished. Steam is added to the water jacket to raise the temperature of the reaction mixture. As the reactor temperature increases, the exothermic reactions add heat to the system, further increasing the reactor temperature. As the reactor temperature begins to increase, the amount of steam added to the reactor is decreased and cooling water is added to the water jacket. Eventually, the steam is cut off, and the cooling water removes the heat generated by the exothermic reactions. Figure 12.12 shows the control signals that are sent to the valves on the steam and the cooling water by the split-range temperature controller. Note that as the error between the remote setpoint for the jacket water temperature and the measured jacket water temperature increases, the control action switches from cooling to heating.

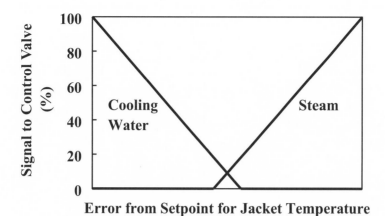

Figure 12.12 The signals to the control valves from the split-range temperature controller as a function of the specified jacket water temperature.

12.5 Summary

Reset windup can occur when a control valve saturates. External reset feedback or turning off the integral action when a control valve saturates eliminates reset windup. Bumpless transfer provides a smooth startup procedure for a control loop by ramping the setpoint from the initial value of the controlled variable to its desired final value. Split-range control uses two or more actuators or manipulated variables in parallel so that the control system operates efficiently over a wide operating range.

12.6 Additional Terminology

Anti-reset windup - approaches that prevent reset windup, e.g., external reset feedback.

Bumpless transfer - a startup procedure used to gradually bring a control loop into service.

Clamping - restricting the output of a controller to less than a maximum amount (e.g., 100%) and greater than a minimum amount (e.g., 0%).

External reset feedback - an anti-windup approach that uses the measured value of the manipulated variable.

Integral windup - the accumulation of the integral of the error from setpoint caused by an uncontrollable error from setpoint.

Internal reset feedback - an anti-windup approach that does not use the measured value of the manipulated variable.

Manipulated variable saturation - a manipulated variable that is either at its maximum or minimum value.

Reset windup - the accumulation of the integral of the error from setpoint caused by an uncontrollable error from setpoint.

Split-range flow control - using two flow control loops in parallel, one with a smaller valve than the other, to provide precise flow metering over a wide range of flow rates.

Windup - the accumulation of the integral of the error from setpoint caused by an uncontrollable error from setpoint.

12.7 Preliminary Questions

12.1 In your own words, explain how windup occurs and what problems it causes.

12.2 Show that internal reset feedback is equivalent to conventional control for a PI controller.

12.3 Explain, in your own words, how external reset feedback eliminates integral windup.

12.4 What advantages does internal reset feedback have over using the velocity form of the PID controller and clamping the controller output?

12.5 What is the advantage of external over internal reset feedback?

12.6 If you were applying an anti-windup strategy that turned off the integral when a control valve saturated, how would you determine whether or not a control valve was saturated?

12.7 What is the primary requirement for applying external reset feedback?

12.8 How can large setpoint changes or starting a control loop far from its setpoint result in unstable operation of the control loop?

12.9 Explain how bumpless transfer is applied and indicate what its advantages are.

12.10 Why do operators prefer bumpless transfer?

12.11 When should you use split-range flow control?

12.12 Explain how the controller outputs shown in Figure 12.10 are responsible for implementing split-range flow control.

12.13 Why is split-range temperature control necessary for the batch reactor shown in Figure 12.11?

12.14 Explain how the controller outputs shown in Figure 12.12 are responsible for implementing split-range temperature control.

PART V

CONTROL OF MIMO PROCESSES

Chapter 13

PID Controllers Applied to MIMO Processes

13.1 Introduction

A multiple-input/multiple-output (MIMO) process has two or more inputs and two or more outputs. A two-input/two-output system is shown schematically in Figure 13.1. Note that c_1 affects both y_1 and y_2 and c_2 affects both y_1 and y_2. When both inputs affect both outputs the process is **coupled**. Coupled MIMO processes are frequently encountered in the CPI.

This chapter considers the application of PID controllers to coupled MIMO processes. A key issue when applying PID controllers to MIMO systems is deciding which manipulated variable should be used to control which controlled variable. This is referred to as choosing the **manipulated/controlled variable pairings** [(c,y) pairings] or the **control configuration**. The factors that affect the choice of (c, y) pairings are analyzed in this chapter. A strategy for tuning PID controllers that are applied to MIMO processes is presented as well as an introduction to decoupling. In this chapter for simplicity, the transfer function $G'(s)$ is used to represent the combined effect of the actuator, process, and sensor [$G_a(s)\ G_p(s)\ G_s(s)$].

13.2 SISO Controllers and (c, y) Pairings

Figure 13.2 shows two **single-loop PID controllers** applied to a two input/two output process (2×2 system). Applying single-loop PID controllers to a MIMO process is called **decentralized control**. Centralized control is addressed in the next chapter. The coupling in this 2×2 system causes the two control loops to interact. That is, while control loop 1 manipulates c_1 to keep y_1 at its setpoint, it upsets control loop 2. Likewise, the operation of control loop 2 acts as an upset for control loop 1. Figure 13.3 shows schematically the coupling effect of control loop 2 (indicted by heavy lines) as an additive disturbance to control loop 1. The coupling effects of control loop 1 are also represented as an additive disturbance to control loop 2. For this

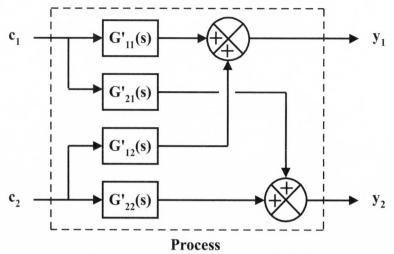

Process

Figure 13.1 Block diagram of a two-input/two-output process.

2×2 example, tuning control loop 1 must include the effects of control loop 2 and vice versa. When tuning single-loop PID controllers applied to a MIMO process, one must take into account the effects of coupling.

The selection of pairings for decentralized control can have a dramatic effect on the resulting overall control performance. Consider the 2×2 system represented by transfer function models shown in Table 13.1. Using c_1 to control y_1 and c_2 to control y_2 has the advantage that the magnitude of coupling is relatively small. The steady-state process gain for the effect of c_1 on y_1 is 1.0 and for the effect of c_2 on y_2 is

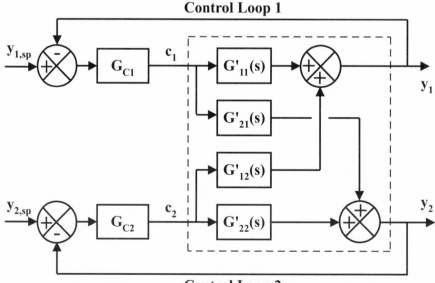

Control Loop 2

Figure 13.2   Block diagram of a 2 × 2 process with single-loop controllers (decentralized control).

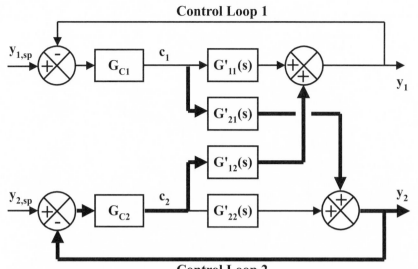

Figure 13.3 A block diagram of a 2 × 2 process with single-loop controllers showing the coupling effect of loop 2 on y_1 for changes in c_1.

2.0 while the gain for the effect of c_1 on y_2 is 0.05 and for the effect of c_2 on y_1 is 0.1. As a result, relatively small changes in c_1 and c_2 are called for by the feedback controllers since the process gains are relatively large and the resulting coupling is relatively low in magnitude. On the other hand, if c_1 were chosen to control y_2 and c_2 to control y_1, large changes in c_1 and c_2 would be required by the feedback controllers due to the low process gains. Then, the resulting coupling is severe.

	Table 13.1 **Transfer Function Models for a Two Input/Two Output Process.**		
		c_1	c_2
y_1		$\dfrac{1.0}{10s+1}$	$\dfrac{0.1}{10s+1}$
y_2		$\dfrac{0.05}{10s+1}$	$\dfrac{2.0}{10s+1}$

Three factors determine the best pairings for a MIMO process: coupling, dynamic response, and the sensitivity to disturbances. Each of these factors is considered separately in the next three sections.

13.3 Steady-State Coupling

Bristol[1] developed the **Relative Gain Array (*RGA*)**, which is a measure of steady-state coupling. The *RGA* for a 2 × 2 system is given by

$$RGA = \begin{pmatrix} \lambda_{11} & \lambda_{12} \\ \lambda_{21} & \lambda_{22} \end{pmatrix}$$

where

$$\lambda_{11} = \frac{\left(\dfrac{\Delta y_1}{\Delta c_1}\right)_{c_2}}{\left(\dfrac{\Delta y_1}{\Delta c_1}\right)_{y_2}} \qquad \lambda_{12} = \frac{\left(\dfrac{\Delta y_1}{\Delta c_2}\right)_{c_1}}{\left(\dfrac{\Delta y_1}{\Delta c_2}\right)_{y_2}}$$

13.1

$$\lambda_{21} = \frac{\left(\dfrac{\Delta y_2}{\Delta c_1}\right)_{c_2}}{\left(\dfrac{\Delta y_2}{\Delta c_1}\right)_{y_1}} \qquad \lambda_{22} = \frac{\left(\dfrac{\Delta y_2}{\Delta c_2}\right)_{c_1}}{\left(\dfrac{\Delta y_2}{\Delta c_2}\right)_{y_1}}$$

where

$$\left(\frac{\Delta y_i}{\Delta c_j}\right)_{c_k}$$

represents the steady-state change in y_i resulting from a change in c_j while keeping c_k constant and

$$\left(\frac{\Delta y_i}{\Delta c_j}\right)_{y_k}$$

represents the steady-state change in y_i for a change in c_j while keeping y_k constant. As a result, **the *RGA* is the ratio of the process gain without coupling to the process gain with coupling**. The numerator of λ_{11} in Equation 13.1 is simply the open-loop gain for the effect of c_1 on y_1, i.e., the steady-state gain in $G_{11}(s)$, and this can be determined by implementing a change in c_1 and measuring the resulting steady-state change in y_1 while control loop 2 is open (Figure 13.4). The denominator of λ_{11} is the gain between c_1 and y_1 while keeping y_2 at its setpoint, which requires that the second loop be closed (Figure 13.5). If no coupling is present, the numerator of λ_{11} equals the

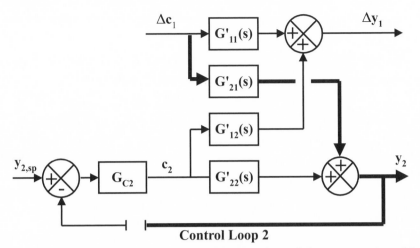

Figure 13.4 Block diagram for the determination of the numerator of λ_{11}.

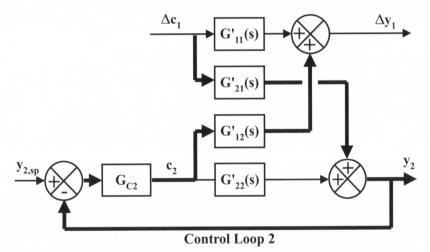

Control Loop 2

Figure 13.5 Block diagram for the determination of the denominator of λ_{11}.

denominator. As a result, the closer λ_{11} is to 1.0, the less steady-state coupling a configuration has.

Consider the system represented by Table 13.1. The steady-state gain matrix for this process is given by

$$K = \begin{pmatrix} K_{11} & K_{12} \\ K_{21} & K_{22} \end{pmatrix} = \begin{pmatrix} 1.0 & 0.1 \\ 0.05 & 2.0 \end{pmatrix}$$

Consider λ_{11}. The numerator is the open-loop gain of the first transfer function, 1.0. The evaluation of the numerator of λ_{11} is shown schematically in Figure 13.4. To calculate the value of

$$\left(\frac{\Delta y_1}{\Delta c_1}\right)_{y_2}$$

consider a change in c_1 of 1.0. From Figure 13.5, the net effect on y_1 is the combined effect of the primary response and the result of coupling. The primary response is the product of Δc_1 and K_{11}, 1.0. The result of coupling is calculated by using the various steady-state gains. The effect of Δc_1 on y_2 is given by

$$\Delta y_2 = \Delta c_1 K_{21} = 0.05$$

The (c_2, y_2) control loop must compensate for this change in y_2; therefore, the required change in c_2 is given by

$$\Delta c_2 = \frac{-\Delta y_2}{K_{22}} = -0.025$$

Finally, the effect of Δc_2 on y_1 is given by

$$\Delta y_1 = \Delta c_2 K_{12} = -0.0025$$

which represents the coupling result for a Δc_1 change.

Therefore, the total effect is the sum of the primary effect and the coupling effect, i.e.,

$$\left(\frac{\Delta y_1}{\Delta c_1}\right)_{y_2} = \frac{1-0.0025}{1.0} = 0.9975$$

Then, λ_{11} is given by

$$\lambda_{11} = \frac{1.0}{0.9975} = 1.0025$$

which indicates that this pairing is highly decoupled.

For a 2×2 system, the value of λ_{11} is expressed as a function of the steady-state gains, i.e.,

$$\lambda_{11} = \frac{K_{11}}{K_{11} - \dfrac{K_{12} K_{21}}{K_{22}}} = \frac{1}{1 - \dfrac{K_{12} K_{21}}{K_{11} K_{22}}} \qquad \text{13.2}$$

In this example, the effect of coupling works in the opposite direction of the primary action, where the primary action in this case is given by K_{11}. As a result, λ_{11} is greater than unity. When the primary action and the coupling effect act in the same direction, λ_{11} is less than one. This can be understood by recognizing that when both effects act in the same direction, the denominator of Equation 13.2 is greater than the numerator.

It can be shown that

$$\lambda_{11} + \lambda_{12} = 1$$

Likewise,

$$\lambda_{21} + \lambda_{22} = 1$$

It can also be shown that

$$\lambda_{11} + \lambda_{21} = 1$$

and

$$\lambda_{12} + \lambda_{22} = 1$$

These results show that the sum of any row or any column is equal to unity. As a result,

$$\lambda_{11} = \lambda_{22}$$

and

$$\lambda_{12} = \lambda_{21} = 1 - \lambda_{11}$$

As a result, determining that

$$\lambda_{11} = 1.0025$$

sets

$$\lambda_{22} = 1.0025$$
$$\lambda_{12} = -0.0025$$
$$\lambda_{21} = -0.0025$$

Therefore, once λ_{11} is determined, all the other λ's are specified for a 2×2 system. As a result, the *RGA* for a 2×2 system is typically reported as a single number (i.e., λ_{11}). In addition, if the pairing of c_1 and c_2 are switched, the *RGA* value is simply one minus the *RGA* (λ_{11}) value for the original pairing.

For the system represented in Table 13.1, if c_1 were used to control y_2 and c_2 were used to control y_1, the steady-state gain matrix would be

$$K = \begin{pmatrix} 0.1 & 1.0 \\ 2.0 & 0.05 \end{pmatrix}$$

Using Equation 13.2 yields

$$\lambda_{11} = \frac{1}{1 - \dfrac{2}{0.005}} = -0.0025$$

which is λ_{12} for the original pairing scheme.

Consider the *RGA* for a 3×3 system

$$RGA = \begin{pmatrix} \lambda_{11} & \lambda_{12} & \lambda_{13} \\ \lambda_{21} & \lambda_{22} & \lambda_{23} \\ \lambda_{31} & \lambda_{32} & \lambda_{33} \end{pmatrix}$$

where

$$\lambda_{12} = \frac{\left(\dfrac{\Delta y_1}{\Delta c_2}\right)_{c_1, c_3}}{\left(\dfrac{\Delta y_1}{\Delta c_2}\right)_{y_2, y_3}}$$

Note that the gain in the numerator is based upon keeping c_1 and c_3 constant while the gain in the denominator is based upon keeping y_2 and y_3 constant. The closer the diagonal elements of the *RGA* are to unity, the more decoupled the process is. The sum of λ's in any row or any column is equal to one. Therefore, for a 3×3 system, the *RGA* requires the determination of four of the nine possible λ's.

13.4 Dynamic Factors in Configuration Selection

For the 2×2 system represented in Table 13.1, all the input/output relationships have the same dynamic behavior; therefore, a steady-state analysis is sufficient. Consider the transfer function representation of a 2×2 system shown in Table 13.2. From Equation 13.2, the steady-state *RGA* (λ_{11}) for this system is 0.94, indicating that the control loop pairings listed in Table 13.2 are proper.

Table 13.2
Transfer Function Representation of a 2×2 System with Dynamic Coupling

	c_1	c_2
y_1	$\dfrac{1.0}{100s+1}$	$\dfrac{0.3}{10s+1}$
y_2	$\dfrac{-0.4}{10s+1}$	$\dfrac{2.0}{100s+1}$

However, notice that the effect of c_1 on y_1 and the effect of c_2 on y_2 have much slower dynamics than the effect of c_1 on y_2 and the effect of c_2 on y_1 (i.e., the coupling). The time constants for the diagonal responses are ten times the time constants for the off-diagonal terms. When changes in c_1 are made to correct for deviations in y_1 from its setpoint, changes in y_2 result long before y_1 can be corrected. Then the (c_2, y_2) control loop makes changes in c_2 to correct for the coupling. Once again, because of the dynamic differences, y_1 responds to the coupling much more quickly than y_2 can be corrected. The (c_1, y_1) control loop responds to these additional changes in y_1 and the coupling process continues. This is an example of **dynamic coupling**. Figure 13.6 shows the dynamic response of y_1 and y_2 for a setpoint change in y_1 for the original (c, y) pairings and for the reverse pairings, i.e., (c_1, y_2) and (c_2, y_1). Even though the steady-state RGA of the reverse pairing is 0.06, the control performance of the reverse pairings is far superior.

The dynamic RGA^2 can be used to assess the effect of dynamics on coupling. The dynamic RGA is calculated by substituting $s = i\omega$ into each transfer function

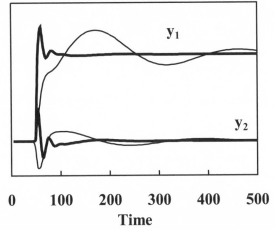

Figure 13.6 Response to a setpoint change in y_1 for the original pairings (thin line) and the reverse pairings (thick line) for the process represented by Table 13.2.

comprising the input/output model. For a specific frequency, the magnitude of each transfer function (Equation 9.1) and the corresponding *RGA* at that frequency is calculated from Equation 13.2 with the transfer function magnitudes used in place of the static gains. In this manner, the *RGA* can be plotted as a function of frequency. At very low frequencies, the dynamic *RGA* approaches the steady-state *RGA* value. Therefore, a comparison of dynamic *RGAs* at intermediate frequencies distinguishes dynamic coupling effects.

Consider the calculation of the dynamic *RGA* for the 2×2 process represented in Table 13.2. Since each of the transfer functions in Table 13.2 is for a first-order process, the magnitude of $G_p(i\omega)$ for a general first-order process is simply A_r and is given by Equation 9.2

$$\left| G_p(i\omega) \right| = \frac{K_p}{\sqrt{\tau_p^2 \omega^2 + 1}}$$

Then, using Equation 13.2, the dynamic *RGA* for the (c_1, y_1) pairing listed in Table 13.2 is given by

$$\lambda_{11}(\omega) = \frac{1}{1 + \dfrac{0.06(100^2 \omega^2 + 1)}{(10^2 \omega^2 + 1)}}$$

Likewise, the dynamic *RGA* for the opposite pairing is given by

$$\lambda_{11}(\omega) = \frac{1}{1 + \dfrac{10^2 \omega^2 + 1}{0.06(100^2 \omega^2 + 1)}}$$

Figure 13.7 shows the dynamic *RGAs* for these two cases. At very low frequencies, which corresponds to the steady-state *RGA*, the original pairing provides superior decoupling, while the reverse pairing is preferred at high frequencies. On the other hand, as shown in Figure 13.6, the configuration with the reverse pairing responds much more quickly. In fact, the frequency corresponding to the time constant of the off-diagonal interaction (i.e., τ_p equal to 10) corresponds to a frequency of 0.1 radians per unit time. At this frequency and higher, the reverse pairing is clearly preferred, as shown in Figure 13.7.

Since transfer function models are not usually available for industrial processes, it is recommended to qualitatively use the results of this section when choosing (c, y) pairings. That is, **when selecting a manipulated variable for a particular controlled variable, choose a manipulated variable that causes the controlled variable to exhibit a relatively fast dynamic response, i.e., choose pairings that have a relatively low effective time constant and a relatively low**

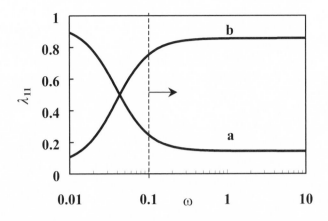

Figure 13.7 Dynamic RGA for (a) the original pairings and (b) the reverse pairings for the process represented in Table 13.2.

effective process deadtime. It is important to remember to use your understanding of the process to guide your analysis.

13.5 Sensitivity to Disturbances

In general, each possible configuration has a different sensitivity to a particular disturbance. Consider the distillation column shown in Figure 13.8. The reflux flow rate, L, is used to control the overhead composition and the boilup rate, V, which is set by the reboiler duty, is used to control the bottom composition. Since L

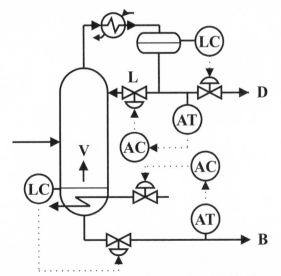

Figure 13.8 Schematic of a distillation column with the (L, V) configuration. Note that control valves represent flow control loops in this figure.

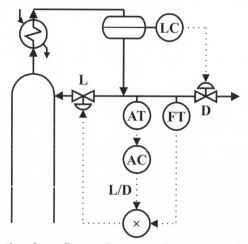

Figure 13.9 Schematic of a reflux ratio controller applied for the control of the overhead composition. Note that control valves represent flow control loops in this figure.

and V are used for composition control, the distillate flow rate, D, is used to control the accumulator level and the bottoms flow rate, B, is used to control the reboiler level. This configuration is referred to as the (L,V) configuration since L is used to control the overhead product composition and V is used to control the bottoms product composition. Consider the $(L/D,\ V/B)$ configuration. Figure 13.9 shows how the reflux ratio, L/D, can be applied to control the overhead product composition. Note that a ratio controller is used for the composition controller and D is used to control the level in the accumulator. In a similar manner, the boilup ratio V/B can be used to control the bottoms product composition. That is, a V/B ratio controller can be used to control the bottoms product composition while the bottoms product flow rate, B, is used to control the level in the reboiler. Figure 13.10 shows the "open-loop" response of a distillation column to a step increase in the light component composition in the feed for the (L,V) and $(L/D,V/B)$ configurations. In this case, open-loop response refers to opening the composition control loops while maintaining the level controllers in

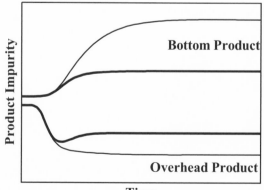

Figure 13.10 The open-loop response of a distillation column with the (L,V) configuration (thick line) and the $(L/D,V/B)$ configuration (thin line) to a step change in feed composition.

closed-loop operation. The (L,V) configuration is less sensitive to feed composition changes than the $(L/D,V/B)$ configuration. As a result, the (L,V) configuration is less affected by feed composition changes than the $(L/D,V/B)$ configuration.

From an analysis of the previous sections it can be concluded that **the combined effect of coupling, dynamic behavior, and sensitivity to disturbances determine the control performance for a particular control configuration for a MIMO process.** Process control engineers typically rely upon their understanding of the process and their experience when selecting a control configuration for a MIMO process.

Example 13.1 Configuration Selection for a C_3 Splitter

Problem Statement. Evaluate the configuration selection problem for a C_3 splitter. A C_3 splitter separates a feed mixture primarily composed of propane and propylene into polymer-grade propylene ($< 0.5\%$ propane) and fuel-grade propane (approximately 2% propylene).

Solution. The nomenclature used here refers to a particular configuration as (c_1, c_2) in which c_1 is the manipulated variable that is used to control the overhead composition and c_2 is the manipulated variable that is used to control the bottoms composition. If we limit ourselves to controlling the overhead composition with L, D, or L/D (the reflux ratio) and the bottoms composition with V, B, or V/B (the boilup ratio), there are a total of nine possible configurations. Here we limit the discussion to the following configurations for illustration purposes: (L, B), (L, V), $(L/D, V/B)$, and (D, V).

The steady-state *RGA*s for each of the configurations considered here are listed below:

Table 13.3 RGA Values for Example 13.1	
Configuration	**RGA (λ_{11})**
(L, B)	0.94
(L, V)	25.3
$(L/D, V/B)$	1.70
(D, V)	0.06

Shinskey[3] recommends *RGA* values between 0.9 and 3.0 for distillation columns, indicating that *RGA* values greater than one are preferred over *RGA* values less than one. Based upon Shinskey's guidelines and the results in Table 13.3, the (L, B) and $(L/D, V/B)$ configurations appear the most promising.

The dynamics of distillation columns can be understood by recognizing that product composition changes result from changes in the vapor/liquid traffic in the column. That is, changing L or V directly affects the column vapor/liquid traffic and has the most immediate effect on the product composition. On the other hand, changes in B and D depend on the level controllers to change the vapor/liquid traffic of the column; therefore, the dynamic response of the product compositions is significantly slower when B and D are changed compared with changing L and V. The dynamic response to changes in L/D and V/B are intermediate between L and V on the fast side and B and D on the slow side. For example, the dynamics of changes in L/D are faster than changes in D but slower than changes in L. Based upon this analysis, (L, B) is expected to perform better for the overhead composition control than for the bottoms, but there is no clear winner between the (L, B) and the $(L/D, V/B)$ configurations with regard to the overall dynamic response.

Table 13.4 shows the relative changes in each manipulated variable for a change in feed composition. This table is based on steady-state results in which the product compositions are maintained at a constant level. A lower relative change for a manipulated variable indicates a reduced sensitivity to feed composition changes for that manipulated variable. L, L/D, and V show the least sensitivity to feed composition changes.

Table 13.4

Relative Changes in the Manipulated Variables to Maintain the Product Purities for a 5 mole % Increase in Feed Composition.

Manipulated Variable	Percentage Change
L	4.2
D	7.4
L/D	-3.0
V	4.4
B	-16.8
V/B	25.5

Table 13.5 lists the integral absolute error (IAE) of each product for each configuration for a feed composition upset. A lower IAE value indicates closer control to setpoint. The (L, B) configuration provided the best overall control performance, especially for the overhead product. This is consistent with the observations that L is dynamically fast and relatively insensitive to feed composition changes coupled with the moderate steady-state coupling as indicated by the RGA.

The (L,V) configuration has the advantages of fast overall dynamics and insensitivity to feed composition upsets. These advantages are negated by the extreme degree of steady-state coupling as indicated by its steady-state RGA value. The control performance of the (L,V) configuration is the poorest of the four configurations listed in Table 13.4. The $(L/D, V/B)$ configuration has a good steady-state RGA and dynamic characteristics, but is particularly sensitive to feed composition upsets for the bottom composition control loop. As a result, its performance is inferior to the (L, B) configuration. The steady-state RGA value of the (D, V) configuration indicates that this configuration will not function properly. Actually, the control performance of the (D,V) configuration is quite reasonable, i.e., the IAEs for the (D,V) configuration are only about 30% larger than those for the (L,B) configuration, which is not a great deal of difference in control performance.

Table 13.5 Control Performance (IAE) for a Step Change in Feed Composition		
Configuration	**IAE for Overhead**	**IAE for Bottoms**
L,B	0.067	1.49
L,V	0.250	13.3
L/D,V/B	0.095	2.00
D,V	0.098	1.91

♠

For complex configuration selection problems, such as distillation columns, the previous analysis is helpful but does not always guarantee that the best configuration is identified. The performance differences between reasonable configuration choices and the best configuration can be substantial. The use of detailed dynamic simulations for the analysis of the control performance of feasible configurations is recommended wherever possible.

13.6 Tuning Decentralized Controllers

The recommended tuning procedure for a single PID loop can be extended to tuning the single-loop PID controllers applied for decentralized control of a MIMO process. The first step in tuning a decentralized controller is to apply ATV tests to each manipulated/controlled variable pair. While an ATV test is being applied to one loop, the other loops should be maintained in an open-loop condition.

Next, determine if any of the loops are significantly faster-responding than the other loops. This can be done by comparing the values of the ultimate periods, P_u, obtained in the ATV tests. If the smallest value of P_u is 20% or less of the next smaller P_u, that loop should be implemented by itself before tuning the other loops. It can be tuned as a single PID loop as discussed in Chapter 7. Then, ATV tests on the remaining loops should be rerun with the tuned fast loop in service (closed-loop operation). Then, the remaining control loops can be tuned using the following procedure.

Consider the tuning of PI controllers for a 2×2 MIMO process. The ATV results are used to select the controller gain and reset time based on an appropriate tuning criterion, e.g., Ziegler-Nichols method. Then, a single tuning factor, F_T, is applied to the tuning parameters for **both control loops**.

$$\left. \begin{array}{l} K_c = K_c^{ZN} / F_T \\[1mm] \tau_I = \tau_I^{ZN} \times F_T \end{array} \right\} \text{ First control loop}$$

$$\left. \begin{array}{l} K_c = K_c^{ZN} / F_T \\[1mm] \tau_I = \tau_I^{ZN} \times F_T \end{array} \right\} \text{ Second control loop} \qquad \textbf{13.3}$$

F_T is adjusted until the dynamic response satisfies the control loop tuning criterion. For example, setpoint changes in y_1 and/or y_2 can be used to select the proper value of F_T. Alternatively, the value of F_T can be adjusted to provide reliable performance of the controllers based on day-to-day controller operating performance. While tuning, if the closed-loop response is sluggish, the value of F_T is decreased. If the controller exhibits periods of ringing, the value of F_T is increased.

After F_T has been adjusted to tune the set of decentralized PI controllers, fine tuning of the controller settings should be used. For example, if one observes that one of the control loops is slow to settle at setpoint in a manner similar to Figure 7.12a, an increase in integral action for that loop should be tested. If one of the loops exhibits ringing, derivative action should be tested to determine if it improves the feedback control performance of that loop. In the latter case, derivative action should be tuned in the manner described in Chapter 7.

13.7 Decouplers

Decouplers are designed to reduce the detrimental effects of coupling. Figure 13.11 shows two decouplers $[D_1(s)$ and $D_2(s)]$ applied to a two-input/two-output process. D_1 is designed to reduce the effects of changes in c_2 on y_1 while D_2 is designed to reduce the effects of changes in c_1 on y_2.

Consider the design of D_1. The effect of changes in c_2 on y_1 is given by

$$G'_{12}(s)C_2(s)$$

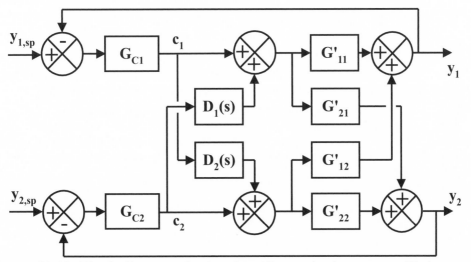

Figure 13.11 Block diagram of a two-input/two-output process with two-way decoupling.

The corrective action on y_1 from D_1 is given by

$$D_1(s)G'_{11}(s)C_2(s)$$

The objective of the decoupler is to eliminate the effect of coupling; therefore, the sum of the previous two terms is set to zero, i.e.,

$$G'_{12}(s)C_2(s) + D_1(s)G'_{11}(s)C_2(s) = 0$$

Solving for $D_1(s)$ yields

$$D_1(s) = \frac{-G'_{12}(s)}{G'_{11}(s)} \qquad\qquad \textbf{13.4}$$

Using a similar analysis

$$D_2(s) = \frac{-G'_{21}(s)}{G'_{22}(s)} \qquad\qquad \textbf{13.5}$$

The decoupler $D_1(s)$ can be viewed as a "feedforward" correction to y_1 for disturbances caused by changes in c_2. Note that Equations 13.4 and 13.5 are similar to the general equation for a feedforward controller (Equation 10.6) where $G'_{12}(s)$ corresponds to $G_d(s)$ and $G'_{11}(s)$ corresponds to $G_p(s)$.

Figure 13.11 shows a 2×2 system with two decouplers, which is referred as a **two-way** or **complete decoupler**. Two-way decouplers are rarely used in industry because, many times, they result in poorer control performance than conventional control without decouplers. This results because two-way decouplers can be sensitive

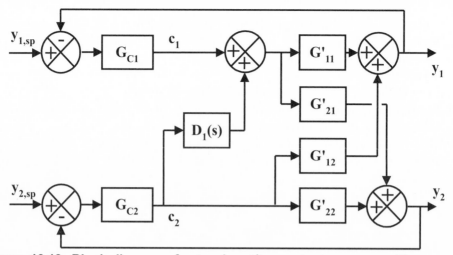

Figure 13.12   Block diagram of a two-input/two-output process with one-way decoupling to reduce the effect of c_2 on y_1.

to nonlinearity and modeling errors in the decouplers. On the other hand, **one-way** or **partial decouplers** (Figure 13.12) are much more reliable and are more frequently used industrially. One-way decouplers are particularly useful when the key controlled variable of a MIMO process suffers from significant coupling.

13.8 Summary

The combined effect of coupling, dynamic behavior, and sensitivity to disturbances determines the best control configuration for a decentralized controller applied to a MIMO process. The steady-state RGA and the dynamic RGA can be used to assess the steady-state and dynamic coupling, respectively, for a particular control configuration. It is desirable to choose (c,y) pairings such that each y responds quickly to changes in the c with which it is paired. Each control configuration for a MIMO process has its own specific sensitivity to disturbances. Once a control configuration is selected, the decentralized controllers can be tuned using an extension of the ATV tuning procedure recommended for a single PID control loop. One-way decouplers can be beneficial when the most important controlled variable in a MIMO process suffers from significant coupling from one or more of the other loops.

13.9 Additional Terminology

Complete decoupling - a decoupler for each controlled variable.
Control configuration - the particular pairing of manipulated and controlled variables for a MIMO process.

Coupling - the effect of one control loop on another in a MIMO process.
Decentralized control - applying single loop PID controllers to a MIMO process.
Dynamic coupling - coupling that includes dynamic differences between various input/output pairs. It can be evaluated using the dynamic RGA.
Manipulated/controlled variable pairings - the choice of which manipulated variable is used to control which controlled variable.
One-way decoupler - a single decoupler applied to a MIMO process.
Partial decoupler - fewer decouplers applied than the number of controlled variables.
RGA - the relative gain array, which indicates the degree of steady-state coupling.
Single-loop PID controllers - PID controllers that are applied to a MIMO process.
Two-way decoupler - two decouplers applied to a 2×2 process.

13.10 References

1. Bristol, E.H., *IEEE Trans Auto. Con.*, AC-11, p. 133 (1966).

2. McAvoy, T.J., *Interaction Analysis*, Instrument Society of America, pp. 190-192 (1983).

3. Shinskey, F.G., *Distillation Control*, 2nd Edition, McGraw-Hill, pp. 154-165 (1984).

13.11 Preliminary Questions

13.1 Explain how coupling occurs in a MIMO process.

13.2 Why is it important to choose a good pairing of manipulated and controlled variables when applying control to a MIMO process?

13.3 Explain how the steady-state *RGA* is a measure of steady-state coupling.

13.4 When is the steady-state *RGA* the best criterion for selecting (c,y) pairings?

13.5 For a 2×2 system, why is the *RGA* given by a single number when the RGA is, in fact, a matrix of numbers?

13.6 What does a negative *RGA* indicate?

13.7 What does an RGA less than unity indicate?

13.8 What does an RGA greater than unity indicate?

13.9 How does one take dynamic coupling into account when comparing control configurations?

13.10 Why is dynamic coupling important to the performance of a control system on a MIMO process?

13.11 Why is the sensitivity of a configuration to disturbances important in the selection of a control configuration for a MIMO process?

13.12 What advantage results from using a control configuration that has a low sensitivity to a disturbance?

13.13 For Example 13.1, what factors contribute to the (L,B) configuration being the best performing configuration considered?

13.14 When tuning decentralized controllers applied to a MIMO process, how does one tune loops that are much faster than the other loops?

13.15 After applying Equation 13.3, what tuning adjustments should be made to a decentralized controller if the response of the process is too sluggish?

13.16 After applying Equation 13.3, what tuning adjustments should be made to a decentralized controller if the response of the process is ringing?

13.17 Assume that after applying Equation 13.3 to tune a decentralized controller on a MIMO process, one of the loop exhibits slow offset removal. What action would you take?

13.18 Assume that after applying Equation 13.3 to tune a decentralized controller on a MIMO process, one of the loops exhibits sluggish response to a setpoint change. What action should be taken?

13.19 When should a one-way decoupler be used?

13.20 Why are two-way decouplers rarely used in industry?

13.12 Analytical Questions and Exercises

13.21 Consider the thermal mixing tank shown in Figure 3.6. Assuming perfect level control, consider that the two manipulated variables are F_1 and F_2 and that the two controlled variables are the total product flow rate and the product temperature. Determine the steady-state RGA for pairing F_1 with the product temperature and F_2 with the total flow rate. Does the dynamic RGA provide additional insight into this problem over the steady-state RGA? What configuration would you recommend and why?

13.22[S] Consider the MIMO version of the endothermic CSTR included with the text. If perfect level control can be assumed, there are two manipulated variables, F and Q, and two controlled variables, T and C_A. Recommend a control configuration for this case and justify your answer using a quantitative analysis.

13.23[S] Using the MIMO version of the CST thermal mixer included with the text, tune a set of decentralized PI controllers for this process using setpoint change in the total flow rate and the product temperature. Test the tuning using a step disturbance upset.

13.24[S] Using the MIMO version of the endothermic CSTR included with the text, tune a set of decentralized PI controllers for this process using setpoint changes in the reactor temperature and the product composition. Test the tuning using a step disturbance upset.

13.25[S] Using the MIMO version of the CST thermal mixer, apply and tune a one-way decoupler to reduce the effect of the product flow rate loop on the product temperature. Retune the decentralized PI controllers and test the controller performance using a step disturbance test.

13.26[S] Using the MIMO version of the endothermic CSTR, apply and tune a one-way decoupler to reduce the effect of the product composition loop on the product temperature.   Retune the decentralized PI controllers and test the controller performance using a step disturbance test.

A superscript "**S**" indicates that the simulators are required.

Chapter 14

Multivariable Controllers

14.1 Introduction

In Chapter 13, the application of conventional PID controllers to a multivariable (MIMO) process was presented. In this chapter, the use of **multivariable controllers** for the control of MIMO systems is considered. Multivariable controllers, also known as **centralized controllers**, can use all available process measurements (i.e., manipulated variables, disturbances, and controlled variables) simultaneously to determine the values of all the manipulated variables for control of a MIMO process. Since multivariable controllers typically use MIMO process models, they are also known as **model-based controllers**. Model-based controllers can also be applied to SISO systems.

A diagram comparing a multivariable controller and a conventional decentralized PI controller is shown in Figure 14.1. The multivariable controller in this case uses y_1 and y_2 and their setpoints to simultaneously calculate u_1 and u_2. The multivariable model used in the multivariable controller considers the effect of u_1 on y_1 and y_2 and the effect of u_2 on y_1 and y_2 when determining the control action; therefore, the multivariable controller provides decoupling. If the multivariable model considers the effect of disturbances on the process, it can also provide feedforward compensation for measured disturbances. If the model used by the multivariable controller is nonlinear, the multivariable controller can directly compensate for the nonlinearity of the process.

This chapter introduces a class of linear multivariable controllers known as **model predictive controllers**. In addition, two nonlinear multivariable controllers are overviewed. Since multivariable controllers normally act as supervisory controllers, in this chapter the controller output is the setpoint for the flow controller on u and is designated as u.

14.2 Model Predictive Control

Model predictive control (**MPC**) is the most widely used form of multivariable control. It has been estimated[1] that there are more than 3,000 industrial

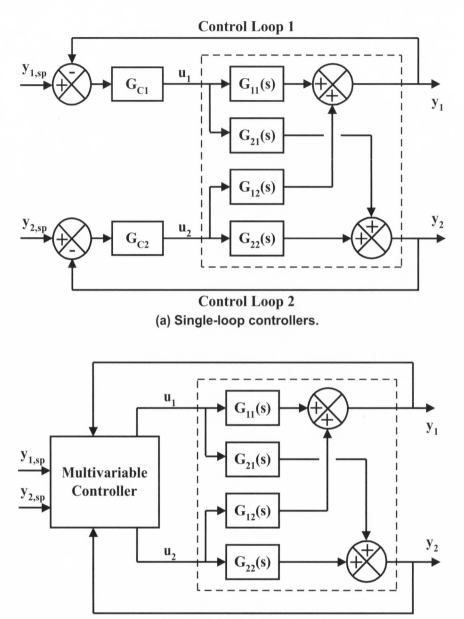

Figure 14.1 A comparison of single-loop PID controllers and a multivariable controller applied to a 2 × 2 MIMO process.

MPC applications worldwide. **Dynamic matrix control**[2] (**DMC**) is the most popular form of MPC. This section considers DMC applied to a SISO process and shows how it can be extended to MIMO processes.

Discrete-Time Step Response Models. DMC uses **discrete-time step response models** of the process to calculate control action. Previously, we used transfer functions to represent the effect of the manipulated variable on the controlled variable, $G_p(s)$. The same information contained in $G_p(s)$ can be represented using a discrete-time step response model. Consider a FOPDT process ($K_p = 1$, $\tau_p = 1$, $\theta_p = 1$). The step response for $\Delta u = 1$ applied at $t = 0$ is shown in Table 14.1 for discrete points in time. Note that these results are based on a fixed sampling time, ΔT_s, of 1.0. Note that, since the step response is complete after 7 sampling time intervals, a_i is constant for i greater than or equal to 7. The generalized discrete-time step response model of a process can be obtained from a step test using the following equation

$$a_i = \frac{y'(t_i)}{\Delta u(t_0)} \qquad 14.1$$

assuming that the process is at steady state at $t = t_0$ and a single step input change is made at $t = t_0$. a_i is called a step response coefficient. The values of the coefficients of the **step response model**, a_i, for this case are also listed in Table 14.1. The equation for the step response model can be obtained by rearranging Equation 14.1.

$$y'(t_i) = y(t_i) - y(t_0) = a_i \Delta u(t_0) \qquad 14.2$$

The flexible form of Equation 14.1 accommodates a wide range of complicated dynamic behavior (e.g., inverse action).

Table 14.1

Step Response and Step Response Coefficients for a FOPDT Process ($K_p = 1$, $\tau_p = 1$, $\theta_p = 1$) for a Step Change in u.

Time	Sample Number, i	$\Delta u(t)$	$y'(t)$	a_i
0	0	1	0	0
1	1	0	0	0
2	2	0	0.63	0.63
3	3	0	0.87	0.87
4	4	0	0.95	0.95
5	5	0	0.98	0.98
6	6	0	0.99	0.99
7	7	0	1.00	1.00
8	8	0	1.00	1.00

The Dynamic Matrix. Equation 14.2 can be used to predict the behavior of $y(t)$ for a series of $\Delta u(t)$ moves by applying the Principle of Superposition. The Principle of Superposition states that the total effect of a number of $\Delta u(t)$ moves on $y(t)$

is equal to the sum of the effect of each individual $\Delta u(t)$. Consider the case in which $y(t_0)$ is known and $y(t)$ is at steady state at $t = t_0$, and that a series of $\Delta u(t_i)$ moves are made into the future. Then, using Equation 14.2 and applying the Principle of Superposition, we get

$$y(t_1) - y(t_0) = a_1 \, \Delta u(t_0)$$
$$y(t_2) - y(t_0) = a_2 \, \Delta u(t_0) + a_1 \Delta u(t_1)$$
$$y(t_3) - y(t_0) = a_3 \, \Delta u(t_0) + a_2 \Delta u(t_1) + a_1 \Delta u(t_2) \qquad\qquad \textbf{14.3}$$
$$\vdots$$
$$y(t_n) - y(t_0) = a_n \Delta u(t_0) + a_{n-1} \Delta u(t_1) + a_{n-2} \Delta u(t_2) + \ldots$$

Consider the equation for $y'(t_3)$. The contribution of $\Delta u(t_0)$ to $y(t_3)$ is the product of a_3 and $\Delta u(t_0)$ in Equation 14.2. To consider the effect of $\Delta u(t_1)$, Equation 14.2 must be shifted backwards in time, ΔT_s. Therefore, the coefficient applied to $\Delta u(t_1)$ is a_2. Another way to consider this problem is that, since $\Delta u(t_1)$ is applied at $t = t_1$, using Equation 14.2 to model the effect of $\Delta u(t_1)$ requires that i in Equation 14.2 be set equal to 2. Similarly, to calculate the effect of $\Delta u(t_2)$ on $y(t_3)$, a_1 should be used. Equation 14.3 can be more compactly expressed by

$$y'(t_n) = y(t_n) - y(t_0) = \sum_{i=1}^{n} a_i \Delta u(t_{n-i}) \qquad\qquad \textbf{14.4}$$

Equation 14.3 and Equation 14.4 can be put into matrix form. Consider the case in which n moves in $\Delta u(t_i)$ are made into the future and the step response models have m coefficients (i.e., a_i's). From Equation 14.3, for $n > m$

$$
\begin{bmatrix} y'(t_1) \\ y'(t_2) \\ y'(t_3) \\ \vdots \\ y'(t_n) \end{bmatrix}
=
\begin{bmatrix}
a_1 & 0 & 0 & \ldots & 0 \\
a_2 & a_1 & 0 & & \\
a_3 & a_2 & a_1 & & \\
\vdots & & & & \\
a_m & a_m & a_m & \ldots & a_1
\end{bmatrix}
\begin{bmatrix} \Delta u(t_o) \\ \Delta u(t_1) \\ \Delta u(t_2) \\ \vdots \\ \Delta u(t_{n-1}) \end{bmatrix}
\qquad\qquad \textbf{14.5}
$$

n is the **prediction horizon** or the number of ΔT_s steps into the future for which the model is used to predict the behavior of the controlled variable and m is the **model horizon** or the number of ΔT_s steps used by the step response model. For a DMC controller, n is sometimes set equal to $1.5m$. Note that a_i for $i > m$ is equal to a_m. Equation 14.5 can also be written as

$$y' = A \, \Delta u \qquad\qquad \textbf{14.6}$$

Table 14.2

Prediction of *y(t)* using a Step Response Model for a Series of Manipulated Variable Changes.

Time	Sample Number, i	$u(t_i)$	$\Delta u(t_i)$	$y(t)$
0	0	1.0	0	1.0
1	1	2.0	1.0	1.0
2	2	3.0	1.0	1.0
3	3	2.0	-1.0	1.63
4	4	2.0	0.0	2.50
5	5	1.0	-1.0	2.19
6	6	0.0	-1.0	2.06
7	7	1.0	1.0	1.39
8	8	2.0	1.0	0.51
9	9	2.0	0.0	0.82
10	10	2.0	0.0	1.57

The matrix A is calculated from the coefficients of the step response model and is dimensioned (n,n), i.e., there are n rows and n columns, and is called the **dynamic matrix**. The dynamic matrix can be used to calculate the dynamic behavior of the process in response to future changes in $\Delta u(t_i)$.

The value of Equation 14.6 stems from the fact that it can be used to calculate the dynamic behavior of y for a series of input changes. Table 14.2 shows how the convolution (i.e., step response) model developed in Table 14.1 is applied to a series of manipulated variable changes using Equation 14.4. Consider the application of Equation 14.4 to calculate $y(t_7)$ for this case

$$y(t_7) = y(t_0) + a_1 \Delta u(t_6) + a_2 \Delta u(t_5) + a_3 \Delta u(t_4) + a_4 \Delta u(t_3)$$
$$+ a_5 \Delta u(t_2) + a_6 \Delta u(t_1) + a_7 \Delta u(t_0)$$

Using the numerical values of these terms results in

$$y(t_7) = 1.39$$

These results are based on assuming that the process is at steady state at $t = t_0$ (i.e., $\Delta u(t_i) = 0$, $i = -7$ to -1 since, based upon Table 14.1, the process takes seven ΔT_s steps to reach steady state). In this manner, the effect of a complicated set of manipulated variable changes on $y(t)$ can be conveniently modeled using discrete-time step response models.

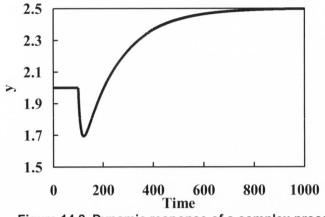

Figure 14.2 Dynamic response of a complex process.

Table 14.3					
Coefficients for Convolution Model of Complex Process Response $(\Delta T_s = 20)$					
i	a_i	i	a_i	i	a_i
1	-0.31	11	0.27	21	0.44
2	-0.26	12	0.30	22	0.45
3	-0.17	13	0.32	23	0.45
4	-0.09	14	0.34	24	0.46
5	-0.02	15	0.36	25	0.46
6	0.05	16	0.38	26	0.47
7	0.10	17	0.40	27	0.47
8	0.15	18	0.41	28	0.48
9	0.20	19	0.42	29	0.48
10	0.23	20	0.43	30	0.48

Figure 14.2 shows a step response for a more complicated process. Table 14.3 lists the coefficients of the step response model for this process. While this modeling approach can be effectively applied to a large number of industrial processes, it is a linear model, and can result in significant **process/model mismatch** for nonlinear processes. Process/model mismatch is the error between the model prediction and the actual process response.

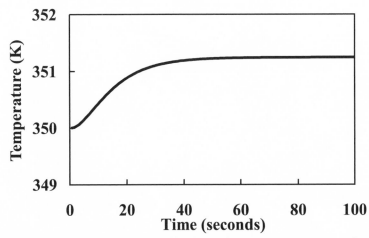

(a) The open-loop response of outlet heat exchanger temperature for a 10% step increase in the heat duty.

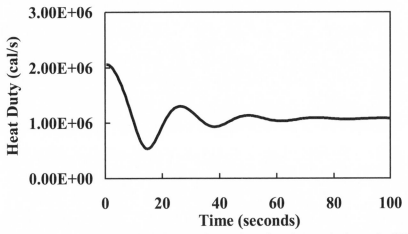

(b) The input profile specified for the heat duty for the endothermic CSTR.

Figure 14.3 Step response and input data specification for the Example 14.1.

Example 14.1 Step Response Model Identification and Prediction

Problem Statement. For the step response shown in Figure 14.3a, which is based on a 10% increase in heat duty for the heat exchanger for the endothermic CSTR (Section 3.5), predict the controlled variable response for the input sequence shown in Figure 14.3b. Assume that the controlled variable is initially at steady state at 350 K.

Solution. First, the step test results should be used to identify the step response model parameters, a_i. The coefficients of the step response model are obtained by applying Equation 14.1 to the step response results. The coefficients of the step response model are listed in Table 14.4.

Table 14.4				
Results for Example 14.1				
Time (sec)	i	a_i	$\Delta u(t_i)$	$y(t_i)$
0	0	0	1.07×10^6	350.00
5	1	2.07×10^{-6}	-7.45×10^6	352.21
10	2	6.10×10^{-6}	-4.87×10^5	354.98
15	3	9.79×10^{-6}	4.09×10^5	354.92
20	4	1.26×10^{-5}	3.43×10^5	354.41
25	5	1.45×10^{-5}	-7.37×10^4	354.56
30	6	1.57×10^{-5}	-2.21×10^5	355.80
35	7	1.65×10^{-5}	-4.54×10^4	356.50
40	8	1.69×10^{-5}	1.23×10^5	356.23
45	9	1.72×10^{-5}	6.55×10^4	356.06
50	10	1.75×10^{-5}	-4.33×10^4	356.40
55	11	1.76×10^{-5}	-5.30×10^4	356.57
60	12	1.77×10^{-5}	9.30×10^3	356.61
65	13	1.77×10^{-5}	3.61×10^4	356.51
70	14	1.77×10^{-5}	8.04×10^3	356.53
75	15	1.77×10^{-5}	1.10×10^3	356.64

Next, the input sequence is approximated by a series of step changes and the results are listed as $\Delta u(t_i)$ in Table 14.4. Then, Equation 14.4 is applied to predict the time behavior of the reactor temperature. The results are also listed in Table 14.4.

♠

Moving Horizon Algorithm. Figure 14.4 illustrates the key features of a moving horizon control algorithm. Note that all the previous controlled variable and manipulated variable values are fixed and known. The manipulated variable moves and the resulting controlled variable values into the future remain unknown at this point. The moving horizon controller chooses the future manipulated variable values to regulate the controlled variable to its setpoint using the step response model and the previous inputs.

After one control interval has expired, a new controlled variable value as well as the last change in manipulated variable value is available. Once again, the controller recalculates the sequence of manipulated variable values into the future to meet the control objective. In this manner, even though the complete sequence of control

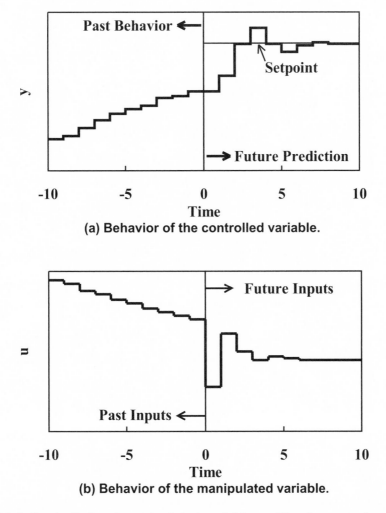

(a) Behavior of the controlled variable.

(b) Behavior of the manipulated variable.

Figure 14.4 Controlled and manipulated variable profiles for a moving horizon controller.

moves into the future is calculated at each control interval, only the first move is actually implemented before a new sequence of inputs is determined. The key feature of this approach is that, at each control interval, a sequence of control moves into the future, as well as the previous input sequence, is considered when determining the next change in the manipulated variable value.

Prediction Vector. Up until this point, we have assumed that $y(t_0)$ is at steady state and that manipulated variable changes are made only for $t \geq t_0$. For a control application, this assumption is not realistic since manipulated variable changes at $t < t_0$ are likely to exist, as shown in Figure 14.4. As a result, the effect of the previous input changes ($\Delta u(t)$ for $t < t_0$) must be taken into account to properly model the future behavior of the controlled variable ($y(t)$ for $t > t_0$).

The **prediction vector, y^P**, contains the values of $y(t)$ for $t > t_0$ if no future manipulated variable changes are made ($\Delta u(t) = 0$ for $t \geq t_0$). The prediction vector contains the effects of previous manipulated variable changes on future controlled variable values.

Assume that the process has a model horizon, m. That is, after m time steps, an input change has had its total steady-state effect on the process. For the step response model listed in Table 14.1, m is equal to 7; therefore, a_i is constant for $i \geq 7$.

Applying Equation 14.4 to calculate the prediction vector at $t = t_1$ results in

$$y^P(t_1) = y(t_{-m}) + a_{m+1}\Delta u(t_{-m}) + a_m\Delta u(t_{-m+1}) + a_{m-1}\Delta u(t_{-m+2})$$
$$+ \ldots\ldots + a_3\Delta u(t_{-2}) + a_2\Delta u(t_{-1}) + a_1\Delta u(t_0)$$

where the negative subscripts indicate the number of sampling intervals before t_0 and assuming that the process is at steady state at $t = t_{-m}$. Note that the coefficients of $\Delta u(t_{-m})$ and $\Delta u(t_{-m+1})$ are both a_m since $a_{m+1} = a_m$. $\Delta u(t_0)$ is zero for the prediction vector; therefore,

$$y^P(t_1) = y(t_{-m}) + a_m\Delta u(t_{-m}) + a_m\Delta u(t_{-m+1}) + a_{m-1}\Delta u(t_{-m+2})$$
$$+ \ldots\ldots + a_3\Delta u(t_{-2}) + a_2\Delta u(t_{-1})$$

Similarly, $y^P(t_2)$ is given by

$$y^P(t_2) = y(t_{-m}) + a_m\Delta u(t_{-m}) + a_m\Delta u(t_{-m+1}) + a_m\Delta u(t_{-m+2}) + a_{m-1}\Delta u(t_{-m+3})$$
$$+ \ldots\ldots + a_4\Delta u(t_{-2}) + a_3\Delta u(t_{-1})$$

In this manner, $y^P(t_n)$ is given by

$$y^P(t_n) = y(t_{-m}) + a_m\Delta u(t_{-m}) + a_m\Delta u(t_{-m+1}) + \ldots\ldots + a_m\Delta u(t_{-2}) + a_m\Delta u(t_{-1})$$

where n is the number of ΔT_s moves into the future that are modeled with $n > m$. The prediction vector, y^P, can be expressed in matrix form as

$$\begin{bmatrix} y^P(t_1) \\ y^P(t_2) \\ \vdots \\ y^P(t_n) \end{bmatrix} = \begin{bmatrix} y(t_{-m}) \\ y(t_{-m}) \\ \vdots \\ y(t_{-m}) \end{bmatrix} + \begin{bmatrix} a_m & a_m & a_{m-1} & a_{m-2} & \ldots\ldots & a_3 & a_2 \\ a_m & a_m & a_m & a_{m-1} & \ldots\ldots & a_4 & a_3 \\ \vdots & & & & & & \\ a_m & a_m & a_m & a_m & \ldots\ldots & a_m & a_m \end{bmatrix} \begin{bmatrix} \Delta u(t_{-m}) \\ \Delta u(t_{-m+1}) \\ \vdots \\ \Delta u(t_{-1}) \end{bmatrix}$$

or $$y^P = y(t_{-m}) + A^P \Delta u^P \qquad\qquad\qquad \textbf{14.7}$$

where $y(t_{-k})$ is the value of the controlled variable at $t = t_o - k\,\Delta T_s$. The values of $y(t)$ for $t > t_o$ can be calculated by combining the prediction vector with the effects of future control moves (Equation 14.6)

$$\boldsymbol{y} \; = \; \boldsymbol{y}^P + A\,\Delta\boldsymbol{u} \qquad\qquad \textbf{14.8}$$

Equation 14.8 is subject to a number of factors that undermine its accuracy: (1) errors in identifying the coefficients of the discrete-time step response model, (2) unmeasured disturbances, (3) nonlinear behavior, and (4) non-steady-state behavior at $t = t_{-m}$. If Equation 14.8 is used for control, offset results due to these sources of process/model mismatch.

Equation 14.7 is used to calculate $y^P(t_0)$ by

$$y^P(t_o) \; = \; y(t_{-m}) + a_m\,\Delta u(t_{-m}) + a_{m-1}\,\Delta u(t_{-m+1}) + \ldots\ldots + a_2\,\Delta u(t_{-2}) + a_1\,\Delta u(t_{-1})$$

The error between the measured value of $y(t_0)$ and the predicted value, $y^P(t_o)$, can be used to adjust Equation 14.8 to make it more accurate. The error between the measured and predicted value of $y(t_0)$ is given as

$$\varepsilon \; = \; y(t_0) - y^P(t_0)$$

Then,

$$\boldsymbol{y} \; = \; \boldsymbol{y}^P + A\,\Delta\boldsymbol{u} + \varepsilon^{\mathsf{T}} \qquad\qquad \textbf{14.9}$$

where

$$\varepsilon \; = \; [\varepsilon \; \varepsilon \; \varepsilon \ldots \varepsilon]$$

so that the predicted value of $y(t)$ agrees with the latest value of the controlled variable $[y(t_0)]$. Using Equation 14.9 in a DMC controller eliminates offset.

DMC Control Law. The DMC control law is based on minimizing the error from setpoint. The objective function, Φ, is the sum of the square of the errors from setpoint for the prediction horizon (i.e., n steps into the future).

$$\Phi \; = \; \sum_{i=1}^{n} \left[y_{sp} - y(t_i) \right]^2 \qquad\qquad \textbf{14.10}$$

Equation 14.9 shows that $y(t_i)$ is made up of three parts: the prediction vector (i.e., the effect of past inputs), the effects of future inputs, and the process/model mismatch correction term. Only the effect of future moves can be changed by the controller; therefore, combining y_{sp}, y^P, and ε into

$$\mathrm{E}(t_i) \; = \; y_{sp} - y^P(t_i) - \varepsilon \qquad\qquad \textbf{14.11}$$

results in

$$\Phi = \sum_{i=1}^{n} [E(t_i) - y_c(t_i)]^2 \qquad \textbf{14.12}$$

where
$$y_c = A \Delta u$$

The objective of the DMC controller is to choose the control moves, $\Delta u(t_i)$ for n moves into the future such that Φ is minimized.

Perfect control (i.e., $\Phi = 0$), which is based upon assuming that $y_c(t_i)$ is the mirror image of $E(t_i)$, is given by

$$\Delta u = A^{-1} E \qquad \textbf{14.13}$$

But, since it assumes that y_c can be moved instantaneously, this result is not realistic. In addition, Equation 14.13 is valid only when the number of dependent variable is equal to the number of input variables. Instead, we can choose the set of control moves that minimizes the sum of the squares of the errors from setpoint. This solution can be obtained analytically by differentiating Equation 14.12 with respect to Δu and setting the result equal to zero,

$$\frac{\partial \Phi}{\partial \Delta u} = A^T (A \Delta u - E) = 0 \qquad \textbf{14.14}$$

Solving for Δu gives

$$\Delta u = (A^T A)^{-1} A^T E \qquad \textbf{14.15}$$

which is the control law for a DMC controller. This equation does not assume instantaneous changes in y_c and can be applied in cases in which the number of dependent variables is different than the number of independent variables. Note that $(A^T A)^{-1} A^T$ is equal to A^{-1} when A is a square matrix. Therefore, once the step response model and the prediction vector are calculated, the DMC controller can be formulated directly using Equation 14.15.

Equation 14.15 results in very aggressive control because it is based on minimizing the deviation from setpoint without regard to the changes in the manipulated variable levels. That is, if Equation 14.15 is applied, excessively sharp changes in u result, which is not desirable operationally. Normal levels of process/model mismatch, combined with the aggressive nature of Equation 14.15, can easily yield unstable control performance. In addition, $(A^T A)^{-1}$ can be ill-conditioned due to process/model mismatch and deadtime in the process model. These problems can be overcome by adding the diagonal matrix, Q^2, to $A^T A$ in Equation 14.15, resulting in

$$\Delta u = (A^T A + Q^2)^{-1} A^T E \qquad \textbf{14.16}$$

where Q is the move suppression matrix and is a diagonal matrix with positive elements, i.e.,

$$Q = \begin{bmatrix} q & 0 & 0 & \dots & 0 \\ 0 & q & 0 & \dots & 0 \\ 0 & 0 & q & \dots & 0 \\ \vdots & \vdots & \vdots & & \\ 0 & 0 & 0 & \dots & q \end{bmatrix}$$

where q is called the **move suppression factor** and is a positive number. The larger the value of q, the more Φ is penalized for changes in the manipulated variable. Therefore, q can be used as a tuning parameter and determines the aggressiveness of the DMC controller. In general, the more nonlinear a process and the larger the magnitude of the disturbances, the larger the value of q that should be used.

Model Identification. In the previous examples, the step response model parameters were calculated directly from a step test. In an industrial setting, it is difficult to conduct a step test while keeping all other inputs constant, particularly for MIMO applications. Moreover, it is better to use a number of step tests to identify "average" coefficients for the step response model, particularly in light of the nonlinearity associated with industrial processes and the presence of unmeasured disturbances.

For model identification, the controlled variable and manipulated variable values are known for a sequence of discrete times. The objective function for identification is given by

$$\Phi = \sum_{i=1}^{k} [y_s(t_i) - y(t_i)]^2 \qquad \textbf{14.17}$$

where k is the number of process measurements available for parameterizing the model, $y_s(t_i)$ is the measured value of the controlled variable at t_i, and $y(t_i)$ is the value of the controlled variable at t_i, calculated from the step response model parameters. The better the step response models of the process, the smaller the resulting value of Φ. The values of the coefficients of the step response model are calculated such that Φ is minimized. Due to the linear nature of $y(t_i)$, the a_i's can be calculated explicitly using matrix algebra.

When implementing the plant tests that are used for model identification, it is not necessary to make a set of complete step tests. In fact, for most MIMO systems, such an approach requires a prohibitive amount of time. Moreover, during plant tests, it is important to keep the controlled variables within specified operating ranges. One way to accomplish this is to make Δu changes at each of the following intervals:

$$\tfrac{1}{4} T_{ss}, \; \tfrac{1}{2} T_{ss}, \; \tfrac{3}{4} T_{ss}, \; T_{ss}, \; \tfrac{5}{4} T_{ss}$$

where T_{ss} is the open-loop time to steady state (the open-loop response time of the process). This approach also develops models for a range of input frequencies. Note that

$$T_{ss} = m \Delta T_s$$

Extension to MIMO Processes. Extending DMC to MIMO processes is relatively straightforward. Partitioned vectors and matrices are used to apply DMC to MIMO processes using Equation 14.16. For example, the partitioned dynamic matrix, A, is given by

$$A = \begin{bmatrix} A_{11} & A_{12} & \cdots & A_{1,j} \\ A_{21} & A_{22} & & A_{2,j} \\ \vdots & & & \\ A_{k,1} & A_{k,2} & \cdots & A_{k,j} \end{bmatrix}$$

where j is the number of manipulated variables and k is the number of controlled variables. Consider a two-input/two-output process. A_{11} is the dynamic matrix for y_1 as affected by u_1 and A_{12} is the dynamic matrix of y_1 as affected by u_2, etc. For illustration purposes, consider

$$A_{11} = \begin{bmatrix} 1 & 2 \\ 3 & 4 \end{bmatrix} \qquad A_{12} = \begin{bmatrix} 5 & 6 \\ 7 & 8 \end{bmatrix}$$

$$A_{21} = \begin{bmatrix} 9 & 10 \\ 11 & 12 \end{bmatrix} \qquad A_{22} = \begin{bmatrix} 13 & 14 \\ 15 & 16 \end{bmatrix}$$

Then, the multivariable dynamic matrix is given by

$$A = \begin{bmatrix} 1 & 2 & 5 & 6 \\ 3 & 4 & 7 & 8 \\ 9 & 10 & 13 & 14 \\ 11 & 12 & 15 & 16 \end{bmatrix}$$

The MIMO manipulated variable vector is given by the following partitioned vector

$$\Delta u = \begin{bmatrix} \Delta u_1 \\ \Delta u_2 \\ \vdots \\ \Delta u_j \end{bmatrix}$$

For example, if

$$\Delta u_1 = \begin{bmatrix} 1 \\ 2 \end{bmatrix} \qquad \Delta u_2 = \begin{bmatrix} 3 \\ 4 \end{bmatrix}$$

then

$$\Delta u = \begin{bmatrix} 1 \\ 2 \\ 3 \\ 4 \end{bmatrix}$$

For the application of the DMC control law, the **A** matrix must be inverted, and the matrix can be quite large for most industrial DMC controllers. Consider the case with 10 manipulated variables, 10 controlled variables, and a prediction horizon of 100 sampling intervals, then the MIMO dynamic matrix is dimensioned 1000×1000. There have been a large number of industrial DMC applications that are considerably larger than this example.

An additional issue that must be addressed when applying DMC to MIMO processes is how to prioritize the various control objectives. DMC controllers use controlled variable weighting, which allows the user to assign a relative weighting to each of the controlled variables. A controlled variable weighting matrix, W, is added to the DMC control law (Equation 14.16)

$$\Delta u = (A^T W^2 A + Q^2)^{-1} A^T W^2 E \qquad\qquad \textbf{14.18}$$

where W is an partitioned matrix, which contains diagonal matrices, W_i. W_i is a diagonal matrix, which contains the same element, w_i, on its diagonal. w_i is the relative weighting factor for the i-th controlled variable.

Application of DMC for Constraint Control. One of the key advantages of DMC is that it can be readily applied for constraint control of multivariable processes. In fact, DMC was developed because conventional overrides were inadequate for maintaining the operation of an FCC unit at its optimum operating conditions[3]. For the optimal operation of an FCC unit, the operative constraints change over time. Each time there is a different combination of operative constraints, a different constraint control configuration with different controller tuning is generally required. As a result, for a complex processes like an FCC unit, there are an extremely large number of different constraint control configurations required, which is well beyond what is practical to maintain industrially. On the other hand, because DMC is a multivariable controller, it is able to automatically switch from controlling one combination of constraints to another.

While DMC treats operative constraints as controlled variables, other forms of MPC explicitly consider the operative constraints of a system. DMC has the advantage that it is much more computationally efficient than the other forms of MPC for constraint control. Since DMC is based on a least squares solution, constraints are added to the control law by adding them to the dynamic matrix. The DMC controller chooses the control action based on a compromise between meeting the objectives for the constraints and the controlled variables. The weighting factors (i.e., the diagonal elements for *W* in Equation 14.18) for the controlled variables and the constraints are part of the controller design and are typically provided in a "lookup table".

Combining a Linear-Based Optimization with DMC. The widespread industrial use of DMC and MPC, in general, is the result of their ability to operate processes in a more profitable fashion. That is, if DMC provided only reduced variability operation, its use by industry would be drastically reduced compared to its current use. The improved profitability of processes for DMC comes from its ability to operate processes at higher production rates for the more highly-valued products. In many cases, this can result by processing the largest feed rate to the process by maintaining the operation against the most advantageous set of constraints, i.e., constraint control.

A linear program (LP) assesses the economics of the process and constraints and specifies to the DMC controller against which constraints to control the process. An LP determines optimum values of the decision variables for a linear economic objective function (i.e., a linear version of Equation 1.1) subject to a set of linear constraints. In the case of an LP, the optimum is located at a vertex, i.e., the intersection of *n* constraints where *n* is the number of decision variables. The LP determines which is the most favorable set of constrains against which to control. In this manner, as the operation of the process or the cost of the feeds and value of the products change, the LP ensures that the process maintains the most profitable operation. Because the process gains used by the LP are identical to the steady-state gains for the step response models used by the DMC controller, the LP and DMC controller work together in a consistent fashion.

14.3 Nonlinear Multivariable Controllers

There is a variety of nonlinear multivariable controllers[3]. In this section, two nonlinear controllers are outlined: generic model control and nonlinear model predictive control. For both cases it is assumed that a SISO nonlinear model is known, i.e.,

$$\frac{dy}{dt} = f(y, u, d, p) \qquad\qquad \textbf{14.19}$$

where *y* is the controlled variable, *f* is a nonlinear function, *u* is the manipulated variable, *d* is the measured disturbance, and *p* is the model parameter.

Generic Model Control. **Generic model control (GMC)**[4] uses the current process conditions along with the nonlinear model (Equation 14.19) to calculate the control action without regard to the future behavior of the process, i.e., a **single-step-ahead controller**.

The GMC control law is given by

$$K_c \left[(y_{sp} - y) + \frac{1}{\tau_I} \int_0^t (y_{sp} - y)\, dt \right] = f(y, u, d, p) \qquad \textbf{14.20}$$

where K_c is the controller gain and τ_I is the reset time. All parameters in Equation 14.20 are known except u; therefore, Equation 14.20 is solved directly to calculate the value of u. K_c and τ_I are analogous to the tuning parameters for a PI controller; therefore, PI tuning techniques can be applied to tune GMC controllers[5].

Using the steady-state values of y, u, and d, the model parameter, p, can be calculated by solving the following equation

$$\frac{dy}{dt} = f(y, u, d, p) = 0 \qquad \textbf{14.21}$$

The extension of GMC to MIMO systems is direct. For MIMO systems, there is an equation similar to Equation 14.20 for each controlled variable. GMC can be effective for the control of processes that exhibit severe nonlinearity in the process gain but have simple, first-order dynamics (e.g., certain CSTRs and batch reactors).

Nonlinear Model Predictive Control. **Nonlinear model predictive control (NLMPC)** is a direct extension of linear MPC except that nonlinear dynamic models are used instead of linear dynamic models. NLMPC is a moving horizon controller that chooses a sequence of inputs that minimize the objective function over the prediction horizon, n, but only implements the first control move at each control interval. NLMPC chooses control moves into the future that minimize the following objective function, Φ

$$\Phi = \sum_{i=0}^{n-1} [y_{sp} - y(t_i)]^2 + \sum_{i=0}^{n-1} q [\Delta u(t_i)]^2 \qquad \textbf{14.22}$$

where q is the move suppression factor, and $y(t_i)$ is calculated using the control action, $\Delta u(t_i)$, and the nonlinear dynamic model (Equation 14.19). The solution of this optimization problem requires a nonlinear optimization algorithm, whereas the objective function for linear MPC can be solved analytically using linear matrix equations. The number of degrees of freedom for the optimization problem for NLMPC is equal to the product of the number of control moves into the future (i.e., n, the prediction horizon) and the number of manipulated variables.

For MIMO problems, the numerical application of NLMPC may not be feasible. The computer time required to minimize Φ and calculate the next control step can be excessively long, rendering NLMPC ineffective. The key factors in this problem are the total number of degrees of freedom for the optimization problem and the computer time required to integrate the model equations over the prediction horizon. NLMPC can be applied to cases that exhibit severe gain and dynamic nonlinearity for which accurate and computationally efficient models are available.

14.4 Summary

Multivariable controllers use measured values of the manipulated variables, the controlled variables, and disturbances to simultaneously calculate all the manipulated variable levels for the control of MIMO processes. Multivariable controllers can provide decoupling, feedforward compensation, and compensation for nonlinear behavior.

DMC is the most popular form of linear multivariable control and is based on discrete-time step response models of the process to calculate control action. The DMC controller uses the coefficients of the step response model, the previous input history, and the latest measured value of the controlled variable to calculate the next manipulated variable value using a moving horizon control approach. A move suppression factor is used to tune the DMC controller to provide reliable control performance.

GMC is a single-step-ahead controller that uses tuning parameters that are analogous to those of conventional PI controllers and is useful for processes that have significant gain nonlinearity with well-behaved dynamics. NLMPC extends MPC to nonlinear control using a moving horizon approach and is a more general nonlinear model-based controller. The computational requirements for NLMPC can pose a limitation for certain industrial applications.

14.5 Additional Terminology

Centralized controller - a controller that uses all the available process information to select control action for a MIMO process.
Discrete-time step response model - the discrete-time behavior of a process to a unit step change in an input variable.
Dynamic matrix control (DMC) - a linear model predictive controller that uses step response models of the process to select control action.
Dynamic matrix - the A matrix in the DMC controller, which is constructed from the coefficients of the step response model.

Generic model control (GMC) - a single-step-ahead nonlinear multivariable controller.

Model-based controller - a controller that chooses control action based upon a model of the process.

Model horizon (m) - the number of sampling intervals used to model a step response of the process.

Moving horizon algorithm - a control approach that calculates future control moves based on a process model and the input history.

Model predictive control (MPC) - a controller that uses a process model to calculate control action by determining a sequence of inputs that regulates the process to setpoint.

Move suppression factor (q) - the tuning factor for a DMC controller that determines the aggressiveness of the controller.

Multivariable controller - a controller that uses all the available process information to select control action for a MIMO process.

Nonlinear model predictive control (NLMPC) - MPC using nonlinear process models.

Prediction vector (y^p) - the future values of the controlled variable if no changes in the manipulated variable are made.

Prediction horizon (n) - the number of sampling intervals into the future in which the model is used to predict the behavior of the controlled variable.

Process/model mismatch - the difference between the model predictions for the controlled variable and the actual process behavior.

Sampling interval - the time period between the calculations of control action.

Single-step-ahead controller - a controller that calculates the current control action without predicting the future behavior of the process.

Step response model - the discrete-time response of a process to a unit step change in an input variable.

14.6 References

1. Quin, S. J. and T. A. Badgwell, "An Overview of Industrial Model Predictive Control Technology", *Proceedings of the Fifth International Conference on Chemical Process Control*, AIChE Symposium Series Number 316, Vol 93, p. 232 (1997).

2. Cutler, C. R. and B. L. Ramaker, "Dynamic Matrix Control - A Computer Control Algorithm", *Proceedings of the Joint Automatic Control Conference*, San Francisco (1980).

3. Bequette, B. W., "Nonlinear Control of Chemical Processes: A Review", *Ind. Eng. Chem. Res.*, Vol 30, p. 1391 (1991).

4. Lee, P. L. and G. R. Sullivan, "Generic Model Control", *Computers Chem. Eng..*, Vol 12, p. 573 (1988).

5.   Flathouse, S. E. and J. B. Riggs, "Tuning GMC Controllers using the ATV Procedure", *Computers Chem. Eng.*, Vol 20, p. 979 (1996).

14.7 Analytical Questions and Exercises

14.1[S]   For each of the following simulators provided with this text, develop a step response model. First, determine the open-loop response time for the process. Then, choose ΔT_s so that m is equal to 10. Finally, develop the step response model for the process.

      a. CST thermal mixer   b. CST composition mixer

      c. Endothermic CSTR   d. Heat exchanger

14.2[S]   Using the results for 14.1, predict the output variable as a function of time for a series of 10 input changes. Use the same series of inputs on the process simulator and plot these results along with the step response model results on the same graph.

A superscript "**S**" indicates that the simulators are required to complete the problem.

Chapter 15

Multiunit Controller Design

15.1 Introduction

The previous material in this text has been concerned with the control of a single control loop or control of a single MIMO process. This chapter addresses the problem of applying the approaches that were developed for SISO and MIMO processes to a multiple-unit process, which is composed of a number of unit operations connected together, forming an overall processing unit. A typical multiple unit process could include a reactor followed by several distillation columns. The reactor converts the feed into products and the distillation columns separate the product from the byproducts and the unconverted feed. The control engineer is responsible for implementing controls on this multiunit process so that the process meets its operational objectives, e.g., a specified production rate with impurity levels less than the specified limits while maintaining maximum profitability in a safe and reliable manner in the face of a variety of process disturbances. To accomplish this task, the control engineer must have a command of the single-unit control techniques, but must also be able to coordinate all the single-unit controls so that the multiunit process functions properly.

In an effort to optimize the designs of plants (i.e., develop designs that maximize profit generation), heat recovery and material recycle are being used frequently in process design. By using product streams to preheat feed streams and by using the condenser of one column to provide reboiler duty for another column, less energy is required to produce the same amount of product. Recycling unreacted feed components increases overall conversion and reduces the material costs for the products. Both heat recovery and material recycle can provide superior steady-state economic performance, but can result in much more difficult processes to control. The following approach to controller design is recommended for both recycle processes and systems that utilize once-through sequential processing. This approach is based on the control design procedure presented by Luyben et. al.[1].

15.2 Approach

Following is the recommended approach for undertaking the control design problem for multiunit processes. This approach is developed assuming that no instrumentation or controls are in place. Obviously, many control projects involve a revamp of existing controls; certain items, such as sensor selection and actuator location can already be completed and are not likely to be modified unless compelling reasons are identified. While this approach was developed for multiunit processes, it can be applied to single-unit systems as well.

1. Identify process objectives. The steady-state and dynamic objectives of the process should first be identified. These include product rate specifications, product variability requirements, process selectivity, product grade specifications, and economic objectives. The control approach chosen should be able to meet each of the process objectives.

2. Identify the process constraints. Process constraints represent limits to normal operation. The specific limits to the operation of the process should be identified with regard to safety, environmental, and equipment constraints. The resulting control configuration must be able to effectively handle all process constraints.

3. Identify significant disturbances. A viable control approach should be able to effectively absorb the full range of process disturbances. Common process disturbances include feed temperature, flow rate, and composition changes, ambient air temperature changes, steam pressure changes and cooling water temperature changes.

4. Determine the type and location of sensors. Ensuring that adequate process measurements are available to meet the operational objectives while satisfying all the process constraints is a prerequisite for controller design. The types of sensors chosen affect the repeatability, dynamic response, and reliability of the process measurements. The location of the sensors determines if the desired process variables are actually being measured and can also affect their measurement delays.

5. Determine the location of control valves. The location of the control valves determines which streams are available to be used as manipulated variables to meet the control objectives while satisfying the process constraints. In the CPI, a control valve is usually applied as a flow control loop.

6. Apply a degree-of-freedom analysis. The total number of manipulated flow streams minus the number of control objectives and active process constraints is equal to the degrees of freedom of the process. If extra degrees of freedom are available, they can be used to improve the economic performance of the process (e.g., through process optimization). When the process is overspecified, all the control objectives cannot be met simultaneously. One approach is to give up on one or more low-priority control objectives until the remaining control objectives and constraints are controllable. It should be pointed out that constraints can change from being active to inactive as operating conditions change. For example, the condenser duty can be an active constraint to a distillation column during the summer when its cooling water temperature is high and is not a factor for the operation (an inactive constraint) during the winter. As a result, the number of degrees of freedom of a process can change as the number of active constraints changes due to changes in the operating conditions.

7. Implement energy management. Energy management involves removing the exothermic heat of reaction or supplying the endothermic heat of reaction occurring within the process and accounting for interactions resulting from process-to-process heat exchanges and heat-integrated unit operations. If the exothermic heat of reaction is not removed, the conditions for a reactor runaway can exist. If the endothermic heat of reaction is not supplied, the reactor does not meet the desired production rate. For all distillation columns, heat must be added in the reboiler and removed in the condenser. Using product streams to preheat feeds and using the overhead stream of one column to provide reboiler duty for another column are effective ways of reducing the overall process energy consumption but tend to result in more highly-coupled processes. Temperature control loops are typically used to control reactors and heat recovery processes.

8. Control process production rate. A change in reactor production rate requires that the selected manipulated variable for production rate control change the reactor conditions that affect the rates of reactions. Production rates can also be set by manipulating the overall feed and relying on the controls of the various unit operations to pass the feed rate through the entire process. The overall process production rate can be changed and the remainder of the process can follow this change, eventually resulting in a corresponding change in the overall process feed rate. For more complicated process systems, selecting the best manipulated variable to control process production rate may require dynamic simulations of the overall process.

9. Select the manipulated variables that meet the control objectives.
An ideal manipulated variable for a particular control objective results in dynamic behavior characterized by a small time constant and deadtime and a large steady-state gain. As a result, it is usually advisable to locate a manipulated variable as close as possible to the control objective of interest. Chapter 13 addresses configuration selection for MIMO processes.

10. Address how disturbances are handled. The sensitivity of the control system to each major disturbance should be considered. Opportunities for cascade, ratio, feedforward, and computed manipulated variable control should be considered to reduce the effects of major disturbances.

11. Develop a constraint handling strategy. Control approaches for each potential constraint should be developed. Override/select control (Chapter 11) can be applied to coordinate manipulated variable action to maintain operation within active constraints. The key is to develop constraint handling strategies that satisfy all known constraints.

12. Control inventories. Inventories include liquid levels and gas pressures. For example, outflow from or inflow to a tank can be manipulated to control its level. Fresh feed streams can be manipulated to control levels, which indicate the amount of the fresh feed in the process. Fresh feed can also be used to control pressure for certain reaction systems or recycle reaction systems. Pressure control on distillation columns usually involves changing condenser duty or using the injection of inert gases or the venting of a portion of the overhead.

13. Check component balances. Component material balances for each component, including inerts, in the process should be formulated to ensure that no component accumulates in the process. This is particularly important for recycle processes. It may be necessary to add a purge stream to prevent the accumulation of a component within the process.

14. Control individual unit operations. The controls for each unit operation should be completed next. That is, each unit operation should be checked to ensure that it is fully controlled. For example, a temperature controller can be applied to maintain the outlet temperature of a process stream leaving a heat exchanger by adjusting the flow rate of steam to the heat exchanger. For distillation columns, control loops are typically applied to control the impurity levels in one or more products. Opportunities for cascade, ratio, and feedforward control should be considered.

15. Apply process optimization. The setpoints for certain controllers that are not otherwise specified can be set according to economic-based process optimization. Choosing the optimum reactor temperature can be a compromise between conversion and selectivity. When a company can sell all the product that it can produce, economic optimization can involve maximizing the product flow rate from the process. The optimization of a distillation column can involve a compromise between product recovery and utility usage. In each of these cases, setpoints to various control loops are selected in such a way that the rate of profit generation for the unit is maximized. The selection of the optimal setpoints can be based on a simple analysis of the process or can involve optimization studies using detailed nonlinear models of the process.

15.3 Distillation Column

Process Description. Consider the design of a control system for an ethylene/ethane (C_2) splitter. The C_2 splitter produces a high-purity polymer-grade ethylene in the overhead and an ethane product in the bottoms. Since ethylene is a saleable product, the overhead is a much more valuable product than the bottoms. Ethane is recycled as feed to the furnaces where it is thermally cracked to yield more ethylene and other cracking products. The feed to the column contains approximately 70 mole percent ethylene, the overhead has a specification of less than 0.1% ethane in the ethylene product, and the setpoint for the ethylene in the ethane product is based on the economic tradeoff between energy usage and ethylene recovery and is generally set around 1% ethylene. Occasionally, small amounts of methane and hydrogen appear in the feed. The low condensing temperature of ethylene requires a refrigerated condenser. The major disturbances to this column are feed flow rate and feed composition upsets.

Identify process objectives. The process objectives are to produce an ethylene product with low variability while satisfying its impurity specification in the face of process disturbances. It is desired to recover as much ethylene as possible while minimizing energy cost.

Identify the process constraints. Upon further examination, it is determined that there is more than adequate reboiler and condenser duty so that, as the feed rate to the column increases, the column eventually floods. The vapor/liquid traffic increases to the point where the tray dimensions do not support that degree of loading and the separation generated by the column becomes compromised. A differential pressure across the column should reliably indicate the onset of flooding.

Identify significant disturbances. The primary disturbances are feed flow rate and feed composition changes.

Determine the type and location of sensors. Figure 15.1 shows the sensors applied to this column. The product streams (D and B), the reboiler steam (S), and the reflux (L) are all equipped with flow sensor/transmitters (FT) since each of these flows is adjusted to meet the control objectives of the column. In addition, a flow sensor/transmitter should also be installed to measure the feed rate since it is a major disturbance to the process. Cost and the type of service indicate the use of orifice plate and differential pressure sensor/transmitter flow indicators. Differential pressure level sensor/transmitters should also be used for the accumulator and bottom of the column since maintaining these levels is essential for reliable operation of the column. A differential pressure sensor/transmitter should also be used to determine the onset of flooding, which has been identified as a process constraint. A pressure indicator should be installed on the top of the accumulator to monitor column pressure. An on-line GC should be used to measure the impurity level in the ethylene product. Since the bottoms product is not a saleable product and it has a "soft" product specification based on the economics for ethylene recovery, it is cost effective to infer composition

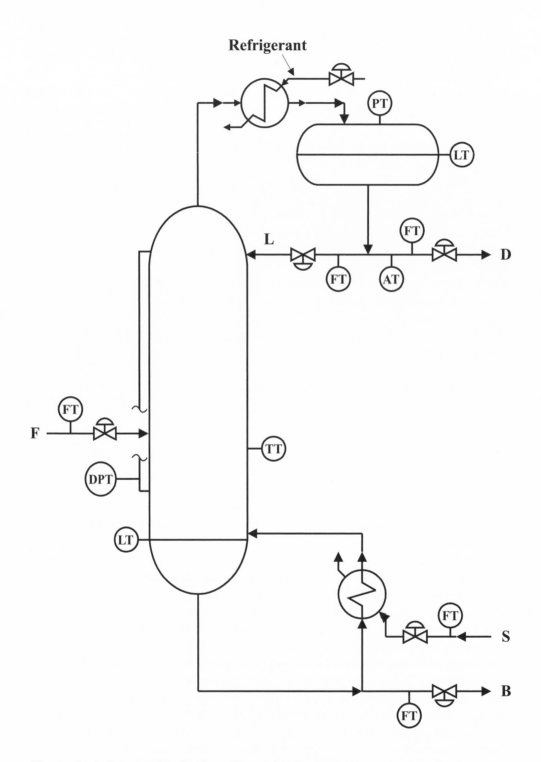

Figure 15.1 Schematic of a C₂ splitter with the sensors and control valves.

using a tray temperature measurement. Laboratory samples of the bottom product taken once every 8 hours are used by the operator to select the proper tray temperature. Using steady-state simulations of the C_2 splitter over the range of operation, the optimal location for the inferential temperature measurement is determined. An RTD temperature sensing element should be used for the tray temperature sensor because of its superior repeatability over TCs.

Determine the location of control valves. Each of the streams equipped with a FT (Figure 15.1) should also have a control valve installed. A control valve is also placed on the refrigerant feed to the condenser.

Apply a degree-of-freedom analysis. There are six control valves indicating that there are six manipulated flow streams. There are five column control objectives: overhead product composition, tray temperature in the stripping section, the level in the accumulator, the level in the reboiler, and the overhead pressure. In addition, the flow rate of the feed to the column can be set. Since the number of controlled variables is equal to the number of manipulated variables, the system is exactly determined. When the column reaches flooding conditions, the differential pressure measurement across the column becomes a constraint and the control problem becomes underdetermined.

Implement energy management. The flow of steam to the reboiler provides the reboiler duty and the flow of refrigerant to the condenser provides the condenser duty for this column.

Control process production rate. The production rate of this column is set by a flow controller on the feed to the column. The operator selects the setpoint for this controller to maintain the level in the column feed tank .

Select the manipulated variables that meet the control objectives. The primary control objective is to maintain the ethylene product on specification. The secondary control objective is the bottom composition control, which is directly related to the control of the tray temperature in the stripping section. Choosing which flow control loop to assign to each of these control objectives is tantamount to choosing the (c,y) pairings for a distillation column. The configuration selection problem for a propylene/propane splitter was addressed in Example 13.1. Since this is a relatively low reflux ratio column with a reflux ratio of approximately 3.5, the (L,V) configuration is a good choice for this application because the (L,V) configuration has a fast dynamic response to manipulated variable changes and is the least sensitive configuration with respect to feed composition upsets. Also, selection of the (L,V) configuration determines that the distillate rate is set by the level controller for the accumulator and the bottoms rate is set by the level controller for the column bottoms. Dynamic simulations of this column for appropriate disturbance tests could be used to check this analysis. Finally, the overhead pressure is controlled by the flow rate of refrigerant to the condenser. This control configuration is shown in Figure 15.2.

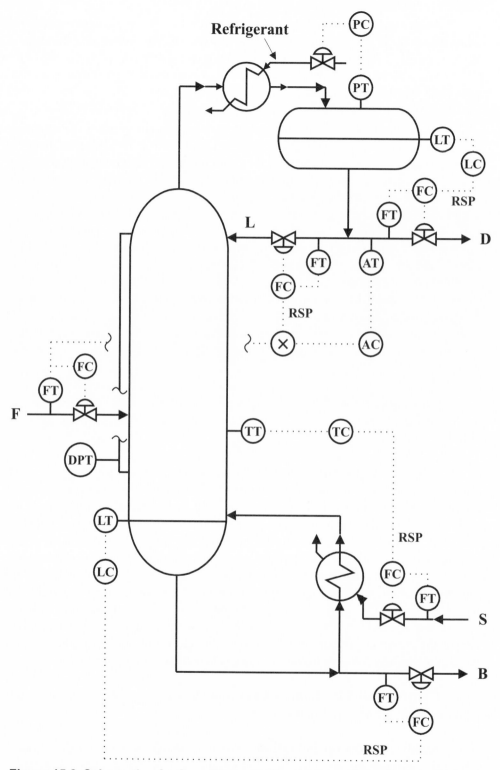

Figure 15.2 Schematic of a C₂ splitter with the (L,V) configuration applied.

Address how disturbances are handled. The feed composition is not measured, but the (L,V) configuration is generally the best configuration with regard to this disturbance. Feed flow rate disturbances are measured and the performance of the (L,V) configuration, particularly for the overhead composition control loop, can be improved by applying ratio control, i.e., L/F control (Figure 15.2).

Develop a constraint handling strategy. The primary constraint is flooding, which occurs when the feed flow is excessive. From the degree-of-freedom analysis, when the column encounters the flooding constraint, one control objective must be discarded. Clearly, the ethylene product purity, as well as the reboiler and accumulator levels, must be maintained. Therefore, when the flooding constraint is encountered, one can no longer expect to maintain the setpoint on the tray temperature in the stripping section (i.e., the purity of the bottoms product). This approach is implemented by combining the output from the tray temperature controller with the output of the differential pressure controller using a low select controller (LS). When the column is not approaching flooding conditions, the differential pressure controller selects a larger steam flow to the reboiler rather than the tray temperature controller. When the flooding constraint is encountered, the differential pressure controller yields a lower steam rate than the tray temperature controller, and the LS transmits the PDT signal to the steam flow control loop. This approach is shown schematically in Figure 15.3.

Control inventories. The level controllers on the reboiler and accumulator handle the liquid inventories. The gas inventories are addressed by the pressure controller on the overhead.

Check component balances. When methane and hydrogen appear in the feed, they accumulate in the overhead because the condenser temperature is not sufficiently low to condense them. Methane and hydrogen buildup decreases the ability to condense the overhead stream and the column pressure increases. A vent line connected to the vapor space on the accumulator provides a means to purge uncondensed light gases that accumulate in the overhead. An override/select controller (S) based on column pressure determines when methane and hydrogen are building up in the overhead and opens the vent to discharge them to a light gas processing unit. The select controller compares the measured pressure with the pressure setpoint used by the pressure controller and, when there is consistent offset between the measured pressure and its setpoint, the select controller opens the valve on the vent line. This select controller is shown schematically in Figure 15.3.

Control individual unit operations. Since this example is a single unit operation, there are no opportunities here.

Apply process optimization. The unassigned setpoints for this process include the setpoint for the ethylene product, the setpoint for the tray temperature controller, the setpoint for the overhead column pressure, and the setpoints for the accumulator and reboiler levels. The setpoints for the levels do not affect steady-state

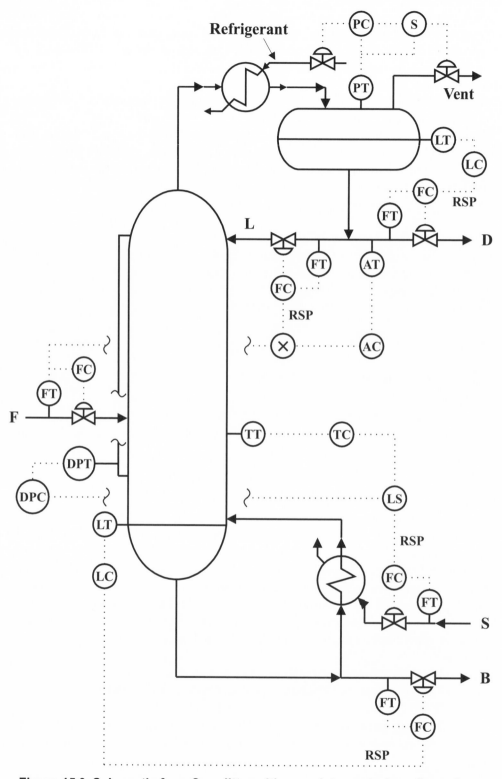

Figure 15.3 Schematic for a C_2 splitter with complete control configuration.

optimization. The impurity setpoint for the ethylene product is based on the product specification and the variability in the ethylene product resulting from the control system. Obviously, the closer the process is operated to the product specifications, the more profitable the operation.

The setpoint for the tray temperature (i.e., the ethylene content in the ethane product) is an optimization problem that requires the comparison of the ethylene recovery with the energy usage for the column. Moderate variations in the ethylene content of the bottoms product do not have a large effect on the economic performance of this column; therefore, the economic benefit from analyzing this optimization problem online to provide the most up-to-date optimal setpoints is low. An off-line estimate of the optimum operating point should be sufficient in this case.

The overhead pressure affects the relative volatility of the separation and, therefore, has a significant effect on the utility usage. The minimum overhead pressure is set by the temperature of the refrigerant. Since relative volatility increases as pressure decreases, this column should be operated near the minimum overhead pressure to obtain the most efficient separation.

15.4 Recycle Reactor Process

Problem Description. Figure 15.4 shows a schematic of a recycle reactor with a stripper[2] that separates the feed from the product. The following endothermic reactions occur

$$A \rightarrow B \rightarrow C$$

The reaction from B to C is much faster than the reaction from A to B; therefore, the product leaving the reactor contains primarily reactant A and product C with low levels of reactant B. The reactor heat exchanger is used to supply heat to drive the endothermic reactions. The reactor product is the feed to the stripper, which separates A from C. Since B is lighter than A, the small amount of B in the product stream from the reactor goes out the overhead of the stripper and is recycled to the reactor. The usual bottleneck of this recycle process is the condenser for the stripper. At other times, an upper limit on the reactor heater duty can limit operation.

Identify process objectives. The overall process objective is to maintain an economically efficient production of product C in a consistent and reliable fashion.

Identify process constraints. The major constraints on this process are the limit for the stripper condenser duty and the limit on the heat duty for the reactor heater.

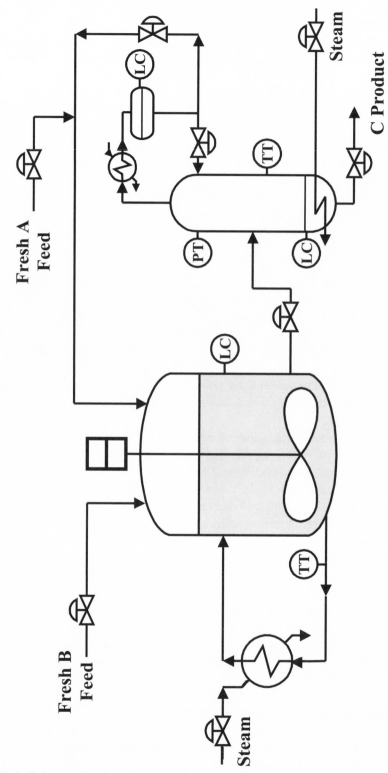

Figure 15.4 Schematic of a recycle reactor process with its sensors and valves.
Note that valve symbols represent flow control loops and level controllers (LC)
represent level indicators and controllers combined.

Identify significant disturbances. Disturbances for this process include steam enthalpy changes for both the reactor heater and the stripper reboiler. The ambient air temperature can significantly affect the available condenser duty, which, in turn, can affect the reactor feed rate.

Determine the type and location of sensors. Figure 15.4 shows the sensors applied to this process. Level indicators are required for the reactor level and for the accumulator and reboiler of the stripper. To measure the reactor temperature, a temperature sensor/transmitter (RTD) is placed in the line that delivers the reaction mixture to the reactor heater. This location was chosen because it is less expensive to install a thermowell in a process line than through the wall of the reactor vessel. Because the fluid velocity should be greater in the process line than inside the reactor, the thermal resistance of the thermowell/RTD system is lower, resulting in a faster-responding temperature sensor.

From an analysis of the stripper, it is determined that a tray temperature measurement in the stripping section of the stripper is a good control point for ensuring that the bottoms product from the stripper meets the product purity specifications for the C product. Steady-state models of the stripper are used to identify the best tray temperature location. An RTD temperature sensor/transmitter should be used for the application. A pressure sensor should also be installed in the top of the stripper to determine when the condenser duty constraint is being encountered. Also, orifice plate/differential pressure flow indicators should be used in each flow control loop.

Determine the location of control valves. Flow control loops, which include a control valve, are shown in Figure 15.5. Flow control loops should be installed on the fresh A feed and fresh B feed lines. Flow control loops should also be installed on the steam lines to the reactor heater and to the stripper reboiler. Flow control loops should be installed on the reactor product line, on the C product line from the stripper, on the stripper reflux line, and on the recycle line to the reactor.

Apply a degree-of-freedom analysis. There are eight flow control valves while there are six controlled variables during unconstrained operation: reactor temperature, reactor level, bottoms and accumulator levels for the stripper, tray temperature in the stripping section of the stripper and the process production rate. Therefore, this system is underdetermined since the stripper reflux rate and the recycle rate (stripper distillate rate) are not used as manipulated variables. When the condenser duty constraint is encountered, a degree-of-freedom is lost, but the system is still underdetermined.

Implement energy management. The steam flow to the reactor heater supplies the energy to drive the endothermic reactions in the reactor. The steam flow to the reboiler supplies the reboiler duty for the stripper while the condenser removes heat from the overhead vapor to condense it.

Control process production rate. The process production rate is set by selecting the setpoint for the flow controller for the fresh B feed. Since virtually all the

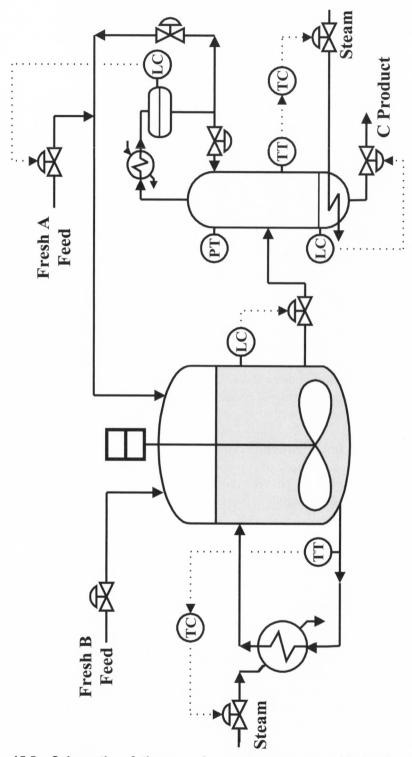

Figure 15.5 **Schematic of the recycle reactor process with basic control configuration implemented. Note that the control valve symbols represent flow control loops and the level controllers (LC) represent combined level indicators and controllers.**

fresh B feed is converted into C product, adjusting the fresh B feed rate to the reactor is a direct means of changing the production rate.

Select manipulated variables that meet the control objectives.   The temperature of the reactor is controlled by adjusting the setpoint for the flow controller on the steam flow to the reactor heater. The reactor level is controlled by adjusting the reactor product flow controller setpoint.

Since the stripper is a low reflux ratio column, the (L,V) configuration is selected. It is well established[2] that a flow rate for an internal liquid stream must be set externally to the recycle to prevent the "snowball" effect. The snowball effect can be understood by considering a level increase in the reactor. The level controller on the reactor increases the reactor product flow rate to lower the reactor level. The increase in the feed to the stripper results in a proportional increase in the distillate rate, which tends to increase the reactor level. The flow rates through the stripper and recycle to the reactor increase until a constraint is encountered. If the reactor level is below setpoint, the reactor product rate decreases and the recycle also decreases, which continues to reduce the loading on the stripper and recycle. To break this feedback system with positive feedback, a constant setpoint for the flow controller on the recycle stream is used. This leaves the accumulator level to be controlled since for the (L,V) configuration, the distillate flow rate (the recycle flow rate in this case) is normally used to control the accumulator level. In this case, the fresh A feed can be used to control the accumulator level. The unused degree of freedom is the setpoint for the reflux flow controller. This control configuration is shown in Figure 15.5.

Address how disturbances are handled. Steam enthalpy changes are handled by the reactor heater and stripper reboiler temperature controllers. The effect of ambient air temperature changes on the condenser duty are addressed in the next section, where constraint handling is considered.

Develop a constraint handling strategy. Two constraints should be considered: the condenser duty and the reactor heater duty. When the condenser duty constraint is encountered, the overhead pressure in the stripper increases. As the pressure of the column increases, the relative volatility between A and C decreases. Therefore, an upper limit on the overhead stripper pressure must be identified and the column must be operated below this upper pressure limit. The most direct way to reduce the pressure in the stripper is to reduce the flow rate of fresh B feed. Normally, the fresh B feed flow controller setpoint is set by the operator to meet the desired production rate for the product C.   A pressure controller is added to the process to adjust this setpoint when the pressure in the stripper overhead is above the specified limit; therefore, a LS controller is used to select the lower between the operator-specified setpoint and the one specified by the stripper overhead pressure controller.

During the winter months, when the condenser duty is at its maximum level, the bottleneck for the process is the reactor heater. When this limit is encountered, the valve on the heater steam saturates; therefore, an override/select controller is used so

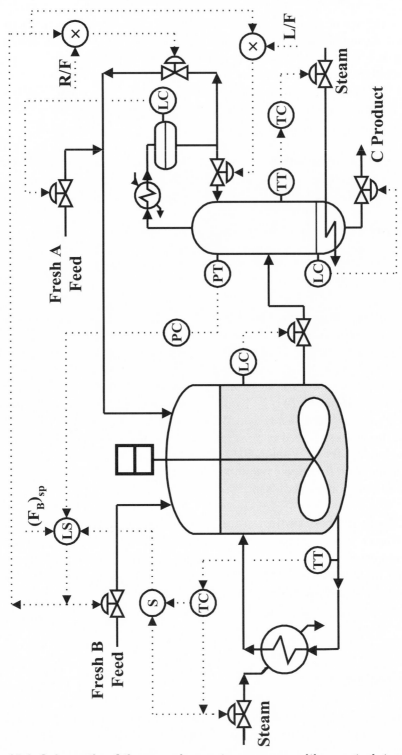

Figure 15.6 Schematic of the recycle reactor process with constraint and ratio controls added. Note that the control valve symbols represent flow control loops and the level controllers represent combined level indicators and controllers.

that, when the heater steam valve saturates, a select controller adjusts the fresh B feed to maintain the temperature of the reactor at its setpoint. This override/select controller is combined with the previous constraint controller by simply sending the output from the select controller to the low select controller, which selects the lowest setpoint for the fresh B feed from among the operator specified value, the value specified by the stripper overhead pressure controller, and the value specified by the reactor temperature override controller. These constraints controls are shown in Figure 15.6.

Control inventories. The reactor level and the stripper accumulator and bottoms levels each have a level controller. There is a pressure controller on the stripper overhead to protect against high-pressure operation.

Check component balances. Components A and B are each recycled to extinction, except for the small amount of A that leaves with the product. Component C is produced in the reactor and removed from the process as the bottom product from the stripper.

Control individual unit operations. During constraint control the feed rate to the stripper can change significantly. Since the recycle rate (stripper distillate rate) and the reflux flow controllers have fixed setpoints, these feed rate changes can cause significant composition upsets in the stripper. In both cases, the ratio of these flow rates to the fresh B feed rate is formed. For the recycle rate, the ratio of recycle rate to fresh B feed rate (R/F) is set by the operator and, when feed rate changes occur, the recycle rate is automatically scaled to the new feed rate. Likewise, the ratio of stripper reflux to fresh B feed (L/F) is set by the operator and, when feed rate changes occur, the stripper reflux is automatically scaled to the new feed rate. In both cases, changes in the fresh B feed rate require dynamic compensation. These additions to the control configuration are shown in Figure 15.6.

Apply process optimization. The reactor temperature setpoint and the ratios R/F and L/F are available as degrees of freedom for process optimization. Since almost complete conversion of B occurs in the reactor, there is little incentive for optimizing the reactor temperature. The value of R/F and L/F can be selected by optimizing the steady-state operation with regard to utility usage while meeting the product impurity specification on the C product.

15.5 Summary

This chapter has presented a procedure for approaching the design of control systems for complex multiunit processes. Using this procedure, the control techniques that have been studied in the previous chapters can be systematically applied to develop effective control schemes for complex chemical processes.

15.6 References

1. Luyben, M.L., B.D. Tyreus, and W.L. Luyben, "Plantwide Control Design Procedure", *AIChE J.*, Vol 43, No.12, pp. 3161-3174 (1997).

2. Tyreus, B.D., and W.L. Luyben, "Dynamics and Control of Recycle Systems. 4. Ternary Systems with One or Two Recycle Streams", *Ind. Eng. Chem. Res.*, Vol 32, pp. 1154-1162 (1993).

Chapter 16

Control Case Studies

16.1 Introduction

This chapter is concerned with the control of heat exchangers, reactors, and distillation columns. The majority of single-unit control problems in the chemical processing industries are represented by these classes of unit operations. The following material is based on various techniques developed in the text, viz., inferential control, selection of the proper mode for a PID controller, and configuration selection, combined with the specific process characteristics of each of these unit operations.

General guidelines concerning recommended control configurations for each of these classes of systems are presented in this chapter. The guidelines are based on the configuration selection analysis procedure presented in Chapter 13. Configuration selection should be based on coupling (for MIMO systems), dynamic response of the controlled variable to manipulated variable changes, and the sensitivity of the configuration to the key disturbances that affect the process.

16.2 Heat Exchanger Control

General Characteristics. Figure 16.1a shows a steam-heated heat exchanger in which the control objective is the outlet temperature of the process fluid being heated. Figure 16.1b shows a liquid/liquid heat exchanger (i.e, a heat exchanger that uses a coolant to extract heat from a hot process stream) in which the control objective is the outlet temperature of the process fluid being cooled. Steam-heated and liquid/liquid heat exchangers are the types of heat exchangers considered here. Both of these systems are self-regulating.

Section 11.3 introduced heat exchanger control by considering the control of a steam-heated heat exchanger. It was demonstrated that changes in the tube side flow rate of the process fluid caused significant changes in the effective process deadtime and process gain (see Table 11.2). As the flow rate decreases, the deadtime and gain both increase. As the number of passes used in the heat exchanger increases (i.e., the tube length increases), the deadtime increases. Industrial heat exchangers can have

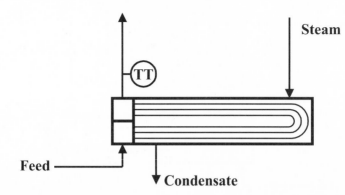

Figure 16.1a   Schematic of a steam-heated heat exchanger.

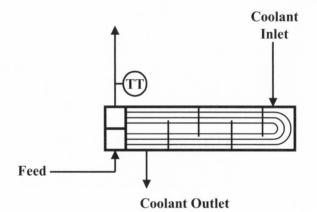

Figure 16.1b   Schematic of a liquid/liquid heat exchanger.

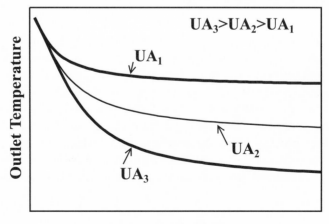

Coolant Flow Rate

Figure 16.2 The static relationship between outlet temperature and coolant flow rate for several liquid/liquid heat exchangers with different heat transfer areas.

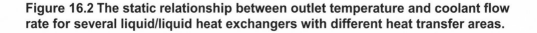

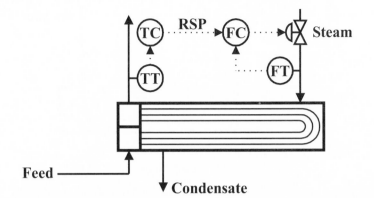

Figure 16.3a Inferior control configuration for a steam-heated heat exchanger, which is based on using steam flow as the manipulated variable. The control valve should be equipped with a positioner.

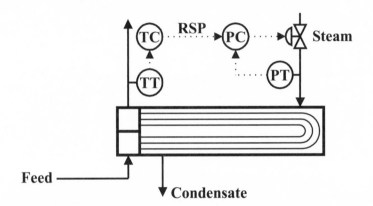

Figure 16.3b Preferred control configuration for a steam-heated heat exchanger, which is based on using steam pressure as the manipulated variable. The control valve should be equipped with a positioner.

deadtime-to-time constant ratios approaching 4.0, depending on the heat exchanger design and the tube side flow rate. Figure 16.2 shows the steady-state temperature change of the outlet process fluid of a liquid/liquid heat exchanger as a function of coolant flow rate for different heat transfer areas. As the coolant flow rate increases from zero, the magnitude of the process gain decreases continuously. Therefore, above a certain cooling water flow rate, no significant change in the product temperature results, i.e., the process gain approaches zero, which renders the process uncontrollable using the cooling water flow rate as the manipulate variable. At a given flow rate, as the heat exchanger area increases, the magnitude of the steady-state gain increases.

Steam-Heated Heat Exchangers. Even though these heat exchanger cases are SISO problems, the configuration selection problem is quite interesting and important. Figures 16.3a and 16.3b show two potential control configurations for steam-heated heat exchangers. The inferior configuration (Figure 16.3a) uses the steam flow as the manipulated variable for the temperature control loop while the

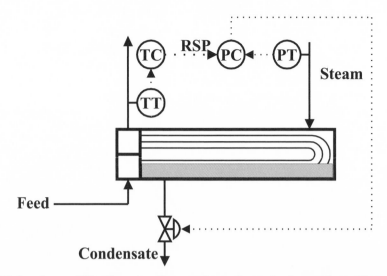

Figure 16.4   A modification to the preferred control configuration for the steam-heated heat exchanger in which the condensate flow is manipulated. Note that the control valve should be equipped with a positioner.

preferred configuration (Figure 16.3b) uses the steam pressure in the heat exchanger as the manipulated variable. Steam pressure is the preferred manipulated variable because it responds directly to changes in the pressure of the steam supply and to changes in the heat duty required to heat the process fluid. A change in steam supply pressure quickly causes a change in the steam pressure inside the exchanger. The pressure controller responds quickly and absorbs this upset efficiently. When the manipulated variable is the steam flow rate, a steam supply pressure upset results in a significant deviation in the control objective from setpoint before corrective action can be taken. When the heat duty requirements change in response to changes in the feed flow rate or inlet temperature, the steam pressure inside the exchanger changes before the outlet temperature begins to change. A steam pressure controller responds much more quickly to heat duty upsets than a steam flow controller. Since the steam pressure control loop responds quickly to the major upsets for a steam-heated heat exchanger, the control configuration based on steam pressure as the manipulated variable is preferred. For the preferred configuration, the steam pressure in the exchanger is a direct measure of the degree of fouling, i.e., the higher the steam pressure for a fixed feed rate and inlet temperature, the more fouling that exists.

Figure 16.4 shows a modification to the preferred control configuration for the steam-heated heat exchanger. The condensate flow controls the level of condensate in the heat exchanger, which determines the heat transfer area available for condensing steam, which is the primary mode of heat transfer for this system. Since the condensate flow, instead of the steam flow, is manipulated, the steam pressure control loop is not as responsive as the steam pressure control loop in Figure 16.3b because level control is an implicit part of the system. On the other hand, since the line size for the condensate is much smaller than for the steam feed, the size of the control valve is much smaller and less expensive. If the configuration using condensate flow as the manipulated variable is used, a steam trap is required downstream of the condensate valve. Choosing between the configurations shown in Figure 16.3b and Figure 16.4 involves a tradeoff between the capital costs and the control performance of these configurations. If control performance is a premium, the configuration shown in Figure 16.3b is preferred. Otherwise, economics likely determine that the configuration shown in Figure 16.4 be chosen.

McMillan[1] offers the following guidelines for scheduling the heat exchanger temperature controller gain and reset time for a change in the flow rate of the process fluid

$$K'_c = K_{c0} \left(\frac{F'}{F_0} \right)^2$$

$$\tau'_I = \tau_{I0} \left(\frac{F'}{F_0} \right)$$

where K_{c0} and τ_{I0} are determined for F_0. Note that the results presented in Chapter 11, which were obtained by tuning a PI controller for a steam-heated heat exchanger at different values of F (Table 10.2), agree with this scheduling function.

Liquid/Liquid Heat Exchangers. Figure 16.5a and 16.5b show two candidate configurations for controlling a liquid/liquid heat exchanger. One uses the coolant flow rate as the manipulated variable for the temperature controller while the other uses the bypass flow rate. When the coolant flow rate is used, the dynamic response of the process (changes in the temperature of the process fluid for changes in the flow rate of the coolant) is relatively slow since the dynamics of the heat transfer inside the exchanger largely determine the dynamic response of this configuration. It also suffers from the type of process nonlinearity described earlier in Figure 16.2 (variations in process deadtime and process gain). When feed bypass is used as the manipulated variable, the process dynamics are considerably faster, with low levels of process deadtime, since the dominant dynamic element for this process is the sensor. This configuration is more linear. Changes in the bypass flow rate create changes in the feed flow rate to the heat exchanger, which cause disturbances for the temperature control loop. However, these disturbances occur at a relatively slow rate so that the temperature controller is able to efficiently absorb them. The feed bypass configuration has the advantage that the coolant flow rate can be maintained at a high value regardless of the feed flow rate, which can significantly reduce the tendency for fouling on the tube-side heat-transfer surface. As a result of these advantages, using the flow rate of the feed bypass as the manipulated variable for a liquid/liquid heat exchanger is generally preferred.

Since the feed bypass configuration for liquid/liquid heat exchangers should have fast dynamics and very low deadtime-to-time constant ratios, derivative action should not be required and the tuning of this loop should be relatively straightforward. The reader is referred to McMillian[1] for more specific details on the application of temperature control to both steam-heated and liquid/liquid heat exchangers.

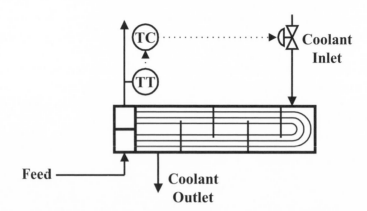

Figure 16.5a Inferior control configuration for a liquid/liquid heat exchanger with the flow rate of the cooling water used as the manipulated variable. The control valve should be equipped with a positioner.

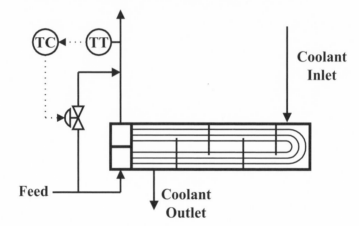

Figure 16.5b Preferred control configuration for a liquid/liquid heat exchanger with the flow rate of the feed bypass used as the manipulated variable. The control valve should have a valve positioner install on it.

16.3 CSTR Temperature Control

General Characteristics. Since reactors convert reactants to products, reactors are the heart of chemical plants. This section considers temperature control for one class of reactors: CSTRs. Reaction rates and equilibrium relations govern the behavior of reactors. Equilibrium relations represent the upper limits on the conversion of a particular reaction system while the rate expressions represent the conversion rates of chemical reactions. Either reaction rate or equilibrium can be controlling. When, the system is far removed from equilibrium constraints, equilibrium limitations can be neglected. When equilibrium limits the rate of reaction, the equilibrium limitations must be included in the rate expression. Catalysts do not participate in the chemical reactions or affect the chemical equilibrium, but do affect the rate of reactions.

One of the major challenges associated with CSTR temperature control is the nonlinearity of these systems. Example 4.18 shows that the gain and time constant of a CSTR are nonlinear functions of temperature when considering an irreversible first-order reaction. The following transfer function was derived by linearizing the nonlinear equation and assuming the reactant concentration, C_A, is constant.

$$G(s) = \frac{T(s)}{Q(s)} = \frac{\cfrac{1}{FC_p + \cfrac{V_r(-\Delta H)C_A k_0 E}{RT_0^2}\exp\left(\cfrac{-E}{RT_0}\right)}}{\left\{\cfrac{V_r \rho C_v}{FC_p + \cfrac{V_r(-\Delta H)C_A k_0 E}{RT_0^2}\exp\left(\cfrac{-E}{RT_0}\right)}s + 1\right\}} = \frac{K_p}{\tau_p s + 1}$$

As temperature increases, the gain and the time constant decrease since the exponential term increases more quickly than the RT_0^2 term. For the results shown in Section 7.4, the process rings when an upset causes the reaction temperature to increase, indicating that the decrease in the time constant outweighs the effect of the decrease in the gain. As the temperature decreases, the gain and time constant increase and the results in Section 7.4 indicate that, since the observed response was sluggish, the time constant effects again prevail. The nonlinear temperature dependence of reaction systems is a major challenge for reactor temperature control. As a rule of thumb for industrial systems, the reaction rate should approximately double each time the reaction temperature is increased by 10°C (18°F).

The most frequent disturbances with which a CSTR is faced are feed flow rate changes, changes in the feed temperature, and changes in the enthalpy of the heating or cooling medium. The most difficult disturbance is a change in the heat-transfer coefficient between the heat-transfer medium and the reaction mixture. Even for a well-mixed CSTR, the linear velocity of the reaction mixture at the heat-transfer surfaces is rarely above 1 ft/s, making the heat-transfer surfaces prone to fouling.

Endothermic CSTRs. Endothermic CSTRs are generally much easier to control than exothermic CSTRs because endothermic reactors are self-regulating. Two candidate control configurations for an endothermic CSTR are shown in Figures 16.6a and 16.6b. Using the flow rate of steam as the manipulated variable (Figure 16.6a) makes the reactor susceptible to heat load changes and steam enthalpy changes that require corrective action by the temperature controller. This configuration has the advantage that it provides a direct measure of the heat load and, as a result, a measure of the conversion in the reactor.

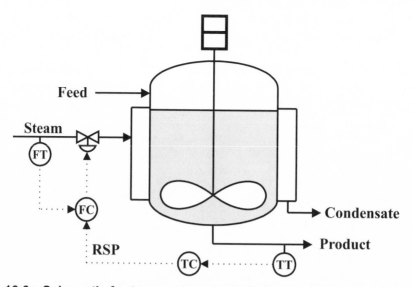

Figure 16.6a Schematic for temperature control of an endothermic CSTR using steam flow rate as the manipulated variable.

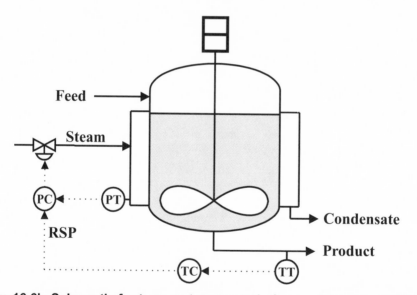

Figure 16.6b Schematic for temperature control of an endothermic CSTR using steam pressure as the manipulated variable. The control valve should be equipped with a positioner.

As in the case of the steam-heated heat exchanger (Figure 16.3b), using the steam pressure in the reactor jacket as the manipulated variable (Figure 16.6b) more effectively absorbs reactor heat duty and steam enthalpy upsets since these changes cause immediate changes in the steam pressure. Controlling steam pressure linearizes the temperature control system compared with controlling steam flow rate[1]. The major disadvantage of using the steam pressure as the manipulated variable is that it does not provide a direct measure of the heat load on the reactor, but this is usually a secondary

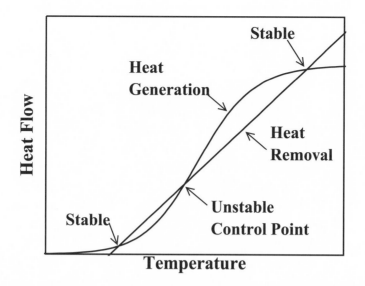

Figure 16.7 Demonstration of multiple steady state operating points for an exothermic CSTR.

consideration and an additional steam flow indicator can be installed if an online measure of the reactor heat duty is necessary.

Chapter 11 demonstrates that scheduling of the controller tuning is required when the system is strongly nonlinear. Excessive nonlinear behavior can be noted when ringing and sluggish behavior are observed for the same set of tuning parameters.

Exothermic CSTRs. Non-self-regulation in exothermic CSTRs arises from the temperature characteristics of heat generation from reaction and heat removal by the coolant. Heat removal is essentially linear with temperature, whereas reaction heat generation exhibits a characteristic "S" shape versus temperature. Low reaction rates result in low heat generation at low temperatures. At intermediate temperatures, the slope of the heat generation curve is steep because of an abundance of reactant and a sufficiently high reaction rate. The slope of the heat generation curves decreases at high temperature because of depletion of the reactant.

Non-self-regulation can result when the slope of the heat generation curve exceeds the slope of the heat removal curve. Figure 16.7 shows the rate of heat generation by reaction and the rate of heat removal by the cooling system as functions of reactor temperature. The intersections of these two curves represent steady-state operating points for the reactor. The low- and high-temperature intersection points are stable operating points since, if the temperature of the reaction mixture increases, the rate of heat removal exceeds the rate of heat generation by reaction and, if the temperature decreases, the rate of heat removal is less than the rate of heat generation. In both cases, the reactor temperature returns to the original operating point.

The operating point corresponding to the intermediate temperature is unstable since, if the reactor temperature increases, the rate of heat generation by reaction exceeds the rate of heat removal and the reactor moves to the stable high-temperature operating point. If the reactor temperature decreases, the rate of heat removal exceeds the rate of heat generation by reaction and the reactor moves to the stable low-temperature operating point. Note that the slope of the heat generation curve is greater than that of the heat removal curve for the unstable operating point, and the slope of the heat generation curve is smaller for the stable points.

A feedback controller must be used to maintain operation at the unstable intermediate temperature operating point that, in many cases, is the desired operating point from an economic point of view. A feedback controller maintains a CSTR at an open-loop unstable operating point by increasing the heat removal rate so that it exceeds the heat generation rate at temperatures above the operating point, and by decreasing the heat removal rate so that it is less than the heat generation at temperatures below the operating point.

A runaway in reactor temperature can occur when the rate of heat generation by reaction exceeds the maximum heat removal rate available from the coolant system and the conversion is much less than 100%. The likelihood of a temperature runaway for an exothermic CSTR can be reduced by replacing a liquid coolant with a boiling coolant (for which the heat-transfer coefficient is tripled), reducing the feed rate of reactants, reducing the concentration of the reactants in the feed, or increasing the ratio of the heat-transfer area to the reactor volume. These changes also increase the controllability of the reactor.

Figures 16.8a and 16.8b show two recommended approaches for controlling the temperature of an exothermic CSTR by cascading the reactor temperature to a coolant temperature controller. Using the setpoint of the coolant temperature as the manipulated variable for temperature control of an exothermic CSTR is recommended because it results in a fast-acting system, and linearizes the process gain[2] (the change in the outlet temperature of the process for a change in the coolant temperature).

In Figure 16.8a, the manipulated variable for the reactor temperature controller is the setpoint for the outlet temperature of the coolant. This configuration has the advantage of providing faster compensation for fouled heat-transfer surfaces, but responds more slowly to changes in the inlet temperature of the coolant or changes in the supply pressure of the coolant.

Figure 16.8b is a schematic of a configuration for controlling the reactor temperature using the setpoint of the inlet temperature of the coolant as the manipulated variable. This configuration has the advantages of a faster response to inlet coolant temperature changes and changes in the supply pressure of the coolant, but responds more slowly to fouling of the heat-transfer surfaces.

The choice between the configurations shown in Figures 16.8a and 16.8b depends upon which is more important: a fast response to coolant upsets or to fouling

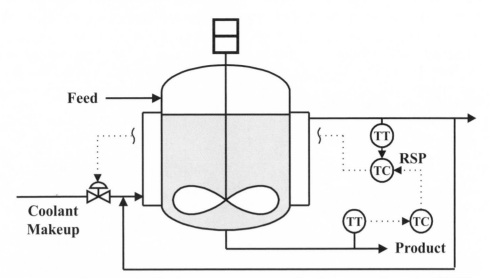

Figure 16.8a Schematic of a temperature controller for an exothermic CSTR in cascade with the outlet temperature of the coolant.

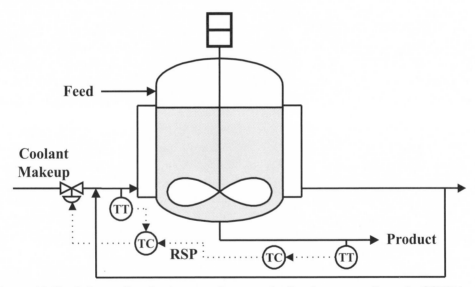

Figure 16.8b Schematic of a temperature controller for an exothermic CSTR in cascade with the inlet temperature of the coolant.

of the heat-transfer surface. As the circulation rate of the coolant increases, the differences between the approaches shown in Figures 16.8a and 16.8b diminishes. At high coolant circulation rates, these approaches provide equivalent performance for the full range of upsets. McMillan[1] presents an analysis of other possible configuration choices.

In certain cases, it is desirable to maximize the production rate of a reactor. Figure 16.9 demonstrates how one of the previous configurations (Figure 16.8a) can be extended to maximize production rate. A **valve position controller (VPC)**

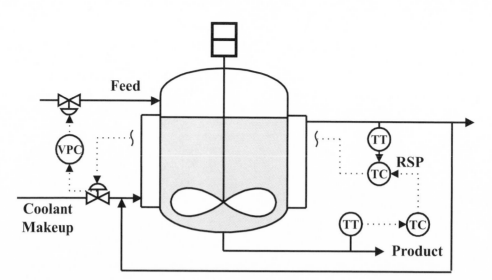

Figure 16.9 Schematic of control system for an exothermic CSTR that is designed to maximize production rate. Note that VPC is a valve position controller.

manipulates the feed until the valve on the coolant makeup is sufficiently open, yet still able to reject disturbances (e.g., 80% open). An integral-only controller is usually used for the valve position controller so that gradual movement to the maximum production rate is ensured.

One of the undesirable aspects of the previous control approaches used to control exothermic CSTRs is that a separate heating system is required for startup. In certain cases, the evaporation of hot condensate can be used as the coolant for exothermic CSTRs. Figure 16.10 is a schematic of such an application. Note that the condensate heats the reactant mixture to initiate reaction and, when the reaction starts, evaporation of the condensate removes heat from the reactor. A steam pressure controller is used as the manipulated variable for the reactor temperature controller since it responds quickly to heat duty changes. The steam produced by cooling the reactor can be added to the low-pressure steam system, which can represent significant energy recovery in certain cases.

Typically, a range of controller gains provides stable operation of an exothermic CSTR operating at an unstable operating point. Since the reactor is open-loop unstable, a minimum amount of feedback control, which corresponds to K_c^{min}, is necessary to stabilize the system. Likewise, there is an upper limit to controller aggressiveness, K_c^{max}, above which the closed-loop process becomes unstable. Therefore, there is a range or window of K_c's that provide stable operation, i.e., for stable operation,

$$K_c^{min} < K_c < K_c^{max}$$

This range of suitable values for K_c is a strong function of the effective deadtime-to-time constant ratio of the process. McMillan[1] indicates that, in general,

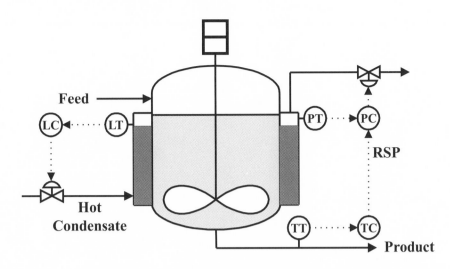

Figure 16.10 Schematic of a control configuration for an exothermic CSTR that uses hot condensate to startup the reactor and cool it.

$$\frac{K_c^{max}}{K_c^{min}} = \frac{1}{\theta_p / \tau_p}$$

and recommends that a reactor not be designed for deadtime-to-time constant ratios exceeding 0.1. The effective deadtime of a temperature loop on a CSTR can be approximated by[1]

$$\theta_p \approx T_{mix} + \tau_{ht} + \tau_{coolant} + \tau_s$$

where T_{mix} is the mixing turnover time, which is approximated by the reactor volume divided by the sum of the feed rate, the recirculation rate, and the pumping rate of the agitator; τ_{ht} is the time constant for heat transfer, which is approximated by the product of the mass of the heat-transfer surface and its heat capacity divided by the product of the heat-transfer coefficient and the area of the heat-transfer surface; $\tau_{coolant}$ is the transportation delay of the coolant, which is approximated by the coolant jacket volume divided by the coolant recirculation rate; and τ_s is the time constant for the temperature sensor system (the thermowell and RTD). Even though each of these elements is a time constant and not a deadtime, their combined effect on the high-order system behaves like deadtime (see Section 5.5). If the deadtime-to-time constant ratio is below 0.1, one can expect excellent reactor temperature control, i.e., peak errors can be expected to be less than the measurement error[1], which is largely offset from the true reading. If inadequate agitator circulation is applied, insufficient heat-transfer area is used, a low coolant flow rate is used, or excessive sensor lag (e.g., a glass thermowell or a thermowell with an excessive air gap between the RTD and the walls of the thermowell) is present, poor control performance or possibly, in the extreme, an uncontrollable process results, irrespective of controller tuning efforts.

The controller tuning for temperature control loops applied to exothermic CSTRs is somewhat different from controller tuning for most other processes. Normal levels of integral action for these systems can lead to an unstable closed-loop system. It is recommended[1] that a reset time greater than 10 min, or approximately 10 times that of normal tuning levels should be used in these cases. It is recommended that the gain be approximately doubled compared with normal tuning and that the derivative time be at least 0.5 min.

16.4 Distillation Control

General Characteristics. Approximately 40,000 distillation columns are operated in the U.S. chemical process industries and they comprise 95% of the separation processes for these industries. Because distillation operation directly affects product quality, process production rates, and utility usage, the economic importance of distillation control is clear.

Distillation control is a challenging problem because of the following factors:

-Process nonlinearity

-Multivariable coupling

-Severe disturbances

-Nonstationary behavior

Distillation columns exhibit static nonlinearity because impurity levels asymptotically approach zero. The impurity level in the overhead product is the concentration of the heavy key, and the impurity level in the bottoms product is the concentration of the light key. Nonlinear dynamics, i.e., variations in time constants with the size and direction of an input change, and static nonlinearity are much more pronounced for columns that produce high-purity products, e.g., columns that have impurity levels less than 1%. Coupling is significant when the composition of both overhead and bottoms products are being controlled. Columns are affected by a variety of disturbances, particularly feed composition and flow upsets. Nonstationary behavior stems from changes in tray efficiencies caused by entertainment or fouling.

Improved distillation control is characterized by a reduction in the variability of the impurities in the products. Meeting the specification requirements on the variability of final products can make the difference between the product being a high value-added product with large market demand and being a low-valued product with a small market demand. For customers who purchase the products produced by distillation columns as feedstocks for their processes, the variability of the feedstocks can directly affect the quality of the products they produce, e.g., the variability in the monomer feed to a polymerization process can directly affect the mechanical properties of the resulting polymer produced. In addition, control performance can affect plant processing rates and utility usage. Figure 1.1 shows that after the

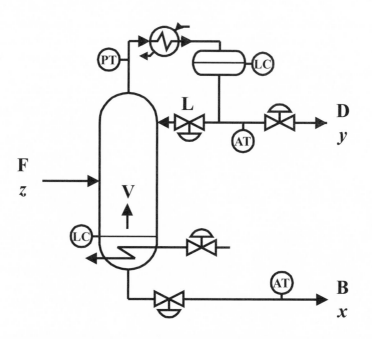

Figure 16.11 Schematic of a two product distillation column. Note that the valves on this figure represent flow control loops.

variability of a product has been reduced, the setpoint for the impurity in the product can be increased, moving the setpoint closer to the specification limit. If this column is the bottleneck for the process, then increasing the average impurity level, i.e., moving the impurity setpoint closer to the specification limit, allows greater plant processing rates. Even if the column in question is not a bottleneck, moving the impurity setpoint closer to the specification limit reduces the utility usage for the column. While each of these factors can be economically important for large-scale processes, the order of economic importance is usually product quality first, followed by process throughput, and finally utility reductions.

Control-Relevant Aspects of Distillation. A schematic of a binary distillation column with one feed and two products is shown in Figure 16.11.

Material balance and energy balance effects. Combining an overall steady-state material balance with the light component material balance for a binary separation yields

$$\frac{D}{F} = \frac{z-x}{y-x}$$

Rearranging results in

$$y = x + \frac{z-x}{D/F}$$

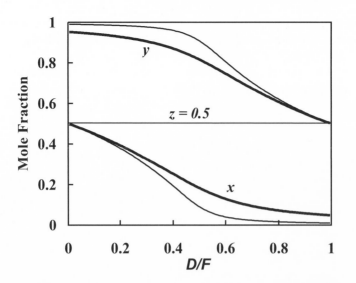

Figure 16.12 Effect of *D/F* and energy input on product purities. The thin line corresponds to a case in which the energy input is increased.

This equation indicates that as the flow rate of the distillate product, D, decreases while keeping F, z, and x constant, the purity of the overhead product, y, increases. Likewise, as D increases, its purity decreases. Because the sum of the product flows must equal the feed rate at steady state, when one product becomes more pure, the other product must get less pure. This is shown graphically in Figure 16.12. This is an example of the **material balance effect** in which the product impurity level varies directly with the flow rate of the corresponding product.

Another key factor that affects product purities is the energy input to the column, which determines the vapor rate, V, up the column. As the energy input to the column increases, the separation of the light and heavy components usually increases (Figure 16.12). One measure of the separation is the separation factor, S, which is given by

$$S = \frac{y}{1-y}\frac{1-x}{x}$$

As the impurity levels in the products decrease (i.e., $y \rightarrow 1$ and/or $x \rightarrow 0$), S increases.

Another way to understand the effect of an increase in energy input to the column is to consider the vapor/liquid traffic inside the column. If V increases while D and B are kept constant, the reflux, L, increases by the same amount as V. As a result, the reflux ratio, L/D, increases. This increase in vapor/liquid traffic inside the column causes a decrease in the impurities in the products for the same D/F ratio (Figure 16.12). When evaluating how a column responds in a control situation, it is helpful to remember that **energy input to the column generally determines the degree of**

separation that the column can achieve while the material balance (i.e., D/F) determines how the separation is allocated between the two products.

Vapor and liquid dynamics. The difference between vapor and liquid dynamics in a distillation column can contribute to interesting composition dynamic behavior. For all but very-high-pressure columns, i.e., those operating near the critical pressure of the light key, a change in V in the reboiler can be observed in the overhead in just a few seconds while a change in the reflux flow rate requires several minutes to reach the reboiler. The hydraulic response of a tray depends on the accumulation or depletion of liquid on it. The hydraulic time constant for flow from a tray typically ranges between 3 and 10 seconds. As a result, for a column with 50 or more trays, the overall hydraulic response time is on the order of several minutes.

As an example of the effect of the difference between liquid and vapor dynamics, consider the overhead product purity for an increase in V for a column in which the accumulator level sets the reflux level and the distillate rate is held constant. Initially, the increase in vapor flow moves up the column rapidly while the liquid flow down the column remains relatively constant since the reflux rate is set by the level controller on the accumulator. In the rectifying section, the L/V ratio determines the separating power of that section. As a result of the increase in V, the concentration of the impurity in the overhead increases initially. The increase in V begins to increase the level in the accumulator, which, after some time, leads to an increase in the reflux flow. As the increased reflux flow slowly makes its way down the rectifying section, L/V increases, causing a decrease in the impurity level in the overhead product. Therefore, for this scenario, an increase in V results in an inverse response in the concentration of the overhead product.

Entrainment. For columns operating at pressures less than about 165 psia, as V increases above 80% of flood conditions, droplets of liquid from the active area of the tray are blown in the vapor to the tray above, thus reducing the separation efficiency of the column. For certain vacuum columns, the tray efficiency can drop as much as 30% as the boilup rate increases above 80% of flood[3]. 100% of flood corresponds to the condition for which an increase in vapor rate results in a decrease in separation for the column. As the tray efficiency decreases because of increased entrainment, the process gain decreases, requiring larger changes in the manipulated variables to obtain the same change in the product impurity levels.

Structure packed columns. Columns that use sections of structured packing offer significant efficiency advantages over trayed columns for low-pressure applications because there is less pressure drop across the structured packing than across a corresponding set of trays. Because of the low liquid holdup on structured packing, these columns have faster composition dynamics than trayed columns. The liquid holdup on the structured packing is low enough that the composition profile through the packing reaches its steady-state profile much more quickly than the reboiler and accumulator. For a column with structured packing, the dynamic lag of the accumulator and the reboiler primarily determine the dynamic response of the product compositions.

Disturbances.   The type and magnitude of disturbances affecting a distillation column have a direct effect on the resulting product variability. An analysis of the major types of disturbances encountered in distillation columns follows.

Feed composition upsets. Changes in the feed composition represent the most significant upsets with which a distillation control system must deal on a continuous basis. A feed composition change shifts the composition profile through the column resulting in a large upset in the product compositions. Most industrial columns do not have a feed composition analyzer; therefore, feed composition upsets appear as unmeasured disturbances. When a feed composition analyzer is available, a feedforward controller can be applied using the online measurements of the feed composition. Since feed composition changes represent a major disturbance for distillation control, the sensitivity of potential control configurations to feed composition upsets is a major issue for configuration selection.

Feed flow rate upsets. The flow rates in a steady-state model of a column with constant tray efficiencies scale directly with column feed rate. Therefore, ratio control (using L/F, D/F, V/F or B/F as composition controller output) is an effective means of handling feed flow rate upsets. Dynamic compensation is normally required to account for the dynamic mismatch between the response of the product compositions to feed flow rate changes and the response to changes in the manipulated variables. When certain ratios (e.g., L/D, V/B) are used as manipulated variables, these ratios, combined with the level control, automatically compensate for feed flow rate changes.

Feed enthalpy upsets. For columns that use a low reflux ratio, feed enthalpy changes can significantly alter the vapor/liquid rates inside the column, causing a major shift in the internal composition profile and, therefore, a significant upset in the product compositions. This upset can be difficult to identify since (1) most industrial columns do not have feed temperature measurements and (2) even if a feed temperature measurement is available, it does not detect feed enthalpy changes for a two-phase feed. This disturbance may be difficult to distinguish from feed composition upsets without a more detailed analysis. It may be necessary to install a feed preheater or cooler to maintain a constant feed enthalpy to a column.

Subcooled reflux changes. When a thundershower passes over a plant, the reflux temperatures for the columns can drop sharply. Columns that use finned-fan coolers as overhead condensers are particularly susceptible to rapid changes in ambient conditions. If internal reflux control (Section 11.5) is not applied, severe upsets in the operation of the columns result because of major shifts in the composition profiles of the columns. When internal reflux control is correctly applied, the impact of a thunderstorm on column operations can be nearly eliminated.

Loss of reboiler steam pressure. When a steep drop in steam header pressure occurs, certain columns (those operating with control valves on the reboiler steam that are nearly fully open) experience a sharp drop in reboiler duty. This results in a sharp increase in the impurity levels in the products. When the steam header pressure returns to its normal level, the composition control system for the column attempts to return to the normal product purities. Because of the severity of this upset, if the composition controllers are not properly tuned, the upset can be amplified by the composition controllers, requiring the operators to take these controllers off-line to stabilize the column, greatly extending the duration of the period of production of off-specification products. This disturbance is, in general, the most severe disturbance that a control system on a distillation column must handle, and may require invoking overrides that gradually bring the operation of the column to its normal operating window instead of expecting the composition controllers to handle this severe upset by themselves.

Column pressure upsets. Column pressure has a direct effect on the relative volatility of the key components in the column. Thus, changes in the column pressure can significantly affect product compositions. A properly implemented pressure control scheme maintains column pressure close to its setpoint, with only short-term and low-amplitude departures. A large class of columns (e.g., refinery columns) is operated at maximum condenser duty to maximize column separation, which minimizes steam usage. For these cases, the column pressure increases during the day, when the cooling water or ambient air temperature is the greatest, and decreases at night, but the resulting pressure changes are usually slow enough that the composition controller can efficiently reject this disturbance.

Regulatory Controls. Improperly functioning flow, level, or pressure controllers can undermine the effectiveness of the product composition controllers.

Flow controllers. Flow controllers are used to control the flow rates of the products, the reflux, and the heating medium used in the reboiler, and their setpoints are determined by the various level and composition controllers. Applying block sine waves (Figure 8.2) and comparing the closed-loop results for the deadband and time constant with the expected performance levels listed in Table 2.3 can be used to assess the performance of a flow control loop.

Level controllers. Level controllers are used to maintain the level in the accumulator, the reboiler, and the intermediate accumulator of a stacked column (i.e., a distillation column composed of two separate columns when there are too many trays for one column). Loose level control on the accumulator and reboiler has been shown[4] to worsen the composition control problem for material balance control configurations (when either D or B is used as a manipulated variable for composition control). When D or B is adjusted, the internal vapor/liquid traffic changes only after the corresponding level controller acts as a result of the change in D or B. On the other hand, if a level controller is tuned too aggressively, it can result in oscillation passed back to the column and contribute to erratic operation. When the reboiler duty is set by the level controller on the reboiler, a level controller that causes oscillation in the reboiler can also cause cycling in the column pressure. Equations 7.15 and 7.16 provide initial estimates for level controllers based on a critically damped response.

Column pressure controllers. The column overhead pressure acts as an integrator and is determined by the net accumulation of material in the vapor phase. Column pressure is controlled by directly changing the amount of material in the vapor

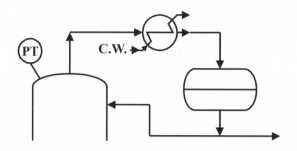

Figure 16.13   Minimum column pressure operation using maximum cooling water flow rate.

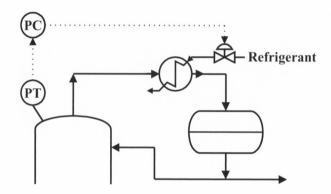

Figure 16.14   Column pressure configuration using refrigerant flow as the manipulated variable.

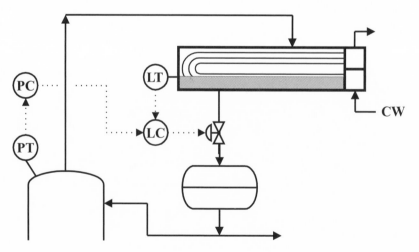

Figure 16.15   Column pressure configuration using the setpoint for the liquid level in the condenser as the manipulated variable for the pressure controller.

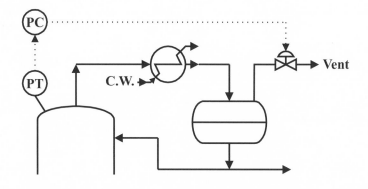

Figure 16.16 Column pressure control configuration using vent flow as the manipulated variable.

phase of the overhead or by changing the rate of condensation of the overhead, which converts low-density vapor to high-density liquid. A variety of approaches can be used to control column pressure including [1] using the maximum cooling water flow rate and allowing the column pressure to float at the minimum pressure level (Figure 16.13), [2] adjusting the flow rate of a refrigerant to the condenser (Figure 16.14), [3] adjusting the level of liquid in the condenser to change the effective heat-transfer area (Figure 16.15), [4] venting vapor from the accumulator (Figure 16.16), and [5] venting vapor from or injecting inert gas into the vapor space in the accumulator (Figure 16.17). Note that [1] - [3] directly affect the rate of vapor condensation to control pressure while [4] and [5] directly adjust the amount of vapor in the overhead of the column for pressure control.

The fastest-responding pressure control configurations (i.e., the approaches that should provide the tightest control to setpoint) are vent flow (Figure 16.16) and vent flow or inert injection (Figure 16.17). The override/select controller in Figure

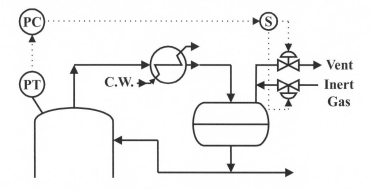

Figure 16.17 Column pressure control configuration using vent flow or inert gas injection as the manipulated variable.

16.17 uses vent flow when the measured pressure is above setpoint and uses the injection of an inert gas when the pressure is below setpoint. The speed of the pressure control loops based on manipulating the flow of a refrigerant (Figure 16.14) and adjusting the effective heat-transfer area (Figure 16.15) respond considerably more slowly since both of these approaches make changes in the rate of heat transfer to change the column pressure. Operating at minimum column pressure (Figure 16.13) allows the column pressure to swing with the maximum pressure normally occurring during the afternoon and the minimum pressure occurring early in the morning. A more extensive coverage of column pressure control is presented by Sloley[5].

Product Composition Measurements.   Product impurity levels (measured either online or in the laboratory) are used by feedback controllers to adjust column operation to meet product specifications. In addition, tray temperatures are used to infer product compositions, where feasible.

Online analyzers. A range of online analyzers commonly used in the CPI is discussed in Section 2.4. A key issue with analyzers is their associated analyzer delay. For columns that have slow-responding composition dynamics, analyzer delay is usually less of an issue. For a propylene/propane splitter (i.e., a high reflux ratio column), the composition dynamics have a time constant of about 2 hours. As the cycle time increases from 5 minutes to 10 minutes, it does not significantly affect the feedback control performance. For an ethane/propane splitter (i.e., a low reflux ratio column), even a five-minute analyzer delay seriously undermines composition control performance because the time constant for this process is less than five minutes. Fortunately, most fast-acting columns have a significant temperature drop across them so that product composition can be effectively inferred from tray temperature measurements. For columns that have a low relative volatility (i.e., less than 1.4), inferential temperature control is not feasible and feedback based on an online analyzer is required, but these columns generally have slow composition dynamics compared to the analyzer delay. For columns with a high relative volatility (i.e., greater than 2.0), inferential temperature control is usually effective.

Inferential temperature control. Inferential temperature control (Section 11.2) is an effective means of maintaining composition control for columns from a control and economic standpoint. That is, it greatly reduces the analyzer deadtime for feedback control and is much less expensive to install and maintain than an online composition analyzer. Because of their superior repeatability, RTDs are usually used for inferential temperature applications .

For multicomponent separations, tray temperatures do not uniquely determine the product composition (see Figure 11.4). As a result, for these cases it is essential that an online analyzer or, at least, periodic laboratory analysis be used to adjust the tray temperature setpoint to the proper level. If feedback based on laboratory analysis is not used, offset between the desired product composition and the actual product composition results.

Column pressure also significantly affects tray temperature measurements. For most systems, a simple linear correction compensates for variations in column pressure.

$$T_{pc} = T_{meas} - K_{pr}\left(P - P_0\right)$$

where T_{pc} is the pressure-compensated temperature that should be used for feedback control, T_{meas} is the measured tray temperature, K_{pr} is pressure correction factor, P is the operating pressure, and P_0 is the reference pressure. K_{pr} can be estimated by applying a steady-state column simulator for two different pressures within the normal operating range and using the following equation

$$K_{pr} = \frac{T_i(P_1) - T_i(P_2)}{P_1 - P_2}$$

where T_i is the value of the tray temperature predicted by the column simulator.

A steady-state column model can also be used to determine the best tray locations for inferential control by finding the trays whose temperatures show the strongest correlation with product composition. The following procedure is recommended.

1. Apply the steady-state column model at the base-case conditions (i.e., x^{BC} and y^{BC}) and record the temperature of each tray as T_i^{BC}.

2. Run the column model for an increase in the impurity level in the bottoms product (i.e., $x^{BC} + \Delta x$, y^{BC}) and record the tray temperatures as $T_i^{\Delta x}$. Δx should be approximately 25-50% of the impurity level at the base-case conditions.

3. Run the column model for an increase in the impurity level in the overhead product (i.e., x^{BC}, $y^{BC} + \Delta y$) and record the tray temperatures as $T_i^{\Delta y}$. Δy should be approximately 25-50% of the impurity level at the base-case conditions.

4. To locate the best tray for inferential control for the stripping section, determine the tray number i that maximizes

$$\Delta T_i^{net} = \left| T_i^{\Delta x} - T_i^{BC} \right| - \left| T_i^{\Delta y} - T_i^{BC} \right|$$

Because the proper tray should not be particularly sensitive to variations in the composition of the overhead product, the effect of Δy is subtracted from the temperature difference caused by changes in the bottom product composition.

5. To locate the best tray for inferential control for the rectifying section, determine the tray number i that maximizes

$$\Delta T_i^{net} = \left| T_i^{\Delta y} - T_i^{BC} \right| - \left| T_i^{\Delta x} - T_i^{BC} \right|$$

6.   Finally, repeat this procedure for a representative range of feed compositions. Then, select the tray that provides the best overall results. Remember that it may not be possible to locate the tray temperature measurement precisely at the optimum tray location.

Table 16.1 shows an example of this approach used to locate the best tray temperature for inferential temperature control in the stripping section of a depropanizer. Note that a temperature measurement anywhere between tray 7 and tray 16 should work well for this application for the assumed feed composition.

For certain columns, the bulk of the temperature change occurs in a few trays, resulting in a very steep temperature profile.   If a single tray temperature is used to infer the product composition in such a case, feed composition changes can move the location of the steep temperature change away from the tray selected for control, leading to a situation in which the chosen tray temperature is insensitive to changes in product impurity levels. This problem can be handled by controlling the average of several tray temperatures that bracket the area where the steep temperature changes occur for feed composition changes. In this manner, when feed changes cause the temperature profile in the column to move, at least one of the tray temperatures used in the average of the temperatures is located on the steep temperature front. The average of the tray temperatures should still be sensitive to product impurity changes over the full range of feed composition changes.

Single Composition Control.   Here the composition of one product is controlled while the composition of the other product is allowed to float.   In the chemical industry over 90% of the columns are operated under single composition control compared to dual composition control, which controls both the overhead and the bottoms product compositions.

Figure 16.18 shows single composition control using the reflux to control the purity of the overhead product while maintaining a fixed reboiler duty. The bottom composition is not controlled directly and can vary drastically as the feed composition changes. The control performance of the overhead product is generally best when reflux, L, rather than either the distillate flow rate, D, or the reflux ratio, L/D is the manipulated variable. As shown in Example 13.1, L is the fastest-acting manipulated variable for the overhead and the least sensitive to feed composition changes. Since the reboiler duty is fixed, coupling is not an issue.

Table 16.1

**Example for Choosing the Proper Tray
Location for Inferential Temperature Control**

	BC	Δx	Δy	
x	0.04	0.02	0.04	
y	0.03	0.03	0.15	
	T_i^{BC}	$T_i^{\Delta x}$	$T_i^{\Delta y}$	ΔT_i^{NET}
T_1	112.4	114.1	111.8	1.1
T_2	105.1	107.5	104.6	1.9
T_3	102.8	105.6	102.2	2.3
T_4	100.8	103.9	100.2	2.5
T_5	99.0	102.4	98.5	2.9
T_6	97.3	101.1	96.8	3.3
T_7	95.6	99.7	95.0	3.5
T_8	94.0	98.4	93.6	4.0
T_9	92.4	97.1	91.7	4.2
T_{10}	90.9	95.8	90.2	4.2
T_{11}	89.4	94.4	88.6	4.2
T_{12}	87.4	93.0	85.6	4.2
T_{13}	86.5	91.6	87.0	4.2
T_{14}	85.1	90.0	85.6	4.0
T_{15}	83.6	88.4	84.6	3.8
T_{16}	82.2	86.7	81.2	3.5
T_{17}	80.7	84.9	79.7	3.2
T_{18}	79.2	83.0	78.1	2.7

When the bottom product is controlled by single composition control, the control configuration shown in Figure 16.19 is recommended. Since the boilup rate, V,

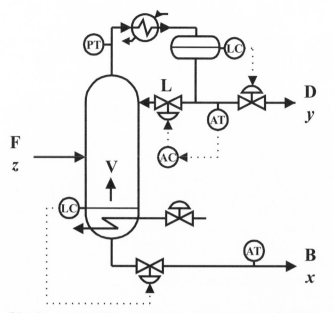

Figure 16.18 Single composition control using L to control the purity of the overhead product. The symbol for a control valve represents a flow control loop.

is faster acting and less sensitive to disturbances than either the bottoms product rate, B, or the boilup ratio, V/B, V is used to control the bottom product composition with the reflux rate fixed, which allows the overhead composition to float.

Single composition control is much easier to implement, tune, and maintain than dual composition control. The choice between single and dual composition

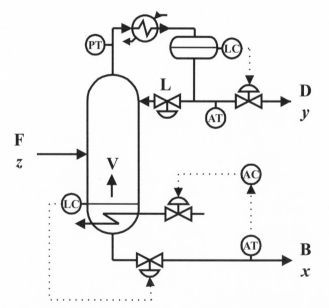

Figure 16.19 Single composition control using V to control the purity of the bottoms product. The symbol for a control valve represents a flow control loop.

control is based on the tradeoff between the additional cost associated with dual composition control (analyzer costs, increased controller maintenance, etc.) and the economic benefit of dual composition control (increased product recovery and reduced utility costs). While single composition control is in widespread use in the chemical industry, dual composition control is generally preferred for refinery columns and columns that produce high-volume chemical intermediates because the energy usage for these columns is much larger.

Dual Composition Control. The choice of the proper configuration for dual composition control is a more challenging problem than for single composition control because there are more viable approaches and the analysis of performance is more complex. There is a variety of choices for manipulated variables ($L, D, L/D, V, B,$ $V/B, B/L$ and D/V) that can be paired to the four control objectives (x, y, reboiler level, and accumulator level), indicating that there are a large number of possible configuration choices, although most of them are not practical. It is assumed that the choice for the control configuration for the column pressure (Figures 16.13-16.17) is made separately from the selection of the composition control configuration. If we limit our choices to $L, D,$ and L/D for controlling y and $V, B,$ and V/B for controlling x, there are nine possible configurations to consider: $(L,V), (D,V), (L/D,V), (L,B), (D,B),$ $(L/D,B), (L,V/B), (D,V/B),$ and $(L/D,V/B)$. In each configuration, the first term is the manipulated variable used to control y and the second term is used to control x.

Figure 16.20 shows the (L,V) configuration. The setpoint for the reflux flow controller is set by the overhead composition controller and the setpoint for the flow controller on the reboiler duty is set by the bottom composition controller. This leaves D to control the accumulator level and B to control the reboiler level. Figure 16.21 shows the (D,B) configuration where D is adjusted to control y and B is changed to control x, which leaves L for the accumulator level and V for the reboiler level. Figure 13.9 shows how the reflux ratio can be used as the manipulated variable for the overhead composition.

Consider the classifications of these nine control configurations. The five configurations that use either D or B as a manipulated variable for composition control are referred to as **material balance configurations** because they use the overall material balance for the column to adjust product compositions. In fact, the (D,B) configuration has been referred to as the super material balance configuration. The four configurations that do not use D or B as manipulated variables are known as **energy balance configurations** because they directly adjust the vapor/liquid traffic in the column for composition control. The $(L/D,V/B)$ configuration is known as the **double ratio configuration**.

Chapter 13 demonstrates that the major factors affecting the composition control performance of a particular configuration are coupling, sensitivity to disturbances, and the response time for changes in the manipulated variable. The most commonly used configuration is (L,V) because it provides good dynamic response, is the least sensitive to feed composition disturbances, and is the easiest to implement, even though it is highly susceptible to coupling. On the other hand, the $(L/D,V/B)$

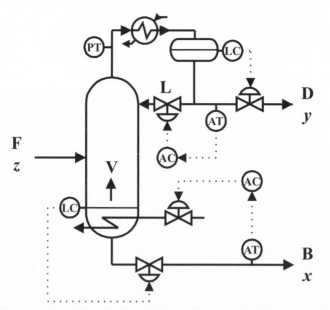

Figure 16.20 Schematic of the (*L,V*) configuration for dual composition control.

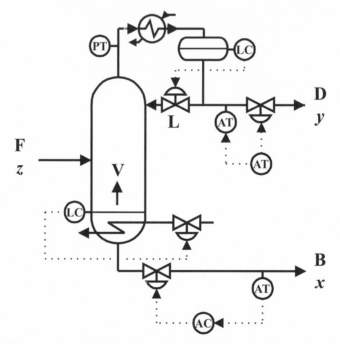

Figure 16.21 Schematic of the (*D,B*) configuration for dual composition control.

configuration is, in general, the least affected by coupling and has good dynamic response, but is quite sensitive to feed composition disturbances and is more difficult to implement. The (*D,B*) configuration has advantages for certain high-purity columns if the levels are tuned tightly, but is open-loop unstable, i.e., non-self-regulating. As a result, there is no clear choice for the best configuration for dual composition control of distillation columns. In fact, there are specific cases for which each of the nine potential configurations listed earlier provides the best control performance.

While it is not possible to *a priori* choose the optimum configuration, there are some guidelines that can reduce the possibility of choosing a poor configuration for a particular column. In general, for high reflux ratio cases ($L/D > 8$), configurations that use material balance manipulated variables (D and B) or ratios (L/D and V/B) are preferred while for low reflux ratio cases ($L/D < 5$), configurations that use energy balance manipulated variables (L and V) or ratios are preferred.

In many cases, the control of one of the two products is more important than control of the other. For these cases, when the overhead product is more important, L is usually the best manipulated variable. When the bottoms product is more important, V is the proper manipulated variable. If the column is a high reflux ratio column, the manipulated variable for the less important product should be a material balance knob (D or B) or a ratio (L/D or V/B). Since a C_3 splitter (see Example 13.1) is a high reflux ratio column and control of the overhead product is more important, the (L,B) or ($L,V/B$) configuration is preferred, which is consistent with simulation studies[6] that have been performed. If the column is a low reflux ratio column, the less important product should be controlled by an energy balance knob (V or L) or a ratio (L/D or V/B). For example, for a low reflux column for which the bottom product is more important, the (L,V) or ($L/D,V$) configuration is preferred.   Table 16.2 summarizes the recommended control configurations for columns in which one product is more important than the other.

Table 16.2 Recommended Control Configurations When One Product is More Important than the Other		
	x more important	**y more important**
Low reflux ratio columns (L/D <5)	(L/D,V); (L,V)	(L,V/B); (L,V)
High reflux ratio columns (L/D > 8)	(L/D,V); (D,V)	(L,V/B); (L,B)

Composition Controller Tuning. For most distillation columns, the effective deadtime-to-time constant ratio is relatively small. Therefore, derivative action is not necessary and PI composition controllers are commonly used. When inferential temperature control is used, fast-acting temperature loops with significant sensor lag may require derivative action because of their effective deadtime-to-time constant ratios. Since most composition and temperature control loops are relatively slow responding, ATV identification with online detuning (Section 7.13) is recommended.

When one product is more important than the other, it is best to tune the important loop first to control to setpoint tightly (a 1/6 decay ratio) and then tune the less important loop loosely (less aggressive, e.g., critically damped). This dynamically decouples the multivariable control problem by providing relatively fast closed-loop dynamics for the important loop and considerably slower closed-loop dynamics for the less important loop. In this manner, the coupling effects of the less important loop are slow enough that the important loop can easily absorb them. As a result, the variability in the important loop can be maintained consistently at a relatively low level. In effect, this approach approximates the performance of single composition control without allowing the less important product composition to suffer large offsets from setpoint.

When the importance of the control of both products is approximately equal, the tuning procedure outlined in Section 13.6 should be used. In this case, both loops must be detuned equally to the point where the effects of coupling are at an acceptable level.

Constraint Control. Some of the most common column constraints include:

Maximum reboiler duty. This constraint can result from (1) an increase in the column pressure that reduces the temperature difference for heat transfer in the reboiler; (2) fouled or plugged heat-exchanger tubes in the reboiler that reduce the maximum heat transfer-rate; (3) an improperly sized steam trap that causes condensate to back up into the reboiler tubes; (4) an improperly sized control valve on the steam to the reboiler that limits the maximum steam flow to the reboiler; or (5) an increase in the column feed rate such that the required reboiler duty exceeds the maximum duty of the reboiler.

Maximum condenser duty. This constraint can be due to (1) an increase in the ambient air temperature that decreases the temperature difference for heat transfer; (2) fouled or plugged tubes in the condenser that reduce its maximum heat duty; (3) an improperly sized coolant flow control valve (Figure 16.14); (4) an increase in coolant temperature; or (5) an increase in column feed rate such that the required condenser duty exceeds the maximum duty of the condenser.

Flooding. Kister[7] discusses in detail the three types of flooding, showing that each type results from excessive levels of vapor/liquid traffic in the column.

Weeping. Weeping results when the vapor flow rate is too low to keep the liquid from draining through a tray onto the tray below.

Maximum reboiler temperature. For certain systems, elevated temperatures in the reboiler can promote polymerization reactions to the level that excessive fouling of the reboiler results.

A reboiler duty constraint can be identified when the steam flow control valve remains fully open and the requested steam flow is consistently above the measured

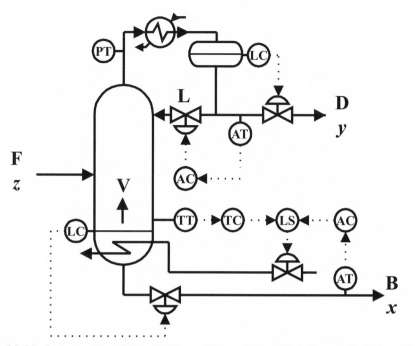

Figure 16.22 Schematic of the (L,V) configuration with LS constraint controls designed to maintain control of the overhead purity when a maximum reboiler temperature constraint is encountered.

flow rate. Condenser duty constraints are usually identified when the column pressure reaches a certain level or when the reflux temperature rises to a certain value. The onset of flooding or weeping is generally correlated to the pressure drop across the column or across a portion of the column. It should be emphasized that it is the reboiler duty that is adjusted to honor each of these constraints, i.e., prevent the process from violating the constraints.

Three approaches can be used for constraint control of a distillation column:

1. Convert from dual composition control to single composition control.

2. Reduce the column feed rate to maintain the purity of the products.

3. Reduce the product impurity setpoints for both products.

Figure 16.22 shows how a low select can be used to switch between constraint control and unconstrained control for a maximum reboiler temperature constraint when the overhead is the more important product. When the bottom product is more important, the combined constrained and unconstrained configuration is more complicated, with more potential configuration choices. Figure 16.23 shows a control configuration for observing the maximum reboiler temperature constraint when the bottoms product is more important. Note that in this case, the reflux flow rate is used to maintain the bottom product composition while the reboiler duty is used to maintain the reboiler temperature. In this configuration, the reboiler temperature control loop

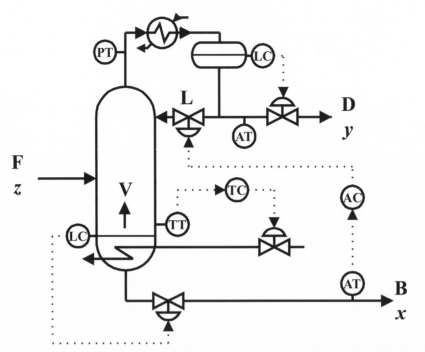

Figure 16.23 Schematic for the configuration of a constraint controller for a maximum reboiler constraint for which the bottom product is most important.

acts relatively quickly while the bottoms composition loop is slower acting since reflux flow is used as the manipulated variable.

Figure 11.17 shows a case for which the column feed rate is used as a manipulated variable to control the bottom product composition when a reboiler duty constraint is encountered. To reduce the impurity setpoints of both products when a constraint is encountered, a steady-state model of the column is usually used to select the proper tradeoff between the two products. This approach is not usually applied using advanced PID controllers.

Multivariable Control. The advantage of model predictive control (MPC) applied to distillation columns is greatest when MPC is applied to a series of columns, e.g., an entire separation train. This results because the MPC controller can efficiently operate the system of columns against the operative constraints to maximize the throughput for the system. For a typical industrial separation train, there is a large complex set of constraints that limit the overall process throughput. As a result, there is a large number of combinations of operative constraints that must be controlled if the controller is to maximize the throughput for the full range of operation. Advanced PID constraint controllers applied to this problem require a separate control configuration for each combination of operative constraints, resulting in an excessively large number of separate control configurations. On the other hand, an MPC controller can directly handle the full range of combinations of operative constraints with a single MPC controller. In addition, the MPC controller is much easier to maintain than a custom-built advanced PID controller for such a complex system. MPC can provide significant control improvements over PID control for a single column in most cases, but these improvements pale in comparison to the economic advantages offered by applying MPC to large-scale processes.

Keys to Effective Distillation Control. For effective distillation control, it is imperative to take care of the basics first.

1. Ensure that the regulatory controls are functioning properly.
2. Evaluate the analyzer deadtime, reliability, and accuracy.
3. Check that RTDs are being used to measure tray temperatures for composition inference and that they are correctly placed. Also, ensure that pressure-corrected tray temperatures are used.
4. Use internal reflux controls for changes in reflux temperature.
5. When L, D, V, and B are used as manipulated variables for composition control, ratio them to the measured feed rate wherever possible.

For configuration selection, use the (L,V) configuration for single composition control. For dual composition control, use an energy balance configuration for low reflux ratio cases and use material balance or ratio configurations for high reflux ratio columns. For many dual composition control cases, the control of one product is much more important than the other. For such cases, one should use L as the manipulated variable when the important product is produced in the overhead and V when it is produced in the bottoms. Additionally, the less important product should be controlled using an energy balance knob (L or V) or a ratio knob $(L/D$ or $V/B)$ for low reflux cases or D, L/D, B, or V/B for high reflux columns. For these cases, it is important to tune the important loop tightly and tune the less important loop much less aggressively. Finally, override and select control should be applied to ensure that all column constraints are honored when they become operative.

16.5 Summary

These case studies have demonstrated that, to identify the proper control configuration, process knowledge must be used to accomplish each of the following tasks:

1. Identify the key process disturbances.
2. Determine the control configurations that most effectively reduce the impact of these disturbances.
3. Identify control configurations that provide fast dynamic response to upsets and have low deadtime-to-time constant ratios.
4. Evaluate the impact of coupling if present.
5. Choose a control configuration that represents the best combination of dynamic response to upsets and sensitivity to coupling.

16.6 References

1. McMillan, G.K., *Advanced Temperature Control*, Instrument Society of America, 1995, pp. 95-132.

2. Shinskey, F.G., *Process Control Systems*, 4th Edition, McGraw-Hill, 1996, p. 325.

3. Kister, H.Z., *Distillation Operation*, McGraw-Hill, 1990, p. 386.

4. Yang, D.R., D.A. Mellichamp, D.E. Seborg, "The Influence of Inventory Control Dynamics on Composition Control", *Proceed 12th World Congress of IFAC*, Vol 4, Sydney, Australia, 1993, pp. 27-32.

5. Sloley, A. W., "Effectively Control Column Pressure", *CEP*, 2001, pp38-48.

6. Hurowitz, S.E., *Superfractionator Process Control*, Ph.D. Dissertation, Texas Tech University, 1998, p, 96.

7. Kister, H.Z., *Distillation Operation*, McGraw-Hill, 1990, pp. 139-150.

Appendix A

Piping and Instrument Diagrams

A.1 Introduction

Piping and Instrument Diagrams (P&IDs) are used by industry to document the control systems for their plants. Even though the Instrument Society of America has established a standard for symbols that are used in P&IDs (ANS/ISA-5.1-1984), the standard is general and, in some cases, open ended. As a result, operating companies in the CPI generally develop their own P&ID standards within their company. This appendix is intended to provide only a brief introduction to P&IDs. Only the elements of P&IDs that relate to the control schematics used in this text are presented. The reader is referred to the aforementioned ISA standard if more detailed information is required.

There are three general types of control diagrams. (1) Simplified diagrams (also known as process flow diagrams) are the simplest type and provide an overview of the process and the primary controls (i.e., the normally operating control loops) without identifying the sensors and controllers by number. (2) Conceptual diagrams present a complete representation of the primary controls, without numbering for sensors and controllers. In principle, these diagrams are closest to the control schematics used in this text. (3) P&IDs show all of the hardware, including block and bypass valves, and all of the controls, including override and startup and shutdown controls. Detailed diagrams provide numbers for the controllers and sensors.

A.2 Loop and Sensor Convention for Acronyms

Table A.1 lists some of the P&ID acronyms for sensors and controllers. These acronyms appear inside a circle, used to represent instruments on a P&ID. Consider a tag for a temperature controller: TC-101. The first letter (i.e., the primary letter) indicates that temperature is involved, and the second letter specifies that it is a controller. The number following the "TC" is the loop number. Therefore, the temperature sensor/transmitter for this loop is represented by TT-101 because each instrument in the control loop has the same number.

One or more letters can follow the primary letter, and indicate the particular function of the instrument. For example, consider a temperature controller that also records the temperature reading. In that case, the controller is represented by

TRC-xxx. A temperature controller that has an indicator attached to it is given by TIC-xxx. FRC-xxx represents a flow controller that records the flow rate on a strip chart. The recorder designation has generally become obsolete for DCSs. For DCSs, FIC is used to represent a flow controller that provides indication of the flow rate.

| **Table A.1** |||
| **Acronyms for Several Commonly Encountered Sensors and Controllers** |||
Letter	**First or Primary Letter**	**Succeeding Letters**
A	Analysis	Alarm
C		Controller
D		Differential
F	Flow rate	Ratio
H		High
I		Indicator
L	Level	Low
P	Pressure	
R		Recorder
S		Switch
T	Temperature	Transmitter
Y		Computation block

FR-xxx indicates that a ratio of flow rates is formed by the denoted instrument. Switches (S) with high (H) and low (L) limits can also be specified for P&IDs. For example, a high-level switch is given by LSH-xxx. A high-pressure switch is given by PSH. The difference between two sensor readings is often used for control purposes. For example, a differential pressure sensor/transmitter (PDT-xxx) is used to indicate the onset of flooding in a column. Note that the schematics in this text represent differential pressure sensor/transmitters as DPTs, and they are known industrially as DP cells. The difference between two temperature readings that is transmitted to a controller and also recorded is given by TDRT-xxx.

One of the most widely used control instrument acronyms, and the most ambiguous, is the computation block (Y). It is used to represent a ratio operation (Section 10.3), a feedforward controller (Section 10.4), or a computed manipulated

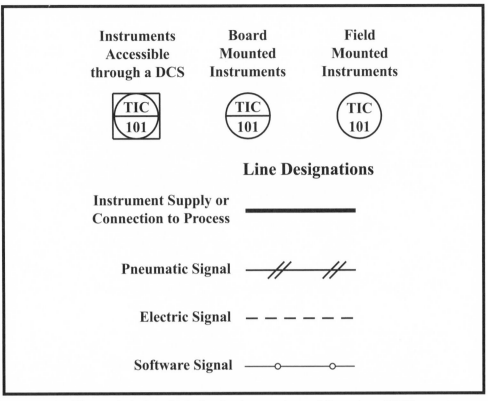

Figure A.1 Symbols for instruments and lines in a P&ID.

variable (Section 11.5). Sometimes a note attached to the computation block explains its function. **Usually, there is a sheet that accompanies P&IDs to define the symbols used.**

A.3 P&ID Symbols

A selected group of P&ID symbols is presented in Figure A.1. A "bubble" with a horizontal line through the middle indicates a sensor reading or a controller that is board-mounted in a control room, e.g., an analog electronic controller. The acronym for the instrument is placed inside the bubble and above the horizontal line, and the loop number associated with the instrument is placed below the line. If a bubble for an instrument does not have a horizontal line, it indicates that the instrument is mounted in the field. A bubble inside a square indicates that the instrument represented by the bubble can be accessed using a DCS or control computer.

A solid line without crosshatching represents instrument supply (e.g.., instrument air lines) or a connection to the process (e.g., the pressure taps from a differential pressure sensor to the process). Pneumatic lines are given by a solid line with pairs of crosshatching. Electric lines are represented by dashed lines. Software

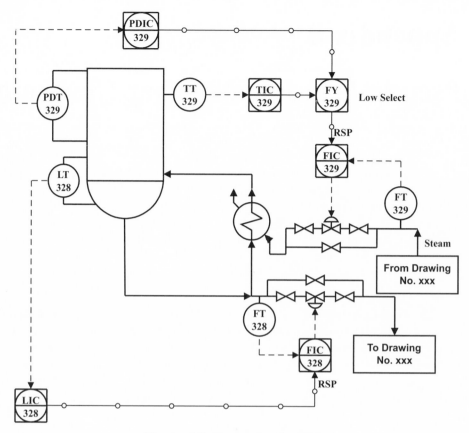

Figure A.2 Example of a P&ID

signals, which are represented by a line connecting small circles, represent the logic flow within a control computer or DCS.

A.4 Example P&ID

Figure A.2 shows a P&ID for the stripping section of the column shown in Figure 1.14. The correspondence between Figure A.2 and Figure 1.14 is good except that the low select is represented by a computation block (FY) and Figure A.2 shows the block and bypass valves around each control valve and Figure 1.14 does not. In addition, the control loop number for the reboiler level is 328 and for the reboiler steam is 329. There are tags to show the connection between this P&ID and other P&IDs. In most cases, a control engineer must use a number of P&IDs to determine the existing control configuration for a single distillation column.

There are field-mounted sensor transmitters for level, flow, and differential pressure. The rest of the instrument functions reside in the DCS.

Appendix B

Pseudo-Random Number Generator

Application of the model for sensor noise presented in Chapter 3 requires a random number, x_n. Considerable work has been done in developing techniques to generate random numbers that have a very nearly perfectly random distribution. For modeling noise, the requirements for a random number generator are not nearly as demanding. A simple pseudo-random number generator[1] will suffice and is given by

$$x_{n+1} = 10^P \, C \, x_n - I(10^P \, C \, x_n)$$

where x_{n+1} is the calculated random number, which is between zero and unity, x_n is the previous random number, which is also between zero and unity, P is the number of significant figures used in x_n, $I(y)$ is the integer value of y, and A and B are constants. To generate a random number, four values are required: A, B, P, and x_n. A is any non-negative integer and B is any number from the set $\{3, 11, 13, 19, 21, 27, 29, 37, 53, 59, 61, 67, 69, 77, 83, 91\}$. C is calculated by the following expression

$$C = 10^{-P} \, (200A + B)$$

The initial random number (x_0), known as the seed, should be between zero and unity and contain the same number of significant figures as x_n such that

$$x_0 = 10^{-P} \, K$$

where K is any integer not divisible by 2 or 5 such that $0 < K < 10^P$.

1. Graybeal, W.T., and U.W. Pooch, *Simulation: Principles and Methods*, Little, Brown, and Company, Boston, MA, Section 4.2.5 (1984).

Appendix C

Signal Filtering

C.1 Introduction

Some degree of noise is associated with all process measurements. This noise can be caused by electrical interference, mechanical vibration, or changes in the process (e.g., variations resulting from turbulent flow). Noise is a high-frequency variation in the process measurement that is not associated with the true process measurement. A controller that is responding to the noise on a measurement makes high-frequency changes to the manipulated variable, causing short-term process variations in the controlled variable. The noise can increase the variability of the controlled variable about its setpoint, but the average value of the controlled variable does not change. In effect, a controller using measured controlled variable values with significant noise levels passes the noise into the process if preventive steps are not taken. Depending on the process gain and time constant, the noise level can be amplified by the controller. When derivative action is used, the feedback system is even more prone to amplifying the noise on the measurement of the controlled variable. Filtering of process measurements is an effective means of reducing the effects of measurement noise.

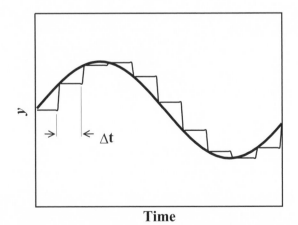

Figure C.1   Comparison between a continuous measurement and the corresponding sample and hold measurement.

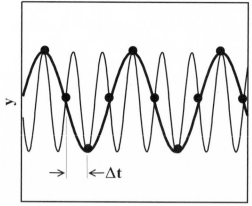

Time

Figure C.2 Signal aliasing resulting from using too large a sampling period. Thin line- the original signal. Thick line- the apparent low-frequency signal resulting from signal aliasing. ● represents the sampled measurement.

C.2 Sampling

The measurement of a controlled variable must be converted into a digital value by the A/D converter before it can be used by the control algorithm in the DCS. A continuous measurement (e.g., a temperature sensor) is sampled by the A/D converter at discrete points in time. After the measurement is sampled, its value is fixed at that level until the next sampling by the A/D converter. Figure C.1 shows a continuous measurement and the discrete sampled measurement. Since the sampled value is fixed at its last measured value, this sampling approach is called the **sample and hold** approach or a **zero-th order hold**. The time between sample points is called the **sampling period**, Δt. The **sampling rate** is $1/\Delta t$ and the **sampling frequency** is $2\pi/\Delta t$.

From Section 7.16, both the control interval and sampling period should be less than $0.05(\tau_p + \theta_p)$ to approach continuous control performance. If this guideline is used, a sample and hold approach to sampling the controlled variable should provide an accurate measure of the process behavior.

C.3 Signal Aliasing

A sampling period that is too long results in a loss of information. Significant variation of the signal can occur during the sampling period and knowledge of the true dynamic behavior is lost. Figure C.2 shows the original signal as a high-frequency sinusoid (thin line). A sampling period (Δt), which is too large to accurately measure the original signal, is applied to the original signal yielding the apparent signal (thick line). The apparent signal is also a sinusoid, but with a much lower frequency. This phenomenon is known as **signal aliasing**. According to Shannon's sampling theorem[1], to prevent signal aliasing, the sampling period must be less than one-half the period of the original signal to accurately reconstruct the original signal.

An industrial sensor reading contains a full range of frequencies, i.e., low frequencies representing true process changes and high frequencies from sensor noise. As a result, the sampling period selected to follow the changes in the true process causes the high-frequency components of the sensor reading (i.e., those with periods twice Δt and smaller) to appear as lower-frequency components due to signal aliasing. The low-frequency components resulting from signal aliasing can affect control performance if their frequencies correspond to the frequencies of the process being controlled. The effects of signal aliasing on control performance can be handled by applying the proper filtering techniques to the sensor reading.

C.4 Filtering Process Measurements

The effects of high-frequency noise on a process measurement can be reduced by filtering the measurement signal. Filtering can be thought of as taking a running average of the measurement readings of the last n samples. In this manner, the high-frequency variations resulting from noise can be "averaged" out. The continuous form of a first-order filter is given by a first-order differential equation

$$\tau_f \frac{dy_f}{dt} + y_f = y_s$$

where y_s is the unfiltered sensor reading, y_f is the filtered value of the sensor reading, and τ_f is the time constant for the filter. Using a first-order backward finite difference approximation of the first derivative yields the equation for a digital filter

$$y_f(t) = \frac{\dfrac{\tau_f}{\Delta t}}{\dfrac{\tau_f}{\Delta t} + 1} y_f(t - \Delta t) + \frac{1}{\dfrac{\tau_f}{\Delta t} + 1} y_s$$

where Δt is the sampling period. This equation can be written in the following simplified form

$$y_f(t) = [1 - f] \, y_f(t - \Delta t) + f \, y_s(t)$$

where f is the filter factor defined by $f = \dfrac{1}{\dfrac{\tau_f}{\Delta t} + 1}$

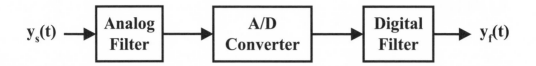

Figure C.3 Schematic showing the sequence of signal processing steps used to filter and sample a continuous measurement for use in a DCS.

Consider the case for which $f = 0.05$. The filter for this case can be viewed as an average of the current sensor reading (y_s) and the previous 19 sensor readings since for $f = 0.05$, 5% of the new filtered value comes from the current measurement and 95% comes from the previous readings.

The smallest control interval for normal control loops on a DCS is 0.5 to 1.0 second. From Shannon's sampling theorem, the components of the noise with periods less than 1.0 second experience signal aliasing. Since analog filters can operate at much higher frequencies (smaller sampling periods) than A/D converters on a DCS, the continuous measurement signal is typically passed through an analog filter to remove the high-frequency noise before it goes to the A/D converter. Analog filters use resistors and capacitors to remove high-frequency noise from electrical signals. The output of the A/D converter has a digital filter which removes the lower-frequency noise. This signal processing sequence is shown schematically in Figure C.3.

1. Astrom, K.J. and B Wittenmark, *Computer Controlled Systems*, Prentice-Hall (1984).

Index

D